BOOK OF HOMILIES

Edited by John Griffiths

REGENT COLLEGE PUBLISHING
Vancouver, British Columbia

Originally published
at the University Press, Oxford, 1859 under the title,
"The Two Books of Homilies Appointed to be Read in Churches"

Reproduced 2008 by

Regent College Publishing
5800 University Boulevard
Vancouver, British Columbia
V6T 2E4 Canada
Web: www.regentpublishing.com
E-mail: info@regentpublishing.com

ISBN-10: 1-57383-391-6
ISBN-13: 978-1-57383-391-2

CONTENTS.

THE EDITOR'S PREFACE.

1. OF THE FIRST BOOK OF HOMILIES.

THE First Book of Homilies was the first work pertaining either to the public worship or to the teaching of the Church of England which was put forth in the reign of Edward the Sixth; and Cranmer seems to have set himself to prepare it as soon as more urgent matters, consequent on the demise of the crown, would allow. Henry the Eighth died on the 28th of January 1547, and the first edition of the Homilies bears date on the last day of July in that year.

It was a work which the Archbishop had long had in view. For there can be no doubt that he had sanctioned and encouraged the publication of the discourses called Postils which were collected and printed by Richard Taverner in 1540; perhaps he had even been a contributor to the volume[a]. And it must have been by his persuasion that "the bishops, in the Convocation holden A.D. 1542, agreed to make certain homilies for stay of such errors as were then by ignorant preachers sparkled among the people[b]." That Convocation sat at intervals from January 20 to April 3 in that year, but did not meet again for business till February 16, 1543, when some homilies, not made by the bishops, but composed by certain dignitaries of the Lower House, were produced by the Prolocutor[c]. Of these nothing further is recorded; but, although the project "took none effect then[d]," some of them may have been pre-

[a] See Dr. Cardwell's Preface to *Taverner's Postils*, page x.

[b] Gardiner's Letter to the Lord Protector Somerset, dated June 10, 1547, in Foxe's *Acts and Monuments*, VI, 41, ed. 1843-9. Since Gardiner in his next letter speaks of that Convocation as "holden five years past," it seems clear that the date "1542" is not to be understood according to the old style.

[c] *Concilia*, Wilkins, III, 860-863.

[d] Gardiner's next Letter to the Protector, without date, in Foxe *ibid.*

served, and turned to account by Cranmer in 1547. Be that as it may, he now tried to carry out the design in the manner then agreed upon, and called upon Gardiner, and probably upon other bishops, to furnish homilies accordingly[e]; and, although Gardiner refused to be bound by an agreement made five years before, the Archbishop seems to have found Bonner more compliant[f], and was aided also by more willing coadjutors.

The book came forth with the following title: "Certain Sermons, or Homilies, appointed by the King's Majesty to be declared and read by all Parsons, Vicars, or Curates every Sunday in their churches where they have cure." It was printed by the King's Printer, Richard Grafton, and began with a Preface, running in the King's name, in which all the clergy having cure of souls were commanded to read it through to their parishioners again and again until the King's pleasure should be further known. The same order was given in the King's Injunctions, which bore date on the same day; and both the Injunctions and the Homilies were together delivered out to the bishops and archdeacons by the King's Commissioners in their visitation of the several dioceses during the summer and autumn of that year.

Cranmer appears to have speedily taken care to have the Homilies, at any rate the first five of them, translated into Latin, and so made known upon the Continent; but the translation is not known to be now extant. At Strasburg in particular it was received with lively interest by the friends of the Reformation; and Bucer, who seems to have then just completed his answer to two scurrilous publications of Gardiner, immediately prefixed to it a few pages of congratulation addressed to the Church of England, in which, while he praised most highly the explanation given in the Homilies of the fundamental doctrines of Christianity, he expressed the utmost joy at the

[e] See Gardiner's Letters cited above.

[f] See the remarks, in the third section of this Preface, on the second and sixth Homilies of the First Book. Yet that the teaching of the whole volume was not to Bonner's liking is clear from the circumstance, related by Foxe (*Acts and Monuments*, v, 742), that, when the King's Commissioners in their visitation at St. Paul's delivered to him a copy of the Injunctions and of the Homilies, he only received them with a protestation, "and immediately he added, with an oath, that he never read the said Homilies and Injunctions."

recognition of the principle, that every one should search the Scriptures for himself as the sole repository of the word of God, and his strong conviction that this would soon issue in the correction of whatsoever was wrong in the administration of Christ's Sacraments or in any other part of the doctrine or discipline of the Church[g].

In this country the demand for the Homilies was necessarily great, and was supplied with great rapidity. The Catalogue of early editions subjoined to this Preface contains a description of six which came from Grafton's press, and of three more printed by Whitchurch, before the end of 1547; whereof Grafton's second was manifestly in type before the first of Whitchurch, though that bears the date of August 20[h]. But, as

[g] "Gratulatio Martini Buceri ad Ecclesiam Anglicanam de Religionis Christi restitutione: Et, Responsio Ejusdem ad duas Stephani Episcopi Vintoniensis Angli conviciatrices Epistolas, De coelibatu sacerdotum et coenobitarum." This tract, which, notwithstanding the division in the title, is all continuous, has at the end the signature of Bucer with the date of November 1547. It was printed in 1548, on the continent I believe, but with no name of place or printer. Of the 82 pages, of which (after excluding the title) the book consists, the "Gratulatio" occupies five. An English translation of it was immediately made by Thomas Hobye, then residing with Bucer as a pupil, and was printed in London (without date of year) by Richard Jugge: the translator's dedication to his brother "Syr Philyppe Hobye knight, M. of y[e] Kinges maiesties ordinaunce," bears date "At Argentyne, Kalendis Februarii." Both are in the Bodleian Library. The "Gratulatio", apart from the Answer to Gardiner, is given among Bucer's *Scripta Anglicana*, p. 171; and there is some account of it in Strype's *Memorials*, Edward VI, I, v, an. 1547.

Bucer does not say that he had become acquainted with the Homilies through a translation, but I think we may draw that inference from a statement which he makes elsewhere, that it was by that help that he studied the Book of Common Prayer on his arrival in England in 1549. See the opening of his "Censura" in *Script. Anglic.* p. 456. In the "Censura" itself, which was written after he had passed a year and a half in this country, he cites, as might be expected, several of the Prayers in English.

The "Gratulatio" makes express mention of the first five Homilies, but contains no certain evidence that he had seen any of the rest.

[h] It is very difficult to account for the great number of editions thus printed on the very first publication of such a book. When a special Form of Prayer is appointed in these days, the Queen's Printer takes care to strike off at once many thousands of copies, so as fully to supply the wants of every place of worship within the pale of the Church. Yet it is not found in 1547 only: the same thing was done on the publication of the Second Book of Homilies, of which there are as many as eight editions dated in 1563, though perhaps two of them were not printed till after that year; and again in 1570, when five distinct editions of the Homily against Rebellion are known to have appeared before it was annexed to the Second Book in the following

was to be expected, they did not find a cordial reception every where. In some parishes the clergy were so illiterate that they could not, in others so hostile to the innovation that they would not, read them in a way to be understood by the people; and often, when pains were taken to utter them plainly, there were persons in the congregation who would neither listen to them themselves nor suffer them to be heard by any of their neighbours. "But how shall he read this book? As the Homilies are read?" asks Latimer in March 1549. "Some," he adds, "call them Homelies; and indeed so they may be well called, for they are homely handled. For, though the priest read them never so well, yet, if the parish like them not, there is such talking and babbling in the church that nothing can be heard; and, if the parish be good and the priest naught, he will so hack it and chop it, that it were as good for them to be without it for any word that shall be understood[i]." In 1550 Ridley found it necessary, in his visitation of his diocese of London, to order "that the Homilies be read orderly, without omission of any part thereof[k]." And in January 1551 Bucer, then at Cambridge, not many weeks before his death, repeated in writing to the Archbishop the complaints concerning the clergy which Latimer in preaching had pressed upon the King[l].

year. Can it be that of all the elements which go to the manufacture of a printed book the compositor's labour was in those days the cheapest?

Strype knew but two of these editions, both by Grafton. The latter of them, he says, "had this advantage, that in some places the English was mended, and the style corrected and much refined, otherwise the same." *Memorials*, ibid. No doubt one was either Grafton's first or second, which do not differ much; the other, one of his four later, which nearly resemble each other, but differ considerably from the former in bulk and appearance, and vary from them also in many places in the text.

[i] Latimer's *Second Sermon before King Edward VI*, p. 121, ed. Park. Soc.

[k] Ridley's *Works*, Injunctions, p. 320, ed. Park. Soc.

[l] "Interea ... utile est recitari puras ex verbo Dei homilias: sed curandum cum primis erit, ut recitentur summa gravitate et religione ad aedificationem fidei in populis efficacem; quod, proh dolor, hodie in perpaucis fit ecclesiis. Nam passim illis praesunt aut homines Epicurei aut Papistae, qui nolunt, etiam si possint, Christi mysteria populis fideliter exponere, aut insigniter indocti, ut, etiam si velint, non queant sacra illa ea perspicuitate recitare, ut a populo salubriter intelligantur. Ingens enim per regnum pastorum numerus est, qui Sacra sic perturbate, leviter, praecipitanter, non recitant, sed impie demurmurant, ut populus non plus ea quae leguntur intelligat quam si lingua recitarentur Turcica aut Indica." Buceri *Censura in Ordin. Minist. Eccles. Anglic.*, *Script. Anglic.* p. 466.

Whether it were with the view of making the reading of the Homilies less distasteful to those who thus disliked it, or of enabling such as wished to profit by them to bear away their lessons more certainly and to digest them better, it was resolved, when the Prayer Book was put forth in March 1549, to divide them into Parts, of which one only should be read at a time. The rubric concerning them stood thus in the Communion Service: "After the Creed ended shall follow the Sermon or Homily, or some portion of one of the Homilies, as they shall be hereafter divided." And the first edition of them in Parts was printed by Grafton in August of that year. Whatever may have been the motive to it, the division did not commend itself to the zeal of Bucer, who appears to have made in this instance too little allowance for the ignorance of the very rudiments of Christian truth in which the uneducated classes in the country had been kept so long, and for the indifference, not to say disrelish, to it thereby engendered. "Indignum est," he says in the Review of the Prayer Book which he wrote at Cranmer's request in January 1551, "Indignum est etiam professione Christiana Homilias tam breves in partes secare. Quid enim illi faciant aut patiantur pro Nomine Servatoris nostri Jesu Christi, qui non sustineant audire erectis animis et cupidis tam breves eas, denique tam salutares, Homilias totas[m]?" It must be admitted however, even by those who think the Homilies were too long to be profitable to the generality of congregations at that time, that the division was not very judiciously made, being determined rather by the quantity of matter in a Homily than by the successive stages of an argument or exhortation, often therefore interrupting the thread of the discourse, and in one place[n] actually cleaving in two a quotation from St. Paul.

For more than five years and a half the use of the Homilies rested upon the sole authority of the King, as "supreme head in earth, next under Christ, of the Church of England[o]," except so far as it received the sanction of Convocation and of Parliament by implication in the rubric above quoted, when the Book of Common Prayer was approved and enacted. At length

[m] Ibid.

[n] At the end of the First Part of the Homily against Contention.

[o] Article 36, an. 155$\frac{2}{3}$; Cardwell's *Synodalia*, I, 31.

in March 155⅔ they obtained the express assent of Convocation in the thirty-fourth of the XLII Articles which were then agreed upon. Yet it is to be observed that that Article does not seem to be drawn as if such assent were considered necessary, but rather for the purpose of finding an effectual remedy for the carelessness or wilfulness of which Latimer and Bucer complained. It ran thus: "The Homilies of late given and set out by the King's authority be godly and wholesome, containing doctrine to be received of all men, and therefore are to be read to the people diligently, distinctly, and plainly [p]."

In the following July King Edward died, and the Church passed through the fire of persecution in the reign of Mary. It was one of the least of the mischiefs of her hostility to the new learning, that careful search was made for all its doctrinal and devotional books in order to their destruction; and yet perhaps in this, as in other far more important matters, we may trace some good resulting from the evil. For it is likely that the preservation of the few copies which still remain, some of them in a sound and even beautiful condition, is due to the very bitterness of this opposition, the owners cherishing them as relics of that first brief period of freedom to the Gospel, and often as memorials of its Confessors and Martyrs. At any rate there is reason to believe that an uninterrupted use of them would have been fully as destructive; for, in the case of the Homilies at least, the editions of Elizabeth's time are, with only two or three exceptions, quite as rare as those which were printed in the reign of Edward.

But, notwithstanding the general changes which were made, the same method of instruction was still employed. Its value was so approved by six years' experience, that in the Letter with Articles sent to all the bishops by Queen Mary in March 155¾ it was ordered, "that by the bishop of the diocese an uniform doctrine be set forth by homilies or otherwise for the good instruction and teaching of all people [q];" and Bonner accord-

[p] Cardwell's *Synodalia*, 1, 30: but I have changed the spelling to our modern fashion. The Article in the original Latin is as follows: "Homiliae nuper Ecclesiae Anglicanae per Injunctiones Regias traditae atque commendatae piae sunt atque salutares, doctrinamque ab omnibus amplectendam continent: quare populo diligenter, expedite, clareque recitandae sunt." Ib. 15.

[q] Cardwell's *Documentary Annals*, 1, 114, Art. 16.

ingly in 1555 put forth a volume of Homilies, amounting ultimately to thirteen[r], to be used in his diocese of London, and others were published by different authors[s].

Elizabeth succeeded to the throne upon the death of her sister on the 17th of November 1558; and in April 1559 a Bill for Uniformity passed both Houses of Parliament with the Book of Common Prayer annexed to it to be in use from the following festival of St. John the Baptist. The Prayer Book, by the rubric in the Communion Service, carried with it the Homilies; and accordingly we find a new edition of them with the date of the same year, which no doubt was ready for use at the same time. It was based upon Whitchurch's edition of 1549, or some later one of that printer, not (as we should expect) on any of Grafton's editions, though these bear more decided marks of authority upon them. But Whitchurch was not followed verbatim. Like the Prayer Book, the Homilies were not simply reprinted: they were first, as the title says, "perused and overseen for the better understanding of the simple people;" and the changes made were numerous. None of them however affected doctrine: all were intended to make the language plainer, some by substituting easy words, especially words of English origin, for such as were thought more difficult or were derived from Latin, others by appending to a harder word some easy synonym by way of explanation. Many of these alterations would be judged unnecessary now, and some few seem to have been thought so then, for they were removed before the next edition was put forth[t]. The supremacy of the sovereign

[r] Bp. Bonner sent out three Homilies first, concerning "the Creation and Fall of Man" and his "Redemption", with a short Preface, dated July 1, 1555, containing a promise of more. Then came three others, concerning "the Sacrament of the Altar" and "Transubstantiation", with no title, name, nor date: these are now found bound up together with the former in a copy at Lambeth, and in another in the Bodleian Library, "Tanner 182." Lastly the whole thirteen appeared, with the name of the writer subjoined to each, and were annexed to his book entitled "A profitable and necessary Doctrine." Of these there were several editions.

[s] "Fyve Homiles of late made by a ryght good and vertuous clerke, called master Leonarde Pollarde, prebendary of the Cathedrall Churche of Woster," printed by Jugge and Cawood in 1556. "Two homilies upon the first, second, and third articles of the Crede, made by maister Iohn Feknam Deane of Paules", printed by Robert Caly without date.

[t] All these were in the First Part of the Exhortation against the Fear of

continued to be expressed in the Homily of Obedience by the title "supreme head over all," but "governor" was put in place of "head" in the next edition, and has remained there since[u]. This indeed seems to be the only change that was made intentionally in the First Book during the reign of Elizabeth after her first edition of 1559; and this itself tends to shew that that edition was prepared for the press, if not actually printed, before the end of April in that year. For it appears from a letter written "April ult. 1559" by Edwin Sandys, afterwards Archbishop of York, to Matthew Parker, then at Cambridge but shortly afterwards Archbishop of Canterbury, that "Mr. Lever" had already "wisely put such a scruple in the Queen's head that she would not take the title of supreme head" in the Bill of Supremacy which was then passing through Parliament[x].

Many editions of this Book were issued in the course of Elizabeth's reign. At first, for more than twenty years, it came out quite separately: afterwards, from 1582, it was printed uniformly with the Second Book, yet still in a distinct volume; for the two were not put together into one till near the end of the reign of James I. But for the particulars of these it is sufficient to refer the reader to the Catalogue which follows this Preface.

2. OF THE SECOND BOOK OF HOMILIES.

The First Book contained but twelve Homilies, of which the first five may be called doctrinal and the other seven practical; and after their division into Parts they supplied no more than thirty-one lections or readings. But Cranmer intended from the first that more should follow, and put a promise to that effect at the end of the Book together with a list of subjects on which they should treat. None however appeared; and Bucer in his review of the Prayer Book observed upon the scantiness

Death: see for example page 91, notes d, e, f, in this volume. But no discrimination was exercised in their removal. For the next edition the printers in that Part simply went back to an earlier copy, and so cancelled all the changes in the Part, even several which they kept elsewhere, in order to be sure of clearing away the few which were absurd.

[u] See page 106, line 22, in this volume.

[x] *Correspondence of Abp. Parker*, p. 66. ed. Park. Soc. See Cardwell's *Documentary Annals*, I, 202, note.

of the published volume, and urged the preparation of more discourses, especially upon certain subjects (nearly twenty in number) which he went on to specify[y]. That the intention continued is evident from the second Prayer Book of King Edward VI, in which the rubric in the Communion Service was altered into the following form, nearly the same as we have it at the present day: "After the Creed, if there be no Sermon, shall follow one of the Homilies already set forth or hereafter to be set forth by common authority." That Prayer Book was approved by both Houses of Parliament before the middle of April 1552; and on the 13th of October following we find the King himself, in a private note of "matters to be considered," setting down among other things concerning religion "The making of more Homelies[z]," but he did not live to see the notion realized.

Burnet indeed, writing at the very end of the seventeenth century, implies, if he does not assert, that the Second Book of Homilies was finished "about the time of his death[a];" and, although Heylyn forty years before did not venture to be so positive, I think we may gather from his words that he knew such an opinion was entertained. "Who they were," he says, "which laboured in this second Book, whether they were the same that drew up the first, or those who in Queen Elizabeth's time reviewed the Liturgy, or whether they were made by the one and reviewed by the other, I have no where found, though I have taken no small pains in the search thereof[b]." Burnet

[y] "Postremo est etiam nimis exiguus Homiliarum numerus, paucique loci religionis nostrae his docentur. Cum itaque Dominus regnum hoc donarit aliquot pereximiis concionatoribus, demandandum illis esset, ut Homilias plures atque de praecipue necessariis locis componerent, quae populis ab iis recitarentur pastoribus qui ipsi meliores non possent adferre. Atque inter alias, etiam aliquot 1 De vera Christi communione atque disciplina," &c. Buceri *Script. Anglic.* p. 466.

[z] This document, "A summary of matters to be considered," entirely in King Edward's handwriting, is preserved in the British Museum, being Lansdowne MS. 1326, fol. 19. Some account of its contents is given by Strype in his *Memorials*, Edward VI, II, xii, an. 1552.

[a] "At the time of the Reformation... there were two Books of Homilies prepared: the first was published in King Edward's time; the second was not finished till about the time of his death, so it was not published before Queen Elizabeth's time." Burnet's *Exposition of the XXXIX Articles* (first published in 1699), Art. XXXV.

[b] *Historia Quinquarticularis* (first published in 1660), xvii, 5. But Heylyn

however, in another part of the same volume, speaks of the "great share" which Jewel had "in compiling the second Book of Homilies[c];" and, although his two statements might possibly be consistent with each other, there is other evidence which seems to refute completely the one first quoted. In the Interpretations of the Queen's Injunctions, drawn up by the Archbishop and Bishops in 1560 according to Strype for the better direction of the clergy, one Item on Injunction XX is as follows; "That there be some long Catechism devised and printed for the erudition of simple curates: Homilies to be made of those arguments which be shewed in the Book of Homilies; or others of some convenient arguments, as of the Sacrifice of the Mass, of the Common Prayer to be in English, that every particular Church may alter and change the public rites and ceremonies of their Church, keeping the substance of the faith inviolably, with such like. And that these be divided to be made by the Bishops, every Bishop two, and the Bishop of London to have four[d]." Surely, if there had been so many discourses nearly or quite ready for publication in 1553, their existence could not have been unknown to the prelates who framed this direction[e].

If that direction had been strictly followed, the Second Book would perhaps have contained a larger number of Homilies than it does, and would certainly have exhibited a greater variety of style. When first published, the number of subjects treated in it was twenty, and the number of discourses (each Part of a Homily being reckoned separately) thirty-eight; but in actual

seems to have supposed that the Second Book was ready for publication at the same time with the First and with the Prayer Book, in the early part of 1559.

c "The first, and indeed the much best writer of Queen Elizabeth's time, was Bishop Jewel;...who had so great share in all that was done then, particularly in compiling the Second Book of Homilies, that I had great reason to look on his works as a very sure commentary on our Articles, as far as they led me." *Exposition*, Preface, page x, ed. Oxf. 1831.

d Strype, *Annals*, Ch. XVII. Cardwell, *Documentary Annals*, I, 204, 30 &c.

e Further evidence to the same effect is contained in the Preface prepared by Bishop Cox on the completion of the Second Book. "And whereas in the said Book of Homilies" [viz. the First] "mention was made of other Homilies concerning certain necessary points of religion that were intended to be annexed to these, her Highness hath caused the same to be faithfully drawn, perused, and hereunto annexed," &c. Strype, *Annals*, Ch. XXX.

bulk it exceeded the First Book much more than these numbers appear to shew, fully in the ratio of five to two. In 1571 the addition of the Homily against Rebellion gave six Parts more, and increased the ratio of bulk so much that it was now almost three to one. It is likely however that but few of the Bishops contributed discourses towards the new volume, or else that Jewel, if he (as is commonly believed) were really its editor, was dissatisfied with some of the contributions; for the internal, though uncertain, evidence of style appears to confirm Burnet's other assertion respecting him by making it probable that he was himself the author of nearly half the volume. On this point something more will be said in the next section of this Preface, when a few remarks are offered concerning the Homilies severally.

Much time passed before the Book was ready; but at length it was submitted, together with the Thirty-nine Articles, to the famous Convocation of 156$\frac{2}{3}$, and received its approbation. Yet we cannot suppose that the Convocation had much to do with either, for its Session only began on the 12th of January, and the Articles, involving the Homilies in the thirty-fifth of them, passed both Houses by the 5th of February. The Articles indeed, being little more than a modification of the Forty-two of 155$\frac{2}{3}$, would not require much discussion; but the Homilies were entirely new matter, some of it in those days very debatable.

The Queen took much longer time for her consideration of them[f], and I think it may be shewn that, like the Articles, they did not come from her hands unaltered.

There is in the British Museum a copy of the first edition, "C. 25. h. 3," which differs considerably from every other copy that I have seen. It is in its original contemporary binding, of the handsomest of the time, and richly gilt; and the pages within are, or at least were when I collated it in 1857, almost

[f] Parker says to Cecil in a letter not dated, but evidently written in 1563 before Midsummer, "For that I intend by God's grace to visit my diocese shortly after Midsummer,... I would gladly the Queen's Majesty would resolve herself in our books of Homilies, which I might deliver to the parishes as I go," &c., where the plural word "books" can hardly mean the Two Books of Homilies, now commonly so called, but rather copies of the Second Book, then ready to be issued. *Correspondence of Abp. Parker*, p. 177, ed. Park. Soc.

as clean and fresh as when the volume left the binder's hands. The Museum has no record of its history, but it is known not to have been acquired in recent times, and there is no reason why it may not be believed to belong to the old Bibliotheca Regia, which dates from the reign of Henry VII, and was given to the nation by King George II. The list of "Faultes escaped in the printying" at the end of the volume is the same as in all other copies. On examining this carefully we observe that full two thirds of the corrections were not occasioned by errors of the printer, but were such changes as an author or editor or critic might make; and a further search will shew that the copy contains as many as twelve cancel leaves. It is plain therefore that the book had been submitted to a pretty close revision after the sheets were printed off; and after such revision it was bound as above described, evidently for the use of some great personage[g]. It is clear too that some of the corrections were not made by the respective authors, but rather by a committee of review, such as Convocation might have been likely to appoint[h].

If now we compare with this volume a perfect copy of the same edition in the state in which it ordinarily occurs, we shall see that the differences between them are sure signs of a further revision. Those differences consist of three particulars: the ordinary copy has on the back of its Title the "Admonition," which the Museum copy has not; it contains all the twelve cancel leaves of the Museum copy, and five more besides[i]; and it has one whole sheet inserted in the middle of signature Ccc. Now the "Admonition," though not actually running in the Queen's name, as was the case with the Preface of the First Book, speaks nevertheless in a tone of authority which could have been assumed by no one else[k]; and it is my

[g] There is evidence, if evidence be needed, that Archbishop Parker took pains about the binding of books which were to be laid before the Queen. In announcing to Cecil the completion of the new edition of the Bible in 1568 he says, on the 22nd of September, "Some ornaments of the same be yet lacking," and, on the 5th of October, "I have caused one book to be bound as ye see, which I heartily pray you to present favourably to the Queen's Majesty." *Ibid.* p. 334.

[h] See, for example, page 186, note g, in this volume.

[i] All these cancel leaves are specified in the description of the edition in the Catalogue which follows this Preface.

[k] The Preface which was drawn up by Bishop Cox on the completion of the Second Book, evidently with the notion of it being prefixed to the two Books

conviction that the other changes likewise, the five additional cancels and the inserted sheet, were made by the Queen's authority alone. Whether however that be so, or not, it will be interesting to see what alterations they effected in the text, and I shall therefore set them before the reader with references both to that edition and to this[1].

1. In the First Part of the Homily against Peril of Idolatry, Gg 1 *b*, line 8, ed. 1; p. 178, l. 20, ed. 1859:

ORIGINAL.	CORRECTED.
"Which place both enforceth that neither the material church or temple ought to have any images in it, (for of it is taken the ground of the argument,) neither that any true Christian ought to have any ado with filthy and dead images, for that he is the holy temple" &c.	"Which place enforceth, both that we should not worship images, and that we should not have images in the temple, for fear and occasion of worshipping them, though they be of themselves things indifferent; for the Christian is the holy temple" &c.

2. In the first sentence of the Third Part of the same Homily, Mm 2 *b*, ed. 1; p. 213, ed. 1859:

ORIGINAL.	CORRECTED.
"Now ye have heard how plainly, how vehemently, and that in many places, the word of God speaketh against not only idolatry and worshipping of images, but also against idols and images themselves; and have heard likewise" &c.	"Now ye have heard how plainly, how vehemently, and that in many places, the word of God speaketh against not only idolatry and worshipping of images, but also against idols and images themselves: I mean always thus herein, in that we be stirred and provoked by them to worship them, and not as though they were simply forbidden by the New Testament without such occasion and danger. And ye have heard likewise" &c.

3. In the Homily of Common Prayer and Sacraments, Kk (for Ppp) 3, ed. 1; p. 355, l. 13, ed. 1859:

ORIGINAL.	CORRECTED.
"And as for the number of them, if they should be considered according	"And as for the number of them, if they should be considered according

united in one volume, runs entirely in the Queen's name, and is in fact based upon her own Preface to the First Book. It is given by Strype in his *Annals*, Ch. xxx.

[1] In these extracts, as throughout the text of this edition, the modern way of spelling is followed.

ORIGINAL.

to the exact signification, as fully so expressed and commended by Christ in the New Testament, there be two, namely, Baptism, and the Supper of the Lord: but in a general acception" &c.

CORRECTED.

to the exact signification of a Sacrament, namely, for visible signs, expressly commanded in the New Testament, whereunto is annexed the promise of free forgiveness of our sin, and of our holiness and joining in Christ, there be but two, namely, Baptism, and the Supper of the Lord. For, although Absolution hath the promise of forgiveness of sin, yet by the express word of the New Testament it hath not this promise annexed and tied to the visible sign, which is imposition of hands. For this visible sign, I mean laying on of hands, is not expressly commanded in the New Testament to be used in Absolution, as the visible signs in Baptism and the Lord's Supper are; and therefore Absolution is no such Sacrament as Baptism and the Communion are. And, though the Ordering of Ministers hath his visible sign and promise, yet it lacks the promise of remission of sin, as all other Sacraments besides do. Therefore neither it nor any other Sacrament else be such Sacraments as Baptism and the Communion are. But in a general acception" &c.

4. In the Sermon of the Nativity, Aaaa 4 *a*, l. 8 up, ed. 1; p. 405, l. 23, ed. 1859:

ORIGINAL.

"We are evidently taught in Scripture, that our Lord and Saviour Christ consisted of two several natures, being, as touching his outward flesh, perfect man, as touching his inward spirit, perfect God."

CORRECTED.

"We are evidently taught in the Scripture, that our Lord and Saviour Christ consisteth of two several natures; of his manhood, being thereby perfect man; and of his Godhood, being thereby perfect God."

5. Near the end of the First Part of the Sermon of the Worthy Receiving of the Sacrament, Iiii 3 *a*, l. antep., ed. 1; p. 445, l. 18, ed. 1859:

ORIGINAL.

"For the unbelievers and faithless cannot feed upon that precious Body:

CORRECTED.

"For the unbelievers and faithless cannot feed upon that precious Body:

ORIGINAL.	CORRECTED.
whereas the faithful have their life, their abiding, in him; their union, and as it were their incorporation, with him. Whereof thus saith St. Augustine: 'He which is at discord with Christ doth neither eat his flesh nor drink his blood, although he receive, to the judgment of his destruction, daily the outward Sacrament of so great a thing.' Wherefore let us" &c. And "Lib. 4. de Trinit." is in the margin.	whereas the faithful have their life, their abiding, in him; their union, and as it were their incorporation, with him. Wherefore let us" &c.

These five are the alterations made by means of cancels. The first two of them bear upon the question of images in such a way that they might seem to have been suggested by the Queen herself, who is known to have retained the crucifix for some time in her own chapel. The third, explaining more fully certain rites of the Church, and the fourth, correcting some inaccuracies concerning the Person of our blessed Saviour, need not necessarily have come from any one but a divine. Yet it must be remembered that both the Queen and some of her Ministers were more competent and more accustomed to discuss questions of divinity than is usual with statesmen and high political personages at the present day. See for instance a letter from Parker to Cecil, dated "4th of June 1571," which shews that the subject of the twenty-ninth Article, a subject connected with the fifth of the alterations here exhibited, had been in debate between them[m]. And that fifth alteration, the omission of the sentence cited from St. Augustine concerning the unworthy partaker of the Holy Communion, when considered together with the suppression of the twenty-ninth Article after it had been approved by the same Convocation[n], is so evidently to be referred to the interference of the Queen, that few, I think, can doubt it.

The only change remaining to be noticed is the insertion of an entire sheet in the middle of signature Ccc, whereby the Homily of Fasting, originally undivided, was so much increased in bulk, that it was judged necessary to break it into two Parts; and an

m *Correspondence of Abp. Parker*, p. 381, ed. Park. Soc.

n See Cardwell, *Synodalia*, 1, 38, note; and 54, note.

examination of the inserted portion, which comprises the first half of the Second Part of the Homily, and is too long to be reprinted here, will shew beyond all question that the Queen's counsellors at least, if not the Queen herself, directed that addition to be made. For not only is it purely secular or political in its character, but, as is shewn in note 1 upon that Part of the Homily[o], it was occasioned by an Act of Parliament which was not even brought in as a Bill till the 9th of March, more than a month after the Homilies had been approved by Convocation[p].

These particulars have served to convince me that the unique volume in the British Museum exhibits the Second Book of Homilies exactly in the state in which it was approved by the two Houses of Convocation, and that it is the identical volume which was presented to Queen Elizabeth when her royal assent was asked.

After all this deliberation and revision the book at length came forth with the following Title: "The Second Tome of Homilies, of such matters as were promised and intituled in the former part of Homilies: set out by the authority of the Queen's Majesty, and to be read in every Parish Church agreeably." The exact date of its publication has not been ascertained: but, even if the Archbishop did not obtain it before Midsummer, as he hoped[q], it must have been issued before the end of July; for in the Form of Prayer which was ordered by the Queen's Letter bearing date on "the first day of August" 1563, on account of the great pestilence then raging, the last of the directions which follow the Prayers speaks of "the seconde Tome of Homylyes now lately set forth by the Quenes Maiesties aucthoritie," and orders Churchwardens to "prouide the same seconde Tome . . . with all speede at the charges of the Paryshe[r]."

[o] See page 289. See also page 293, note o.

[p] See Sir Simonds D'Ewes' *Journal*, p. 87.

[q] See before, page xvii, note f.

[r] Sign. C 3 *b*, ed. 1563. Reprinted in the *Remains of Bp. Grindal*, p. 94, ed. Park. Soc.

One of the copies of "the Seconde Tome" in the Library of St. John's College, Cambridge, "Qq. II. 13," has on its title page the merchant's mark and name of its first owner, Ansell Beckett, with a note that he bought it on the "20 daye of augste 1563."

The demand for it, as for the First Book in 1547, was necessarily great, and the printers took great pains to satisfy it. Five editions followed the first with great rapidity, each printed half at one office and half at another, doubtless for the sake of saving time; and even after that, when the first requirements of the country had been met, two more editions came out, each bearing the date of 1563[s]. Nevertheless Strype asserts, on the authority of "a journal of a Minister of London of that time," that "all the churches hardly came to be fully supplied" with the book till 1564[t].

No changes analogous to the division of the First Book into Parts have ever been made in the Second Book, and the only material alteration which took place in it during the reign of Elizabeth was one which has been already mentioned, the addition of the Homily against Wilful Rebellion. That Homily was written early in 1570, was first published separately, passed rapidly through five editions, and in 1571 was annexed to the Second Book by the addition of its title at the end of the Article "Of Homilies" when the Thirty-nine Articles were again approved and confirmed by Convocation.

Editions of either Book separately came out from time to time according as they were wanted, and in 1582 (for the first time so far as is known) they were printed uniformly, so that they might more suitably be bound in one volume. But, although it is likely that some editions have wholly perished in lapse of time, for which allowance must be made, there is good reason still to suppose that the intervals between the publications became gradually longer. Indeed it was to be expected that such would be the case in proportion as both the ability and the desire to deliver sermons of their own composition should increase among the clergy.

At first it had been found necessary to enjoin the clergy to read the Homilies "orderly, without omission of any part thereof[u];" "diligently, plainly, and distinctly, that they may

[s] All these editions are particularly described in the Catalogue which follows this Preface.

[t] *Annals*, Ch. XXXIX.

[u] Bp. Ridley's *Injunctions*, cited before, page x, note k.

be understanded of the people[x];" "gravely and aptly, without any glosing of the same or any additions[y]:" for there were then many, as has been already observed, so strongly attached to popery and so suspicious of the new doctrine that they would not read in such a way that the congregation could gather instruction or profit from what they heard. But in process of time the aspect of things was vastly changed, and, as has been the case with other documents of our Church, protection had to be sought in the Homilies against dangers from the opposite quarter. Before Elizabeth had been on the throne ten years there were parts of the kingdom in which "puritanism, and not popery, was the opponent to be dreaded[z];" and in less than ten years more she judged it necessary to give orders for the suppression of the Exercises called Prophesyings, for lessening the number of licensed preachers, and for the more general reading of the authorised Homilies in accordance with the Injunctions issued at the beginning of her reign[a]. The number however and the power of the puritan party continued to grow, notwithstanding the endeavours of the Queen and of Archbishop Whitgift, and afterwards of James I and Bancroft, to check it; Abbot's primacy is believed to have encouraged them; and at length the liberty used by preachers in their sermons was so alarming that James, like Elizabeth, deemed it necessary to limit them, and like her also sought assistance in the Homilies. In a letter bearing date on the 4th of August 1622 he sent to Archbishop Abbot certain "Directions concerning Preachers," of which the first commands all preachers under the dignity of bishops or deans to confine their sermons to such subjects as are "comprehended and warranted in essence, substance, effect, or natural inference within some one of the" Thirty-nine Articles, "or in some of the Homilies set forth by authority in the Church of England, not only for a help of the nonpreaching,

[x] Article XXXIV, ann. 155 2/3 and 156 2/3.

[y] Advertisements of Archbishop Parker and Bishops in commission with him in 1564, Cardwell's *Documentary Annals*, I, 291, 16.

[z] Cardwell, *ibid.* I, 303, 16. This was in 1567.

[a] *Ibid.* I, 373, 379. The Queen spoke to Abp. Grindal on this subject before the end of 1576. Concerning the Exercises see pages 354 and 367 of the same volume.

but withal for a pattern and a boundary, as it were, for the preaching ministers; and, for their further instruction for the performance thereof, that they forthwith read over and peruse diligently the said book of Articles and the two books of Homilies;" and the fourth orders "that no preacher" whatsoever "shall presume to meddle with" such "matters of state" as pertain to the relations between sovereign princes and their subjects "otherwise than as they are instructed and presidented in the Homily of Obedience and in the rest of the Homilies and Articles of Religion, set forth (as before is mentioned) by public authority, but rather confine themselves [*thus*] wholly to those two heads of faith and good life which are all the subject of the ancient sermons and homilies [b]."

There can be no doubt that these "Directions" gave occasion to the edition which was published in 1623, the first that was printed in folio. In this for the first time the two Books are united in one volume. Each indeed has still its separate register and pagination, and the Second has its own Title prefixed to it; but the Title of the First is made to serve for both by alterations which bring it to the following form: "Certain Sermons or Homilies, appointed to be read in Churches in the time of the late Queen Elizabeth of famous memory, and now thought fit to be reprinted by authority from the King's most excellent Majesty:" a form which appears very plainly to imply that they had not been reprinted since the accession of James to the throne in March 1603, twenty years before. Throughout both Books in this edition many changes are found in the text, a large number of them in all probability owing to the carelessness of the printer, which was very great, but most nevertheless having been purposely introduced by the King's authority. In making these the same principle was followed on which the revision of the First Book was conducted in 1559 by command of Queen Elizabeth: none of them affect doctrine in any way, but all were intended solely for the amendment of the language by substituting easier words for such as still were difficult or had become obsolete, and replacing a few coarse or unseemly expressions by terms or phrases more suitable to the age. I believe there is but one change of a different character, namely,

[b] *Ibid.* II, 149, 150.

the addition of two side notes concerning St. Ambrose and the Emperor Theodosius in the Second Part of the Homily of the Right Use of the Church[c].

This seems to be the latest edition in which changes were made in the text with any semblance of authority. It was followed at intervals by others, of which it is not necessary here to speak particularly. The reader will find a sufficient description of such as were published before the end of that century in the Catalogue subjoined to this Preface.

3. OF THE HOMILIES SEVERALLY.

Before I proceed to give an account of the present edition, I venture to offer a few remarks upon the several Homilies in both Books, addressing myself chiefly to matters which, if fully examined, might help to tell us by whom they were written. Very little is known on this question. The external evidence discovered at present is very scanty; and the internal evidence of style, which is always doubtful, is here the less serviceable, because most of the persons whom we should consider likely to have been contributors have left but small remains of their written works[d]. Heylyn, as we have seen, had failed two centuries ago to learn who were the persons concerned in the Second Book; and even thirty years ago no discourse in either Book had been assigned to its author with any certainty. But the attention which has been given of late to the English divines of the sixteenth century has furnished us with positive information concerning some few of the Homilies, and it is reasonable to expect that a further amount of critical research will enable us at the least to form probable conjectures about others.

[c] See page 165, lines 5 and 7, in this volume.

[d] For example, I have not ventured to ascribe any Homily in these two Books to the famous Dean of St. Paul's, Alexander Nowell, the author of the Homily concerning the Justice of God, which accompanied the special Form of Prayer set forth on occasion of the great pestilence in the summer of 1563. Yet, if Grindal really undertook to furnish the four Homilies which the agreement of the bishops assigned to him, it is likely that he called upon his Dean to help him make up his quota, as he certainly required him in the pestilence "to write an homily meet for the time." See his Letter to Sir William Cecil dated "30 July 1563" among his *Remains*, p. 258, ed. Park. Soc.

The Homilies of the First Book.

1. Exhortation to the reading of holy Scripture. Probably written by Cranmer. This conjecture has been often made, by some from a general similarity of style, by others from a supposed special resemblance to his Preface to the Bible. But I do not know that it has been observed, that of the passages cited from the Fathers in this Homily five are extracted under the head "Sacrae Scripturae intellectus et utilitas" in his Common Place Book, now preserved in the British Museum (Reg. MSS. 7. B. XI and XII), vol. I, pp. 9–12.

2. Of the Misery of Man. By John Harpesfeld or Harpsfield, Archdeacon of London. It is the second of the thirteen Homilies set forth by Bishop Bonner in 1555 "to be read within his diocesse of London[e]," and in that volume has Harpsfield's name appended to it as the author. Many variations are there found, the greater part of no importance, but several evidently meant to bring the Homily, or possibly to restore it, to a Romish cast of thought[f].

3, 4, 5. Of Salvation. Of Faith. Of Good Works. By Cranmer. See Jenkyns' edition of his Works, vol. II, p. 138, note.

6. Of Charity. By Bonner. At least it occurs, with a long preamble but with few other variations, in Bonner's volume cited above, under the title, "An Homely of Christian love, or Charitye," with his own initials, "E. B.," appended to it. It is the fifth Homily of the thirteen. The passage in it which speaks of the "two offices" of Charity, page 71 of this volume, shews that the author could easily reconcile his notions of this

e See before, page xiii, note r.

f See for example the following places in page 22 of this volume. In "And all these heavenly treasures are given us[, not for our own deserts, merits, or good deeds, which of ourselves we have none, but] of his mere mercy freely," the part within [ ] is omitted in Bonner's volume. In "Of whom only it may be truly said, that he did all things well" &c. "only" is omitted. For "None but he alone may say, The prince of this world came, and in me he hath nothing," Bonner has "Likewise he may say" &c. For "And he alone may say also, Which of you shall reprove me of any fault?" Bonner puts "He may say also" &c. In "He is the alone Mediator between God and man" Bonner leaves out "alone."

grace with the strictest requirements of the most rigorous justice.

7. Of Swearing. Some of the thoughts in this Homily are found in Becon's "Invective against Swearing," and some of the quotations also, but these for the most part are handled differently. It appears to me to have been composed by a calmer writer, making such use of the "Invective" as he thought fit. If Becon were the author, he would most likely have reprinted it, like the Homily against Adultery, among his collected Works.

8. Of Falling from God.

9. Of the Fear of Death. A resemblance has been pointed out to me, by one who has paid much attention to the writings of this age, between several passages in this Homily and several in Ridley's "Farewell to the Prisoners in Christ's Gospel's cause[g]." It is highly probable that Ridley took part with Cranmer in preparing the First Book, and I could readily believe him to be the author both of this and of the one before this. But, since his "Farewell" was written within a fortnight of his death in October 1555, more than eight years after the First Book had been published for constant use in the Church, I fear there is not in such resemblance any sufficient proof of authorship; especially as one of the similar passages, a third of the whole in bulk, is drawn from the twelfth chapter of the Epistle to the Hebrews. Bishop Pilkington in his Exposition upon Haggai has adopted[h] in one place some thoughts and some

[g] Ridley's *Works*, Letter XXXIII, ed. Park. Soc. Compare four passages, p. 95, l. 19 &c. and l. 34 &c., p. 96, l. 16 &c., and p. 97, l. 25 &c., in this volume with passages in pp. 424–426 of the Works.

[h] Pilkington's *Works*, pp. 94, 95, 66, ed. Park. Soc.

Read as they were over and over again in Church, the Homilies could not fail to leave many of their thoughts and phrases impressed upon the minds of the hearers. That Bishop Pilkington and other divines imbued with their spirit should also, though unconsciously, adopt some of their language is a thing that will surprise no one. But there is a very familiar passage in Shakespeare, which shews their influence upon the poet likewise:

Who steals my purse steals trash; 'tis something, nothing;
'Twas mine, 'tis his, and has been slave to thousands:
But he that filches from me my good name
Robs me of that which not enriches him
And makes me poor indeed. *Othello* III, 3.

"And many

very remarkable words from the Homily of the Misery of Man, which was written by Harpsfield, and in another place a few words from the Homily of Charity, which is Bonner's, doubtless because frequent use had made them familiar both to himself and to his readers.

10. Of Obedience.

11. Against Adultery. By Thomas Becon, who was one of Cranmer's Chaplains. He declared himself the author by placing it in the Second Part of his collected Works, printed by John Day in 1560–1564.

12. Against Contention. If Latimer wrote any of the Homilies, as many have thought likely, probably this one, as many likewise have supposed, was contributed by him. But there is no proof that he did, beyond the uncertain evidence of style. He speaks of the Homilies more than once[i], but gives no intimation whether he took part in writing them or no.

The Homilies of the Second Book.

1. Of the Right Use of the Church. Probably the first three Homilies in this Book were written by the same person. The second begins with a summary of the first, and contains a reference to the third[k]: one phrase, "church or temple," "church and temple," occurs in all three very often; indeed the word "church" is scarcely used of the material building in any of them without having the word "temple" connected with it.

2. Against Peril of Idolatry. This Homily is based upon a document which was first printed, imperfectly and with alterations, by Foxe at the end of his "Acts and Monuments" under the title of "A Treatise of Master Nicholas Ridley, in the name, as it seemeth, of the whole Clergy, to King Edward the Sixth, concerning Images not to be set up nor worshipped in Churches."

"And many times cometh less hurt of a thief than of a railing tongue: for the one taketh away a man's good name; the other taketh but his riches, which is of much less value and estimation than is his good name." *Homily against Contention*, p. 137, l. 15.

[i] See his *Sermons*, pp. 61, 121, ed. Park. Soc. The latter passage has been cited before in page x.

[k] See p. 261, l. 3.

It is almost a waste of words to shew that the treatise was never addressed to King Edward. After the first few months of his reign the most earnest hater of image worship would have seen no cause for exhorting either the King himself or his advisers against it; and during those few months he was too young for the personal appeals which are made at the end of the document. Moreover the Caroline Books, which are cited in it, were not in print, nor was their tenor known, before 1549[l]; and Sir John Cheke's Translation of Leo's Tactica, which is also cited, though finished in 1544 and then dedicated and doubtless presented to Henry VIII, was actually not in print till after King Edward's death[m]. Since Foxe then is wrong in that part of his statement, his authority need not weigh with us concerning the author of the treatise.

It was really presented to Queen Elizabeth by Archbishop Parker and the other Prelates, probably in 1560. A copy of it in its complete form, but without signatures, is among the Parker MSS. at Corpus Christi College, Cambridge, from which it has been printed for the Parker Society among the Archbishop's "Correspondence" at pp. 79–95. The editors describe the MS. as a "Copy," meaning, I presume, that it is not in his own handwriting.

This document however, strictly speaking, was not from the first an original composition. It was taken by abridgment from Bullinger's treatise "De Origine Erroris in Divorum et Simulacrorum Cultu," which was first published in 1528, and was again put out in 1539 so greatly enlarged that, as he says in his Preface, it would hardly be known to be the same book except

l "Opus Inlustrissimi ... Viri, Caroli Magni, ... contra Synodum quae in partibus Graeciae pro adorandis imaginibus stolide sive arroganter gesta est. Item, Paulini Aquileiensis Episcopi adversus Felicem Urgelitanum et Eliphandum Toletanum Episcopos libellus. Quae nunc primum in lucem restituuntur. Anno salutis M.DXLIX." In 8vo, printed at Paris, but without name of place or printer. The Preface has this heading: "Eli. Phili. Christiano Lectori S." The editor was Jean Dutillet or du Tillet, Bishop of Meaux, disguising his name under the words "Elias Philyra" or "Philyras", a fanciful translation of its Latin form, "Ioannes Tilius". See a Letter of Flacius Illyricus to Abp. Parker dated "Ienae, 22 Maii, 1561," *Correspondence of Abp. Parker*, p. 141, ed. Park. Soc. See also p. 206 in this volume.

m "Leonis Imperatoris de Bellico Apparatu Liber, e Graeco in Latinum conversus, Ioan. Checo Cantabrigiensi Interp. Basileae, apud Mich. Isingrinium, M.D.LIIII." in 8vo.

in spirit[n]. And the writer of the Homily did not merely take the terse memorial of the Bishops and expand it for general use by topics of his own, but he again availed himself largely of the treatise, taking nearly all his historical statements and most of his quotations from the Fathers out of chapters 21, 24–31, and 33–35 of Bullinger. His reasoning however seems to be his own; and in the Third Part especially, which indeed consists of little else, it is cast into the severe form of logical argument, nearly after the fashion of the old Disputations in the Schools.

The subject of the Homily is one which has long ceased to have much interest for us, but at the time there was scarcely any question that was practically more important; and, as the discourse is far the longest in the volume, being in bulk about one quarter of the Second Book as first published, so it is by far the most argumentative and elaborate. And it is my conviction that, just as in the beginning of Edward's reign the vital question of Justification was most carefully and ably treated by Archbishop Cranmer in three Homilies, making just a quarter of the First Book, so in the beginning of Elizabeth's reign the stirring question of Image worship was handled with equal force and at corresponding length by the then great champion of the Church of England, Bishop Jewel. He felt the importance of the matter very strongly, more strongly (so at least he himself thought) than Archbishop Parker and some others did[o].

[n] Bullinger printed it a third time with some amendments in 1568. The estimation in which the work was held in England may be gathered from what is said of Abp. Cranmer in the note on n°. 20 below; and Abp. Grindal expresses his own great obligation to it in a letter addressed to Bullinger himself on the 8th of February 1567, printed in the Parker Society's first series of *Zurich Letters*, p. 108 of the original Latin, p. 182 of the Translation.

[o] "Nunc ardet lis illa crucularia [the dispute about the use of the crucifix]. Vix credas in re fatua quantum homines qui aliquid sapere videbantur insaniant. Ex illis quos quidem tu noris praeter Coxum nullus est. Crastino die instituetur de ea re disputatio. Arbitri erunt ex senatu selecti quidam viri. Actores inde Cantuariensis et Coxus, hinc Grindallus Londinensis Episcopus et ego. Eventus *ἐν κριτῶν γούνασι κεῖται*. Rideo tamen, cum cogito quibus illi et quam gravibus et solidis rationibus defensuri sint suam cruculam. Sed, quicquid erit, scribam posthac pluribus; nunc enim 'sub judice lis est:' tamen, quantum auguror, non scribam posthac ad te episcopus. Eo enim jam res pervenit, ut aut cruces argenteae et stanneae, quas nos ubique confregimus, restituendae sint, aut episcopatus relinquendi." Jewel's *Letter to Peter Martyr* dated "Londini, 4 Februarii, 1560."

He had been for some time resident at Zurich, in intimate acquaintance with Bullinger, and regarded him with gratitude and love as a protector and a friend, and with reverence as a teacher of Christ's truth[p]. The method of reasoning is like Jewel's; the occasional bursts of indignation, and many details of the style, even to single words, resemble his; and there is one remarkable quotation from a work of Jacopo Nachianti, Bishop of Chioggia, which he probably noted during his stay at Padua soon after the book from which it comes was published, that is given, I believe, by no other English writer[q].

3. For Repairing and Keeping Clean of Churches. See the remarks on n°. 1.

4. Of Fasting. This Homily, as has been stated before, was originally undivided. The necessity for breaking it into two Parts arose from a large addition which was made to it after it had passed Convocation. This inserted matter begins with the prayer immediately before the end of the First Part, p. 287, l. 8, and extends beyond the middle of the Second Part, ending p. 293, l. 4. The occasion and subject of it have been already noticed at page xxii. That this is really an insertion may be easily seen by any one who has access to the first edition of the Second Book, the additional matter being there all contained in an extraordinary sheet, which comes exactly in the middle of signature Ccc and begins with the words "for the use of fasting," which words at the top of the page on which they were originally printed (then the fifth, now the thirteenth, page of that signature) have been struck out with a pen. And any one who reads the Homily with care in any edition will see that the summary of what has been said in it, with which its last paragraph begins, does not comprise the subjects treated of in the inserted portion, and that that portion closes with a summary of its own.

Possibly the writer of the Homily as it stood at first was Bishop Grindal, who was strongly persuaded of the value of fasting[r]. At any rate it was not written by the author of any

[p] See his Letters to Peter Martyr as well as to Bullinger himself.

[q] See p. 237, l. 36, in this volume: and compare Jewel's *Reply to Harding*, Art. XIV, "Of Adoration of Images," Div. 12, "Latria, Doulia"; and *Defence of the Apology*, Part VI, Ch. xii, Div. 2.

[r] "By outward appearance it seemeth that this order of fast" [the weekly fast appointed on account of the great pesti-

one of the first three Homilies: in those the Vulgate translation of the Bible is used; in this the quotations of Scripture are made from the Hebrew or the Greek. But the inserted portion is from another pen, possibly Archbishop Parker's[s]. The form "Moyses" occurs in it four times, whereas "Moses" is the name in the original part of the Homily.

5. Against Gluttony and Drunkenness. A few sentences in this Homily are taken from Bishop Pilkington's Exposition upon Haggai, which was published in 1560; and a large portion of the remainder is translated or adapted from Peter Martyr's discourse "De Vino et Ebrietate" in his Commentary on the Book of Judges. See notes 3–6, 9, and 12 on the Homily.

6. Against Excess of Apparel. A few sentences in this Homily also are taken from the same Exposition. See note 5. The two Homilies apparently are from one pen, and Dr. Corrie assigns them both to Pilkington. Considering what was said of that writer at page xxviii, it is some confirmation of Dr Corrie's opinion to find a strong resemblance between a sentence in the former of the two, "Certainly that sin" &c. p. 298, l. 7, and one in the Homily against Contention, "It must needs be a great fault" &c. p. 137, l. 33.

7. 8. 9. Concerning Prayer. Of the Place and Time of Prayer. Of Common Prayer and Sacraments. These three are probably by one author. The quotations from Scripture seem to be made from the Vulgate; and each of the three exhibits the same misapprehension of one text, 1 Tim. III, 8, which an accurate knowledge of the Greek would have prevented. Each enters more or less into the controversy with popery. The second of them, nº. 8, contains arguments and phrases which we have had before in nºs. 1–3 concerning churches; one passage beginning p. 343, l. 30, nearly the same with one in nº. 1 at p. 154, l. 2; and another beginning p. 347, l. 38, very similar to one in nº. 2, p. 209, l. 23, and p. 210, l. 19, concerning the progress of the Turks. I should ascribe them all to Jewel.

lence in 1563] "is generally embraced. Surely my opinion hath been long, that in no one thing the adversary hath more advantage against us than in the matter of fast, which we utterly neglect: they have a shadow." Grindal's *Letter to Sir William Cecil*, dated 21 August, 1563, p. 265, ed. Park. Soc.

[s] See what he says of fasting in a *Letter to Cecil* written June 3, 1564, *Correspondence*, p. 216, ed. Park. Soc.

10. Of Certain Places of Scripture. A few sentences near the beginning of this Homily are translated from a tract of Erasmus. See note 1. The author uses the old form "mought" for "might," a peculiarity which occurs but once besides, p. 530, l. 23.

11. Of Almsdeeds. The writer of this Homily was largely indebted to Cyprian's treatise "De Opere et Eleemosynis." He quoted from the Vulgate. See note 4 on the Third Part, p. 397.

12. Of the Nativity.

13. Of the Passion, for Good Friday. From Taverner's Postils, under the title "The passion on Palme sonday," pp. 173–181, ed. Cardwell.

14. The Second Sermon of the Passion. Perhaps this and n°. 12 are by one author, and he perhaps one of the older fathers of the Reformation in England. Their simplicity and earnestness savour much of the Homilies in the First Book, or even of Taverner's Postils.

15. Of the Resurrection. From Taverner, pp. 189–199, ed. Cardwell. Apparently by a different author from n°. 13. A collation of the original form of both is given among the Various Readings at the foot of each page. It will be seen that the changes in this are much more numerous than in n°. 13, but not many of them are important. The omission of the words "that the stone of the grave was removed from the entrance thereof, and shewed them" in p. 430, l. 28, was probably an oversight. But the omission of the words "in form of bread" in p. 433, l. 22, was doubtless intentional, and ought to be borne in mind, when attempts are made to found an argument for the presence of Christ in the consecrated elements upon the retention of the words "under the form of bread and wine" in the promise of more Homilies which closes the First Book: for its import is shewn by another omission, "now received in this holy Sacrament," in p. 435, l. 18.

16. 17. Concerning the Sacrament. For Whitsunday. These two have been ascribed to Jewel: and the style, the method of argument, the handling of controverted points, the references to history, especially to the history of Popes, the citations from Scripture and from the Fathers, all go to establish the conjecture.

18. For Rogation Week.

I. The first three Parts form one discourse, with which the fourth Part (so called) has no connection. The former first appeared separately, without date, but certainly before the publication of the Second Book, and probably in 1560 or 1561. Queen Elizabeth's Injunctions, issued in 1559, permit the customary perambulation of the bounds of parishes, but direct that the parishioners shall, "at their return to the church, make their Common Prayers," and also "that the Curate in their said common perambulations, used heretofore in the days of Rogations, at certain convenient places shall admonish the people to give thanks to God, in the beholding of God's benefits, for the increase and abundance of his fruits upon the face of the earth, with the saying of the 103rd Psalm, *Benedic, anima mea,*" &c., and shall "inculcate these or such sentences [*thus*], *Cursed be he which translateth the bounds and doles of his neighbour* [Deut. XXVII, 17], or such other order of prayers as shall be hereafter appointed[t]." In the Interpretations of the Injunctions drawn up by the Bishops in 1560 the direction upon the nineteenth is "that in the procession [in Rogation Week] they sing or say the two Psalms beginning *Benedic, anima mea, Domino* [CIII and CIV], with the Litany and Suffrages thereto, with some Sermon or a Homily of thanksgiving to God and moving to temperancy in their drinkings[u]." And it is likely that our

t Cardwell's *Documentary Annals*, I, 187, Inj. XVIII and XIX.

u Ibid. p. 204. See Bp. Grindal's direction to the Archdeacon of Essex "for avoiding of superstitious behaviour and for uniformity to be had in the Rogation Week, now at hand," dated 13 May 1560, among his *Remains*, p. 240, ed. Park. Soc. And compare with the "Interpretation" of 1560, on which this note is added, the "Item" upon the same subject among the "Advertisements" prepared by the Bishops in 1565, *Docum. Ann.* I, 293; and Abp. Grindal's Injunctions at York for the Laity, item 18, at p. 141 of his *Remains*.

Much curious and interesting information about "Parochial Perambulations in Rogation week," comprising an account of harmless customs still kept in some places as well as of old superstitions and abuses, is given in Sir Henry Ellis' edition of Brand's *Popular Antiquities*, I, 116–124. One of the superstitious practices is mentioned by Tyndale in his *Answer to Sir Thomas More*, p. 62, ed. Park Soc., "the saying of Gospels to the corn in the field in the Procession week, that it should the better grow:" and it is curious to observe that the "Sermon in the Crosse Dayes or Rogation Weke" among Taverner's *Postils*, pp. 278–282, ed. Cardwell, approves this practice as sure to be effectual, provided we "intreate and heare the word of God wyth deuoute and religiouse myndes."

Homily, in three Parts, was thereupon composed and set forth.

The writer has one peculiarity, which is scarcely found elsewhere in the volume. He often omits to mark the third person singular of a verb by the usual inflexion, writing "take," "consider," where others would use "taketh," "considereth [x]." This is found still more frequently in the first and separate edition, as is shewn in the Various Readings at the foot of the pages; for the printers gradually removed it, so that in successive editions of the Second Book it disappeared almost entirely. This peculiarity, the use of certain words, the obscurity of the style in some parts, and the devout earnestness and solemnity of the tone throughout, together lead me to believe that the author was Archbishop Parker [y]. But, whoever was the writer, we do not seem to have the composition exactly as it, or its different portions, stood at first. It seems to be made up from several sermons, written originally upon different texts. One such text is plainly Rom. XI, 16, cited in page 471, and again, near the end of the Homily, in page 492. Another, upon which much of the Third Part appears to have been founded, is Ephes. V, 15, 16. See note 6 on that Part.

II. The Exhortation to be used at the perambulation of boundaries, which is called the Fourth Part of the Homily, may possibly be by the same author, though it does not exhibit all the characteristics above mentioned. It was evidently written for the purpose to which it is addressed. It contains a few very rare words, chiefly concerning agriculture, which perhaps were even then provincial.

19. Of Matrimony. Half of this Homily is translated from a Hortatory Address of Veit Dietrich of Nuremberg, and half from a Homily of St. Chrysostom. See notes 1 and 8 upon it. Dietrich, otherwise called Theodor, was born at Nuremberg in

[x] See the item, "Verbs in the third person singular," in the article "Words" &c. in the General Index.

[y] The words, *brittle*, *casualty*, *contentation*, *expend*, *nurture*, *otherwhere*, *otherwhiles*, *sequester*, *stayed*, *in worth*, *self* for *selves*, which occur either frequently or in peculiar uses in the Homily are found similarly in the Archbishop's *Correspondence* before cited. The difficulty of his style must be felt by any one who reads the "Correspondence", and even at the time Bp. Sandys complained of his "sundry dark sentences, hard to scan forth." *Correspondence* of Abp. Parker, p. 124.

1507, studied at Wittemberg, where he won the esteem of Luther and Melancthon, became Pastor of St. Sebald's in his native city, and died there so early as 1549[z]. He wrote Sermons for Children, "Kinder Postilla," on the Gospels for the Sundays and Holy Days throughout the year, a folio volume, which purports to have been printed at Nuremberg in 1556, though his Preface or Dedication is dated ten years earlier; and several single sermons and tracts by him are also extant. His great celebrity as a preacher is recorded by Joachim Camerarius the elder in his Life of Melancthon, pp. 256, 257, ed. 1655.

20. Against Idleness. Perhaps by Jewel. There is not indeed much in the Homily that is characteristic: but the blended quotation from St. Bernard and Peter of Blois in page 519, (where see note 4), was doubtless taken from some Florilegium; and most of the quotations concerning pride in the Homily for Whitsunday (n°. 17) in page 465, together with the numerous epithets of the Spirit in page 468, are to be found in several such Collections[a].

21. Of Repentance. Two thirds of the First Part of this Homily are translated from Rodolph Gualther. See note 1 upon it. Instead of "since" used argumentatively the writer has "sith that." This occurs nine times in this Homily, but nowhere else throughout the volume.

22. Against Rebellion. This was not in the Second Book as first published. It was occasioned by the Rising in the North, which began in November 1569, and came to an end before the ensuing Christmas[b]; and it was no doubt written and set forth

[z] See Zedler's *Universal Lexicon*, XLIII, 743.

[a] To suppose that Jewel was content to make quotations at second hand in a book intended for popular use and printed without his name is no disparagement either to his learning or his industry. His studied and acknowledged works give most ample proof of both. It was the custom of the time, and it has been common enough in all times since, to rely too much on published books. If a person familiar with Bullinger's treatise "De Origine Erroris" examines Cranmer's Common Place Book, he may follow him in his perusal of that work by the patristic extracts which he has transcribed from it; but the remainder of the two large volumes, and the Notes on Justification preserved at Lambeth, give abundant evidence that Cranmer was very well acquainted with the actual writings of the Fathers.

[b] Some information concerning the Rebellion is furnished in the notes at pp. 559, 570, 581, 582, 594. But there is a letter from Bishop Jewel to Bullinger, dated "7 Augusti, 1570", which touches so many points in the Homily,

in the early part of 1570. Five editions of it at the least were published separately[c], till in 1571 it was counted as the last Homily in the Second Book by the Convocation which then ratified the Thirty-nine Articles, and thenceforward it was printed in that volume accordingly.

4. OF THIS EDITION.

It only remains to give some account of what has been done in the present volume.

Text. The eminent scholar who prepared the Oxford edition of 1822, the earliest critical edition of the Homilies, formed his text "for the most part on the principle of adhering to the last recension published by public authority, that is to say, to the edition of 1623," thinking that it "was not only reprinted, as stated in the title-page, but also revised by authority of the crown," and that it "has some claim to be considered as the standard text" inasmuch "as no later recension has ever been made by public authority:" but he was well aware of "the numerous errors of every sort by which that edition is defiled,"

that I think it well to give some extracts from it here.

"Quod vulgo apud vos obscuris rumoribus ferebatur de mutatione status nostri, nihil erat. ... Duo quidem comites nostrates, et juvenes, et fatui, et obaerati, et perditi, quibus alea magis quam religio curae esset, sub extremum autumnum in ultimis Angliae finibus aliquot millia rusticorum conscripserunt. Ea freti multitudine, edicta etiam ausi sunt publicare homines levissimi, velle se nescio quos (neque enim quenquam nominabant) e sacro reginae senatu submovere, et avitam religionem constituere. Quid quaeris? Non mora: excitantur in castris altaria: comburuntur sacra biblia: dicuntur missae. Post aliquot hebdomadas mittitur in illos comes Sussexius, vir bonus et strenuus et magni consilii, cum exigua manu. Illi se paulatim recipere et retro cedere. Sussexius insequi prudenter atque acriter, et urgere cedentes. Ad extremum miseri, cum hostes infestis signis sibi viderent imminere, homines imperiti rerum, qui hostem nunquam prius viderant, non ausi experiri fortunam belli, perculsi conscientia sceleris, amentes et caeci, destituunt exercitum sine duce, et relictis castris clam noctu cum paucis profugiunt in Scotiam. Habes historiam nostrarum rerum ....

"Omnes istas turbas nobis dedit sanctissimus pater. Is enim pro sua sanctitate et sapientia submiserat in Angliam ad suos bullam (aureamne dicam an plumbeam?) magni ponderis. Ea menses aliquot inter paucos obscure ferebatur. Significabat videlicet bonus pater, Elizabetham reginam Angliae non esse; sibi enim illius instituta non placere; itaque mandare se, ne quis illam agnoscat principem, neve illi obtemperet imperanti; qui secus fecerit, illum se omnibus diris devovere atque exitio dedere .... Mitto ad te exemplar illius putidissimae atque inanissimae bullae, ut intelligas quam illa bestia solenniter hoc tempore atque impudenter insaniat."

[c] They are described in the Catalogue which follows.

and that "the early editions of Queen Elizabeth's recension exhibit a much better text;" nay, he even printed the Homily against Rebellion from what he believed to be the first edition of it, and intimated his opinion that a future editor might perhaps think it "advisable to restore the text of Queen Elizabeth throughout the whole volume with the exception of some particular expressions [d]." Had he but known how very many editions earlier than 1623 are still extant, and observed how each, with scarcely an exception, is a reprint from its immediate predecessor, but introduces deviations, evidently arbitrary, which are mostly repeated and perpetuated by those which succeeded it, that opinion of his would certainly have been confirmed. Take one of the earliest editions, and compare it with the edition of 1623, and you will find so many differences, that, knowing the latter to have had some changes made in it by authority, you will be inclined to ascribe the same authority to all. If however you trace these variations through the intermediate editions, and notice how many of them, not fewer than thirty on an average, originate in each, and that not one of all the editions exhibits the accuracy and regularity which betoken the care bestowed by a good editor of the present day, you will see that far the largest number of their differences must be referred either to the negligence or the wilfulness of the printers [e], and that the earliest edition of all is likely to give the purest text.

It is upon this principle, and in accordance with Dr. Elmsley's opinion above recorded, that the text of this edition has been formed. Adhering slavishly to no single edition, it is yet based upon the earliest of each portion of the volume. In the First Book indeed Cranmer himself admitted so great a change in 1549 by dividing the several Homilies into Parts, and the revision at the beginning of Elizabeth's reign altered so many words and phrases throughout, that it has not been thought right to print it from the first, nor even from any Edwardian, edition. The text of 1559 therefore, the earliest known Elizabethan text,

[d] *Advertisement* prefixed to the edition of 1822.

[e] Upwards of thirty variations have been caused by injudicious attempts to correct errors made in previous editions, such as the following:

p. 17,l.23. were; wer; we; be.
215,l. 9. a finite; an infinite; a small.
298,l.18. sweating; swearing; swilling.
561,l.12. region; religion; realm.

has been followed, except in two respects. On the one hand an endeavour has been made by means of the earliest editions to get rid of the many unauthorised changes which had crept into the successive editions of King Edward's time, and which were not removed in 1559; and on the other hand later editions of Queen Elizabeth have been followed in omitting the changes in the First Part of the Homily of the Fear of Death, which were not retained after 1559, and in substituting "governor" for "head" as the title of the Sovereign in the First Part of the Homily of Obedience[f]. The bulk of the Second Book has been reprinted from the first edition, except where the second supplies a word or two which seem to have been added by authority, and where the previous edition of the Homily for Rogation Week gives a manifestly better text[g]. Of the Homily against Rebellion the second edition has been followed, as being the first which exhibits it in six Parts; but here also a small addition has been admitted from the third[h]. It must be observed however that throughout the volume erroneous readings have been set right wherever any later edition, as far down as the year 1623, has been found to correct them, and that some also have been amended upon other authority than that of actual editions of the Homilies, and two or three upon no external authority at all[i].

[f] The words which were added by way of explanation in 1559 are placed within ( ), thus, "under pretence (or colour)", "admit (or receive)", p. 60, ll. 20, 23. I should have been glad to omit them altogether.

[g] See page 357, note a; page 490, note k; page 491, note x.

[h] See page 596, note g.

[i] In p. 118 a marginal abstract is supplied from Becon's edition of his collected Works, and another in p. 127. In p. 190, l. 26, "error" is printed for "errors" in accordance with the passage of St. Jerome there cited, as well as with the context; and in a similar way the words "are reckoned" are supplied in p. 527, l. 32, as the rendering of "censentur" in the passage there translated from Gualther. In p. 280, l. 29, "through" is printed for "though", and in p. 397, l. 3, "it is not more hard" for "it is more hard", on the authority of Abp. Whitgift's Selection of Homilies put forth in 1586 together with a Form of Prayer for use in the Diocese of Canterbury; the latter correction being also found in his own handwriting in the copy of the second edition of the Second Book at Lambeth. And in p. 581, l. 32, "printed" is restored for "painted" from the very first edition of the Homily against Rebellion.

For omitting "if" before "we shall heap" in p. 136, l. 38, and "as" before "they first came" in p. 246, l. 32, there is no ancient authority to vouch, but the former change has been made by Dr. Corrie. In p. 186, l. 35, "born" is

In thus recovering the text the editor has had to use a discretion, of which he does not flatter himself that every exercise will be approved by every reader. But he has used it honestly, with no bias, not seeking to produce such sense or such English as he might himself think best, but only wishing and trying to determine the true reading in every instance by the actual evidence before him, "neque id reponere quod scribere debuerat auctor, sed quod scripsit[j]." The more he considers the principle on which he has been working, the more strongly he is convinced of its soundness; and he ventures to think that on the whole he has succeeded in putting together a more genuine text, nearer to the words actually written by the authors of the several Homilies or by the authorised editors and revisers of them[k], than is contained in any other edition whatever, not excepting the very earliest.

The authorities upon which it is constructed may be gathered from the Various Readings given at the foot of each page. To these reference is made in the text by the letters of the small alphabet. They are intended to exhibit, and no pains have been spared in the attempt to make them exhibit faithfully, the entire succession of changes in the text to the end of the reign of James I. For this purpose they supply a complete collation of Various Readings.

omitted, as in the actual text of the first edition, although the Corrections at the end of it direct that the word shall be inserted, and although it has been printed in every subsequent edition accordingly; for it is plain that the words "of a Jew" there are equivalent to "from being a Jew", or, as we should now say, "from Judaism". It is no wonder that strange uses of the word "of" perplex modern readers, as in our Lord's precept that we should *make to ourselves friends of the mammon of unrighteousness*, Luke xvi, 9, or in David's entreaty, *Hold not thy tongue, O God, of my praise*, Ps. cix, 1, *Deus, laudem meam ne tacueris*, Vulg., printed in all our Prayer Books since 1632 *O God of my praise* with *Deus laudum* at the head of the Psalm; but it is curious to see a critic of that time destroying the sense of a passage because he did not understand it himself.

[j] Wyttenbach, *Praefat. ad Plutarch. Moral.* IV.

[k] Some may think that Dr. Elmsley's opinion ought to have been closely followed throughout, and that it would have been better to alter "some particular expressions" in accordance with the edition of 1623, adopting the revision of that year as well as the one made in 1559. But it must be observed, not only that we have the Homilies upon the authority of Queen Elizabeth rather than of King James I, but also that that edition is so full of errors, many of them errors of omission, that it really is not possible to determine with certainty which of the changes in it were intended by the editor and which are due to the carelessness of the printer.

the edition of 1623 at one end of the period and of the first edition of every portion of the volume at the other, and intermediately between the two extreme points they specify the particular edition in which each variation is first found. They also give a complete collation of the first Elizabethan edition of the First Book, printed in 1559, of the Homilies for Good Friday and for Easter Day from that edition of Taverner's Postils which was reprinted at the University Press in 1841, of the first edition of the Homily for Rogation Week or rather of the first three Parts of it (so called), and of the second edition (which indeed may be considered practically as the first) of the Homily against Rebellion[1]. But they do not, except in a very few instances, shew such variations as were merely transient, being found in only a few editions, and disappearing before the close of the period in question: that would have required a verbatim collation of every edition, an amount of labour from which no adequate benefit seemed likely to result. And they contain no collation whatever of any edition later than the year 1623.

Great pains have been taken to state the variations clearly, but it may be well to say here, for example, that a reading specified as "*from* 1547 G 6" is found for the first time in Grafton's sixth edition of the First Book, and is continued in all editions afterwards, and that a reading said to be "*till* 1547 G 6" is found in Grafton's first five editions, but not in his sixth nor in any one later. Only those expressions must not be understood to comprise any of Whitchurch's editions of the First Book in 1547, nor Grafton's edition of it in 1551, nor either of the octavo editions, nor the editions of both Books printed in 1587 and 1595. These editions were not followed by those which came after them; they contribute nothing to the succession of the text; a full collation of them therefore would only encumber the page, and the reader is not to suppose them to be included any where unless they are expressly named.

Among the Various Readings will be found a few notes on matters otherwise concerning the text. Of some words or phrases, which are either ungrammatical or in any respect such

[1] The editions of which a complete collation is given are precisely indicated in the "List of the Copies used for this Edition" which is subjoined to this Preface.

that a reader might reasonably suspect them to be errors of this edition, I have thought fit to state that they are "*so in all*" the editions collated. I have said the same of a few other words, which do not appear to me to be genuine, though found in all editions; and in some few cases of this kind I have ventured to go further, and to suggest the word which perhaps the author wrote.

Paragraphs. Punctuation.

The ancient editions will not serve as guides in the division of the text into Paragraphs, nor in the Punctuation. Very few of them agree with each other in these particulars; none is even consistent with itself; and none appears to represent the mind of the several authors. Liberty has therefore been taken to arrange these throughout in the way that seemed best for the argument and the sense, and it is hoped that several places which have been difficult or even unmeaning will now be found clear and effective.

Italic character.

The Italic character in the text is strictly confined to quotations from Scripture. It has been used in preference to inverted commas, partly in compliance with old custom, but chiefly because the commas are commonly understood to mark quotations made verbatim without alteration of any kind, whereas the Italic character serves to indicate the whole extent of an adopted passage, even when some slight change has been made in its form to fit it to the sentence into which it is woven.

Spelling.

In reprinting any book so old as the Homilies it is confessedly a difficult matter to determine how far the antique modes of spelling shall be retained and how far they may be altered to the modern fashion, and I fear that in this volume they have not been treated from first to last with exact uniformity. Upon the whole the rule followed is nearly this, to disregard the final e, the interchange of i and y, and such other little things as belong to the spelling only, and do not affect the sense or the etymology of words[m], but to retain scrupulously every

[m] The following words, which have been made modern in the text, are given here, because some persons may doubt whether I have done right in altering them all. Several of them occur in the old editions in their modern form. *accompt, accompted, compted; auctority, aucthority; capitayne; christen* for *christian*, especially in the plural number; *commeth*, &c.; *counterfaict* for *counterfeit; crepe* for *creep; crouch* for *crutch; damosel; elles* for *else; emperial; errour; falshed; farder* for *further; furth* for *forth; geve, forgeve*, &c.; *hable, ha-*

ancient form and likewise every particular of orthography by which the meaning of a word may be more clearly seen or its derivation better traced. Many of these old forms are only found in the earliest editions, having passed out of use long before the end of the reign of James I. They have been restored to the text in this edition, not from any mere love of archaisms, but from the conviction that they will tend to refute the very common opinion that the Second Book was all written by one author, Bishop Jewel, and in the hope that they may even help some student by and by to discover some of the other writers[n]. The form "mought," for example, occurs four times in the Homily concerning Certain Places in Scripture and only once besides; we find "sith that" nine times in the Homily of Repentance, but no where else: shall we attribute this to the caprice of the printers, or rather to the peculiar usage of the several authors?

These archaisms are included in the article, "Words obsolete or rare in form, meaning, or construction," in the General Index; an article, which persons who are well acquainted with the progress of our language may think needlessly copious, but which may perhaps lead some readers to consider how greatly

bility; hole for *whole, holsomely; hundreth* for *hundred; intertained; lenger* for *longer; maister* and *mayster* for *master; marchaunt, marchaundise; mary* for *marrow; middest; moneth; obreyde, obreydeth,* for *upbraid; onless; perfite* and *perfitte* for *perfect; person* for *parson; querels* for *quarrels, quereled; raunsome; reken* for *reckon; rendre, suffre,* &c.; *slea* for *slay; sterres* for *stars; then* for *than; venime* for *venom.* The old editions always have *drawen, knowen,* &c. for *drawn, known,* &c., and in some places *doen* for *done.*

I have adopted the modern distinction between *divers* and *diverse,* between *doth* and *doeth,* between *travail* and *travel,* between *altogether* and *all together.* The old editions most commonly have *al* for *all,* and it is sometimes difficult to settle this last distinction; but in the only passage in which it is of serious importance, a passage affecting essentially the doctrine of Justification, p. 26, l. 29, several of the earliest editions rightly have "all together".

[n] It is for this reason that in words which really begin with the Latin prepositive "in", but which in English have been spelt with i or with e according as the writers took them directly from the Latin or mediately through the French, I have generally printed that form (whether "increase" or "encrease", for example) which I found in the earliest edition. But I have now come to the conclusion that I need not have been so particular, that, even if the several writers observed any certain rule, the printers have from the first neglected it, and that the modern usage in all such words may as well be adopted in future editions.

the usage and signification of even the commonest words become changed in lapse of time[o].

Great pains were taken with the Marginal References to Scripture in the Oxford edition of 1840, and much was then accomplished in the way both of verifying them and of making them complete by the addition of the verses; but without the help of the earliest editions and the use of the Vulgate translation it was impossible to set them right. Even in the first editions there are errors, not all owing to the printers' carelessness[p]; every edition in its turn added to their number; and the difficulty of correcting them was at the same time increased by their being allowed to slip to points in the margin away from the words to which they belong, so that at length in several instances the reference and the quotation stood on different pages. They have now been revised throughout; and it is hoped that here also, as well as in the text, the intentions of the writers are better represented than they have ever been before. And care has been taken to lessen the risk of error in future editions by using the letters of the small Greek alphabet to direct the reader to the right reference in the margin wherever the number or the uncertainty of quotations seemed likely to cause any mistake. It has not however been thought desirable to print the references exactly as they stand in the early editions, with the names of the different books taken from the Vulgate, 1 Regum for 1 Samuel, Paralipomena for Chronicles, Sapientia for Wisdom, and the like; but the usage of modern editors has been followed, and the convenience of modern readers consulted, by adopting the titles of the books from our Authorised Version. A few undoubted errors also have been tacitly corrected, but in all other respects they are given with scrupulous fidelity, hooks [ ] being used to shew that the numbers of the verses, the Hebrew numeration of the Psalms wherever they are cited according to the Vulgate reckoning, many additional

Marginal References.

o One item in that article is "his = its". The word "its" was not invented even when our Authorised Translation of the Bible was made under James I; but a passage in p. 289, l. 14, "the thing, which of the own nature is indifferent", with the various reading, "of it own nature", shews curiously how the want of it was felt half a century before.

p See for instance p. 529, n. 8.

references[q], and a few remarks besides, are matter for which the editor alone is responsible.

With other notes or references in the margin no liberty whatever has been assumed: all are printed just as the early editions give them.

Notes. The Notes at the foot of pages, to which reference is made in the text by means of Arabic numerals, are not included within hooks, inasmuch as there is no mixture of matter among them, and it seemed to be better to state here once for all that they are wholly supplied by the editor. The largest portion of them consists of the original Latin or Greek of passages cited in the Homilies from the Fathers and other writers; and in this part of my work I have been much helped by the Cambridge edition of 1850, the only one hitherto in which such passages have been given. Yet I have nowhere rested upon that or any other compilation; I have examined every passage for myself in the original authors; and it will be seen that I do not in all places acquiesce in the selection made by the learned editor. The labour has not been perfectly successful: one passage cited as "St. Augustine's words," with "In Epist. ad Julianum Comitem 30" in the margin, p. 538, l. 15, has baffled all research; the marginal reference "Chrysostom" in p. 165 is very unsatisfactorily answered in note 8 there; and the import of "Dialogorum Lib. iii" in the margin of p. 465 has not been discovered[r]. No one who has had experience in similar work will be surprised at these failures; and any reader who observes how the Fathers and other writers are quoted, often by name only, and seldom with precise reference, will be ready to make allowance for the difficulty of the task. It is but by a happy accident that a sentence cited in p. 144, l. 11, as "that which is written" has been found, not in the Bible, but in the Decretum, extracted by Gratian from a Sermon of St. Augustine.

[q] In the Homilies for Good Friday and Easter Day I have supplied from Taverner's Postils several references which are omitted in all editions of the Homilies, but I have not thought it necessary to place these within hooks.

[r] I suspect the explanation of this last reference is to be found in the fact that all the quotations in p. 465 were taken at second hand from some Florilegium or other book which contained also a quotation from the Dialogues ascribed to Pope Gregory the Great, and that the reference was transcribed although the quotation was rejected. See before, page xxxvii, no. 20.

Similar to these are the notes in which short extracts are given from the Vulgate. That is the form in which all the writers of the Homilies best knew the Bible, and from which most of them appear to have made their quotations, translating it on each occasion for themselves[s]. Well educated persons continued to be familiar with it down to the time of Lord Bacon or later, but the New Translation of King James displaced it gradually, and to members of the Church of England it is now almost wholly unknown. This in fact is the chief obstacle to the frequent use of the Homilies in our churches, and a clergyman intending to read any of them publicly would do well to put the quotations from Scripture into language with which his people are familiar, the language of the Authorised Version. Wherever I have noticed a discrepancy between that Version and the quotations given in the Homilies, and have been able to trace it to the Vulgate, I have subjoined the extract from this in a foot note, with the double object of justifying the Homilist and helping the reader to follow him[t]. Quotations from the Greek of the New Testament are also given in a few places where it seemed expedient to supply them.

There are a few notes in which some explanation is attempted of obsolete and very rare words, and a very few which give some account of such obsolete ceremonies and customs as are mentioned or alluded to in the Homilies. Others again, not many in number, are concerned with historical statements, correcting in some instances certain errors in matters of fact, most of which were discovered very many years ago, and none of which have ever been thought by unprejudiced minds to impair the usefulness of the volume, or to falsify the character given of it in the thirty-fourth Article. But there are none which deal with doctrine. Although I have felt it my duty to furnish the reader with means for guarding against false interpretations of Scripture, and to obviate mistakes in history by placing before him statements drawn from authentic sources, I have judged it better, if there be any enunciations of doctrine which seem to

[s] This will account for the misapprehension of several passages of Scripture, for example, of Matth. vi, 33, repeatedly.

[t] The edition from which I have made my quotations is one of the Louvain recension, put forth "ex officina Christophori Plantini" at Antwerp in 1565.

him incautiously or inadequately uttered, that he should try such passages for himself by the test to which the Homilies from first to last appeal, the written word of God.

It is no new thing, in bringing a literary undertaking to a close, to have to acknowledge much ready assistance, given not only by personal friends, but also by many with whom the author or editor had previously little or no acquaintance. I have received this in many departments of my work. But the greatest help, the most essential service, has been rendered by those who have liberally trusted me with copies of rare editions from their respective libraries, His Grace the Lord Archbishop of Canterbury, the Societies of Exeter, Corpus Christi, and Wadham Colleges in Oxford, the Master and Senior Fellows of St. John's College in Cambridge, the Reverend Dr. Cardwell, the Reverend Dr. Corrie, who edited the Cambridge edition and has furthered this in various ways, the late Reverend Dr. Bliss, the late Reverend Robert Riland Mendham, and his cousin and heir the Reverend John Mendham. For it would not have been possible to make a sufficient examination of the various editions, in order to a true restoration of the text, without bringing together a much larger number of copies than is yet to be found in any single library, nor without having many of them at hand for use from the beginning to the end of the undertaking. To all these therefore I am bound to express my gratitude, and glad to avow my obligations. Yet I do not doubt but they would think themselves best rewarded, if the volume to which they have thus lent their aid should help at all towards the object which I have kept in view throughout the labour of preparing it, the furthering of the glory of God by setting in clearer light the agreement of the Church of England with the Gospel of our Blessed Lord and Saviour.

JOHN GRIFFITHS.

ST. GILES', OXFORD,
March 19, 1859.

A DESCRIPTIVE CATALOGUE

OF EDITIONS OF THE HOMILIES

TO THE END OF THE SEVENTEENTH CENTURY.

---

1. I count a distinct *edition*, when the bulk of a book has been set up in type afresh, although a few pages, or even a sheet or two, of the former edition may have been kept standing. By the term, distinct *impression*, I mean that the bulk of the book remains the same, although a few pages, or even a sheet or two, may have been set up afresh either with or without alterations.

2. For the *recto* and *verso* of a leaf I use the letters *a* and *b*.

3. Under each edition within the sixteenth century I have set down the Public Libraries (including those of corporate bodies) in which it may be seen, but I have not thought it right to specify such copies as I have found in private hands. There is no edition earlier than 1623 of which I know so many as ten copies, and there are very few of which I know so many as five.

4. Every edition before the year 1683 is printed in Black Letter.

THE FIRST BOOK SEPARATELY.

1547 G 1. FIRST EDITION. GRAFTON. QUARTO.

Title: "Certain | Sermons, or Homi | lies, appoynted by the | Kynges Maiestie, to be | declared and redde, by all | Persones, Uicars, or | Curates, euery Sō | day in their Chur | ches, where thei | haue Cure. | Anno. 1547." "Anno" in Roman Capitals, the rest in Black Letter. The figure of a Leaf stands before "Certain" in the same line, and a Maltese Cross between two Leaves forms a line immediately below "have Cure." Forming each side of the Title-frame is a terminal horned figure with foliage and carved work, a male figure on the right or outer side, a female on the left.

Collation. In all 26½ sheets, the first having for signature a Maltese Cross, the next 5½ a Leaf, the remaining 20 A–U of the large alphabet. No pagination. The back of the Title is blank, the Preface is on the third, fourth, and fifth pages, the Table on the sixth, Grafton's large rebus with "Incitum" in the legend on the seventh, and the eighth is blank. The second signature comprises six leaves, and just contains the first Homily: the odd half sheet in it is not an inset, but follows the entire sheet. The sixth signature has its last three pages blank. The Homily of Faith begins on the first page of the seventh signature, A 1.

Colophon on U 4 *a*: "Imprynted at London, | the laste daye of Iulii, in the fyrste yere | of the reigne of our souereigne lord | Kynge Edward the. VI: By | Rychard Grafton Printer | to his moste royall | Maiestie. | In the yere of our Lord. | M.D.XLVII. | Cum priuilegio ad impri | mendum solum." The first line Black Letter, the rest Italic. A Sinister Hand inverted begins the first line, a Leaf begins the last but one. On U 4 *b* is Grafton's rebus, as before.

This edition contains on O 4, towards the end of the Homily of Obedience, a passage, about a page in length, "Our sauior Christ—— to cherishe well doers," which is found in no other. See page 115, note k, of this volume.

Where. There is a beautiful copy at *Oxford* in the *Bodleian Library*, "4°. I. 6. Th. Seld.," in the original contemporary binding, with the "Injunctions" of Edward VI*, which came from Grafton's press on the

* It seems to have been a common thing to bind these Injunctions (and the King's Visitation Articles as soon as they were published, see the next note) with the Homilies, whether of Grafton's or of Whitchurch's editions; and, as the Injunctions came first in the volume, their colophon has often been preserved when the colophon of the Homilies has been lost. The

same day; and another in the Library of *Corpus Christi College*, likewise in the original binding, from which something, probably the "Injunctions," has been cut away.

1547 G 2. GRAFTON'S SECOND EDITION. QUARTO.

Title and Title-frame the very same as in G 1.

Collation. In all 26 sheets, or 25 entire with a half sheet at either end, the first half sheet having for signature a Maltese Cross, the 25 sheets A–Bb, the final half sheet Cc. No pagination. The Preface begins on the back of the Title, and occupies the next two pages also. The first Homily begins on the first page of A 1. The Table is on Cc 2 *a*; and the Colophon, which is the very same as in G 1, is on Cc 2 *b*.

This edition differs in many places from G 1; for example, the words "wrought in faith" were now inserted in the last sentence of the Homily of Good Works. But the revision seems to have been made hastily. Indeed it would appear that the order to omit from the Homily of Obedience the passage, "Our sauior Christ" &c., was given while this edition was passing through the press, and even after the next Homily, or at least the first sheet of it, was printed off. For the last few lines of the Homily of Obedience are spread by a strange display over U 3 *a* so as to leave a few words only (from "for us all") to come at the top of U 3 *b*, and then U 4 *a* (a right hand page) is blank, and the Homily against Adultery begins on U 4 *b*, a left hand page, such as it begins upon in G 1. Hence it may be inferred that this edition and Whitchurch's first were passing through the press about the same time, but that this was the earlier of the two, and was published about or soon after the middle of August. For Whitchurch follows G 1, not this edition, as he surely would have done if it had appeared before he began to print. And he follows G 1 page for page till near that omitted passage, when he begins to prepare for its omission and for saving half a sheet in consequence, shewing clearly that the order to leave it out reached him before he came to the place. See below, 1547 W 1.

Where. *Cambridge: University Library*, with the King's Injunctions.

1547 G 3. GRAFTON'S THIRD KNOWN EDITION. QUARTO.

Title: "Certayne | Sermons, or Homi | lies, appoynted by the kyn | ges Maiestie, to bee decla |*red and redde, by all per | sones, Uicars, or

words of the two colophons are nearly the same, but they differ in *type*. In all editions of the Injunctions Grafton printed the colophon in small Roman Capitals; but in all his editions of the Homilies he used the Italic character, except for the first line, which he put in Black Letter.

Cu | rates, euery Son | daye in their | churches, | where | thei haue | cure. | Anno 1547." "Certayne" in Italic Capitals, "Anno" Roman, the rest in Black Letter. Title-frame architectural, consisting of a square column on each side, each having a riband and a tablet with projecting ends, an architrave with one head in the centre, and a base with three heads on it.

Collation. In all 23 sheets, A–Z. No pagination. The Table is on the back of the Title, the Preface occupies the next three pages, and the first Homily begins on the sixth page. The headings of the pages are in Roman Capitals, as also in G 4.

Colophon on Z 4 *a*: "Imprinted at London, | the laste daie of Iulii, in the firste yere | of the reigne of our souereigne | lorde kyng Edward the . VI: | By Rychard Grafton | printer to his moste | royall Ma | iestie. | In the yere of our Lorde. | M.D.XLVII. | Cum priuilegio ad impri | mendum solum." The first line begins with a Half Moon and is in Black Letter, the rest Italic. On Z 4 *b* is Grafton's large rebus with "Incitum."

Before this edition was printed the text had been revised throughout, and many verbal changes were made.

Where. *British Museum*, "C. 25. g. 5." *Cambridge: C. C. C.*, Archbishop Parker's copy, in the original parchment wrapper, with the King's Injunctions and Visitation Articles* prefixed.

1547 G 4. GRAFTON'S FOURTH KNOWN EDITION. QUARTO.

Title, Collation, Colophon, and final page, all as in G 3, except these words in the Title, "Homelies †," "Uicares," "they."

Where. *British Museum*, "T. 1033"/1, wanting the final leaf. *Sion College. Norwich Cathedral.*

1547 G 5. GRAFTON'S FIFTH KNOWN EDITION. QUARTO.

Title, Collation, and Colophon as in G 3, except these words in the

* King Edward's Visitation Articles were printed by Grafton without date. It seems to have been a common thing to bind them between the Injunctions and the Homilies, and hence we get some evidence to shew that at any rate they were not issued till near the end of August 1547. For no known copy of Grafton's first or second editions of the Homilies or of Whitchurch's first edition seems to have been bound with them: those editions are found with the Injunctions only, and in one copy of Whitchurch's edition (British Museum, "697. f. 1") the ink of the Title of the Homilies has come off upon the last page of the Injunctions, shewing plainly that they were bound together wet from the press with nothing between them. Archbishop Parker's copy of the Homilies is the earliest in which the Visitation Articles have been found.

† "Some call them Homelies," says Latimer, adding, "and indeed so they may well be called, for they are homely handled" [by the bad reading of the clergyman or the "talking' and babbling" of the congregation]. Second Sermon before King Edward the Sixth, p. 121, ed. Park. Soc.

Title, "Homelies," "be," "they," "Cure," except also that the headings of the pages are in Black Letter, as they are in G 6 likewise. On the last page is the rebus with "Insitum."

Where. *British Museum*, "C. 25. g. 6," with a final leaf belonging to the Injunctions, not to any edition of the Homilies. *Oxford: Bodl.*, "4°. P. 16. Th. Seld.," imperfect.

1547 G 6. Grafton's sixth known edition. Quarto.

Title, Collation, Colophon, and final page, all precisely as in G 5, from which edition this can only be distinguished by variations in the text. Some of those variations will be mentioned immediately.

Where. *Lincoln Cathedral.* In the British Museum is a volume, "C. 25. h. 2," which consists of 9 sheets from G 4 with the headings of the pages in Roman Capitals, and 14 sheets from this G 6 with the headings in Black Letter. The condition of the volume is such as to make one think it was so made up from the waste of the two editions by Grafton himself.

That the four editions G 3–6 are later than G 2 is clear from the compression of them into smaller bulk, and from the revision of the text in them throughout, of which one instance may here suffice. The two versions of the quotation from St. Basil, near the beginning of the Second Part of the Homily of Salvation (see page 28, note o, in this volume), which were carelessly allowed to remain together in G 1, remain also in G 2, but the second only is retained in these and all later editions.

The order of the four among themselves is determined by the succession of variations in the text, as may be seen in a few specimens:

Page and line in edd. 1547 G 3–6 and 1548.				
A 3 *b*, 8 *up*.	savor G 1–5,	favor G 6, &c.		
B 2 *a*, 1 *or* 2.	an (*before* astronomer) G 1–4,	and G 5 *and* 6, &c.		
C 2 *a*, 5.	were G 1,	wer G 3–5,	we G 6,	be 1548, &c.
C 3 *b*, 6.	forgiveness G 1–5,	righteousness G 6, &c.		
D 4 *b*, 8 *or* 9 *up*.	justified in the law G 1–4,	justified by the law G 5 *and* 6, &c.		
E 1 *b*, 7 *up*.	thereby G 1–5,	therefore G 6, &c.		
F 2 *a*, 7.	hereof G 1–3,	thereof G 4–6, &c.		
P 3 *b*, 3 *up*.	chasten G 1–4,	chastise G 5 *and* 6, &c.		
Q 2 *a*, 20.	believeth him G 1–3,	believeth on him G 4–6, &c.		
Q 2 *b*, 2.	righteous G 1–3,	righteousness G 4–6,	righteous 1548, &c.	

1547 W 1. Whitchurch's first edition. Quarto.

Title: "Certayne | Sermons, or Homi | lies, appoynted by the | Kynges Maiestie, to be | declared and redde, by all | Persones, Uycars, or | Curates, euery Sō | day in their Chur | ches, where they | haue Cure. | Anno, 1547." "Certayne" Roman, "Anno" Roman Capitals, the rest Black Letter. The figure of a Leaf erect stands by itself immediately below "haue Cure." Title-frame architectural, having a column on each side, a sun on the architrave above, and on the base two Cupids seated supporting a tablet on which is Whitchurch's monogram.

Collation. In all 26 sheets, 25 entire and 2 halves, the first sheet having for signature a Maltese Cross, the next 5½ a Half Moon, the remaining 19½ (of which the half sheet comes last) A–U of the large alphabet. No pagination. The Table is on the back of the Title, with "Finis" at the end of it in Roman Capitals; the Preface is on the third, fourth, and fifth pages; a list of "Faultes escaped" (20 in number) is on the sixth and seventh; and the eighth is blank. The second signature has six leaves, and just contains the first Homily: the odd half sheet in it is not an inset, but follows the entire sheet. The sixth signature has its last three pages blank. The Homily of Faith begins on the first page of the seventh signature, "A 1."

Colophon on U 2 *b*: "Imprinted | at London, in Flete strete, | at the signe of the | Sunne, ouer agaynste | the Conduyte, | by Edwarde | Whit | churche, the . xx. daye of Au | gust, in the yeare of | oure Lorde. | 1547. | Cum priuilegio ad imprimen | dum solum." Lines 1, 4, 13, Roman; 2, 12, Italic; the rest, Black Letter. "Imprinted" has a Half Moon before it and a Leaf after it.

This edition is evidently printed from Grafton's first, which it follows closely in its Register. The saving of half a sheet at the end is made by the omission of the passage "Our sauior" &c. on O 4 and some compression afterwards. See before, 1547 G 2.

Three impressions of it are known.

The first, which is as described above, occurs in the *British Museum*, $\frac{\text{"697 . f . 1"}}{2}$, and at Oxford in *Exeter College* and *All Souls' College*.

In the second impression the beginning of the small alphabet, *a–e*, is used for the five signatures which follow the first, except that the Half Moon still remains on the odd half sheet after *a*; and about half the "Faultes" are corrected in the text, but not the same faults in all copies. It is found in the *British Museum*, $\frac{\text{"225 . a . 16"}}{2}$, and in *Abp. Tenison's Library*.

The third impression has the characteristics of the second, but the list of "Faultes escaped" does not appear in it, and it has the Table on the sixth page. The *Bodleian Library* contains a copy, "Tanner 216," wanting the Title and the fourth leaf, which no doubt was blank.

1547 W 2. WHITCHURCH'S SECOND KNOWN EDITION. QUARTO.

Title just as in W 1.

Collation. In all 25 sheets, the first without signature, then A–Bb omitting Z. No pagination. The Table is on the back of the Title, with "Finis" in Roman character, large, but not in Capitals; the Preface is on the next three pages; the sixth is blank; and the first Homily begins on the seventh page.

Colophon on Bb 4 *b*, the very same as in W 1.

In this edition the text throughout has been revised fully as much as in G 3–6, but it differs from them very frequently, and many of its readings seem to be in themselves the better of the two. This is especially the case in the Homilies of the Misery of Mankind, of Charity, and against Adultery, in which, where it varies from G 3–6, it usually agrees with Bonner's and Becon's own editions. And there is one place (see page 20, note p, of this volume) where that which is undoubtedly the true reading has been preserved in no edition of the Homilies but this and W 3, which was printed from this. Nevertheless none of these editions of Whitchurch in 1547 is concerned in the succession of the text, as will be stated under 1549 W.

Where. *Cambridge: University Library; Jesus College.*

1547 W 3. WHITCHURCH'S THIRD KNOWN EDITION. QUARTO.

Title just as in W 1 and 2, except the second line, which is "Sermons or homi-."

Collation and general description the same as in W 2.

Colophon on Bb 4 *b*: "Imprinted at | London, in Flete strete, | at the signe of the | Sunne, ouer agaynste | the Conduyte, | by Edwarde | Whit | churche, the . v . daye of No | uember, in the yeare of | oure Lord. | 1547. | Cum priuilegio ad imprimen | dum solum." Lines 1, 4, 13, Roman; 2, 12, Italic; the rest, Black Letter. The first line begins with a Half Moon.

This edition closely follows W 2, but is not so carefully printed.

Where. *Oxford: Exeter College.*

1548. GRAFTON. QUARTO.

Title as in 1547 G 5 and 6, except the date, which is "Anno. M.D.XLVIII." all in Roman Capitals. Title-frame as in 1547 G 3–6, except that the columns are changed over, producing an impossible perspective.

Collation and general description the same as in 1547 G 3–6.

Colophon also the same, except line 2, which is "the . xxi . daye of

Iune, in the seconde yere", and the date of the year, which is "M.D.XLVIII." On the last page is the rebus with "Insitum."

This edition closely follows 1547 G 6.

Where. *British Museum*, "C. 25. g," two copies, one perfect, the other wanting the final leaf. *Lambeth*. *Oxford: Exeter College*. *Durham: Dr. Routh's Library*.

1549 G. FIRST EDITION IN PARTS. GRAFTON. QUARTO.

Title: "Certayne | Sermons, or Home | lies, appointed by the kyn | ges Maiestie, to be decla | red and redde, by all per | sones, Uicars, or Cu | rates, euery Son | daye in their | churches, | wher | they haue | Cure | Newly imprinted and by | the Kynges highnes | aucthorite deuided. | Anno M.D.XLIX." The first and last lines in Roman Capitals, the rest in Black Letter. Title-frame as in 1547 G 3–6, except that the base has no heads upon it and does not fit the sides.

Collation. In all 24 sheets, A–Aa. No pagination. Table, Preface, &c., on the same pages as in 1547 G 3–6.

Colophon at the foot of Aa 3 *b*: "Excusum Londini, in ædibus Richardi Graftoni | Regii Impressoris. | Mense Augustij. M.D.xlix. | Cum priuilegio ad imprimendum solum." All Italic. On Aa 4 *a* is the rebus with "Insitum:" Aa 4 *b* in blank.

This edition seems to have been printed in haste and carelessly: see, for instance, the opening of the Third Part of the Homily of Salvation on E 3 *b*, given in page 32, note n, of this volume.

Where. *Oxford: Bodl.* "4°. C. 127. Th."; *C. C. C.*

1549 W. WHITCHURCH. QUARTO.

Title: "Certayne | sermõs appoynted by y^e | kinges Maiestie, to be | declared and reade, | by al persons, ui | cars or Cu | rates, euery Sonday and holy | daye in theyr Churches, | where they haue Cure: | Newely Imprinted in | partes, according as | is mẽcioned in the | boke of commõ | prayer. | An. D. 1549." "Certayne" Italic Capitals, "An. D." Italic, the rest Black Letter. Title-frame as in 1547 W 1–3.

Collation. In all 25 sheets, A–Bb. No pagination.

Colophon on Bb 3 *b*: "Imprinted at London | in Flete strete at the signe of the | Sunne, by Edwarde | Whitchurche. | Cum priuilegio ad imprimendum solum. | An. Do. 1549." Line 1, Roman; 2, 3, 4, Black Letter; 5, 6, Italic. Line 5 begins with a Half Moon. On Bb 4 *a* is a cut representing a scene from the Apocalypse, the woman crowned standing on the moon, &c., with these legends; on the left, "All fayre and whyte arte thou my Churche, and no spot is in thee.";

at the top, "*Thus sayeth the Lorde.*"; on the right, "*I haue hated the Malignaunt Congregacion.*"; all Italic. Bb 4 *b* is blank.

In this edition Whitchurch did not follow either of his own texts of 1547, but Grafton's of 1548 or 1549, introducing into it however many variations, which have remained to modern times. For it was this edition, or some later one by Whitchurch, not any one of Grafton's, which was followed in 1559.

Where. *Oxford : Bodl.*, "4°. N. 27. Jur."; *Christ Church*, imperfect. *Cambridge : St. John's College*, "Qq. 11. 12," wanting the last leaf.

1549. Oswen, at Worcester. Quarto.

Title, the same words as in 1549 W, in 19 lines, the last line in Italic Capitals, the rest in Black Letter. Between blocks of the Title-frame on either side is a legend from Mark xvi, 15, 16, in Italic character.

Collation. In all 25 sheets, A–Bb. No pagination.

Colophon on Bb 4 *a* : "Imprinted the | eyghte daye of October, | Anno. Do. M.D.XLIX. | At Worceter by | Ihon Oswen. | They be also to sell at Shrewesbury. | Cum priuilegio ad imprimendum solum." The third line Italic Capitals, the last Italic, the rest Black Letter. Bb 4 *b* is blank.

This edition closely follows 1549 W.

Where. *British Museum*, "C. 25. g."

1551. Grafton. Quarto.

Title : "Certain | Sermones, or Home | lies, appoincted by the kyn | ges Maiestie, to bee decla | red and read, by all Perso | nes, Uicars, or Cura | tes, euery Son | daie in their | churches, | where | thei haue | Cure. | Newly imprinted, and by | the kynges highnes au | cthoritee diuided. | Anno. 1551." "Anno" Italic, the rest Black Letter. A Half Moon before "Certain" and before "Newly."

Collation, Colophon, and final leaf, all as in 1549 G, except that the date in the Colophon is omitted.

In this edition Grafton followed his own text of 1549, not Whitchurch's ; and therefore, as Whitchurch, not Grafton, was followed in 1559, this edition is not concerned in the succession of the text.

Cambridge : St. John's College, "Qq. 11. 13," wanting the first two sheets. *Durham : Dr. Routh's Library*, wanting the final leaf and otherwise imperfect.

1552? Grafton. Octavo, pocket size.

Title, and therefore Date, not known.

Collation. In all 17 sheets, A–R. No pagination.

Colophon at the foot of R 8 *b*: "Excusum Londini, in ædibus Richar | di Graftoni Regii Impressoris. | Cum priuilegio ad imprimendum solum." All Italic.

This edition seems to follow the Quarto of 1551.

Where. *British Museum*, $\frac{\text{“}3932.\ \text{a,”}}{1}$ wanting Title and C 8.

1559. FIRST KNOWN EDITION UNDER QUEEN ELIZABETH. JUGGE AND CAWOOD. QUARTO.

Title: "¶ Certayne Sermons appoynted by | the Quenes Maiestie, | to be declared and read, | by all Persones, Uycars, and | Curates, euery Sonday and | holy daye, in theyr Churches: | And by her Graces aduyse | perused & ouersene, for | the better understan | dyng of the simple | people. | Newly Imprynted in partes, | accordyng as is menci | oned in the booke | of Commune | prayers. | (:) | Anno. M.D.Lix. | Cum priuilegio Regiæ | Maiestatis." Lines 1, 2, 19, 20, Italic; the rest Black Letter, lines 3–11 being in larger type than 12–18. The Title-frame is composed of four blocks of scroll foliage, the foot-block having in its centre "R. I." within a circle with "Omnia Desuper" as a motto round it.

Collation. In all 24 sheets, A–Aa. No pagination. The catchword at the end of sheet "R" is "kynges," as the text stood under Edward VI, whereas the first word of sheet "S" is "quenes," to suit the reign of Elizabeth. This curious error is continued in the quarto editions of 1562 and 1563, which successively followed this page for page.

Colophon on Aa 4 *a*: "Imprynted at London in Powles | Churchyarde by Richarde Iugge and | Iohn Cawood printers to the | Quenes Maiestie. | Cum priuilegio Regiæ Maiestatis." The first line Black Letter, the rest Italic. Aa 4 *b* is blank.

This edition was based upon 1549 W, or some later one of Whitchurch, not upon any one from Grafton's press. But many verbal changes were made in the text, partly by substitution, partly by addition, all intended, as the Title says, to make the language plainer. Probably they were made by different hands; and such as were introduced into the First Part of the Homily against the Fear of Death, many of which were unnecessary and some absurd, were afterwards struck out and are only found in this edition. This also is the only edition after the accession of Elizabeth in which the title, "supreme head over all," is retained in the Homily of Obedience for the Sovereign. See page 106, note r, of this volume.

There appear to have been several impressions or issues of it. I have examined four copies, and do not find one of them printed from the same fount of type throughout; and three of the four contain one sheet, "U," and one of them contains another, "Q," quite different from the corresponding sheets in the fourth copy, which I take to be the oldest *.

Where. *British Museum*, $\frac{\text{"C. 15. a. 16."}}{1}$

1562, 8vo. JUGGE AND CAWOOD. OCTAVO, POCKET SIZE.

Title in 17 lines, ending "M.D.LXII.": the first Roman, the rest Black Letter. The Title-frame has the royal arms with supporters at the top, terminal figures of a Fawn and a Nymph at the sides, and at foot within a circle a crowned figure holding what seems to be a sceptre in the right hand and two dogs by a leash with the left.

Collation. In all 17 sheets, A–R. No pagination.

Colophon at the foot of R 8 *b*: "Imprinted at London in Powles | Churchyarde, by Richard Iugge, and | Iohn Cawood Printers to the | Queenes Maiestyes. | Cum priuilegio Regiæ Maiestatis." Lines 1–4 Black Letter, 5 Roman.

From variations in the text it appears that this is earlier than either of the two Quarto editions, A and B, of the same year: of thirty-four places in which ed. 1559 differs from ed. 1562 A, this agrees in twenty-five with ed. 1559, and only in nine with ed. 1562 A. And this is the only edition after King Edward's reign which retains the sentence, "Let us look upon our feet" &c., at the end of the First Part of the Homily of the Misery of Man, which was first dropped in 1549 W. See page 20, note i, of this volume.

Where. *British Museum*, "695. a. 21."

1562 A. JUGGE AND CAWOOD? QUARTO.

Title in 15 lines, ending "Anno M.D.LXII.": lines 1–3 Roman, 4–14 Black Letter of three sizes (4 and 5 large, 12–14 small), 15 Italic. Title-frame architectural, having pilasters of false proportion at the sides, in the centre of the architrave a medallion with a man's head looking towards his right, in the centre of the base a shield bearing Cawood's merchant's mark.

Collation. In all 24 sheets, A–Aa. No pagination.

I cannot give the Colophon, because the only copy I have seen wants the final leaf, on which it should be.

* Strype (*Life of Parker*, B. II, Ch. iii) says there was an edition printed "Anno M.D.LX.," "and added at the end of the quarto edition of the Book of Common Prayer" which was printed by Jugge and Cawood in that year. He may have seen the two bound together in one volume, as has been done with later editions, for example, with the Oxford editions of 1683 described below; but the Prayer Book of 1560 was a complete book by itself with its own Title and Colophon, and no doubt the Homilies formed a complete book likewise. I have not discovered a copy of the edition. It is plain that Strype had not seen the edition of 1559.

1562 B. JUGGE AND CAWOOD. QUARTO.

Title in 18 lines, ending "1562. | Cum priuilegio Regiæ Maiestatis." : line 1 Italic Capitals, 2 Italic, 3–16 Black Letter, date "1562." between black lines which reach nearly across the page, line 18 Roman. Title-frame quasi-architectural, consisting of an architrave with fruit and vases and with Jugge's monogram in the centre supported by two terminal figures, a male and a female, and a base on which is an oval tablet between two lions couchant.

Collation. In all 24 sheets, A–Aa. No pagination.

Colophon on Aa 4 *a*: "Imprinted at Lon | don in Powles Churcheyarde, by Richard | Iugge, and Iohn Cawood Prynters | to the Quenes Maiestie. | Cum priuilegio Regiæ Maiestatis." Lines 1–4 Black Letter, 5 Italic: the first line begins with a Leaf inverted. Aa 4 *b* is blank.

Where. *Lambeth. Lincoln Cathedral,* wanting title, and otherwise imperfect.

The order of the two editions 1562 A and B is determined by the following and several other variations.

Page	Line	In 1562 A and all earlier.	In 1562 B and all later.
B 3 *a*,	14.	palace	place
D 2 *b*,	13.	receive by	receive of
H 2 *b*,	8.	acceptable	accepted
M 1 *a*,	8 *up*.	or local	and local
U 2 *b*,	19.	a nearer	any nearer

1563. JUGGE AND CAWOOD. QUARTO.

Title in 17 lines: 1 Italic Capitals; 2 and 17 Italic; 3–15 Black Letter; 16, the date "1563.", between black lines. Title-frame the same as in 1562 A.

Collation. In all 24 sheets, A–Aa. No pagination.

Colophon on Aa 4 *a*: "Imprinted at London | in Powles Churcheyard, by Richard | Iugge, and Iohn Cawood Prin | ters to the Quenes | Maiestie. | Cum priuilegio Regiæ Maiestatis." All Roman, line 1 in Capitals. Aa 4 *b* is blank.

Where. *Oxford: Bodl.,* "Douce, HH. 256"; *Wadham College. Cambridge: University Library.*

1569. JUGGE AND CAWOOD. QUARTO IN EIGHTS*.

Title in 17 lines: 1, Roman Capitals; 2, 4, 11, 13, 15, Roman; 3 and 17, Italic; 5–10, 12, 14, Black Letter; 16, the date "1569.", be-

* The description "quarto in eights" does not mean that the book is made up of large double sheets folded each into eight leaves of 4to size, but that each signature, when full, comprises two separate sheets, one of which is an inset

tween black lines which reach nearly across the page. Title-frame the same as in 1562 A.

Collation. In all 23 sheets in 13 signatures, A–N; the last of one sheet (four leaves) only. No pagination. The Preface is in Roman character except "Homily" and "Homilies".

Colophon at the foot of N 4 *a*: "¶ Imprinted at London in Paules Church | Yarde, by Richarde Iugge and Iohn Ca | wood, Printers to the Que | nes Maiestie. | Cum priuilegio Regiæ Maiestatis." Lines 1–4 Roman, 5 Italic. N 4 *b* is blank.

Where. *British Museum*, $\frac{\text{“1026 . e . 15”}}{\text{1}}$; in this copy the tail of the "9" in the Title is gone, so that the date seems at first to be "1560"†. *Oxford: C.C.C. York Cathedral.*

1574. R. Jugge. Quarto in eights.

Title in 16 lines: 1, Italic; 2, Black Letter large; 3–13, Black Letter small; 14, the date "1574."; 15, 16, Roman. Title-frame the same as in 1562 B.

Collation, as in 1569.

Colophon at the foot of N 4 *a*: "¶ Imprinted at London by Newgate | market, next unto Christes Churche, | by Richard Iugge, Printer to the Queenes Maiestie. | Cum priuilegio Regiæ Maiestatis." Lines 1 and 3–6 Roman, 2 Italic. N 4 *b* is blank.

Where. *Oxford: Bodl.*, "4°. N. 27 *. Jur.", in its original binding; *New College.*

1576. R. Jugge. Quarto in eights.

Title in 17 lines: 1 and 3–11, Italic; 2, 16, 17, Roman; 12–14, Black Letter small; 15, the date "1576." Title-frame of Elizabethan carved work, with a little foliage and fruit on a cord over the top and down the sides and a bird on each side at the top pecking at it, in the base on a wreath a bush or tree with two stems intertwined and a nightingale sitting in it, and below "Omne. Bonū. Supernae."

Collation, as in 1569.

Colophon at the foot of N 4 *a*: "¶ Imprinted at London by Ri-

to the other, so that the outer one consists of ff. 1, 2, 7, and 8, and the inner one of ff. 3–6. Therefore in closely collating different copies of such books it is necessary to compare both halves of each signature. Perhaps the earliest example of this practice occurs in the sheet inserted in the middle of sign. "Ccc" in the first edition (1563 A) of the Second Book of Homilies: at least it is not found in any edition of either Book before that date, and it is found in every 4to edition after it. The practice continues to this day in folio volumes for convenience in binding, a single signature often comprising two, three, or even four sheets; and a familiar instance of it is seen in the *Times* newspaper.

† This copy was so entered in the Old Catalogue, and a collation of Cranmer's three Homilies in it is given with that date in the Parker Society's edition of Cranmer's Works.

chard | Iugge, Printer to the Queenes | Maiestie. | Cum priuilegio Regiæ Maiestatis." Lines 1 and 3 Roman, 2 and 4 Italic. N 4 *b* is blank.

Where. *Prayer Book and Homily Society.*

THE SECOND BOOK SEPARATELY.

1563 A. FIRST EDITION. JUGGE AND CAWOOD. QUARTO.

Title: "The seconde | Tome of Homelyes, of | such matters as were pro | mysed and Intituled in | the former part of Ho | melyes, set out by | the aucthoritie | of the Quenes | Maiestie : | And to be read in | euery paryshe | Churche | agrea | blye. | 1563." All Black Letter. Title-frame the same as in ed. 1562 B of the First Book.

Collation. In all 74 sheets: first a half sheet without signature; then 72 entire sheets, Bb–Ddddd (Kk and Ll being used a second time for Ppp and Qqq), with an extra sheet inserted in the middle of sign. "Ccc"; and lastly a half sheet at the end, Eeeee. No pagination. The Admonition is on the back of the Title. The Table is on the next two pages. The first Homily begins on "Bb. i." After the last Homily is a list of "Faultes escaped in the printyng." The inserted sheet in Ccc comes into the Homily of Fasting, which originally was not divided into two Parts. There is a signature, "Ccc. iii.", printed on its first leaf, but no other leaf of it is marked in that manner; whereas the original "Ccc", like every other sheet in the volume, bears a signature on each of its first three leaves. The first words of the original "Ccc. iii." (now the seventh leaf of that signature), "for the use of fastyng", are struck out with a pen. Seventeen leaves in the volume are cancels, namely, these twelve, Dd 4, Qq 2, Ss 2, Bbb 4, Lll 1, Ll (for Qqq) 1, Rrr 2, Ffff 3 and 4, Gggg 4, Hhhh 1, and Kkkk 1, and these five (of which more is said in the Preface to this volume), Gg 1, Mm 2, Kk (for Ppp) 3, Aaaa 4, Iiii 3; and copies are apt to be defective in these places.

Colophon at the foot of the last page, after the list of "Faultes": "Imprinted at London in Powles | Churchyarde, by Richard Iugge, and | Iohn Cawood, Printers to the | Quenes Maiestie. | ¶ Cum priuilegio Regiæ Maiestatis." The last line Italic, the rest Black Letter. The first line begins with a Half Moon.

Such is a description of the book as it usually occurs, and as it is found in the collection of the *Prayer Book and Homily Society*, and at *Cambridge*, in *St. John's College*, "Qq. II. 7", and "Qq. II. 13" (imperfect), and in *Trinity College* (wanting the Table). But there is a copy in the *British Museum*, "C. 25. h. 3" (formerly "1026. e. 16"), which I believe to be unique, and of which I have given a full account in my

Preface at pages xvii–xxii. It is without the Admonition, having the back of the Title blank; it is without the inserted sheet in "Ccc"; of the 17 leaves specified above the five last mentioned are the original leaves, not the cancels; and the last line of the Colophon has "Ræegie", an error which I have seen in one other copy. It is cited in this volume as "1563 A 1."

1563 B. THE SECOND KNOWN EDITION. JUGGE AND CAWOOD. QUARTO IN EIGHTS*.

Title: "The seconde | Tome of Homelyes of | such matters as were pro | mised and Intituled in | the former part of Ho | melyes, set out by | the aucthoritie of | the Quenes | Maiestie: | And to be read in euery | paryshe Churche | agreablye. | 1563." All Black Letter. Title-frame the same as in A.

Collation. In all 73½ sheets in 38 signatures, Aa–Ppp, Ss and Tt having only four leaves each and Ppp only six. Leaves numbered, *Fol.* 1—*Fol.* 292, "*Fol.* 1" being "Aa. iii." On the back of the Title is the Admonition: the initial "F" is large, with a sphinx and scroll foliage, and with 14 short lines of text against it and 17 long lines below, none of them set in. The Table is on the next two pages: the heading begins with a quincunx of small figures which may all be called stars, although there are no rays to any but the central one; n°s. 14–17 have "*Fol.* 2005" &c. in accordance with the error on the leaves themselves mentioned below. The first Homily begins on "*Fol.* 1".

The book was printed at two presses, perhaps at two offices, the former half probably by Jugge, the latter (beginning from "Uu") by Cawood. The division was made at the end of sign. Nnn of the first edition; but in making it the bulk of matter was miscalculated, and hence "Ss" and "Tt", which are the last two signatures of the former half, have but four leaves each, and the matter is spread very wide on ff. 136 and 137 in "Ss". The former half is in a sharper and clearer type, and is printed better in every way†, than the latter. In the former half the signatures are made thus, "Aa (iii)", "Tt (i)", and the first four leaves only are marked in each; in the latter half they are made thus, "Uu. i.", "Ppp. v.", and five leaves in each are marked. The leaves are marked "*Fol.* 1", "*Fol.* 2", &c., uniformly throughout the first half; in the second half "*Fo.*" occurs frequently for "*Fol.*" The same division into halves for printing was made in the other editions of 292 leaves, C, D, E, and F, in order no doubt to supply more quickly the large demand for the new Tome; and these remarks apply equally to those editions also.

* See note * on ed. 1569 of the First Book.

† Of 259 variations which I have noted among the seven editions B–H only 25 occur within the first half of B–F.

In this edition nearly all the 37 leaves following "*Fol.* 200" are numbered with a superfluous cypher, 2001–2037; and two have two cyphers too many, "20011," "20013." The last page of text, fol. 292 *a*, has these readings: "*of Repentaunce*", "*Fo.* 292.", "Christ", "inheritaũce", "kingdome", "heauen.", "Christ", "honour": below "Amen." is a Leaf within "( )" having its stalk to the left, and then a black line across the page; lower down is the figure of a Pediment.

Colophon on fol. 292 *b*: "Imprinted at Lon | don in Powles Churcheyarde, | by Rychard Iugge, and Ihon Ca | wood, Pryntersto the | Quenes Maie | stie. | Cum priuilegio Regiæ Maiestatis." Lines 1–6 Black Letter, 7 Italic. A black line above "Imprinted" &c., also above and below "Cum priuilegio" &c. A Pediment underneath.

Where. *Lambeth.** *Oxford: Wadham College. Cambridge: St. John's College*, "T. 9. 15."

1563 C. The third known edition. Jugge and Cawood. Quarto in eights.

Title, Admonition, and Table the very same as in B.

Collation also the same, except as follows. The leaves following "*Fol.* 200" are numbered correctly. The last page of text has these readings: "*of Repentance.*", "*Fol.* 292.", "Christ", "inherytaunce", "kingdome", "heauen.", "Chryst", "honoure": below "Amen." is a Dexter Hand pointing, then a black line and a Pediment as in B.

Colophon as in B, but with "Richard" and "Printers" instead of "Rychard" and "Prynters." The three black lines and Pediment as in B.

Where. *British Museum*, $\frac{\text{"C. 15. a. 16"}}{2}$. *Cambridge: St. John's College*, "Qq. 11. 12," very imperfect. Each of these copies has two or three sheets belonging to B.

1563 D. The fourth known edition. Jugge and Cawood. Quarto in eights.

Title and Admonition the very same as in B and C. The Table also the same, except that the heading begins with a Half Moon instead of the quincunx of Stars, and that Nos. 14–17 have "*Fol.* 205" &c. correctly, as the leaves themselves have.

Collation likewise the same, except as follows. The last page of text has these readings: "*of Repentaunce*", "*Fol.* 292.", "Chryst", "in-

* The Lambeth copy of 1563 B contains marks and writing of Abp. Whitgift throughout ff. 89–102 and on fol. 179 *a*, the former being his directions for abridging and slightly altering the Homily of Fasting to accompany the Form of Prayer which he put out for the use of his diocese in 1586, while the latter is the correction of an error in the Homily of Almsdeeds on the same occasion, which nevertheless has remained in every edition of the Homilies till now. See page 397, note q, in this volume.

heritaunce", "kyngdome", "heauen,", "Chryst", "honour": below "Amen." is a Dexter Hand pointing, but no black line and no Pediment.

Colophon as in C, but with no black lines and no Pediment below. The second line does not range well, being too far to the left.

Where. *British Museum*, "1026. e. 17," wanting the first two leaves.

1563 E. THE FIFTH KNOWN EDITION. JUGGE AND CAWOOD.

QUARTO IN EIGHTS.

Title and Admonition the very same as in B, C, and D, except that the letter "i" has dropped out from the words, "committed," "edification," "consider," "office," in lines 18, 25, 26, 28 of the Admonition. The Table the same as in D.

Collation also the same, except as follows. The last page of text has these readings: "*of repentaunce*", "*Fo.* 292.", "Chryst", "inheritaunce", "kyngdome", "heauen.", "Chryst", "honour": below "Amen." is a Dexter Hand pointing inverted, with no black line, but with a Pediment underneath.

Colophon precisely as in D.

Where. *Cambridge: University Library*, wanting ff. 102, 103.

1563 F. THE SIXTH KNOWN EDITION. JUGGE AND CAWOOD.

QUARTO IN EIGHTS.

Title the very same as in B–E. The Admonition has its heading in two lines, its initial "F" small, on foliage, with six short lines against it, then eight long lines, and then the lines begin to be set in. The Table is the same as in D and E.

Collation likewise the same, except as follows. The last page of text has these readings: "*of Repentaunce.*", "*Fol.* 292", "Christ", "inheritance", "kingdome", "heauen,", "Christ", "honor": below "Amen." is a Leaf with its stalk to the left, with no black line and no Pediment.

Colophon as in C, with the three black lines, but with no Pediment underneath. Lines 4–6 do not range well.

Where. *Oxford: Bodl.*, "Tanner 214"; *New College.*

Of E I have seen no more than one copy. On the whole it seems to be prior to F, yet in several sheets F is the earlier. Therefore in the short table of variations given immediately after 1563 H, and likewise in the Various Readings throughout the Book, I have thought it safer for the most part to quote "1563 E F" jointly, and not to specify the two editions separately.

1563 G. THE SEVENTH KNOWN EDITION. JUGGE AND CAWOOD. QUARTO IN EIGHTS.

Title in 11 lines besides the date "1563." : lines 1, 3, 5, 7, 9, Black Letter; 2, 8, 10, 11, Roman; 4, 6, Italic. Title-frame the same as in A–F.

Collation. In all 72 sheets in 36 signatures, Aa–Nnn. "Aa (iii)" is marked "Fol. 1."; the following leaves are numbered only. The last number is "287", but ought to be "285", for "167" and "182" have been omitted by error. The final leaf, Nnn 8, is not marked. The back of the Title is blank. The Admonition is on the third page, the Table on the fourth.

The first demand having been supplied by six editions, this was printed more leisurely at one press, probably in Jugge's office. It follows B–F sheet for sheet and mostly page for page to the end of sign. "Rr", f. 134, and then begins to come into less compass.

Colophon on Nnn 8 *a* : "Imprinted at Lon | don in Powles Church-yarde | by Richarde Iugge and Iohn | Cawood, Printers to the Queenes | Maiestie. | Cum priuilegio Regiæ Maiestatis." Line 1, Roman Capitals; 2, 4, 5, 6, Roman; 3, Italic. Line 1 begins with a Leaf. On Nnn 8 *b* is Jugge's device, exhibiting a pelican in her piety, with "Pro Lege Rege, et Grege" over her head on the inner oval, and "Love kepyth the Lawe, obeyeth the Kynge, and is good to the Commen Welthe." in an outer oval round her, a figure of "Prudencia" on one side and of "Iusticia" on the other, and at the bottom Jugge's monogram.

Where. *British Museum,* "C. 25. g," wanting the final leaf. *Prayer Book and Homily Society. Oxford: Bodl.* "Douce, HH 256."

1563 H. THE EIGHTH KNOWN EDITION. JUGGE AND CAWOOD. QUARTO IN EIGHTS.

Title in 11 lines besides "(.·.)" and the date "1563.": line 1, Roman Capitals; 2, 4, 6, 8, 9, 11, Black Letter; 3, 10, Roman; 5, 7, Italic. The first line begins with a Leaf. Title-frame the same as in ed. 1562 A of the First Book.

Collation. In all 69½ sheets in 35 signatures, Aa–Mmm, the last of six leaves only. Leaves marked as in G, the last being "276."

This also was printed all at one press, perhaps in Cawood's office; and the compression in it begins much earlier than in G, and makes a greater saving. Perhaps both this and G, though bearing the date of 1563, were really printed after that year.

Colophon at the foot of fol. 276 *b*: "Imprinted at London | in

Paules Churchyarde by Richard | Iugge and Iohn Cawood, Prin | ters to the Queenes | Maiestie. | Cum priuilegio Regiæ Maiestatis." Line 1, Roman Capitals; 2, 6, Roman; 3, 5, Black Letter; 4, Italic. The first line begins with a Leaf.

Where. *Oxford: Exeter College.*

Among these eight editions, 1563 A–H, the priority of A is shewn by unquestionable tokens. The order of B–H is determined by the succession of variations in the text, of which a few specimens are here given; and the compression into smaller compass is a further proof that G is later than B–F, and H than G.

Page and line in edd. B–F.					
Fol. 70 *a*,	7.	fell down A-G,	fall down H, &c.		
71 *b*,	6 *up*.	Antoninus Verus A–D,	Antonius Verus E–H, &c.		
106 *b*,	16.	horrible A–F,	terrible G, H, &c.		
139 *a*,	12.	in the week A–D,	of the week E–H, &c.		
146 *b*,	6.	attone A–F,	atone G,	at one H, &c.	
163 *b*,	21.	if he thirst A, B;	if he be thirst C;	if he be thirsty D–H, &c.	
174 *b*,	6 *up*.	effectually A–F;	especially G, H, &c.		
177 *b*,	9 *up*.	medicine A–C;	remedy D–H, &c.		
210 *a*,	10.	bold A, B;	bould C;	bound D, E;	bold F–H, &c.
250 *b*,	14.	delectation A, B;	declaration C–H, &c.		

Of variations thus affecting the succession of the text I have noted 24 beginning in C, 23 in D, 29 in E or F, 109 in G, and only 3 in H.

1567, but 1563 in the Title. THE FIRST KNOWN EDITION WITH PAGES NUMBERED. JUGGE AND CAWOOD. QUARTO IN EIGHTS.

Title in 16 lines besides the date "1563.": lines 1, 3, 5, 7, 8, Roman; 2, 9, Italic; 4, 6, 10–16, Black Letter. Title-frame the same as in 1563 A–G.

Collation. In all 68 sheets in 34 signatures, A–Ll, making pp. 543 besides the final page. On the back of the Title, p. 2, is the Table; the Admonition, all in Roman character, is on p. 3; and the first Homily begins on p. 4 or A 2 *b*.

Colophon on the last page: "Imprinted at London in Powles | Churchyarde by Richarde Iugge and | Iohn Cawood, printers to the | Queenes Maiestie. | Ann. 1567. The .xvii. of October. | Cum priuilegio Regiæ Maiestatis." All Roman. The first line begins with a Leaf. Below is a device resembling the one in 1563 G, but smaller, and with "Cogita . Mori" at the top of it.

Where. *Cambridge: St. John's College*, "Qq. 11. 5," wanting the Title.

1570. JUGGE AND CAWOOD. QUARTO IN EIGHTS.

Title in 13 lines besides the date "1570": lines 1, 3, 5, 7, 8, Roman; 2, 9, Italic; 4, 6, 10–13, Black Letter. Title-frame the same as in 1567.

Collation also the same.

Colophon on the last page: "¶ Imprinted at London in Powles | Church yarde by Rychard Iugge and Iohn | Cawood printers to the Queenes | Maiestie. Anno. 1570. | The .23. of Iune. | Cum priuilegio Regiæ Maiestatis." Line 2, Italic; the rest, Roman. Below is the same device as in 1563 G.

Where. *British Museum*, "1026. e. 15"/2. *York Cathedral.*

1571. THE FIRST EDITION THAT CONTAINS THE HOMILY AGAINST REBELLION. JUGGE AND CAWOOD. QUARTO IN EIGHTS.

Title in 12 lines besides the date "1571.": lines 1, 3, 5, 7, 8, Roman; 2, Italic; 4, 6, 9–12, Black Letter. Title-frame the same as in 1567.

Collation. In all 77 sheets in 39 signatures, A–Qq, the last with four leaves only: pp. 616 as marked, besides the final leaf, which contains the Thanksgiving; but the last number marked ought to be 614, for 591 and 600 are left out. The Homily against Rebellion begins on p. 544, which was the final page in 1567 and 1570.

Colophon at the foot of Qq 4*b*: "¶ Imprinted at London in Poules | Churchyarde, by Richarde Iugge, and | Iohn Cawood, Printers to the Queenes | Maiestie." Lines 1, 3, 4, Roman; 2, Italic.

Where. *British Museum*, "4455. b." *Oxford: C. C. C.*

1574. R. JUGGE. QUARTO IN EIGHTS.

Title in 13 lines besides the date "1574.": lines 1, 3–7, Roman; 2, Italic; 8–13, Black Letter. Title-frame the same as in ed. 1576 of the First Book.

Collation the same as in 1571. It should be observed that this edition is not uniform with the edition of the First Book printed in the same year. They differ in title-frame, pagination, type, and length of page.

Colophon at the foot of Qq 4 *b*: "Imprinted at London by Newgate | Market next unto Christes Church, | by Richard Iugge, Printer to the Queenes | Maiestie. | Cum priuilegio Regiæ Maiestatis." Lines 1, 3–5, Roman; 2, Italic.*

Where. *Oxford: Bodl.*, "4°. N. 27. Jur." Between this copy and

* The variation recorded in page 158, note c, of this volume makes it probable that there was an edition of Book II after 1574 in which "noon" in that place was printed "none;" and the variation specified in page 191, note p, seems to

Dr. Corrie's, which by his kind permission I have examined, there is a variation in page 123, lines 13 and 14; as is specified in page 243, note y, of this volume.

THE HOMILY FOR THE ROGATION DAYS SEPARATELY.

THE FIRST KNOWN EDITION. JUGGE AND CAWOOD. QUARTO. 1561 or 1562? certainly earlier than the first edition of the Second Book.

No Title. Heading: "An Homylye deui | ded into three partes, for the dayes | of Rogation weke. | That all good thynges commeth from God." Lines 1–3 Black Letter, 4 Italic. The first line begins with a Half Moon.

Collation. In all 4½ sheets in 4 signatures made by Half Moons, the last with six leaves. No pagination.

Colophon on the last page: "Imprinted at London in Powles | Churchyarde by Richard Iugge and | Iohn Cawood, Printers to the | Queenes Maiestie. | Cum priuilegio Regiæ Maiestatis." Lines 1–4 Black Letter, 5 Italic.

Where. *Lambeth. Cambridge: Sidney Sussex College,* "S. 6. 20."

THE HOMILY AGAINST REBELLION SEPARATELY.

A. FIRST EDITION. JUGGE AND CAWOOD. QUARTO. 1570?

No Title. Heading: "An Homelie against | disobedience and wylfull rebellion." Line 1 Roman, 2 Italic. Then, "¶ The first part.", Roman.

Collation. In all 10 sheets, A–K. No pagination. The Homily is divided into five Parts only. The fifth Part begins on G 4 *a*, and ends on K 2 *a*. The Thanksgiving fills the next two pages, K 2 *b* and K 3 *a*.

prove that there was an edition printed in 1577. Queen Elizabeth's letter to the Bishops, dated May 7, 1577, in which she ordered a more general use of the Homilies in accordance with her Injunctions, is another reason for expecting to find an edition of that year. Cardwell's *Documentary Annals*, I, 373.

Probably that edition introduced many of the readings which are now found first in 1582, if at least it were printed by Christopher Barker, who succeeded Jugge as Queen's Printer in that very year. But I have searched for it in vain. If any collector has a copy, and will do me the favour of letting me examine it, I shall be much obliged to him. And I take this opportunity for saying that I shall be grateful to any one who will send me any correction or addition to this List.

Colophon at the top of K 3 *b*: "¶ Imprinted at Lon | don in Powles Churchyarde by | Richard Iugge and Iohn Cawood, | printers to the Queenes Ma | iestie. | Cum priuilegio Regiæ Maiestatis." Line 2 Italic, the rest Roman. Below is the same device as in ed. 1563 G of the Second Book. At the top of K 4 *a* is a statement of "Faultes escaped," comprised in six lines. The remainder of that page, and the whole of the final page, K 4 *b*, is blank.

Where. *Cambridge: St. John's College*, "Hh. 9. 15."

B. The second known edition. Jugge and Cawood. Quarto. 1570?

No Title. Heading: "An Homilie against | disobedience and wylful rebellion." Line 1 Roman, 2 Italic. Then, "The first part.", Roman.

Collation. In all 10 sheets, A–K. No pagination. The Homily is now divided into six Parts. The initial "W" on G 4 *a* (the beginning of Part 5) is large with 11 short lines against it. The Notice "Thus have you heard" &c. at the bottom of H 3 *b* (the end of Part 5) is in small type, there being scarcely room to get it in. The sixth Part begins on H 4 *a*, and ends on K 2 *b*. The Thanksgiving is on K 3.

Colophon and device, the same as in ed. A, on K 4 *a*. K 4 *b* is blank.

C. The third known edition. Jugge and Cawood. Quarto. 1570?

No Title. Heading: "An Homilie a | gainst disobedience and wyl | full rebellion." Lines 1, 3, Roman; 2, Italic: the first line begins with a Leaf. Then, "¶ The first part.", Roman.

Collation the same as in ed. B, except that the initial "W" on G 4 *a* is smaller and has only 8 short lines against it, whereby the space of two lines is gained, there is no crowding at the bottom of H 3 *b*, and the Notice there is in the same type as the rest. Several other pages likewise shew that the printer took more pains with this edition than with B, especially in making the number of lines in a page 32 uniformly.

Colophon, device, &c., precisely as in ed. B.

Where. *British Museum*, "225. e. 34."

D. The fourth known edition. Jugge and Cawood. Quarto. 1570?

No Title. Heading: "¶ An Homilie a | gaynst disobedience and wyl | ful rebellion." Lines 1, 3, Roman; 2, Italic. Then, "The first part", Roman, with a cinquefoil before it.

Collation the same as in ed. C. In the Notice at the foot of H 3 *b* "the sixt part" is printed by error for "the fifth part"; and there are several other errors throughout the Homily.

Colophon at the top of K 4 *a*: "Imprinted at Lon | don in Powles Churchyarde, by Ri | charde Iugge and Iohn Cawood, | Printers to the Queenes | Maiestie. | ¶ Cum priuilegio Regiæ Maiestatis." Line 2 Italic, the rest Roman: line 1 begins with a Leaf. Below is the same device as in the earlier editions. K 4 *b* is blank.

Where. *Lambeth.*

E. THE FIFTH KNOWN EDITION. JUGGE AND CAWOOD. QUARTO.

1570?

No Title. Heading the same as in ed. D, except that the last line is "¶ The first part."

Collation, Colophon, &c., the same as in ed. D, with the same error at the bottom of sign. H 3 *b*, which also remains in ed. 1571 of the Second Book.

Where. *British Museum,* $\frac{\text{"1026. e. 15"}}{3}$.

Among these five editions the priority of A is clear. The order of B–E is determined by the succession of variations in the text, of which a few specimens are here given.

Page and line in edd. C–E.			
A 4 *a*,	12, 13.	constitute A, B;	constituted C–E, &c.
C 3 *a*,	14.	furdest A–D;	furthest E, &c.
D 2 *b*,	16.	with words A–D;	worth words E, 1571.
G 1 *b*,	17.	possiblie A–C;	possible D, E, &c.
H 2 *a*,	16.	this ambition A–C;	his ambition D, E, &c.
K 1 *a*,	21.	the clergy A, B;	the Romish clergy C–E, &c.

THE TWO BOOKS UNIFORMLY, BUT WITH SEPARATE TITLES AND REGISTERS.

1582. CHR. BARKER. QUARTO IN EIGHTS.

No pagination. The pages are much broader than in any previous edition of either Book, and contain 39 lines each. Title-frame an Elizabethan border, exhibiting the Royal Arms at the top, figures of Justice and Religion? at the upper corners, the Royal supporters at the lower corners, and the initial letters "C. B." in the centre of the lowest scrollwork.

Book I. Title in 15 lines: lines 1, 3, 5–8, 14, 15, Italic; the rest, Roman. There are in all 16 sheets in 8 signatures, A–H. Colophon at the bottom of H 7 *b*: "Imprinted at London by Christopher | Barker, Printer to the Queenes | most excellent Maiestie. | Cum priuilegio Regiæ Maiestatis." Lines 1–3 Roman, 4 Italic. The last leaf, H 8, is blank.

Book II. Title in 12 lines: line 2, Italic; 3, Black Letter; the rest, Roman, "Anno" in Capitals. There are in all 49½ sheets in 25 signatures, A a—B b b, the last with six leaves only. Colophon on B b b 6 *a*: "¶ Imprinted at London by Christopher | Barker, Printer to the Queenes | Maiestie. | Cum priuilegio Regiæ Maiestatis." Line 2 Italic, the rest Roman. The last page, B b b 6 *b*, is blank.

This edition differs in many places from all before it.

Where. *Durham: Bp. Cosin's Library.*

1587. R. JUGGE? QUARTO IN EIGHTS.

No pagination. The pages are not of uniform width, but all narrower than in the former 4to. editions and nearer to the modern 8vo. shape. Title-frame of light Elizabethan tracery; at the top, in the centre, the Royal Arms within the Garter; at the bottom, in the centre a pelican in her piety; in the left corner a Cupid bearing in his right hand the letter "R," in the right corner a bush with a nightingale in it and "Iugge" on a scroll above.*

In Book I the Title ends thus: "prayers. | 1587. | Cum priuilegio Regiæ | Maiestatis." There are in all 24 sheets in 12 signatures, A–M.

In Book II the Title ends thus: "...agreea | bly. | Anno Domini. | 1587." There are in all 76 sheets in 38 signatures, A–Pp.

There is no Colophon to either Book. The last three pages in each are blank.

In the latter half of Book I this edition follows ed. 1582, but in the former half it seems to be printed from one much earlier, perhaps ed. 1559. In Book II it follows ed. 1582. But in both Books there are many variations, some of which shew great carelessness. It is of no value in regard to the succession of the text, nor is ed. 1595, which follows it; for ed. 1623 is based upon ed. 1582, not upon either of these.

Where. *British Museum*, $\frac{\text{"C. 15. a. 17"}}{\text{1, 2}}$. *Prayer Book and Homily Society. Oxford: Christ Church.*

1595. EDW. ALLDE. QUARTO IN EIGHTS.

No pagination. The pages are not of uniform width, but mostly

* Ames supposes that this edition was printed by Joan Jugge, widow of Richard.

narrower even than in 1587. The Title-frame is Elizabethan: at the top, between figures of Fame and Victory? seated, are the Royal Arms within the Garter and with the Crest; at the bottom, in the corners, are the Royal Supporters, a Lion crowned and a Griffin; immediately below the Title are the Arms of the Stationers' Company, and still lower, in a blank space between the letters "H" and "D", is the date "1595."

The Title in Book I ends thus: "prayer. | Cum priuilegio Regiæ Maiestatis. | Imprinted at London by | Edward Allde." In Book II thus: "Imprinted at London by Edward Allde." No Colophon to either. In both Books this edition is reprinted sheet for sheet, perhaps page for page, from ed. 1587, and its registers are the same; but it has a few special readings of its own.

Where. *Lambeth. Prayer Book and Homily Society. Oxford: Bodl.*, "4°. F. 40. Th." *Colchester: Abp. Harsnett's Library.*

THE TWO BOOKS IN ONE VOLUME.

1623. FIRST FOLIO EDITION. JOHN BILL. FOLIO IN SIXES.

Title: "Certaine Sermons or Homilies appointed to be read in Churches, In the time of the late Queene Elizabeth of famous memory. And now thought fit to bee reprinted by Authority from the Kings most Excellent Maiestie. London, Printed by John Bill, Printer to the Kings most Excellent Maiestie, 1623." Title-frame an arch supported by pillars, &c.: on the base are the words "Cum priuilegio." Before Book II is the old Title with "late" inserted before "Queenes", with the Royal Arms below, and then the Imprint, "London—1623.", but with no Title-frame.

Collation. Each Book has a separate register and pagination. Register of Book I: a, of four leaves only, not paged, containing the Title, Preface, and Table, and having the second, sixth, and eighth pages blank; then A—I, the last with two leaves only, making pp. 98 besides the last leaf, which is blank. Register of Book II: two leaves without signature and not paged, containing the Title, Table, and Admonition, each on one page, and having the fourth page blank; then Aa—Ddd, making pp. 320 besides the last two leaves, of which the former contains the Thanksgiving, the latter has on its first page the Colophon, "London—1623.", and the last page is blank.

This is the latest edition in which changes were made with any semblance of authority. They were merely verbal, and were intended, like the changes in the First Book in 1559, to make the language plainer. None of them affect doctrine, and the only alteration which was not verbal was the introduction of the two marginal notes concerning the Emperor Theodosius given at page 165 of this volume. The Preface has this heading, "The Preface as it was published in the yeere 1562," although any other year in Elizabeth's reign from 1559 might have been specified with equal truth. Probably the reason for naming the year "1562" rather than any other was because the earliest copy of any Elizabethan edition of the First Book in the Lambeth Library was then, as now, a copy of ed. 1562 B.

There were two impressions or issues of this edition, the first two signatures (A and B) or 24 pages having been reprinted.

In the first, 1623 a, the marginal abstracts on those pages are nearly all in the Roman character, whereas through the rest of the volume nearly all are in Italic.

In the second, 1623 b, the Italic character is used in the abstracts on the first 24 pages, as throughout the volume, and not fewer than 13 important variations occur in the text of those pages, two of which serve to shew the priority of 1623 a.

Page.	Line.	Old edd.	1582.	1623 a.	1623 b.
5,	19.	nedeth	endeth	endeth	tendeth
19,	15.	deserve	discern	discern	deserve

There is a copy of each impression at *Lambeth*, the earlier one being on large paper; and copies of one or other are so plentiful that I do not think it necessary to specify the Libraries which contain them. There are as many as ten in *Oxford*.

1633. Folio in sixes.

Colophon: "London. Printed by John Norton, for Joyce Norton, and Richard Whitaker...1633."

Collation of registers, pagination, &c., the same as in 1623, except that the first signature is "*a*", not "a". The Preface before Book I is in Italic character: the Admonition before Book II is (as in 1623) on one page.

1633 and 1635. Folio in sixes.

Colophon: "London. Printed by John Norton, for Joyce Norton, and Richard Whitaker...1633."

Collation of registers, pagination, &c., the same as in 1623. The Preface is in Roman character: the Admonition is on two pages.

There are two impressions. In the first the date in the first Title is "1633", as in the Colophon, but the date in the second Title is "1635". In the second the date in the first Title is "1635", but the date in the Colophon remains the same, and there seems to be no other change throughout the volume.

1640. Folio in sixes.

Colophon: "London, Printed by John Norton, for Richard Whitaker: ...1640."

Collation. The register is continuous, A—M m in sixes, N n of eight leaves: but the pagination is still separate. Sign. "A" has its first leaf blank, the Title on its second, the Preface beginning on its third, which is falsely signed "A 2," the Table on its fifth, the first Homily and the pagination of Book I beginning on its sixth. The First Book ends on I 6 *b*, p. 98. Sign. "K" has the second Title on its first leaf, the Admonition and Table on its second, and the first Homily and the pagination of Book II beginning on its third. Book II ends on N n 6 *b*, p. 320, and this is the last page marked; N n 7 contains the Thanksgiving; the Colophon is on N n 8 *a*, and N n 8 *b* is blank.

1673. FOLIO IN FOURS.

"London, Printed by T. R. for Andrew Crooke, Samuel Mearne, and Robert Pawlet, MDCLXXIII. Cum Privilegio."

Collation. The register and pagination are continuous, the latter beginning from B 1 *a*; namely, A—M in fours, containing Book I, pp. 88; N, a single sheet, containing the Title, Admonition, and Table of Book II, pp. 89—92; and O—D d d in fours, containing Book II, pp. 93—388. No Colophon.

1676. FOLIO IN FOURS.

"London, Printed by T. R. for Samuel Mearne Stationer to the King's most Excellent Majesty, and for Robert Pawlet. MDCLXXVI. Cum Privilegio." Collation the same as in 1673.

1683. FOLIO IN FOURS.

"London, Printed for Ann Mearn, and Blanch Pawlet, 1683. Cum Privilegio." Collation the same as in 1673. This is the latest known edition in Black Letter.

1683. FOLIO IN FOURS.

Two editions, being the first known to have been printed at Oxford, the first also in other than Black Letter.

1. "Oxford, Printed at the Theatre; and are to be sold by Peter Parker at the Leg and Star over against the Royal Exchange in Cornhil, London. 1683."

2. "Oxford, Printed at the Theatre, and are to be sold by Thomas Guy at the Oxford Arms on the West side of the Royal Exchange, London 1683."

By using figures to distinguish these two editions I do not mean to assert that n°. 1 is the earlier. Of n°. 2 another impression occurs with a different bookseller's name in the imprint, being "to be sold by Moses Pitt at the Angel in St. Paul's Church-yard." That they are two impressions or issues of the same edition, and not two distinct editions, is shewn by the identity of figures, at the foot of pages, indicating the office-number of the press at which any form was worked off, and by the identity of errors, as in the numbering of pages 256 and 384.

The Collation of the two editions is the same: indeed they run page for page with one another. The register is continuous: first there is a half sheet without signature containing the Title only; then one sheet, A, containing on its first two pages the Preface (which belongs properly to the First Book), on its third page the Admonition (which belongs properly to the Second Book), and on its fourth page a Table formed by throwing the Tables of both Books into one; then B—Ddd in fours, except N, which is a single sheet. The pagination begins from B 1 *a*, and ends on Ddd 2 *b*, which is page 388; but the numbers 91—94, which would have been the middle numbers of sign. N had it contained four leaves like the rest, are omitted; the last two leaves also of Ddd are not paged. The First Book begins on B 1 *a*, p. 1, and ends on N 1 *b*, p. 90. The Second Book begins on N 2 *a*, p. 95, and ends on Ddd 2 *b*, p. 388. The last two leaves of sign. Ddd are filled with the Thirty-nine Articles and the Table of Affinity. There is no Colophon.

No doubt these editions were specially intended for use in Churches, and sometimes they were bound up with the Prayer Book *, as in the British Museum "3406. f." No doubt also the original sign. A contained the Title, Preface, and Table of the First Book; and the inset sheet of sign. N, which supplied the missing pp. 91—94, contained the Title, Admonition, and Table of the Second Book: but the convenience of having a single Table of Contents in a volume intended for such use was afterwards perceived, and those sheets were cancelled.

1687 †. DUODECIMO.

"Certain Sermons or Homilies appointed to be read in Churches in the time of Queen Elizabeth of famous memory: and now reprinted for the use of private families. In two Parts. London: Printed for George Wells at the Sun, Abel Swall at the Unicorn, in St. Paul's Church-yard, and George Pawlett at the Bible in Chancery-Lane. 1687." Register, A—Ee, A having six leaves only; pp. 646.

* It was usual to read the Homilies from the Desk, not from the Pulpit.

† In 1685 was published a folio broadsheet, printed on both sides, with this heading: "Godly and wholsome Doctrine, and necessary for these Times: being the Second Part of the Homily concerning the Holy Ghost; dissolving this Doubt" &c., and with this as a Colophon: "London, Printed for Sam. Thomason. 1685."

A LIST OF THE COPIES USED FOR THIS EDITION.

Of the editions here marked with an asterisk a complete collation is given in the Various Readings, except that the collation of "1549 G" is only complete for the sentences then added at the beginning of Parts.

BOOK I.

*1547 G 1 .... Bodl., "4°. I. 6. Th. Seld."
1547 G 2 .... Cambr. Univ. Libr.
1547 G 3 .... Brit. Mus., "C. 25. g. 5."
1547 G 4 .... Sion College.
1547 G 5 .... Brit. Mus., "C. 25. g. 6."
1547 G 6 .... Rev. John Mendham.
1547 W 1 .... Exeter College.
1547 W 2 .... Cambr. Univ. Libr.
1547 W 3 .... Exeter College.
1548 .... Exeter College.
*1549 G .... C. C. C., Oxford.
1549 W.......... Bodl., "4°. N. 27. Jur."
1551 .... St. John's College, Cambridge, "Qq. 11. 13."
*1559 .... Rev. John Griffiths.
1562 A .... Rev. Dr. Corrie.
1562 B .... Lambeth.
1563 .... Wadham College.
1569 .... C. C. C., Oxford.
1574 .... Bodl., "4°. N. 27*. Jur."
1576 .... Prayer Book and Homily Society.
1582 .... Rev. Dr. Corrie.
1587 .... Rev. Dr. Cardwell.
1595 .... Lambeth.
*1623 .... Lambeth.
*1623 a, pp. 1–24,.. Christ Church, Oxford.

ALSO IN BOOK I.

BON. .... Bp. Bonner's Homilies, 4°. 1555; Bodl., "4°. P. 16. Th. BS."
BEC. .... Becon's Works, II, 157–162, ed. 1560–4, Bodl., "V. 7. 13. Th."

BOOK II.

*1563 A 1 .... Brit. Mus., "C. 25. h. 3."
*1563 A .... St. John's College, Cambridge, "Qq. 11. 7."
1563 B .... Lambeth.
1563 C .... Rev. Dr. Corrie.

1563 D.......... Rev. Dr. Corrie.
1563 E.......... Cambr. Univ. Libr.
1563 F.......... Rev. John Mendham.
1563 G.......... Brit. Mus., "C. 25. g."
1563 H.......... Exeter College.
1567 .... Rev. John Griffiths.
1570 .... Brit. Mus., "$\frac{1026.\ e.\ 15}{2}$".
1571 .... C. C. C., Oxford.
1574 .... Bodl., "4°. N. 27. Jur."
1582 .... Rev. Dr. Corrie.
1587 .... Rev. Dr. Cardwell.
1595 .... Lambeth.
*1623 .... Lambeth.

Homily for the Rogation Days.

*Ed. 1............ Lambeth.

Homily against Rebellion.

*A .... St. John's College, Cambridge, "Hh. 9. 15."
*B .... Rev. John Griffiths.
C .... Brit. Mus., "225. e. 34."
D .... Lambeth.
E .... Brit. Mus., "$\frac{1026.\ e.\ 15}{3}$".

ALSO IN BOOK II.

WHITGIFT...... Homilies (selected and abridged) issued by Abp. Whitgift in 1586, with a Form of Prayer for use in the Diocese of Canterbury. St. John's Coll., Cambridge, "Hh. 9. 15."

*TAV............ Taverner's Postils as edited by Dr. Cardwell, 8vo. Oxford, 1841; pp. 173–181, and 189–199.

A LIST OF THE EDITIONS

FROM WHICH THE AUTHORS HERE NAMED ARE QUOTED IN THE NOTES.

St. Ambrose	ed. Benedict. Paris. 1686–90.
St. Augustine	ed. Benedict. Paris. 1689 &c.
St. Basil	ed. Benedict. Paris. 1721 &c.
St. Bernard	ed. Benedict. Paris. 1719.
St. Chrysostom	ed. Benedict. Paris. 1718 &c.
Clemens Romanus, the "Recognitiones" ascribed to,	ed. Coteler. Amst. 1724.
St. Jerome	ed. Vallars. Veron. 1734 &c.
Origen	ed. Benedict. Paris. 1733 &c.
Tertullian	ed. Oehler, Lips. 1853.

When other Authors are cited by volume and page, the edition is also mentioned.

ADDITIONS AND CORRECTIONS.

Page 30, note i. *for* 1547 G 2 *read* 1547 G 3.
48, note g. *after* 1547 G 1 *add* *and* 2.
90, note m. *for* 1547 G 2 *read* 1547 G 3.
201, note 46. *add* Compare with Foxe's story a statement made by Abp. Parker to Lord Burghley in a letter indorsed "6th October 1572", printed among his *Correspondence*, p. 401, ed. Park. Soc.
226, note 26. *add at the end of the first paragraph* Bishop Voysey of Exeter cautioned his diocesē against the same superstitious worship of St. Loy in his Admonition of October 17, 1539; but Wilkins has printed "saint Lewis's day" for "saint Loy's day" in *Concilia* III, 846, the name in the Bishop's Register, vol. II, fol. 83, being "looys".
407, marg., π. *for* Luke ii, 79 *read* Luke i, 79.

Certain Sermons

appointed by the Queen's Majesty to be declared and read by all Parsons, Vicars, and Curates every Sunday and Holy Day in their Churches, and by Her Grace's advice perused and overseen for the better understanding of the simple people.

Newly imprinted in Parts according as is mentioned in the Book of Common Prayers.[a]

[a] CERTAIN — PRAYERS.] *Such, with the date and generally the words,* Cum privilegio Regiae Majestatis, *below, was the Title of the First Book throughout the reign of Elizabeth.*

In 1547 *and* 1548 *the Title was this:* Certain Sermons or Homilies appointed by the King's Majesty to be declared and read by all Parsons, Vicars, or Curates every Sunday in their Churches where they have Cure. *In Grafton's editions of* 1549 *and* 1551 *it was the same, with these words added,* Newly imprinted and by the King's Highness' authority divided. *In the editions of Whitchurch and Oswen in* 1549 *the form was altered by the omission of* or Homilies, *the insertion of* and Holy

A TABLE OF THE SERMONS

CONTAINED[a] IN THIS PRESENT VOLUME.

Finis Tabulae[b].

Day *after* Sunday, *and the substitution of these words at the end,* Newly imprinted in Parts, according as is mentioned in the Book of Common Prayer.

In 1623 *the Title at the beginning of the volume, serving in fact for both Books, ran thus:* Certain Sermons or Homilies, appointed to be read in Churches in the time of the late Queen Elizabeth of famous memory, and now thought fit to be reprinted by authority from the King's Most Excellent Majesty.

[a] SERMONS CONTAINED] SERMONS OR HOMILIES CONTAINED 1547–1551 *except* 1549 W.

[b] Tabulae] *added in* 1559.

THE PREFACE.[a]

CONSIDERING how necessary it is that the word of God, which is the only food of the soul, and that most excellent light that we must walk by in this our most dangerous pilgrimage, should at all convenient times be preached unto the people, that thereby they may both learn their duty towards God, their Prince, and their neighbours, according to the mind of the Holy Ghost expressed in the Scriptures, and also to avoid the manifold enormities which heretofore by false doctrine have crept into the Church of God; and how that all they which are appointed ministers have not the gift of preaching sufficiently to instruct the people which is committed unto them, whereof great inconveniences might rise, and ignorance still be main-

[a] THE PREFACE.] THE PREFACE, as it was published in the year 1562. *Ed.* 1623.

The Preface above is that which was set before the First Book of Homilies by Queen Elizabeth. King Edward's Preface was as follows:

THE King's Most Excellent Majesty, by the prudent advice of his most dear beloved uncle Edward Duke of Somerset, Governor of His Majesty's person and Protector of all His Highness' realms, dominions, and subjects, with the rest of his most honourable counsel, most graciously considering the manifold enormities which heretofore have crept into His Grace's realm through the false usurped power of the Bishop of Rome and the ungodly doctrine of his adherents, not only unto the great decay of Christian religion, but also (if God's mercy were not) unto the utter destruction of innumerable souls, which through hypocrisy and pernicious doctrine were seduced and brought from honouring of the alone true, living, and eternal God unto the worshipping of creatures, yea, of stocks and stones, from doing the commandments of God unto voluntary works and phantasies invented of men, from true religion unto popish superstition; considering also the earnest and fervent desire of his dearly beloved subjects to be delivered from all errors and superstitions[a] and to be truly and faithfully instructed in the very word of God, that lively food of man's soul, whereby they may

[a] superstitions] superstition 1547 G 1.

tained, if some honest remedy be not speedily found and provided; the Queen's Most Excellent Majesty, tendering the soul health of her loving subjects and the quieting of their consciences in the chief and principal points of Christian religion, and willing also by the true setting forth and pure declaring of God's word, which is the principal guide and leader unto all godliness and virtue, to expel and drive away as well all corrupt, vicious, and ungodly living, as also erroneous and poisoned doctrines tending to superstition and idolatry, hath, by the advice of her most honourable counsellors, for her discharge in this behalf, caused a Book of Homilies, which heretofore was set forth by her most loving brother, a Prince of most worthy memory, Edward the Sixth, to be printed anew; wherein are contained certain wholesome and godly exhortations, to move the people to honour and worship Almighty God, and diligently to serve him, every one according to their degree, state, and vocation. All which Homilies Her Majesty commandeth and straitly chargeth all Parsons, Vicars, Curates, and all other having spiritual cure, every Sunday and Holy Day in the year, at the ministering of the Holy Communion, or, if there be no

---

learn unfeignedly, and according to the mind of the Holy Ghost expressed in the Scriptures, to honour God and to serve their King with all humility and subjection, and godly and honestly to behave themselves toward all men; again, calling to remembrance that the next and most ready way to expel and avoid as well all corrupt, vicious, and ungodly living, as also erroneous doctrine tending to superstition and idolatry, and clearly to put away all contention which hath heretofore risen through diversity of preaching, is the true setting forth and pure declaring of God's word, which is the principal guide and leader unto all godliness and virtue; finally, that all Curates, of what learning soever they be, may have some godly and fruitful lessons in a readiness to read and declare unto their parishioners for their edifying, instruction, and comfort; hath caused a Book of Homilies to be made and set forth, wherein is contained[b] certain wholesome and godly exhortations, to move the people to honour and worship Almighty God, and diligently to serve him, every one according to their degree, state, and vocation. The which Homilies His Majesty commandeth and straitly chargeth all Parsons, Vicars, Curates, and all other having spiritual cure, every Sunday in[c] the year, at the Communion[d], when the people

[b] is contained] *so in all.* [c] Sunday in] Sunday and Holy Day in 1549 W. [d] the Communion] High Mass 1547, 1548.

Communion ministered that day, yet after the Gospel and Creed, in such order and place as is appointed in the Book of Common Prayers, to read and declare to their parishioners plainly and distinctly one of the said Homilies in such order as they stand in the Book; except there be a Sermon according as it is injoined in the book of her Highness' Injunctions [1], and then for that cause only, and for none other, the reading of the said Homily to be differred[b] unto the next Sunday or Holy Day following. And, when the foresaid Book of Homilies is read over, Her Majesty's pleasure is, that the same be repeated and read again in such like sort as was before prescribed.

Furthermore Her Highness commandeth, that, notwithstanding this order, the said ecclesiastical persons shall read Her Majesty's Injunctions at such times and in such order as is in the book thereof appointed [2]; and that the Lord's Prayer, the Articles of the Faith, and the Ten Commandments be openly read unto the people as in the said Injunctions is specified [3]; that all her people, of what degree or condition soever they be, may learn how to invocate and call upon the Name of God,

[b] differred] deferred *from* 1569.

[1] See *Cardwell's Documentary Annals*, I, 180, Inj. III, IV; 182, Inj. VIII.

[2] Ibid. 185, Inj. XIV.

[3] Ibid. 181, Inj. V.

---

be most gathered together, to read[e] and declare to their parishioners plainly and distinctly in such order as they stand in the Book; except any Sermon be preached, and then for that cause only, and for none other, the reading of the said Homily to be differred unto the next Sunday following. And, when the foresaid Book of Homilies is read over, the King's Majesty's pleasure is, that the same be repeated and read again, in such like sort as was before prescribed, unto such time as His Grace's pleasure shall further be known in this behalf.

Also His Majesty commandeth that the said ecclesiastical persons, upon the first Holy Day falling in the week time of every quarter of the year, shall read his Injunctions openly and distinctly to the people in manner and form in the same expressed [1]. And upon every other Holy and Festival Day through the year, likewise falling in the week time, they shall recite the Pater Noster, the Articles of our Faith, and the Ten Commandments in English openly before all the people, as in the

[e] at the Communion—to read] at the celebration of the Communion, in such order and place as is appointed in the Book of Common Prayer, to read 1549 W.

[1] See *Cardwell's Documentary Annals*, I, 12, 30-35.

know[c] what duty they owe both to God and man; so that they may pray, believe, and work according to knowledge while they shall live here, and after this life be with Him that with his blood hath bought us all. To whom, with the Father and the Holy Ghost, be all honour and glory for ever. Amen.

[c] God, know] God, and know *from* 1574.

---

said Injunctions is specified[2]; that all degrees and all ages may learn to know God and to serve him according to his holy word. Amen.

2 See *Cardwell's Documentary Annals*, I, 7, 19–27.

A FRUITFUL EXHORTATION

TO THE READING AND KNOWLEDGE

OF HOLY SCRIPTURE.

The praise of holy Scripture.

UNTO a Christian man there can be nothing either more necessary or profitable than the knowledge of holy Scripture; forasmuch as in it is contained God's true word, setting forth his glory and also man's duty. And there is no truth nor doctrine necessary for our justification and everlasting salvation, but that is or may be drawn out of that fountain and well of truth. Therefore as many as be desirous to enter into the right and perfect way unto God must apply their minds to know holy Scripture; without the which they can neither sufficiently know God and his will, neither their office and duty. And, as drink is pleasant to them that be dry, and meat to them that be hungry, so is the reading, hearing, searching, and studying of holy Scripture to them that be desirous to know God or themselves, and to do his will. And their stomachs only do loathe and abhor the heavenly knowledge and food of God's word, that be so drowned in worldly vanities, that they neither savour[a] God nor any godliness: for that is the cause why they desire such vanities rather than the true knowledge of God. As they that are sick of an ague, whatsoever they eat or drink[b], though it be never so pleasant, yet it is as bitter to them as wormwood, not for the bitterness of the meat, but for the corrupt and bitter humour that is in their own tongue and mouth; even so is the sweetness of God's word bitter, not of itself, but only unto them that have their minds corrupted with long custom of sin and love of this world.

The perfection of holy Scripture.

The knowledge of holy Scripture is necessary.

To whom the knowledge of holy Scripture is sweet and pleasant.

Who be enemies to holy Scripture.

An apt similitude, declaring of whom the Scripture is abhorred.

Therefore, forsaking the corrupt judgment of fleshly[c] men, which care[d] not but for their carcase, let us reverently hear and read holy Scriptures, which[e] is the food of the soul[α]. Let us diligently search for the well of life in the books of the New and Old[h] Testament, and not run to the stinking puddles of men's

An exhortation unto the diligent reading, hearing, and[f] searching of the holy Scriptures[g].

α Matt. iv, [4].

[a] savour] favour *from* 1547 G 6 *till* 1623 b. [b] or drink] and drink *from* 1563. [c] fleshly] carnal *till* 1559. [d] care] came 1623 b. [e] Scriptures, which] Scripture, which 1623 b. [f] reading, hearing, and] reading and *from* 1547 G 6. [g] the holy Scriptures] the holy Scripture *from* 1563. [h] New and Old] Old and New 1623 b.

traditions, devised by man's[i] imagination, for our justification and salvation. For in holy Scripture is fully contained what we ought to do and what to eschew, what to believe, what to love, and what to look for at God's hands[k] at length. In those[l] books we shall find the Father, from whom, the Son, by whom, and the Holy Ghost, in whom, all things have their being and keeping up[m]; and these three Persons to be but one[n] God and one substance. In these books we may learn to know ourselves, how vile and miserable we be; and also to know God, how good he is of himself, and how he maketh us and all creatures partakers of his goodness[o]. We may learn also in these books to know God's will and pleasure, as much as for this present time is convenient for us to know. And, as the great clerk and godly preacher St. John Chrysostom saith[1], "whatsoever is required to salvation of man is fully contained in the Scripture of God. He that is ignorant may there learn and have knowledge. He that is hardhearted and an obstinate sinner shall there find everlasting[p] torments prepared of God's justice, to make him afraid, and to mollify (or soften[q]) him. He that is oppressed with misery in this world shall there find relief in the promises of everlasting[r] life, to his great consolation and comfort. He that is wounded by the devil unto death shall find there medicine, whereby he may be restored again unto health." "If[2] it shall require[s] to teach any truth or reprove false doctrine, to rebuke any vice, to commend any virtue, to give good counsel, to comfort, or to exhort[t], or to do any other thing requisite for our salvation; all those things," saith St. Chrysostom, "we may learn plentifully of the Scripture." "There is,"

The holy Scripture is a sufficient doctrine for our salvation.

What things we may learn in the holy Scripture.

[i] man's] men's 1582, 1623. [k] hands] hand 1623 b. [l] those] these *from* 1574. [m] keeping up] conservation *till* 1559. [n] be but one] be one 1547 G 1 *and* W 1–3. [o] how he maketh us and all creatures partakers of his goodness] how he communicateth his goodness unto us and to all creatures *till* 1559. [p] everlasting] eternal *till* 1559. [q] or soften] *added in* 1559. [r] everlasting] eternal *till* 1559. [s] require] be requisite 1623 b. [t] or to exhort] or exhort 1623 b.

1 Quidquid quaeritur ad salutem, totum jam adimpletum est in Scripturis. Qui ignarus est inveniet ibi quod discat. Qui contumax est et peccator inveniet ibi futuri judicii flagella quae timeat. Qui laborat inveniet ibi glorias et promissiones vitae perpetuae, quas manducando amplius excitetur ad opus..... Qui percussus est a diabolo et vulneratus est in peccatis inveniet ibi medicinales cibos, qui eum per poenitentiam revocent ad salutem. *Scriptor. Incert. in Matth. Hom.* XLI, *Chrysost. Opp. ad calc. Tom.* VI, *p.* CLXXiv B.

2 **Πρὸς διδασκαλίαν**· εἴ τι μαθεῖν, εἴ τι ἀγνοῆσαι χρὴ, ἐκεῖθεν εἰσόμεθα· εἰ ἐλέγξαι τὰ ψευδῆ, καὶ τοῦτο ἐκεῖθεν· εἰ ἐπανορθωθῆναι καὶ σωφρονισθῆναι, πρὸς παράκλησιν, πρὸς παραμυθίαν, φησὶ, **πρὸς ἐπανόρθωσιν**, τουτέστιν, εἴ τι λείπει καὶ χρὴ προστεθῆναι. **ἵνα ἄρτιος ᾖ ὁ τοῦ Θεοῦ ἄνθρωπος**· διὰ τοῦτό, φησι, γέγονεν ἡ τῶν γραφῶν παράκλησις, **ἵνα ἄρτιος ᾖ ὁ τοῦ Θεοῦ ἄνθρωπος**. Chrysost. in Epist. II ad Tim. Hom. IX; Opp. XI, 714 E.

Holy Scripture ministereth sufficient doctrine for all degrees and ages.

saith Fulgentius[3], "abundantly enough both for men to eat and children to suck. There is whatsoever is meet[u] for all ages and for all degrees and sorts of men."

What commodities and profits the knowledge of holy Scripture bringeth.

These books therefore ought to be much in our hands, in our eyes, in our ears, in our mouths, but most of all in our hearts. For the Scripture of God is the heavenly meat of our souls[β]: *the hearing and keeping of it* maketh us *blessed*[γ], *sanctifieth*[δ] us, and maketh us holy: *it turneth*[x] *our souls*[ε]: *it is a light lantern to our feet: it is* a *sure, steadfast, and everlasting*[y] instrument of salvation: *it giveth wisdom to the humble and lowlyhearted*[z]: *it* comforteth, *maketh glad,* cheereth, and cherisheth *our consciences*[a]: *it is* a *more excellent* jewel or treasure *than any gold or precious stone*[4]: *it is more sweet*[b] *than honey or honeycomb:* it is called *the best part,* which *Mary did choose*[ϛ][5]; for it hath in it everlasting comfort. The words of holy Scripture be called *words of everlasting*[c] *life*[ζ]; for they be God's instrument, ordained for the same purpose. They have power to turn[d] through[e] God's promise, and they be effectual[η] through God's assistance; and, being received in a faithful heart, they have ever an heavenly spiritual working in them. They are *lively, quick, and mighty in operation, and sharper than any two-edged sword, and entereth through*[f] *even unto the dividing asunder of the soul and the spirit, of the joints and the marrow.* Christ calleth[θ] him a wise builder that buildeth upon his word, upon his sure and substantial foundation. By this word of God we shall be judged; for *the word*[g] *that I speak*[h], saith Christ, *is it that shall judge in the last day.* He that keepeth the word of Christ is promised[ι] the love and favour of God, and that he shall be the dwellingplace[i] or temple of the blessed Trinity. This word whosoever is diligent

β Matt. iv, [4.]
γ Luke xi, [28.]
δ John xvii, [17.]
ε Ps. xix, [7–10; cxix, 105, 130.]
ϛ Luke x, [39, 42.]
ζ John vi, [68.]
η Col. i, [5, 6, 25–28.]
Heb. iv, [12.]
θ Matt. vii, [24.]
John xii, [48.]
ι John xiv, [23.]

[u] meet] convenient *till* 1559. [x] turneth] converteth *till* 1559. [y] steadfast, and everlasting] a constant, and a perpetual *till* 1559. [z] lowlyhearted] lowly hearts *from* 1547 G 2, *except* 1547 G 4. [a] consciences] conscience *from* 1548. [b] more sweet] more sweeter *till* 1559. [c] comfort. The words of holy Scripture be called words of everlasting] *omitted* 1623 b. [d] turn] convert *till* 1559. [e] turn through] turn thorough 1559. [f] entereth through] entereth thorough 1623. [g] for the word] for the words 1559–1569. [h] speak] spake 1547 G 1. [i] dwellingplace] mansion place *till* 1559.

3 In quibus denuo mandatis, tanquam ditissimis ferculis, sic coelestium deliciarum copia spiritalis exuberat, ut in verbo Dei abundet quod perfectus comedat, abundet etiam quod parvulus sugat. Ibi est enim simul et lacteus potus quo tenera fidelium infantia nutriatur, et solidus cibus quo robusta perfectorum juventus spiritalia sanctae virtutis accipiat incrementa. Ibi prorsus ad salutem consulitur universis quos Dominus salvare dignatur: ibi est quod omni aetati congruat, ibi quod omni professioni conveniat. *Fulgent. Serm.* I, § 1; *Opp. ed. Paris.* 1684, *p.* 546.

4 Desiderabilia super aurum et lapidem pretiosum multum. *Psal.* XVIII (*Heb.* XIX), 10, *Vulg.*

5 Maria optimam partem elegit. *Vulg.*

to read, and in his heart to print that he readeth, the great affection to the transitory things of this world shall be minished in him, and the great desire of heavenly things, that be therein promised of God, shall increase in him. And there is nothing that so much strengtheneth[k] our faith and trust in God, that so much keepeth up[l] innocency and pureness of the heart and also of outward godly life and conversation, as continual reading and recording[m] of God's word. For that thing which, by continual[n] use of reading of holy Scripture and diligent searching of the same, is deeply printed and graven in the heart, at length turneth almost into nature. And moreover the effect and virtue of God's word is to illuminate the ignorant, and to give more light unto them that faithfully and diligently read it; to comfort their hearts, and to encourage them to perform that which of God is commanded. It teacheth patience in all adversity, in prosperity humbleness; what honour is due unto God, what mercy and charity to our neighbour. It giveth good counsel in all doubtful things. It sheweth[κ] of whom we shall look for aid and help in all perils, and that God is the only Giver of victory in all battles and temptations of our enemies, bodily and ghostly. And in reading of God's word he most profiteth not always that is most ready in turning of the book, or in saying of it without the book; but he that is most turned into it, that is most inspired with the Holy Ghost, most in his heart and life altered and changed[o] into that thing which he readeth; he that is daily less and less proud, less wrathful[p], less covetous, and less desirous of worldly and vain pleasures; he that daily, forsaking his old vicious life, increaseth in virtue more and more. And, to be short, there is nothing that more maintaineth godliness of the mind, and driveth away[q] ungodliness, than doth the continual reading or hearing of God's word, if it be joined with a godly mind and a good affection to know and follow God's will. For without a single eye, pure intent, and good mind nothing is allowed for good before God. And, on the other side, nothing more darkeneth[r] Christ and the glory of God, nor bringeth in[s] more blindness and all kinds of vices, than doth the ignorance of God's word[λ].

κ 1 Sam. xiv, [6–23:] 2 Chron. xx, [1–30:] 1 Cor. xv, [57:] 1 John v, [4.]

Who profit most in reading God's word.

λ Isai. v, [13, 24:] Matt. xxii, [29:] 1 Cor. xiv.

What incommodities[t] the ignorance of God's word bringeth.

[k] strengtheneth] establisheth *till* 1559. [l] keepeth up] conserveth *till* 1559. [m] recording] meditation *till* 1559. [n] continual] perpetual *till* 1559. [o] changed] transformed *till* 1559. [p] wrathful] ireful *till* 1559. [q] driveth away] expelleth *till* 1559. [r] darkeneth] obscureth *till* 1559. [s] bringeth in] induceth *till* 1559. [t] incommodities] discommodities 1582, 1623.

THE SECOND PART OF THE SERMON OF THE HOLY[u] SCRIPTURE.

IN the first part of this Sermon[x], which exhorteth to the knowledge of holy Scripture, was declared wherefore the knowledge of the same is necessary and profitable to all men, and that by the true knowledge and understanding of Scripture the most necessary points of our duty towards God and our neighbours are also known. Now as concerning the same matter you shall hear what followeth.[y]

God's word excelleth all sciences.

If we profess Christ, why be we not ashamed to be ignorant in his doctrine, seeing that every man is ashamed to be ignorant in that learning which he professeth? That man is ashamed to be called a philosopher which readeth not the books of philosophy; and to be called a lawyer, an astronomer[z], or a physician[a], that is ignorant in the books of law, astronomy, and physic. How can any man then say that he professeth Christ and his religion, if he will not apply himself, as far forth as he can or may conveniently, to read and hear, and so to know, the books of Christ's Gospel and doctrine? Although other sciences be good and to be learned, yet no man can deny but this is the chief, and passeth all other incomparably. What excuse shall we therefore make at the last day before Christ, that delight to read or hear men's phantasies and inventions more than his most holy Gospel; and will find no time to do that which chiefly, above all things, we should do; and will rather read other things than that for the which we ought rather to leave reading of all other things? Let us therefore apply ourselves, as far forth as we can have time and leisure, to know God's word by diligent hearing and reading thereof, as many as profess God, and have faith and trust in him.

Vain excuses dissuading from the knowledge of God's word. The first. The second.

But they that have no good affection to God's word, to colour this their fault, allege commonly two vain and feigned excuses. Some go about to excuse them by their own frailness and fearfulness, saying[b] that they dare not read holy Scripture, lest through their ignorance they should fall into any error. Other pretend that the difficulty to understand it, and the hardness

[u] THE HOLY] THE KNOWLEDGE OF HOLY *from* 1576. [x] this Sermon] this Homily 1549 G.
[y] THE SECOND PART —— what followeth.] *not in* 1547 *or* 1548, *the Homily not being then divided.*
[z] an astronomer] and astronomer *from* 1547 G 5. [a] or a physician] or physician 1582, 1623.
[b] saying] feigning 1623 b.

thereof, is so great, that it is meet to be read only of clerks and learned men.

Matt. xxii, [29.]

As touching the first, ignorance of God's word is the cause of all error, as Christ himself affirmed to the Sadducees, saying, that *they erred, because they knew not the Scripture.* How should they then eschew error that will be still ignorant? and how should they come out of ignorance that will not read nor hear that thing which should give them knowledge? He that now hath most knowledge was at the first ignorant: yet he forbare not to read, for fear he should fall into error; but he diligently read, lest he should remain in ignorance, and through ignorance in error. And, if you will not know the truth of God (a thing most necessary for you), lest you fall into error, by the same reason you may then lie still, and never go, lest, if you go, you fall in the mire; nor eat any good meat, lest you take a surfeit; nor sow your corn, nor labour in your occupation, nor use your merchandise, for fear you lose your seed, your labour, your stock: and so, by that reason, it should be best for you to live idly, and never to take in hand to do any manner of good thing, lest peradventure some evil thing may chance thereof. And, if you be afraid to fall into error by reading of holy Scripture, I shall shew you how you may read it without danger of error. Read it humbly with a meek and a lowly [c] heart, to the intent you may glorify God, and not yourself, with the knowledge of it; and read it not without daily praying to God, that he would direct your reading to good effect; and take upon you to expound it no further than you can plainly understand it. For, as St. Augustine saith [6], the knowledge of holy Scripture is a great, large, and a high palace [d], but the door is very low; so that the high and arrogant man cannot run in, but he must stoop low and humble himself that shall enter into it. Presumption and arrogancy is

How most commodiously, and without all peril, the holy Scripture is to be read.

[c] and a lowly] and lowly 1582, 1623.

[d] palace] place *from* 1562 B.

6 Itaque institui animum intendere in Scripturas sanctas, ut viderem quales essent. Et ecce video rem non compertam superbis, neque nudatam pueris, sed incessu humilem, successu excelsam, et velatam mysteriis; et non eram ego talis ut intrare in eam possem, aut inclinare cervicem ad ejus gressus. *Augustin. Confess.* III, 5; *Opp.* I, 91 A. Cum primo puer ad divinas Scripturas ante vellem afferre acumen discutiendi quam pietatem quaerendi, ego ipse contra me perversis moribus claudebam januam Domini mei: quum pulsare deberem, ut aperiretur, addebam, ut clauderetur. Superbus enim audebam quaerere quod nisi humilis non potest invenire. *Augustin. Serm.* LI, 6; *Opp.* V, 285 G.

the[e] mother of all error: and humility needeth[f] to fear no error. For humility will only search to know the truth; it will search and will bring together[g] one place with another; and, where it cannot find out the meaning[h], it will pray, it will ask[i] of other that know, and will not presumptuously and rashly define any thing which it knoweth not. Therefore the humble man may search any truth boldly in the Scripture without any danger of error. And, if he be ignorant, he ought the more to read and to search holy Scripture, to bring him out of ignorance. I say not nay, but a man may prosper[k] with only hearing; but he may much more prosper[l] with both hearing and reading.

This have I said as touching the fear to read through[m] ignorance of the person. And concerning the hardness[n] of Scripture, he that is so weak that he is not able to brook strong meat[μ], yet he may suck the sweet and tender milk[7], and defer[o] the rest until he wax stronger and come to more knowledge. For God receiveth the learned and unlearned, and casteth away none, but is indifferent unto all. And the Scripture is full, as well of low valleys, plain ways, and easy for every man to use and to walk in, as also of high hills and mountains, which few men can climb[q] unto. And "whosoever giveth his mind to holy Scriptures with diligent study and burning[r] desire, it cannot be," saith St. John[s] Chrysostom[8], "that he should be left without[u] help. For either God Almighty will send him some godly doctor to teach[v] him, as he did to instruct Eunuchus[x], a nobleman of Ethiope, and treasurer unto queen Candace; who

μ [1 Cor. iii, 2; Heb. v, 12-14.]

Scripture in some places is easy, and in some places hard to be understand[p].

God leaveth no man untaught that hath a good[t] will to know his word.

[e] is the] are the 1623 b. [f] needeth] nedeth *till* 1582; endeth 1582, 1623 a; tendeth 1623 b. [g] bring together] confer *till* 1559. [h] find out the meaning] find the sense *till* 1559. [i] ask] inquire *till* 1559. [k], [l] prosper] profit 1623 b. [m] through] thorough 1559–1623 a. [n] hardness] difficulty *till* 1559. [o] defer] differ 1547 G 3–1563. [p] understand] understood 1623. [q] climb] ascend *till* 1559. [r] burning] fervent *till* 1559. [s] John] *omitted* 1582, 1623. [t] hath a good] hath good 1582, 1623. [u] left without] destitute of *till* 1559. [v] teach] instruct *till* 1559. [x] Eunuchus] the Eunuch 1623 b.

7 See the passage before cited from Fulgentius, p. 9, n. 3.

8 Οὐδὲ γάρ ἐστι τὸν μετὰ σπουδῆς καὶ πολλοῦ πόθου τοῖς θείοις ἐντυγχάνοντα περιοφθῆναί ποτε· ἀλλὰ, κἂν ἄνθρωπος ἡμῖν μὴ γένηται διδάσκαλος, αὐτὸς ὁ Δεσπότης ἄνωθεν ἐμβατεύων ταῖς καρδίαις ταῖς ἡμετέραις φωτίζει τὴν διάνοιαν, καταυγάζει τὸν λογισμὸν, ἐκκαλύπτει τὰ λανθάνοντα, διδάσκαλος ἡμῖν γίνεται τῶν ἀγνοουμένων.... Καὶ γὰρ ὁ εὐνοῦχος ἐκεῖνος ὁ βάρβαρος ὁ τῆς βασιλίσσης Αἰθιόπων...τὸν Προφήτην ἔχων μετὰ χεῖρας πολλὴν ἐποιεῖτο τὴν σπουδὴν πρὸς τὴν ἀνάγνωσιν, καὶ ταῦτα οὐκ εἰδὼς τὰ ἐγκείμενα.... Διὰ τοῦτο ὁ φιλάνθρωπος Δεσπότης ὁρῶν αὐτοῦ τὸν πόθον οὐ περιεῖδεν, ...ἀλλ' εὐθέως αὐτῷ τὸν διδάσκαλον ἔπεμψε. Chrysost. in Genes. Hom. XXXV; Opp. IV, 349 E—350 E. There is a similar passage in Conc. III de Laz., Opp. I, 740, which is cited by Cranmer in his Preface to the Bible.

having a great[y] affection to read the Scripture, although he understood it not, yet, for the desire that he had unto God's word, God sent his Apostle Philip to declare unto him the true sense of the Scripture that he read; or else, if we lack a learned man to instruct and teach us, yet God himself from above will give light unto our minds, and teach us those things which are necessary for us, and wherein we be ignorant." And in another place Chrysostom saith[9], that "man's human and worldly wisdom or science needeth not[a] to the understanding of Scripture, but the revelation of the Holy Ghost, who inspireth the true meaning[b] unto them that with humility and diligence do search therefore." *He that asketh shall have, and he that seeketh shall find, and he that knocketh shall have the door open.* If we read once, twice, or thrice, and understand not, let us not cease so, but still continue reading, praying, asking of other; and so, by still knocking, at the last the door shall be opened, as St. Augustine saith[10]. Although many things in the Scripture be spoken in obscure mysteries, yet there is nothing spoken under dark mysteries in one place but the selfsame thing in other places is spoken more[d] familiarly and plainly[11] to the capacity both of learned and unlearned. And those things in the Scripture that be plain to understand and necessary for salvation, every man's duty is to learn them, to print them in memory, and effectually to exercise them; and, as for the dark[g] mysteries, to be contented to be ignorant in them until such time as it shall please God to open those things unto him. In the mean season, if he lack either aptness or opportunity, God will not impute it to his folly: but yet it

How the knowledge of Scripture[z] may be attained unto.

Matt. vii, [8.]

A good rule for the understanding of the Scripture[c].

No man is excepted[e] from the knowledge of God's will[f].

[y] a great] *omitted* 1582, 1623. [z] knowledge of Scripture] knowledge of the Scripture *from* 1574. [a] needeth not] is not needful 1623 b. [b] meaning] sense *till* 1559. [c] understanding of the Scripture] understanding of Scripture *from* 1549 W. [d] more] *not in* 1547 G 1. [e] excepted] except 1547 G 1 *and* W 1–3. [f] God's will] God's word 1623 b. [g] the dark] the obscure *till* 1559.

9 *Οὐδὲ γὰρ σοφίας ἀνθρωπίνης δεῖται ἡ θεία γραφὴ πρὸς τὴν κατανόησιν τῶν γεγραμμένων, ἀλλὰ τῆς τοῦ Πνεύματος ἀποκαλύψεως, ἵνα τὸν ἀληθῆ νοῦν τῶν ἐγκειμένων καταμαθόντες πολλὴν ἐκεῖθεν δεξώμεθα τὴν ὠφέλειαν· ... μόνον ἐὰν νήφωμεν, καὶ μὴ ἁπλῶς παρατρέχωμεν, ἀλλὰ συντείνοντες ἡμῶν τὸν λογισμὸν κατοπτεύσωμεν ἅπαντα μετὰ ἀκριβείας.* Chrysost. in Genes. Hom. XXI; Opp. IV, 181 A.

10 Non enim quod in Scripturis sanctis tegitur ideo clausum est ut negetur, et non potius ut pulsanti aperiatur, dicente ipso Domino, *Petite, et accipietis; quaerite, et invenietis; pulsate, et aperietur vobis. Augustin. Serm.* CCLXX, *In Die Pentec.* IV; *Opp.* V, 1096 C. Augustine often uses this figure concerning obscurity in holy Scripture: see for instance *Enarrat.* I *in Psalm.* XXXIII, § 1; *in Psalm.* XCIII, § 1; *in Psalm.* CXLVI, § 12; *Opp.* IV, 208 D, E; 997 G; 1645 A.

11 Nihil enim de illis obscuritatibus eruitur quod non planissime dictum alibi reperiatur. *Augustin. de Doctr. Christian.* II, § 8; *Opp.* III, 22 A.

behoveth not that such as be apt should set aside reading, because some other be unapt to read. Nevertheless, for the hardness[h] of such places the reading of the whole ought not to be set apart. And briefly to conclude: as St. Augustine saith[12], by the Scripture all men be amended, weak men be strengthened, and strong men be comforted. So that surely none be enemies to the reading of God's word but such as either be so ignorant that they know not how wholesome a thing it is, or else be so sick that they hate the most comfortable medicine that should heal them, or so ungodly that they would wish the people still to continue in blindness and ignorance of God.

What persons would have ignorance to continue.

Thus we have briefly touched some part of the commodities of God's holy word, which is one of God's chief and principal benefits given and declared to mankind here in earth. Let us thank God heartily for this his great and special gift, beneficial favour, and fatherly providence. Let us be glad *to revive*[13] *this precious gift*[v] of our heavenly Father. Let us hear, read, and know these holy rules, injunctions, and statutes of our Christian religion, and upon that we have made profession to God at our baptism. Let us with fear and reverence lay up in the chest of our hearts these necessary and fruitful lessons. Let us *night and day* muse and *have meditation* and contemplation *in them*. Let us ruminate and as it were chew the cud, that we may have the sweet juice, spiritual effect, marrow, honey, kernel, taste, comfort, and consolation of them. Let us stay, quiet, and certify our consciences with the most infallible certainty, truth, and perpetual assurance of them. Let us pray to God, the only Author of these heavenly studies[i], that we may speak, think, believe, live, and depart hence according to the wholesome doctrine and verities of them. And by that means in this world we shall have God's defence[k], favour, and grace, with the unspeakable solace of peace and quietness of conscience, and after this miserable life we shall enjoy the endless bliss and glory of heaven. Which he grant us all that died for us all, Jesus Christ: to whom with the Father and Holy[l] Ghost be all honour and glory both now and everlastingly. Amen.[m]

The holy Scripture is one of God's chief benefits.

v [2 Tim. i, 6.]

The right reading, use, and fruitful studying in holy Scripture.

Ps. i, [2.]

h hardness] difficulty *till* 1559. i studies] meditations *till* 1559. k defence] protection *till* 1559. l and Holy] and the Holy *from* 1559. m Amen.] *omitted* 1623.

12 His salubriter et prava corriguntur, et parva nutriuntur, et magna oblectantur ingenia. Ille huic doctrinae inimicus est animus, qui vel errando eam nescit esse saluberrimam, vel odit aegrotando medicinam. *Augustin. Epist.* CXXXVII, § 18; *Opp.* II, 409 G.

13 'Αναμιμνήσκω σε ἀναζωπυρεῖν τὸ χάρισμα τοῦ Θεοῦ.

A SERMON[a]

OF THE MISERY OF ALL MANKIND AND OF HIS CONDEMNATION TO DEATH EVERLASTING BY HIS OWN SIN.

THE Holy Ghost, in writing the holy Scripture, is in nothing more diligent than to pull down man's vainglory and pride; which of all vices is most universally grafted in all mankind, even from the first infection of our first father Adam. And therefore we read in many places of Scripture many notable lessons against this old rooted vice, to teach us the most commendable virtue of humility, how to know ourselves, and to remember what we be of ourselves.

In the book of Genesis Almighty God giveth us all a title and name in our great-grandfather Adam, which ought to warn[b] us all to consider what we be, whereof we be, from whence we came, and whither we shall, saying thus: *In the sweat of thy face shalt thou eat thy bread*[c], *till thou be turned again into the ground; for out of it wast thou taken; inasmuch as thou art dust, and into*[d] *dust shalt thou be turned again.* Here, as it were in a glass, we may learn to know ourselves to be but ground, earth, and ashes, and that to earth and ashes we shall return. Also the holy patriarch Abraham did well remember this name and title, *dust*, earth, *and ashes*, appointed and assigned by God to all mankind; and therefore he calleth himself by that name[α], when he maketh his earnest prayer for Sodom and Gomorre. And we read that Judith, Hester, Job, Hieremy[β], with other holy men and women in the Old Testament, did use sackcloth, and to cast dust and ashes upon their heads, when they bewailed their sinful living. They called and cried to God for help and mercy with such a ceremony of sackcloth, dust, and ashes, that thereby they might declare to the whole world what an humble and lowly estimation they had of themselves, and how well they remembered their name and title aforesaid, their vile, corrupt, frail nature, dust, earth, and ashes.

Gen. iii, [19.]

α [Gen. xviii, 27.]

β Jud. iv, [10, 11;] and ix, [1: Esth. xiv, 2:] Job xlii, [6:] Jer. vi, [26;] and xxv, [34.]

a A SERMON] AN HOMILY *till* 1549 W. b warn] admonish *till* 1559. c eat thy bread] eat bread 1547 G 1. d dust, and into] dust, into *from* 1574.

The book of Wisdom also, willing to pull down our proud [Wisd. vii, [1–6.]] stomachs, moveth us diligently to remember our mortal and earthly generation, which we have all *of him that was first made;* and that *all men*, as well kings as subjects, *come into this world and go out of the same in like sort*, that is, as of ourselves, full miserable, as we may daily see. And Almighty God commanded his Prophet Esay to make a proclamation and cry to the whole world: and Esay asking, *What shall I cry?* the Lord [Isai. xl, [6, 7.]] answered, Cry that *all flesh is grass, and* that *all the glory thereof*[e] *is but as the flower of the field: when the*[f] *grass is withered, the flower falleth away, when the wind of the Lord bloweth upon it. The people surely is grass, the which drieth up, and the flower fadeth away.* And the holy Prophet[g] Job, having in himself great experience of the miserable and sinful estate of man, doth open the same to the world in these words. *Man*, [Job xiv, [1–4.]] saith he, *that is born of a woman, living but a short time, is full of manifold miseries. He springeth up like a flower, and fadeth again, vanishing*[h] *away as it were a shadow, and never continueth in one state. And dost thou judge it meet, O Lord, to open thine eyes upon such a one, and to bring him to judgment with thee? Who can make him clean that is conceived of an unclean seed?*[1] And all men, of their evilness and natural proneness, were[i] so universally given to sin, that, as the Scripture saith[γ], [γ Gen. vi, [6.]] *God repented that ever he made man:* and by sin his indignation was so much provoked against the world, that he drowned[δ] [δ Gen. vii.] all the world with Noe's flood, except Noe himself and his little household.

It is not without great cause that the Scripture of God doth so many times call all men here in this world by this word, *Earth. O thou earth, earth, earth,* saith Jeremy, *hear the word* [Jer. xxii, [29.]] *of the Lord.* This our right name, calling[k], and title, *Earth, Earth, Earth*, pronounced by the Prophet, sheweth what we be indeed, by whatsoever other style, title, or dignity men do call us. Thus he plainly nameth[l] us, who knoweth best both what we be, and what we ought of right to be called. And thus he setteth us forth[m], speaking by his faithful Apostle St. Paul: *All men, Jews and Gentiles, are under sin. There is none right-* [Rom. iii, [9–18.]] *eous, no, not one. There is none that understandeth; there is*

[e] glory thereof] glory of man thereof *till* 1559. [f] field: when the] field: the BON. [g] holy Prophet] holy man 1623. [h] vanishing] vanisheth 1582, 1623. [i] were] wer 1547 G 3–5, we 1547 G 6, be *from* 1548. [k] calling] vocation *till* 1559. [l] nameth] named *all except* 1547 W *and* BON. [m] setteth us forth] describeth us *till* 1559.

1 Quis potest facere mundum de immundo conceptum semine? *Vulg.*

none that seeketh after God. They are all gone out of the way; they are all unprofitable: there is none that doeth good, no, not one. Their throat is an open sepulchre; with their tongues they have used craft and deceit; the poison of serpents is under their lips. Their mouth is full of cursing and bitterness; their feet are swift to shed blood. Destruction and wretchedness are in their ways, and the way of peace have they not known: there is no fear of God before their eyes. And in another place St. Paul writeth thus: *God*[ε] *hath wrapped all nations in unbelief, that he might have mercy on all. The Scripture*[ζ] *shutteth up*[n] *all under sin, that the promise by the faith of Jesus*[o] *Christ should be given unto them that believe.* St. Paul in many places painteth us out in our colours, calling us[η] *the children of the wrath of God when we be born;* saying also[θ] that *we cannot think a good thought of ourselves,* much less we can[p] say well or do well of ourselves. And the Wise Man saith in the book of Proverbs, *The just man falleth seven times a day*[2].

ε Rom. xi, [32.] ζ Gal. iii, [22.] η Ephes. ii, [3.] θ [2 Cor. iii, 5.] Prov. xxiv, [16.]

The most tried and approved man Job *feared all his works*[3]. St. John the Baptist, being sanctified in his mother's womb, and praised before he was born[ι], called[q] *an angel*[4] and *great before the Lord, filled*[r] *even from his birth with the Holy Ghost, the preparer of the way for* our Saviour *Christ,* and commended of our Saviour Christ to be *more than a prophet* and *the greatest that ever was born of a woman,* yet he plainly granteth that he *had need to be washed of Christ*[κ]; he worthily extolleth and glorifieth his Lord and Master Christ, and humbleth himself as *unworthy to unbuckle his shoes*[λ], and giveth all honour and glory to God. So doth St. Paul both oft and evidently confess himself what[s] he was of himself[μ], ever giving, as a most faithful servant, all praise to his Master and Saviour. So doth blessed St. John the Evangelist, in the name of himself and of all other holy men, be they never so just, make this open confession: *If we say we have no sin, we deceive ourselves, and the truth is not in us. If we knowledge*[t] *our sins, God is faithful and just to forgive us our*[u] *sins, and to cleanse us from all unrighteousness.*

[Job ix, 28.] ι Luke i, [15, 76: Mal. iii, 1: Matth. xi, 9–11.] κ Matt. iii, [11, 14.] λ [Mark i, 7, 8.] μ [1 Cor. xv, 8–10: 1 Tim. i, 11–17.] 1 John i, [8–10.]

n shutteth up] concludeth *till* 1559. o Jesus] Jesu 1559–1576. p we can] can we *from* 1547 G 6: we can BON. q born, called] born, being called *from* 1549 W, *but not* BON. r filled] replenished *till* 1559. s what] that 1623. t knowledge] acknowledge 1623. u forgive us our] forgive our 1582, 1623.

2 Septies enim cadet (*al.* enim in die cadet) justus. *Vulg.*

3 Verebar omnia opera mea, sciens quod non parceres delinquenti. *Vulg.*

4 Hic est enim de quo scriptum est (*sc. Mal.* iii, 1), Ecce ego mitto angelum meum ante faciem tuam, qui praeparabit viam tuam ante te. *Matth.* xi, 10, *Vulg.*

If we say we have not sinned, we make him a liar, and his word is not in us. Wherefore the Wise Man, in the book called Ecclesiastes, maketh this true and general confession: *There is not one just man upon the earth that doeth good and sinneth not.* And St. David[x] is ashamed of his sin, but not to confess his sin[ν]: How oft, how earnestly and lamentably, doth he desire God's great mercy for his great offences, and that God should[ξ] *not enter into judgment with him!* And again, how well weigheth this holy man his sins, when he confesseth[o] that they be so many in number and so hid and hard to understand, that it is in manner[y] unpossible to know, utter, or number them! Wherefore, he having a true, earnest, and deep contemplation and consideration of his sins, and yet not coming to the bottom of them, he maketh supplication to God *to forgive him his privy, secret, hid sins,* to the knowledge of the which he[z] cannot attain.[a] He weigheth rightly his sins from the original root and spring-head, perceiving inclinations, provocations, stirrings, stingings, buds, branches, dregs, infections, tastes, feelings, and scents of them to continue in him still. Wherefore he saith[π], *Mark and behold, I was conceived in sins*[5]. He saith not *sin*, but in the plural number *sins*; forasmuch as out of one, as fountain[b], springeth all the rest.

And our[c] Saviour Christ saith[ρ] *there is none good but God,* and that *we can do nothing* that is good *without him,* nor no *man can come to the Father but by him.* He commandeth[σ] us all[d] to say that *we be unprofitable servants, when we have done all that we can do.* He preferreth[τ] the penitent Publican before the proud, holy, and glorious Pharisee. He calleth[υ] himself a *Physician, but not to them that be whole, but to them that be sick,* and have need of his salve for their sore. He teacheth[φ] us in our prayers to reknowledge ourselves sinners, and to ask forgiveness[e] and deliverance from all evils at our heavenly Father's hand. He declareth[χ] that the sins of our own hearts do defile our own selves. He teacheth that an evil word or thought deserveth condemnation, affirming[ψ] that *we shall give an account*[f] *for every idle word.* He saith[ω] *he came not to save but the sheep that were* utterly *lost* and cast away. Therefore few of the proud, just, learned, wise, perfect, and holy Pharisees

Eccles. vii, [20.]
ν Ps. li.
ξ Ps. cxlii [cxliii, 2.]
o Ps. xix, [12; xl, 12.]
π Ps. li, [5.]
ρ [Matt. xix, 17:] Mark x, [18:] Luke xviii, [19:] John xv, [5; xiv, 6.]
σ Luke xvii, [10.]
τ Luke xviii, [14.]
υ Matt. ix, [12.]
φ [Matt. vi, 12, 13: Luke xi, 4.]
χ [Matt. xv, 19, 20.]
ψ Matt. xii, [36.]
ω Matt. xv, [24.]

x And St. David] And David 1623. y in manner] in a manner 1623. z of the which he] of which we 1623. a attain.] attain unto, *all except* 1547 W 2 *and* 3, *and* BON. b as fountain] as a fountain 1623. c rest. And our] rest. Our *from* 1549 W, *but not* BON. d us all] us also 1623. e forgiveness] righteousness *from* 1547 G 6, *but not* BON. f give an account] give account 1623.

5 Ecce enim in iniquitatibus conceptus sum. *Vulg.*

were saved by him; because they justified themselves by their counterfeit holiness before men. Wherefore, good people, let us beware of such hypocrisy, vainglory, and justifying of ourselves. Let us look upon our feet; and then down peacock's[g] feathers, down proud heart, down vile[h] clay, frail and brittle vessels[i].

THE SECOND PART OF THE SERMON OF THE MISERY OF MAN.

FORASMUCH as the true knowledge of ourselves is very necessary to come to the right knowledge of God, ye have heard in the last reading how humbly all godly[k] men always have thought of themselves, and so to think and judge of themselves are taught of God their Creator by his holy word. For[l] of ourselves we be crabtrees, that can bring forth no apples. We be of ourselves of such earth as can bring forth but[m] weeds, nettles, brambles, briars, cockle, and darnel. Our fruits be declared in the fifth chapter to the Galathians. We have neither faith, charity, hope, patience, chastity, nor any thing else that good is, but of God; and therefore these virtues be called there *the fruits of the Holy Ghost*, and not the fruits of man.

Gal. v, [19–23.]

Let us therefore acknowledge ourselves before God, as we be indeed, miserable and wretched sinners. And let us earnestly repent, and humble ourselves heartily, and cry to God for mercy. Let us all confess with mouth and heart that we be full of imperfections. Let us know our own works, of what imperfection they be; and then we shall not stand foolishly and arrogantly in our own conceits, nor challenge any part of justification by our merits or works[n]. For truly there be[o] imperfections in our best works: we do not love God so much as we are bound to do, with all our heart, mind, and power; we do not fear God so much as we ought to do; we do not pray to God but with great and many imperfections; we give, forgive, believe, love[p], and hope unperfectly; we speak, think, and do unperfectly[q]; we fight against the devil, the world, and the flesh unperfectly[r]. Let us therefore not be ashamed to confess plainly our state of imperfection; yea, let us not be ashamed to confess imperfec-

[g] down peacock's] down our peacock's BON. [h] vile] vain 1547 W 2 *and* 3, *and* BON. [i] Let us look—vessels] *omitted in* 1549 W *and all from* 1559 *except the* 8vo. *edition of* 1562. [k] godly] good 1623 b. [l] THE SECOND PART—word. For] *not in* 1547 *or* 1548, *the Homily not being then divided; nor in* BON. [m] bring forth but] but bring forth 1623 b. [n] nor challenge—or works] *omitted in* BON. [o] there be] there is 1547 G 1, 1547 W, BON. [p] believe, love] believe, live *all except* 1547 W 2 *and* 3, *and* BON. [q] do unperfectly] do imperfectly 1623. [r] flesh unperfectly] flesh imperfectly 1623.

tion even in all our own best[s] works. Let none of us be ashamed to say with holy St. Peter, *I am a sinful man.* Luke v, [8.] Let us all say with the holy Prophet David[t], *We have sinned with our fathers; we have done amiss, and dealt wickedly.* Ps. cvi, [6.] Let us all make open confession with the prodigal son to our Father, and say with him, *We have sinned against heaven and before thee, O Father; we are not worthy to be called thy sons.* Luke xv, [18, 19.] Let us all say with holy Baruch[u], *O Lord our God, to us is worthily ascribed shame and confusion, and to thee righteousness: we have sinned, we have done wickedly, we have behaved ourselves ungodly in all thy righteousness.* Baruch ii, [6, 12.] Let us all say with the holy Prophet Daniel, *O Lord, righteousness belongeth to thee; unto us belongeth confusion. We have sinned, we have been naughty, we have offended, we have fled from thee, we have gone back from all thy precepts and judgments.* Dan. ix, [7, 5.] So we learn of all good men in holy Scripture[x] to humble ourselves, and to exalt, extol, praise, magnify, and glorify God.

Thus we have heard how evil we be of ourselves; how, of ourselves and by ourselves, we have no goodness, help, nor salvation, but contrariwise sin, damnation, and death everlasting: which if we deeply weigh and consider, we shall the better understand the great mercy of God, and how our salvation cometh only by Christ. For in ourselves, as of ourselves[α], we find nothing whereby we may be delivered from this miserable captivity, into the which we were cast, through the envy of the devil, by breaking[y] of God's commandment in our first parent Adam. We are all become unclean[β]: but we all are not able to cleanse ourselves, nor to make one another of us clean. We are *by nature the children of God's wrath*[γ]: but we are not able to make ourselves the children and inheritors of God's glory. We are *sheep that run astray*[δ]: but we cannot of our own power come again to the sheepfold; so great is our imperfection and weakness. In ourselves therefore may not we[z] glory, which of ourselves are nothing but sinful. Neither we may[a] rejoice in any works that we do; which all be so unperfect and unpure that they are not able to stand before the righteous judgment seat[b] of God, as the holy Prophet David saith: *Enter not into judgment with thy servant, O Lord; for no man that liveth shall be found righteous in thy sight.* Ps. cxliii, [2.]

α 2 Cor. iii, [5.]
β Ps. l [li, 1–10.]
γ Ephes. ii, [3.]
δ 1 Pet. ii, [25.]

[s] our own best] our best 1623. [t] us all say—David] us say—David *from* 1569. [u] all say—Baruch] also say—Baruch 1623 b. [x] Scripture] Scripturs 1559, Scriptures *from* 1562 A. [y] breaking] transgressing *till* 1559. [z] not we] we not 1582, 1623. [a] we may] may we BON., *and from* 1569. [b] judgment seat] throne *till* 1559.

To God therefore must we flee[c]; or else shall we never find peace, rest, and quietness of conscience in our hearts. For he is *the Father of mercies, and God of all consolation*[ε]. He is the Lord with whom *is plenteous redemption*[ζ]. He is the God which *of his own mercy saveth us*[η]; and setteth out his charity and exceeding love toward[d] us, in that of his own voluntary goodness, when we were perished, he saved us, and provided an everlasting kingdom for us. And all these heavenly treasures are given us, not for our own deserts, merits, or good deeds, which of ourselves we have none, but of his mere mercy freely. And for whose sake? Truly for Jesus Christ's[e] sake, that *pure and undefiled Lamb*[θ] of God. He is that dearly beloved Son for whose sake God is fully pacified, satisfied, and set at one with man. He is *the Lamb of God, which taketh away the sins of the world*[ι]: of whom only it may be truly spoken, that[κ] he did *all things well*, and *in his mouth was found no craft* nor subtilty. None but he alone may say, *The prince of the world came, and in me he hath nothing*[λ]. And he alone may say also[f], *Which of you shall reprove me of any fault*[μ]*?* He is *that high*[g] *and everlasting Priest*[ν], *which hath offered himself once for all* upon the altar of the cross, and *with that one oblation hath made perfect for evermore them that are sanctified.* He is the *alone Mediator between God and man*[ξ]; which *paid our ransom to God with his own blood;* and *with that hath he cleansed us all from sin.* He is the Physician *which healeth all our diseases*[ο]. He is that Saviour which *saveth his people from all their sins*[π]. To be short, he is that flowing and most plenteous fountain *of whose fulness all we have received*[ρ]. For *in him alone are all the treasures of the wisdom and knowledge of God hidden*[σ]; and in him, and by him, have we from God the Father all good things[τ] pertaining either to the body or to the soul.

ε 2 Cor. i, [3.]
ζ Ps. cxxx, [7.]
η [Tit. iii, 5: Rom. v, 8.]
θ [1 Pet. i, 19.]
ι John i, [29.]
κ [Mark vii, 37:] 1 Pet. ii, [22.]
λ John xiv, [30.]
μ John viii, [46.]
ν Heb. vii, [24–27; x, 14.]
ξ [1 Tim. ii, 5, 6: Rev. v, 9; i, 5:] 1 John i, [7.]
ο [Ps. ciii, 3.]
π Matt. i, [21.]
ρ John i, [16.]
σ [Col. ii, 3.]
τ [Rom. viii, 32.]

O how much are we bound to this our heavenly Father for his great mercies, which he hath so plenteously declared unto us in Christ Jesu our Lord and Saviour! What thanks worthy and sufficient can we give to him? Let us all with one accord burst out with joyful voices[h], ever praising and magnifying this Lord of mercy for his tender kindness shewed to[i] us in his dearly beloved Son Jesus Christ our Lord.

Hitherto have we heard what we are of ourselves; verily[k],

c flee] fly 1563, 1569, 1623 b. d toward] towards *from* 1547 G 3. e Christ's] Christ 1547 G 1. f say also] also say *from* 1562 B. g that high] the high *from* 1569. h voices] voice 1582, 1623. i shewed to] shewed unto *from* 1574. k verily] very *from* 1574.

sinful, wretched, and damnable. Again, we have heard how that, of ourselves and by ourselves, we are not able either to think a good thought, or work a good deed: so that we can find in ourselves no hope of salvation, but rather whatsoever maketh unto our destruction. Again, we have heard the tender kindness and great mercy of God the Father toward[l] us, and how beneficial he is to us for Christ's sake, without our merits or deserts, even of his own mere mercy and tender goodness. Now, how these exceeding great mercies of God, set abroad in Christ Jesu for us, be obtained, and how we be delivered from the captivity of sin, death, and hell, it shall more at large, with God's help, be declared in[m] the next Sermon[n]. In the mean season, yea, and at all times, let us learn to know ourselves, our frailty and weakness, without any cracking[o] or boasting of our own good deeds and merits. Let us also knowledge the exceeding mercy of God toward[p] us, and confess that, as of ourselves cometh all evil and damnation, so likewise of him cometh all goodness and salvation; as God himself saith by the Prophet Osee: *O Israel, thy destruction cometh of thyself, but in me only is thy help* and comfort. If we thus humbly submit ourselves in the sight of God, we may be sure that in the time of his visitation he will lift us up unto the kingdom of his dearly beloved Son Christ Jesu our Lord. To whom with the Father and the Holy Ghost be all honour and glory for ever. Amen.

Hos. xiii, [9.]

[l] toward] towards *from* 1547 G 5. [m] declared in] declared to you in 1547 G 1. [n] Sermon] Homily *till* 1549 W. [o] cracking] ostentation *till* 1559. [p] God toward] God towards *from* 1547 G 3.

A SERMON[a]

OF THE SALVATION OF MANKIND BY ONLY CHRIST OUR SAVIOUR FROM SIN AND DEATH EVERLASTING.

BECAUSE all men be sinners and offenders against God, and breakers of his law and commandments, therefore can no man by his own acts, works, and deeds, seem they never so good, be justified and made righteous before God; but every man of necessity is constrained to seek for another righteousness or justification, to be received at God's own hands, that is to say, the remission, pardon, and[b] forgiveness of his sins and trespasses in such things as he hath offended. And this justification or righteousness, which we so receive by[c] God's mercy and Christ's merits, embraced by faith, is taken, accepted, and allowed of God for our perfect and full justification.

For the more full understanding hereof, it is our parts and duty[d] ever to remember the great mercy of God; how that, all the world being wrapped in sin by breaking of the law, God sent his only Son our Saviour Christ into this world to fulfil the law for us, and by shedding of his most precious blood to make a sacrifice and satisfaction or (as it may be called) amends to his Father for our sins, to assuage his wrath and indignation conceived against us for the same. Insomuch that infants, being baptized and dying in their infancy, are by this sacrifice washed from their sins, brought to God's favour, and made his children and inheritors of his kingdom of heaven. And they which in act or deed[e] do sin after their baptism, when they turn[f] again to God unfeignedly, they are likewise washed by this sacrifice from their sins in such sort that there remaineth not any spot of sin that shall be imputed to their damnation. This is that justification or righteousness which St. Paul speaketh of when he saith[a], *No man is justified by the works of the law, but freely by*

The efficacy of Christ's passion and oblation.

a Rom. iii, [20, 22, 24.]

[a] A SERMON] AN HOMILY *till* 1549 W. [b] remission, pardon, and *omitted after* 1549 G. [c] receive by] receive of *from* 1562 B. [d] duty] duties *from* 1576. [e] in act or deed] actually *till* 1559. [f] they turn] they convert and turn *till* 1559.

faith in Jesus Christ. And again he saith[β], *We believe in Christ Jesus*[g], *that we be justified* freely *by the faith of Christ, and not by the works of the law; because that no man shall be justified by the works of the law.* β [Gal. ii, 16.]

And, although this justification be free unto us, yet it cometh not so freely unto[h] us that there is no ransom paid therefore at all.

An objection[i]. But here may man's reason be astonied, reasoning after this fashion. If a ransom be paid for our redemption, then it is[k] not given us freely: for a prisoner that payeth[l] his ransom is not let go freely; for, if he go freely, then he goeth without ransom; for what is it else to go freely than to be set at liberty without payment[m] of ransom?

An answer[n]. This reason is satisfied by the great wisdom of God in this mystery of our redemption; who hath so tempered his justice and mercy together, that he would neither by his justice condemn us unto the everlasting[o] captivity of the devil and his prison of hell, remediless for ever without mercy, nor by his mercy deliver us clearly without justice or payment of a just ransom, but with his[p] endless mercy he joined his most upright and equal justice. His great mercy he shewed unto us in delivering us from our former captivity without requiring of any ransom to be paid or amends to be made upon our parts; which thing by us had been impossible to be done. And, whereas it lay not in us that to do, he provided a ransom for us, that was, the most precious body and blood of his own most dear and best beloved Son Jesu Christ; who, besides his ransom[q], fulfilled the law for us perfectly. And so the justice of God and his mercy did embrace together, and fulfilled the mystery of our redemption. And of this justice and mercy of God knit together speaketh St. Paul in the third chapter to the Romans: *All have offended and have need of the glory of God*[1], *but are*[r] *justified freely by his grace by redemption which is in Jesu Christ; whom God hath set*[s] *forth to us for a reconciler and peacemaker*[2] *through faith in his blood, to shew his righteousness.* Rom. iii, [23-25.]

And in the tenth chapter: *Christ is the end of the Law unto* Rom. x, [4.]

[g] Christ Jesu] Jesu Christ *from* 1548. [h] freely unto] freely to 1547 G 1. [i] An objection] Objection *from* 1547 G 5. [k] then it is] then is it *from* 1547 G 5. [l] payeth] payed 1582, 1623. [m] without payment] without paying *from* 1576. [n] An answer] Answer *from* 1576. [o] everlasting] perpetual *till* 1559. [p] with his] without his 1623 b. [q] his ransom] this ransom *from* 1559. [r] but are] *inserted in* 1559. [s] set] sent *from* 1574.

[1] Egent gloria Dei. *Vulg.*

[2] Ὃν προέθετο ὁ Θεὸς ἱλαστήριον. Quem proposuit Deus propitiationem (*al.* propitiatorem): *Vulg.*

righteousness to every man that believeth. And in the eighth chapter: *That which was impossible by the Law, inasmuch as it was weak by the flesh, God sending his own Son in the similitude of sinful flesh by sin*[3] *damned sin in the flesh, that the righteousness of the Law might be fulfilled in us, which walk not after the flesh, but after the Spirit.*

Rom. viii, [3, 4.]

Three things must go together in our justification.

In these foresaid places the Apostle toucheth specially three things, which must go[t] together in our justification: upon God's part, his great mercy and grace; upon Christ's part, justice, that is, the satisfaction of God's justice, or the price of our redemption by the offering of his body and shedding of his blood with fulfilling of the law perfectly and throughly; and upon our part, true and lively faith in the merits of Jesu[u] Christ; which yet is not ours but by God's working in us. So that in our justification is not only God's mercy and grace, but also his justice, which the Apostle calleth *the justice of God*[4][γ]; and it consisteth in paying our ransom and fulfilling of the law. And so the grace of God doth not shut out[x] the justice of God in our justification, but only shutteth out[y] the justice of man, that is to say, the justice of our works, as to be merits of deserving our justification. And therefore St. Paul declareth here nothing upon the behalf of man concerning his justification, but only a true and lively faith; which nevertheless is *the gift of God*[δ], and not man's only work without God. And yet that faith doth not shut out[z] repentance, hope, love, dread, and the fear of God, to be joined with faith in every man that is justified; but it shutteth them out[b] from the office of[c] justifying. So that, although they be all present together in him that is justified, yet they justify not all together. Nor that[d] faith also doth not shut[e] out[f] the justice of our good works, necessarily to be done afterward[g] of duty towards God, (for we are most bounden to serve God in doing good deeds commanded by him in his holy Scripture all the days of our life;) but it excludeth them so that we may not do them to this intent, to be made good[h] by doing of them. For all the good works that we can

γ [Rom. iii, 21, 22, 25, 26.]

δ [Eph. ii, 8.]

How it is to be understand[a] that faith justifieth without works.

[t] must go] must concur and go *till* 1559. [u] of Jesu] of Jesus *from* 1576. [x] shut out] exclude *till* 1559. [y] shutteth out] excludeth *till* 1559. [a] understand] understood 1587, 1595, 1623. [b] shutteth them out] excludeth them *till* 1559. [c] office of] office or 1582, 1623. [d] Nor that] Nor the 1569–1623 a. [e] Nor that faith also doth not shut] Neither doth faith shut 1623 b. [f] shut out] exclude *till* 1559. [g] afterward] afterwards *from* 1574. [h] made good] made just 1623 b.

3 Καὶ περὶ ἁμαρτίας. Et de peccato; *Vulg.*
4 Δικαιοσύνη Θεοῦ. Justitia Dei: *Vulg.*

do be unperfect, and therefore not able to deserve our justification: but our justification doth come freely, by the mere mercy of God; and of so great and free mercy that, whereas all the world was not able of their selves to pay any part towards their ransom, it pleased our heavenly Father, of his infinite mercy, without any our desert or deserving, to prepare for us the most precious jewels of Christ's body and blood, whereby our ransom might be fully paid, the law fulfilled, and his justice fully satisfied. So that Christ is now the righteousness of all them that truly do believe in him. He for them paid their ransom by his death. He for them fulfilled the law in his life. So that now in him and by him every true Christian man may be called a fulfiller of the law; forasmuch as that which their infirmity lacketh[i] Christ's justice hath supplied.

THE SECOND PART OF THE SERMON OF SALVATION.

YE have heard of whom all men ought to seek their justification and righteousness, and how also this righteousness cometh unto men by Christ's death and merits. Ye heard also how that three things are required to the obtaining of our righteousness; that is, God's mercy, Christ's justice, and a true and a lively faith, out of the which faith springeth good works. Also[j] before was declared at large that no man can be justified by his own good works, because[k] that no man fulfilleth the law according to the full request[l] of the law. And St. Paul in his
Epistle to the Galathians proveth the same, saying thus: *If* Gal. iii, [21.]
there had been any law given which could have justified[5], *verily*
righteousness should have been by the law. And again he saith,
If righteousness be by the law, then Christ died in vain. And [Gal. ii, 21.]
again he saith, *You that are justified in the*[m] *law*[6] *are fallen* [Gal. v, 4.]
away from grace. And furthermore he writeth to the Ephesians
on this wise: *By grace are ye saved through faith; and that not* Eph. ii, [8,
of yourselves, for *it is the gift of God;* and *not of works, lest any* 9.]
man should glory. And, to be short, the sum of all Paul's dis-

[i] lacketh] lacked *from* 1574. [j] THE SECOND PART——works. Also] *not in* 1547 *or* 1548, *the Homily not being then divided.* [k] because] *omitted after* 1549 G. [l] full request] strict rigour 1623 b. [m] in the] by the *from* 1547 G's.

5 Νόμος ὁ δυνάμενος ζωοποιῆσαι. Lex quae posset vivificare: *Vulg.*
6 Ἐν νόμῳ. In lege: *Vulg.*

e [Rom. xi, 6.]

putation is this: that[e], if justice come of works, then it cometh not of grace; and, if it come of grace, then it cometh not of works. And to this end tendeth all the Prophets, as St. Peter saith in the tenth of the Acts. *Of Christ all the Prophets*, saith St. Peter, *do witness, that through his Name all they that believe in him shall receive the remission of sins.*

Acts x, [43.]

Faith only justifieth, is the doctrine of old doctors.

And after this wise to be justified, only by this true and lively faith in Christ, speaketh[n] all the old and ancient authors, both Greeks and Latins. Of whom I will specially rehearse three, Hilary, Basil, and Ambrose. St. Hilary saith these words plainly in the ninth Canon upon Matthew[7]: "Faith only justifieth." And St. Basil, a Greek author, writeth thus[8]: "This is a[o] perfect and a whole[p] rejoicing in God, when a man avaunteth[q] not himself for his own righteousness, but knowlegeth himself to lack true justice and righteousness, and to be justified by the only faith in Christ. And Paul," saith he, "doth glory in the contempt of his own righteousness, and that he looketh for *the*[r] *righteousness of God by faith.*" These be the very words of St. Basil. And St. Ambrose, a Latin author, saith these words[9]: "This is the ordinance of God, that he which believeth[s] in Christ should be saved without works, by faith only, freely receiving remission of his sins[t]." Consider diligently these words. Without works, by faith only, freely we receive remission of our sins. What can be spoken more plainly than to say that freely, without works, by faith only, we obtain remission of our sins?

Phil. iii, [9.]

These and other like sentences, that we be justified by faith

n speaketh] speak 1623 b. o thus: This is a] thus: This is a perfect and an whole glorying in God, when a man doth not boast himself for his own justice, but knoweth himself certainly to be unworthy of true justice, but to be justified by only faith in Christ. This is a 1547 G 1 *and* 2 *and* W 1, *so giving two versions of the same passage.* p and a whole] and whole 1623. q avaunteth] avaunceth 1547 G 2, 1548–1569, advaunceth 1574, 1576, advanceth 1582, 1623. r for the] for his *till* 1547 G 6. s that he which believeth] that he which believe 1559, 1562; that which believe 1563; that they which believe *from* 1569, *except* 1587 *and* 1595, *where* that we which believe. t his sins] their sins *from* 1569, *except* 1587 *and* 1595.

7 Fides enim sola justificat. *Hilar. Pictav. Comment. in Matth.* c. VIII, § 6; *Opp.* 646 D, *ed. Paris.* 1693.

8 Αὕτη γὰρ δὴ ἡ τελεία καὶ ὁλόκληρος καύχησις ἐν Θεῷ, ὅτε μήτε ἐπὶ δικαιοσύνῃ τὶς ἐπαίρεται τῇ ἑαυτοῦ, ἀλλ' ἔγνω μὲν ἐνδεῆ ὄντα ἑαυτὸν δικαιοσύνης ἀληθοῦς, πίστει δὲ μόνῃ τῇ εἰς Χριστὸν δεδικαιωμένον. καὶ καυχᾶται Παῦλος ἐπὶ τῷ καταφρονῆσαι τῆς ἑαυτοῦ δικαιοσύνης, ζητεῖν δὲ τὴν διὰ Χριστοῦ, τὴν ἐκ Θεοῦ δικαιοσύνην ἐπὶ τῇ πίστει. Basil. Homil. XX, De Humilitate, § 3; Opp. II, 158 E.

9 Quia hoc constitutum est a Deo, ut qui credit in Christum salvus sit sine opere, sola fide, gratis accipiens remissionem peccatorum. *Hilar. Diac. Comment. in Epist.* 1 *ad Cor.* I, 4; *Ambros. Opp.* II, *Append.* 112 D. The passage is here given as Erasmus edited it in 1527. The Benedictine editors put a colon after opere, and read accipit instead of accipiens.

Faith alone, how it is to be understand[y].

only, freely, and without works, we do read ofttimes in the most[u] best and ancient writers. As, beside Hilary, Basil, and St. Ambrose before rehearsed, we read the same in Origen, St. Chrysostom, St. Cyprian, St. Augustine, Prosper, Oecumenius, Photius[x], Bernardus, Anselm[10], and many other authors, Greek and Latin. Nevertheless, this sentence, that we be justified by faith only, is not so meant of them, that the said justifying faith is alone in man, without true repentance, hope, charity, dread, and fear[z] of God, at any time or season[a]. Nor when they say that we be justified freely, they mean not that we should or might afterward be idle, and that nothing should be required on our parts afterward; neither they mean not so[b] to be justified without our good[c] works that we should do no good works at all, like as shall be more expressed at large hereafter. But this saying[d], that we be justified by faith only, freely, and without works, is spoken for to take away clearly all merit of our works, as being unable[e] to deserve our justification at God's hands; and thereby most plainly to express the weakness of man and the goodness of God, the great infirmity

u most] *omitted* 1623 b. x Photius] Phocius 1547 G 2–1576; Procius 1582, 1623 a; Proclus 1623 b. y understand] understood 1623. z and fear] and the fear *from* 1547 G 6. a or season] and season *from* 1547 G 6. b they mean not so] mean they that we are so 1623 b. c without our good] without good 1623. d saying] proposition *till* 1559. e unable] insufficient *till* 1559.

10 See *Origen. Comment. in Epist. ad Rom. Lib.* III; *Opp.* IV, 517 *b* C, E:

Chrysost. in Epist. ad Rom. Hom. VII, §§ 3, 4; *Opp.* IX, 487 B, 488 E:

Rufin. Expositio in Symbolum Apostolorum, and *Arnold. Carnotens. Sermo de Ablutione Pedum*, both formerly ascribed to Cyprian, and still appended to his works; *pp.* 27, 46, *ed. Oxon.*; *coll.* ccxxvi (§ 40), cxxii, *ed. Paris.*: *Cyprian. Epist.* LXIII *ad Caecil.*, *Opp. p.* 149 *ed. Oxon.*, *p.* 105 *ed. Paris.*:

Augustin. Enarrat. II *in Psal.* XXXI, § 6; *De Fide et Oper.* § 21; *De Spir. et Lit.* §§ 11, 16, 45; *Opp.* IV, 174 C; VI, 177 C; X, 90 D, 93 B, 109 D:

Prosper. Aquitan. ad Rufin. de Grat. et Lib. Arbitr. §§ 8, 10:

Oecumen. in Epist. ad Rom. IV, 16, *Comment. cap.* V, *p.* 253 D *ed. Paris.* 1631:

Photius ap. Oecumen. in Epist. ad Rom. V, 2, *Comment. cap.* VI, *p.* 258 A:

Bernard. in Cantica Serm. LXVII, § 10; *Opp.* I, 1506 C, D:

Herv. Dolens. in Epist. ad Rom. III, 28, IV, 1–3, *int. Anselm. Opp.* II, 24 A, 25 C, *ed. Colon.* 1612: (see *Cave, Litt. Hist. an.* 1130).

The passages here cited from Rufinus and Arnoldus Carnotensis are placed, as extracts from Cyprian, under the head "Sola Fides" in the second volume of Cranmer's *Collectiones ex S. Scriptur. et Patribus*, preserved in the British Museum, Reg. MSS, 7 B, XII. The passage from Photius also is placed there under the same head. The other passages (except the one from Cyprian), together with many more of similar import, are comprised in the collection first published by Dr. Jenkyns in his edition of Cranmer's Works, vol. II, pp. 121–137, with the title "Notes on Justification, with Authorities from Scripture" &c., from a MS in Cranmer's hand at Lambeth. No extract on this subject from the genuine works of Cyprian is contained in either collection.

of ourselves and the might and power of God, the imperfectness of our own works and the most abundant grace of our Saviour Christ; and thereby wholly[f] for to[g] ascribe the merit and deserving of our justification unto Christ only and his most precious bloodshedding.

The profit of the doctrine of Faith only justifieth.

This faith the holy Scripture teacheth: this[h] is the strong rock and foundation of Christian religion: this doctrine all old and ancient authors of Christ's Church do approve: this doctrine advanceth[i] and setteth forth the true glory of Christ, and beateth down[j] the vain glory of man: this whosoever denieth is not to be[k] counted[l] for a true Christian[m] man, nor for[n] a setter forth of Christ's glory, but for an adversary of[o] Christ and his Gospel, and for a setter forth of men's vainglory.

What they be that impugn the doctrine of Faith[p] only justifieth.

And, although this doctrine be never so true, as it is most true indeed, that we be justified freely without all merit of our own good works (as St. Paul doth express it), and freely by this lively and perfect faith in Christ only (as the ancient authors use to speak it), yet this true doctrine must be also truly understand[q] and most plainly declared; lest carnal men should take unjustly occasion thereby to live carnally after the appetite and will of the world, the flesh, and the devil. And, because no man should err by mistaking of this doctrine[r], I shall[s] plainly and shortly so declare the right understanding of the same, that no man shall justly think that he may thereby take any occasion of carnal liberty to follow the desires of the flesh, or that thereby any kind of sin shall be committed, or any ungodly living the more used.

A declaration of this doctrine, Faith[t] without works justifieth.

First, you shall understand that in our justification by Christ it is not all one thing, the office of God unto man, and the office of man unto God. Justification is not the office of man, but of God. For man[u] cannot make himself righteous[x] by his own works, neither in part, nor in the whole; for that were the greatest arrogancy and presumption of man that Antichrist could set up[y] against God, to affirm that a man might by his own works take away and purge his own sins, and so justify

[f] thereby wholly] therefore wholly *from* 1547 G 6. [g] wholly for to] wholly to *from* 1547 G 3. [h] teacheth: this] teacheth us: this 1623. [i] advanceth] avaunceth 1547 G 2–1569. [j] beateth down] suppresseth *till* 1559. [k] not to be] not be 1623 a. [l] counted] reputed *till* 1559, accounted 1623. [m] a true Christian] a Christian *from* 1547 G 6. [n] nor for] not for 1559–1569, 1587. [o] adversary of] adversary to *from* 1547 G 6. [p] What... doctrine of Faith] What... doctrine, Faith 1623 b. [q] understand] understood 1587, 1595, 1623. [r] mistaking of this doctrine] mistaking of this true doctrine 1547 G 1. [s] I shall] I will 1623 b. [t] doctrine, Faith] doctrine of Faith 1563–1623 a. [u] For man] or man 1582, 1623. [x] make himself righteous] justify himself 1547–1551, making himself righteous 1559–1563, 1587. [y] set up] erect *till* 1559.

himself. But justification[z] is the office of God only; and is not a thing which we render unto him, but which we receive of him; not which we give to him, but which we take of him, by his free mercy, and by the only merits of his most dearly beloved Son, our only Redeemer, Saviour, and Justifier, Jesus Christ. So that the true understanding of this doctrine, We be justified freely by faith without works, or that we be justified by faith in Christ only, is not that this our own act, to believe in Christ, or this our faith in Christ, which is within us, doth justify us and deserve[a] our justification unto us; for that were to count ourselves to be justified by some act or virtue that is within ourselves. But the true understanding and meaning thereof is, that, although we hear God's word and believe it, although we have faith, hope, charity, repentance, dread, and fear of God within us, and do never so many good works[b] thereunto, yet we must renounce the merit of all our said virtues of faith, hope, charity, and all our other[c] virtues and good deeds, which we either have done, shall do, or can do, as things that be far too weak and insufficient and unperfect to deserve remission of our sins and our justification; and therefore we must trust only in God's mercy, and in that[d] sacrifice which our High Priest and Saviour Christ Jesus, the Son of God, once offered for us upon the cross, to obtain thereby God's grace, and remission, as well of our original sin in baptism, as of all actual sin committed by us after our baptism, if we truly repent and turn[e] unfeignedly to him again. So that, as St.[f] John Baptist, although he were never so virtuous and godly a man, yet in this matter of forgiving of sin he did put the people from him, and appointed them unto Christ, saying thus unto them, *Behold, yonder is the Lamb of God, which taketh away the sins of the world;* even so, as great and as godly a virtue as the lively faith is, yet it putteth us from itself, and remitteth or appointeth us unto Christ, for to have only by him remission of our sins or justification. So that our faith in Christ, as it were, saith unto us thus: It is not I that take away your sins, but it is Christ only; and to him only I send you for that purpose, forsaking[g] therein all your good virtues, words, thoughts, and works, and only putting your trust in Christ.

Justification is the office of God only.

John i, [29.]

[z] But justification] But in justification 1559–1576. [a] deserve] merit *till* 1559. [b] many good works] many works 1623. [c] all our other] all other 1582, 1623. [d] and in that] and that *from* 1559. [e] turn] convert *till* 1559. [f] that, as St.] that St. 1623 b. [g] forsaking] renouncing *till* 1559.

THE THIRD PART OF THE SERMON OF SALVATION.

IT hath been manifestly declared unto you that no man can fulfil the law of God; and therefore by the law all men are condemned: whereupon it followed[h] necessarily that some other thing should be required for our salvation than the law; and that is a true and a lively faith in Christ, bringing forth good works and a life according to God's commandments. And also you heard the ancient authors' minds[i] of this saying[k], Faith in Christ only justifieth man, so plainly declared, that you see[l] that the very true meaning[m] [n] of this proposition (or saying[o]), We be justified by faith in Christ only, according to the meaning of the old ancient authors, is this: We put our faith in Christ, that we be justified by him only, that we be justified by God's free mercy and the merits of our Saviour Christ only, and by no virtue or good work[p] of our own that is in us, or that we can be able to have or to do, for to deserve the same, Christ himself only being the cause meritorious thereof.

Here you perceive many words to be used, to avoid contention in words with them that delight[q] to brawl about words, and also to shew the true meaning, to avoid evil taking[r] and misunderstanding: and yet peradventure all will not serve with them that be contentious; but contenders will ever forge matter[s] of contention, even when they have none occasion thereto. Notwithstanding, such be the less to be passed upon, so that the rest may profit, which will be more[t] desirous to know the truth than, when it is plain enough, to contend about it, and with contentious[u] and captious cavillations[x] to obscure and darken it. Truth it is that our own works do not justify[y] us, to speak properly of our justification; that is to say, our works do not merit or deserve remission of our sins, and make us, of unjust, just before God; but God of his mere[z] mercy, through the only merits and deservings[a] of his Son Jesus Christ, doth justify us. Nevertheless, because faith doth directly send us to

[h] followed] followeth *from* 1574. [i] minds] mind 1549 G. [k] this saying] this proposition *till* 1559. [l] THE THIRD PART——that you see] Thus you do see 1547 *and* 1548, *the Homily not being then divided.* [m] true meaning] true sense *till* 1559. [n] declared, that you see that the very true meaning] declared, that you see the very true sense, &c. Thus you do see that the very true sense 1549 G, 1551. [o] or saying] *added in* 1559. [p] work] works 1582, 1623. [q] delight] delighteth 1547 G 1. [r] taking] talking 1547 G 2–1549 G, 1595. [s] matter] matters *from* 1569. [t] more] the most 1623. [u] contentious] contentions 1547 G 1 *and* 2. [x] cavillations] cavillation *from* 1569. [y] do not justify] doth not justify 1547 G 1. [z] mere] own *from* 1574. [a] and deservings] or deserving 1547 G 1.

Christ for remission of our sins, and that by faith given us of God we embrace the promise of God's mercy and of the remission of our sins, which thing none other of our virtues or works properly doeth, therefore Scripture[b] useth to say, that faith without works doth justify. And, forasmuch that it is all one sentence in effect to say, Faith without works, and, Only faith, doth justify us, therefore the old ancient fathers of the Church from time to time have uttered our justification with this speech, Only faith justifieth us; meaning none other thing than St. Paul meant when he said, Faith without works justifieth us. And, because all this is brought[c] to pass through the only merits and deservings of our Saviour Christ, and not through our merits, or through the merit of any virtue that we have within us, or of any work that cometh from us, therefore, in that respect of merit and deserving, we forsake[d] as it were altogether again faith, works, and all other virtues. For our own imperfection is so great, through the corruption of original sin, that all is imperfect[e] that is within us, faith, charity, hope, dread, thoughts, words, and works, and therefore not apt to merit and deserve[f] any part of our justification for us. And this form of speaking we use[g] in the humbling of ourselves to God, and to give all the glory to our Saviour Christ, which is best worthy to have it.

Here you have heard the office of God in our justification, and how we receive it of him freely, by his mercy, without our deserts, through true and lively faith. Now you shall hear the office and duty of a Christian man unto God, what we ought on our part[h] to render unto God again for his great mercy and goodness. Our office is not to pass the time of this present life unfruitfully and idly after that we are baptized or justified, not caring how few good works we do to the glory of God and profit of our neighbours: much less it is[i] our office, after that we be once made Christ's members, to live contrary to the same, making ourselves members of the devil, walking after his inticements and after the suggestions of the world and the flesh; whereby we know that we do serve the world and the devil, and not God. For that faith which bringeth forth, without repentance, either evil works or no good works is[k] not a right, pure, and lively faith, but a dead, devilish, counterfeit,

They that preach, Faith only justifieth, do not teach carnal liberty, or that we should do no good works.

[b] therefore Scripture] therefore the Scripture 1623 b. [c] this is brought] this brought 1582, 1623. [d] forsake] renounce *till* 1559. [e] imperfect] unperfect *from* 1574. [f] deserve] discern 1582, 1623 a. [g] we use] use we *from* 1547 G 6. [h] part] party 1547 G 1 *and* 2. [i] it is] is it *from* 1559. [k] works is] work is 1623 b.

ϛ [2 Tim. iii, 5: Tit. i, 16: James ii, 17–20, 26. *See below, p. 36.*]

The devils have faith, but not the true faith.

and feigned faith, as St. Paul and St. James call it[ϛ]. For even the devils know and believe that Christ was born of a virgin, that he fasted forty days and forty nights without meat and drink, that he wrought all kind of miracles, declaring himself very God. They believe also that Christ for our sakes suffered most painful death, to redeem us[l] from everlasting[m] death, and that he rose again from death the third day: they believe that he ascended into heaven, and that he sitteth on the right hand of the Father, and at the last end of this world shall come again and judge both the quick and the dead. These articles of our faith the devils believe; and so they believe all things that be written in the New and Old Testament to be true: and yet for all this faith they be but devils, remaining still in their damnable estate, lacking the very true Christian faith. For the right and true Christian faith is, not only to believe that holy Scripture and all the foresaid articles of our faith are true, but also to have a sure trust and confidence in God's merciful promises to be saved from everlasting damnation by Christ; whereof doth follow a loving heart to obey his commandments. And this true Christian faith neither any devil hath, nor yet any man which, in the outward profession of his mouth and in his outward receiving of the Sacraments, in coming to the church and in all other outward appearances, seemeth to be a Christian man, and yet in his living and deeds sheweth the contrary. For how can a man have this true faith, this sure trust and confidence in God, that by the merits of Christ his sins be forgiven[n], and he[o] reconciled to the favour of God, and to be partaker of the kingdom of heaven by Christ, when he liveth ungodly and denieth Christ in his deeds? Surely no such ungodly man can have this faith and trust in God. For, as they know Christ to be the only Saviour of the world, so they know also that wicked men shall not enjoy[p] the kingdom of God. They know that God *hateth unrighteousness*[ζ], that *he will destroy all those that speak untruly;* that *those that*[q] *have done good works*[η], which cannot be done without a lively faith in Christ, *shall come forth into the resurrection of life, and those that have done evil shall come unto the resurrection*[r] *of judgment.* And very[s] well they know also that *to them that be contentious*[θ], *and to them that will not be obedient unto the truth, but will*

What is the true and justifying faith.

They that continue in evil living have not true faith.

ζ Ps. v, [5, 6.]

η [John v, 29.]

θ [Rom. ii, 8, 9.]

[l] us] *omitted* 1582, 1623. [m] everlasting] eternal *till* 1559. [n] forgiven] remitted *till* 1559. [o] and he] and be 1582, 1623 a. [p] enjoy] possess *till* 1559. [q] that those that] that those which 1582, 1623. [r] unto the resurrection] unto resurrection *all except* 1547 W 2 *and* 3, 1582, *and* 1623. [s] And very] Very *from* 1559.

obey unrighteousness, shall come indignation, wrath, and affliction, &c.

Therefore, to conclude, considering the infinite benefits of God shewed and given[t] unto us mercifully without our deserts; who hath not only created us of nothing, and from a piece of vile clay, of his infinite goodness, hath exalted us, as touching our soul, unto his own similitude and likeness; but also, whereas we were[u] condemned to hell and death everlasting[x], hath given his own natural Son (being God eternal, immortal, and equal unto himself in power and glory) to be incarnated, and to take our mortal nature upon him with the infirmities of the same, and in the same nature to suffer most shameful and painful death for our offences, to the intent to justify us and to restore us to life everlasting; so making us also his dear beloved[y] children, brethren[ι] unto his only Son our Saviour Christ, and inheritors for ever with him of his eternal kingdom of heaven: these great and merciful benefits of God, if they be well considered, do neither minister unto us occasion to be idle and to live without doing any good works, neither yet stirreth us by[z] any means to do evil things; but contrariwise, if we be not desperate persons, and our hearts harder than stones, they move us to render ourselves unto God wholly with all our will, hearts, might, and power; to serve him in all good deeds, obeying his commandments during our lives; to seek in all things his glory and honour, not our sensual pleasures and vainglory; evermore dreading willingly to offend such a merciful God and loving Redeemer in word, thought, or deed. And the said benefits of[a] God, deeply considered, do move[b] us for his sake also to be ever ready to give ourselves to our neighbours, and, as much as lieth in us, to study with all our endeavour to do good to every man. These be the fruits of the true[c] faith: to do good, as much as lieth in us, to every man; and, above all things and in all things, to advance[d] the glory of God, of whom only we have our sanctification, justification, salvation, and redemption. To whom be ever glory, praise, and honour world without end. Amen.

ι [Heb. ii, 11.]

[t] given] exhibited *till* 1559. [u] were] have 1623 b. [x] death everlasting] death eternal *till* 1559. [y] beloved] *omitted after* 1551, *except in* 1587 *and* 1595. [z] us by] us up by *from* 1574. [a] said benefits of] said benefits to 1623 b. [b] considered, do move] considered, move *from* 1548. [c] of the true] of true *from* 1574. [d] advance] avaunce 1547, G 3–1563.

A SHORT DECLARATION

OF THE TRUE, LIVELY, AND CHRISTIAN FAITH.

Faith.

THE first coming[a] unto God, good Christian people, is through faith; whereby, as it is declared in the last Sermon, we be justified before God. And, lest any man should be deceived for lack of right understanding thereof[b], it is diligently to be noted that faith is taken in the Scripture two manner of ways.

A dead faith. James ii, [17, 19.]

There is one faith which in Scripture is called a *dead* faith; which bringeth forth no good works, but is idle, barren, and unfruitful. And this faith by the holy Apostle St. James is compared to the faith of *devils*; which *believe* God to be true and just, *and tremble* for fear, yet they do nothing well, but all evil. And such a manner of faith have the wicked and naughty Christian people; which *confess God*, as St. Paul saith, *in their mouth, but deny him in their deeds, being abominable and without the right faith and to all*[c] *good works reproveable*[1]. And this faith is a persuasion and belief in man's heart, whereby he knoweth that there is a God, and agreeth[d] unto all truth of God's most holy word contained in holy[e] Scripture. So that it consisteth only in believing of the[f] word of God, that it is true. And this is not properly called faith: but, as he that readeth Cesar's Commentaries, believing the same to be true, hath thereby a knowledge of Cesar's life and notable[g] acts, because he believeth the history of Cesar, yet it is not properly said that he believeth in Cesar, of whom he looketh for no help nor benefit; even so he that believeth that all that is spoken of God in the Bible is true, and yet liveth so ungodly that he cannot look to enjoy the promises and benefits of God, although it may be said that such a man hath a faith and belief to the words of God, yet it is not properly said that he believeth in

Tit. i, [16.]

[a] coming] entry *till* 1559. [b] hereof] thereof *from* 1547 G 4. [c] to all] in all 1547 G 1 *and* 2. [d] agreeth] assenteth *till* 1559. [e] in holy] in the holy 1582, 1623. [f] believing of the] believing in the 1547 G 6–1623 a, believing the 1623 b. [g] notable] noble *till* 1559.

1 'Απειθεῖς καὶ πρὸς πᾶν ἔργον ἀγαθὸν ἀδόκιμοι. Incredibiles et ad omne opus bonum reprobi: *Vulg.*

God, or hath such a faith and trust in God whereby he may surely look for grace, mercy, and everlasting[h] life at God's hand, but rather for indignation and punishment according to the merits of his wicked life. For, as it is written in a book intituled to be of Didymus Alexandrinus[i], "forasmuch[2] as faith without works is dead, it is not now faith; as a dead man is not a man." This dead faith therefore is not that sure[k] and substantial faith which saveth sinners.

A lively faith.

Another faith there is in Scripture, which is not, as the foresaid faith, idle, unfruitful, and dead, but *worketh by charity*, as St. Paul declareth Gal. v: which, as the other vain faith is called a dead faith, so may this be called a quick or lively faith. And this is not only the common belief of the articles of our faith, but it is also a sure[l] trust and confidence of the mercy of God through our Lord Jesus Christ, and a steadfast hope of all good things to be received at God's hand; and that, although we through infirmity or temptation of our ghostly enemy do fall from him by sin, yet, if we return again unto him by true repentance, that he will forgive and forget our offences for his Son's sake our Saviour Jesus Christ, and will make us inheritors with him of his everlasting kingdom; and that in the mean time, until that kingdom come, he will be our protector and defender in all perils and dangers, whatsoever do chance; and that, though sometime he doth[m] send us sharp adversity, yet that evermore he will be a loving Father unto us, correcting us for our sin, but not withdrawing his mercy finally from us, if we trust in him, and commit ourselves wholly unto[n] him, hang only upon him, and call upon him, ready to obey and serve him. This is the true, lively, and unfeigned Christian faith, and is not in the mouth and outward profession only, but it liveth, and stirreth inwardly in the heart. And this faith is not without hope and trust in God, nor without the love of God and of our neighbours, nor without the fear of God, nor without the desire to hear God's word, and to follow the same in eschewing evil and doing gladly all good works. This faith, as St. Paul describeth it, is the sure ground and foundation of the benefits which we ought to look for and trust to receive of God,

[Gal. v, 6.]

Heb. xi, [1.]

[h] everlasting] eternal *till* 1559. [i] Alexandrinus] Alexandrius 1582, 1623 a. [k] that sure] the sure *from* 1559. [l] a sure] a true *from* 1563, *except* 1587 *and* 1595. [m] doth] do 1547 G 1. [n] wholly unto] wholly to 1547 G 1.

[2] Notandum scilicet quia, cum fides mortua sit praeter opera, jam neque fides est. Nam neque homo mortuus homo est. *Didym. Alexandr. in Epist. Jacob. c.* II, *Interpr. Epiphan. Scholast.*

a certificate and sure looking for[o] them, although they yet sensibly appear not unto us. And after he saith, *He that cometh to God must believe both that he is, and that he is a merciful rewarder of well doers.* And nothing commendeth good men unto God so much as this assured faith and trust in him.

Ibid. [6.]

Three things are to be noted of faith.

Of this faith three things are specially to be noted: first, that this faith doth not lie dead in the heart, but is lively and fruitful in bringing forth good works; second[p], that without it can no good works be done, that shall be acceptable and pleasant to God; third[q], what manner of good works they be that this faith doth bring forth.

Faith is full of good works.

For the first. As[r] the light cannot be hid, but will shew forth itself at one place or other; so a true faith cannot be kept secret, but, when occasion is offered, it will break out and shew itself by good works. And, as the living body of a man ever exerciseth such things as belongeth[s] to a natural and living body for nourishment and preservation of the same, as it hath need, opportunity, and occasion; even so the soul that hath a lively faith in it will be doing alway some good work, which shall declare that it is living, and will not be unoccupied.

Therefore, when men hear in the Scriptures so high commendations of faith, that it maketh us to please God, to live with God, and to be the children of God; if then they phantasy that they be set at liberty from doing all good works, and may live as they list[t], they trifle with God, and deceive themselves. And it is a manifest token that they be far from having the true and lively faith, and also far from knowledge what true faith meaneth. For the very sure and lively Christian faith is not only to believe all things of God which are contained in holy Scripture, but also is[u] an earnest trust and confidence in God, that he doth regard us, and that he is careful over[x] us, as the father is over[y] the child whom he doth love, and that he will be merciful unto us for his only Son's sake; and that we have our Saviour Christ our perpetual Advocate and Priest[z]; in whose only merits, oblation, and suffering we do trust that our offences be continually washed and purged, whensoever we, repenting truly, do return to him with our whole heart, steadfastly determining with ourselves, through his[a] grace, to obey

[o] looking for] expectation of *till* 1559. [p] second] Secondly 1623 b. [q] third] Thirdly 1623 b. [r] As] that 1582, 1623. [s] belongeth] belong 1623 b. [t] list] lust 1549 W, 1559—1623 a. [u] also is] also to have 1623 b. [x] that he is careful over] hath cure of *till* 1559. [y] is over] of *till* 1559. [z] Priest] Prince 1623 b. [a] through his] thorough his 1559—1563.

and serve him in keeping his commandments, and never to turn back again to sin. Such is the true faith that the Scripture doth so much commend: the which[b], when it seeth and considereth what God hath done for us, is also moved, through continual assistance of the Spirit of God, to serve and please him, to keep his favour, to fear his displeasure, to continue his obedient children, shewing thankfulness again by observing (or keeping[c]) his commandments; and that freely, for true love chiefly, and not for dread of punishment or love of temporal reward, considering how clearly without our deservings[d] we have received his mercy and pardon freely.

This true faith will shew forth itself, and cannot long be idle. For, as it is written, *The just man doth[e] live by his faith*[f], he neither[g] sleepeth nor is idle, when he should[h] wake and be well occupied. And God by his Prophet Jeremy saith, that *he is a happy and blessed man which hath faith and confidence in God: for he is like a tree set by the water side, that spreadeth*[i] *his roots abroad toward the moisture, and feareth not heat when it cometh; his leaf will be green, and will not cease to bring forth his fruit.* Even so faithful men, putting away all fear of adversity, will shew forth the fruit of their good works, as occasion is offered to do them.

Hab. ii, [4.]

Jer. xvii, [7, 8.]

THE SECOND PART OF THE SERMON OF FAITH.

YE have heard in the first part of this Sermon that there be two kinds of faith, a dead and an unfruitful faith, and a faith lively *that worketh by charity;* the first to be unprofitable, the second necessary for the obtaining of our salvation; the which faith hath charity always joined unto it, and is fruitful, bringing[k] forth all good works. Now as concerning the same matter you shall hear what followeth.[l]

[Gal. v, 6.]

The Wise Man saith, *He that believeth in God will hearken unto his commandments.* For, if we do not shew ourselves faithful in our conversation, the faith which we pretend to have is but a feigned faith; because the true Christian faith is manifestly shewed by good living, and not by words only, as St. Au-

Ecclus. xxxii, [24.]

[b] the which] that which 1623 b. [c] or keeping] *added in* 1559. [d] without our deservings] without deservings 1582, 1623. [e] doth] shall 1623 b. [f] by his faith] by faith 1623 b. [g] neither] never 1582, 1623. [h] should] would *from* 1569. [i] that spreadeth] and spreadeth 1582, 1623. [k] bringing] and bringeth 1582, 1623. [l] THE SECOND PART——what followeth.] *not in* 1547 *or* 1548, *the Homily not being then divided.*

Lib. de Fide et Operibus, cap. 2. Serm. de Lege et Fide.

gustine saith[3], "Good living cannot be separated from true *faith, which worketh by love.*" And St. Chrysostom saith[4], "Faith of itself is full of good works: as soon as a man doth believe, he shall be garnished with them."

Heb. xi. α Gen. iv, [4, 5.] β Gen. vi, [22:] Ecclus. xliv, [17.] γ Gen. xi, [31; xii, 1–5.]

How plentiful this faith is of good works, and how it maketh the work of one man more acceptable to God than of another, St. Paul teacheth at large in the eleventh chapter to the Hebrews, saying that faith made the oblation of Abel[α] better than the oblation of Cain. This made Noe[β] to build the ark. This made Abraham[γ] to forsake his country and all his friends, and to go unto[m] a far country, there to dwell among strangers. So did also Isaac and Jacob, depending (or hanging[n]) only of the help and trust that they had in God. And, when they came to the country which God promised them, they would build no cities, towns, nor houses; but lived like strangers in tents, that might every day be removed. Their trust was so much in God that they set but little by any worldly thing; for that God had prepared for them better dwellingplaces in heaven of his own foundation and building. This faith made Abraham[δ] ready at God's commandment to offer his own son and heir Isaac, whom he loved so well, and by whom he was promised to have innumerable issue, among the which one should be born in whom all nations should be blessed; trusting so much in God, that though he were slain, yet that God was able by his omnipotent power to raise him from death, and perform his promise. He mistrusted not the promise of God, although unto his reason every thing seemed contrary. He believed verily that God would not forsake him in dearth[o] and famine, that was in the country. And, in all other dangers that he was brought unto, he trusted ever that God would be[p] his God and his protector and defender[q], whatsoever he saw to the contrary. This faith

δ Gen. xxii, [1–18:] Ecclus. xliv, [20.]

[m] go unto] go into *from* 1559. [n] or hanging] *added in* 1559. [o] dearth] death 1582, 1623. [p] would be] should be 1582, 1623. [q] and defender] *added in* 1559.

3 Sicut in Evangelio [*Joan.* v, 28, 29] Dominus loquitur: *Veniet hora, in qua omnes qui sunt in monumentis audient vocem ejus, et procedent qui bene fecerunt in resurrectionem vitae, qui autem male egerunt in resurrectionem judicii.* Neque hic dictum est, hoc *qui crediderunt*, illud autem *qui non crediderunt;* sed hoc *illi qui bene egerunt*, illud *qui male egerunt.* Inseparabilis est quippe bona vita a fide *quae per dilectionem operatur:* imo vero ea ipsa est bona vita. *Augustin. de Fide et Oper.* § 42; *Opp.* VI, 188 A.

4 Οὐκοῦν ἅμα ἐπίστευσας, ἅμα καὶ τοῖς ἔργοις ἐκόμησας. οὐχ ὅτι δὲ ἐλλείπῃ πρὸς τὰ ἔργα, ἀλλ' ὅτι καθ' ἑαυτὴν πίστις πλήρης ἐστὶν ἀγαθῶν ἔργων. Scriptor. Incert. Serm. de Fide et Lege Nat., int. Chrysost. Opp. I, 826 B. See more of the context cited in note 11 on the next Homily.

wrought so in the heart of Moses[ε], that he *refused to be taken for king Pharao his daughter's son*, and to have great inheritance in Egypt; *thinking it better with the people of God to have affliction* and sorrow, *than* with naughty men *in sin to live pleasantly for a time. By faith he cared not for the threatening of king Pharao:* for his trust was so in God, that he passed not of the felicity of this world, but looked for the reward to come in heaven; setting his heart upon *the invisible God, as if he had seen him ever present* before his eyes. *By faith the children of Israel passed through the Red Sea*[ζ]. *By faith the walls of Hierico fell down* without stroke[η]; and many other wonderful miracles have been wrought. In all good men that heretofore have been, faith hath brought forth their good works, and obtained the promises of God. Faith hath *stopped the lions' mouths*[θ]: faith hath *quenched the force of fire*[ι]: faith hath *escaped the sword's edges:* faith hath given weak men strength, victory in battle; *overthrown the armies of infidels;* raised the dead to life. Faith hath made good men to take adversity in good part: *some have been mocked and whipped, bound and cast in prison;* some have lost all their goods, and lived in great poverty; *some have wandered in mountains, hills, and wilderness;* some have been racked, some slain, *some stoned, some sawn,* some rent in pieces, some headed[r], some brent[s] without mercy, and would not be delivered, because they looked to rise again to a better state.

ε Exod. ii, [11: Heb. xi, 24–27.]

ζ Exod. xiv, [22: Heb. xi, 29.]

η Josh. vi, [20: Heb. xi, 30.]

θ Dan. vi, [16–23: Heb. xi, 33.]

ι Dan. iii, [13–28: Heb. xi, 34.]

All these fathers, martyrs, and other holy men, whom St. Paul spake of, had their faith surely fixed in God, when all the world was against them. They did not only know God to be the Lord[t], Maker, and Governor of all men in the world; but also they had a special confidence and trust that he was and would be their God, their comforter, aider, helper, maintainer, and defender. This is the Christian faith; which these holy men had, and we also ought to have. And, although they were not named Christian men, yet was it a Christian faith that they had; for they looked for all benefits of God the Father through the merits of his Son Jesu Christ, as we now do. This difference is between them and us; for[u] they looked when Christ should come, and we be in the time when he is come. Therefore saith St. Augustine[5], "The time is altered and changed[v],

In Joan. Tract. XLV.

[r] headed] beheaded 1623. [s] brent] burnt 1595. [t] be the Lord] be Lord 1547 G 1. [u] us; for] us; that 1623. [v] and changed] *added in* 1559.

5 Ante adventum Domini nostri Jesu Christi, quo humilis venit in carne,

but not the faith. For we have both one faith in one Christ." 2 Cor. iv, [13.] The same Holy Ghost also that we have, had they, saith St. Paul. For, as the Holy Ghost doth teach us to trust in God, and to call upon him as our Father, so did he teach them to say, as it is written, Isai. lxiii, [16.] *Thou, Lord, art our Father and Redeemer, and thy Name is without beginning and everlasting.* God gave them then grace to be his children, as he doth us now. But now, by the coming of our Saviour Christ, we have received more abundantly the Spirit of God in our hearts, whereby we may conceive a greater faith and a surer trust than many of them had. But in effect they and we be all one: we have the same faith that they had in God, and they the same that we have. And St. Paul so much extolleth their faith, because we should no less, but rather more, give ourselves wholly unto Christ, both in profession and living, now when Christ is come, than the old fathers did before his coming. And by all the declaration of St. Paul it is evident that the true, lively, and Christian faith is no dead, vain, or unfruitful thing, but a thing of perfect virtue, of wonderful operation (or working[x]) and strength, bringing forth all good motions and good works.

All holy Scripture agreeably beareth witness that a true lively faith in Christ doth bring forth good works: and therefore every man must examine and try[y] himself diligently, to know whether he have the same true lively faith in his heart unfeignedly or not; which he shall know by the fruits thereof. Many that professed the faith of Christ were in this error, that they thought they knew God and believed in him, when in their life they declared the contrary. Which error St. John in his first Epistle confuting writeth in this wise[κ]: *Hereby we are certified that we know God, if we observe his commandments. He that saith he knoweth God, and observeth not his commandments, is a liar, and the truth is not in him.* And again he saith[λ], *Whosoever sinneth doth not see God, nor know him. Let no man deceive you, well beloved children.* And moreover he saith[μ], *Hereby we know that we be of the truth, and so we shall persuade our hearts before him. For, if our own hearts reprove us, God is above our hearts, and knoweth all things. Well beloved, if our hearts reprove us not, then have we confidence in God, and shall*

κ 1 John ii, [3, 4.]

λ 1 John iii, [6, 7.]

μ Ibid. [19–22.]

x or working] *added in* 1559.

y and try] *added in* 1559.

praecesserunt justi, sic in eum credentes venturum, quo modo nos credimus in eum qui venit. Tempora variata sunt, non fides. *Augustin. in Joan. Evang. Tract.* XLV, § 9; *Opp. Tom.* III, *Par.* II, 597 F.

have of him whatsoever we ask, because we keep his commandments, and do those things that please him. And yet further he saith[υ], *Every man that believeth that Jesus is Christ is born of God:* and, *We know that whosoever*[z] *is born of God doth not sin; but the generation of God purgeth him*[a] [6], *and the devil doth not touch him.* And finally he concludeth, and shewing the cause why he wrote this Epistle saith[b] [ξ], *For this cause have I thus written unto you, that you may know that you have*[c] *everlasting life which do believe in the Son of God*[7]. And in his third Epistle he confirmeth the whole matter of faith and works in few words, saying, *He that doeth well is of God, and he that doeth evil knoweth not God.* And as St. John saith that the[d] lively knowledge and faith of God bringeth forth good works, so saith he likewise of hope and charity that they cannot stand with evil living. Of hope he writeth thus[ο]: *We know that when God shall appear, we shall be like unto him, for we shall see him even as he is. And whosoever hath this hope in him doth purify himself, like as God is pure.* And of charity he saith these words[π]: *He that doth keep God's word* or commandment[e], *in him is truly the perfect love of God.* And again he saith[ρ], *This is the love of God, that we should keep his commandments.*

υ 1 John v, [1, 18.]
ξ Ibid. [13.]
3 John [11.]
ο 1 John iii, [2, 3.]
π 1 John ii, [5.]
ρ 1 John v, [3.]

And St. John wrote not this as a subtile saying[f] devised of his own phantasy, but as a most certain and necessary truth, taught unto him by Christ himself, the eternal and infallible Verity; who in many places doth most clearly affirm that faith, hope, and charity cannot consist (or stand[g]) without good and godly works. Of faith he saith[σ], *He that believeth in the Son hath everlasting life; but he that believeth not in the Son shall not see that life, but the wrath of God remaineth upon him.* And the same he confirmeth with a double oath, saying[τ], *Forsooth and forsooth*[h] *I say unto you, He that believeth in me hath everlasting life.* Now, forasmuch as *he that believeth in Christ hath everlasting life,* it must needs consequently follow that he that hath this faith must have also good works, and be studious to observe God's commandments obediently. For to them that have evil

σ John iii, [36.]
τ John vi, [47.]

[z] whosoever] whatsoever 1559–1595. [a] the generation of God purgeth him] he that is begotten of God purgeth himself 1623. [b] shewing . . . saith] sheweth . . . saying *from* 1582. [c] you have] ye have 1549 W, 1559–1569. [d] And as St. John saith that the] And as St. John saith that as the 1547 G 2, *and all from* 1547 G 5; And St. John saith that as the 1547 G 3. [e] or commandment] and commandment *from* 1574. [f] saying] proposition *till* 1559. [g] or stand] *added in* 1559. [h] Forsooth and forsooth] Verily, verily 1623.

6 Ἀλλ' ὁ γεννηθεὶς ἐκ τοῦ Θεοῦ τηρεῖ ἑαυτόν. Sed generatio Dei conservat eum: *Vulg.*

7 Haec scribo (*al.* scripsi) vobis, ut sciatis quoniam vitam habetis aeternam qui creditis in nomine Filii Dei. *Vulg.*

works, and lead their life in disobedience and transgression (or breaking[i]) of God's commandments, without repentance, pertaineth not everlasting life, but everlasting death, as Christ himself saith[v]: *They that do well shall go into life eternal, but they that do evil shall go into the everlasting*[k] *fire*[l]. And again[m] he saith[ϕ], *I am the first letter and the last, the beginning and the ending. To him that is athirst I will give of the well of the water of life freely. He that hath the victory shall have all things, and I will be his God, and he shall be my Son: but they that be fearful, mistrusting God and lacking faith, they that be cursed people, and murderers, and fornicators, and sorcerers, and idolaters*[n], *and all liars, shall have their portion in the lake that burneth with fire and brimstone, which is the second death.* And, as Christ undoubtedly affirmeth that true faith bringeth forth good works, so doth he say likewise of charity[χ]: *Whosoever hath my commandments and keepeth them, that is he that loveth me.* And after he saith, *He that loveth me will keep my word:* and, *He that loveth me not keepeth not my words.*

v Matt. xxv, [46: John v, 29.]

ϕ Rev. xxi, [6–8.]

Charity bringeth forth good works.

χ John xiv, [21, 23, 24.]

And, as the love of God is tried by good works, so is the fear of God also; as the Wise Man saith: *The dread of God putteth away sin.* And also he saith, *He that feareth God will do good works.*

Ecclus. i, [21;] xv, [1.]

THE THIRD PART OF THE SERMON OF FAITH.

YOU have heard in the second part of this Sermon, that no man should think that he hath that lively faith which Scripture commandeth, when he liveth not obediently to God's laws; for all good works spring out of that faith. And also it hath been declared unto you by examples, that faith maketh men steadfast[o], quiet, and patient in all afflictions[p]. Now as concerning the same matter you shall hear what followeth.[q]

A man may soon deceive himself, and think in his own phantasy that he by faith knoweth God, loveth him, feareth him, and belongeth to him, when in very deed he doeth nothing less. For the trial of all these things is a very godly and Christian life. He that feeleth his heart set to seek God's honour, and studieth to know the will and commandments of God and to frame[r]

[i] or breaking] *added in* 1559. [k] into the everlasting] into everlasting 1582, 1623. [l] everlasting fire] eternal fire *till* 1559. [m] And again] Again 1547 G 1. [n] and idolaters] *omitted* 1582, 1623. [o] men steadfast] men constant *till* 1559. [p] afflictions] affliction 1549 W, *and from* 1559. [q] THE THIRD PART—what followeth.] *not in* 1547 *or* 1548, *the Homily not being then divided.* [r] frame] conform *till* 1559.

himself thereunto, and leadeth not his life after the desire of his own flesh, to serve the devil by sin, but setteth his mind to serve God for God's own[s] sake, and for his sake also to love all his neighbours, whether they be friends or adversaries, doing good to every man, as opportunity serveth, and willingly hurting no man; such a man may well rejoice in God, perceiving by the trade[8] of his life that he unfeignedly hath the right knowledge of God, a lively faith, a steadfast[t] hope, a true and unfeigned love and fear of God. But he that casteth away the yoke of God's commandments from his neck, and giveth himself to live without true repentance, after his own sensual mind and pleasure, not regarding to know God's word, and much less to live according thereunto; such a man clearly deceiveth himself, and seeth not his own heart, if he thinketh that he either knoweth God, loveth him, feareth him, or trusteth in him.

Some peradventure phantasy in themselves that they belong to God, although they live in sin; and so they come to the church, and shew themselves as God's dear children. But St. John saith plainly[ψ], *If we say that we have any company with God, and walk in darkness, we do lie.* Others do vainly think that they know and love God, although they pass not of his[u] commandments. But St. John saith clearly[ω], *He that saith, I know God, and keepeth not his commandments, he is a liar.* Some falsely persuade themselves that they love God, when they hate their neighbours. But St. John saith manifestly[α], *If any man say, I love God, and yet hateth his brother, he is a liar. He that saith that he is in the light, and hateth his brother, he is still in darkness. He that loveth his brother dwelleth in the light: but he that hateth his brother is in darkness, and walketh in darkness, and knoweth not whither he goeth, for darkness hath blinded his eyes.* And moreover he saith[β], *Hereby we manifestly know the children of God from the children of the devil: he that doeth not righteously is not the child of God, nor he that hateth his brother.*

ψ 1 John i, [6.]

ω 1 John ii, [4.]

α 1 John iv, [20;] ii, [9-11.]

β 1 John iii, [10.]

Deceive not yourselves therefore, thinking that you have faith in God, or that you love God, or do trust in him, or do fear him, when you live in sin; for then your ungodly and sinful life declareth the contrary, whatsoever ye[x] say or think. It pertaineth to a Christian man to have this true Christian faith, and to try himself whether he hath it or no, and to know what

s God's own] his own *from* 1574. t a steadfast] a constant *till* 1559. u not of his] not of the *from* 1547 G 6. x ye] you *from* 1559.

8 trade: trodden way, regular course. See note 23 on the next Homily.

belongeth to it, and how it doth work in him. It is not the world that we can trust to: the world, and all that is therein, is but vanity. It is God that must be our defence and protection against all temptation of wickedness and sin, errors, superstition, idolatry, and all evil. If all the world were on our side, and God against us, what could the world avail us? Therefore let us set our whole faith and trust in God, and neither the world, the devil, nor all the power of them, shall prevail against us.

Let us therefore, good Christian people, try and examine our faith, what it is: let us not flatter ourselves, but look upon our works, and so judge of our faith, what it is. Christ himself
Matth. xii, [33.] speaketh of this matter, and saith, *The tree is known by the fruit.* Therefore let us do good works, and thereby declare our faith to be the lively Christian faith. Let us, by such virtues as ought to spring out of faith, shew our election to be sure and
2 Pet. i, [10.] stable; as St. Peter teacheth: *Endeavour yourselves*[9] *to make your calling and choosing*[y] *certain by good works.* And also he
Ibid. [5–7.] saith, *Minister* or declare *in your faith virtue, in virtue knowledge, in knowledge temperance, in temperance patience, again*[z] *in patience godliness, in godliness brotherly charity, in brotherly charity love.* So shall we shew indeed that we have the very lively Christian faith; and may so both certify our conscience the better that we be in the right faith, and also by these means confirm other men. If these fruits do not follow, we do but mock with God, deceive ourselves, and also other men. Well may we bear the name of Christian men, but we do lack the true faith that doth belong thereunto. For true faith doth
James ii, [18.] ever bring forth good works; as St. James saith, *Shew me thy faith by thy deeds.* Thy deeds and works must be an open testimonial of thy faith; otherwise thy faith, being without good works, is but the devils' faith, the faith of the wicked, a phantasy of faith, and not a true Christian faith. And, like as the devils and evil people be nothing the better for their counterfeit

[y] choosing] election 1547–1551, 1623. [z] again] *omitted after* 1574.

9 Endeavour yourselves: σπουδάσατε, satagite, *Vulg.*; mettez-vous en devoir. Of seventeen places, in which the verb occurs in the Homilies, there is but one where it is not reflexive. It is reflexive also in the Collect for the Second Sunday after Easter, in the Preface to the Confirmation Service, and in an Answer made to the Bishop in each of the Ordination Services. So in *Stat.* 2 *&* 3 *Philip and Mary, c.* 8: "Upon the said days the parochians shall endeavour themselves to the amending of the said ways." The old French idiom, Se mettre en devoir, is rendered literally, "he put hym in devoyr," meaning *he endeavoured,* in Fabyan's Chronicle, ann. 1484–5.

faith, but it is unto them the more cause of damnation, so they that be christened[a], and have received knowledge of God and of Christ's merits, and yet of a set purpose do live idly, without good works, thinking the name of a naked faith to be either sufficient for them, or else setting their minds upon vain pleasures of this world do live in[b] sin without repentance, not uttering the fruits that do belong to such an high profession; upon such presumptuous persons and wilful sinners must needs remain the great vengeance of God, and eternal punishment in hell, prepared for the devil and[c] wicked livers.

Therefore, as you profess the name of Christ, good Christian people, let no such phantasy and imagination of faith at any time beguile you: but be sure of your faith; try it by your living; look upon the fruits that cometh of it; mark the increase of love and charity by it toward[d] God and your neighbour; and so shall you perceive it to be a true lively faith. If you feel and perceive such a faith in you, rejoice in it, and be diligent to maintain it and keep it still in you: let it be daily increasing and more and more by[e] well working: and so shall ye[f] be sure that you shall please God by this faith; and at the length, as other faithful men have done before, so shall you, when his will is, come to him, and receive *the end* and final reward *of your faith*, as St. Peter nameth it, *the salvation of your souls*. The which God grant us, that hath promised the same unto his faithful. To whom be all honour and glory world without end. Amen.

1 Pet. i, [9.]

[a] christened] Christians 1582, 1623. [b] do live in] living in 1547 W 2 *and* 3. [c] the devil and] the and 1563, the unjust and *from* 1569. [d] toward] towards *from* 1547 G 3. [e] more by] more be 1547 W. [f] ye] you 1549 W *and from* 1559.

A SERMON[a]

OF GOOD WORKS ANNEXED UNTO FAITH.

No good work can[c] be done without faith.

John xv, [4, 5.]

Heb. xi, [5, 6.]

Rom. xiv, [23.]

IN the last Sermon was declared unto you what the lively and true faith of a Christian man is, that it causeth not a man to be idle, but to be occupied in bringing forth good works, as occasion serveth. Now, by God's grace, shall be declared the second thing that before was noted of faith, that without it can no good work be done, acceptable[b] and pleasant unto God. For, *as a branch cannot bear fruit of itself,* saith our Saviour Christ, *except it abide in the vine, so cannot you, except you abide in me. I am the vine, and you be the branches. He that abideth in me, and I in him, he bringeth forth much fruit: for without me you can do nothing.* And St. Paul proveth that Enoch[d] had faith, because *he pleased God:* for, *without faith,* saith he, *it is not possible to please God.* And again to the Romans he saith, *Whatsoever work is done without faith, it is sin.*

Faith giveth life to the soul; and they be as much dead to God that lack faith, as they be to the world whose bodies lack souls. Without faith all that is done of us is but dead before God, although the work seem never so gay and glorious before man. Even as the picture[e] graven or painted is but a dead representation of the thing itself, and is without life or any manner of moving, so be the works of all unfaithful persons before God. They do appear to be lively works, and indeed they be but dead, not availing to the everlasting[f] life. They be but shadows and shews of lively and good things, and not good and lively things indeed. For true faith doth give life to the works[g]; and out of such faith come good works, that be very good works indeed; and without it no[h] work is good before God.

In Praefat. Ps. xxxi.

As saith St. Augustine[1]: "We must set no good works before

[a] A SERMON] AN HOMILY OR SERMON *till* 1549 W. [b] acceptable] accepted *from* 1562 B. [c] work can] works can 1582, 1623. [d] that Enoch] the Eunoch 1559–1569, that the Eunuch *from* 1574. [e] the picture] a picture 1547 G 1. [f] everlasting] eternal *till* 1559. [g] to the works] to the work 1547 G 1. [h] without it no] without, no 1559–1576, without faith no *from* 1582.

[1] Quid ergo? Debemus nulla opera praeponere fidei, id est, ut ante fidem quisquam dicatur bene operatus. Ea enim ipsa opera quae dicuntur ante

faith, nor think that before faith a man may do any good work[i]. For such works, although they seem unto men to be praiseworthy, yet indeed they be but vain," [illegible] allowed before God. "They be as the course of a horse[k] that runneth out of the way, which taketh great labour, but to no purpose. Let no man therefore," saith he, "reckon upon his good works before his faith: where as faith was not, good works were not. The intent," saith he, "maketh the good works; but faith must guide and order the intent of man." And Christ saith, *If thine*[l] *eye be naught, thy whole body is full of darkness.* "The eye doth signify the intent," saith St. Augustine[2], "wherewith a man doeth a thing." So that he which doeth not his good works with a godly intent and a true *faith that worketh by love*[a], the whole body beside (that is to say, all the whole number of his works) is dark, and there is no light in it[m]. For good deeds be not measured by the facts themselves, and so dissevered[n] from vices, but by the ends and intents for the which they be done[o] [3]. If a heathen man clothe the naked, feed the hungry, and do such other like works; yet, because he doeth them not in faith for the honour and love of God, they be but dead, vain, and fruitless works to him[4]. Faith is it that doth commend the work[p] to God: "for," as St. Augustine saith[5], "whether thou wilt or no, that work that cometh not of faith is naught." Where the faith of Christ is not the foundation, there is no good work, what building soever we make. There is one work

Matt. vi, [23.]

In Praefat. Ps. xxxi.

a [Gal. v, 6.]

[i] good work] good works *from* 1574. [k] a horse] an horse 1547 W *and from* 1582. [l] thine] thy 1547 G 1 *and* 2. [m] in it] in them 1549 W *and from* 1559. [n] dissevered] dissered 1547 G 6, discerued (*sic*) 1548, discerned *from* 1549. [o] be done] were done 1582, 1623. [p] the work] the word 1559–1563, 1587.

fidem, quamvis videantur hominibus laudabilia, inania sunt. Ita mihi videntur esse ut magnae vires et cursus celerrimus praeter viam. Nemo ergo computet bona opera sua ante fidem: ubi fides non erat, bonum opus non erat. Bonum enim opus intentio facit, intentionem fides dirigit. *Augustin. Enarrat.* II *in Ps.* XXXI, § 4; *Opp.* IV, 172 C. The Benedictine editors put a ? after operatus.

2 Aut ergo intellige quod ait Dominus, *Si oculus tuus nequam est, totum corpus tuum tenebrosum erit*, ... et hunc *oculum* agnosce intentionem qua facit quisque quod facit; et per hoc disce eum qui non facit opera bona intentione fidei bonae (hoc est, ejus *quae per dilectionem operatur*), *totum* quasi *corpus* quod illis (velut membris) operibus constat, *tenebrosum* esse, hoc est, plenum nigredine peccatorum. *Augustin. contra Julian.* IV, § 33; *Opp.* X, 602 B. See also *De Serm. Dom.* II, § 45; *Opp. Tom.* III, *Par.* II, 218.

3 Noveris itaque non officiis sed finibus a vitiis discernendas esse virtutes. Officium est autem quod faciendum est; finis vero propter quod faciendum est. *Augustin. contra Julian.* IV, § 21; *Opp.* X, 596 A.

4 See *Augustin. ibid.* §§ 30–33, *coll.* 600–602.

5 *Omne* enim, velis nolis, *quod non ex fide, peccatum est* [Rom. xiv, 23.] Ibid. § 32, col. 601 F.

in the which be all good works, that is, *faith which worketh by charity*[6]. If thou have it, thou hast the ground of all good works; for the virtues of strength, wisdom, temperance, and justice be all referred unto this same faith[7]. Without this faith we have not them, but only the names and shadows of them; as St. Augustine saith[8]: "All the life of them that lack the true faith is sin; and nothing is good without him that is the Author of goodness: where he is not, there is but feigned virtue, although it be in the best works." And St. Augustine, [Ps. lxxxiv, 3.] declaring this verse of the Psalm, *The turtle hath found a nest where she may keep her young birds*, saith[9] that Jews, heretics, and pagans do good works; they clothe the naked, feed the poor, and do other works[q] of mercy; but, because they be not done in the true faith, therefore the birds be lost. But, if they remain in faith, then "faith is the nest" and safeguard "of their birds," that is to say, safeguard of their good works, that the reward of them be not utterly lost.

And this matter, which St. Augustine at large in many books disputeth, St. Ambrose concludeth in few words, saying[10], "He that by nature would withstand vice, either by natural will or [De Vocatione Gentium, Lib. 1, cap. 3.]

q other works] other good works 1623.

6 Opus ergo unum est in quo sunt omnia, *fides quae per dilectionem operatur*. Augustin. Enarrat. in Ps. LXXXIX, § 17; Opp. IV, 961 D.

7 Ideo *justus ex fide* Christi *vivit* [Rom. i, 17.] Ex hac enim fide prudenter, fortiter, temperanter, et juste, ac per hoc his omnibus veris virtutibus recte sapienterque vivit, quia fideliter vivit. *Augustin. contra Julian.* IV, § 19; *Opp.* X, 594 E.

8 Omnis infidelium vita peccatum est, et nihil est bonum sine Summo Bono. Ubi enim deest agnitio aeternae et incommutabilis Veritatis, falsa virtus est, etiam in optimis moribus. *Prosper. Lib. Sententt. ex Augustin. Delibatt.* § 106; *Augustin. Opp. Tom. X, Append.* 230.

9 Quam multi etiam pagani pascunt esurientem, vestiunt nudum, suscipiunt hospitem, visitant aegrotum, consolantur inclusum! Quam multi haec faciunt! quasi videtur parere *turtur*, sed non *sibi invenit nidum*. Quam multa multi haeretici non in Ecclesia operantur, non *in nido pullos ponunt!* Conculcabuntur et conterentur; non servabuntur, non custodientur. . . . . Permanendo ergo in fide, ipsa fides nidus est pullorum tuórum. . . . In ista fide pone pullos tuos; in isto nido operare opera tua. *Augustin. Enarrat. in Ps.* LXXXIII, § 7; *Opp.* IV, 882 E, 883 A, B.

10 His ergo atque aliis malis in naturam humanam irruentibus, fide perdita, spe relicta, intelligentia obcaecata, voluntate captiva, nemo in se unde repararetur invenit: quia, etsi fuit qui naturali intellectu conatus sit vitiis reluctari, hujus tantum temporis vitam steriliter ornavit, ad veras autem virtutes aeternamque beatitudinem non profecit. Sine cultu enim veri Dei etiam quod virtus videtur esse peccatum est; nec placere ullus Deo sine Deo potest. *De Vocatione Gentium*, I, 7.

This treatise was formerly printed among the works of Ambrose, to whom three MSS ascribe it. Other MSS, older, better, and more numerous, name the author Prosper, but do not describe him further. Some modern critics have assigned it to Pope Leo the Great. It is comprised in the later editions of the works both of Prosper of Aquitaine and of Pope Leo.

reason, he doth in vain garnish the time of this life, and attaineth not the very true virtues: for without the worshipping of the true God that which seemeth to be virtue is vice."

And yet most plainly to this purpose writeth St. John[r] Chrysostom in this wise[11]. "You shall find many which have not the true faith and be not of the flock of Christ, and yet, as it appeareth, they flourish in good works of mercy; you shall find them full of pity[s], compassion, and given to justice; and yet, for all that, they have no fruit of their works, because the chief work lacketh." "For, when the Jews asked of Christ what they should do to work good works, he answered, *This is the work of God, to believe in him whom he sent:* so that he called faith *the work of God.* And as soon as a man hath faith, anon he shall flourish in good works: for faith of itself is full of good works, and nothing is good without faith." And for a similitude he saith that "they which glister and shine in good works without faith in God be like dead men, which have goodly and pre-

In Sermone de Fide, Lege, et Spiritu Sancto.

John vi, [29.]

[r] John] *omitted* 1623.

[s] pity] piety 1559–1582.

11 Εὑρήσεις γοῦν πολλοὺς καὶ ἐκτὸς τοῦ λόγου τῆς ἀληθείας ἔργοις ἀγαθοῖς κατὰ τὸ φαινόμενον διαλάμποντας· εὑρήσεις ἄνδρας συμπαθεῖς, ἐλεήμονας, δικαιοσύνῃ προσέχοντας· ἀλλ' οὐδεὶς καρπὸς τοῖς ἔργοις, ἐπειδὴ ἠγνόησαν τὸ ἔργον τῆς ἀληθείας. καλὰ μὲν γὰρ καὶ τὰ ἔργα, ἀλλὰ δεῖ προηγεῖσθαι τὸ ἔργον τὸ ἀνώτατον. καὶ γὰρ Ἰουδαίων ποτὲ λεγόντων πρὸς τὸν Κύριον, Τί ποιήσομεν, ἵνα ἐργασώμεθα τὰ ἔργα τοῦ Θεοῦ; ἀπεκρίνατο πρὸς αὐτούς, Τοῦτό ἐστι τὸ ἔργον τοῦ Θεοῦ, ἵνα πιστεύσητε εἰς ὃν ἀπέστειλεν ἐκεῖνος. ὅρα πῶς τὴν πίστιν ἔργον ἐκάλεσεν. οὐκοῦν ἅμα ἐπίστευσας, ἅμα καὶ τοῖς ἔργοις ἐκόμησας. οὐχ ὅτι δὲ ἐλλείπῃ πρὸς τὰ ἔργα, ἀλλ' ὅτι καθ' ἑαυτὴν πίστις πλήρης ἐστὶν ἀγαθῶν ἔργων.... Οὐδέν ἐστιν ἔξω πίστεως ἀγαθόν. ἐοίκασι δέ μοι, ἀδελφοί, ἵνα εἰκόνι τινὶ χρήσωμαι τοῦ λόγου, ἐοίκασιν οἱ ἔργοις κομῶντες ἀγαθοῖς, καὶ τὸν Θεὸν τῆς εὐσεβείας ἀγνοήσαντες, λειψάνοις νεκρῶν, καλὰ μὲν ἐνδεδυμένοις, αἴσθησιν δὲ τῶν καλῶν οὐκ ἔχουσι.... Οὐ δεῖ μὲν τὴν πίστιν γυμνὴν εἶναι τῶν ἔργων, ἵνα μὴ ὑβρίζηται· πλὴν ἀνωτέρα τῶν ἔργων ἡ πίστις. Ὥσπερ γὰρ ἐν τιμῇ τοῖς ἀνθρώποις ἔδει πρῶτον προηγεῖσθαι τὸ ζῆν, καὶ οὕτω τὸ τρέφεσθαι· τὸ γὰρ συνέχον τὴν ζωὴν ἡμῶν ἐστιν ἡ τροφή· οὕτω δεῖ προηγεῖσθαι ἡμῶν τῆς ζωῆς τὴν εἰς Χριστὸν ἐλπίδα, τρέφεσθαι δὲ καὶ τοῖς ἔργοις τοῖς ἀγαθοῖς. τὸν μὴ τρεφόμενον ἐγχωρεῖ ζῆν πολλάκις, τὸν δὲ μὴ ζῶντα οὐκ ἐγχωρεῖ τρέφεσθαι.... δεῖ μὲν τοῖς ἔργοις τρέφεσθαι· δεῖ δὲ πρὸ τῶν ἔργων τὴν πίστιν ἐνδύεσθαι. ἄνευ πίστεως τὸν ἐργαζόμενον ἔργα δικαιοσύνης οὐ δύνῃ παραστῆσαι ζήσαντα· ἄνευ δὲ ἔργων τὸν πιστὸν δύναμαι δεῖξαι καὶ ζήσαντα καὶ βασιλείας ἀξιωθέντα. οὐδεὶς ἄνευ πίστεως ἔζησεν· ὁ δὲ λῃστὴς πιστεύσας μόνον ἐδικαιώθη. καὶ μή μοι λέγε, Οὐκ ἔσχε καιρὸν πολιτεύεσθαι· οὐδὲ γὰρ ἐγὼ τοῦτο φιλονεικῶ· ἀλλ' ἐκεῖνο παρέστησα, ὅτι ἡ πίστις καθ' ἑαυτὴν ἔσωσεν. εἰ γὰρ ἐπέζησε τῇ πίστει, καὶ ἔργων ἠμέλησεν, ἐξέπιπτε τῆς σωτηρίας. τὸ δὲ σκοπούμενον νῦν καὶ ζητούμενον, ὅτι καὶ ἡ πίστις καθ' ἑαυτὴν ἔσωσεν, ἔργα δὲ καθ' ἑαυτὰ οὐδαμοῦ τοὺς ἐργάτας ἐδικαίωσε. Scriptor. Incert. Serm. de Fide et Lege Nat., int. Chrysost. Opp. I, 826 A–D. But the translation in the Homily was made from the Latin version, as appears especially in these places. Sicut enim hominibus, qui hominis nomen merentur, opus est primum ut praecedat vita et sic enutriantur, ... ita &c. Fidelem autem absque operibus possum monstrare et vixisse et regnum coelorum assecutum. Latro autem credidit duntaxat, et justificatus est a misericordissimo Deo.

cious tombs, and yet it availeth them nothing." "Faith may not be naked without works[t]; for then it is no true faith: and, when it is adjoined to works, yet it is above the works. For, as men, that be very men indeed, first have life, and after be nourished; so must our faith in Christ go before, and after be nourished with good works. And life may be without nourishment, but nourishment cannot be without life." "A man must needs be nourished by good works, but first he must have faith. He that doeth good deeds, yet without faith he hath not life[u]. I can shew a man that by faith without works lived and came to heaven: but without faith never man had life. The thief that was hanged when Christ suffered did believe only, and the most merciful God did justify[x] him. And, because no man shall say again[y] that he lacked time to do good works, for else he would have done them, truth it is, and I will not contend therein: but this I will surely affirm, that faith only saved him. If he had lived, and not regarded faith and the works thereof, he should have lost his salvation again. But this is the effect that I say, that faith by itself saved him, but works by themselves never justified any man." Here ye have heard the mind of St. Chrysostom; whereby you may perceive, that neither faith is without works, having opportunity thereto, nor works can avail to everlasting[z] life without faith.

THE SECOND PART OF THE SERMON OF GOOD WORKS.

OF the three[a] things which were in the former Sermon specially[b] noted of lively faith, two be declared unto you. The first was, that faith is never idle, without good works, when occasion serveth; the second, that good works acceptable to God cannot be done without faith.[c] Now to go forth[d] to the third part, that is, what[e] manner of works they be which spring out of true faith, and lead faithful men unto everlasting[f] life.

What works they are that spring of[g] faith.

This cannot be known so well as by our Saviour Christ himself, who was asked of a certain great man the same question.

[t] without works] without good works *from* 1547 G 3. [u] not life] no life *from* 1547 G 5. [x] did justify] justified *from* 1559, *except* 1587 *and* 1595. [y] say again] object *till* 1559. [z] everlasting] eternal *till* 1559. [a] Of the three] Of three *from* 1559. [b] specially] especially 1623. [c] THE SECOND PART—without faith.] *not in* 1547 *or* 1548, *the Homily not being then divided.* [d] go forth] proceed *till* 1559, go forward 1623. [e] part, that is, what] part which in the former Sermon was noted of faith, that is to say, what 1547–1551, *except* 1549 W. [f] unto everlasting] unto eternal *till* 1559. [g] spring of] spring out of *from* 1574.

What works shall I do, said a prince, *to come to everlasting life?* To whom Jesus answered, *If thou wilt come to the everlasting*[h] *life, keep the commandments.* But the prince, not satisfied herewith, asked further, *Which commandments?* The Scribes and Pharisees had made so many of their own laws and traditions to bring men to heaven beside[i] God's commandments, that this man was in doubt whether he should come to heaven by those laws and traditions or by the laws[k] of God; and therefore he asked Christ which commandments he meant. Whereunto Christ made him a plain answer, rehearsing the commandments of God, saying, *Thou shalt not kill, Thou shalt not commit adultery, Thou shalt not steal, Thou shalt not bear false witness, Honour thy father and mother*[l], and, *Love thy neighbour*[m] *as thyself.* By which words Christ declared that the laws of God be the very way that doth[n] lead to everlasting[o] life, and not the traditions and laws of men. So that this is to be taken for a most true lesson taught by Christ's own mouth, that the works of the moral commandments of God be the very true works of faith which lead to the blessed life to come.

Matt. xix, [16–19.]

The works that lead to heaven be the works[p] of God's commandments.

But the blindness and malice of man, even from the beginning, hath ever been ready to fall from God's commandments. As Adam the first man, having but one commandment, that he should not eat of the fruit forbidden, notwithstanding God's commandment, he gave credit unto the woman seduced by the subtle persuasion of the serpent, and so followed his own will, and left God's commandment. And ever since that time all that came of him[r] hath been[s] so blinded through original sin, that they have been ever ready to fall[t] from God and his law, and to invent a new way unto salvation by works of their own device; so much that almost all the world, forsaking the true honour of the only eternal living God, wandered about in their[u] own phantasies, worshipping some the sun, the moon, the stars, some Jupiter, Juno, Diana, Saturnus, Apollo, Neptunus, Ceres, Bacchus, and other dead men and women. Some, therewith not satisfied, worshipped divers kinds of beasts, birds, fish, fowl, and serpents; every country[x], town, and house in a manner[y] being divided, and setting up images of such things as they

Man, from his first falling from God's commandments, hath ever been ready to do the like, and to devise[q] works of his own phantasy to please God withal.

The devices and idolatry of the Gentiles.

[h] to the everlasting] to the eternal *till* 1559, to everlasting 1582, 1623. [i] beside] besides *from* 1547 G 3. [k] the laws] the law *from* 1559. [l] and mother] and thy mother *from* 1574. [m] neighbour] neighbours 1559–1569. [n] doth] do 1547–1551, *except* 1549 W. [o] to everlasting] to eternal *till* 1559. [p] be the works] be works *from* 1574. [q] to devise] doth devise *from* 1569. [r] that came of him] his succession *till* 1559. [s] hath been] have been 1582, 1623. [t] fall] decline 1547–1551, *except* 1549 W. [u] about in their] about their *from* 1547 G 2. [x] country] region *till* 1559. [y] in a manner] in manner *from* 1547 G 3.

liked, and worshipping the same. Such was the rudeness of the people after they fell to their own phantasies, and left the eternal living God and his commandments, that they devised innumerable images and gods. In which error and blindness they did remain until such time as Almighty God, pitying the blindness of man, sent his true Prophet Moses into the world, to reprove and rebuke[z] this extreme madness, and to teach the people to know the only living God, and his true honour and worship.

But the corrupt inclination of man was so much given to follow his own phantasies[a], and (as you would say) to favour his own bird that he brought up himself, that all the admonitions, exhortations, benefits, and threatenings of God could not keep him from such his inventions. For, notwithstanding all the benefits of God shewed unto the people of Israel, yet, when Moses went up into the mountain to speak with Almighty God, he had tarried there but a few days when the people began to invent new gods[β]; and, as it came into[b] their heads, they made a calf of gold, and kneeled down and worshipped it. And after that they followed the Moabites[γ], and worshipped Beelphegor the Moabites' god. Read the book of Judges, the books[d] of the Kings, and the Prophets; and there you shall find[e] how unsteadfast[f] the people were, how full of inventions, and more ready to run after their own phantasies than God's most holy commandments. There shall you read[δ] of Baal, Moloch, Chamos, Melchom[g], Baalpeor, Astaroth, Bel, the Dragon, Priapus[12], the Brazen Serpent, the Twelve Signs, and many other; unto whose images the people with great devotion invented pilgrimages, preciously[h] decking and censing them, kneeling down and offering to them, thinking that an high merit before God, and to be esteemed above the precepts and commandments of God. And, where at that time God commanded no sacrifice to be made but in Jerusalem only, they did clean contrary; making altars and sacrifices every where, in hills, in woods, and in houses; not regarding God's commandments, but esteeming

The devices and idolatry of the Israelites[c].

β Exod. xxxii, [1–6.]

γ [Num. xxv, 1–3.]

δ [Judg. ii, 13: Amos v, 26: 1 Kings xi, 5, 7, 33: Hos. ix, 10: 2 Kings xviii, 4; xxiii, 5, 13.]

[z] reprove and rebuke] reprehend *till* 1559. [a] his own phantasies] his own phantasie 1574, 1576; his own fantasie 1582, 1623. [b] came into] came in *from* 1547 G 2. [c] Israelites] Gentiles *till* 1549 W. [d] books] book 1547 G 6—1551, *and from* 1574. [e] you shall find] shall you find 1547 G 3—1562. [f] unsteadfast] inconstant *till* 1559. [g] Melchom] Mechom *till* 1574. [h] preciously] precious *from* 1559.

12 Insuper et Maacham matrem suam amovit, ne esset princeps in sacris Priapi et in luco ejus, quem consecraverat. 3 *Reg.* xv, 13, *Vulg.* Sed et Maacham matrem Asa regis ex augusto deposuit imperio, eo quod fecisset in luco simulacrum Priapi. 2 *Paralip.* xv, 16, *Vulg.*

their own phantasies and devotion[i] to be better than them[k]. And the error hereof was so spread abroad that not only the unlearned people, but also the priests and teachers of the people, partly by glory and covetousness[l] were corrupted, and partly by ignorance blindly deceived[m] with the same abominations; so much that, king Achab[e] having but only Helias a true teacher and minister of God, there were eight hundred and fifty priests that persuaded him to honour Baal and to do sacrifice in the woods or groves. And so continued that horrible error, until the three noble kings, as Josaphat, Ezechias, and Josias, God's chosen[n] ministers, destroyed the same clearly[ζ], and brought again[o] the people from such their feigned inventions unto the very commandments of God: for the which thing their immortal reward and glory doth and shall remain with God for ever.

[e] 1 Kings xviii, [19, 22.]

[ζ] [2 Chron. xvii, 3–6; xxx, 14; xxxi, 1; xxxiv, 2–7.]

Religions and sects among the Jews.

And, beside the foresaid inventions, the inclination of man to have his own holy devotions devised new sects and religions, called Pharisees, Sadducees, and Scribes; with many holy and godly traditions and ordinances, as it seemed by the outward appearance and goodly glistering of the works, but in very deed all tending to idolatry, superstition, and hypocrisy; their hearts within being full of malice, pride, covetousness, and all wickedness[p]. Against which sects, and their pretensed[q] holiness, Christ cried out more vehemently than he did against any other persons, saying and often rehearsing[r] these words: *Woe be to you, Scribes and Pharisees, ye hypocrites! for you make clean the vessel without, but within you be*[s] *full of ravine and filthiness. Thou blind Pharisee* and hypocrite, *first make the inward part clean.* For, notwithstanding all the goodly traditions and outward shew[t] of good works devised of their own imagination, whereby they appeared to the world most religious and holy of all men, yet Christ, who saw their hearts, knew that they were inwardly in the sight of God most unholy, most abominable, and furthest from God of all men. Therefore said he unto them, *Hypocrites, the Prophet Esay spake full truly of you when he said, This people honour me with their lips, but their heart is far from me: they worship me in vain that teach doctrines*

Matt. xxiii, [25, 26.]

Matt. xv, [7–9:] Isai. xxix, [13, 14.]

[i] devotion] devotions *from* 1574. [k] than them] than they 1549 W, *and from* 1559. [l] and covetousness] and avarice *till* 1559. [m] deceived] seduced *till* 1559. [n] chosen] elect *till* 1559. [o] brought again] reduced *till* 1559. [p] wickedness] iniquity *till* 1559. [q] pretensed] pretended *from* 1574. [r] rehearsing] repeating *till* 1559. [s] you be] ye be *from* 1574. [t] shew] shews *from* 1547 G 3.

and commandments of men. For you leave the commandments of God to keep your own traditions.

Man's laws must be observed and kept, but not as God's laws.

And, though Christ said *they worship God*[u] *in vain that teach doctrines and commandments of men*, yet he meant not thereby to overthrow all men's commandments; for he himself was ever obedient to the princes and their laws, made for good order and governance of the people: but he reproved the laws and traditions made by the Scribes and Pharisees, which were not made only for good order of the people (as the civil laws were), but they were set up so high[x] that they were made to be a right[y] and pure[z] worshipping of God, as they had been equal with God's laws, or above them; for many of God's laws could not be kept, but were fain to give place unto them. This arrogancy God detested, that man should so advance his laws, to make them equal with God's laws, wherein the true honouring and right worshipping of God standeth, and to make his laws for them to be left off[a]. God hath appointed his laws, whereby his pleasure is to be honoured. His pleasure is also that all man's[b] laws, being not[c] contrary to his[d] laws, shall be obeyed and kept, as good and necessary for every commonweal, but not as things wherein principally his honour resteth. And all civil and man's laws either be or should be made, to bring in men[e] the better to keep[f] God's laws; that consequently (or followingly[g]) God should be the better honoured by them. Howbeit, the Scribes and Pharisees were not content that their laws should be no higher esteemed than other positive and civil laws, nor would not have them called by the name of other temporal laws; but called them holy and godly traditions, and would have them esteemed, not only for a right and true worshipping of God (as God's laws be indeed), but also to be the[h] most high honouring of God, to the which the commandments of God should give place. And for this cause did Christ so vehemently speak against them, saying, *Your traditions, which men esteem so high, be abomination before God.*

Holy traditions were esteemed as God's laws.

Luke xvi, [15.]

Holiness of man's device is commonly occasion that God is offended.

For commonly of such traditions followeth the transgression (or breaking[i]) of God's commandments, and a more devotion in the keeping[k] of such things, and a greater conscience in break-

[u] worship God] worshipped God *till* 1559. [x] set up so high] so highly extolled *till* 1559. [y] be a right] be right 1582, 1623. [z] pure] sincere *till* 1559. [a] left off] omitted *till* 1559. [b] all man's] all men's *from* 1559. [c] being not] not being *from* 1569. [d] to his] unto his *from* 1569. [e] bring in men] induce men *till* 1559, bring men 1623. [f] keep] observe *till* 1559. [g] or followingly] *added in* 1559. [h] also to be the] also to the 1569, also for the *from* 1574. [i] or breaking] *added in* 1559. [k] in the keeping] in the observing *till* 1559, in keeping *from* 1569.

ing of them, than of the commandments of God. As the Scribes and Pharisees so superstitiously and scrupulously kept the Sabbath, that they were offended[η] with Christ because he healed sick men, and with his Apostles because they, being sore hungry, gathered the ears of corn to eat, upon that day. And, because his disciples washed not their hands[θ] so often as the traditions required, the Scribes and Pharisees quarrelled with Christ, saying, *Why do thy disciples break the traditions of the seniors?* But Christ laid to their charge[l], that they, for to keep[m] their own traditions, did teach men to break the very commandments of God. For they taught the people such a devotion, that they offered their goods into the treasure house of the temple, under the pretence of God's honour, leaving their fathers and mothers (to whom they were chiefly bound) unholpen; and so[ι] *they brake the commandments of God, to keep*[m] *their own traditions.* They esteemed more[κ] an oath made by the gold or oblation in the temple than an oath made in the name of God himself or of the temple. They were more studious to pay their tithes of small things[λ] than to do the greater things commanded of God, as works of mercy, or to do justice, or to deal sincerely, uprightly, and faithfully with God and man. *These,* saith Christ, *ought to be done, and the other not left undone*[n]. And, to be short, they were of so blind judgment, that they stumbled at a straw and leaped over a block: they would, as it were, nicely take a fly out of their cup[μ], and drink down a whole camel. And therefore Christ called them *blind guides,* warning his disciples from time to time to eschew their doctrine. For, although they seemed to the world to be most perfect men, both in living and teaching, yet was their life but hypocrisy, and their doctrine but sour leaven mingled[o] with superstition, idolatry, and overthwart[p] judgment, setting up the traditions and ordinances of man in the stead[q] of God's commandments.

η Matt. xii. [1–14.]
θ Matt. xv. [1–6.]
ι [Mark vii. 9.]
κ Matt. xxiii. [16–22.]
λ Ibid. [23.]
μ Ibid. [24.]

THE THIRD PART OF THE SERMON OF GOOD WORKS.

THAT all men might rightly judge of good works, it hath been declared in the second part of this Sermon what kind of good

l laid to their charge] objected against them *till* 1559. m keep] observe *till* 1559. n left undone] omitted *till* 1559. o mingled] mixed *till* 1559. p overthwart] preposterous *till* 1559. q in the stead] in stead *from* 1576.

works they be that God would have his people to walk in, namely, such as he hath commanded in his holy Scripture, and not such works as men have studied out[r] of their own brain, of a blind zeal and devotion, without the word of God. And by mistaking the nature of good works man hath most highly displeased God, and hath gone from his will and commandment[s]. So that thus[t] you have[u] heard how much the world, from the beginning until Christ's time, was ever ready to fall from the commandments of God, and to seek other means to honour and serve him after a devotion found out[x] of their own heads, and how they did set up[y] their own traditions as high or above God's commandments. Which hath happened also in our times (the more it is to be lamented) no less than it did among the Jews; and that by the corruption, or at the least[z] by the negligence, of them that chiefly ought to have preferred God's commandments, and to have[a] preserved the pure[b] and heavenly doctrine left by Christ.

Sects and religions[c] among Christian[d] men.

What man, having any judgment or learning joined with a true zeal unto God, doth not see and lament to have entered into Christ's religion such false doctrine, superstition, idolatry, hypocrisy, and other enormities and abuses; so as by little and little, through the sour leaven thereof, the sweet bread of God's holy word hath been much hindered and laid apart? Never had the Jews in their most blindness so many pilgrimages unto images, nor used so much kneeling, kissing, and censing of them as hath been used in our time. Sects and feigned religions were neither the forty[e] part so many among the Jews, nor more superstitiously and ungodly abused than of late days they have been among us. Which sects and religions had so many hypocritical and feigned works[f] in their state of religion (as they arrogantly named it), that their lamps, as they said, ran always over, able to satisfy, not only for their own sins, but also for all other their benefactors, brothers and sisters of their religion[g], as most ungodly and craftily they had persuaded the multitude of ignorant people; keeping in divers places as it were marts or markets of merits, being full of their holy reliques, images, shrines, and works of overflowing abundance[h] ready to be sold.

[r] studied out] imagined *till* 1559. [s] commandment] commandments *from* 1574. [t] So that thus] So thus 1549 G, 1551. [u] THE THIRD PART—thus you have] Thus have you 1547, 1548, *the Homily not being then divided.* [x] found out] imagined *till* 1559. [y] did set up] extolled *till* 1559. [z] at the least] at least 1582, 1623. [a] preferred God's commandments, and to have] *omitted after* 1563. [b] pure] sincere *till* 1559. [c] and religions] and religion *from* 1559. [d] among Christian] amonges Christian *or* amongst Christian *from* 1559. [e] forty] fortieth *from* 1574. [f] hypocritical and feigned works] hypocritical works *till* 1559. [g] of their religion] of religion *from* 1559. [h] overflowing abundance] supererogation *till* 1559.

And all things which they had were called holy, holy cowls, holy girdles, holy pardoned beads[i] [13], holy shoes, holy rules, and all full of holiness. And what thing can be more foolish, more superstitious, or ungodly, than that men, women, and children should wear a frier's coat to deliver them from agues or pestilence, or, when they die or when they be buried, cause it to be cast upon them in hope thereby to be saved[14]? Which superstition, although, thanks be to God, it hath been little used in this realm, yet in divers other realms it hath been and yet is[k] used among[l] many, both learned and unlearned.

The three chief vows of religion.

But, to pass over the innumerable superstitiousness that hath been in strange apparel, in silence, in dormitory, in cloister, in chapter, in choice of meats and drinks[m], and in such[n] like things, let us consider what enormities and abuses have been in the three chief principal points, which they called the three essentials (or three chief foundations[o]) of religion, that is to say, obedience, chastity, and wilful poverty. First, under pretence (or colour[p]) of obedience to their father in religion (which obedience they made themselves), they were made free[q] by their rules[r] and canons from the obedience of their natural father and mother, and from the obedience of emperor and king and all temporal power, whom of very duty by God's laws they were bound to obey. And so the profession of their obedience not due was a forsaking[s] of their due obedience. And how their profession of chastity was kept[t], it is more honesty to pass over in silence, and let the world judge of that which is well known,

[i] holy pardoned beads] holy pardones, beads *from* 1548, *except* 1549 G *and* 1551, *which have* holy pardones, holy beads. [k] yet is] yet it is 1582, 1623. [l] used among] used both among *till* 1574, *except* 1547 W 2 *and* 3. [m] and drinks] and in drinks *till* 1574. [n] and in such] and such 1547 G 1. [o] or three chief foundations] *added in* 1559. [p] or colour] *added in* 1559. [q] made free] exempted *till* 1559. [r] their rules] their rule 1582, 1623. [s] forsaking] renunciation *till* 1559. [t] kept] observed *till* 1559.

13 "Pardoned beads" were such as had a grant of pardon assured to all who used them. Becon in his *Reliques of Rome* has preserved a (not very grammatical) notice which had been appended to some beads so privileged, beginning thus: "To all good Christen people disposed to say our Ladyes Psaulter within this church or churchyard on any of these beades, the which bene pardoned at the holye place of Shene, shal have ten thousande yeres of pardon. Also for every word the Pater Noster, Ave, and Credo xxiii dayes of pardon totiens quotiens. Also they are pardoned at Sion, and by that ye shall have for every Pater Noster, Ave, and Credo sayde on them three hundred dayes of pardon. Also unto all those" &c. &c. *Becon's Works,* III, 358 b, *ed.* 1564.

14 "Some of those that have been learned, the more was the pity, have died in an Observant or Grey Friar's cowl, and afterward been buried in the same, and so thought themselves well prepared." *Grindal's Funeral Sermon, Remains, p.* 30, *ed. Park. Soc.*

See *Wordsworth's Ecclesiastical Biography, vol.* II, *p.* 18, *n.* 5, *ed.* 1810, in the Life of Thomas Bilney; and compare *Milton, Par. Lost,* III, 468–470.

than with unchaste words by expressing of their unchaste life to offend chaste and godly ears. And as for their wilful poverty, it was such that, when in possessions, jewels, plate, and riches they were equal or above merchants, gentlemen, barons, earls, and dukes, yet by this subtile sophistical term, Proprium in communi[u] [15], that is to say, Proper in common[x], they mocked[y] the world, persuading that, notwithstanding all their possessions and riches, yet they kept[z] their vow and were in wilful poverty. But, for all their riches, they might neither[a] help father nor mother, nor other that were indeed very needy and poor, without the licence of their father abbot, prior, or warden. And yet they might take of every man, but they might not give aught to any man, no, not to them whom the laws of God bound them to help. And so through their traditions and rules the laws of God could bear no rule with them; and therefore of them might be most truly said that which Christ spake unto the Pharisees: *You break the commandments of God by your traditions. You honour God with your lips, but your hearts be far from him.* And the longer prayers they used by day and by night, under pretence (or colour[b]) of such holiness to get the favour of widows and other simple folks, that they might sing trentals[16] and service for their husbands and friends, and admit (or receive[c]) them into their prayers[d], the more truly is verified of them the saying of Christ: *Woe be to you*[e], *Scribes and Pharisees, hypocrites! for you devour widows' houses under colour of long prayers: therefore your damnation shall be the*

Matt. xv, [3, 8.]

Matt. xxiii, [14, 15.]

[u] communi] commune *from* 1576. [x] that is to say, Proper in common] *added in* 1559. [y] mocked] deluded *till* 1559. [z] kept] observed *till* 1559. [a] neither] never *from* 1559. [b] or colour] *added in* 1559. [c] or receive] *added in* 1559. [d] their prayers] their suffrages *till* 1559. [e] to you] unto you *from* 1574.

15 The phrase Proprium in communi has not been found elsewhere, but the following quotations will help to explain it. Illud etiam statui debere prospeximus, ut nullus monachorum aliquid sibi proprium absque societate fratrum audeat vindicare .... Quicquid ergo secum rerum detulerit ..., statim cognoscat omnia in communionem transiisse; et hoc tantum judicet proprium, quicquid cum fratribus possederit indivisum. *Regula S. Ferreoli cap.* 10; *Holsten. Codex Regularum, par.* II, *pag.* 75, *ed. Paris.* 1663. "*Ye shall know them by their fruits.* First, thorns bear no grapes, nor briers figs. Also, if thou see goodly blossoms in them, and thinkest there to have figs, grapes, or any fruit for the sustenance or comfort of man, go to them in time of need, and thou shalt find naught at all. Thou shall find, 'Forsooth I have no goods, nor any thing proper, or that is mine own. It is the convent's. I were a thief if I gave it my father, whatsoever need he had.'" *Tyndale, Expos. of Matth.* VII. See also *Du Cange, v.* Proprietates.

16 A "trental" was a set of thirty masses said for some dead person. See the section "Of Trentals for souls departed" in *Becon's Reliques of Rome, Works,* III, 365 a, 366 b, *ed.* 1564.

greater. Woe be to you, Scribes and Pharisees, hypocrites! for you go about by sea and by land to make mo novices and new brethren, and when they be let in or received[f] *of your sect you make them the children of hell worse than yourselves be.*

Honour be to God, who did put light in the heart of his faithful and true minister of most famous memory, King Henry the Eighth, and gave him the knowledge of his word, and an earnest affection to seek his glory, and to put away all such superstitious and pharisaical sects by Antichrist invented and set up against[g] the true word of God and glory of his most blessed Name; as he gave the like spirit unto the most noble and famous princes, Josaphat, Josias, and Ezechias. God grant all us, the Queen's[h] Highness' faithful and true subjects, to feed of the sweet and savoury bread of God's own word, and, as Christ commanded[v], to eschew all our pharisaical and papistical leaven of man's feigned religion. Which, although it were before God most abominable, and contrary to God's commandments and Christ's pure religion, yet it was praised[i] to be a most godly life and highest state of perfection; as though a man might be more godly and more perfect by keeping the rules, traditions, and professions of men than by keeping the holy commandments of God.

[v] [Matth. xvi, 6, 12: Luke xii, 1.]

Other devices and superstitions.

And, briefly to pass over the ungodly and counterfeit religions[k], let us rehearse some other kinds of papistical superstitions and abuses, as of Beads, of Lady Psalters and Rosaries[17],

[f] let in or received] admitted *till* 1559. [g] against] again *from* 1562 A. [h] Queen's] King's 1547–1551, 1623. [i] praised] extolled *till* 1559. [k] religions] religion *from* 1574.

17 The great Rosary or Lady Psalter consists of the Ave Maria rehearsed a hundred and fifty times, according to the number of the Psalms of David, divided into fifteen decades by the insertion of a Pater Noster, and into three sections containing five decades each by a Credo. The recitation of each decade should be accompanied by meditations on one of the fifteen principal Mysteries of the history of our Lord and of his mother, five joyous, five dolorous, and five glorious. This method of honouring the Virgin is said to have been devised by St. Dominic, to whom is also ascribed the institution of the Society of the Rosary.

But the Rosary contained in the *Horae Beatissimae Mariae Virginis ad usum Sarum* is compressed into one third of this compass, and consists of fifty Aves with as many distichs on the history of our Saviour divided into decades by five Pater Nosters. It begins thus:

Suscipe rosarium, Virgo, deauratum,
Jesu per compendium vita decoratum:
Ave.
Quem Virgo carens vitio de Flamine concepisti,
Dum Gabriele nuncio humillime consensisti:
Ave.

The name Rosary is also given to a string of beads, commonly fifty-five in

of Fifteen Os[18], of St. Bernard's Verses[19], of St. Agathe's Letters[20], of Purgatory, of Masses Satisfactory, of Stations and Jubilees[21], of feigned Reliques, of hallowed[1] Beads, Bells, Bread,

[1] of hallowed] or hallowed *from* 1576.

number, five of which are larger than the rest and divide them into sets of ten, whereby the votary may count his Aves as he says them. And it may be questioned which use of the word was the earlier; whether it first signified the Aves themselves thus rehearsed, as being "a spiritual garland made of certain mystical words, as it were roses, taken out of the Gospel" (*The Society of the Rosary, p.* 170), and was then applied to the instrument by means of which they were rehearsed; or whether, having previously signified a *sertum* or chaplet of roses, and then a *sertum* of any kind, it was applied specially to beads thus *strung* for purposes of devotion, and thence to the devotional service in which they were used.

See *Du Cange, vv.* Capellina 1 and Rosarium 1, and *The Society of the Rosary*, a little book printed without date, a copy of which is in the Bodleian Library, "8vo. R 35 Th."

18 The various editions of the *Horae* cited in note 17 contain the "Quindecim Orationes beatae Brigittae," and in several this rubric is prefixed. "These be the xv Oos the which the holy virgin St. Brygitta was wont to say daily before the holy rood in St. Paul's church at Rome. Whoso say this a whole year, he shall deliver xv souls out of purgatory of his next kindred, and convert other xv sinners to good life, and other xv righteous men of his kindred shall persevere in good life; and what he desire of God, he shall have it, if it be to the salvation of his soul." Some editions contain also "The xv Oos in English." They are prayers addressed to our blessed Saviour, each beginning "O Jesu" or "O Domine Jesu." In the rehearsal of them each is followed by a Pater Noster and an Ave, and the last by a Credo also.

19 The same volume contains the "Versus Sancti Bernardi," to which in some editions this rubric is prefixed. "When St. Bernard was in his prayers, the devil said unto him, 'I know that there be certain verses in the Psalter, who that say them daily shall not perish, and he shall have knowledge of the day that he shall die:' but the fiend would not shew them to St. Bernard. Then said St. Bernard, 'I shall say daily the whole Psalter.' The fiend, considering that St. Bernard shall do so much profit to labour so, he shewed him these verses." But the verses are eight in number in some editions, twelve in others.

20 St. Agatha, called Agas or Agasse in some of our old calendars and by several writers, is said to have suffered martyrdom at Catana about the year of our Lord 252; and her legend tells how, on the first anniversary of her death, her veil, or the cloth which covered her tomb, sheltered the town from perishing by fire from an eruption of mount Etna. Hence, as we read in the *Third Part of the Homily against Peril of Idolatry*, "instead of Vulcan and Vesta, the Gentiles' gods of the fire, our men have placed St. Agatha, and make letters on her day for to quench fire with." Tyndale, in his *Answer to Sir Thomas More, p.* 61, *ed. Park. Soc.*, says that, in order to be effectual, they ought to be "written in the Gospel time," that is, as the context seems to shew, during the time of the reading of the Gospel on her day. The editor has failed to ascertain what the letters were. Bishop Pilkington, who in his tract on the Burning of Paul's Church, sect. VI, speaks of them as "charms for burning of houses," appears to say that the Breviary or the Missal contains them or gives directions for making them; but they have not been found in any edition of those or of any other Service Books. St. Agatha's day is February 5: her name remains in our Calendar.

21 "In the name of our Lord, Amen. These are the stations of the churches of the city of Rome, which Pope Gregory, Pope Cornelius, and their successors have ordained and appointed to be used of all Catholics for the remission of their

Water, Palms[m], Candles, Fire, and such other[22], of superstitious Fastings, of Fraternities (or Brotherheads[n]), of Pardons, with such like merchandise; which were so esteemed and abused to the great prejudice of God's glory and commandments, that they were made most high and most holy things, whereby to attain to the everlasting[o] life or remission of sin. Yea also vain inventions, unfruitful ceremonies, and ungodly laws, decrees, and Councils of Rome were in such wise advanced, that nothing was thought comparable in authority, wisdom, learning, and godliness unto them: so that the laws of Rome, as they said, were to be received of all men as the four Evangelists; to the which all laws of princes must give place; and the laws of God also partly were left off[p] and less esteemed, that the said laws, decrees, and Councils, with their traditions and ceremonies, might be more duly kept[q], and had in greater reverence. Thus was the people through ignorance so blinded with the goodly[r] shew and appearance of those things, that they thought the keeping of them[s] to be a more holiness, a more perfect service and honouring of God, and more pleasing to God, than the keeping of God's commandments. Such hath been the corrupt inclination of man, ever superstitiously given to make new honouring of God of his own head, and then to have more affection and devotion to keep that[t], than to search out God's holy commandments and to keep them; and furthermore to take God's commandments for men's commandments, and men's commandments for God's commandments, yea, and for the highest and most perfect and holy of all God's commandments. And so was all confused, that scant well learned men, and but a small number of them, knew (or at the least would know) and durst affirm the truth, to separate (or sever[u]) God's commandments from the commandments of men: whereupon did grow

Decrees and Decretals.

[m] Palms] Psalms 1582, 1623. [n] or Brotherheads] *added in* 1559. [o] everlasting] eternal *till* 1559. [p] left off] omitted *till* 1559. [q] kept] observed *till* 1559. [r] goodly] godly 1582, 1623. [s] keeping of them] observing of them *till* 1559. [t] keep that] observe that *till* 1559. [u] or sever] *added in* 1559.

sins through the great indulgence and pardon that is there to be found.

"Imprimis, in the Circumcision of our Lord, the stations are to the church of our Lady trans Tiberim."

And so on. *The Monstruous Marchandise of the Romish Bishops, Becon's Works*, III, *f.* 203 b, *ed.* 1564. On Jubilees also as well as Stations see *Becon's Reliques of Rome, Works*, III, 358.

22 Becon gives forms of hallowing Water, Bread, Candles, Palms, Fire, "Beads to say our Lady's Psalter on," and Bells, in the section "Of Benedictions and Consecrations," in *The Monstruous Marchandise of the Romish Bishops*, at *ff.* 207–214, 232 b, 233.

much error, superstition, idolatry, vain religion, overthwart[x] judgment, great contention, with all ungodly living.

An exhortation[y] to the keeping of God's commandments.

Wherefore, as you have any zeal to the right and pure honouring of God, as you have any regard to your own souls, and to the life that is to come, which is both without pain and without end, apply yourselves chiefly above all things[z] to read and to hear[a] God's word: mark diligently therein what his will is you shall do, and with all your endeavour apply yourselves to follow the same. First you must have an assured faith in God, and give yourselves wholly unto him, love him in prosperity and adversity, and dread to offend him evermore. Then, for his sake, love all men, friends and foes; because they be his creation and image, and redeemed by Christ, as ye are. Cast in your minds how you may do good unto all men unto your powers, and hurt no man. Obey all your superiors and governors, serve your masters faithfully and diligently, as well in their absence as in their presence, not for dread of punishment only, but for conscience sake, knowing that you are bound so to do by God's commandments. Disobey not your fathers and mothers, but honour them, help them, and please them to your power. Oppress not, kill not, beat not, neither slander nor hate any man; but love all men, speak well of all men, help and succour every man as you may, yea, even your enemies that hate you, that speak evil of you, and that do hurt you. Take no man's goods nor covet your neighbour's goods wrongfully, but content yourselves with that which ye get truly, and also bestow your own goods charitably, as need and case requireth. Flee all idolatry, witchcraft, and perjury. Commit no manner of adultery, fornication, nor other[b] unchasteness, in will nor in deed, with any other man's wife, widow, maid[c], or otherwise. And travailing continually during your life[d] thus in the keeping[e] the commandments of God, wherein standeth[f] the pure, principal, and right[g] honour of God, and which, wrought in faith[h], God hath ordained to be the right trade[23] and path-

A brief rehearsal of God's commandments.

[x] overthwart] preposterous *till* 1559. [y] exhortation] hortation 1559. [z] things] thing *till* 1582. [a] and to hear] and hear 1582, 1623. [b] nor other] or other *from* 1576. [c] widow, maid] widow, or maid *from* 1569. [d] your life] this life 1623. [e] in the keeping] in the observing *till* 1559, in keeping *from* 1582. [f] standeth] consisteth *till* 1559. [g] right] direct *till* 1559. [h] wrought in faith] *not in* 1547 G 1 *or* W 1.

23 trade: see before, p. 45, n. 8.

Or I'll be buried in the king's highway,
Some way of common trade, where subjects' feet
May hourly trample on their sovereign's head:

way unto heaven, you shall not fail, as Christ hath promised, to come to that blessed and everlasting[i] life where you shall live in glory and joy with God for ever. To whom be praise[k], honour, and impery[l] for ever and ever. Amen.

[i] everlasting] eternal *till* 1559. [k] praise] laud *till* 1559. [l] impery] empery 1574, 1623.

For on my heart they tread now whilst I live ;
And, buried once, why not upon my head?
Shakespeare, Rich. II, III, 3.

A SERMON[a]

OF CHRISTIAN LOVE AND CHARITY.

OF all things that be good to be taught unto Christian people, there is nothing more necessary to be spoken of and daily called upon than charity; as well for that all manner of works of righteousness be contained in it, as also that the decay thereof is the ruin (or fall[b]) of the world, the banishment of virtue, and the cause of all vice. And forsomuch as almost every man maketh and frameth to himself charity[c] after his own appetite, and, how detestable soever his life be both unto God and man, yet he persuadeth himself still that he hath charity; therefore you shall hear now a true and plain description (or setting forth[d]) of charity, not of men's imagination, but of the very words and example of our Saviour Jesus Christ. In which description (or setting forth[e]) every man, as it were in a glass, may consider himself, and see plainly without error whether he be in the true charity or not.

What charity is. The love of God.

Charity is to love God with all our heart, all our life, and[f] all our powers and strength. With all our heart: that is to say, that our heart's mind[g] and study be set to believe his word, to trust in him, and to love him above all other things that we love best in heaven or in earth. With all our life: that is to say, that our chief joy and delight be set upon him and his honour, and our whole life given unto the service of him above all things, with him to live and die, and to forsake all other things rather than him; for, *he that loveth his father or mother, son or daughter*, house or land, *more than me,* saith Christ, *is not worthy to have me.* With all our powers: that[h] is to say, that with our hands and feet, with our eyes and ears, our mouths and tongues, and with all other parts[i] and powers both of body and soul, we should be given to the keeping and fulfilling of his commandments. This is the first and prin-

Matt. x, [37; xvi, 24–27; xix, 29.]

[a] A SERMON] AN HOMILY *till* 1549 W. [b] or fall] *added in* 1559. [c] himself charity] himself a charity BON. [d e] or setting forth] *added in* 1559. [f] life, and] soul, and 1623. [g] heart's mind] heart, mind *from* 1574. [h] powers: that] power: that 1582, 1623. [i] other parts] our parts *from* 1569.

The love of thy neighbour.

cipal part of charity, but it is not the whole: for charity is also to love every man, good and evil, friend and foe; and, whatsoever cause be given to the contrary, yet nevertheless to bear good will and heart unto every man, to use ourselves well unto them as well in words and countenance[j] as in all our outward acts and deeds. For so Christ himself taught, and so also he performed in deed.

Matt. xxii, [37.]

Of the love of God he taught in this wise unto a doctor of the law, that asked him which was the great and chief commandment in the law. *Love thy Lord God,* said Christ, *with all thy heart, with all thy life*[k], *and with all thy mind.* And of the love that we ought to have among ourselves each to other he teacheth us thus: *You have heard it taught in times past, Thou shalt love thy friend, and hate thy foe: but I tell you, Love your enemies, speak well of them that diffame you and*[l] *speak evil of you, do well to them that hate you, pray for them that vex and persecute you; that you may be the children of your Father that is in heaven; for he maketh his sun to rise both upon the evil and good, and sendeth rain to just*[m] *and unjust. For, if you love them that love you, what reward shall you have? do not the publicans likewise? And, if you speak well only of them that be your brethren and dear beloved friends, what great matter is that? do not the heathen the same also?* These be the very words of our Saviour Christ himself touching the love of our neighbour. And forasmuch as the Pharisees, with their most pestilent traditions, false[n] interpretations, and gloses[o], had corrupted and almost clearly stopped up this pure well of God's lively word, teaching that this love and charity pertained only to a man's friends, and that it was sufficient for a man to love them which do love him, and to hate[p] his foes; therefore Christ opened this well again, purged it, and scoured it, by giving unto his godly law of charity a true and clear interpretation, which is this, that we ought to love every man, both friend and foe; adding thereto what commodity we shall have thereby, and what incommodity by doing the contrary. What thing can we wish so good for us as the eternal heavenly Father to reckon[q] and take us for his children? And this shall we be sure of, saith Christ, if we love every man without exception. And if we do otherwise, saith he, we be no better than the

Matt. v, [43-47.]

j countenance] countenances *from* 1562 A. k thy life] thy soul 1623. l diffame you and] defame and 1623. m to just] to the just 1582, 1623. n traditions, false] traditions, and false *from* 1548. o gloses] glosses 1623. p and to hate] and hate 1582, 1623. q reckon] repute *till* 1559.

Pharisees, publicans, and heathen, and shall have our reward with them, that is, to be shut out[r] from the number of God's chosen[s] children and from his everlasting inheritance in heaven.

Thus of true charity Christ taught, that every man is bound to love God above all things, and to love every man, friend and foe. And thus[t] likewise he did use himself, exhorting his adversaries, rebuking the faults of his adversaries, and, when he could not amend them, yet he prayed for them. First he loved God his Father above all things, so much that he sought not his own glory and will, but the glory and will of his Father.

John v, [30.] *I seek not*, said he, *mine own will, but the will of him that sent me.* Nor he refused not to die, to satisfy his Father's will, saying,

Matt. xxvi, [39, 42.] *If it may be, let this cup of death go*[u] *from me; if not, thy will be done, and not mine.* He loved also not[x] only his friends, but also his enemies; which in their hearts bare exceeding great hatred against him, and in their tongues[y] spake all evil of him, and in their acts and deeds pursued him with all their might and power even unto death. Yet, all this notwithstanding, he withdrew not his favour from them; but still loved them, preached unto them, of love rebuked[z] their false doctrine, their wicked living, and did good unto them, patiently taking[a] whatsoever they spake or did against him. When they gave him evil words, he gave none evil again; when they did strike him, he did not smite again[b]; and when he suffered death, he did not slay them, nor threaten them, but prayed for them, and did put[c] all things to his Father's will. And, as a

a Isai. liii, [7:] Acts viii, [32.] sheep[a] that is led unto the shambles to be slain and as a lamb that is shorn of his fleece make[d] no noise nor resistance, even so went he unto[e] his death without any repugnance or opening of his mouth to say any evil.

Thus have I set forth[f] unto you what charity is, as well by the doctrine as by the example[g] of Christ himself. Whereby also every man may without error know himself, what state and condition he standeth in, whether he be in charity, and so the child of the Father in heaven, or not. For, although almost every man persuadeth himself to be in charity, yet let him ex-

[r] shut out] excluded *till* 1559. [s] chosen] elect *till* 1559. [t] And thus] And this 1582, 1623. [u] go] pass *from* 1576. [x] loved also not] loved not *all except* 1547 W *and* BON. [y] in their tongues] with their tongues 1582, 1623. [z] preached unto them, of love rebuked] *This is the punctuation in* 1547 W *and in* BON. *See below, p.* 72, *ll.* 22, 23. [a] taking] accepting *till* 1559. [b] smite again] smite him again 1623. [c] did put] referred *till* 1559. [d] make] maketh 1549 W *and from* 1559. [e] went he unto] he went unto 1574, 1576; he went to 1582, 1623. [f] set forth] described *till* 1559. [g] example] examples *from* 1563.

amine none other man, but his own heart, his life and conversation, and he shall not be deceived, but truly decern[h] and judge whether he be in perfect charity or not. For he that followeth not his own appetite and will, but giveth himself earnestly to God, to do all his will and commandments, he may be sure that he loveth God above all things: and else, surely he loveth him not, whatsoever he pretend. As Christ said, *If ye love me, keep my commandments.* For, *He that knoweth my commandments and keepeth them, he it is,* saith Christ[i], *that loveth me.* And again he saith, *He that loveth me, will keep my word; and my Father will love him, and we will both come to him and dwell with him.* And, *He that loveth me not will not keep my words.* And likewise he that beareth good[k] heart and mind, and useth well his tongue and deeds, unto every man, friend and foe, he may know thereby that he hath charity. And then[l] he is sure also that[m] Almighty God taketh him for his dear beloved son; as St. John saith, *Hereby manifestly are known the children of God from the children of the devil: for whosoever doth not love his brother belongeth not unto God.*

John xiv, [15, 21, 23, 24.]

1 John iii, [10.]

THE SECOND PART OF THE SERMON OF CHARITY.

YOU have heard a plain and a fruitful setting forth[n] of charity, and how profitable and necessary a thing charity is; how charity stretcheth[o] itself both to God and man, friend and foe, and that by the doctrine and example of Christ; and also who may certify himself whether he be in perfect charity or not. Now as concerning the same matter it followeth.

Against carnal men, that will not forgive their enemies.

The perverse[p] nature of man, corrupt with sin, and destitute of God's word and grace, thinketh it against all reason that a man should love his enemy, and hath many persuasions which bring[q] him to the contrary. Against all which reasons we ought as well to set the teaching as the living of our Saviour Christ, who, loving us when we were his enemies, doth teach us to love our enemies. He did patiently take for us many reproaches, suffered beating and most cruel death. Therefore we be no

h decern] discern *from* 1574. i saith Christ] said Christ 1547 G 2—1569. k beareth good] beareth a good *from* 1582. l then] when *from* 1574. m sure also that] sure that 1623. n setting forth] description *till* 1559. o stretcheth] extendeth *till* 1559. p THE SECOND PART— The perverse] But the perverse 1547, 1548, *the Homily not being then divided.* q bring] induceth 1547 G 1 *and* W, *and* BON.; induce 1547 G 2—1551.

members of him if we will not follow him. *Christ,* saith St. Peter, *suffered for us, leaving an example, that we should follow him.* [1 Pet. ii, [21.]] Furthermore, we must consider that to love our friends is no more but that which thieves, adulterers, homicides, and all wicked persons do; insomuch that Jews, Turks, infidels, and all brute beasts do love them that be their friends, of whom they have their living or any other benefits: but to love enemies is the proper condition only[r] of them that be the children of God, the disciples and followers of Christ. Notwithstanding, man's froward and corrupt nature weigheth over deeply many times the offence and displeasure done unto him by enemies, and thinketh it a burden intolerable to be bound to love them that hate him. But the burden should be easy enough, if on the other side every man would consider what displeasure he hath done to his enemy again, and what pleasure he hath received of his enemy. And, if we find no equal[s] (or even[t]), recompence neither in receiving pleasures of our enemy nor in requiting[u] displeasures unto[v] him again, then let us ponder the displeasures which we have done against[x] Almighty God, how often and how grievously we have offended him; whereof if we will have of God forgiveness, there is none other remedy but to forgive[y] the offences done unto us, which be very small in comparison of our offences done against God. And, if we consider that he which hath offended us deserveth not to be forgiven of us, let us consider again that we much less deserve to be forgiven of God. And, although our enemy deserve not to be forgiven for his own sake, yet we ought to forgive him for God's love; considering how great and many benefits we have received of him without our deserts, and that Christ hath deserved of us that for his sake we should forgive them their trespasses committed against us.

A question.[z] But here may rise a necessary question to be dissolved. If charity require to think, speak, and do well unto every man, both good and evil, how can magistrates execute justice upon malefactors (or evildoers[a]) with charity? How can they cast evil men in prison, take away their goods, and sometime their lives, according to laws, if charity will not suffer them so to do?

An answer.[b] Hereunto is a plain and a brief answer: that plagues and

[r] only] *omitted* 1623. [s] equal] egall 1547 G 1 *and* W. [t] or even] *added in* 1559. [u] requiting] rendering *till* 1559. [v] displeasures unto] displeasure unto 1547 G 1 *and* W, *and* BON. [x] done against] done unto 1623. [y] there is none other remedy but to forgive] there is none other mean but to forgive 1547 G 1, we must needs forgive 1547 G 2. [z] A question.] *not in* 1547 G 1 *or* 2. [a] or evildoers] *added in* 1559. [b] An answer.] *not in* 1547 G 1 *or* 2, Answer. *from* 1576.

punishments be not evil of themselves, if they be well taken of the harmless[c]; and to an evil man they are both good and necessary, and may be executed according to charity, and with charity should be executed.

Charity hath two offices.

For declaration whereof you shall understand that charity hath two offices, the one contrary to the other, and yet both necessary to be used upon men of contrary sort and disposition. The one office of charity is to cherish good and harmless men[d]; not to oppress them with false accusations, but to encourage them with rewards to do well and to continue[e] in well doing, defending them with the sword from their adversaries. And the[f] office of bishops and pastors is to praise good men for well doing, that they may continue[g] therein, and to rebuke and correct by the word of God the offences and crimes of all evil-disposed persons. The other[h] office of charity is to rebuke, correct, and punish vice without regard[i] of persons; and this is to[k] be used against them only that be evil men and malefactors (or evildoers[l]). And that it is as well the office of charity to rebuke, punish, and correct them that be evil, as it is to cherish and reward them that be good and harmless[m], St. Paul declareth (writing to the Romans), saying that *the high powers are ordained of God*, not to be dreadful to them that do well, but unto malefactors, to draw the sword *to take vengeance of him that committeth the sin*. (Rom. xiii, [1-4.]) And St. Paul biddeth Timothy stoutly and earnestly[n] to rebuke sin by the word of God. (1 Tim. v, [20.]) So that both offices should be diligently executed, to fight against[o] the kingdom of the devil, the preacher with the word, and the governor[p] with the sword: else they love neither[q] God nor them whom they govern, if, for lack of correction, they wilfully suffer God to be offended, and them whom they govern to perish. For, as every loving father correcteth his natural son when he doeth amiss, or else he loveth him not, so all governors of realms, countries, towns, and houses should lovingly correct them which be offenders under their governance, and cherish them which live innocently, if they have any respect either unto God and their office or love unto them of whom they have governance. And such rebukes and punishments of them that offend must

[c] the harmless] innocents *till* 1559. [d] harmless men] innocent men *till* 1559. [e], [g] continue] persevere *till* 1559. [f] And the] as the *from* 1574. [h] The other] For the other *till* 1574, *except* 1547 W *and* BON. [i] regard] acceptation *till* 1559. [k] and this is to] and this to 1547 G 3—1551, and is to *from* 1559. [l] or evildoers] *added in* 1559. [m] harmless] innocent *till* 1559. [n] stoutly and earnestly] constantly and vehemently *till* 1559. [o] fight against] impugn *till* 1559. [p] governor] governors 1582, 1623. [q] love neither] neither love 1582, 1623.

be done in due time, lest by delay the offenders fall headlings[r] into all manner of mischief, and not only be evil themselves, but also do hurt unto many men, drawing other by their evil example to sin and outrage after them: as one thief may both rob many men, and also make many thieves; and one seditious person may allure many, and noy[s] a whole town or country. And such evil persons, that be so great offenders of God[t] and the commonweal, charity requireth to be cut off[u] from the body of the commonweal, lest they corrupt other good and honest persons; like as a good surgeon cutteth away a rotten[x] and festered member for love he hath to the whole body, lest it infect other members adjoining to it[y].

Thus it is declared unto you what true charity or Christian love is, so plainly that no man need to be deceived. Which love whosoever keepeth, not only toward[z] God, whom he is bound to love above all things, but also toward[a] his neighbour, as well friend as foe, it shall surely keep him from all offence of God and just offence of man. Therefore bear well away this one short lesson, that by true Christian charity God ought to be loved above all things, and all men ought to be loved[b], good and evil, friend and foe; and to all such we ought, as we may, to do good; those that be good, of love to encourage and cherish, because they be good; and those that be evil, of love to procure and seek[c] their correction and due punishment, that they may thereby either be brought to goodness, or at the least that God and the commonwealth may be the less[d] hurt and offended. And, if we thus direct our life by Christian love and charity, then Christ doth promise and assure us that he loveth us, that we be the children of our heavenly Father, reconciled to his favour, very members of Christ, and that, after this short time of this present and mortal life, we shall have with him everlasting life[e] in his everlasting kingdom of heaven. Therefore to him with the Father and the Holy Ghost be all honour and glory now and ever[f]. Amen.

[r] headlings] headlongs 1549 W, 1559–1576; headlong *from* 1582. [s] noy] annoy 1595, 1623. [t] of God] to God *from* 1574. [u] off] *omitted* 1582, 1623. [x] rotten] putrified *till* 1559. [y] to it] unto it *from* 1569. [z] only toward] only towards *from* 1547 G 3. [a] also toward] also towards 1547 G 3—1569. [b] above all things, and all men ought to be loved] *omitted after* 1562. [c] and seek] *added in* 1559. [d] be the less] be less *from* 1569. [e] everlasting life] eternal life *till* 1559. [f] and ever] and for ever 1582, 1623.

AGAINST[a] SWEARING AND PERJURY.

ALMIGHTY God, to the intent his most holy Name should be had in honour and evermore be magnified of the people, commandeth that no man should take his Name vainly in his mouth, threatening punishment unto him that unreverently abuseth it by swearing, forswearing, and blasphemy. To the intent therefore that this commandment may be the better known and kept, it shall be declared unto you both how it is lawful for Christian people to swear, and also what peril and danger it is vainly to swear or to be forsworn.

How and in what causes it is lawful to swear.

First, when judges require oaths of the people for declaration (or opening[b]) of the truth or for execution of justice, this manner of swearing is lawful. Also, when men make faithful promises with calling to witness[c] of the Name of God to keep[d] covenants, honest promises, statutes, laws, and good customs; as Christian princes do in their conclusions of peace for conservation of commonwealths; and private persons promise their fidelity in matrimony, or one to another in honest[e] and true friendship; and all men, when they do swear to keep common laws, or local[f] statutes and good customs, for due order to be had and continued among men; when subjects do swear to be true and faithful to their king and sovereign lord, and when judges, magistrates, and officers swear truly to execute their offices; and when a man would affirm the truth to the setting forth of God's glory for the salvation of the people in open preaching of the Gospel, or in giving of good counsel privately for their souls' health: all these manner of swearings[g] for causes necessary and honest be lawful. But, when men do swear of custom, in reasoning, buying and selling, or other daily communication[h], as many be common and great swearers, such kind of swearing is ungodly, unlawful, and forbidden[i] by the commandment of God: for such swearing is nothing else but taking of God's holy Name in vain.

And here is to be noted that lawful swearing is not forbidden[k],

[a] AGAINST] A SERMON AGAINST *from* 1574. [b] or opening] *added in* 1559. [c] calling to witness] attestation *till* 1559. [d] keep] observe *till* 1559. [e] in honest] in honeste 1548, 1549; in honestie *from* 1559. [f] or local] and local *from* 1562 B. [g] swearings] swearing *from* 1574. [h] communication] communications *from* 1574. [i] and forbidden] and prohibited *till* 1559. [k] not forbidden] not forbid 1547 G 1.

but commanded, of[l] Almighty God. For we have examples of Christ and godly men in holy Scripture, that did swear themselves, and required oaths of other[m] likewise. And God's commandment is[α], *Thou shalt dread thy Lord God, and shalt swear by his Name.* And Almighty God by his Prophet David saith, *All men shall be praised that swear*[n] *by him.*

[α] Deut. vi, [13.]
Ps. lxii [lxiii, 11.]

Thus did our Saviour Christ swear divers times, saying, *Verily, Verily*[β]. And St. Paul sweareth thus, *I call God to witness*[γ]. And Abraham, waxing old, required an oath of his servant[δ] that he should procure a wife for his son Isaac, which should come of his own kinred: and the servant did swear that he would perform his master's will. Abraham also, being required, did swear[ε] unto Abimelech the king of Geraris that he should not hurt him nor his posterity: and so likewise[o] did Abimelech swear unto Abraham. And David[ς] did swear to be and continue a faithful friend to Jonathas: and Jonathas did swear to become a faithful friend unto David.

[β] John iii, [3, 5, 11.]
[γ] 2 Cor. i, [23.]
[δ] Gen. xxiv, [1–9.]
[ε] Gen. xxi, [22–31.]
[ς] [1 Sam. xviii, 3; xx, 12–17, 42.]

Also God once commanded[η] that if a thing were laid to pledge to any man or left with him to keep, if the same thing were stolen or lost, that the keeper thereof should be sworn before judges, that he did not convey it away, nor used any deceit in causing the same to be conveyed away by his consent or knowledge. And St. Paul saith[θ] that in all matters of controversy between two persons, where as one saith yea, and the other nay, so as no due proof can be had of the truth, the end of every such controversy must be an oath ministered by a judge.

[η] [Exod. xxii, 10, 11.]
[θ] Heb. vi, [16.]

And moreover God by the Prophet Jeremy saith, *Thou shalt swear, The Lord liveth, in truth, in judgment, in righteousness.* So that, whosoever[p] sweareth when he is required of a judge, let him be sure in his conscience that his oath have these three[q] conditions[1], and he shall never need to be afraid of perjury. First, he that sweareth must swear *truly*[u]; that is, he must, setting apart[x] all favour and affection to the parties, have the truth only before his eyes, and for love thereof say and speak that which he knoweth to be truth, and no further. The second is, he that taketh an oath must do it *with judgment*; not

Jer. iv, [2.]
What conditions[r] a lawful oath[s] ought to have.
The first.[t]
The second.[y]

[l] commanded, of] commanded, by *from* 1574. [m] of other] of others 1582, 1623. [n] that swear] that sweareth 1547 G 1. [o] and so likewise] and likewise 1582, 1623. [p] whosoever] whoso 1547 G 1. [q] have these three] have three 1623. [r] What conditions] What condition *from* 1562 A. [s] a lawful oath] an oath *from* 1563. [t] The first.] *not in* 1547 G 1, 1576, 1582, 1623. [u] must swear truly] must swear that he sweareth truly 1547 G 1 *and* 2, may swear truly *from* 1574. [x] setting apart] secluding *till* 1559. [y] The second.] *not in* 1547 G 1.

[1] See Article XXXIX, "Of a Christian man's Oath."

rashly and unadvisedly, but soberly, considering what an oath is. The third is, he that sweareth must swear *in righteousness*[a]; that is, for the very zeal and love which he beareth to the defence of innocency, to the maintenance of the truth, and to[b] the righteousness[c d] of the matter or cause, all profit, disprofit, all love and favour unto the person for friendship or kinred, laid apart. Thus an oath, if it have[e] with it these three conditions, is a part of God's glory which we are bound by his commandment[f] to give unto him: for he willeth that we shall swear only by his Name. Not that he hath pleasure in our oaths[g]: but, like as he commanded the Jews to offer sacrifices unto him, not for any delight that he had in them, but to keep the Jews from committing of idolatry, so he, commanding us to swear by his holy Name, doth not teach us that he delighteth in swearing, but he thereby forbiddeth all men to give his glory[t] to any creature in heaven, earth, or water.

The third.[a]

Why we be willed in Scripture to swear by the Name of God.

[t] Isai. xlii, [8:] Ps. cl, [6.]

Hitherto you see that oaths lawful are commanded of God, used of Patriarchs and Prophets, of Christ himself, and of his Apostle Paul. Therefore Christian people must think lawful oaths both godly and necessary. For by lawful promises[h] and covenants, confirmed by oaths, princes and their countries are confirmed in common tranquillity and peace. By holy promises with calling the Name of God to witness[i] we be made lively members of Christ, when we profess his religion, receiving the Sacrament of Baptism. By like holy promise the sacrament of matrimony knitteth man and wife in perpetual love, that they desire not to be separated for any displeasure or adversity that shall after happen. By lawful oaths which kings, princes, judges, and magistrates do swear common laws are kept inviolate, justice is indifferently ministered, harmless[k] persons, fatherless children[l], widows, and poor men are defended from murderers, oppressors, and thieves, that they suffer no wrong, nor take any harm. By lawful oaths mutual society, amity, and good order is kept continually in all commonalties, as boroughs, cities, towns, and villages. And by lawful oaths malefactors are searched out, wrong doers are punished, and they which sustain wrong are restored to their right. Therefore lawful swearing cannot be evil, which bringeth unto us so many godly, good, and necessary commodities.

Commodities had by lawful oaths made and observed.

[a] The third.] *not in* 1547 G 1. [d] righteousness] rightwiseness 1547 G 1. [b] and to] and of *from* 1569. [c] to the righteousness] to righteousness *till* 1547 G 5. [e] it have] it hath 1547 G 1 *and* 2. [f] commandment] commandments 1582, 1623. [g] in our oaths] in oaths 1623. [h] lawful promises] lawful promise *from* 1562 B. [i] with calling the Name of God to witness] with attestation of God's Name *till* 1559. [k] harmless] innocent *till* 1559. [l] fatherless children] orphans *till* 1559.

Vain swearing is forbidden[m].

Wherefore, when Christ so earnestly forbad swearing, it may not be so[n] understanded[o] as though he did forbid all manner of oaths: but he forbiddeth all vain swearing and forswearing both by God and by his[p] creatures, as the common use of swearing in buying, selling, and in our daily communication; to the intent every Christian man's word should be as well regarded in such matters, as if he should confirm his communication with an oath. For "every Christian man's word," saith St. Hierome[2], "should be so true, that it should be regarded as an oath." And Chrysostom, witnessing the same, saith[3], "It is not convenient to swear: for what needeth us to swear, when it is not lawful for one of us to make a lie unto another?"

An objection.

Peradventure some will say, I am compelled to swear, for else men that do common[q] with me, or do buy and sell with me, will not believe me.

An answer.

To this answereth St. Chrysostom[4], that he that thus saith sheweth himself to be an unjust and a deceitful person: for, if he were a trusty man, and his deeds taken to agree with his words, he should not need to swear at all. For he that useth truth and plainness in his bargaining and communication, he shall have no need by such vain swearing to bring himself in credence with his neighbours, nor his neighbours will not mistrust his sayings. And, if his credence be so much lost indeed that he thinketh no man will believe him without he swear, then he may well think his credence is clean gone. For truth it is, as Theophylactus writeth[5], that "no man is less trusted than he that

m Vain swearing is forbidden] Vain swearing forbidden 1547 G 1. n not be so] not so be 1547 G 5—1595, not be 1623. o understanded] understood 1623. p and by his] and his 1547 G 1. q do common] do commen 1547 G 1, do commune *from* 1574.

2 Evangelica autem veritas non recipit juramentum, cum omnis sermo fidelis pro jurejurando sit. *Hieron. in Matth.* v, 34–37; *Opp.* VII, 30 D.

3 Jurare nos prorsus non convenit. Quid enim unicuique nostrum jurare necesse est, cum nobis mentiri omnino non liceat; quorum verba ita vera semper, ita debent esse fidelissima, ut pro juramento habeantur? *Chromatii in Matth. Tractat.* IX, 11; *Galland. Biblioth. Patr.* VIII, 344. No doubt the error of referring this passage to Chrysostom arose from the identity of the first three letters in the two names. The same error with another passage of Chromatius was made by Gratian, or perhaps by some earlier compiler, in *Decret.* II, xxii, 5, *Juramenti,* whence the passage is cited as Chrysostom's by Becon in his Invective against Swearing.

4 Ἀπιστούμεθά, φησιν. ἀπιστούμεθα, ἐπειδὴ βουλόμεθα· ἐξῆν γὰρ ἀπὸ τοῦ τρόπου πιστεύεσθαι μᾶλλον ἡμᾶς ἢ ἀπὸ τῶν ὅρκων. διὰ τί γάρ, εἰπέ μοι, τοῖς μὲν οὐδὲ ὀμνύουσι πιστεύομεν, τοὺς δὲ καὶ χωρὶς ὅρκων πιστοὺς ἡγούμεθα; ὁρᾷς ὅτι οὐδαμοῦ χρεία ὅρκων. Chrysost. in Epist. ad Ephes. Hom. II; Opp. xi, 13 E. See also Ad Pop. Antioch. Hom. VII, and In Act. Apost. Hom. IX; Opp. II, 91 A, and IX, 79 B; the former of which two passages is cited by Becon in his Invective against Swearing as Chrysostom's answer to a similar plea.

5 Οὐδεὶς γὰρ οὕτως ἀπιστεῖται, ὡς ὁ προχείρως ὀμνύων. Theophylact. in Matth. v, 37.

useth much to swear." And Almighty God by the Wise Man saith, *That man which sweareth much shall be full of sin, and the scourge of God shall not depart from his house.*

Ecclus. xxiii, [11.]

Another objection.

But here some men will say, for excusing of their many oaths in their daily talk, Why should I not swear when I swear truly?

An answer.

To such men it may be said that, though they swear truly, yet, in swearing often, unadvisedly, for trifles, without necessity, and when they should not swear, they be not without fault, but do take God's most holy Name in vain. Much more ungodly and unwise men are they that abuse God's most holy Name, not only in buying and selling of small things daily in all places, but also in eating [r], drinking, playing, commoning [s], and reasoning; as if none of these things might be done, except in doing of them the most holy Name of God be commonly used and abused, vainly and unreverently talked of, sworn by and forsworn, to the breaking of God's commandment, and procurement of his indignation.

THE SECOND PART OF THE SERMON OF SWEARING.

YOU have been taught in the first part of this Sermon against swearing and perjury, what great danger it is to use the Name of God in vain; and that all kind of swearing is not unlawful, neither against God's commandment; and that there be three things required in a lawful oath; first, that it be made for the maintenance of the truth; second [t], that it be made with judgment, not rashly and unadvisedly; thirdly, for the zeal and love of justice. Ye heard also what commodities cometh of lawful oaths, and what danger cometh of rash and unlawful oaths. Now, as concerning the rest of the same matter, ye shall [u] understand that as [x] well they use the Name of God in vain that by an oath make lawful [y] promises of good and honest things and perform them not, as they which do promise evil and unlawful things and do perform the same.

Lawful oaths and promises would be better regarded.

Of such men that regard not their godly promises bound [z] by an oath, but wittingly and wilfully breaketh them, we do read in holy Scripture two notable punishments. First, Josue and the people of Israel made a league [k] and faithful promise of perpetual

[k] Josh. ix.

[r] also in eating] also eating *all except* 1547 W 2 *and* 3, *and from* 1574. [s] commoning] communing *from* 1574. [t] second] secondly 1623. [u] ye shall] you shall 1582, 1623. [x] THE SECOND PART——that as] And as 1547, 1548, *the Homily not being then divided.* [y] make lawful] make unlawful *from* 1576. [z] bound] confirmed *till* 1559.

amity and friendship with the Gabaonites: notwithstanding, afterward in the days of wicked Saul many of these Gabaonites were murdered, contrary to the said faithful promise made. Wherewith Almighty God was so sore[a] displeased[λ], that he sent an universal hunger[b] upon the whole country, which continued by the space of three years; and God would not withdraw his punishment, until the said offence was revenged by the death of seven sons or next kinsmen of king Saul. Also[c], whereas Sedechias king of Jerusalem had promised[μ] fidelity to the king of Chaldea, afterward, when Sedechias, contrary to his oath and allegiance, did rebel against king Nabuchodonozor, this heathen king, by God's permission and sufferance[d], invading the land of Jewry and besieging the city of Jerusalem, compelled the said king Sedechias to flee, and in fleeing took him prisoner, slew his sons before his face, and put out both his eyes, and binding him with chains led him prisoner miserably into Babylon. Thus doth God shew plainly how much he abhorreth breakers of honest promises bound[e] by an oath made in his name.

λ 2 Sam. xxi, [1–14.]

μ [2 Kings xxiv, 17–xxv, 7.]

Unlawful oaths and promises are not to be kept.

And of them that make wicked promises by an oath, and will perform the same, we have example in the Scripture[f], chiefly of Herod, of the wicked Jews, and of Jephthah. Herod *promised by an oath* unto the damsel which danced before him *to give unto her whatsoever she would*[g] *ask*, when she was *instructed before of her* wicked *mother* to ask the head of St. John Baptist. Herod, as he took a wicked oath, so he more wickedly performed the same, and cruelly slew the most holy Prophet. Likewise *did* the malicious Jews *make an oath, cursing themselves if they did either eat or drink until they had slain St. Paul.* And Jephthah[ν], when God had given to him victory of the children of Ammon, promised, of a foolish devotion unto God, to offer for a sacrifice unto him that person which of his own house should first meet with him after his return home. By force of which fond and unadvised oath he did slay his own and only daughter, which came out of his house with mirth and joy to welcome him home. Thus the promise, which he made most foolishly to God, against God's everlasting[h] will and the law of nature most cruelly he performed, so committing against God double[i] offence. Therefore, whosoever maketh any promise binding himself thereunto by an oath, let him foresee that the thing which he pro-

Matt. xiv, [6–11.]

Acts xxiii, [12.]

ν Judg. xi, [30–39.]

[a] was so sore] was sore 1549 G, 1551, *and from* 1576. [b] hunger] famine *till* 1559. [c] Also] And *from* 1574. [d] and sufferance] *added in* 1559. [e] bound] confirmed *till* 1559. [f] Scripture] Scriptures 1582, 1623. [g] she would] she should 1547 G 3–1559. [h] everlasting] eternal *till* 1559. [i] God double] God a double 1623.

miseth be good, honest[k], and not against the commandment of God, and that it be in his own[l] power to perform it justly: and such good promises must all men keep evermore assuredly. But, if a man at any time shall, either of ignorance or of malice, promise and swear to do anything which is either against the law of Almighty God or not in his power to perform, let him take it for an unlawful and ungodly oath.

Against perjury.

Now something to speak of perjury. To the intent you should know how great and grievous an offence against God this wilful perjury is, I will shew you what it is to take an oath before a judge upon a book. First, when they, laying their hands upon the Gospel book, do swear truly to inquire and to make a true presentment of things wherewith they be charged, and not to let from saying the truth and doing truly for favour, love, dread, or malice[m] of any person, as God may help them and the holy contents of that book, they must consider that in that book is contained God's everlasting truth, his most holy and eternal word, whereby we have forgiveness of our sins, and be made inheritors of heaven, to live for ever with God's angels and his saints[n] in joy and gladness. In the Gospel book is contained also God's terrible threats to obstinate sinners, that will not amend their lives, nor believe the truth of God, his holy word, and the everlasting pain prepared in hell for idolaters, hypocrites, for false and vain swearers, for perjured men, for false witness bearers, for false condemners of innocent and guiltless men, and for them which for favour hide[o] the crimes of evildoers[p], that they should not be punished. So that, whosoever wilfully forsweareth himself[q] upon Christ's holy Evangely, they utterly forsake God's mercy, goodness, and truth, the merits of our Saviour Christ's nativity, life, passion, death, resurrection, and ascension; they refuse the forgiveness of sins promised to all penitent sinners, the joys of heaven, the company with angels and saints for ever; all which benefits and comforts are promised unto true Christian persons in the Gospel. And they, so being forsworn upon the Gospel, do betake themselves to the devil's service, the master of all lies, falsehood, deceit, and perjury, provoking the great indignation and curse of God against them in this life, and the terrible wrath and judgment of our Saviour Christ at the great day of the last judgment, when he shall justly judge both the

An oath before a judge.

[k] good, honest] good and honest 1623. [l] his own] our own 1547 G 1. [m] or malice] nor malice *till* 1547 G 5. [n] and his saints] and saints 1623. [o] hide] hideth 1547 G 1. [p] evildoers] malefactors *till* 1559. [q] forsweareth himself] forsweareth themself 1576, forswear themselves *from* 1582.

quick and the dead according to their works. For whosoever forsaketh the truth for love or displeasure of any man, or for lucre and profit to himself, doth forsake Christ, and with Judas betrayeth[r] him. And, although such perjured men's falsehood be now kept secret, yet it shall be opened at the last day, when the secrets of all men's hearts shall be manifest to all the world; and then the truth shall appear, and accuse them; and their own conscience, with all the blessed company of heaven, shall bear witness truly against them; and Christ, the righteous[t] Judge, shall then justly condemn them to everlasting shame and death.

Though perjury do escape here unespied[s] and unpunished, it shall not do so ever.

This sin of perjury Almighty God by the Prophet Malachy doth threaten to punish sore, saying unto the Jews, *I will come to you in judgment, and I will be a swift witness* and a sharp judge *upon sorcerers, adulterers, and perjured persons.* Which thing to the Prophet Zachary God declareth in a vision, wherein the Prophet saw a book flying[u], which was twenty cubits long and ten cubits broad, God saying then unto him, *This is the curse that shall go forth upon the face of the earth for falsehood, false swearing, and perjury; and this curse shall enter into the house of the false man and into the house of the perjured man, and it shall remain in the midst of his house, and consume him, the*[x] *timber and stones of his house.* Thus you see how much God doth hate perjury, and what punishment God hath prepared for false swearers and perjured persons.

Mal. iii, [5.]

Zech. v, [1-4.]

Thus you have heard how and in what causes it is lawful for a Christian man to swear; ye have heard what properties and conditions a lawful oath must have, and also how such lawful oaths are both godly and necessary to be observed; ye have heard that it is not lawful to swear vainly, that is, other ways than in such causes and after such sort as is declared; and finally ye have heard how damnable a thing it is either to forswear ourselves[y] or to keep an unlawful and unadvised[z] oath. Wherefore let us earnestly call for grace, that, all vain swearing and perjury set apart, we may only use such oaths as be lawful and godly, and that we may truly, without all fraud, keep[a] the same, according to God's will and pleasure. To whom with the Son and Holy[b] Ghost be all honour and glory. Amen.

[r] betrayeth] betray *from* 1562 A. [s] unespied] unspied *from* 1582. [t] righteous] rightwise 1547 G 1, 1547 W. [u] flying] fleeing *from* 1562 A, *except* 1569, 1595. [x] house, and consume him, the] house, consume him, and the *from* 1582. [y] ourselves] ourself *till* 1547 G 5. [z] and unadvised] and an unadvised *from* 1547 G 2. [a] keep] observe *till* 1559. [b] and Holy] and the Holy 1559, *and from* 1569.

A SERMON,

HOW DANGEROUS A THING IT IS TO FALL[a] FROM GOD.

OF our going from God, the Wise Man saith that pride was the first beginning: for by it man's heart was turned from God his Maker. *For pride*, saith he, *is the fountain of all sin: he that hath it shall be full of cursings, and at the end it shall overthrow him*[1]. (Ecclus. x, [12, 13.]) And, as by pride and sin we go from God, so shall God, and all goodness with him, go from us. And the Prophet Osee doth plainly affirm that they which go away still from God by vicious living, and yet would go about to pacify him otherwise by sacrifice, and entertain him thereby, they labour in vain: for, notwithstanding all their sacrifice, yet he goeth still away from them. Forsomuch, saith the Prophet, as *they do not apply their minds*[b] *to return to God, although they go about with whole flocks and herds to seek the Lord, yet they shall not find him; for he is gone away from them.* (Hos. v, [4, 6.])

But as touching our turning to God, or from God, you shall understand that it may be done divers ways. Sometimes directly by idolatry, as Israel and Juda then did[α]. (α [Hos. iv, 12; v, 5.]) Sometimes men go from God by lack of faith and mistrusting of God, whereof Esay speaketh in this wise: *Woe to them that go down into Egypt to seek for help, trusting in horses, and having confidence in the number of chariots and puissance* (or power[c]) *of horsemen: they have no confidence in the holy God of Israel, nor seek for the Lord.* (Isai. xxxi, [1, 3.]) But what followeth? *The Lord shall let his hand fall upon them, and down shall come both the helper and he that is holpen: they shall be destroyed all together.*

Sometime men go from God by the neglecting of his commandments concerning their neighbours, which commandeth them to express hearty love towards every man: as Zachary said unto the people in God's behalf, *Give true judgment, shew* (Zech. vii, [9–14.])

[a] FALL] DECLINE 1547–1551, *except* 1549 W: *and the heading of the pages is* OF DECLINING FROM GOD *in* 1547–1551, *but* OF FALLING FROM GOD *in* 1549 W. [b] minds] mind 1547 G 1. [c] or power] *added in* 1559.

1 Initium superbiae hominis apostatare a Deo: quoniam ab eo qui fecit illum recessit cor ejus. Quoniam initium omnis peccati est superbia: qui tenuerit illam adimplebitur maledictis, et subvertet eum ad finem. *Vulg.*

mercy and compassion every one to his brother, imagine no deceit towards widows, or children fatherless and motherless, towards stranger[d], *or the poor; let no man forge evil in his heart against his brother. But these things they passed not of; they turned their backs, and went their way; they stopped their ears, that they might not hear; they hardened their hearts as an adamant stone, that they might not listen to the law, and the words that the Lord had sent through his Holy Spirit by his ancient Prophets. Wherefore the Lord shewed his great indignation upon them. It came to pass,* saith the Prophet, *even as I told them: as they would not hear, so when they cried they were not heard, but were scattered*[e] *into all kingdoms which they never knew, and their land was made desolate.*

And, to be short, all they that may not abide the word of God, but, following the persuasions and stubbornness of their own Jer. vii, [24.] hearts, *go backward and not forward* (as it is said in Jeremy), they go and turn away from God. Insomuch that Origen saith[2], Origen. super Exod. Hom. XII. "He that with mind, with study, with deeds, with thought and care, applieth and giveth[f] himself to God's word, and thinketh upon his laws day and night, giveth himself wholly to God, and in his precepts and commandments is exercised, this is he that is turned to God." And on the other part he saith, "Whosoever is occupied with fables and tales, when the word of God is rehearsed, he is turned from God. Whosoever in time of reading God's word is careful in his mind of worldly business, of money, or of lucre, he is turned from God. Whosoever is entangled with the cares of possessions, filled with covetousness of riches, whosoever studieth for the glory and honour of this world, he is turned from God." So that, after his mind, whosoever hath not a special mind to that thing that is commanded or taught of God; he that doth not listen unto it, embrace, and

[d] stranger] strangers *from* 1582. [e] scattered] dispersed *till* 1559. [f] and giveth] *added in* 1559.

2 Sed et hoc ipsum, converti ad Dominum, quale sit videamus. Et ut evidentius scire possimus quid sit conversus, dicendum nobis prius est quid sit aversus. Omnis qui cum recitantur verba Legis communibus fabulis occupatur aversus est. Omnis qui cum legitur Moyses de negotiis saeculi, de pecunia, de lucris solicitudinem gerit aversus est. Omnis qui possessionum curis stringitur et divitiarum cupiditate distenditur, qui gloriae saeculi et mundi honoribus studet, aversus est. Sed et qui ab his quidem videtur alienus, assistit autem et audit verba Legis, et, vultu atque oculis intentus, corde tamen et cogitationibus evagatur, aversus est. Quid est converti? Si his omnibus terga vertamus, et studio, actibus, mente, solicitudine verbo Dei operam demus, et in Lege ejus die ac nocte meditemur, omissis omnibus Deo vacemus, exerceamur in testimoniis ejus, hoc est conversum esse ad Dominum. *Origen. in Exod. Homil.* XII, § 2; *Opp.* II, 172 b, D.

print it in his heart, to the intent that he may duly fashion his life thereafter; he is plainly turned from God, although he do other things of his own devotion and mind, which to him seems[g] better and more to God's honour.

Which thing to be true we be taught and admonished in the holy Scripture by the example[h] of king Saul[β]; who, being commanded of God by Samuel, that he should kill all the Amalechites and destroy them clearly with their goods and cattals[i][3], yet he, being moved partly with pity and partly (as he thought) with devotion unto God, saved Agag their king[k], and all the chief of their cattle, therewith to make sacrifice unto God. Wherewithal God being displeased highly said unto the Prophet Samuel, *I repent that ever I made Saul a king*[l]*; for he hath forsaken me, and not followed my words;* and so he commanded Samuel to shew him. And, when Samuel asked wherefore contrary to God's word he had saved the cattle, he excused the matter partly by fear, saying he durst do none other, for that the people would have it so; partly, for that they were goodly beasts, he thought God would be content, seeing it was done of a good intent and devotion to honour God with the sacrifice of them. But Samuel, reproving all such intents and devotions (seem they never so much to God's honour), if they stand not with his word, whereby we may be assured of his pleasure, said in this wise: *Would God have sacrifices and offerings, or rather that his word should be obeyed? To obey him is better than offerings, and to listen to him is better than to offer the fat of rams. Yea, to repugn*[m] *against his voice is as evil as the sin of soothsaying*[n]*, and not to agree to it is like abominable idolatry*[4]*. And now, forasmuch as thou hast cast away the word of the Lord, he hath cast away thee, that thou shouldest not be king.*

β 1 Sam. xv, [1–24.]

The turning of God from man.

By all these examples of holy Scripture we may know that, as we forsake God, so shall he ever forsake us. And, what miserable state doth consequently and necessarily follow there-

g seem] seemeth 1547 G 1. h by the example] by example 1547 G 1 *and* 2. i cattals] cattels 1549 W, 1559; cattel *or* cattell *from* 1562 A. k their king] the king 1549 W *and from* 1559. l Saul a king] Saul king *from* 1569. m repugn] repine *till* 1559. n soothsaying] divination *till* 1559.

3 cattals: moveable or personal property, now written chattels. See *Du Cange, v.* Catallum. "Cattle" is the same word with its meaning limited by use, and was often written cattall or cattail, as in this very sentence in many of the early editions, but I think never cattals.

4 Quoniam quasi peccatum ariolandi est repugnare, et quasi scelus idololatriae nolle acquiescere. *Vulg.*

upon, a man may easily consider by the terrible threatenings of God. And, although he consider not all the said misery to the uttermost, being so great that it passeth any man's capacity in this life sufficiently to consider the same, yet he shall soon perceive so much thereof that, if his heart be not more than stony, or harder than the adamant, he shall fear, tremble, and quake to call the same to his remembrance.

First, the displeasure of God toward us[o] is commonly expressed in the Scripture by these two things, by shewing his fearful countenance upon us, and by turning his face or hiding it from us. By shewing his dreadful countenance is signified his great wrath; but by turning his face or hiding thereof is many times more signified, that is to say, that he clearly forsaketh us and giveth us over. The which significations be taken of the properties of men's manners. For men towards them whom they favour commonly bear a good, a cheerful, and a loving countenance; so that by the face or countenance of a man it doth commonly appear what will or mind he beareth towards other. So, when God doth shew his dreadful countenance towards us, that is to say, doth send dreadful plagues of sword, famine, or pestilence upon us, it appeareth that he is greatly wroth with us. But, when he withdraweth from us his word, the right doctrine of Christ, his gracious assistance and aid, which is ever joined to his word, and leaveth us to our own wit, our own will and strength, he declareth then that he beginneth to forsake us. For, whereas God hath shewed to all them that truly believe his Gospel his face of mercy in Jesus Christ, which doth so lighten their hearts that they, if they behold it as they ought to do, be transformed to his image[γ], be made partakers of the heavenly[p] light and of his Holy Spirit, and be fashioned to him in all goodness requisite to the children of God; so, if they after do neglect the same, if they be unthankful unto him, if they order not their lives according to his example and doctrine and to the setting forth of his glory, he will take away from them his kingdom[δ], his holy word, whereby he should reign in them, because they bring not forth the fruit thereof, that he looketh for.

γ [2 Cor. iii, 18; iv, 4, 6.]

δ [Matth. xxi, 43.]

Nevertheless, he is so merciful and of so long sufferance that he doth not shew upon us that great wrath suddenly. But, when we begin to shrink from his word, not believing it, or not ex-

o toward us] towards us *from* 1547 G 3.

p the heavenly] that (*contracted*) heavenly 1547 G 1, that (*in full*) heavenly 1547 W.

pressing it in our livings, first he doth send his messengers, the true preachers of his word, to admonish and warn[q] us of our duty; that, as he for his part, for the great love he bare unto us, delivered his own Son to suffer death, that we by his death might be delivered from death and be restored to the life everlasting[r], evermore to dwell with him, and to be partakers and inheritors with him of his everlasting glory and kingdom of heaven, so again that we for our parts should walk in a godly life, as becometh his children to do. And, if this will not serve, but still we remain disobedient to his word and will, not knowing him, not loving[s] him, not fearing him, not putting our whole trust and confidence in him; and, on the other side, to our neighbours behaving ourselves[t] uncharitably by disdain, envy, malice, or by committing murder, robbery, adultery, gluttony, deceit, lying, swearing, or other like detestable works and ungodly behaviour; then he threateneth us by terrible comminations[e], swearing in great anger that *whosoever doeth these works shall never enter into his rest*, which is the kingdom of heaven.

[e] Heb. iv, [1–13:] Gal. v, 21:] Ps. xcv, [11.]

THE SECOND PART OF THE SERMON OF FALLING[u] FROM GOD.

IN the former part of this Sermon ye have learned how many manner of ways men fall from God; some by idolatry, some for lack of faith, some by the neglecting[x] of their neighbours, some by not hearing God's[y] word, some by the pleasure they take in the vanities of worldly things. Ye have also learned in what misery that man is which is gone from God; and how that God yet of his infinite goodness, to call again man from that his misery, useth first gentle admonitions by his preachers, after he layeth on terrible threatenings.[z]

Now, if this gentle monition and threatening[a] together do not serve, then God will shew his terrible countenance upon us; he will pour intolerable plagues upon our heads; and after he will take away from us all his aid and assistance, wherewith before he did defend us from all such manner of calamity. As the evangelical Prophet Esay, agreeing with Christ's parable, doth teach us, saying that God had made a goodly[b] vineyard for his

Isai. v, [1–6:] Matt. xxi, [33–41.]

[q] and warn] *added in* 1559. [r] life everlasting] life eternal *till* 1559. [s] not loving] nor loving *from* 1582. [t] ourselves] us *till* 1559. [u] FALLING] DECLINING 1549 G, 1551. [x] by the neglecting] by neglecting 1623. [y] hearing God's] hearing of God's 1549 W *and from* 1559. [z] THE SECOND PART—terrible threatenings.] *not in* 1547 *or* 1548, *the Homily not being then divided.* [a] threatening] commination *till* 1559. [b] goodly] godly 1559–1574.

beloved children; *he hedged it,* he walled it round about, *he planted it with chosen vines, and made a turret in the middes*[c] *thereof, and therein also a winepress*[d]*; and, when he looked that it should bring him forth good grapes, it brought forth wild grapes.* And after it followeth: *Now shall I shew you,* saith God, *what I will do with my vineyard. I will pluck down the hedges, that it may perish; I will break down the walls, that it may be trodden under foot: I will let it lie waste; it shall not be cut, it shall not be digged, but briers and thorns shall overgrow it; and I shall command the clouds that they shall no more rain upon it.*

By these threatenings we are monished and warned[e] that, if we, which are the chosen vineyard of God, bring not forth good grapes, that is to say, good works, that may be delectable and pleasant in his sight, when he looketh for them, when he sendeth his messengers to call upon us for them, but rather bring forth wild grapes, that is to say, sour works, unsweet[f], unsavoury, and unfruitful, then will he pluck away all defence, and suffer grievous plagues of famine and battle[g], dearth and death, to light upon us: finally, if these do not yet serve[h], he will let us lie waste; he will give us over; he will turn away from us; he will dig and delve no more about us; he will let us alone, and suffer us to bring forth even such fruit as we will, to bring forth brambles, briers, and thorns, all naughtiness, all vice, and that so abundantly that they shall clean overgrow us, choke[i], strangle, and utterly destroy us.

But they that in this world live not after God, but after their own carnal liberty, perceive not this great wrath of God towards them, that he will not dig nor delve any more about them, that he doth let them alone even to themselves: but they take this for a great benefit of God, to have all at their[k] own liberty; and so they live, as carnal[l] liberty were the true liberty of the Gospel. But God forbid, good people, that ever we should desire such liberty. For, although God suffer sometimes the wicked to have their pleasure in this world, yet the end of ungodly living is at length endless[m] destruction. The murmuring Israelites[ζ] had that they longed for: they had quails enough, yea, till they were weary of them. But what was the end thereof? Their sweet meat had sour sauce: even[η] *whiles the meat was in their mouths,* the plague of God lighted upon them, and suddenly they

ζ Numb. xi, [4-6, 31-33.]

η [Ps. lxxviii, 30, 31.]

[c] middes] middest 1587, 1595, 1623. [d] winepress] vinepress *from* 1582. [e] and warned] *added in* 1559. [f] unsweet] *omitted after* 1574. [g] famine and battle] famine, battle *from* 1582. [h] do not yet serve] serve not *from* 1582. [i] choke] suffocate *till* 1559. [k] all at their] all their *from* 1547 G 5. [l] as carnal] as if carnal 1623. [m] endless] eternal *till* 1559.

died. So, if we live ungodly, and God suffereth us to follow our own wills, to have our own delights and pleasures, and correcteth us not with some plague, it is no doubt but he is almost utterly displeased with us.

And, although it be[n] long or[5] he[o] strike, yet many times, when he striketh such persons, he striketh them at once for ever. So that when he doth not strike us, when he ceaseth to afflict us, to punish or beat us, and suffereth us to run headlings[p] into all ungodliness and pleasures of this world that we delight in, without punishment and adversity, it is a dreadful token that he loveth us no longer, that he careth no longer for us, but hath given us over to our own selves. As long as a man doth proine[q][6] his vines, doth dig at the roots, and doth lay fresh earth to them, he hath a mind to them, he perceiveth some token of fruitfulness that may be recovered in them: but, when he will bestow no more such cost and labour about them, then it is a sign that he thinketh they will never be good. And the father, as long as he loveth his child, he looketh angerly, he correcteth him, when he doeth amiss: but, when that serveth not, and upon that he ceaseth from correction of him and suffereth him to do what he list himself, it is a sign that he intendeth to disinherit him, and to cast him away for ever.

So surely nothing should pierce our heart so sore, and put us in such horrible fear, as when we know in our conscience that we have grievously offended God and do so continue, and that yet he striketh not, but quietly suffereth us in the naughtiness that we have delight in. Then specially it is time to cry, and to cry again, as David did, *Cast*[θ] *me not away from thy face, and take not away thy Holy Spirit from me. Lord*[ι], *turn not away thy face from me; cast not thy servant away in displeasure. Hide*[κ] *not thy face from me, lest I be like to them*[r] *that go down into hell*[s]. The which lamentable prayers of him, as they do certify us what horrible danger they be in from whom God turneth his face, for that time[t] and as long as he so doth, so should they move and stir[u] us to cry upon God with all our heart, that we may not be brought into that state; which doubtless is so sorrowful, so miserable, and so dreadful, as no tongue

θ Ps. l [li, 11.]

ι Ps. xxvi [xxvii, 9.]

κ Ps. cxlii [cxliii, 7.]

n it be] he be *from* 1574. o or he] ere he *from* 1582. p headlings] headlongs 1559–1576, headlong *from* 1582. q proine] prune 1623. r like to them] like unto them *from* 1547 G 2. s into hell] to hell *from* 1547 G 2. t that time] the time *from* 1562 A. u and stir] *added in* 1559.

5 or: ere, before. So in *Psal.* lviii, 8 (Prayer Book Version), and *Dan.* vi, 24.

6 proine: now written prune. Tyrwhitt in his *Glossary on Chaucer* derives the word from the French "provigner," to propagate vines by layers.

can sufficiently express or any[x] heart can think. For what deadly grief may a man suppose it is to be under the wrath of God; to be forsaken of him; to have his Holy Spirit, the Author of all goodness, to be taken from him; to be brought to so vile a condition that he shall be left meet for no better purpose than to be for ever condemned to hell[y]! For not only such places of David do shew[z] that upon the turning of God's face from any persons they shall be left bare from all goodness and far from hope of remedy, but also the place rehearsed[a] last before of Esay doth mean the same; which sheweth that God at length doth so forsake his unfruitful vineyard, that he will not only suffer it to bring forth weeds, *briers, and thorns*, but also, further to punish the unfruitfulness of it, he saith he will not cut it, he will not delve it, and he *will command the clouds that they shall not rain upon it;* whereby is signified the teaching of his holy word (which St. Paul after a like manner expresseth[b] by planting and watering[λ]), meaning that he will take that away from them. So that they shall be no longer of his kingdom; they shall be no longer governed by his Holy Spirit; they shall be put from[c] the grace and benefits that they had, and ever might have enjoyed, through Christ; they shall be deprived of the heavenly light and life, which they had in Christ whiles they abode in him; they shall be (as they were once) as men *without God in this world*[μ], or rather in worse taking; and, to be short, they shall be given into the power of the devil, which beareth the rule in all them that be cast away from God, as he did in Saul, and Judas[ν], and generally in all such as work after their own wills, *the children*[ξ] *of mistrust and unbelief*[d][7].

λ [1 Cor. iii, 6–8.]

μ [Eph. ii, 12.]

ν 1 Sam. xv, [23–35; xvi, 14: Luke xxii, 3: John xiii, 2, 27.]

ξ [Ephes. ii, 2: Col. iii, 6.]

Let us beware therefore, good Christian people, lest that we, rejecting (or casting away[e]) God's word, by the which we obtain and retain true faith in God, be not at length cast off so far, that we become as the children of unbelief[f]. Which be of two sorts, far diverse, yea, almost clean contrary, and yet both be very far from returning to God. The one sort, only weighing their sinful and detestable living with the right judgment and straightness of God's righteousness, be so without[g] counsel, and be so comfortless, (as all they[h] must needs be from whom

[x] or any] nor any *from* 1569. [y] to hell] in hell 1595, 1623. [z] do shew] doth shew 1547 G 1. [a] rehearsed] recited *till* 1559. [b] expresseth] expressed *from* 1559. [c] put from] frustrated of *till* 1559. [d] mistrust and unbelief] diffidence and infidelity *till* 1559: *see note* 7 *below*. [e] or casting away] *added in* 1559. [f] unbelief] infidelity *till* 1559. [g] so without] so destitute of *till* 1559. [h] all they] they all *from* 1574.

7 Ἀπειθείας, rendered in the *Vulgate* by diffidentiae in *Eph.* ii, 2, by incredulitatis in *Col.* iii, 6. See note d above.

the Spirit of counsel[o] and comfort is gone,) that they will not be persuaded in their hearts but that either God cannot, or else that he will not, take them again to his favour and mercy. The other, hearing the loving and large promises of God's mercy, and so not conceiving a right faith thereof, make those promises larger than ever God did; trusting that, although they continue in their sinful and detestable living never so long, yet that God at the end of their life will shew his mercy upon them, and that then they will return. And both these two sorts of men be in a damnable state: and yet nevertheless God, who *willeth not the death of the wicked*[r], hath shewed means whereby both the same, if they take heed in season, may escape.

[o] [Isai. xi, 2.]

[r] Ezek. xviii, [23, 32;] and xxxiii, [11.]

Against desperation.

The first, as they do dread God's rightful justice in punishing sinners, (whereby they should be dismayed, and should despair indeed, as touching any hope that may be in themselves,) so, if they would constantly (or steadfastly[i]) believe that God's mercy is the remedy appointed against such despair and distrust, not only for them, but generally for all that be sorry and truly repentant and will therewithal stick to God's mercy, they may be sure they shall obtain mercy, and enter into the port or haven of safeguard; into the which whosoever doth come, be they beforetime never so wicked, they shall be out of danger of everlasting damnation. As God by Ezechiel saith: *What time soever the wicked doth*[k] *return*, and take earnest and true repentance, I will forget all his wickedness.

Ezek. xxxiii, [12, 14–16, 19.]

Against presumption.

The other, as they be ready to believe God's promises, so they should be as ready to believe the threatenings of God. As well they should believe the Law as the Gospel; as well that there is an hell and everlasting fire, as that there is an heaven and everlasting joy. As well they should believe damnation to be threatened to the wicked and evildoers, as salvation to be promised to the faithful in word and works. As well they should believe God to be true in the one as in the other. And the sinners that continue in their wicked living ought to think that the promises of God's mercy and the Gospel pertain not unto them, being in that state, but only the Law and those Scriptures which contain the wrath and indignation of God and his threatenings: which should certify them that, as they do overboldly presume of God's mercy and live dissolutely, so doth God still more and more withdraw his mercy from them; and

[i] or steadfastly] *added in* 1559. [k] the wicked doth] the which doth 1559–1563; the sinner doth 1569–1576; a sinner doth *from* 1582.

he is so provoked thereby to wrath at length, that he destroyeth such presumers many times suddenly. For of such St. Paul said 1 Thess. v, [3.] thus: *When they shall say, It is peace, There is no danger; then shall sudden destruction come upon them.* Let us beware therefore of such naughty boldness to sin. For God, which hath promised his mercy to them that be truly repentant, although it be at the latter end, hath not promised to the presumptuous sinner, either that he shall have long life, or that he shall have true repentance at his last[l] end. But for that purpose hath he made every man's death uncertain, that he should not put his hope in the end, and in the mean season, to God's high displeasure, live ungodly.

Wherefore let us all follow[m] the counsel of the Wise Man: [Ecclus. v, 7.] let us *make no tarrying to turn unto the Lord;* let us *not put off from day to day: for suddenly shall his wrath come, and in time of vengeance he shall destroy*[n] the wicked[8]. Let us therefore Hos. xiv, [2.] turn betimes: and, when we turn, let us pray to God as Osee teacheth, saying, *Forgive us all*[o] *our sins, receive us graciously.* And, if we turn to him with an humble and a very penitent heart, he will receive us to his favour and grace for his holy Name's sake, for his promise sake, for his truth and mercy's[p] sake, promised to all faithful believers in Jesus Christ his only natural Son. To whom, the only Saviour of the world, with the Father and the Holy Ghost, be all honour, glory, and power world without end. Amen.

[l] his last] the last *from* 1547 G 2. [m] us all follow] us follow *from* 1547 G 2. [n] shall (*before* destroy)] shal 1547 G 3–5, wal 1547 G 6, will *from* 1548. [o] forgive us all] forgive all *from* 1569. [p] mercy's] mercy 1547 G 1.

8 Subito enim veniet ira illius, et in tempore vindictae disperdet te. *Vulg.*

AN EXHORTATION

AGAINST THE FEAR OF DEATH.

It is not to be marvelled that worldly men do fear to die. For death depriveth them of all worldly honours, riches, and possessions: in the fruition whereof the worldly man counteth himself happy, so long as he may enjoy them at his own pleasure; and otherwise, if he be dispossessed of the same without hope of recovery, then he can none other[a] think of himself but that he is unhappy, because he hath lost his worldly joy and pleasure. Alas, thinketh this carnal[b] man, shall I now depart for ever from all my honours, all my treasures[c], from my country, friends, riches, possessions, and worldly pleasures, which are my joy and heart's delight? Alas, that ever that day shall come, when all these I must bid fare well at once, and never to enjoy any of them after! Wherefore it is not without great cause spoken of the Wise Man, *O death, how bitter and sour is the remembrance of thee to a man that liveth in peace and prosperity in his substance, to a man living at ease, leading his life after his own mind without trouble, and is therewithal well pampered and fed!* Ecclus. xli. [1.]

There be other men, whom this world doth not so greatly laugh upon, but rather vex and oppress with poverty, sickness, or some other adversity; yet they do fear death, partly because the flesh abhorreth naturally his own sorrowful dissolution, which death doth threaten unto them, and partly by reason of sicknesses and painful diseases, which be most strong pangs and agonies in[d] the flesh, and use commonly to come to sick men before death, or at the least accompany death[e], whensoever it cometh.

Although these two causes seem great and weighty to a worldly man, whereupon he is moved to fear death, yet there is another cause much greater than any of these afore rehearsed, for which indeed he hath just cause to fear death; and that is the state and condition whereunto at the last end death bringeth all them that have their hearts fixed upon[f] this world without

[a] none other] none otherwise *from* 1574. [b] carnal] fleshly 1559. [c] treasures] treasure *from* 1559. [d] agonies in] agonies or battles and in 1559, *where* and *is by error*. [e] accompany death] accompany or affellowship death 1559. [f] fixed upon] fixed or nailed upon 1559.

repentance and amendment. This state and condition is called [Rev. xxi, 8.] *the second death;* which unto all such shall ensue after[g] this bodily death. And this is that death which indeed ought to be dread and feared: for it is the[h] everlasting loss, without remedy, of the grace and favour of God, and of everlasting joy, pleasure, and felicity. And it is not only the loss for ever of all these eternal[i] pleasures, but also it is the condemnation both of body and soul, without either appellation or hope of redemption, unto everlasting pains in hell. Unto this state death sent the unmerciful and ungodly[k] rich man that Luke speaketh of in his [Luke xvi, [19-31.]] Gospel; who, living in all wealth and pleasure in this world, and cherishing himself daily with dainty fare and gorgeous apparel, despised poor Lazarus, that lay pitifully[l] at his gate, miserably plagued, and *full of sores,* and also grievously pined with hunger. Both these two were arrested of death; which sent Lazarus, the poor miserable man, by angels anon unto Abraham's bosom, a place of rest, pleasure, and consolation. But the unmerciful rich man descended[m] down into hell; and *being in torments* he cried for comfort, complaining of the intolerable pain that he suffered in that flame of fire: but it was too late. So unto this place bodily death sendeth all them that in this world have their joy and felicity, all them that in this world be unfaithful unto God and uncharitable unto their neighbours, so dying without repentance and hope of God's mercy. Wherefore it is no marvel that the worldly man feareth death: for he hath much more cause so to do than he himself doth consider.

Thus we see three causes why worldly men fear death; one, [The first.] because they shall lose thereby their worldly honours, riches, [The second[n].] possessions, and all their heart's desires; another, because of the painful diseases and bitter pangs which commonly men [The third[o].] suffer either before or at the time of death; but the chief cause above all other is the dread of the miserable state of eternal damnation both of body and soul, which they fear shall follow after their departing out of[p] the worldly pleasures of this present life. For these causes be all mortal men which be given to the love of this world both in fear and state of death through sin, as the holy Apostle saith[a], so long as they live here in this world. [a Heb. ii, [15.]]

But, everlasting thanks be to Almighty God for ever, there

[g] ensue after] ensue and follow after 1559. [h] for it is the] for it is an *from* 1547 G 2. [i] eternal] everlasting 1559. [k] and ungodly] and the ungodly *from* 1569. [l] pitifully] pitifull 1623. [m] descended] went 1559. [n] The second] Second *from* 1562 A. [o] The third] Third *from* 1562 A. [p] departing out of] departing of 1569, departing from *from* 1574.

is never one[q] of all these causes, no, nor yet they all[r] together, that can make a true Christian man afraid to die, which is[s] the very member of Christ, the temple of the Holy Ghost[β] (β 1 Cor. iii, [16; vi, 19.]), the son of God, and the very inheritor of the everlasting kingdom of heaven; but, plainly contrary, he conceiveth great and many causes, undoubtedly grounded upon the infallible and[t] everlasting truth of the word of God, which move[u] him, not only to put away the fear of bodily death, but also, for the manifold benefits and singular commodities which ensue unto every faithful person by reason of the same, to wish, desire, and long heartily for it. For death shall be to him no death at all, but a very deliverance from death, from all pains, cares, and sorrows, miseries, and wretchedness of this world, and the very entry into rest, and a beginning of everlasting joy, a tasting of heavenly pleasures, so great that neither tongue is able to express, neither eye to see[γ] (γ [1 Cor. ii, 9.]), nor ear to hear them, no, nor for any[v] earthly man's heart to conceive them. So exceeding great benefits they be which God our heavenly Father, by his mere mercy, and for the love of his Son Jesus Christ, hath laid up in store and prepared for them that humbly submit themselves to God's will, and evermore unfeignedly love him from the bottom of their hearts.

And we ought to believe that death, being slain by Christ, cannot keep any man that steadfastly trusteth in Christ under his perpetual[x] tyranny and subjection, but that he shall rise from death again unto glory at the last day, appointed by Almighty God, like as Christ our Head did rise again, according to God's appointment, the third day. For St. Augustine saith, the Head going before, the members trust to follow and come after[1]. And St. Paul saith, if Christ be risen from the dead, we shall rise also from the same. ([1 Cor. xv, 20–23.]) And, to comfort all Christian persons herein, holy Scripture calleth this bodily death *a sleep*[δ] (δ [John xi, 11, 13: Acts vii, 60: 1 Thess. iv, 13–18.]); wherein man's senses be, as it were, taken from him for a season, and yet, when he awaketh, he is more fresh than he was when he went to bed. So, although we have our souls separated from our bodies for a season, yet at the general resur-

q never one] never a one 1623. r they all] them all *from* 1582. s which is] who is 1623. t infallible and] infallible or undeceivable and 1559. u move] moveth *from* 1574. v nor for any] nor any *from* 1569. x perpetual] everlasting 1559.

1 Resurrectionem enim Christiani novimus in Capite nostro jam factam et in membris futuram. Caput Ecclesiae Christus est, membra Christi Ecclesia. Quod praecessit in Capite sequetur in corpore. Haec est spes nostra. *Augustin. Enarrat. in Psal.* LXV, § 1; *Opp.* IV, 640 E.

rection we[y] shall be more fresh, beautiful, and perfect, than we be now. For now we be mortal, then we shall be immortal[z]; now infect[a] with divers infirmities, then clearly void of all mortal[b] infirmities; now we be subject to all carnal desires, then we shall be all spiritual, desiring nothing but God's glory and things eternal.

Thus is this bodily death a door or entering unto life; and therefore not so much dreadful, if it be rightly considered, as it is comfortable; not a mischief, but a remedy of[c] all mischief; no enemy, but a friend; not a cruel tyrant, but a gentle guide; leading us, not to mortality, but to immortality, not to sorrow and pain, but to joy and pleasure, and that to endure for ever; if it be thankfully taken and accepted[d] as God's messenger, and patiently borne of us for Christ's love, that suffered most painful death for our love, to redeem us from death eternal[e]. According hereunto St. Paul saith *our life is hid with Christ in God, but, when our Life shall appear, then shall we also appear with him in glory.* Col. iii, [3, 4.]

Why then shall we fear to die, considering the manifold and comfortable promises of the Gospel and of holy Scriptures? *God the Father hath given us everlasting life*, saith St. John, *and this life is in his Son. He that hath the Son hath life; and he that hath not the Son hath not life.* [1 John v, [11–13.] And, *This I wrote*[f], saith St. John, *to you that believe in the Name of the Son of God, that you may know that you have everlasting life, and that you do believe*[2] *upon the Name of the Son of God.* And our Saviour Christ saith, *He that believeth in me hath life everlasting, and I will raise him from death to life at the last day.* John vi, [40, 47.] St. Paul also saith[ε] that *Christ is ordained and made of God our righteousness, our holiness*[g] *and redemption, to the intent that he which will glory should glory in the Lord.* ε 1 Cor. i, [30, 31.] St. Paul did contemn and set little by *all other things*[ς], *esteeming them as dung, which before he had in very great price, that he might be found in Christ,* to have everlasting life, true holiness, righteousness, and redemption. ς [Phil. iii, 7–11.] Finally, St. Paul maketh a plain argument in this wise[η]: *If our heavenly Father would not spare his own natural Son, but did give him to death for us, how can it be that with him he should not give us all things?* η Rom. viii, [32.] Therefore, if we have Christ, then have we with

y resurrection we] resurrection and rising again we 1559. z we shall be immortal] shall we be immortal *from* 1582. a infect] infected 1623. b all mortal] all immortal *from* 1574. c remedy of] remedy for *from* 1574. d accepted] received 1559. e death eternal] death everlasting 1559. f wrote] write *from* 1576. g our holiness] or holiness 1582, 1587, 1623.

2 Καὶ ἵνα πιστεύητε.

him and by him all good things, whatsoever we can in our hearts wish or desire; as, victory over death, sin, and hell; we have the favour of God, peace with him, holiness, wisdom, justice, power, life, and redemption; we have by him perpetual[h] health, wealth, joy, and bliss everlasting.

THE SECOND PART OF THE SERMON OF[i] THE FEAR OF DEATH.

IT hath been heretofore shewed you that there be three causes wherefore men do commonly fear death; first, the sorrowful departing from worldly goods and pleasures[k]; the second, the fear of the pangs and pains that come with death; last and principal cause is the horrible fear of extreme misery and perpetual damnation in time to come. And yet none of these three causes troubleth good men; because they stay themselves by true faith, perfect charity, and sure hope of the endless[l] joy and bliss everlasting.[m]

All those therefore have great cause to be full of joy that be joined to Christ with true faith, steadfast hope, and perfect charity, and not to fear death nor everlasting damnation. For death cannot deprive them of Jesu Christ, nor any sin can condemn[θ] them that are graffed surely in him, which is their only joy, treasure, and life. Let us repent our sins, amend our lives, trust in his mercy and satisfaction, and death can neither take him from us nor us from him. For then, as St. Paul saith[ι], *whether we live or die, we be the Lord's own.* And again he saith, *Christ did die, and rose again, because he should be Lord both of the dead and quick.* Then, if we be the Lord's own when we be dead, it must needs follow that such temporal death not only cannot harm us, but also that it shall much be[n] to our profit, and join us unto God more perfectly. And thereof the Christian heart may surely be certified by the infallible (or undeceivable[o]) truth of holy Scripture. *It is God,* saith St. Paul[κ], *which hath prepared us unto immortality, and the same is he which hath given us an earnest of the Spirit. Therefore let us be always of good comfort: for we know that, so long as we be in the body, we be as it were far from God* in a strange country, subject to many

θ [Rom. viii, 1.]

ι Rom. xiv, [8, 9.]

κ [2 Cor. v, 5–8.]

h perpetual] everlasting 1559. i SERMON OF] SERMON AGAINST 1623. k pleasures] pleasure 1549 W, 1559, 1562. l endless] perpetual *till* 1559. m THE SECOND PART—bliss everlasting.] *not in* 1547 *or* 1548, *the Homily not being then divided.* n much be] be much 1582, 1623. o or undeceivable] *added in* 1559.

perils, *walking without* perfect *sight* and knowledge of Almighty God, *only* seeing him *by faith* in holy Scriptures; *but we have a courage, and desire rather to be at home with God and our Saviour Christ, far from the body,* where *we may behold his Godhead as he is*[λ], *face to face,* to our everlasting comfort. These be St. Paul's words in effect: whereby we may perceive that the life in this world is resembled and likened[p] to a pilgrimage in a strange country far from God; and that death, delivering us from our bodies, doth send us straight home into our own country, and maketh us to dwell presently with God for ever in everlasting rest[q] and quietness. So that to die is no loss, but profit and winning, to all true Christian people.

λ [1 John iii, 2: 1 Cor. xiii, 12.]

What lost the thief, that hanged on the cross with Christ, by his bodily death? Yea, how much did he gain by it! Did not our Saviour say unto him[μ], *This day thou shalt be with me in Paradise?* And Lazarus[ν], that pitiful person, that lay before the rich man's gate, pained with sores and pined with hunger, did not death highly profit and promote him, which by the ministry of angels sent him unto Abraham's bosom, a place of rest, joy, and heavenly consolation? Let us think none other, good Christian people, but Christ hath prepared, and made ready before[r], the same joy and felicity for us that he prepared for Lazarus and the thief. Wherefore let us stick unto his salvation and gracious redemption, and believe his word, serve him from our hearts, love and obey him; and, whatsoever[s] we have done heretofore contrary to his most holy will, now let us repent in time, and hereafter study to correct our life, and doubt not but we shall find him as merciful unto us, as he was either to Lazarus or to the thief: whose examples are written in holy Scripture for the comfort of them that be sinners, and subject to sorrows, miseries, and calamities in this world; that they should not despair in God's mercy, but ever trust thereby to have forgiveness of their sins and life everlasting, as Lazarus and the thief had.

μ Luke xxiii, [43.]
ν Luke xvi, [20–22.]

Thus I trust every Christian man perceiveth by the infallible (or undeceivable[t]) word of God, that bodily death cannot harm nor hinder them that truly believe in Christ, but contrary[u] shall profit and promote the Christian souls which, being truly penitent for their offences, depart hence in perfect charity, and in sure trust that God is merciful to them, forgiving their sins for the merits of Jesus Christ his only natural Son.

p and likened] *added in* 1559. q everlasting rest] perpetual rest *till* 1559. r and made ready before] *added in* 1559. s whatsoever] whatever 1559. t or undeceivable] *added in* 1559. u contrary] contrarily 1623.

The second cause why some do fear death.

The second cause why some do fear death is sore sickness and grievous pains, which partly come before death, and partly accompanieth[x] (or cometh with[y]) death, whensoever it cometh. This fear is the fear of the frail flesh, and a natural passion belonging unto the nature of a mortal[z] man. But true faith in God's promises, and regard of the pains and pangs which Christ upon the cross suffered for us miserable sinners, with consideration of the joy and everlasting life to come in heaven, will mitigate and assuage less[a] those pains, and moderate (or bring into a mean[b]) this fear, that it shall never be able to overthrow the hearty desire and gladness that the Christian soul hath to be separated from this corrupt body, that it may come to the gracious presence of our Saviour Jesus Christ. If we believe steadfastly the word of God, we shall perceive that such bodily sickness, pangs of death, or whatsoever dolorous pains we[c] suffer either before or with death, be nothing else in Christian men but the rod of our heavenly and loving Father; wherewith he mercifully correcteth us, either to try and declare the faith of his patient children, that they may be found laudable, glorious, and honourable in his sight, when Jesus Christ shall be openly shewed to be the Judge of all the world, or else to chasten[d] and amend in them whatsoever offendeth his fatherly and gracious goodness, lest they should perish everlastingly. And this his correcting rod is common to all them[e] that be truly his.

Heb. xii, [1-11.]

Therefore *let us cast away the burden of sin that lieth so*[f] *heavy* in our necks, and return unto God by true penance and amendment of our lives. *Let us with patience run this course that is appointed;* suffering, for his sake that died for our salvation, all sorrows and pangs of death, and death itself joyfully, when God sendeth it to us; *having our eyes fixed* and set fast[g] ever *upon the Head and Captain of our faith, Jesus Christ; who, considering the joy that he should come unto,* cared neither for the shame nor pain of death, but willingly conforming and framing[h] his will to his Father's will, *most patiently suffered the* most shameful and painful *death of the cross,* being innocent and harmless[i]; and now therefore[g] he is exalted in heaven, *and* everlastingly *sitteth on the right hand of the throne of God* the Father. Let us call to our remembrance therefore the life and joys of heaven, that are kept for all them that patiently do suffer here with

[g] Phil. ii, [9.]

[x] accompanieth] accompany 1623. [y] or cometh with] *added in* 1559, or come with 1623. [z] of a mortal] of mortal 1559. [a] and assuage less] *added in* 1559. [b] or bring into a mean] *added in* 1559. [c] pains we] pangs we *from* 1563. [d] chasten] chastise *from* 1547 G 5. [e] to all them] to all men *from* 1582. [f] so] to (*then the usual way of spelling* too) 1548–1576, too *from* 1582. [g] and set fast] *added in* 1559. [h] and framing] *added in* 1559. [i] and harmless] *added in* 1559.

Christ; and *consider that Christ suffered* all his painful passion *by sinners*, and for sinners; and then we shall with patience, and the more easily, suffer such sorrows and pains when they come. *Let us not set at light the chastising of the Lord;* nor grudge at him, *nor fall from him, when of him we be corrected: for the Lord loveth them whom he doth correct, and beateth every one whom he taketh to be his*[k] *child. What child is that*, saith St. Paul, *whom the father* loveth, and *doth not chastise? If ye be without God's correction, which all his well beloved and true children have, then be you but bastards*, smally regarded of God, *and not his true children. Therefore, seeing that, when we have in earth our carnal fathers to be our correctors, we do fear them and reverently take their correction, shall we not much more be in subjection to God our spiritual Father, by whom we shall have everlasting life*[l]*? And our carnal fathers sometime correct us, even as pleaseth*[m] *them*, without cause: *but this Father* justly correcteth us, either for our sin, to the intent we should amend, or *for our commodity and wealth, to make us thereby partakers of his holiness. Furthermore, all correction* which God sendeth us *in this present time seemeth to have no joy* and comfort, *but sorrow* and pain; yet it bringeth with it a taste of God's mercy and goodness towards them that be so corrected, and a sure hope of God's everlasting consolation in heaven.

If then these sorrows, diseases, and sicknesses, and also death itself, be nothing else but our heavenly Father's rod, whereby he certifieth us of his love and gracious favour, whereby he trieth and purifieth us, whereby he giveth unto us holiness, and certifieth us that we be his children, and he our merciful Father; shall not we then with all humility, *as obedient* and loving *children*[o], joyfully kiss our heavenly Father's rod, and ever say in our heart with our Saviour Jesus Christ, *Father, if this* anguish and sorrow which I feel, and death, which I see approach, *may not pass*, but that thy will is that I must suffer them, *thy will be done?*

o [1 Pet. i, 14.]
Matt. xxvi, [42.]

THE THIRD PART OF THE SERMON OF THE FEAR OF DEATH.

IN this Sermon[n] against the Fear of Death two causes were declared, which commonly move worldly men to be in much

k to be his] to his *from* 1569. l everlasting life] eternal life *till* 1559. m as pleaseth] as it pleaseth *from* 1582. n Sermon] Homily 1549 G, 1551.

fear to die; and yet the same do nothing trouble the faithful and good livers when death cometh, but rather giveth them occasion greatly to rejoice, considering that they shall be delivered from the sorrow and misery of this world, and be brought to the great joy and felicity of the life to come.[o]

Now the third and special cause why death indeed is to be feared is the miserable state of the worldly and ungodly people after their death. But this is no cause at all why the godly and faithful people should fear death; but rather contrariwise their godly conversation in this life, and belief in Christ, cleaving continually to his merits[p], should make them to long sore after that life that remaineth for them undoubtedly after this bodily death. Of this immortal state, after this transitory life, where we shall live evermore in the presence of God, in joy and rest, after victory over all sickness, sorrows, sin, and death, there be many both[q] plain places of holy Scripture, which confirm the weak conscience against the fear of all such dolours, sicknesses, sin, and bodily death[r], to assuage such trembling and ungodly fear, and to encourage us with comfort and hope of a blessed state after this life. St. Paul wisheth unto the Ephesians *that God the Father of glory would give unto them the spirit of wisdom and revelation, that the eyes of their hearts might have light*[s] *to know him*, and to perceive how great things he had called them unto, and how rich inheritance he hath prepared after this life for them that pertain unto him. And St. Paul himself declareth *the desire* of his heart, which was *to be dissolved* and loosed from his body *and to be with Christ*[3], which, as he said, was *much better for him, although to them it was more necessary that he should live*, which he refused not for their sakes. Even like as St. Martin said[4], "Good Lord, if I be necessary for thy people, to do good unto them, I will refuse no labour: but else, for mine own self, I beseech thee to take my soul."

The third cause why death is to be feared.

Ephes. i, [17, 18.]

Phil. i, [23–26.]

Now the holy fathers of the old Law, and all faithful and righteous men which departed before our Saviour Christ's ascension into heaven, did by death depart from troubles unto rest, from the hands of their enemies into the hands of God, from

[o] THE THIRD PART—life to come.] *not in* 1547 *or* 1548, *the Homily not being then divided.* [p] merits] mercies *from* 1576. [q] both] *omitted* 1623. [r] bodily death] death corporal *till* 1559. [s] have light] give light 1559–1576, give life *from* 1582.

3 Τὴν ἐπιθυμίαν ἔχων εἰς τὸ ἀναλῦσαι καὶ σὺν Χριστῷ εἶναι. Desiderium habens dissolvi et esse cum Christo. *Vulg.*

4 Domine, si adhuc populo tuo sum necessarius, non recuso laborem; fiat voluntas tua. *Sulpic. Sever. Epist. ad Bassulam de Obitu B. Martini.*

sorrows and sicknesses unto joyful refreshing, into Abraham's[t] bosom, a place of all comfort and consolation; as Scriptures[u] do plainly by manifest words testify. The Book of Wisdom
Wisd. iii, [1-3.] saith *that the righteous men's souls be in the hand of God, and no torment shall touch them. They seemed to the eyes of foolish men to die; and their death was counted miserable, and their departing out of this world wretched: but they be in rest.* And
[Ibid. v, 15, 16.] another place saith *that the righteous shall live for ever, and their reward is with the Lord, and their minds be with God, who is above all*[5]*: therefore they shall receive a glorious kingdom, and a beautiful crown at the Lord's hand.* And in another place the
Ibid. iv, [7.] same Book saith, *The righteous, though he be prevented with sudden death, nevertheless he shall be there where he shall be refreshed*[6]. Of Abraham's bosom Christ's words be so plain[p] that
p [Luke xvi, 22–25.] a Christian man needeth[x] no more proof of it.

Now then, if this were the state of the holy fathers and righteous men before the coming of our Saviour, and before he was glorified, how much more then ought all we to have a steadfast faith and a sure hope of this blessed state and condition after our death; seeing that our Saviour now hath performed the whole work of our redemption, and is gloriously
John [xiv, 2, 3;] xvii, [24; xii, 26.] ascended into heaven, *to prepare our dwellingplaces* with him, and said unto his Father, *Father, I will that where I am my servants shall be with me.* And we know that, whatsoever Christ will, his Father will the same: wherefore it cannot be but, if we be his faithful servants, our souls shall be with him after our departing[y] out of this present life.

St. Stephen, when he was stoned to death, even in the midst
Acts vii, [55-59.] of his torments, what was his mind most upon? *When he was full of the Holy Ghost,* saith holy Scripture, *having his eyes lifted up into heaven, he saw the glory of God, and Jesus standing on the right hand of God.* The which truth after he had confessed boldly before the enemies of Christ, *they drew him out of the city, and there they stoned him; who cried unto God, saying, Lord Jesu Christ, take my spirit.* And doth not our Saviour say
John v, [24.] plainly in St. John's Gospel, *Verily, verily, I say unto you, He that heareth my word, and believeth him*[z] *that sent me*[7], *hath*

[t] into Abraham's] in Abraham's *from* 1574. [u] as Scriptures] as the Scriptures *from* 1574. [x] needeth] needs 1547 G 1. [y] departing] departure 1623. [z] believeth him] believeth on him] *from* 1547 G 4.

[5] Καὶ ἡ φροντὶς αὐτῶν παρὰ ὑψίστῳ. Et cogitatio illorum apud Altissimum. *Vulg.*

[6] Δίκαιος δὲ ἐὰν φθάσῃ τελευτῆσαι, ἐν ἀναπαύσει ἔσται. Justus autem si morte praeoccupatus fuerit, in refrigerio erit. *Vulg.*

[7] Καὶ πιστεύων τῷ πέμψαντί με.

everlasting life, and cometh not into judgment, but shall pass from death to life[8]? Shall we not then think that death to be precious, by the which we pass unto life? Therefore it is a true saying of the Prophet[σ], *The death of the holy and righteous men is precious in the Lord's sight.* Holy Simeon, after that he had his heart's desire in seeing our Saviour, that he ever longed for all his[a] life, *he embraced* (or took[b]) *him in his arms, and said, Now, Lord, let me depart in peace, for mine eyes have beholden that Saviour which thou hast prepared for all nations.* It is truth therefore that the death of the righteous is called *peace*, and *the benefit of the Lord*, as the Church saith in the name of the righteous departed out of this world, *My soul*[τ], *turn thee to thy rest, for the Lord hath been good to thee and rewarded thee*[9]. And we see by holy Scripture, and other ancient histories of Martyrs, that the holy, faithful, and righteous, ever since Christ's ascension (or going up[c]), in their death did not doubt but that they went to be with[d] Christ in spirit, which is our life, health, wealth, and salvation.

σ Ps. cxvi, [15.]

Luke ii, [28-31.]

τ Ps. cxiv [cxvi, 7.]

John in his holy Revelation saw a hundred[e] forty and four thousand virgins and innocents, of whom he said, *These follow the Lamb* Jesu Christ *wheresoever he goeth.* And shortly after in the same place he saith, *I heard a voice from heaven saying unto me, Write, Happy and blessed are the dead which die in the Lord: from henceforth surely, saith the Spirit, they shall rest from their pains and labours*[10]*: for their works do follow them.* So that then they shall reap with joy and comfort that which they sowed with labours and pains. *They that sow*[υ] *in the spirit*[11], *of the spirit shall reap everlasting life. Let us therefore never be weary of well doing: for, when the time* of reaping or reward *cometh, we shall reap without any weariness*[12] everlasting joy. *Therefore, while we have time*, as St. Paul exhorteth us, *let us do good to all men;* and *not lay up*[φ] *our treasures in earth,*

Rev. xiv, [1-5, 13.]

υ Gal. vi, [8-10.]

φ Matt. vi, [19.]

a for all his] for his 1582–1595, for in his 1623. b or took] *added in* 1559, and took *from* 1574. c or going up] *added in* 1559. d be with] *omitted after* 1563. e a hundred] an hundred 1549 W *and from* 1559.

8 Ἀλλὰ μεταβέβηκεν ἐκ τοῦ θανάτου εἰς τὴν ζωήν. Sed transiet (*al.* transiit) a morte in vitam. *Vulg.*

9 Convertere, anima mea, in requiem tuam, quia Dominus benefecit tibi. *Vulg.*

10 Μακάριοι οἱ νεκροὶ οἱ ἐν Κυρίῳ ἀποθνήσκοντες ἀπάρτι· Ναί, λέγει τὸ Πνεῦμα· ἵνα ἀναπαύσωνται ἐκ τῶν κόπων αὐτῶν. Beati mortui qui in Domino moriuntur. Amodo jam dicit Spiritus, ut requiescant a laboribus suis. *Vulg.*

11 Εἰς τὸ πνεῦμα. In spiritu. *Vulg.*

12 Καιρῷ γὰρ ἰδίῳ θερίσομεν, μὴ ἐκλυόμενοι. Tempore enim suo metemus non deficientes. *Vulg.*

James v, [3.] *where rust and moths corrupt it;* which *rust,* as St. James saith, *shall bear witness against us* at the great day, condemn us, *and shall like* most brenning[f] *fire torment our flesh.*

Ibid. v, [1-4.] Let us beware therefore, as we tender our own wealth, that we be not in the number of those miserable, covetous, and wretched[g] men, which St. James biddeth mourn and lament for their greedy gathering and ungodly keeping of goods. Let us be wise in time, and learn to follow the wise example of the

x Luke xvi, [1-9.] wicked Steward[x]. Let us so wisely order[h] our goods and possessions, committed unto us here by God for a season, that we may truly hear and obey this commandment of our Saviour Christ[i]: *I say unto you,* saith he, *Make you friends of the wicked mammon, that they may receive you into everlasting tabernacles* (or dwellings[k]). Riches he calleth[l] *wicked,* because the world abuseth them unto all wickedness; which are otherwise the good gift[m] of God, and the instruments whereby God's servants do truly serve him in using of the same. He commanded them not to make them rich friends, to get high dignities and worldly promotions[n], to give great gifts to rich men that have no need thereof; but to make them friends of poor and miserable men, unto whom whatsoever they give, Christ taketh[o] it as given to himself. And to these friends Christ in the Gospel giveth so great honour and preeminence, that he saith *they shall receive* them that do good unto them[p] *into everlasting houses:* not that men shall be our rewarders for our well doing, but that Christ will reward us, and take it to be done unto himself, whatsoever is done to such friends. Thus making poor wretches our friends we make our Saviour Christ our friend, whose members they are: whose misery as he taketh for his own misery, so their relief, succour, and help he taketh for his succour, relief, and help; and will as much thank us and reward us for our goodness shewed to them, as if he himself had received like benefit at our

Matt. xxv, [40; x, 42; xviii, 6.] hands; as he witnesseth in the Gospel, saying, *Whatsoever ye have done to any of these simple persons which do believe in me, that have ye done to myself.*

Therefore let us diligently foresee that our faith and hope, which we have conceived in Almighty God and in our Saviour Christ, wax not faint, nor that the love which we bear in

[f] brenning] burning *from* 1574. [g] and wretched] *added in* 1559. [h] wisely order] prudently dispose *till* 1559. [i] of ... Christ] of ... Christ's *all Grafton's editions.* [k] or dwellings] *added in* 1559. [l] he calleth] be called *from* 1569. [m] gift] gifts *from* 1574. [n] promotions] possessions *till* 1559. [o] taketh] accepteth *till* 1559. [p] them that do good unto them] their benefactors *till* 1559.

hand[q] [13] to bear to him wax not cold; but let us study daily and diligently to shew ourselves to be the true honourers and lovers of God by keeping of his commandments, by doing of good deeds unto our needy neighbours, relieving by all means that we can their poverty with our abundance and plenty[r], their ignorance with our wisdom and learning, and comfort[s] their weakness with our strength and authority, calling all men back from evildoing by godly counsel and good example, persevering still in well doing so long as we live. So shall we not need to fear death for any of those three causes aforementioned, nor yet for any other cause that can be imagined. But contrary[t], considering the manifold sicknesses, troubles, and sorrows of this present life, the dangers of this perilous pilgrimage, and the great encombrance which our spirit hath by this[u] sinful flesh and frail body, subject to death; considering also the manifold sorrows and dangerous deceits of this world on every side, the intolerable pride, covetousness, and lechery in time of prosperity, the impatient murmuring of them that be worldly in time of adversity, which cease not to withdraw and pluck us from God, our Saviour Christ, from our life, wealth, or everlasting[x] joy, and salvation; considering also the innumerable assaults of our ghostly enemy the devil, with all his fiery darts of ambition, pride, lechery, vainglory, envy, malice, detraction (or backbiting[y]), with other his innumerable deceits, engines, and snares, whereby he goeth busily about to catch all men under his dominion, ever, *like*[z] *a roaring lion*, by all means *searching whom* 1 Pet. v. [8]
he may devour: the faithful Christian man which considereth all these miseries, perils, and incommodities, whereunto he is subject so long as he here liveth upon earth, and on the other part considereth that blessed and comfortable state of the heavenly life to come, and the sweet condition of them that depart in the Lord, how they are delivered from the continual encombrances of their mortal and sinful body, from all the malice, crafts, and deceits of this world, from all the assaults of

[q] bear in hand] pretend *till* 1559. [r] and plenty] *added in* 1559. [s] and comfort] *so in all*. [t] contrary] contrarily 1623. [u] by this] by his 1562 B—1595. [x] everlasting] eternal *till* 1559. [y] or backbiting] *added in* 1559. [z] ever, like] even like 1549 G, 1551.

13 bear in hand: profess, pretend, hold out.

> Your daughter, whom she bore in hand to love
> With such integrity, she did confess
> Was as a scorpion to her sight. *Shakespeare, Cymb.*, v, 5.

To bear another person in hand is a different phrase, which also occurs in the Homilies.

their ghostly enemy the devil, to live in peace, rest, and endless[a] quietness, to live in the fellowship of innumerable Angels[ψ], and with the congregation of perfect just men, as Patriarchs, Prophets, Martyrs, and Confessors, and finally unto the presence of Almighty God and our Saviour Jesus Christ: he that doth consider all these things, and believeth them assuredly, as they are to be believed, even from the bottom of his heart, being stablished[b] in God in this true faith, having a quiet conscience in Christ, a firm hope and assured trust in God's mercy through[c] the merits of Jesu Christ to obtain this quietness, rest, and everlasting[d] joy, shall not only be without fear of bodily death when it cometh, but certainly, as St. Paul did, so shall he gladly, according to God's will, and when it please[e] God to call him out of this life, greatly desire it in[f] his heart[ω], that he may be rid from all these occasions of evil, and live ever to God's pleasure, in perfect obedience of his will, with our Saviour Jesus Christ: to whose gracious presence the Lord of his infinite mercy and grace bring us, to reign with him in life everlasting. To whom with our heavenly Father and the Holy Ghost be glory in worlds without end. Amen.

ψ [Heb. xii, 22, 23.]

ω Phil. i, [23.]

[a] endless] perpetual *till* 1559. [b] stablished] established *from* 1547 G 2. [c] through] thorough 1559. [d] and everlasting] and eternal *till* 1559. [e] please] pleaseth *from* 1547 G 2. [f] desire it in] desire in *from* 1547 G 2.

AN EXHORTATION

CONCERNING GOOD ORDER AND OBEDIENCE TO RULERS AND MAGISTRATES.

ALMIGHTY God hath created and appointed all things, in heaven, earth, and waters, in a most excellent and perfect order. In heaven he hath appointed distinct (or several[a]) orders and states of archangels and angels. In earth he hath assigned and appointed[b] kings and princes[c], with other governors under them, all in[d] good and necessary order. The water above is kept, and raineth down in due time and season. The sun, moon, stars, rainbow, thunder, lightning, clouds, and all birds of the air, do keep their order. The earth, trees, seeds, plants, herbs, corn, grass, and all manner of beasts, keep themselves[e] in their order[f]. All the parts of the whole year, as winter, summer, months, nights, and days, continue in their order. All kinds of fishes in the sea, rivers and waters, with all fountains and springs[g], yea, the seas themselves, keep their comely course and order. And man himself also hath all his parts both within and without, as soul, heart, mind, memory, understanding, reason, speech, with all and singular corporal members of his body, in a profitable, necessary, and pleasant order. Every degree of people, in their vocation, calling, and office, hath appointed to them their duty and order. Some are in high degree, some in low; some kings and princes, some inferiors and subjects; priests and laymen, masters and servants, fathers and children, husbands and wives, rich and poor; and every one have need of other. So that in all things is to be lauded and praised the goodly order of God: without the which no house, no city, no commonwealth can continue and endure (or last[h]); for, where there is no right order, there reigneth all abuse, carnal liberty, enormity, sin, and Babylonical confusion. Take away kings, princes, rulers, magistrates, judges, and such estates[i] of God's

[a] or several] *added in* 1559, and several *from* 1574. [b] and appointed] *added in* 1559. [c] kings and princes] kings, princes *all except* 1547 W. [d] all in] in all *from* 1569. [e] keep themselves] keep them *till* 1559. [f] keep . . . in their order] keep . . . in order *from* 1582. [g] fountains and springs] fountains, springs *all except* 1547 W. [h] or last] *added in* 1559. [i] estates] states *till* 1559.

order, no man shall ride or go by the highway unrobbed; no man shall sleep in his own house or bed unkilled; no man shall keep his wife, children, and possessions[k] in quietness; all things shall be common; and there must needs follow all mischief and utter destruction both of souls, bodies, goods, and commonwealths.

But blessed be God that we in this realm of England feel not the horrible calamities, miseries, and wretchedness which all they undoubtedly feel and suffer that lack this godly order. And praised be God that we know the great excellent benefit of God shewed toward[l] us in this behalf. God hath sent us his high gift, our most dear Sovereign Lady Queen Elizabeth[m], with godly[n], wise, and honourable counsel, with other superiors and inferiors, in a beautiful order and goodly[o]. Wherefore let us subjects do our bounden duties, giving hearty thanks to God, and praying for the preservation of this godly order. Let us all obey, even from the bottom of our hearts, all their godly proceedings, laws, statutes, proclamations, and injunctions, with all other their godly[p] orders. Let us consider the Scriptures of the Holy Ghost, which persuade and command us all obediently to be subject, first and chiefly to the Queen's[q] Majesty, Supreme Governor[r] over all, and next[s] to her[t] honourable counsel, and to all other noblemen, magistrates, and officers, which by God's goodness be placed and ordered.

For Almighty God is the only author and provider of[u] this forenamed state and order; as it is written of God in the Book of the Proverbs: *Through[x] me kings do reign; through[y] me counsellors make just laws: through[z] me do princes bear rule, and all judges of the earth execute judgment*[1]*: I am loving to them that love me.* Here let us mark well and remember, that the high power and authority of kings, with their making of laws, judgments, and officers[a], are the ordinances, not of man, but of God; and therefore is this word, *Through me,* so many times repeated. Here is also well to be considered and remembered, that this good order is appointed of[b] God's wisdom,

Prov. viii, [15-17.]

[k] possessions] possession 1623. [l] toward] towards *from* 1547 G 3. [m] Lady Queen Elizabeth] Lord King Edward the Sixth 1547-1551, Lord King James 1623. [n] with godly] with a godly *from* 1574. [o] and goodly] *added in* 1559, and godly *from* 1574. [p] other their godly] other godly *from* 1547 G 3. [q] Queen's] King's 1547-1551, 1623. [r] Governor] Head *till* 1562 A. [s] and next] and the next *from* 1569. [t] her] his 1547-1551, 1623. [u] provider of] provider for *from* 1574. [x y z] through (*in the full quotation*)] thorough *from* 1574. [a] and officers] and offices *from* 1562 A. [b] appointed of] appointed by 1623.

1 Per me reges regnant, et legum conditores justa decernunt. Per me principes imperant, et potentes decernunt justitiam. *Vulg.*

favour, and love specially[c] for them that love God; and therefore he saith, *I love them that love me.*

Also in the Book of Wisdom we may evidently learn that a king's power, authority, and strength is a great benefit of God, given of his great mercy to the comfort of our great misery. For thus we read there spoken to kings: *Hear, O ye kings, and understand; learn, ye that be judges of the ends of the earth; give ear, ye that rule the multitudes: for the power is given*[d] *you of the Lord, and the strength from the Highest.* Let us learn also here by the infallible and undeceivable[e] word of God, that kings and other supreme and higher[f] officers are ordained of God, who is Most Highest; and therefore they are here diligently taught[g] to apply and give[h] themselves to knowledge and wisdom, necessary for the ordering of God's people to their governance committed (or whom to govern they are charged of God[i]). And they be here also taught by Almighty God, that they should reknowledge[k] themselves to have all their power and strength, not from Rome, but immediately of God Most Highest.

Wisd. vi, [1-3.]

We read in the Book of Deuteronomy that all punishment pertaineth to God by this sentence: *Vengeance is mine, and I will reward*[2]. But this sentence we must understand to pertain also to[l] the magistrates, which do exercise God's room in judgment and punishing by good and godly laws here in earth. And the places of Scripture which seem to remove from among all Christian men judgment, punishment, or killing ought to be understand[m], that no man of his own private authority may be judge over other, may punish, or may[n] kill, but we must refer all judgment to God, to kings and rulers, and judges[o] under them, which be God's officers to execute justice, and by plain words of Scripture have their authority and use of the sword granted from God; as we are taught by St. Paul, the dear[p] and chosen[q] Apostle of our Saviour Christ, whom we ought diligently to obey, even as we would obey our Saviour Christ if he were present. Thus St. Paul writeth to the Romans: *Let every*

Deut. xxxii, [35.]

Rom. xiii, [1-6.]

[c] specially] especially *from* 1574. [d] power is given] power given *from* 1582. [e] and undeceivable] *added in* 1559. [f] supreme and higher] their 1547 G 1. [g] diligently taught] taught diligently *from* 1574. [h] and give] *added in* 1559. [i] or whom to govern they are charged of God] *added in* 1559. [k] reknowledge] acknowledge 1623. [l] also to] also unto *from* 1547 G 3. [m] be understand] be understood 1623. [n] punish, or may] punish, may 1547 G 1 *and* 2. [o] rulers, and judges] rulers, judges *from* 1563. [p] the dear] that dear *from* 1562 A. [q] chosen] elect *till* 1559.

2 Mea est ultio, et ego retribuam. *Vulg.* See *Rom.* XII, 19; *Heb.* X, 30.

soul submit himself unto the authority of the higher powers. For there is no power but of God: the powers that be be ordained of God. Whosoever therefore withstandeth[r] *the power withstandeth*[s] *the ordinance of God: but they that resist* (or are against[t]) *shall receive to themselves damnation. For rulers are not fearful to them that do good, but to them that do evil. Wilt thou be without fear of the*[u] *power? do well then, and so shalt thou be praised of the same: for he is the minister of God for thy wealth. But and if*[3] *thou do that which is evil, then fear: for he beareth not the sword for naught; for he is the minister of God, to take vengeance on him that doeth evil. Wherefore ye must needs obey, not only for fear of vengeance, but also because of conscience. And even for this cause pay ye tribute: for they are God's ministers, serving for the same purpose.* Here let us all learn[x] of

[Acts ix, 15.] St. Paul, the *chosen*[y] *vessel* of God, that all persons having souls, (he excepteth none, nor exempteth none, neither priest, apostle, nor prophet, saith St.[z] Chrysostom[4],) do owe, of bounden duty and even in conscience, obedience, submission, and subjection to the high[a] powers which be set[b] in authority by God; forasmuch as they be God's lieutenants, God's presidents, God's officers, God's commissioners, God's judges, ordained of God himself, of whom only they have all their power and all their authority. And the same St. Paul threateneth no less pain than everlasting damnation to all disobedient persons, to all resisters against this general and common authority; forasmuch as they resist not man, but God; not man's device and invention, but God's wisdom, God's order, power, and authority.

THE SECOND PART OF THE SERMON OF OBEDIENCE.

FORASMUCH as God hath created and disposed all things in a comely order, we have been taught, in the first part of

r s withstandeth] resisteth *till* 1559. t or are against] *added in* 1559, or are against it *from* 1576. u fear of the] fear of that *from* 1569. x us all learn] us learn *from* 1582. y chosen] elect *till* 1559. z St. (*before* Chrysostom)] *not in* 1547 G 1. a high] higher 1547 G 1. b which be set] to men being constitute 1547 G 1, which be constituted 1547 G 2–1551.

3 But and if: *and* is here used for *an*, which is itself equivalent to *if*; but the reduplication was not uncommon. It occurs also in 1 Pet. iii, 14.

4 Καὶ δεικνὺς ὅτι πᾶσι ταῦτα διατάττεται, καὶ ἱερεῦσι καὶ μοναχοῖς, οὐχὶ τοῖς βιωτικοῖς μόνον, ἐκ προοιμίων αὐτὸ δῆλον ἐποίησεν, οὕτω λέγων, Πᾶσα ψυχὴ ἐξουσίαις ὑπερεχούσαις ὑποτασσέσθω, κἂν ἀπόστολος ᾖς, κἂν εὐαγγελιστὴς, κἂν προφήτης, κἂν ὁστισοῦν. Chrysost. in Epist. ad Rom. Homil. XXIII, Opp. IX, 686 B.

this[c] Sermon[d] concerning good Order and Obedience, that we also ought in all commonwealths[e] to observe and keep a due order, and to be obedient to the powers, their ordinances and laws; and that all rulers are appointed of God, for a godly[f] order to be kept in the world; and also how the magistrates ought to learn how to rule and govern according to God's laws; and that all subjects are bounden[g] to obey them as God's ministers, yea, although they be evil, not only for fear, but also for conscience sake.[h]

And here, good people, let us[i] all mark diligently, that it is not lawful for inferiors and subjects in any case to resist (or stand against[j]) the superior powers: for St. Paul's words be plain, that *whosoever withstandeth*[k] *shall get to themselves damnation; for whosoever withstandeth*[l] *withstandeth*[m] *the ordinance of God.* [Rom. xiii, 2.] Our Saviour Christ himself and his Apostles received many and divers injuries of the unfaithful and wicked men in authority: yet we never read that they, or any of them, caused any sedition or rebellion against authority. We read oft that they patiently suffered all troubles, vexations, slanders, pangs, and pains, and death itself obediently, without tumult or resistance. They *committed their cause to him that judgeth righteously*, [1 Pet. ii, 23.] and prayed for their enemies heartily and earnestly. They knew that the authority of the powers was God's ordinance; and therefore, both in their words and deeds, they taught ever obedience to it, and never taught nor did the contrary. The wicked judge Pilate said to Christ, *Knowest thou not that I have power to crucify thee, and have power also to loose thee? Jesus answered, Thou couldest have no power at all against me, except it were given thee from above.* John xix, [10, 11.] Whereby Christ taught us plainly that even the wicked rulers have their power and authority from God. And therefore it is not lawful for their subjects by force[n] to withstand[o] them, although they abuse their power: much less then it is lawful for subjects to withstand[p] their godly and Christian princes, which do not abuse their authority, but use the same to God's glory and to the profit and commodity of God's people.

The holy Apostle St. Peter[q] commandeth servants to be obedient to their masters, *not only if they be good and gentle, but* 1 Pet. ii, [18-21.]

[c] of this] of the *from* 1562 A. [d] Sermon] Homily 1549 G, 1551. [e] commonwealths] commonweals *from* 1582. [f] godly] goodly *from* 1562 A. [g] bounden] bound *from* 1574. [h] THE SECOND PART—conscience sake.] *not in* 1547 *or* 1548, *the Homily not being then divided.* [i] us] *omitted* 1559. [j] or stand against] *added in* 1559, and stand against *from* 1582. [k l m] withstandeth] resisteth *till* 1559. [n] by force] *omitted after* 1574. [o p] withstand] resist *till* 1559. [q] Apostle St. Peter] Apostle Peter 1582, 1623.

also if they be evil and *froward*, affirming that the vocation and calling of God's people is to be patient and of the suffering side[r]. And there he bringeth in the patience of our Saviour Christ, to persuade obedience to governors, yea, although they be wicked and wrong doers. But let us now hear St. Peter himself speak, for his own words[s] certify best our conscience. Thus he uttereth them in his first Epistle: *Servants, obey your masters with fear, not only if they be good and gentle*[t], *but also if they be froward. For it is thankworthy, if a man for conscience toward God suffereth grief, and suffereth*[u] *wrong undeserved. For what praise is it, when ye be beaten for your faults, if ye take it patiently? But when ye do well, if you then suffer wrong, and take it patiently, then is there cause to have thank of God. For hereunto verily were ye called: for so did Christ suffer for us, leaving us an example, that we should follow his steps.* All these be the very words of St. Peter.

α 1 Sam. xviii, xix, and xx.

St.[x] David also teacheth us a good lesson in this behalf[α]: who was many times most cruelly and wrongfully persecuted of king Saul, and many times also put in jeopardy and danger of his life by king Saul and his people; yet he never[y] withstood[z], neither used any force or violence against, king Saul, his mortal (or deadly[a]) enemy, but did ever to his liege lord and master king Saul most true, most diligent, and most faithful service. Insomuch that, when the Lord God had given king Saul into David's hands in his own cave[β], he would not hurt him, when he might, without all bodily peril, easily have slain him; no, he would not suffer any of his servants once to lay their hands[b] upon king Saul, but prayed to God in this wise: *Lord, keep me from doing that thing unto my master, the Lord's anointed; keep me that I lay not my hand upon him, seeing he is the anointed of the Lord. For, as truly as the Lord liveth, except the Lord smite him, or except his day come, or that he go down to war, and in battle perish*[c], *the Lord be merciful unto me, that I lay not my hand upon the Lord's anointed*[5]. And that David might have

β 1 Sam. xxiv.

[r] side] sides *from* 1563. [s] his own words] his words *from* 1563. [t] gentle] ientle 1559. [u] suffereth grief, and suffereth] endureth grief, and suffer *from* 1574. [x] St. (*before* David)] *omitted* 1587, 1595; Holy 1623. [y] he never] he neither *from* 1562 A. [z] withstood] resisted *till* 1559. [a] or deadly] *added in* 1559, and deadly *from* 1574. [b] their hands] their hand *from* 1582. [c] in battle perish] perish in battle *from* 1574.

[5] Propitius sit mihi Dominus ne faciam hanc rem domino meo, christo Domini, ut mittam manum meam in eum, quia christus Domini est. Vivit Dominus, quia, nisi Dominus percusserit eum, aut dies ejus venerit ut moriatur, aut descendens in praelium perierit, propitius mihi sit Dominus ut non mittam manum meam in christum Domini. *Vulg.*, but not in all MSS.

killed his enemy king Saul it is evidently proved in the first Book of the Kings, both by the cutting off the lap of Saul's garment, and also by the plain[d] confession of king Saul. Also another time, as it is[e] mentioned in the same Book[γ], when the most unmerciful and most unkind king Saul did persecute poor David, God did again give king Saul into David's hands by casting of king Saul and his whole army into a dead sleep; so that David and one Abisai with him came in the night into Saul's host, where *Saul lay sleeping, and his spear stack in the ground at his head. Then said Abisai unto David, God hath delivered thine enemy into thy hands at this time: now therefore let me smite him once with my spear to the earth, and I will not smite him again the second time;* meaning thereby to have killed him with one stroke, and to have made him sure for ever. *And David* answered and *said to Abisai, Destroy him not: for who can lay his hands on the Lord's anointed, and be guiltless? And David said furthermore, As sure as the Lord liveth, the Lord shall smite him, or his day shall come to die, or he shall descend* (or go down[f]) *into battle and there perish. The Lord keep me from laying my hands upon the Lord's anointed: but take thou now the spear that is at his head, and the cruse of water, and let us go:* and so he did. Here is evidently proved that we may not withstand[g] nor in any ways[h] hurt an anointed king; which is God's lieutenant, vicegerent, and highest minister in that country where he is king.

[γ] [1 Sam. xxvi, 7–12.]

But peradventure some here would say that David in his own defence might have killed king Saul lawfully and with a safe conscience. But holy David did know that he might in no wise withstand[l], hurt, or kill his sovereign lord and king: he did know that he was but king Saul's subject, though he were in great favour with God, and his enemy king Saul out of God's favour. Therefore, though he were never so much provoked, yet he refused[m] utterly to hurt the Lord's anointed. He durst not, for offending God and his own conscience, (although he had occasion and opportunity,) once lay[n] his hands upon God's high officer the king, whom he did know to be a person reserved and kept[o] for his office sake only to God's punishment and judgment. Therefore he prayeth so oft and so earnestly, that he lay not his hands upon the Lord's anointed. And by these two

Objection[i]. Answer[k].

[d] by the plain] by plain *from* 1562 A. [e] as it is] as is *from* 1562 A. [f] or go down] *added in* 1559. [g, l] withstand] resist *till* 1559. [h] ways] wise *from* 1574. [i] Objection] An objection *from* 1562 A. [k] Answer] An answer *from* 1562 A. [m] refused] refuseth 1547 G 1. [n] once lay] once to lay 1547 G 1. [o] and kept] *added in* 1559.

examples St. David, being named in Scripture *a man after God's own heart*[δ], giveth a general rule and lesson to all subjects in the world not to withstand[p] their liege lord and king, not to take a sword by their private authority against their king, God's anointed; who only beareth the sword by God's authority, for the maintenance of the good and for the punishment of the evil; who only by God's law hath the use of the sword at his commandment[q], and also hath all power, jurisdiction, regiment, coercion, and punishment[r], as supreme governor of all his realms and dominions, and that even by the authority of God and by God's ordinances.

δ Ps. lxxxviii [lxxxix, 3, 20–26: 1 Sam. xiii, 14: Acts xiii, 22.]

Yet another notable story and doctrine is in the second Book of the Kings[ε], that maketh also for this purpose. When an Amalechite, by king Saul's own consent and commandment, had killed king Saul, he went to David, supposing to have had great thank[s] for his message that he had killed David's deadly[t] enemy; and therefore he made great haste to tell to David the chance, bringing with him king Saul's crown that was upon his head, and his bracelet that was upon his arm, to persuade his tidings to be true. But godly David was so far from rejoicing at these news[u], that immediately and forthwith[x] he rent his clothes off his back, he mourned and wept, and said to the messenger, *How is it that thou wast not afraid to lay thy hand*[y] *on the Lord's anointed to destroy him?* And by and by David made one of his servants to kill the messenger, saying, *Thy blood be on thy*[z] *own head; for thy*[a] *own mouth hath testified and witnessed*[b] *against thee, granting that thou hast slain the Lord's anointed.*

ε 2 Sam. i, [1–16.]

These examples being so manifest and evident, it is an intolerable ignorance, madness, and wickedness for subjects to make any murmuring, rebellion, resistance (or withstanding[c]), commotion, or insurrection against their most dear and most dread Sovereign Lord and King, ordained and appointed of God's goodness for their commodity, peace, and quietness.

Yet let us believe undoubtedly, good Christian people, that we may not obey kings, magistrates, or any other, though they be our own fathers, if they would command us to do any thing contrary to God's commandments. In such a case we ought to

p withstand] resist *till* 1559. q his commandment] his command 1623. r regiment, coercion, and punishment] regiment, and coercion *till* 1559, regiment, correction, and punishment *from* 1562 A. s thank] thanks 1549 G, 1551, *and from* 1582. t deadly] mortal *till* 1559. u these news] this news 1623. x and forthwith] *added in* 1559. y hand] hands *from* 1547 G 3. z on thy] on thine *all except* 1547 G 1 *and* 1562 A—1569. a for thy] for thine 1547 W, 1623. b and witnessed] *added in* 1559. c or withstanding] *added in* 1559.

say with the Apostles[d], *We must rather obey God than man.* But nevertheless in that case we may not in any wise withstand[e] violently or rebel against rulers, or make any insurrection, sedition, or tumults, either by force of arms or other ways[f], against the anointed of the Lord or any of his appointed officers[g]; but we must in such case patiently suffer all wrongs and injuries, referring the judgment of our cause only to God. Let us fear the terrible punishment of Almighty God against traitors or rebellious[h] persons by the example of Core, Dathan, and Abiron[ζ], which repugned[i] and grudged against God's magistrates and officers, and therefore the earth opened and swallowed them up alive. Other, for their wicked murmuring and rebellion, were by a sudden fire[η], sent of God, utterly consumed. Other, for their froward behaviour to their rulers and governors, God's ministers, were suddenly stricken with a foul leprosy[θ]. Other were stinged to death with wonderful strange fiery serpents[ι]. Other were sore plagued, so that there was killed in one day the number of fourteen thousand and seven hundred[κ], for rebellion against them whom God had appointed to be in authority. Absalon[λ] also, rebelling against his father King David, was punished with a strange and notable death.

Acts v, [29.]

ζ [Numb. xvi, 1–33.]

η Numb. xi, [1.]

θ Ibid. xii, [1–10.]

ι Ibid. xxi, [5, 6.]

κ Ibid. xvi, [41–49.]

λ 2 Sam. xviii, [9, 10.]

THE THIRD PART OF THE SERMON OF OBEDIENCE.

YE have heard before, in this Sermon[k] of good Order and Obedience, manifestly proved both by Scriptures[l] and examples, that all subjects are bounden to obey their magistrates, and for no cause to resist (or withstand[m]), rebel[n], or make any sedition against them, yea, although they be wicked men.[o] And let no man think that he can escape unpunished that committeth treason, conspiracy, or rebellion against his Sovereign Lord the King, though he commit the same never so secretly, either in thought, word, or deed, never so privily in his privy chamber by himself, or openly communicating and consulting with other[p]. For treason will not be hid; treason will out at the length[q].

d Apostles] Apostle *from* 1582. e withstand] resist *till* 1559. f other ways] otherwise *from* 1569. g his appointed officers] his officers 1623. h or rebellious] and rebellious *from* 1574. i which repugned] which repined *till* 1559, which he repugned 1623. k Sermon] Homily 1549 G, 1551. l by Scriptures] by the Scriptures *from* 1582. m or withstand] *added in* 1559. n withstand, rebel] withstand, or rebel *from* 1582. o THE THIRD PART—wicked men.] *not in* 1547 *or* 1548, *the Homily not being then divided.* p with other] with others 1623. q at the length] at length 1547 W 2 *and* 3, 1549 G, 1551, *and from* 1582.

God will have that most detestable vice both opened and punished; for that it is so directly against his ordinance and against his high principal judge and anointed in earth. The violence and injury that is committed against authority is committed against God, the common weal, and the whole realm; which God will have known, and condignly (or worthily[r]) punished one way or other. For it is notably written of the Wise Man in Scripture, in the book called Ecclesiastes, *Wish the king no evil in thy thought, nor speak*[s] *no hurt of him in thy privy chamber; for a bird*[t] *of the air shall betray thy voice, and with her feathers shall she*[u] *bewray thy words.*

Eccles. x, [20.]

These lessons and examples are written for our learning. Let us all therefore[x] fear the most detestable vice of rebellion, ever knowing and remembering that he that resisteth (or withstandeth[y]) common authority resisteth (or withstandeth[z]) God and his ordinance, as it may be proved by many other mo places of holy Scripture.

And here let us take heed that we understand not these or such other like places, which so straitly command obedience to superiors, and so straitly punisheth[a] rebellion and disobedience to the same, to be meant in any condition of the pretensed (or coloured[b]) power of the bishop of Rome. For truly the Scripture of God alloweth no such usurped power, full of enormities, abusions, and blasphemies: but the true meaning of these and such places be to extol and set forth God's true ordinance, and the authority of God's anointed kings, and of their officers appointed under them. And concerning the usurped power of the bishop of Rome, which he most wrongfully challengeth as the successor of Christ and Peter, we may easily perceive how false, feigned, and forged it is, not only in that it hath no sufficient ground in holy Scripture, but also by the fruits and doctrine thereof. For our Saviour Christ and St. Peter teach[c], most earnestly and agreeably[d], obedience to kings, as to the chief and supreme rulers in this world next under God: but the bishop of Rome teacheth, that they that are under him are free from all burdens and charges of the commonwealth and obedience towards[e] their prince[f], most clearly against Christ's doctrine and

[r] or worthily] *added in* 1559. [s] thought, nor speak] thought or speech 1547 G 1 *and* W 1; thought, or speak *all Grafton's other editions.* [t] a bird] the bird *from* 1574. [u] she] he 1549 G, 1551; *omitted in* 1549 W *and after* 1551. [x] Let us all therefore] Therefore let us all 1549 W *and from* 1559. [y], [z] or withstandeth] *added in* 1559. [a] punisheth] punished *from* 1569. [b] or coloured] *added in* 1559. [c] teach] teacheth *from* 1547 G 2. [d] agreeably] agreeable 1559. [e] towards] toward *from* 1582. [f] that they that are——towards their prince] immunities, privileges, exemptions, and disobedience *till* 1559.

St. Peter's. He ought therefore rather to be called Antichrist and the successor of the Scribes and Pharisees, than Christ's vicar or St. Peter's successor; seeing that not only in this point, but also in other weighty matters of Christian religion, in matters of remission and forgiveness[g] of sins and of salvation, he teacheth so directly against both St. Peter and against our Saviour Christ: who not only taught obedience to kings, but also practised obedience in their conversation and living; for we read that they both paid tribute[μ] to the king. And also we read that the holy Virgin Mary, mother to our Saviour Christ, and Joseph, who was taken for his father, at the Emperor's commandment went to the city of David[ν], named Bethleem, to be taxed among other, and to declare their obedience to the magistrates for God's ordinances' sake. And here let us not forget the blessed Virgin Mary's obedience: for, although she was highly in God's favour, and Christ's natural mother, and was also great with child that same[h] time, and so nigh her travail that she was delivered in her journey, yet she gladly, without any excuse or grudging, for conscience sake did take that cold and foul winter journey; being in the mean season so poor that she lay in the stable[i], and there she was delivered of Christ.

μ Matt. xvii, [24–27.]

ν Luke ii, [4–7.]

And according[k] to the same lo how St. Peter agreeth, writing by express words in his first Epistle. *Submit yourselves* (or be subject[l]), saith he, *unto kings, as unto the chief heads, or unto*[m] *rulers, as unto them that are sent of him for the punishment of evil doers and for the*[n] *praise*[o] *of them that do well: for so is the will of God.* I need not to expound these words, they be so plain of themselves. St. Peter doth not say, *Submit yourselves unto* me as supreme head of the Church; neither he saith[p],

1 Pet. ii, [13–15.]

g and forgiveness] *added in* 1559. h that same] at the same *from* 1574. i the stable] a stable *from* 1574.

k *Between* of Christ. *and* And according *is the following passage in* 1547 G 1 *only*:
Our Saviour Christ refused the office of a worldly judge, and so he did the office of a worldly king; commanding his disciples, and all that believe in him, that they should not contend for superiority neither for worldly dominion in this world. For ambition and pride is detestable in all Christian persons of every degree. And the Apostles in that place do not represent the persons of bishops and priests only, but also (as ancient authors do write) they represent the persons of kings and princes, whose worldly rule and governance they then ambitiously desired. So that in that place Christ teacheth also Christian emperors, kings, and princes, that they should not rule their subjects by will, and to their own commodity and pleasure only, but that they should govern their subjects by good and godly laws. They should not make themselves so to be lords over the people, to do with them and their goods what they list, and to make what laws they list, without dread of God and of his laws, without consideration of their honour and office, whereunto God hath called them, (as heathen kings and princes do,) but to think themselves to be God's officers, ordained by God to be his ministers unto the people, for their salvation, common quietness and wealth, to punish malefactors, to defend innocents, and to cherish well doers.
And at the beginning of the passage the margin has Luce xii, Johan. vi, *and* Mat. xviii, *meaning* Luke xii, 13, 14; John vi, 15; *and* Matth. xviii, 1–9.

l or be subject] *added in* 1559, and be subject *from* 1574. m or unto] and unto *from* 1574. n the (*before* praise)] *not in* 1547 G 1–6, 1547 W 1, 1548, 1549 W. o praise] laud *till* 1559. p neither he saith] neither saith he *from* 1582.

Submit yourselves from time to time to my successors in Rome: but he saith, *Submit yourselves unto your king, your supreme head,* and unto those that he appointeth in authority under him; *for,* that ye[q] shall so shew your obedience, *it is the will of God;* God will that you be in subjection to your head and king. This[r] is God's ordinance, God's commandment, and God's holy will, that the whole body of every realm, and all the members and parts of the same, shall be subject to their head, their king; and that, as St. Peter writeth[g], *for the Lord's sake,* and, as St. Paul writeth, *for conscience sake,* and not for fear only.

[g] 1 Pet. ii, [13:] Rom. xiii, [5.]

Thus we learn by the word of God to yield to our king[o] that is due to our king, that is, honour, obedience, payments of due taxes, customs, tributes, subsidies, love, and fear.

[o] Matt. xxii, [21:] Rom. xiii, [7.]

Thus we know partly our bounden duties to common authority: now let us learn to accomplish the same. And let us most instantly and heartily pray to God, the only author of all authority, for all them that be in authority; according as St. Paul willeth, writing thus to Timothy in his first Epistle. *I exhort therefore that, above all things, prayers, supplications, intercessions, and giving of thanks be done for all men, for kings, and for all that be in authority, that we may live a quiet and a peaceable life with all godliness and honesty: for that is good and accepted*[s] (or allowable[t]) *in the sight of God our Saviour.* Here St. Paul maketh an earnest and an especial exhortation concerning giving of thanks and prayer for kings and rulers, saying, *Above all things,* as he might say, In any wise principally and chiefly, *let prayer be made for kings.* Let us heartily thank God for his great and excellent benefit and providence concerning the state of kings. Let us pray for them that they may have God's favour and God's protection. Let us pray that they may ever in all things have God before their eyes. Let us pray that they may have wisdom, strength, justice, clemency, zeal[u] to God's glory, to God's verity, to Christian souls, and to the common wealth. Let us pray that they may rightly use their sword and authority for the maintenance and defence of the catholic faith contained in holy Scripture and of their good and honest subjects, and for[x] the fear and punishment of the evil and vicious people. Let us pray that they may faithfully[y] follow the most faithful[z] kings and captains in the Bible, David, Ezechias, Josias,

1 Tim. ii, [1-3.]

[q] ye] *omitted* 1563, you *from* 1569. [r] This] That 1547 G 4–1569. [s] accepted] acceptable 1551. [t] or allowable] *added in* 1559. [u] clemency, zeal] clemency, and zeal *from* 1574. [x] subjects, and for] subjects, for *from* 1569. [y] may faithfully] may most faithfully *from* 1582. [z] most faithful] *omitted after* 1576.

Moses[a], with such other. And let us pray for ourselves that we may live godly in holy and Christian conversation: so we shall have[b] God of our[c] side[w]; and then let us not fear what man can do against us: so we shall live in true obedience, both to our most merciful King in heaven, and to our most Christian Queen[d] in earth: so shall we please God, and have the exceeding benefit, peace of conscience, rest, and quietness, here in this[e] world; and after this life we shall enjoy a better life, rest, peace, and the everlasting[f] bliss of heaven. Which he grant us all that was *obedient* for us all, *even to the death of the cross,* Jesus Christ: to whom with the Father and the Holy Ghost be all honour and glory both now and ever. Amen.

[w] Judith v, [17, 21: Ps. cxviii, 6: Heb. xiii, 6.]

[Phil. ii, 8.]

[a] Josias, Moses] Josias and Moses *from* 1548. [b] we shall have] shall we have *from* 1582. [c] of our] on our *from* 1574. [d] Queen] King 1547–1551, 1623. [e] in this] in the 1559–1574. [f] everlasting] eternal *till* 1559.

A SERMON

AGAINST[a] WHOREDOM AND UNCLEANNESS.

ALTHOUGH there want not, good Christian people, great swarms of vices worthy to be rebuked, unto such decay is true godliness and virtuous living now come, yet[b] above other vices the outrageous seas of adultery (or breaking of wedlock[c]), whoredom, fornication, and uncleanness have not only brast[d] in, but also overflowed almost the whole world, unto the great dishonour of God, the exceeding infamy of the name of Christ, the notable decay of true religion, and the utter destruction of the public wealth; and that so abundantly that, through the customable use thereof, this vice is grown into[e] such an height, that in a manner among many it is counted no sin at all, but rather a pastime, a dalliance, and but a touch of youth; not rebuked, but winked at; not punished, but laughed at. Wherefore it is necessary at this present to intreat of the sin of whoredom and fornication, declaring unto you the greatness of this sin, and how odious, hateful, and abominable it is and hath alway been reputed before God and all good men, and how grievously it hath been punished both by the law of God and the laws of divers princes; again, to shew you certain remedies whereby ye may, through the grace of God, eschew this most detestable sin of whoredom and fornication, and lead your lives in all honesty and cleanness.

[How grievous a sin whoredom is in the sight of God.][f]

Exod. xx, [14.]

And, that ye may perceive that fornication and whoredom are in the sight of God most abominable sins, ye shall call to remembrance this commandment of God, *Thou shalt not commit adultery*. By the which word *adultery*, although it be properly understand[g] of the unlawful commixtion (or joining together[h]) of a married man with any woman beside his wife, or of a wife with any man beside her husband, yet thereby is signified also all unlawful use of those parts which be ordained for generation. And this one commandment forbidding adultery doth sufficiently paint and set out before our eyes the greatness of this

[a] A SERMON AGAINST] AN HOMILY OF 1547–1551, *except* 1549 W. [b] come, yet] come to, yet 1547 G 1. [c] or breaking of wedlock] *added in* 1559. [d] brast] burst 1623. [e] grown into] grown unto 1559–1569. [f] How grievous a sin whoredom is in the sight of God.] *in* BEC. *only*. [g] understand] understood 1587, 1595, 1623. [h] or joining together] *added in* 1559.

sin of whoredom, and manifestly declareth how greatly it ought to be abhorred of all honest and faithful persons. And, that none of us all shall think himself excepted from this commandment, whether we be old or young, married or unmarried, man or woman, hear what God the Father saith by his most excellent Prophet Moses: *There shall be no whore among the daughters of* Deut. xxiii, [17.] *Israel, nor no whoremonger*[i][1] *among the sons of Israel.* Here is whoredom, fornication, and all uncleanness[k] forbidden to all kinds of people, all degrees, and all ages, without exception.

And, that we shall not doubt but that this precept (or commandment[l]) pertaineth to us indeed, hear what Christ, the perfect Teacher of all truth, saith in the New Testament. *Ye have* Matt. v, [27, 28.] *heard,* saith Christ, *that it was said to them of the old*[m] *time, Thou shalt not commit adultery: but I say unto you, Whosoever seeth a woman, to have his lust of her, hath committed adultery with her already in his heart.* Here our Saviour Christ doth not only confirm and stablish the law against adultery given in the Old Testament of God the Father by his servant Moses, and maketh[n] it of full strength, continually to remain among the professors of his Name in the new law; but he also, condemning the gross interpretation of the Scribes and Pharisees, which taught that the aforesaid[o] commandment only required to abstain from the outward adultery and not from the filthy desires and unpure lusts, teacheth us an exact and full perfection of purity and cleanness of life, both to keep our bodies undefiled, and our hearts pure and free from all evil thoughts, carnal desires[p], and fleshly consents. How can we then be free from this commandment, where so great charge is laid upon us? May a servant do what he will in any thing, having a commandment[q] of his master to the contrary? Is not Christ our Master? are not we his servants? How then may we neglect our Master's will and pleasure, and follow our own will and phantasy? *Ye are my friends,* saith Christ, *if you*[r] *keep those things* John xv, [14.] *that I command you.* Now hath Christ our Master commanded us that we should forsake all uncleanness and lechery[s] both in body and spirit: this therefore must we do, if we look to please God.

In the Gospel of St. Matthew we read, that the Scribes and Matt. xv, [1–20.]

[i] whoremonger] whoremongers *till* 1574. [k] all uncleanness] all other uncleanness 1623. [l] or commandment] *added in* 1559. [m] of the old] of old *from* 1576. [n] maketh] make *from* 1547 G 5. [o] aforesaid] foresaid *from* 1574. [p] desires] desire 1559. [q] having a commandment] having commandment 1623. [r] if you] if thou 1559. [s] lechery] filthiness 1623.

[1] Scortator. *Vulg.*

Pharisees were grievously offended with Christ because his disciples did not keep the traditions of the forefathers, for they washed not their hands when they went to dinner or supper; and among other things Christ answered and said, *Hear and understand. Not that thing which entereth into the mouth defileth the man, but that which cometh out of the mouth defileth the man. For those things which proceed out of the mouth come forth from the heart, and they defile the man. For out of the heart proceed evil thoughts, murders, breaking of wedlock, whoredom, thefts, false witness, blasphemies. These are the things which defile a man.* Here may we see that not only murder, theft, false witness, and blasphemy defile men, but also evil thoughts, breaking of wedlock, fornication, and whoredom. Who is now of so little wit, that he will esteem whoredom and fornication to be things of small importance and of no weight before God? Christ, which is[t] *the Truth*[α] and *cannot lie*, saith that evil thoughts, breaking of wedlock, whoredom, and fornication defile a man, that is to say, corrupt both the body and soul of man, and make them, of the temples of the Holy Ghost, the filthy dunghill or dungeon of all unclean spirits; of the house[u] of God, the dwellingplace of Satan.

α John xiv, [6:] Tit. i, [2.]

John viii, [11.]

Again, in the Gospel of St. John, when the woman taken in adultery was brought unto Christ, said not he unto her, *Go thy way, and sin no more?* Doth not he here call whoredom sin? And what is *the reward of sin* but everlasting *death*[β]*?* If whoredom be sin, then is it[x] not lawful for us to commit it. For St. John saith[γ], *He that committeth sin is of the devil.* And our Saviour saith[δ], *Every one that committeth sin is the servant of sin.* If whoredom had not been sin, surely St. John Baptist would never have rebuked king Herod for taking his brother's wife: but he told him plainly[ε], that it was not lawful for him to take his brother's wife. He winked not at that[y] whoredom of Herod, although he were a king of great[z] power; but boldly reproved him for his wicked and abominable living, although for the same he lost his head. But he would rather suffer death, than see God so dishonoured by the breaking of his holy precept (or commandment[a]), than to suffer whoredom to be unrebuked, even in a king. If whoredom had been but a pastime, a dalliance, and a thing[b] not to be passed of[c], as many count it

β Rom. vi, [23.]

γ 1 John iii, [8.]

δ John viii, [34:] Rom. vi, [16.]

ε [Matt. xiv, 3–10.]

[t] which is] who is 1623. [u] house] mansion *till* 1559. [x] then is it] then it is *from* 1576. [y] at that] at the *from* 1547 G 5. [z] great] *omitted* 1623. [a] or commandment] *added in* 1559, and commandment *from* 1574. [b] a thing] *omitted after* 1563. [c] passed of] passed off 1623.

now a days, truly John had been more than twice mad, if he would have had the displeasure of a king, if he would have been cast into[d] prison and lost his head, for a trifle. But John knew right well how filthy, stinking[e], and abominable the sin of whoredom is in the sight of God: therefore would not he[f] leave it unrebuked, no, not in a king. If whoredom be not lawful in a king, neither is it lawful in a subject. If whoredom be not lawful in a public (or common[g]) officer, neither is it lawful in a private person. If it be not lawful neither in king nor subject, neither in common officer nor private person, truly then is it[h] lawful in no man nor woman, of whatsoever[i] degree or age they be.

Furthermore, in the Acts of the Apostles we read that, when the Apostles and elders with the whole congregation were gathered together to pacify the hearts of the faithful dwelling at Antioch, which were disquieted through the false doctrine of certain Jewish preachers, they sent word to the brethren, that it seemed good to the Holy Ghost and to them to charge them with no more than with necessary things; among other, they willed them to abstain from idolatry and fornication; *from which*, said they, *if ye keep yourselves, ye shall do well.* Note here how these holy and blessed fathers of Christ's Church would charge the congregation with no mo things than were necessary. Mark also how, among those things from the which they commanded the brethren of Antioch to abstain, fornication and whoredom is numbered. It is therefore necessary, by the determination and consent of the Holy Ghost, and the Apostles and elders with the whole congregation, that, as from idolatry and superstition, so likewise we must abstain from fornication and whoredom. Is it necessary unto salvation to abstain from idolatry? So[k] is it to abstain from whoredom. Is there any nigher way to lead unto[l] damnation than to be an idolater? No. Even so neither is there a nearer[m] way to damnation than to be a fornicator and an[n] whoremonger. Now where are those people which so lightly esteem breaking of wedlock, whoredom, fornication, and adultery? It is necessary, saith the Holy Ghost, the blessed Apostles, the elders, with the whole congregation of Christ; it is necessary to salvation, say they, to abstain from

Acts xv, [22-29.]

[d] into] in *from* 1574. [e] filthy, stinking] filthy and stinking 1623. [f] not he] he not 1559, 1562 A. [g] or common] *added in* 1559. [h] then is it] then it is *from* 1569. [i] whatsoever] what 1559. [k] Is it—idolatry? So] It is—idolatry? So 1549 G, 1559, 1574; It is—idolatry: So 1551, *and from* 1576. [l] lead unto] lead into 1559–1569. [m] a nearer] any nearer *from* 1562 B. [n] and an] and a 1623.

whoredom. If it be necessary unto salvation, then woe be to them which, neglecting their salvation, give their minds[o] to so filthy[p] and stinking sin, to so wicked vice, to[q] such detestable abomination.

THE SECOND PART OF THE SERMON AGAINST ADULTERY.

YOU have been taught in the first part of this Sermon against Adultery, how that vice at this day reigneth most above all other vices, and what is meant by this word Adultery, and how holy Scripture dissuadeth (or discounselleth[r]) from doing that filthy sin, and finally what corruption cometh to man's soul through[s] the sin of adultery.

Now, to proceed further, let us hear[t] what the blessed Apostle St. Paul saith to this matter. Writing to the Romans he hath these words: *Let us cast away the works of darkness, and put on the armours*[u] *of light. Let us walk honestly, as it were in the daytime, not in eating and drinking, neither in chamberings*[x] *and wantonness, neither in strife and envying: but put ye on the Lord Jesus*[y] *Christ, and make not provision for the flesh, to fulfil the lusts of it.* Here the holy Apostle exhorteth us to cast away the works of darkness; which, among other, he calleth gluttonous eating, drinking, chambering, and wantonness; which all[z] are ministers unto that vice, and preparations to induce and bring in the filthy sin of the flesh. He calleth them the deeds and works of darkness, not only because they are customably done[a] in darkness or in the nighttime, (*for*[ζ] *every one that doeth evil hateth the light, neither cometh he to the light, lest his works should be reproved,*) but that they lead the right way unto that *utter darkness*[η] *where weeping and gnashing of teeth shall be.* And he saith in another place of the same Epistle[θ], *They that are in the flesh cannot please God. We are debtors, not to the flesh, that*[b] *we should live after the flesh: for, if ye live after the flesh, ye shall die.*

Again he saith[ι], *Fly*[c] *from whoredom. For every sin that a*

Rom. xiii, [12–14.]

ζ John iii, [20.]

η Matt. xiii, [42, 50; xxii, 13; xxv, 30.]

θ Rom. viii, [8, 12, 13.]

ι 1 Cor. vi, [18–20.]

[o] minds] mind 1547 W *and* BEC. [p] to so filthy] to filthy 1547 G 1 *and* W 1–3, *and* BEC. [q] vice, to] vice, and to 1549 G, 1551, 1623. [r] or discounselleth] *added in* 1559, *but* discounselled *by error till* 1569. [s] through] thorough 1549 W, 1559–1563. [t] THE SECOND PART—let us hear] Now let us hear 1547, 1548, *the Homily not being then divided.* [u] armours] armour *from* 1574. [x] chamberings] chambering *from* 1574. [y] Jesus] Jesu 1559, 1562. [z] all are] are all *from* 1559. [a] done] *omitted after* 1574. [b] not to the flesh, that] to the flesh not that *till* 1559. [c] Fly] Flee *from* 1569.

man committeth is without his body; but whosoever committeth whoredom sinneth against his own body. Do ye not know that your members are the temple of the Holy Ghost which is in you, whom also ye have of God, and ye are not your own? for ye are dearly bought. Glorify God in your body[d], *&c.* And a little afore[e] he saith[κ], *Do ye not know that your bodies are the members of Christ? Shall I then take the members of Christ and make them the members of an*[f] *whore? God forbid. Do ye not know that he which cleaveth to an*[g] *whore is made one body with her? There shall be two in one flesh, saith he. But he that cleaveth to the Lord is one spirit.* What godly reasons[h] doth the blessed Apostle St. Paul bring forth here, to dissuade (or discounsel[i]) us from whoredom and all uncleanness! *Your members,* saith he, *are the temple of the Holy Ghost: which whosoever doth defile, God will destroy him*[2], as saith St. Paul[λ]. If we be the temple of the Holy Ghost, how unfitting then is it to drive that Holy Spirit from us through whoredom, and in his place to set the wicked spirits of uncleanness and fornication, and to be joined and do service to them! *Ye are dearly bought,* saith he: *therefore glorify God in your bodies.* Christ, that innocent Lamb of God, hath bought us from the servitude of the devil, *not*[μ] *with corruptible gold and silver, but with his most precious* and dear heart *blood.* To what intent? That we should fall again unto[k] our old uncleanness and abominable living? Nay verily: but that we should *serve him*[ν] *all the days of our life in holiness and righteousness,* that we should *glorify him in our bodies* by purity and cleanness of life. He declareth also that *our bodies are the members of Christ.* How unseemly a thing is it then to cease to be incorporate (or embodied[l]) and one[m] with Christ, and through whoredom to be joined[n] and made all one with an[o] whore! What greater dishonour or injury can we do to Christ, than to take away from him the members of his body, and to join them to whores, devils, and wicked spirits? And what more dishonour can we do to ourselves, than through uncleanness to lose so excellent a dignity and freedom, and to become bondslaves and miserable captives to the spirits[p] of darkness? Let us therefore consider first the glory of Christ,

κ 1 Cor. vi, [15–17.]

λ [1 Cor. iii, 17.]

μ 1 Pet. i, [18, 19.]

ν Luke i, [74, 75:] Isai. xxxviii, [20.]

[d] body] bodies *all except* 1547 W *and* BEC. [e] afore] before *from* 1547 G 5. [f g] an] a 1623. [h] reasons] reason 1559, words *from* 1562 B. [i] or discounsel *added in* 1559, and discounsel *from* 1582. [k] unto] into *from* 1582. [l] or embodied] *added in* 1559. [m] and one] and made one *from* 1582. [n] joined] enjoined *from* 1559. [o] with an] with a 1623. [p] the spirits] the spirit 1559.

2 Οὐκ οἴδατε ὅτι ναὸς Θεοῦ ἐστε, καὶ τὸ πνεῦμα τοῦ Θεοῦ οἰκεῖ ἐν ὑμῖν; εἴ τις τὸν ναὸν τοῦ Θεοῦ φθείρει, φθερεῖ τοῦτον ὁ Θεός. 1 Cor. iii, 16, 17.

and then[q] our estate[r], our dignity, and freedom, wherein God hath set us by giving us his Holy Spirit; and let us valiantly defend the same against Satan and all his crafty assaults, that Christ may be honoured, and that we lose not our liberty (or freedom[s]), but still remain in one spirit with him.

Ephes. v, [3–5.] Moreover, in his Epistle to the Ephesians the blessed Apostle willeth us to be so pure and free from adultery, *fornication, and all uncleanness, that we not once name them among us, as it becometh saints; nor filthiness, nor foolish talking, nor jesting, which are not comely; but rather giving of thanks. For this ye know,* saith he, *that no whoremonger, either[t] unclean person, or covetous person, which is an[u] idolater, hath any inheritance* ξ *in the kingdom of Christ and God*[x]. ξ Gal. v, [19–21.] And, that we should remember to be holy, pure, and free from all uncleanness, the holy Apostle calleth us *saints,* because we are sanctified ° and made holy in[y] the blood of Christ through the Holy Ghost. ° 1 Cor. vi, [11.] Now, if we be saints, what have we to do with the manners of the heathen? 1 Pet. i, [15:] Lev. xi, [44;] and xix, [2.] St. Peter saith, *As he which called you is holy, even so be ye holy also in all your[z] conversation; because it is written, Be ye holy, for I am holy.*

Hitherto have we heard how grievous a sin fornication and whoredom is, and how greatly God doth abhor it throughout the whole Scripture. How can it any otherwise be than a sin of most abomination, seeing it once may not[a] be named among the Christians, much less it may in any point be committed? And surely, if we would weigh[b] the greatness of this sin, and consider it in the right kind, we should find the sin of whoredom to be that most filthy lake, foul puddle, and stinking sink, whereinto[c] all kinds of sins and evils flow, where also they have their resting place and abiding. For hath not the adulterer a pride in his whoredom? [Prov. ii, 14.] As the Wise Man saith: *They are glad when they have done evil, and rejoice in things that are stark naught*[3]. Is not the adulterer also idle, and delighteth in no godly exercise, but only in that his most filthy and beastly pleasure? Is not his mind plucked[d] and utterly drawn away from all virtuous studies and fruitful labours, and only given to carnal and fleshly[e] imaginations[f]? Doth not the whoremonger give

[q] Christ, and then] Christ, then *from* 1582. [r] estate] state *till* 1559. [s] or freedom] *added in* 1559. [t] either] neither 1582, 1623. [u] is an] is any 1559. [x] and God] and of God *from* 1574. [y] holy in] holy by *from* 1582. [z] in all your] in your *from* 1582. [a] it once may not] it may not once *from* 1574. [b] weigh] weight 1559–1563. [c] whereinto] whereunto *from* 1559. [d] plucked] abstract *till* 1559. [e] and fleshly] *added in* 1559. [f] imaginations] imagination *from* 1559.

[3] Qui laetantur cum malefecerint, et exultant in rebus pessimis. *Vulg.*

his mind to gluttony, that he may be the more apt to serve his lusts and carnal pleasures? Doth not the adulterer give his mind to covetousness and to polling and pilling of other, that he may be the more able to maintain his harlots and whores, and to continue in his filthy and unlawful love? Swelleth he not also with envy against other, fearing that his prey should be allured and taken away from him? Again, is he not ireful, and replenished with wrath and displeasure, even against his best beloved, if at any time his beastly and devilish request be letted? What sin or kind of sin is it that is not joined with fornication and whoredom? It is a monster of many heads. It receiveth all kinds of vices, and refuseth all kinds of virtues. If one several sin bringeth damnation, what is to be thought of that sin which is accompanied with all evils, and hath waiting on it whatsoever is hateful to God, damnable to man, and pleasant to Satan?

Great is the damnation that hangeth over the heads of fornicators and adulterers. What shall I speak of other incommodities which issue and flow out of this stinking puddle of whoredom? Is not that treasure which before all other is most regarded of honest persons, the good fame and name of man and woman, lost through whoredom? What patrimony (or livelihood[g]), what substance, what goods, what riches doth whoredom shortly consume and bring to naught! What valiantness and strength is many times made weak and destroyed with whoredom! What wit is so fine, that is not doted[h] and defaced through[i] whoredom! What beauty, although it were never so excellent, is not disfigured[k] through whoredom! Is not whoredom an enemy to the pleasant flower of youth? and bringeth it not grey hairs and old age before the time? What gift of nature, although it were never so precious, is not corrupted with whoredom? Come not the French pocks, with other diverse[l] diseases, of whoredom? From whence come so many bastards and misbegotten children, to the high displeasure of God and dishonour of holy wedlock, but of whoredom? How many consume all their substance and goods, and at the last fall into such extreme poverty, that afterward they steal, and so are hanged, through whoredom! What contention and manslaughter cometh of whoredom! How many maidens be deflowered, how many

[g] or livelihood] *added in* 1559, or livelode *from* 1569. [h] doted] besotted 1623. [i] through (*after* defaced)] thorough *from* 1569. [k] disfigured] obscured *till* 1559. [l] the French pocks, with other diverse] many foul and most loathseme 1623.

wives corrupted, how many widows defiled, through whoredom! How much is the public and common[m] weal impoverished and troubled through whoredom! How much is God's word contemned and depraved by[n] whoredom and whoremongers!

Of this vice cometh a great part of the divorces which now a days be so commonly accustomed and used by men's private authority, to the great displeasure of God, and the breach of the most holy knot and bond of matrimony. For, when this most detestable sin is once crept into the breast of the adulterer, so that he is entangled with unlawful and unchaste love, straightways his true and lawful wife is despised; her presence is abhorred; her company stinketh and is loathsome; whatsoever she doeth is dispraised; there is no quietness in the house so long as she is in sight: therefore, to make short tale[o], must she[p] away, for her husband can brook her no longer. Thus through whoredom is the honest and harmless[q] wife put away, and an harlot received in her stead: and in like sort it happeneth many times in the wife towards her husband. O abomination! Christ our Saviour, very God and man, coming to restore the law of his heavenly Father unto the right sense, understanding, and meaning, among other things reformed the abuse of this law of God. For, whereas the Jews used, of a[r] long sufferance, by custom, to put away their wives at their pleasure for every cause, Christ, correcting that evil custom, did teach[ς] that, if any man put away his wife, and marrieth another, for any cause except only for adultery (which then was death by the law), he was an adulterer; and forced also his wife, so divorced, to commit adultery, if she were joined to any other man; and the man also, so joined with her, to commit adultery. In what case then are those[s] adulterers which for the love of an whore put away their true and lawful wife against all law, right, reason, and conscience? O damnable[t] is the state[u] wherein they stand! Swift destruction shall fall on them, if they repent not and amend not. For God will not ever[x] suffer holy wedlock thus to be dishonoured, hated, and despised. He will once punish this fleshly[y] and licentious manner of living, and cause that his[z] holy ordinance shall be had in reverence and honour. For surely *wedlock*, as the Apostle saith, *is honourable among all*

ς Matt. xix, [8, 9.]

Heb. xiii, [4.]

[m] and common] *added in* 1559. [n] depraved by] depraved through *from* 1582. [o] tale] work 1623. [p] must she] she must *from* 1562 A. [q] harmless] innocent *till* 1559. [r] used of a] used a *from* 1582. [s] those] these *from* 1582. [t] O damnable] O how damnable 1623. [u] state] estate 1582, 1623. [x] ever] *omitted* 1623. [y] fleshly] carnal *till* 1559. [z] that his] that this 1549 G, 1551, *and from* 1574.

men, and the bed undefiled; but whoremongers and fornicators God will judge, that is to say, punish and condemn.

But to what purpose is this labour taken to describe and set forth the greatness of the sin of whoredom, and the incommodities[a] that issue and flow out of it, seeing that breath and tongue shall sooner fail any man, than he shall or may be able to set it out according to the abomination and heinousness thereof? Notwithstanding, this is spoken to the intent that all men should flee whoredom, and live in the fear of God. God grant that it may not be spoken in vain!

THE THIRD PART OF THE SERMON AGAINST ADULTERY.

IN the second part of this Sermon against Adultery, that was last read, you have learned how earnestly the Scripture warneth us to avoid the sin of adultery and to embrace cleanness of life; and that through adultery we fall into all kinds of sins[b] and are made bondslaves to the devil, through cleanness[c] of life we are made members of Christ; and finally how far adultery bringeth a man from all goodness, and driveth him headlong into all vices, mischief, and misery.[d] Now will I declare unto you in order with what grievous punishments God in times past plagued adultery, and how certain worldly princes also did punish it, that ye may perceive that whoredom and fornication be sins no less detestable in the sight of God and all[f] good men than I have hitherto uttered.

[Punishments appointed for whoredom.[e]]

In the first book of Moyses we read that, when mankind began to be multiplied upon the earth, the men and women gave their minds so greatly to fleshly delight[g] and filthy pleasure, that they lived without all fear of God. God, seeing this their beastly and abominable living, and perceiving that they amended not, but rather increased daily more and more in their sinful and unclean manners, repented that he ever[h] had made man: and, to shew how greatly he abhorred[i] adultery, whoredom, fornication, and all uncleanness, he made all the

Gen. vi, [and vii.]

[a] incommodities] commodities 1582–1595, discommodities 1623. [b] of sins] of sin 1623. [c] through cleanness] thorough cleanness 1549 G, 1551, 1559. [d] THE THIRD PART——and misery.] *not in* 1547 *or* 1548, *the Homily not being then divided.* [e] Punishments appcinted for whoredom.] *in* BEC. *only.* [f] God and all] *so* BEC.; God, and of all 1547–1563, *except* 1547 W 2 *and* 3; God, and to all 1569–1576; God, to all *from* 1582. [g] fleshly delight] carnal delectation *till* 1559. [h] he ever] ever he *from* 1562 A. [i] abhorred] abhorreth *from* 1563.

fountains of the deep earth to burst out, and the sluices of heaven to be opened, so that the rain came down upon the earth by the space of forty days and forty nights; and by this means destroyed the[k] whole world and all mankind, eight persons only excepted, that is to say, Noe, the *preacher of righteousness* (as St. Peter calleth him), and his wife, his three sons and their wives. O what a grievous plague did God cast here upon all living creatures for the sin of whoredom! For the which God took vengeance not only of man, but also of beasts[l], fowls, and all living creatures. Manslaughter was committed before[π]; yet was not the world destroyed for that: but for whoredom all the world, few only except, was overflowed with waters, and so perished. An example worthy to be remembered, that ye may learn to fear God.

[2 Pet. ii, 5.]

π Gen. iv.

We read again that for the filthy sin of uncleanness Sodom and Gomorre[ρ], and the other cities nigh unto them, were destroyed with[m] fire and brimstone from heaven, so that there was neither man, woman, child, nor beast, nor yet any thing that grew upon the earth, there left undestroyed. Whose heart trembleth not at the hearing of this history? Who is so drowned in whoredom and uncleanness that will not now for ever after leave this abominable living, seeing that God so grievously punisheth uncleanness, to rain fire and brimstone from heaven, to destroy whole cities, to kill man, woman, and child, and all other living creatures there abiding, to consume with fire all that ever grew? What can be more manifest tokens of God's wrath and vengeance against uncleanness and impurity of life? Mark this history, good people, and fear the vengeance of God.

ρ Gen. xix, [1–29.]

Do we[n] not read[σ] also that *God did smite Pharao and his house with great plagues,* because that he ungodly desired Sara the wife of Abraham? Likewise read we of Abimelech[τ] king of Gerar[o], although he touched her not by carnal knowledge.

σ Gen. xii, [14–19.]

τ Gen. xx.

These plagues and punishments did God cast upon[p] filthy and unclean persons before the Law was given, the law of nature only reigning in the hearts of men, to declare how great love he had to matrimony (or wedlock[q]), and again how much he abhorred adultery, fornication, and all uncleanness. And, when the law that forbade whoredom was given by Moses to the Jews, did not God command that the breakers[r] thereof should be put

[k] destroyed the] destroyed of the 1559. [l] but also of beasts] but of all beasts *from* 1582. [m] destroyed with] destroyed by *from* 1582. [n] Do we] Do you *from* 1574. [o] Gerar] Gerat 1559. [p] cast upon] cast on upon 1582, 1587, 1623. [q] or wedlock] *added in* 1559, and wedlock *from* 1562 A. [r] breakers] transgressors *till* 1559.

to death? The words of the law be these[υ]: *Whoso committeth adultery with any man's wife shall die the death, both the man and the woman, because he hath broken wedlock with his neighbour's wife.* In the Law also it was commanded[φ], that a damsel and a man taken together in whoredom should be both stoned to death. In another place[χ] we also read that God commanded Moses to take all the head rulers and princes of the people, and to hang them upon gibbets openly, that every man might see them, because they either committed or did not punish whoredom. Again, did not God send[ψ] such a plague among the people for fornication and uncleanness, that they died in one day three and twenty thousand?

υ Lev. xx, [10.]

φ [Deut. xxii, 23, 24.]

χ Numb. xxv, [4.]

ψ [Ibid. 9: 1 Cor. x, 8.]

I pass over, for lack of time, many other histories of the holy Bible which declare the grievous vengeance and heavy displeasure of God against whoremongers and adulterers. Certes this extreme punishment appointed of God sheweth evidently how greatly God hateth whoredom. And let us not doubt but that God at this present abhorreth all manner of uncleanness no less than he did in the old Law, and will undoubtedly punish it both in this world and in the world to come. For he is a God that can abide no[s] wickedness[ω]: therefore ought it to be eschewed of all that tender the glory of God and the salvation[t] of their own souls. St. Paul saith[α] *all these things are written for our example,* and to teach us the fear of God and the obedience to his holy law. For, *if God[β] spared not the natural branches,* neither will he spare us that be but grafts, if we commit like offence. If God destroyed many thousands of people, many cities, yea, the whole world, for whoredom, let us not flatter ourselves, and think we shall escape free and without punishment. For he hath promised in his holy law to send most grievous plagues upon them that transgress (or break[u]) his holy commandments.

ω Ps. v, [4.]

α 1 Cor. x, [6, 11.]

β [Rom. xi, 21, 22.]

Thus have we heard how God punisheth the sin of adultery. Let us now hear certain laws which the civil magistrates devised in divers[y] countries for the punishment thereof, that we may learn how uncleanness hath ever been detested in all well ordered cities and commonwealths and among all honest persons. The law among the Lepreians was this, that, when any were taken in adultery, they were bound and carried three days through[z] the city, and afterward, as long as they lived, were they despised, and with shame and confusion counted[a] as per-

Laws devised for punishment[x] of whoredom.

[s] abide no] abide none 1559–1563. [t] salvation] salvations 1547 G 1 *and* W 1–3, 1548, 1549 G, 1551. [u] or break] *added in* 1559. [x] for punishment] for the punishment *from* 1569. [y] divers] their 1582, 1623. [z] through] thorough *from* 1569. [a] counted] reputed *till* 1559.

sons void[b] of all honesty. Among the Locrensians[c] the adulterers had both[d] their eyes thrust out. The Romans in times past punished whoredom, sometime by fire, sometime by sword. If a[e] man among the Egyptians had been taken in adultery, the law was that he should openly, in the presence of all the people, be scourged naked with whips unto the number of a thousand stripes: the woman that was taken with him had her nose cut off, whereby she was known ever after to be an[f] whore, and therefore to be abhorred of all men. Among the Arabians they that were taken in adultery had their heads stricken from their bodies. The Athenians punished whoredom by death in like manner. So likewise did the barbarous Tartarians. Among the Turks even at this day they that be taken in adultery, both man and woman, are stoned straightways[g] to death without mercy[4].

Thus see we[h] what godly acts were devised in times past of the high powers for the putting away of whoredom, and for the maintaining of holy matrimony (or wedlock[i]) and pure conversation. And the authors of these acts were not[k] Christians, but heathen[l]: yet were they so inflamed with the love of honesty and pureness of life, that, for the maintenance and conservation (or keeping up[m]) of that, they made godly statutes suffering neither fornication nor adultery[n] to reign in their realms unpunished.

Matt. xii, [41.] Christ said to the people, *The Ninivites shall rise at the judgment with this nation,* meaning the unfaithful Jews, *and shall condemn them: for they repented at the preaching of Jonas; but behold,* saith he, *a greater than Jonas is here,* meaning himself, and yet they repent[o] not. Shall not, think you, likewise the Locrensians[p], Arabians, Athenians, with such other, rise up at[q] the judgment and condemn us; forasmuch as they ceased from

[b] void] desolate *till* 1559. [c, p] Locrensians] Locreusians *all Grafton's editions.* [d] had both] hath both 1547 G 6—1549 G, have both 1549 W *and from* 1559. [e] If a] If any *from* 1582. [f] an] a *from* 1582. [g] straightways] straightway *from* 1582. [h] see we] we see *from* 1569. [i] or wedlock] *added in* 1559. [k] were not] were no *from* 1547 G 3. [l] but heathen] but the heathen *from* 1582. [m] or keeping up] *added in* 1559. [n] nor adultery] or adultery *from* 1582. [o] repent] repented 1547 W 2 *and* 3, *and* BEC. [p] *see note* c. [q] up at] up in 1623.

4 See, for the Lepreians, *Heracl. Pont. de Rebus Publicis Fragm.* XIV, *ed. Koeler,* 1804: for the Locrensians, *Aelian. Var. Hist.* XIII, 14: for the Romans, *Jul. Capitol. Opilius Macrinus c.* 12; and *Virg. Aen.* VI, 612: for the Egyptians, *Diod. Sic.* I, 78: for the Athenians, *Plutarch. Solon, Opp.* I, 90 F, *ed.* 1599: for the Arabians, Tartarians, and Turks, *Joan. Boem. de Omnium Gentium Ritibus* II, 1, 10, and 11. The Homilist may have taken most of his instances from the large collection of such penalties gathered by *Tiraquellus* (André Tiraqueau) in *Leg. Connubial.* XIII, 6–25; but he seems to have found several for himself in *Joannes Boemus,* who, for example, says of the Turks, In adulterio deprehensus cum adultera absque misericordia absque mora lapidatur.

whoredom[r] at the commandment of man, and we have the law and manifest precepts and commandments[s] of God, and yet forsake we not our filthy conversation? Truly, truly, it shall be easier at the day of judgment to those[t] heathen than to us, except we repent and amend. For, although[u] death of body[x] seemeth to us a grievous punishment in this world for whoredom, yet is that pain nothing in comparison of the grievous torments which adulterers, fornicators, and all unclean persons shall suffer after this life. For all such shall be[y] excluded and shut out of the kingdom of heaven, as St. Paul saith: *Be not deceived; for neither whoremongers, nor worshippers of images, nor adulterers, nor softlings[z], nor sodomites, nor thieves, nor covetous persons, nor drunkards, nor cursed speakers, nor pillers, shall inherit the kingdom of God.* And St. John in his Revelation saith that *whoremongers shall have their part* with murderers, sorcerers, enchanters, liars, idolaters, and such other, *in the lake which burneth with fire and brimstone, which is the second death.* The punishment of the body, although it be death, hath an end; but the punishment of the soul, which St. John calleth *the second death*, is everlasting: there shall be *fire and brimstone; there shall be weeping and gnashing of teeth*[γ]; *the worm* that shall there[a] gnaw the conscience of the damned *shall never die.* O whose heart distilleth not even drops of blood, to hear and consider these things? If we tremble and shake at the hearing and naming of these pains, O what shall they do that shall feel them, that shall suffer them, yea, and ever shall suffer, worlds without end? God have mercy on[b] us! Who is now so drowned in sin and past all godliness, that he will set more by a filthy[c] and stinking pleasure, which soon passeth away, than by the loss of everlasting glory? Again, who will so give himself to the lusts of the flesh, that he feareth nothing at all the pains[d] of hell fire?

1 Cor. vi, [9, 10:] Gal. v, [19–21:] Eph. v, [5.]

Rev. xxi, [8.]

γ Matt. xiii, [42: Mark ix, 43–48:] Luke iii, [17: Is. lxvi, 24.]

But let us hear how we may eschew the sin of whoredom and adultery, that we may walk in the fear of God, and be free from those most grievous and intolerable torments which abide all unclean persons. To avoid[e] fornication, adultery, and all uncleanness, let us provide that above all things we may keep our hearts pure and clean from all evil thoughts and carnal lusts;

Remedies whereby to avoid fornication and adultery.

[r] from whoredom] from the whoredom 1623. [s] and commandments] *added in* 1559. [t] those] these *all except* 1547 W 2 *and* 3, *and* BEC. [u] although] though *from* 1569. [x] of body] of the body 1547 W 2 *and* 3, *and* BEC. [y] such shall be] such be 1547 W *and* BEC. [z] softlings] weaklings 1574–1595, effeminate persons 1623. [a] shall there] there shall *from* 1582. [b] on] upon *from* 1547 G 2. [c] by a filthy] by filthy *from* 1574. [d] the pains] the pain *from* 1582. [e] To avoid] Now to avoid 1623.

for, if that be once infected and corrupt, we fall headlong into all kind of ungodliness. This shall we easily do, if, when we feel inwardly that Satan our old enemy tempteth us unto whoredom, we by no means consent to his crafty suggestions, but valiantly resist and withstand him by strong faith in the word of God, alleging[f] against him always in our heart this commandment of God: Scriptum est, *Non moechaberis;* It is written, *Thou shalt not commit whoredom.* It shall be good also for us ever to live in the fear of God, and to set before our eyes the grievous threatenings of God against all ungodly sinners; and to consider in our mind how filthy, beastly, and short that pleasure is whereunto Satan moveth[g] us, and again how the pain appointed for that sin is intolerable and everlasting. Moreover, to use a temperance and sobriety in eating and drinking, to eschew unclean communication, to avoid all filthy company, to flee idleness, to delight in reading of holy[h] Scripture[i], to watch in godly prayers and virtuous meditations[k], and at all times to exercise some godly travails, shall help greatly unto the eschewing of whoredom.

[Exod. xx, 14: Matt. iv, 4, 7, 10.]

And here are all degrees to be monished, whether they be married or unmarried, to love chastity and cleanness of life. For the married are bound by the law of God so purely to love one another, that neither of them seek any strange love. The man must only cleave to his wife, and the wife again only to her husband. They must so delight one in another's company, that none of them covet any other. And, as they are bound thus to live together in all godliness and honesty, so likewise it is[l] their duty virtuously to bring up their children, and to provide[m] that they fall not into Satan's snare nor into any uncleanness, but that they come pure and honest unto holy wedlock when time requireth. So likewise ought all masters and rulers to provide that no whoredom, nor any point of uncleanness, be used among their servants. And again, they that are single, and feel in themselves that they cannot live without the company of a woman, let them get wives of their own, and so live godly together. *For it is better to marry than to burn:* and, *to avoid fornication,* saith the Apostle, *let every man have his own wife, and every woman her own husband.* Finally, all

1 Cor. vii, [2, 9.]

[f] alleging] objecting *till* 1559. [g] Satan moveth] Satan continually stirreth and moveth *from* 1582. [h] reading of holy] reading holy 1547–1576, *except* 1547 W 2 *and* 3, *and* BEC.; reading the holy 1623. [i] Scripture] Scripturs 1563, Scriptures *from* 1569. [k] meditations] meditation *from* 1582. [l] likewise it is] likewise is *all except* 1547 W 2 *and* 3, BEC., *and* 1623. [m] and to provide] and provide 1623.

such as feel in themselves a sufficiency and ability, through the working[n] of God's Spirit, to lead a sole and continent life, let them praise God for his gift, and seek all means possible to maintain the same; as by reading of holy Scriptures, by godly meditations, by continual prayers, and such other virtuous exercises.

If we all on this wise will endeavour ourselves to eschew fornication, adultery, and all uncleanness, and lead our lives in all godliness and honesty, serving God with a pure and clean heart, and glorifying him in our bodies by leading[o] an innocent and harmless[p] life, we may be sure to be in the number of those of whom our Saviour Christ speaketh in the Gospel on this manner: *Blessed are the pure in heart, for they shall see God.* To Matt. v, [8.] whom alone be all glory, honour, rule, and power, worlds without end. Amen.

[n] working] operation *till* 1559. [o] by leading] by the leading 1582, 1623. [p] and harmless] *added in* 1559.

A SERMON[a]

AGAINST CONTENTION AND BRAWLING.

THIS day, good Christian people, shall be declared unto you the unprofitableness and shameful unhonesty of contention, strife, and debate; to the intent that, when you shall see, as it were in a table painted before your eyes, the evilfavouredness and deformity of this most detestable vice, your stomachs may be moved to rise against it, and to detest and abhor that sin, which is so much to be hated, and so pernicious[b] and hurtful to all men.

But among all kinds of contention none is more hurtful than
1 Tim. i, [4:] 2 Tim, ii, [23, 24.] is contention in matters of religion. *Eschew*, saith St. Paul, *foolish and unlearned questions, knowing that they breed strife. It becometh not the servant of God to fight* or strive, *but to be meek toward all men.* This contention and strife was in St. Paul's time among the Corinthians, and is at this time among us Englishmen. For too many there be which, upon the ale benches or other places, delight to set forth[c] certain questions, not so much pertaining to edification as to vain glory and shewing forth of their cunning[d]; and so unsoberly to reason and dispute, that, when neither party[e] will give place to other, they fall to chiding and contention, and sometime from hot[f] words to further inconvenience. St. Paul could not abide to hear among
1 Cor. [i, 12;] iii, [4.] the Corinthians these words of discord or dissension: *I hold of Paul, I of Cephas, and I of Apollo.* What would he then say, if he heard these words of contention, which be now almost in every man's mouth: He is a Pharisee, He is a Gospeller, He is of the new sort, He is of the old faith, He is a new-broached brother, He is a good catholic father, He is a papist, He is an heretic? O how the Church is divided! O how the cities be cut and mangled! O how the coat of Christ, that was without seam, is all to[1] rent and torn! O body mystical of Christ, where

[a] A SERMON] AN HOMILY *till* 1549 W. [b] and so pernicious] and pernicious *from* 1563. [c] set forth] propound *till* 1559. [d] shewing forth of their cunning] ostentation *till* 1559. [e] party] part *from* 1559. [f] hot] hote *till* 1569.

1 all to: thoroughly, entirely, altogether; in which last word alone the phrase, once very common, has maintained its ground. It occurs again in p. 140, l. 33, "all to naught." It occurs also in Judges ix, 53, "and all to brake his skull," that is, broke (or crushed) in, where the Vulgate has confregit.

is that holy and happy unity, out of the which whosoever is, he is not in Christ? If one member be pulled from another, where is the body? If the body be drawn from the head, where is the life of the body? We cannot be jointed[g] to Christ our Head[a], except we be glued with concord and charity one to another. For he that is not in this[h] unity is not of the Church of Christ; which is a congregation or unity together, and not a division.

[a] [Eph. iv, 15, 16.]

St. Paul saith that, *as long as emulation* (or envying[i]), *contention, and factions* (or sects[j]) *be among us, we be carnal, and walk according to the fleshly man.* [1 Cor. iii, [3.]] And St. James saith, *If you*[k] *have bitter emulation* (or envying[l]) *and contention in your hearts, glory not of it. For, where as contention is, there is unsteadfastness*[m] *and all evil deeds.* [James iii, [14, 16.]] And why do we not hear St. Paul, which prayeth us, whereas he might command us, saying; *I beseech you in the name of our Lord Jesus Christ, that you will speak all one thing, and that there be no dissension among you, but that you will be one whole body, of one mind, and of one opinion* in the truth. [1 Cor. i, [10.]] If his desire be reasonable and honest, why do we not grant it? if his request be for our profit, why do we refuse it? And, if we list not to hear his petition or prayer[n], yet let us hear his exhortation, where he saith, *I exhort you that you walk as it becometh the vocation in the which*[o] *you be called, with all submission and meekness, with lenity*[p] *and softness of mind, bearing one another by charity, studying to keep the unity of the Spirit by the bond of peace: for there is one body, one Spirit, one faith, one baptism.* [Eph. iv, [1-5.]] There is, he saith, but[q] *one body:* of the which he can be no lively member that is at variance with the other members. There is *one Spirit,* which joineth and knitteth all things in one: and how can this one Spirit reign in us, when we among ourselves be divided? There is but *one faith:* and how can we then say, He is of the old faith, and, He is of the new faith? There is but *one baptism:* and then shall not all they which be baptized be one? Contention causeth division: wherefore it ought not to be among Christians, whom one faith and baptism joineth in an unity. But, if we contemn St. Paul's request and exhortation, yet at the least let us regard his earnest entreating[r]; in the which he doth very earnestly

[g] jointed] joined *from* 1559. [h] in this] of this *from* 1582. [i], [l] or envying] *added in* 1559. [j] or sects] *added in* 1559. [k] If you] If ye *from* 1574. [m] unsteadfastness] inconstancy *till* 1559. [n] or prayer] of prayer *from* 1547 G 2. [o] in the which] in which *from* 1569. [p] lenity] levity 1559. [q] he saith, but] saith he, but *from* 1574. [r] earnest entreating] obtestation *till* 1559.

charge us, and, as I may so speak, conjure us, in this form and manner: *If there be any consolation in Christ, if there be any comfort of love, if you have any fellowship*[s] *of the Spirit, if you have any bowels of pity and compassion, fulfil my joy, being all like affected, having one charity, being of one mind, of one opinion, that nothing be done by contention or vain glory.* Who is he, that hath any bowels of pity, that will not be moved with these words so pithy? Whose heart is so stony, that the[t] sword of these words, which be *more sharp than any two-edged*[u] *sword*[β], may not cut and break asunder? Wherefore, let us endeavour ourselves to fulfil St. Paul's joy here in this place, which shall be at length to our great joy in another place.

Phil. ii, [1-3.]

β [Heb. iv, 12.]

How we should read the Scripture.

Let us so read the Scripture, that by reading thereof we may be made the better livers, rather than the more contentious disputers. If any thing is[x] necessary to be taught, reasoned, or disputed, let us do it with all meekness, softness, and lenity. If any thing shall chance to be spoken uncomely, let one bear another's frailty. He that is faulty, let him rather amend than defend that which he hath spoken amiss, lest he fall by contention from a foolish error into an obstinate heresy. For it is better to give place meekly than to win the victory with the breach of charity; which chanceth where every[y] man will defend his opinion obstinately. If we be Christian[z] men, why do we not follow Christ, which saith, *Learn of me, for I am meek and lowly in heart?* A disciple must learn the lesson of his schoolmaster, and a servant must obey the commandment of his master. *He that is wise and learned*, saith St. James, *let him shew his goodness by his good conversation and soberness of his wisdom. For, where there is envy and contention, that wisdom cometh not from God, but is worldly wisdom, man's wisdom, and devilish wisdom. For the wisdom that cometh from above,* from the Spirit of God, *is chaste* and pure, corrupted with no evil affections; *it is* quiet, meek, and *peaceable*, abhorring all desire of[a] contention; *it is tractable,* obedient, not grudging to learn, and to give place to them that teach better for their[b] reformation. For there shall never be an end of striving and contention, if we contend who in contention shall be master, and have the overhand: we[c] shall heap error upon error, if we continue to

Matt. xi, [29.]

James iii, [13-17.]

[s] fellowship] communion *till* 1559. [t] stony, that the] stony but that the 1547–1551, *although the error is corrected among the "Faultes escaped" in* 1547 W 1; stony the 1559–1569. [u] two-edged] two-handed 1547 G 1 *and* 2. [x] thing is] thing be 1551, *and from* 1574. [y] where every] when every *from* 1582. [z] be Christian] be the Christian 1623. [a] desire of] desire and 1623. [b] for their] for the 1623. [c] overhand: we] overhand: if we *all*.

defend that obstinately which was spoken unadvisedly. For truth it is that stiffness in maintaining an opinion breedeth contention, brawling, and chiding; which is a vice, among all other, most pernicious and pestilent to common peace and quietness.

And, as[d] it standeth betwixt two persons and parties, (for no man commonly doth chide with himself,) so it comprehendeth two most detestable vices: the one is picking of quarrels with sharp and contentious words; the other standeth in froward answering and multiplying evil words again. The first is so abominable, that St. Paul saith, *If any that is called a brother be a worshipper of idols, a brawler* or picker[e] of quarrels, *a thief* or an extortioner, *with him that is such a man see that ye eat not.* Now here consider that St. Paul numbereth a scolder, a brawler, or a picker of quarrels among thieves and idolaters. And many times cometh[f] less hurt of a thief than of a railing tongue: for the one taketh away a man's good name; the other taketh but his riches, which is of much less value and estimation than is his good name. And a thief hurteth but him from whom he stealeth; but he that hath an evil tongue troubleth all the town where he dwelleth, and sometime the whole country. And a railing tongue is a pestilence so full of contagiousness[g], that St. Paul willeth Christian men to forbear the company of such, and neither to eat nor drink with them. And, whereas he will not[y] that a Christian woman should forsake her husband, although he be an infidel, nor that[h] a Christian servant should depart from his master, which is an infidel and heathen, and so suffereth[i] a Christian man to keep company with an infidel, yet he forbiddeth us to eat or drink with a scolder or a quarrel picker[k]. And also in the sixth chapter to the Corinthians he saith thus: *Be not deceived; for neither fornicators, neither worshippers of idols, neither thieves nor drunkards, neither cursed*[l] *speakers, shall dwell in the kingdom of heaven.* It must needs be a great fault that doth move and cause the father to disherit his natural son: and how can it otherwise be but that this cursed speaking must needs be a most damnable sin, the which doth cause God, our most merciful and loving Father, to deprive us of his most blessed kingdom of heaven?

Against the other sin, that standeth in requiting taunt for

Against quarrel picking.

1 Cor. v, [11.]

y [1 Cor. vii, 13: 1 Tim. vi, 1.]

1 Cor. vi, [9, 10.]

Against froward answering.

[d] as] *omitted* 1623. [e] or picker] a picker *from* 1562 A. [f] times cometh] times there cometh 1623. [g] contagiousness] contagion *till* 1559. [h] nor that] or that *from* 1563. [i] suffereth] suffer *all except* 1547 W. [k] or a quarrel picker] or quarrel picker *from* 1582. [l] neither cursed] nor cursed *from* 1574.

taunt, speaketh Christ himself. *I say unto you*, saith our Saviour Christ, *Resist*[m] *not evil; but love your enemies, and say well by them that say evil by you, do well unto them that do evil to you*[n], *and pray for them that do hurt and persecute*[o] *you; that you may be the children of your Father which is in heaven, who suffereth his sun to rise both upon good and evil, and sendeth his rain both to*[p] *the just and unjust.* To this doctrine of Christ agreeth very well the teaching of St. Paul, that *chosen*[q] *vessel*[δ] of God, who ceaseth not to exhort and call upon us, saying, *Bless them that curse you; bless, I say, and curse not. Recompense to no man evil for evil. If it be possible, as much as lieth in you, live peaceably with all men.*

Matt. v, [39, 44, 45.]

δ [Acts ix, 15.]

Rom. xii, [14, 17, 18.]

THE SECOND PART OF THE SERMON AGAINST[r] CONTENTION.

IT hath been declared unto you in this Sermon against strife and brawling, what great inconvenience cometh thereby, and specially[s] of such contention as groweth in matters of religion; and how, when as no man will give place to another, there is none end of contention and discord, and that unity which God requireth of Christians is utterly thereby neglected and broken; and that this contention standeth chiefly in two points, as in picking of quarrels and making froward[t] answers.

Now you[u] shall hear St. Paul's words, saying[x], *Dearly beloved, avenge not yourselves, but rather give place unto wrath: for it is written*[ε], *Vengeance is mine, I*[y] *will revenge, saith the Lord. Therefore, if thine enemy hunger, feed him; if he thirst, give him drink. Be not overcome with evil, but overcome evil with goodness.* All these be the words of St. Paul.

[Rom. xii, 19–21.]

ε Deut. xxxii, [35.]

An objection[z].

But they that be so full[a] of stomach, and set so much by themselves, that they may not abide so much as one evil word to be spoken of them, peradventure will say, If I be evil reviled[b], shall I stand still, like a goose or a fool, with my finger in my mouth? Shall I be such an idiot and dizzard to suffer every

[m] himself. I say unto you, saith our Saviour Christ, Resist] himself, saying, I say unto you, Resist *from* 1582. [n] to you] unto you *from* 1562 A. [o] persecute] pursue *till* 1559. [p] both to] both upto (*by error for* unto) 1569, both upon *from* 1574. [q] chosen] elect *till* 1559. [r] AGAINST] OF 1549 G, 1551. [s] thereby, and specially] thereby, specially *from* 1559. [t] making froward] making of froward *from* 1562 A. [u] Now you] Now ye *from* 1559. [x] THE SECOND PART—words, saying] *not in* 1547 *or* 1548, *the Homily not being then divided.* [y] mine, I] mine, and I *from* 1582. [z] An objection] Objection 1549 G, 1551, 1559. [a] be so full] be full *from* 1569. [b] be evil reviled] be reviled *from* 1582.

man to speak upon me what they list, to rail what they list, to spew out all their venom against me at their pleasures? Is it not convenient that he that speaketh evil should be answered accordingly? If I shall use this lenity and softness, I shall both increase mine enemy's frowardness, and provoke other to do like. Such reasons make they that can suffer nothing for the defence of their impatience. And yet, if by froward answering to a froward person there were hope to remedy his frowardness, he should less offend that should so[d] answer, doing the same not of ire or malice, but only of that intent, that he that is so froward or malicious may be reformed: but he that cannot amend another man's fault, or cannot amend it without his own fault, better it were that one should perish than two. Then, if he cannot quiet him with gentle words, at the least let him not follow him in wicked and uncharitable words. If he can pacify him with suffering, let him suffer; and if not, it is better to suffer evil than to do evil, to say well than to say evil: for to speak well against evil cometh of the Spirit of God; but to render evil for evil cometh of the contrary spirit. And he that cannot temper ne[e] rule his own anger[f] is but weak and feeble, and rather more like a woman or a child than a strong man: for the true strength and manliness is to overcome wrath, and to despise injury[g] and other men's foolishness. And besides this, he that shall despise the wrong done unto him by his enemy, every man shall perceive that it was spoken or done without cause; whereas, contrary[h], he that doth fume and chafe at it shall help the cause of his adversary, giving suspicion that the thing is true. And so in[i] going about to revenge evil we shew ourselves to be evil; and, while we will punish and revenge another man's folly, we double and augment our own folly.

An answer[c].

But many pretences find they that be wilful to colour their impatience. Mine enemy, say they, is not worthy to have gentle words or deeds, being so full of malice or frowardness. The less he is worthy, the more art thou allowed[k] of God, the[l] more art thou commended of Christ, for whose sake thou shouldest render good for evil, because he hath commanded thee and also deserved that thou shouldest so do. Thy neighbour[m] hath peradventure with a word offended thee: call thou to thy remembrance with how many words and deeds, how grievously, thou

[c] An answer] Answer 1549 G, 1551, 1559. [d] should so] so should *from* 1574. [e] ne] nor *from* 1582. [f] anger] ire *till* 1559. [g] injury] injuries *from* 1569. [h] contrary] contrarily 1623. [i] so in] in so *from* 1562 A. [k] thou allowed] thou therefore allowed *from* 1582. [l] God, the] God, and the *from* 1582. [m] Thy neighbour] Thine neighbour *till* 1559.

hast offended thy Lord God. What was man when Christ died for him? Was he not his enemy, and unworthy to have his favour and mercy? Even so with what gentleness and patience doth he forbear and tolerate and suffer[n] thee, although he is daily offended by thee! Forgive therefore a light trespass to thy neighbour, that Christ may forgive thee many thousands of trespasses, which art every day an offender. For, if thou forgive thy brother, being to thee a trespasser, then hast thou a sure sign and token that God will forgive thee, to whom all men be debtors or[o] trespassers. How wouldest thou have God merciful to thee, if thou wilt be cruel unto thy brother? Canst thou not find in thine heart to do that toward[p] another, that is thy fellow, which God hath done to thee, that art but his servant? Ought not one sinner to forgive another, seeing that Christ, which was no sinner, did pray to his Father for them that without mercy and despitefully put him to death? *Who*[ζ]*, when he was reviled, did*[q] *not use reviling words again; and, when he suffered wrongfully, he did not threaten; but gave all vengeance to the judgment of his Father, which judgeth rightfully.* And what crackest thou of thy Head, if thou labour not to be in the body? Thou canst be no member of Christ, if thou follow not the steps of Christ: who, as the Prophet saith[η], was *led to death like a lamb*, not opening his mouth to reviling, but opening his mouth to praying for them that crucified him, saying[θ], *Father, forgive them, for they cannot tell what they do.* The which example, anon after Christ, St. Stephen did follow[ι], and after St. Paul. *We be evil spoken of*, saith he[κ], *and we speak*[r] *well; we suffer persecution, and take it patiently; men curse us, and we gently entreat.* Thus St. Paul taught that he did, and he did that he taught. *Bless you*, saith he[λ], *them that persecute you; bless you, and curse not.* Is it[s] a great thing to speak well to thine[t] adversary, to whom Christ doth command thee to do well? David, when Semei did call him all to[2] naught, did not chide again, but said patiently[μ], *Suffer him to speak evil, if perchance the Lord will have mercy on me.*

ζ 1 Pet. ii, [23.]
η Is. liii, [7.]
θ Luke xxiii, [34.]
ι Acts vii, [60.]
κ 1 Cor. iv, [12, 13.]
λ [Rom. xii, 14.]
μ [2 Sam. xvi, 11, 12.]

Histories be full of examples of heathen men, that took very meekly both opprobrious and reproachful[u] words, and injurious

[n] and suffer] *added in* 1559. [o] debtors or] debtors and *from* 1574. [p] toward] towards *from* 1547 G 5. [q] reviled, did] reviled, he did 1623. [r] and we speak] and speak 1547 G 3—1574. [s] Is it] It is 1547 G 1-4, *but with ? at the end of the sentence.* [t] to thine] *so from* 1548; to thy 1547 G 1-4 *and* W 1-3; to of and thine 1547 G 5 *by error;* to and of thine 1547 G 6 *and among the corrections of "Faultes escaped" in* 1547 W 1. [u] and reproachful] *added in* 1559.

[2] all to: see note 1 on this Homily.

or wrongful[x] deeds. And shall those heathen men excel[y] in patience us, that profess Christ, the teacher and example of all patience? Lysander, when one did rage against him in reviling of him, he was nothing moved, but said, "Go to, go to, speak against me as much and as oft as thou wilt, and leave out nothing; if perchance by this means thou mayest discharge thee of those naughty things with the which it seemeth that thou art full laden."[3] Many men speak evil of all men, because they can speak well of no man. After this sort this wise man avoided[z] from him the reproachful[a] words spoken unto him, imputing and laying them to the natural sickness of his adversary. Pericles, when a certain scolder or a railing[b] fellow did revile him, he answered not a word again, but went into a gallery[4]; and after, toward[c] night, when he went home, this scolder followed him, raging still more and more because he saw the other to set nothing by him; and, after that he came to his gate, being dark night, Pericles commanded one of his servants to light a torch and to bring the scolder home to his own house. He did not only with quietness suffer this brawler patiently, but also recompensed an evil turn with a good turn, and that to his enemy. Is it not a[d] shame for us, that profess Christ, to be worse than heathen people in a thing chiefly pertaining to Christ's religion? Shall philosophy persuade them more than God's word shall persuade us? Shall natural reason prevail more with them than religion shall do with[e] us? Shall man's wisdom lead them to that thing[f] whereunto the heavenly doctrine cannot lead us? What blindness, wilfulness, or rather madness is this! Pericles, being provoked to anger with many villanous[g] words, answered not a word. But we, stirred but with one little word, what foul work do we make[h]! how do we fume, rage, stamp, and stare like mad men! Many men of every trifle will make a great matter, and of the spark of a little word will kindle a great fire, taking all things in the worst part. But how much better is it, and more like to the example and doctrine of Christ, to make rather of a great fault in our neighbour a small fault, reasoning

[x] or wrongful] *added in* 1559. [y] heathen men excel] heathen excel *from* 1559. [z] avoided] avoideth *from* 1582. [a] the reproachful] the injurious *till* 1559. [b] or a railing] or railing 1549 G, 1551, *and from* 1574. [c] toward] towards *from* 1582. [d] Is it not a] It is a 1549 G, 1551. [e] shall do with] shall with *from* 1569. [f] that thing] that things 1563, those things *from* 1569. [g] villanous] contumelious *till* 1559. [h] foul work do we make] tragedies do we move *till* 1559.

3 See *Plutarch. Apophthegm. Lacon., Lysandr.* XIII, p. 229 E.

4 Λοιδορούμενος γοῦν ποτε καὶ κακῶς ἀκούων ὑπό τινος τῶν βδελυρῶν καὶ ἀκολάστων ὅλην ἡμέραν ὑπέμεινε σιωπῇ κατ' ἀγορὰν ἅμα τι τῶν ἐπειγόντων καταπραττόμενος· ἑσπέρας δ' ἀπῄει κοσμίως οἴκαδε κ.τ.λ. Plutarch. Pericl., Opp. I, 154 C, ed. 1599.

with ourselves after this sort: He spake these words, but it was in a sudden heat; or the drink spake them, and not he; or he spake them at the motion of some other; or he spake them being ignorant of the truth; he spake them not against me, but against him whom he thought me to be.

Reasons to move men from quarrel picking.

But as touching evil speaking, he that is ready to speak evil against other men, first let him examine himself, whether he be faultless and clear of the fault which he findeth in another. For it is a shame when he that blameth another for any fault is guilty himself, either in the same fault, either in a[i] greater. It is a shame for him that is blind to call another man blind: and it is more shame for him that is whole blind to call him blinkard[k] that is but poreblind[l]; for this is to see a straw in another man's eye, when a man hath a block in his own eye. Then let him consider, that he that useth to speak evil shall commonly be evil spoken of again, and he that speaketh what he will for his pleasure shall be compelled to hear that[m] he would not to his displeasure. Moreover, let him remember that saying, that we *shall give an account for every idle word.* How much more then shall we make a reckoning[n] for our sharp, bitter, brawling, and chiding words, which provoke our brother to be angry, and so to the breach of his charity!

Matt. xii, [36.]

Reasons to move men from froward answering.

And as touching evil[o] answering, although we be never so much provoked by other men's evil speaking, yet we shall not follow their frowardness by evil answering, if we consider that anger is a kind of madness, and that he which is angry is, as it were, for the time in a phrensy. Wherefore let him beware lest in his fury he speak any thing whereof afterward he may have just cause to be sorry. And he that will defend that anger is no[p] fury, but that he hath reason even when he is most angry, then let him reason thus with himself when he is angry: Now I am so moved and chafed, that within a little while after I shall be otherways[q] minded: wherefore then should I now speak any thing in mine anger, which hereafter, when I would fainest, cannot be changed? Wherefore shall I do any thing now, being (as it were) out of my wit, for the which, when I shall come to myself again, I shall be very sad? Why doth not reason, why doth not godliness, yea, why doth not Christ obtain that thing now of me which hereafter time shall obtain of me?

[i] either in a] or in a 1623. [k] blinkard] winkard 1549 G, 1551. [l] poreblind] poureblind 1562–1576, purblind *from* 1582. [m] hear that] hear what 1623. [n] make a reckoning] make reckoning 1623. [o] touching evil] touching ill 1547 G 1. [p] is no] is not *from* 1574. [q] otherways] otherwise *from* 1569.

If a man be called an adulterer, usurer, drunkard, or by any other shameful[r] name, let him consider earnestly whether he be so called truly or falsely. If truly, let him amend his fault, that his adversary may not after worthily charge him with such offences. If these things be laid against him falsely, yet let him consider whether he hath given any occasion to be suspected of such things; and so he may both cut off that suspicion whereof this slander did arise, and in other things shall live more warily. And thus using ourselves we may take no hurt, but rather much good, by the rebukes and slanders of our enemy. For the reproach of an enemy may be to many men a quicker spur to the amendment of their life than the gentle monition of a friend. Philippus the king of Macedony[s], when he was evil spoken of by the chief rulers of the city of Athens[t], he did thank them heartily, because by them he was made better both in his words and deeds: "for I study," said[u] he, "both by my sayings and doings to prove them liars[v]."[5]

THE THIRD PART OF THE SERMON AGAINST[x] CONTENTION.

YE heard in the last lesson of the Sermon against strife and brawling, how we may answer them which maintain their froward sayings in contention, and that will revenge with words such evil as other men do to them[y]; and finally how we may according to God's will order ourselves, and what to consider towards them, when we are provoked to contention and strife[z] with railing words. Now, to proceed in the same matter, you shall know the right way how to disprove and overcome your adversary and enemy.[a]

This is the best way to improve[b][6] a man's adversary: so to live, that all which shall know his honesty may bear witness that he is slandered unworthily. If the fault whereof he is slandered be such that for the defence of his honesty he must needs make answer, yet[c] let him answer quietly and softly on

[r] shameful] contumelious *till* 1559. [s] Macedony] Macedones 1547 G 1. [t] Athens] Arthens 1559–1563. [u] said] saith *from* 1576. [v] liars] lies 1547 G 1. [x] AGAINST] OF 1549 G, 1551. [y] do to them] do them *from* 1582. [z] and strife] *added in* 1559. [a] THE THIRD PART ——and enemy.] *not in* 1547 *or* 1548, *the Homily not being then divided.* [b] improve] refel *till* 1559. [c] yet] *omitted after* 1569.

5 See *Plutarch. Apophthegm. Regg. et Ducc., Philipp. Alex. Patr.* VII, *p.* 177 E.
6 to improve: to disprove, a literal rendering of *improbare.*

this fashion, that those faults be laid against him falsely. For it is truth that the Wise Man saith: *A soft answer assuageth anger, and a hard and sharp answer doth stir up rage and fury.* The sharp answer of Nabal[ξ] did provoke[d] David to cruel vengeance; but the gentle words of Abigail quenched the fire again, that was all in a flame. And a special remedy against malicious tongues is to arm ourselves with patience, meekness, and silence; lest with multiplying words with the enemy we be made as evil as he.

Prov. xv, [1.]
ξ 1 Sam. xxv, [10–35.]

An objection[e].

But they that cannot bear one evil word, peradventure, for their own excuse[f] will allege that which is written: "He that despiseth his good name is cruel."[7] Also we read[o], *Answer a fool according to his foolishness.* And our Lord Jesus did hold his peace[π] at certain evil sayings, but to some he answered diligently. He heard men call him[ρ] *a Samaritan, a carpenter's son, a wine drinker,* and he held his peace: but, when he heard them say, *Thou hast a devil*[g] *within thee,* he answered to that earnestly.

o Prov. xxvi, [5.]
π John xix, [9.]
ρ [Matt. xi, 19; xiii, 55: John viii, 48.]

Answer[h].

Truth it is indeed, that there is a time when it is convenient to *answer*[τ] *a fool according to his foolishness, lest he should seem in his own conceit to be wise.* And sometime it is not profitable[υ] to *answer a fool according to his foolishness,* lest the wise man be made like to the fool. When our infamy (or the reproach that is done unto us[i]) is joined with the peril of many, then it is[k] necessary in answering to be quick and ready. For we read that many holy men of good zeals[l] have sharply and fiercely both spoken and answered tyrants and evil men; which sharp words came[m] not of anger, rancour, or malice, or desire[n] of vengeance, but of a fervent desire to bring them to the true knowledge of God and from ungodly living by an earnest and sharp rebuke[o] and chiding. In this zeal St. John Baptist called the Pharisees *adders' brood*[φ]*;* and St. Paul called the Galathians *fools*[χ]*;* and the men of Crete he called[ψ] *liars, evil beasts,* and *sluggish bellies;* and the false apostles he called[ω] *dogs* and *crafty workmen.* And this[p] zeal is godly and to be allowed, as

τ [Prov. xxvi, 5.]
υ [Ibid. 4.]
φ Matt. iii, [7.]
χ Gal. iii, [1.]
ψ Tit. i, [12.]
ω Phil. iii, [2.]

d did provoke] provoked *from* 1582. e An objection] Objection 1549 G, 1551, 1559. f excuse] excusation *till* 1559. g a devil] the devil *from* 1569. h Answer] An answer 1548, 1549 W, 1562–1574. i or the reproach that is done unto us] *added in* 1559. k then it is] then is it 1547 G 5–1563. l zeals] zeal 1623. m came] proceeded *till* 1559. n or desire] or appetite *till* 1559. o rebuke] objurgation *till* 1559. p And this] And his *from* 1582.

7 Qui, fidens conscientiae suae, negligit famam suam crudelis est. *Augustin. Serm.* 355 (al. *de Divers.* 49), *De Vit. et Mor. Cler.* I; *Opp.* V, 1380 B: cited by Gratian in *Decret.* II, xii, 1, c. 10 *Nolo.* Compare *Augustin. de Bono Viduitatis, cap.* XXII; *Opp.* VI, 384, 385.

it is plainly proved by the example of Christ; who, although he were the fountain and spring of all meekness, gentleness, and softness, yet he calleth[q] the obstinate Scribes and Pharisees[α] *blind guides, fools, painted graves, hypocrites, serpents, adders' brood, a corrupt and wicked generation.* Also he rebuketh Peter eagerly, saying[β], *Go behind me, Satan.* Likewise St. Paul reproveth Elymas, saying[γ], *O thou full of all craft and guile, enemy to all justice, thou ceasest not to destroy the right ways of God: and now, lo, the hand of the Lord is upon thee, and thou shalt be blind, and not see for a time.* Also St. Peter[r] reprehendeth Ananias very sharply, saying[δ], *Ananias, how is it that Satan hath filled thy heart, that thou shouldest lie unto the[s] Holy Ghost?*

α Matt. xxiii, [16–33; xii, 39.]
β Matt. xvi, [23.]
γ Acts xiii, [10, 11.]
δ Acts v, [3.]

This zeal hath been so fervent in many good men, that it hath stirred them not only to speak bitter and eager words, but also to do things which might seem to some to be crnel; but indeed they be very just, charitable, and godly, because they were not done of ire, malice, or contentious mind, but, of a fervent mind to the glory of God and the correction of sin, executed by men called to that office. For in this zeal our Lord Jesus Christ did drive[ε] with a whip the buyers and sellers out of the temple. In this zeal Moses brake the two tables[ζ] which he had received at God's hand, when he saw the Israelites dancing about a calf[t], and caused to be killed twenty and three[u] thousand of his own people[8]. In this zeal Phinees the son of Eleazar did thrust through[η] with his sword[9] Zambri and Cozbi, whom he found together joined in the act of lechery[x].

ε John ii, [15.]
ζ Exod. xxxii, [15–19, 27, 28.]
η Numb. xxv, [8, 14, 15.]

But these examples are not to be followed of every body, but as men be called to office, and set in authority.

Wherefore now to return again to contentious words, and specially in matters of religion and God's word, which would be used with all modesty, soberness, and charity[y], the words of St. James ought to be well marked and borne in memory, where he saith[θ] that of contention riseth all evil. And the wise King Solomon saith, *Honour is due to a man that keepeth himself from contention, and all that mingle themselves therewith be fools.* And, because this vice is so much hurtful to the society of a commonwealth, in all well ordered cities these common brawlers

θ James iii, [16.]
Prov. xx, [3.]

q calleth] called *from* 1563. r Also St. Peter] And St. Peter *from* 1547 G 5. s unto the] upon the 1559. t a calf] the calf *from* 1582. u twenty and three] *so* 1549 G *and* 1551; xxiii. 1547, 1548, 1549 W, 1559, 1562 A, 1563, 1569; xxiiii. 1562 B, *and from* 1574. x lechery] uncleanness 1623. y charity] chastity *from* 1569.

8 Feceruntque filii Levi juxta sermonem Moysi, cecideruntque in die illa quasi viginti (*al.* triginta) tria millia hominum. *Exod.* XXXII, 28, *Vulg.*

9 Arrepto pugione. *Vulg.*

and scolders be punished with a notable kind of pain, as to be set on the cucking stool, pillory[10], or such like. And they be unworthy to live in a commonwealth the which do as much as lieth in them with brawling and scolding to disturb the quietness and peace of the same. And whereof cometh this contention, strife, and variance, but of pride and vainglory? Let us therefore *humble*[ι] *ourselves under the mighty hand of God*, which hath promised to rest upon them that be humble and low in spirit[κ]. If we be good and quiet Christian men, let it appear in our speech and tongues. If we have forsaken the devil, let us use no more devilish tongues. He that hath been a railing scolder, now let him be a sober counsellor. He that hath been a malicious slanderer, now let him be a loving comforter. He that hath been a vain railer, now let him be a ghostly teacher. He that hath abused his tongue in cursing, now let him use it in blessing. He that hath abused his tongue in evil speaking, now let him use it in speaking well. *All bitterness*[λ], *anger, railing, and blasphemy, let it be avoided from you.* If you may, and it be[11] possible, in no wise be angry. But, if you may not be clean void of this passion, then yet so temper and bridle it, that it stir you not to contention and brawling. If you be provoked with evil speakiug, arm yourself with patience, lenity, and silence; either speaking nothing, or else being very soft, meek, and gentle in answering. Overcome thine adversaries[z] with benefits and gentleness. And above all things keep peace and unity: be no peace breakers, but peace makers. And then there is no doubt but that God, the Author of comfort and peace, will grant us peace of conscience, and such concord and agreement, *that with one mouth*[μ] *and mind we may glorify God, the Father of our Lord Jesus Christ.* To whom be all glory now and ever[a]. Amen.

ι 1 Pet. v, [6.]
κ Luke i, [52: Is. lvii, 15.]
λ [Eph. iv, 31.]
μ [Rom. xv, 6.]

z adversaries] adversary *from* 1582.
a and ever] and for ever *from* 1582.

10 The Cucking Stool, though obsolete, is still a legal instrument for punishing scolds. There is an excellent article upon it, written by F. A. Carrington, Esq., in the *Wiltshire Archaeological Magazine, vol.* 1, *p.* 68. See also the note on "Kukstole" in Mr. Albert Way's edition of the *Promptorium Parvulorum*.

The punishment of the Pillory was abolished by Act of Parliament in 1837. There is a very good article upon it in the *Penny Magazine*.

11 and it be: an it be, if it be.

HEREAFTER shall follow Sermons[b] of Fasting, Praying, Alms[c] deeds; of the Nativity, Passion, Resurrection, and Ascension of our Saviour Christ; of the due receiving of his blessed body and blood under the form of bread and wine; against Idleness, against Gluttony and Drunkenness, against Covetousness, against Envy, Ire, and Malice; with many other matters as well fruitful as necessary to the edifying of Christian people and the increase of godly living. Amen.[d]

GOD SAVE THE QUEEN[e].

[b] Sermons] Homilies *till* 1549 W. [c] Alms] Almose *all Grafton's editions*, Almese 1559–1569.
[d] Amen.] *omitted after* 1569. [e] QUEEN] KING 1547–1551, 1623.

The Second Tome

of Homilies,

of such matters as were promised and intituled

in the former part of Homilies:

set out by the authority of the Queen's[a] Majesty,

and to be read in every Parish Church

agreeably.

[a] the Queen's] the late Queen's 1623.

AN ADMONITION

TO ALL MINISTERS ECCLESIASTICAL[a].

FOR that the Lord doth require of his *servant whom he hath set over his household* to shew both faithfulness and prudence in his office, it shall be necessary that ye, above all other, do behave yourself[b] most faithfully and diligently in your so high a function; that is, aptly, plainly, and distinctly to read the sacred Scriptures, diligently to instruct the youth in their Catechism, gravely and reverently to minister his most holy Sacraments, prudently also to choose out such Homilies as be most meet for the time and for the more agreeable instruction of the people committed to your charge, with such discretion, that where the Homily may appear too long for one reading, to divide the same to be read part in the forenoon and part in the afternoon. And, where it may so chance some one or other chapter of the Old Testament to fall in order to be read upon the Sundays or Holy Days which were better to be changed with some other of the New Testament of more edification[1], it shall be well done to spend your time to consider well of such chapters beforehand, whereby your prudence and diligence in your office may appear; so that your people may have cause to glorify God for you, and be the readier to embrace your labours, to your better commendation, to the discharge of your consciences and their own.

[Matt. xxiv, 45.]

[a] AN ADMONITION &c.] *The Admonition is not in* 1563 A 1. [b] yourself] yourselves *from* 1582.

1 See *Cardwell's Documentary Annals, No.* LV, *vol.* I, *p.* 260, *ed.* 1839: *History of Conferences, ch.* I, *note* t, *p.* 31, *ed.* 1840.

THE TABLE OF HOMILIES ENSUING.[a]

I. Of[b] the right use of the Church, &c.[c]

II. Against peril of Idolatry. Three Parts.[d]

III. For repairing and keeping clean the Church.

IV. Of Good Works. And first of Fasting. Two Parts.[e]

V. Against Gluttony and Drunkenness.

VI. Against excess of Apparel.

VII. An Homily of Prayer. Three Parts.

VIII. Of the place and time of Prayer. Two Parts.

IX. Of Common Prayer and Sacraments.

X. An Information for them[f] which take offence at certain places of holy Scripture. Two Parts.

XI. Of Alms deeds. Three Parts.

XII. Of the Nativity.

XIII. Of the Passion. For Good Friday. Two Homilies.

XIV. Of the Resurrection. For Easter Day.

XV. Of the worthy receiving of the Sacrament. Two Parts.

XVI. An Homily concerning the coming down of the Holy Ghost. For Whitsunday. Two Parts.

XVII. An Homily for Rogation Week. Four[g] Parts.

XVIII. Of the state of Matrimony.

XIX. Against Idleness.

XX. Of Repentance and true reconciliation unto God. Three Parts.

XXI. An Homily against Disobedience and wilful Rebellion. Six Parts.[h]

[a] THE TABLE &c.] *The Table is on the back of the Title, and of course precedes the Admonition, after* 1563. [b] Of] First, Of 1563. [c] &c.] *omitted after* 1563 F. [d] Three Parts.] *The number of Parts in a Homily is not stated in* 1623. [e] Two Parts.] *not in* 1563 A, *the Homily not being divided at first.* [f] for them] of them *from* 1582. [g] Four] Three 1574–1595. [h] XXI. An Homily——Six Parts.] *not in the Table till* 1571.

AN HOMILY

OF THE RIGHT USE OF THE CHURCH OR TEMPLE OF GOD, AND OF THE REVERENCE DUE UNTO THE SAME.

THE FIRST PART[a].

WHERE there appeareth at these days great slackness and negligence of a great sort of people in resorting to the church, there to serve God their heavenly Father according to their most bounden duty; as also much uncomely and unreverent behaviour of many persons in the same, when they be there assembled; and thereby may just fear arise of the wrath of God and his dreadful plagues hanging over our heads for our grievous offence[b] in this behalf, amongst other many and great sins which we daily and hourly commit before the Lord: therefore, for the discharge of all our consciences and the[c] avoiding of the common peril and plague hanging over us, let us consider what may be said out of God's holy book concerning this matter; whereunto I pray you give good audience, for that it is of great weight, and concerneth you all.

Although the eternal and incomprehensible Majesty of God, the *Lord of heaven and earth*[α], whose *seat is heaven and the earth his footstool,* cannot be enclosed *in temples* or houses *made with* man's *hand,* as in dwellingplaces able to receive or contain his Majesty; (according as is evidently declared of[d] the Prophet Esay[β], and by the doctrine of St. Stephen and St. Paul in the Acts of the Apostles, and where king Salomon, who builded unto the Lord the most glorious temple that ever was made, saith[γ], *Who shall be able to build a meet or worthy house for him? if heaven, and the heaven above all heavens, cannot contain him, how much less can that which I have builded!* and further confesseth, *What am I, that I should be able to build thee an house, O Lord? but yet*[1] *for this purpose only it is made that*

α [Matt. xi, 25.]

β Isai. lxvi, [1:] Acts vii, [48, 49;] and xvii, [24.]

γ 1 Kings viii, [27:] 2 Chron. ii, [6;] and vi, [18, 19.]

a PART] CHAPTER *from* 1582. b offence] offences *from* 1563 B. c and the] and for the *from* 1567, *except* 1574. d declared of] declared by *from* 1567.

1 Sed ad hoc tantum facta est, ut respicias orationem servi tui et obsecrationem ejus. 2 *Paralip.* VI, 19, *Vulg.*

thou mayest regard the prayer of thy servant and his humble supplication; much less then be our churches meet dwellingplaces to receive the incomprehensible Majesty of God:) and indeed the chief and special temples of God, wherein he hath greatest pleasure, and most delighteth to dwell and continue in, are the bodies and minds of true Christians and the chosen people of God; (according to the doctrine of the holy Scripture, declared 1 Cor. iii, [16, 17.] in the first Epistle to the Corinthians: *Know ye not,* saith St. Paul, *that ye be the temple of God, and that the Spirit of God doth dwell*[e] *in you? if any man defile the temple of God, him will God destroy; for the temple of God is holy, which ye are:* and Ibid. vi, [19, 20.] again in the same Epistle: *Know ye not that your body is the temple of the Holy Ghost dwelling in you, whom ye have given you of God, and that ye be not your own? for ye be dearly*[f] *bought: glorify ye now therefore God in your body and in your spirit, which are God's:*) and therefore, as our Saviour Christ teacheth John iv, [23, 24.] in the Gospel of St. John, they that *worship* God *the Father in spirit and truth,* in what place soever they do it, worship him aright; *for such worshippers doth* God *the Father look for: for God is a Spirit; and those which*[g] *worship him must worship him in Spirit and truth,* saith our Saviour Christ: yet, all this notwithstanding, the material church or temple is a place appointed, as well by the usage and continual examples expressed in the Old Testament as in the New, for the people of God to resort together unto, there to hear God's holy word, to call upon his holy Name, to give him thanks for his innumerable and unspeakable benefits bestowed upon us, and duly and truly to celebrate his holy Sacraments; in the unfeigned doing and accomplishing of the which standeth that true and right worshipping of God aforementioned. And the same church or temple is by the Scriptures[h], both of the Old Testament and the New[i], called the house and temple of the Lord, for the peculiar service there done to his Majesty by his people, and for the effectuous presence of his heavenly grace, wherewith he, by his said holy word, endueth his people so there assembled. And to the said house or temple of God, at times[k] by common order appointed, are all people that be godly indeed bound with all diligence to resort, unless by sickness or other most urgent causes they be letted therefro. And all the same so resorting

[e] doth dwell] dwelleth *from* 1563 B. [f] be dearly] are dearly *from* 1563 B. [g] those which] those that *from* 1567. [h] the Scriptures] the holy Scriptures 1623. [i] and the New] and New 1623. [k] at times] at all times *from* 1563 B. *See pp.* 159, 31; 160, 10; 165, 31; 167, 16.

thither ought with all quietness and reverence there to behave themselves in doing their bounden duty and service to Almighty God in the congregation of his saints. All which things are evident to be proved by God's holy word, as hereafter shall plainly appear.

And first of all I will declare by the Scriptures, that it is called, as it is indeed, *the house of God* and *temple of the Lord*. *He that sweareth by the temple*, saith our Saviour Christ, *sweareth by it, and him that dwelleth therein*, meaning God the Father: which he also expresseth plainly in the Gospel of St. John, saying, *Do not make the house of my Father the house of merchandise*. And in the book of the Psalms the Prophet David saith, *I will enter into thine house, I will worship in thy holy temple in thy fear*. And it is in almost[l] infinite places of the Scripture, specially in the Prophets and book of Psalms, called *the house of God*, or *the house*[m] *of the Lord*. Sometime it is named *the tabernacle*[δ] *of the Lord*[2]; and sometime *the sanctuary*[ε], that is to say, the holy house or place[n], *of the Lord*.

Matt. xxiii, [21.] John ii, [16.] Ps. v, [7.] δ Ps. cxxxi [cxxxii, 5, 7.] ε Exod. xxv, [8:] Levit. xix, [30.]

And it is in like wise[o] called *the house of prayer*. As Salomon, who builded the temple of the Lord at Jerusalem, doth oft[ζ] call it the house of the Lord in the which the Lord's name should be called upon. And Esay in the fifty-sixth[p] chapter: *My house shall be called the house of prayer amongst all nations*: which text our Saviour Christ allegeth in the New Testament, as doth appear in three of the Evangelists[η]. And in the parable of the Pharisee and the Publican which went to pray; in which parable our Saviour Christ saith[θ], they *went up into the temple to pray*. And Anna, the holy widow and prophetess, *served*[ι] *the Lord in fasting and prayer in the temple night and day*. And in the story of the Acts[κ] it is mentioned, how that *Peter and John went up into the temple at the hour of prayer*. And St. Paul[λ], praying in the temple at Jerusalem, was rapt in spirit[q], and did see Jesus speaking unto him. And, as in all convenient places prayer may be used of the godly privately, so is it[r] most certain that the church or temple is the due and appointed place for common and public prayer.

ζ 1 Kings viii, [29–49:] 2 Chron. ii, [4;] and vi, [10, 20–40.] Isai. lvi, [7.] η Matt. xxi, [13:] Mark xi, [17:] Luke xix, [46.] θ Luke xviii, [10.] ι Luke ii, [37.] κ Acts iii, [1.] λ Acts xxii, [17, 18.]

Now that it is likewise the place of thanksgiving unto the

[l] in almost] almost in *from* 1582. [m] or the house] or house *from* 1582. [n] house or place] place or house 1623. [o] is in like wise] is likewise *from* 1582. [p] fifty-sixth] *either* l. *or* 50 *in all except* 1571 *and* 1623. [q] in spirit] in the spirit *from* 1570. [r] so is it] so it is *from* 1563 B.

[2] Tabernaculum Deo Jacob. Introibimus in tabernaculum (*al.* tabernacula) ejus. *Psal.* CXXXI (CXXXII), 5, 7, *Vulg.*

Lord for his innumerable and unspeakable benefits bestowed upon us, appeareth notably in the latter end of the Gospel of St. Luke and the beginning of the story of the Acts; where it is written, that the Apostles and disciples, after the ascension of the Lord, *continued with one accord daily in the temple, always praising and blessing God.*

Luke xxiv, [53:] Acts ii, [46.]

And it is likewise declared in the first Epistle to the Corinthians, that the church is the due place appointed for the reverent[s] use of the Sacraments.

1 Cor. xi, [20–34.]

It remaineth now to be declared, that the church or temple is the place where the lively word of God (and not man's inventions) ought to be read and taught, and that the people are bound thither with all diligence to resort; and this proof likewise to be made by the Scriptures, as hereafter shall appear.

Acts xiii, [5, 14–41.]

In the story of the Acts of the Apostles we read, that Paul and Barnabas *preached the word of God in the temples of the Jews* at Salamin. And, when *they came to Antiochia, they entered on the sabbath day into the synagogue* or church, *and sat down; and after the lesson* or reading *of the Law and the Prophets, the ruler*[t] *of the temple sent unto them, saying, Ye men and brethren, if any of you have any exhortation to make unto the people, say it. And so Paul, standing up, and making silence with his hand, said, Ye men that be Israelites, and ye that fear God, give ear,* and so forth[u], preaching to them a sermon out of the Scriptures, as there at large appeareth. And in the same story of the Acts, the seventeenth chapter, is testified how Paul preached Christ *out of the Scriptures* at Thessalonica. And in the fifteenth chapter James the Apostle, in that holy council and assembly of his fellow Apostles, saith: *Moses of old time hath in every city certain that preach him in the synagogues* or temples, *where he is read every sabbath day.* By these places ye may see the usage of reading of the[v] Scriptures of the Old Testament among the Jews in their synagogues every sabbath day, and sermons usually made upon the same. How much more then is it convenient that the Scriptures of God, and specially the Gospel of our Saviour Christ, should be read and expounded to us, that be Christians, in our churches; specially our Saviour Christ and his Apostles allowing this most godly and necessary usage, and by their examples confirming[x] the same!

Ibid. xvii, [1–3.]

Ibid. xv, [21.]

It is written in the stories of the Gospels, in divers places[µ],

µ Matt. iv, [23;] ix, [35:]

[s] reverent] *omitted after* 1574. [t] ruler] *so in all.* [u] and so forth] &c. 1623. [v] reading of the] reading the 1623. [x] confirming] confirm 1623.

that *Jesus went round about all Galilee, teaching in their synagogues, and preaching the Gospel of the kingdom;* in which places is his great diligence in continual preaching and teaching of the people most evidently set forth. In Luke ye read[v] how Jesus, *according to his accustomed use, came into the temple,* and how *the book of Esay the Prophet was delivered him;* how he read a text therein, and made a sermon upon the same. And in the nineteenth is expressed how he taught daily in the temple. And it is thus written in the eighth of John: *Jesus came again early in the morning into the temple, and all the people came unto him, and he sat down and taught them.* And in the eighteenth of John our Saviour testifieth before Pilate, that he *spake openly unto the world,* and that he *always taught in the synagogue and in the temple, whither all the Jews resorted, and* that *secretly* he *spake nothing.* And in St. Luke: *Jesus taught in the temple, and all the people came early in the morning unto him, that they might hear him in the temple.* Here ye see, as well the diligence of our Saviour in teaching the word of God in the temple daily, and specially on the sabbath days, as also the readiness of the people resorting all together, and that early in the morning, into the temple to hear him.

Mark i, [14, 39:] Luke iv, [15, 44:] Matt. xiii, [54:] Mark vi, [2:] Luke xiii, [10.] v Luke iv, [16–22.] Ibid. xix, [47.] John viii, [2.] Ibid. xviii, [20.] Luke xxi, [37, 38.]

The same example of diligence in preaching the word of God in the temple shall ye find in the Apostles, and the people resorting unto them (Acts the fifth); how[y] the Apostles, although they had been whipped and scourged the day before, and by the high priest commanded that they should preach no more in the name of Jesus, yet the day following *they entered early in the morning into the temple,* and *did not cease to teach and declare Jesus Christ.* And in sundry other places of the story of the Acts ye shall find like diligence, both in the Apostles in teaching, and in the people in coming to the temple to hear God's word.

[Acts v, 21, 28, 40, 42.] Acts xiii; xv; xvii.

And it is testified in the first of Luke, that when Zachary, the holy priest, and father to John Baptist, did sacrifice within the temple, *all the people stood without a long time praying:* such was their zeal and fervency at that time. And in the second of Luke appeareth what great journeys men, women, yea, and children took, to come to the temple on the feast day, there to serve the Lord; and 'specially the example of Joseph, the blessed Virgin Mary, mother to our Saviour Christ[z], and of our Saviour Christ himself, being yet but a child; whose examples are wor-

Luke i, [9, 10.] Luke ii, [41–44.]

y ; how] . Where 1623. z to our Saviour Christ] to our Saviour Jesus Christ *from* 1567.

thy for us to follow. So that, if we would compare our negligence in resorting to the house of the Lord, there to serve him, to the[a] diligence of the Jews in coming daily, very early, sometime great[b] journeys, to their temple, and, when the multitude could not be received within the temple, the fervent zeal that they had, declared in standing long without and praying, we may justly in this comparison condemn our slothfulness and negligence, yea, plain contempt, in coming to the Lord's house (standing so near unto us) so seldom, and scarcely at noon[c] time; so far is it from a great many of us to come early in the morning, or give attendance without, who disdain to come into the temple. And yet we abhor the very name of the Jews, when we hear it, as of a most wicked and ungodly people. But it is to be feared, that in this point we be far worse than the Jews, and that they shall rise at the day of judgment to our condemnation, who, in comparison to them, shew such slackness and contempt in resorting to the house of the Lord, there to serve him, according as we are of duty most bound.

And, besides this most horrible dread of God's just judgment in the great day, we shall not in this life escape his heavy hand and vengeance for this contempt of the house of the Lord and his due service in the same, according as the Lord himself threateneth in the first chapter of his Prophet[d] Aggeus after this sort: *Because you have left my house desert and without company, saith the Lord, and ye have made haste every man to his own house; for this cause are the heavens stayed over you, that they should give no dew, and the earth is forbidden that it shall bring forth his fruit*[e]*; and I have called drought upon the earth, and upon the mountains, and upon corn, and upon wine, and upon oil, and upon all things that the earth bringeth forth, and upon men, and upon beasts, and upon all things that men's hands labour for.* Behold, if we be such worldlings that we care not for the eternal judgments of God, (which yet of all other are most dreadful and horrible,) we shall not escape the punishment of God in this world by drought and famine and the taking away of all worldly commodities, which we as worldlings seem only to regard and care for.

Hag. i, [9-11.]

Whereas, on the contrary part, if we would amend this fault of[f] negligence, slothfulness, and contempt of the house of the Lord and his due service there, and with diligence resort thither

[a] to the] with the 1623. [b] sometime great] sometime by great *from* 1582. [c] noon] none 1563 A–F, 1571; noone 1563 G—1570, 1574; any *from* 1582. [d] his Prophet] the Prophet 1623. [e] his fruit] her fruit 1623. [f] fault of] fault or *from* 1563 B.

together, to serve the Lord with one accord and consent in all holiness and righteousness before him, we have promises of benefits both heavenly and worldly. *Wheresoever two or three be* Matt. xviii, [20.]
gathered in my name, saith our Saviour Christ, *there am I in the middle*[g] *of them.* And what can be more blessed than to have our Saviour Christ amongst[h] us? Or what again can be more unhappy or mischievous than to drive our Saviour Christ from amongst us, and to[i] leave a place for his and our most ancient and mortal enemy, the old dragon and serpent, Satan the devil, in the middle[k] of us? In the second of Luke it is written, how Luke ii, [46.]
that the mother of Christ, and Joseph, when they had long sought Christ, whom they had lost, and could find him no where, that at the last *they found him in the temple, sitting in the middle*[l] *of the doctors.* So, if we lack Jesus Christ, that is to say, the Saviour of our souls and bodies, we shall not find him in the market place, or in the guild hall[m], much less in the alehouse or tavern amongst good fellows (as they call them), so soon as we shall find him in the temple, the Lord's house, amongst the teachers and preachers of his word, where indeed he is to be found. And as concerning worldly commodities, we have a sure Matt. vi, [33.]
promise of our Saviour Christ: *Seek ye first the kingdom of God and the righteousness thereof*[3], *and all these things shall withal be given unto you.*

And thus we have in the first part of this Homily declared by God's word, that the temple or church is the house of the Lord, for that the service of the Lord (as teaching and hearing of his holy word, calling upon his holy Name, giving thanks to him for his great and innumerable benefits, and due ministering of his Sacraments) is there used. And it is likewise declared already[n] by the Scriptures, how all godly and Christian men and women ought, at times appointed, with diligence to resort unto the house of the Lord, there to serve him and to glorify him, as he is most worthy and we most bound. To whom be all glory and honour world without end. Amen.

g, k, l middle] middest *from* 1567. h amongst] among *from* 1582. i us, and to] us, to *from* 1582. m guild hall] yelde hall 1563 A. n already] *omitted after* 1574.

3 Ζητεῖτε δὲ πρῶτον τὴν βασιλείαν τοῦ Θεοῦ καὶ τὴν δικαιοσύνην αὐτοῦ. Quaerite ergo primum regnum Dei et justitiam ejus. *Vulg.*

THE SECOND PART OF THE HOMILY

OF THE RIGHT USE OF THE CHURCH &c.[a]

IT was declared in the first part of this Homily by God's word, that the temple or church is the house of the Lord, for that the service of the Lord (as teaching and hearing of his holy word, calling upon his holy Name, giving thanks to him for his great and innumerable benefits, and due ministering of his Sacraments[b]) is there used. And it is likewise already declared by the Scriptures, how all godly and Christian men and women ought, at times appointed, with diligence to resort unto the house of the Lord, there to serve him and to glorify him, as he is most worthy and we most bounden. Now it remaineth, in this second part of the Homily concerning the right use of the temple of God, to be likewise declared by God's word, with what quietness, silence, and reverence those that resort to the house of the Lord ought there to use and behave themselves.

It may teach us sufficiently how well it doth become us Christian men reverently to use the church and holy house of our prayers, by considering in how great reverence and veneration the Jews in the old law had their temple; which appeareth by sundry places, whereof I will note unto you certain. In the twenty-sixth of Matthew it was laid[c] to our Saviour Christ's
Matt. xxvi, [61.] charge before a temporal[d] judge, as a matter worthy death, by the two false witnesses, that he had said he could destroy the temple of God, and in three days build it again; not doubting but, if they might make men to believe that he had said any thing against the honour and majesty of the temple, he should seem to all men most worthy of death. And in the twenty-first
Acts xxi, [27, 28.] of the Acts, when the Jews found Paul in the temple, they *laid hands upon him, crying, Ye men Israelites, help: this is that man who teacheth all men every where against the people and the law and against this place; besides that, he hath brought the Gentiles into the temple, and hath profaned this holy place.* Behold how they took it for a like offence to speak against the temple of God, as to speak against the law of God; and how they judged it convenient that none but godly persons and the true worship-

[a] OF THE RIGHT USE OF THE CHURCH &c.] *not in* 1563 A: &c. *omitted after* 1563. [b] his Sacraments] the Sacraments *from* 1567. [c] was laid] is laid *from* 1582. [d] temporal] *so in all.*

pers of God should enter into the temple of God. And the same fault is laid to Paul's charge by Tertullus, an eloquent man, and by the Jews, in the twenty-fourth of the Acts, before a temporal judge, as a matter worthy death[e], that he *went about* Acts xxiv,[6.] *to pollute the temple* of God. And in the twenty-seventh of Matthew, when the chief priests had received again the pieces of silver at Judas' hand, they said, *It is not lawful to put them* Matt. xxvii, [6.] *into Corban,* (which was the treasure house of the temple,) *because it is the price of blood.* So that they could not abide that not only any unclean person, but also any other dead thing that was judged unclean, should once come into the temple or any place thereto belonging.

And to this end is St. Paul's saying in the second Epistle to the Corinthians, the sixth chapter, to be applied: *What fellow-* 2 Cor. vi, [14–16.] *ship is there betwixt righteousness and unrighteousness? or what communion between light and darkness? or what concord between Christ and Belial? or what part can the faithful have with the unfaithful? or what agreement can there be between the temple of God and images?* Which sentence, although it be chiefly referred to the temple of the mind of the godly, yet, seeing that the similitude and pith of the argument is taken from the material temple, it enforceth that no ungodliness, specially of images or idols, may be suffered in the temple of God, which is the place of worshipping God, and therefore can no more be suffered to stand there, than light can agree with darkness, or Christ with Belial; for that the true worshipping of God and the worshipping of images are most contrary, and the setting of them up in the place of worshipping may give great occasion to the worshipping of them.

But to return[f] to the reverence that the Jews had to their temple. You will say they[g] honoured it superstitiously and a great deal too much, crying out, *The temple of the Lord, The* Jer. vii, [1–15.] *temple of the Lord,* being notwithstanding most wicked in life, and be therefore most justly reproved of Jeremy, the Prophet of the Lord. Truth it is, that they were superstitiously given to the honouring of their temple. But I would we were not as far too short from the due reverence of the Lord's house, as they overshot themselves therein. And, if the Prophet justly reprehended them, hearken also what the Lord requireth at our hands, that we may know whether we be blameworthy or no.

[e] worthy death] worthy of death 1623. [f] return] turn *from* 1567. [g] say they] say that they *from* 1582.

Eccles. iv, [17, v, 1, *Vulg.*, but v, 1, 2, *Eng. Vers.*]

It is written in Ecclesiastes, the fourth chapter: *When thou dost enter into the house of God*, saith he[1], *take heed to thy feet; draw near that thou mayest hear: for obedience is much more worth than the sacrifice of fools, which know not what evil they do. Speak nothing rashly there, neither let thine heart be swift to utter words before God: for God is in heaven, and thou art upon the earth; therefore let thy words be few.* Note, well-beloved, what quietness in gesture and behaviour, what silence in talk and words, is required in *the house of God*, for so he calleth it. See whether they *take heed to their feet* (as they be here warned) which never cease from uncomely walking and jetting[2] up and down and overthwart the church[3], shewing an evident signification of notable contempt both of God and all good men there present: and what heed they take to their tongues and speech which do not only *speak words swiftly and rashly before the Lord*, (which they be here forbidden,) but also oftentimes speak filthily, covetously, and ungodly, talking of matters scarce honest or fit for the alehouse or tavern in the house of the Lord; little considering that they speak *before God*, who dwelleth *in heaven*, (as is here declared,) when they be but vermins here creeping *upon the earth* in comparison to his eternal Majesty; and less regarding that they must *give an account at the great day of every idle word*[a], wheresoever it be spoken, much more of filthy, unclean, or wicked words spoken in the Lord's house to the great dishonour of his Majesty and offence of all that hear them.

a Matt. xii, [36.]

And indeed, concerning the people and multitude, the temple is prepared for them to be hearers rather than speakers; considering that as well the word of God is there read or taught, whereunto they are bound to give diligent ear with all reverence and silence, as also that common prayer and thanksgiving are rehearsed and said by the public minister in the name of the people and the whole multitude present, whereunto they giving their ready audience should assent, and should say[h] *Amen*, as St. Paul teacheth in the first Epistle to the Corinthians; and in another place[β], *Glorifying God with one spirit and mouth*, which cannot be when every man and woman, in severate[i] pretence of

1 Cor. xiv, [16.]

β [Rom. xv, 6.]

h and should say] and say *from* 1567.   i severate] severat 1567–1571, severall *from* 1574.

1 Custodi pedem tuum ingrediens domum Dei, et appropinqua ut audias: multo enim melior est obedientia quam stultorum victimae, qui nesciunt quid faciunt mali. *Eccles.* IV, 17, *Vulg.*

2 jetting: strutting.

3 See *Cardwell's Documentary Annals, No.* LXI, *vol.* I, *p.* 277, 20–30.

devotion, prayeth privately, one asking, another giving thanks, another reading doctrine, and forceth not[k] to hear[4] the common prayer of the minister. And peculiarly, what due reverence is to be used in the ministering of the Sacraments in the temple, the same St. Paul teacheth in his Epistle[l] to the Corinthians, rebuking such as did unreverently use themselves in that behalf. *Have ye not houses to eat and drink in?* saith 1 Cor. xi, [22.] he. *Do ye despise the Church* or congregation *of God? What shall I say to you? Shall I praise you? In this I praise you not.*

And God requireth not only this outward reverence of behaviour and silence in his house, but all inward reverence in cleansing of the thoughts of our hearts; threatening by his Prophet Ose, in the ninth chapter, that *for the malice of the inven-* Hosea ix, [15.] *tions*[5] and devices of the people he *will cast them out of his house;* whereby is also signified the eternal casting of them out of his heavenly house and kingdom, which is most horrible. And therefore in the nineteenth of Leviticus God saith, *Fear* Lev. xix, [30.] *you with reverence my sanctuary, for I am the Lord.* And according to the same the Prophet David saith, *I will enter into* Ps. v, [7.] *thine house, I will worship in thy holy temple in thy fear;* shewing what inward reverence and humbleness of mind the godly men ought to have in the house of the Lord.

And to allege somewhat concerning this matter out of the New Testament, in what honour God would have his house or temple kept, and that by the example of our Saviour Christ,

k forceth not] not regarding 1623.

l in his Epistle] *omitted after* 1574.

4 forceth not to hear: does not care to hear, thinks the hearing of no force or importance, allows no force to the hearing. "No force," meaning *No matter*, and "to do" or "yeve (give) no force," meaning *to care nothing*, are forms of expression which occur several times in Chaucer, having their origin perhaps in a rare French phrase, which has long been obsolete.

De fruit avoir ne fait-il force,

or, as the older editions give the line,

Que de fruit avoir ne fait force,

(*Le Roman de la Rose*, 4401 *ed.* 1814, but 4491 *ed.* 1735), is rendered by Chaucer,

Fruicte to get
They yeve no force.

The Romaunt of the Rose, 4825, 6. But he does not use the verb, to force, in this sense. It occurs three times in the Homilies, once (p. 169, l. 7) impersonally, "It forceth not, whether"—. Jamieson, under "Fors," gives instances of its use in Scottish writers; and our lexicographers, from Johnson downwards, cite from Camden, "I force not of such fooleries." Shakespeare also has it in *Love's Labour Lost*, v, 2:

Your oath once broke, you force not to forswear.

But it must have become obsolete before the end of the reign of James I, for each of the three places in which it is printed in this volume was altered in the edition of 1623.

5 Propter malitiam adinventionum eorum de domo mea ejiciam eos. *Vulg.*

whose authority ought of good reason with all true Christians to be of most weight and estimation. It is written of all the four Evangelists[γ], as a notable act, and worthy to be testified by many holy witnesses, how that our Saviour Jesus Christ, that merciful and mild Lord, compared for his meekness to a sheep[δ] suffering with silence his fleece to be shorn from him, and to a lamb led without resistance to the slaughter, which[ε] *gave his body to them that did smite him*, answered not him that reviled, *nor turned away his face from them that did reproach him and spit upon him*[6], and according to his own example gave precepts[ζ] of mildness and sufferance to his disciples, yet, when he seeth the temple and holy house of his heavenly Father misordered, polluted, and profaned, useth great severity and sharpness, overturneth the tables of the exchangers, subverteth the seats of them that sold doves, maketh a whip of cords and scourgeth out those wicked abusers and profaners of the temple of God, saying, *My house shall be called the house of prayer, but ye have made it a den of thieves;* and in the second of John, *Do not ye make the house of my Father the house of merchandise.* For, as it is the house of God when God's service is duly done in it, so, when we wickedly abuse it with wicked talk or covetous bargaining, we make it a den of thieves or house[m] of merchandise. Yea, and such reverence would Christ should be shewed[n] therein, that *he would not suffer any vessel to be carried through the temple.* And, whereas our Saviour Christ (as is before mentioned out of St. Luke) could be found no where, when he was sought, but only in the temple amongst the doctors, and now again exerciseth[o] his authority and jurisdiction, not in castles and princely palaces amonges[p] soldiers, but in the temple, ye may hereby understand in what place his spiritual kingdom, which he denieth to be *of this world*[η], is soonest to be found and best to be known of all places in this world.

γ Matt. xxi, [12, 13:] Mark xi, [15, 17:] Luke xix, [45, 46:] John ii, [15.]
δ Is. liii, [7:] Acts viii, [32.]
ε Is. l, [6:] 1 Pet. ii, 23.]
ζ Matt. v, [38-48.]
John ii, [16.]
Mark xi, [16.]
[Luke ii, 46.]
η [John xviii, 36.]

And, according to this example of our Saviour Christ, in the primitive Church (which was most holy and godly, and in the which due discipline with severity was used against the wicked) open offenders were not suffered once to enter into the house of the Lord, nor admitted to common prayer and the use of the

m or house] or an house *from* 1570. n shewed] *omitted after* 1563 A. o again exerciseth] again he exerciseth 1623. p amonges] amongst *from* 1563 B.

6 Corpus meum dedi percutientibus .... : faciem meam non averti ab increpantibus et conspuentibus. *Isai.* L, 6, *Vulg.*

holy Sacraments with other true Christians, until they had done open penance before the whole Church. And this was practised not only upon mean persons, but also upon the rich, noble, and mighty persons, yea, upon Theodosius, that puissant and mighty Emperor, whom, for committing* a grievous and wilful murder, St. Ambrose, bishop of Millain, reproved sharply, and† did also excommunicate the said Emperor, and brought him to open penance[7]. And they that were so justly exempted and banished (as it were) from the house of the Lord were taken (as they be indeed) for men divided and separated from Christ's Church[8] and in most dangerous estate, yea, as St. Paul saith[θ], even *given unto Satan* the devil for a time; and their company was shunned and avoided of all godly men and women, until such time as they by repentance and public penance were reconciled. Such was the honour of the Lord's house in men's hearts and outward reverence also at that time; and so horrible a thing was it to be shut out of the church and house of the Lord in those days, when religion was most pure, and nothing so corrupt as it hath been of late days. And yet we willingly either, by absenting ourselves from the house of the Lord, do, as it were, excommunicate ourselves from the Church and fellowship of the saints of God; or else, coming thither, by uncomely and unreverent behaviour there, by hasty, rash, yea, unclean and wicked thoughts and words before the Lord our God, horribly dishonour his holy house, the Church of God, and his holy Name and Majesty, to the great danger of our souls, yea, and certain damnation also, if we do not speedily and earnestly repent us of this wickedness.

Chrysostom.

θ 1 Cor. v, [5: 1 Tim. i, 20.]

Thus ye have heard, dearly beloved, out of God's word, what reverence is due to the holy house of the Lord, how all godly persons ought with diligence at times appointed thither to repair, how they ought to behave themselves there with reverence

* The people's fault was most grievous: the sentence executed otherwise and more cruel than it should. *Marginal note* 1623. † He was only dehorted from receiving the Sacrament, until by Repentance he might be better prepared. *Marginal note* 1623.

7 See *Ambros. Epist.* 51, and *De Obitu Theodos.* § 34; *Opp.* II, 997–1001, 1207 A: *Sozom. Hist. Eccles.* VII, 25: *Theodoret. Hist. Eccles.* V, 17, 18.

8 The word "Chrysostom" in the margin stands against this sentence in all the early editions. The passage intended may perhaps be the opening of *Chrysost. De Dav. et Saul. Hom.* III, *Opp.* IV, 768–771, but it does not contain all the statements of this sentence. It would fit very well with the first sentence of this paragraph.

If the reference stood against the beginning of the second sentence, the passage might be the noble address to the clergy as ministrants of the Sacrament of the Lord's Supper, *κἂν στρατηγός τις ᾖ κ.τ.λ.*, in *Hom.* LXXXII (*al.* LXXXIII) *in Matth.*, *Opp.* VII, 789 C.

and dread before the Lord, what plagues and punishments, as well temporal as eternal, the Lord in his holy word threateneth, as well to such as neglect to come to his holy house, as also to such who, coming thither, do unreverently by gesture[q] or talk there behave themselves. Wherefore, if we desire to have seasonable weather, and thereby to enjoy the good fruits of the earth; if we will avoid drought and barrenness, thirst and hunger, which are plagues threatened unto such as make haste to go to their own houses[ι], to alehouses, and to taverns[r], and leave the house of the Lord empty and desolate; if we abhor to be scourged, not with whips made of cords out of the material temple only (as our Saviour Christ served the defilers of the house of God in Jerusalem), but also to be beaten and driven out of the eternal temple and house of the Lord (which is his heavenly kingdom) with the iron rod of everlasting damnation, and *cast into outward*[s] *darkness*[κ], *where is weeping and gnashing of teeth;* if we fear, dread, and abhor this, I say, as we have most just cause so[t] to do, then let us amend this our negligence and contempt in coming to the house of the Lord, this our unreverent behaviour in the house of the Lord; and, resorting thither diligently together, let us there, with reverent hearing of the Lord's holy word, calling on the Lord's holy Name, giving of hearty thanks unto the Lord for his manifold and inestimable benefits daily and hourly bestowed upon us, celebrating also reverently of the[u] Lord's holy Sacraments, serve the Lord in his holy house, as becometh the servants of the Lord, *in holiness*[λ] *and righteousness before him all the days of our life:* and then we shall be assured after this life to *rest in his holy hill*[μ], and to *dwell in his tabernacle*, there to *praise* and magnify *his* holy *Name in the congregation of his saints*[ν], in the holy house of his eternal kingdom of heaven[ξ], which he hath purchased for us by the death and shedding of the precious blood of his Son our Saviour Jesus Christ. To whom with the Father and the Holy Ghost, one immortal Majesty of[x] God, be all honour, glory, praise, and thanksgiving world without end. Amen.

ι [Hag. i, 9–11.]
κ [Matt. viii, 12; xxii, 13; xxv, 30.]
λ [Luke i, 75.]
μ Ps. [xv, 1.]
ν [Ps. cxlix, 1, 3.]
ξ Eph. [ii, 21;] iii, [21.]

q gesture] iesture 1563–1574. r and to taverns] and taverns 1623. s outward] outter 1571, utter *from* 1574. t so] *omitted after* 1563 A. u reverently of the] reverently the 1623. x Majesty of] *omitted* 1623.

AN HOMILY

AGAINST PERIL OF IDOLATRY AND SUPERFLUOUS DECKING OF CHURCHES.

THE FIRST PART.

IN what points the true ornaments of the church or temple of God do consist and stand, hath been declared in the two last Homilies, intreating of the right use of the temple or house of God, and of the due reverence that all true Christian people are bound to give unto the same. The sum whereof is, that the church or house of God is a place appointed by the holy Scriptures, where the lively word of God ought to be read, taught, and heard, the Lord's holy Name called upon by public prayer, hearty thanks given to his Majesty for his infinite and unspeakable benefits bestowed upon us, his holy Sacraments duly and reverently ministered; and that therefore all that be godly indeed ought both with diligence at times appointed to repair together to the said church, and there with all reverence to use and behave themselves before the Lord; and that the said church, thus godly used by the servants of the Lord in the Lord's true service, for the effectuous[a] presence of God's grace (wherewith he doth by his holy word and promises endue his people there present and assembled, to the attainment as well of commodities worldly, necessary for us, as also of all heavenly gifts and life everlasting), is called by the word of God (as it is indeed) *the temple of the Lord* and *the house of God;* and that therefore the due reverence thereof is stirred up in the hearts of the godly by the consideration of these true ornaments of the said house of God, and not by any outward ceremonies or costly and glorious decking of the said house or temple of the Lord. Contrary to the which most manifest doctrine of the Scriptures, and contrary to the usage of the primitive Church, which was most pure and uncorrupt, and contrary to the sentences and judgments of the most ancient, learned, and godly doctors of the Church (as hereafter shall appear), the corruption of these latter days hath brought into the church infinite multitudes of images; and the same, with other parts of the temple also, have[b]

[a] effectuous] effectual 1623. [b] have] *so in all.*

decked with gold and silver, painted with colours, set them with stone and pearl, clothed them with silks and precious vestures, phantasing[c] untruly that to be the chief decking and adorning of the temple or house of God, and that all people should be the more moved to the due reverence of the same, if all corners thereof were glorious and glistering with gold and precious stones: whereas indeed they by the said images and such glorious decking of the temple have nothing at all profited such as were wise and of understanding; but have thereby greatly hurt the simple and unwise, occasioning them thereby to commit most horrible idolatry, and the covetous persons, by the same occasion, seeming to worship, and peradventure worshipping indeed, not only the images, but also the matter of them, gold and silver, as that vice is of all others in the Scriptures peculiarly called *idolatry*[α] or worshipping of images.

α Eph. v, [5:] Col. iii, [5.]

Against the which foul abuses and great enormities shall be alleged unto you, first, the authority of God's holy word, as well out of the Old Testament as of the New; and, secondly, the testimonies of the holy and ancient learned fathers and doctors, out of their own works and ancient histories ecclesiastical; both that you may at once know their judgments, and withal understand what manner of ornaments were in the temples in the primitive Church in those times which were most pure and sincere: thirdly, the reasons and arguments made for the defence of images or idols and the outrageous decking of temples and churches with gold, silver, pearl, and precious stone shall be confuted, and so this whole matter concluded.

But, lest any should take occasion by the way of doubting by words or names, it is thought good here to note first of all, that, although in common speech we use to call the likeness or similitudes of men or other things images, and not idols, yet the Scriptures use the said two words, *idols* and *images*, indifferently for one thing alway. They be words of diverse tongues and sounds, but one in sense and signification in the Scriptures. The one is taken of the Greek word εἴδωλον[d], an idol, and the other of the Latin word Imago, an image; and so both used as English terms in the translating of Scriptures indifferently, according as the Septuaginta have in their translation in Greek εἴδωλα, and St. Hierome in his translation of the same places in Latin hath Simulacra, in English *images*. And, in the New Testament, that which St. John calleth εἴδωλον[β] St. Hierome like-

β 1 John v, [21.]

[c] phantasing] fancying 1623.

[d] word εἴδωλον] word εἴδωλα *from* 1574.

wise translateth Simulacrum, as in all other like places of Scripture usually he doth so translate. And Tertullian, a most ancient doctor, and well learned in both the tongues, Greek and Latin, interpreting this place of St. John, *Beware of idols,* "that is to say," saith Tertullian, "of the images themselves," the Latin words which he useth be Effigies and Imago[1], to say, an image. And therefore it forceth[e] not[2], whether in this process we use the one term or the other, or both together, seeing they both (though not in common English speech, yet in Scripture) signify one thing. And though some, to blind men's eyes, have heretofore craftily gone about to make them to be taken for words of diverse signification in matters of religion, and have therefore usually named the likeness or similitude of a thing set up amongst the heathen in their temples or other places to be worshipped an Idol, but the like similitude with us set up in the church, the place of worshipping, they call an Image; as though these two words, *idol* and *image,* in Scripture did differ in propriety and sense, which (as is aforesaid) differ only in sound and language, and in meaning be indeed all one, specially in the Scriptures and matters of religion; and our images also have been, and be, and, if they be publicly suffered in churches and temples, ever will be also worshipped, and so idolatry committed to them, as in the last part of this Homily shall at large be declared and proved: wherefore our images in temples and churches be indeed none other but idols, as unto the which idolatry hath been, is, and ever will be committed.

Lib. de Corona Militis.

And, first of all, the Scriptures of the Old Testament, condemning and abhorring as well all idolatry or worshipping of images, as also the very idols or images themselves, specially in temples, are so many and plentiful, that it were almost an infinite work, and to be contained in no small volume, to record all the places concerning the same. For, when God had chosen to himself a peculiar and special people from amongst all other nations, that knew not God, but worshipped idols and false gods, he gave unto them certain ordinances and laws to be kept and observed of his said people: but concerning none other matter did he give either mo, or more earnest and express, laws to his said people, than those that concerned the true worshipping of him, and the avoiding and fleeing of idols and images

e forceth] skilleth 1623.

1 See note 2 on the Second Part of this Homily.
2 it forceth not: it is of no force or importance. See before, p. 163, n. 4.

and idolatry; for that, that both[f] the said idolatry is most repugnant to the right worshipping of him and his true glory above all other vices, and that he knew the proneness and inclination of man's corrupt kind and nature to that most odious and abominable vice. Of the which ordinances and laws, so given by the Lord to his people concerning that matter, I will rehearse and allege some that be most special for this purpose, that you by them may judge of the rest.

In the fourth chapter in[g] the book named Deuteronomy is a notable place, and most worthy with all diligence to be marked, Deut. iv, [1, 2.] which beginneth thus: *And now, Israel, hear the commandments and judgments which I teach thee*, saith the Lord, *that thou doing them mayest live, and enter and possess the land which the Lord God of your fathers will give you. Ye shall put nothing to the word which I speak to you, neither shall ye take any thing from it. Keep ye the commandments of the Lord your God, which I command you.* And, by and by after, he repeateth the same sentence three or four times before he come to the matter that he would specially warn them of, as it were for a preface, to [Ibid. 9.] make them to take the better heed unto it. *Take heed to thyself*, saith he, *and to thy soul with all carefulness, lest thou forgettest the things which thine eyes have seen, and that they go not out of thy*[h] *heart all the days of thy life: thou shalt teach them to thy children and nephews*[3] or posterity. And shortly after: [Ibid. 12.] *The Lord spake unto you out of the middle of fire: you*[i] *heard the voice* or sound *of his words, but you did see no form* or shape [Ibid. 15-19.] *at all.* And by and by followeth: *Take heed therefore diligently unto your souls: you saw no manner of image in the day in the which the Lord spake unto you in Horeb out of the midst of the fire: lest peradventure you being deceived should make to yourselves any graven image or likeness of man or woman, or the likeness of any beast which is upon the earth, or of the birds that fly*[k] *under heaven, or of any creeping thing that is moved on the earth, or of the fishes that do continue in the waters; lest peradventure thou, lifting up thine eyes to heaven, do see the sun and the moon and the stars of heaven, and so thou, being deceived by error, shouldest honour and worship them, which the Lord thy God hath created to serve all nations that be under heaven.* And again: [Ibid. 23-28.] *Beware that thou forget not the covenant of the Lord thy God,*

f for that, that both] for that both 1623. g chapter in] chapter of *from* 1563 B. h of thy] of thine 1623. i fire: you] fire: but you *from* 1570. k fly] flee *from* 1563 B.

3 Nepotes. *Vulg.*

which he made with thee, and so make to thyself any carved image of them which the Lord hath forbidden to be made : for the Lord thy God is a consuming fire, and a jealous God. If thou have children and nephews, and do tarry in the land, and, being deceived, do make to yourselves any similitude, doing evil before the Lord your God, and provoke him to anger; I do this day call upon heaven and earth to witness, that ye shall quickly perish out of the land which you shall possess : you shall not dwell in it any long time; but the Lord will destroy you, and will scatter you amongst all nations; and ye shall remain but a very few amongst the nations whither the Lord will lead you away; and then shall you serve gods which are made with man's hands, of wood and stone, which see not, nor hear[l] *not, neither eat nor smell :* and so forth. This is a notable chapter, and intreateth almost altogether of this matter; but, because it is too long to write out the whole, I have noted you certain principal points out of it: first, how earnestly and oft he calleth upon them to mark and to take heed, and that upon the peril of their souls, to the charge which he giveth them; then, how he forbiddeth, by a solemn and long rehearsal of all things in heaven, in earth, and in the water, any image or likeness of any thing at all to be made; thirdly, what penalty and horrible destruction he solemnly, with invocation of heaven and earth for record, denounceth and threateneth to them, their children and posterity, if they, contrary to this commandment, do make or worship any image[m] or similitude, which he so straitly hath forbidden. And when they, this notwithstanding, partly by inclination of man's corrupt nature, most prone to idolatry, and partly occasioned by the Gentiles and heathen people dwelling about them, who were idolaters, did fall to the making and worshipping of images, God, according to his word, brought upon them all those plagues which he threatened them with; as appeareth in the Books of the Kings and the Chronicles in sundry places at large.

And agreeable hereunto are many other notable places in the Old Testament. Deuteronomy xxvii : *Cursed be he that maketh a carved image or a cast* or molten *image, which is abomination before the Lord, the work of the artificer's hand, and setteth it up in a secret corner : and all the people shall say, Amen.* [Deut. xxvii, 15.]

Read the thirteenth and fourteenth chapters of the Book of Wisdom, concerning idols or images, how they be made, set up,

l nor hear] and hear *from* 1571.

m image] images *from* 1570.

called upon, and offered unto; and how he praiseth the tree whereof the gibbet is made, as happy in comparison to the tree that an image or idol is made of, even by these very words: [Wisd. xiv, 7, 8.] *Happy is the tree wherethrough righteousness cometh,* meaning the gibbet; *but cursed is the idol that is made with hands, yea, both it, and he that made it:* and so forth. And by and by he sheweth how that the things which were the good *creatures of God* before, as trees or stones, when they be once altered and [Ibid. 11–14.] fashioned into images to be worshipped, *become abomination, a temptation unto the souls of men, and a snare for the feet of the unwise.* And why? *The seeking out of images is the beginning of whoredom,* saith he; *and the bringing up of them is the destruction of life. For they were not from the beginning, neither shall they continue for ever. The wealthy idleness of men hath found them out upon earth: therefore shall they come shortly to an end.* And so forth to the end of the chapter, containing these points: how idols or images were first invented and [Ibid. 16.] offered unto; how *by an ungracious custom* they were established; how tyrants compel men to worship them; how the ignorant and the common people are deceived by the cunning of the workman and the beauty of the image to do honour unto it, and so to err from the knowledge of God; and of other great and many mischiefs that come by images. And for a conclu- [Ibid. 27, 28.] sion he saith, that *the honouring of abominable images is the cause, the beginning, and end of all evil,* and that the worshippers of them be *either mad* or most wicked. See and view the whole chapter with diligence, for it is worthy to be well considered, specially that is written of the deceiving of the simple and unwise common people by idols and images, and repeated twice or thrice lest it should be forgotten. And in the chapter [Wisd. xv, [4–6.] following be these words[4]: *The painting of the picture and carved image with divers colours inticeth the ignorant, so that he honoureth and loveth the picture of a dead image that hath no soul. Nevertheless, they that love such evil things, they that trust in them, they that make them, they that favour them, and they that honour them, are all worthy of death:* and so forth.

In the book of Psalms the Prophet curseth the image ho-

4 Non enim in errorem induxit nos ... umbra picturae, labor sine fructu, et effigies [*al.* fructu, effigies] sculpta per varios colores; cujus aspectus insensato dat concupiscentiam, et diligit mortuae imaginis effigiem sine anima. Malorum amatores digni sunt morte, qui [*al.* sunt, qui] spem habent in talibus, et qui faciunt illos, et qui diligunt, et qui colunt. *Vulg.*

nourers[n] in divers places. *Confounded be all they that worship* Ps. xcvi [xcvii, 7;] *carven*[o] *images, and that delight* or glory *in them. Like be they* cxv, [8;] *unto the images that make them, and all they that put their trust* cxxxiv [cxxxv, 18.] *in them.*

And in the Prophet Esay saith the Lord: *Even I am the Lord,* Is. xlii. [8.] *and this is my name; and my glory will I give to none other, neither my honour to graven images.* And by and by: *Let them be* [Ibid. 17.] *confounded with shame that trust in idols* or images, *or say to them, You are our gods.* And in the fortieth chapter, after he hath set forth the incomprehensible Majesty of God, he asketh, *To whom then will ye make God like? or what similitude will ye* Is. xl, [18–21.] *set up unto him? Shall the carver make him a carved image? And shall the goldsmith cover him with gold, and cast him into a form of silver plates? And for the poor man shall the image maker frame an image of timber, that he may have somewhat to set up also?* And after this he crieth out, O wretches, *heard ye never of this? Hath it not been preached unto you since the beginning?* and so forth, how by the creation of the world and the greatness of the work they might understand the Majesty of God, the Creator and Maker of all, to be greater than that it could[p] be expressed or set forth in any image or bodily similitude.

And, besides this preaching, even in the law of God, *written with his own finger* (as the Scripture speaketh[γ]), and that in the first table, and the beginning thereof[δ], is this doctrine aforesaid against images, not briefly touched, but at large set forth and preached, and that with denunciation of destruction to the contemners and breakers of this law and their posterity after them. And, lest it should yet not be marked or not remembered, the same is written and reported, not in one, but in sundry places of the word of God[ε], that by oft reading and hearing of it we might once learn and remember it. As you also hear daily read in the church: *God spake these words and said, I am the Lord thy God. Thou shalt have none other gods but me. Thou shalt not make to thyself any graven image, nor the likeness of any thing that is in heaven above, or in the*[q] *earth beneath, nor in the water under the earth: thou shalt not bow down to them, nor worship them: for I the Lord thy God am a jealous God, and visit the sin*[r] *of the fathers upon the children unto the third and fourth generation of them that hate me, and shew mercy unto thousands in them that love me and keep my commandments.* All

γ [Exod. xxxi, 18.]

δ Exod. xx, [4, 5.]

ε Exod. xx, [23:] Lev. xix, [4:] Deut. v, [8, 9.]

n honourers] honourer *till* 1570. o carven] carved *from* 1571. p could] should *from* 1563 B. q or in the] or the 1563 A, nor in the *from* 1582. r sin] *so in all. So likewise in the Prayer Books of* 1552 *and* 1559.

this notwithstanding, neither could the notableness of the place, being the very beginning of the living[s] Lord's law, make us to mark it; nor the plain declaration by recounting of all kind of similitudes cause us to understand it; nor the oft repeating and reporting of it in divers and sundry places, the oft reading and hearing of it, could cause us to remember it; nor the dread of the horrible penalty to ourselves and our[t] children and posterity after us fear us from transgressing of it; nor the greatness of the reward to us and our children after us move us any thing to obedience and the observing of this the Lord's great law: but, as though it had been written in some corner, and not at large expressed, but briefly and obscurely touched; as though no penalty to the transgressors, nor reward to the obedient, had been adjoined unto it; like blind men without all knowledge and understanding, like unreasonable beasts without dread of punishment or respect of reward, have[u] diminished and dishonoured the high Majesty of the living God by the baseness and vileness of sundry and divers images of dead stocks, stones, and metals.

Places of the Scripture against idols or images.

And, as the Majesty of God, whom we have left, forsaken, and dishonoured, and therefore the greatness of our sin and offence against his Majesty, cannot be expressed, so is the weakness, vileness, and foolishness in device of the images whereby we have dishonoured him expressed at large in the Scriptures; namely, the Psalms, the Book of Wisdom, the Prophet Esay, Ezechiel, and Baruch; specially in these places and chapters of them, Psalm cxv and cxxxiv[5], Esay xl and xliv, Ezechiel vi[x], Wisdom xiii, xiv, xv, Baruch vi. The which places, as I exhort you often and diligently to read, so are they too long at this present to be rehearsed in an homily. Notwithstanding, I will make you certain brief or short notes out of them, what they say of these idols or images. First, that they be made but of small pieces of wood, stone, or metal; and therefore they cannot be any similitudes of the great Majesty of God, whose *seat is heaven*[ζ], *and the earth his footstool.* Secondarily, that they be dead, *have eyes and see not*[η], *hands and feel not, feet and cannot go*, &c.; and therefore they cannot be fit similitudes of the living God. Thirdly, that they have no power to do good nor harm to others; though some of them have an axe, some a sword, some

ζ [Is. lxvi, 1.]
η [Ps. cxv, 5, 7.]

s the living] the loving 1582, the very loving 1623. t ourselves and our] ourselves, our *from* 1567. u have] *so, without* we, *in all.* x Ezechiel vi] Ezechiel the vi *from* 1571.

5 Psalm cxxxiv in the *Vulgate* is cxxxv in our versions.

a spear in their hands, yet do thieves come into their temples and rob them, and they cannot once stir to defend themselves from the thieves; nay, if the temple or church be set afire, that their priests can run away and save themselves, but they cannot once move, but tarry still, like blocks as they are, and be burned; and therefore they can be no meet figures of the puissant and mighty God, who alone is able both to save his servants and to destroy his enemies everlastingly. They be trimly decked in gold, silver, and stone, as well the images of men as of women, like wanton wenches (saith the Prophet Baruch) that love paramours; Bar. vi, [9, 11.] and therefore can they not teach us, nor our wives and daughters, any soberness, modesty, and chastity. And therefore, although it is now commonly said that they be the laymen's books[6], yet we see they teach no good lesson, neither of God, nor godliness, but all error and wickedness.

Therefore God by his word, as he forbiddeth any idols or images to be made or set up, so doth he command such as we find made and set up to be pulled down, broken, and destroyed. And it is written in the book of Numbers, the twenty-third chapter, that there was *no idol in Jacob*[7], nor there was *no image* Numb. xxiii, [21.] *seen in Israel*, and that *the Lord God* was *with that*[y] *people.* Where note, that the true Israelites, that is, the people of God, have no images among them; but that God was with them, and that therefore their enemies cannot hurt them, as appeareth in the process of that chapter. And as concerning images already set up, thus saith the Lord in Deuteronomy: *Overturn their* Deut. vii, [5, 6.] *altars, and break them to pieces, cut down their groves, burn their images: for thou art an holy people unto the Lord.* And the same is repeated more vehemently again in the twelfth chapter Ibid. xii, [2, 3.] of the same book. Here note[z], what the people of God ought to do to images, where they find them. But, lest any private persons, upon colour of destroying of images[a], should make any stir or disturbance in the commonwealth, it must always be remembered, that the redress of such public enormities appertaineth[b] to the magistrates and such as be in authority only, and

[y] with that] with the *from* 1574. [z] Here note] Here not 1623. [a] destroying of images] destroying images 1623. [b] appertaineth] pertaineth 1623.

6 This argument for the use of images, which was commonly urged at the time of the Reformation, may be traced to the *Epistle of Pope Gregory the Great* cited in note 30 on the Second Part of this Homily. It suggested to Roger Hutchinson the latter part of the title to his treatise, "The Image of God or Layman's Book," as he states in his Dedicatory Epistle.

7 Non est idolum in Jacob, nec videtur simulacrum in Israel. Dominus Deus ejus cum eo est. *Vulg.*

θ 1 Kings xv, [11-14:] 2 Chron. xiv, [2-5;] xv, [8, 16;] xxxi, [1, 20; xvii, 3-6; xxxiv, 2-7.]

ι [1 Kings xiv, 9; xvi, 30-33: 2 Chron. xxiv, 17-24: 2 Kings xiii, 11.]

κ [Lev. xxvi, 30:] Numb. i: Mic. i, [3-7:] Hab. ii, [18, 19.]

Ezek. vi, [3-7.]

[Ibid. 9, 12.]

not to private persons. And therefore the good kings of Judaθ, Asa, Ezechias, Josaphat, and Josias[c], are highly commended for the breaking down and destroying of the altars, idols, and images; and the Scriptures declare, that they specially in that point *did that which was right before the Lord.* And contrariwiseι Hieroboam, Achab, Joas, and other princes, which either set up or suffered such altars or images undestroyed, are by the word of God reported to have *done evil before the Lord.* And if any, contrary to the commandment of the Lord, will needs set up such altars or images, or suffer them undestroyed amongst them, the Lord himself threatenethκ in the first chapter of the book of Numbers[d], and by[e] his holy Prophets Ezechiel, Micheas, and Abacuc, that he will come himself and pull them down. And how he will handle, punish, and destroy the people that so set up or suffer such altars, images, or idols undestroyed, he denounceth by his prophet Ezechiel on this manner: *I myself, saith the Lord, will bring a sword over you, to destroy your high places; I will cast down your altars, and break down your images; your slain men will I lay before your gods, and the dead carcases of the children of Israel will I cast before their idols; your bones will I strow*[f] *round about your altars and dwellingplaces; your cities shall be desolate, the hill chapels laid waste, your altars destroyed and broken, your gods cast down and taken away, your temples laid even with the ground, your own works clean rooted out; your slain men shall lie amongst you: that ye may learn to know how that I am the Lord:* and so forth to the chapter's end, worthy with diligence to be read, that *they that be near shall perish with the sword, they that be far off with the pestilence,* they that flee[g] into holds or wilderness with hunger, and, if any be yet left, that they shall be carried away prisoners to servitude and bondage. So that, if either the multitude or plainness of the places might make us to understand, or the earnest charge that God giveth in the said places move us to regard, or the horrible plagues, punishments, and dreadful destruction threatened to such worshippers of images or idols, setters up or maintainers of them, might ingender any fear in our hearts, we w uld once leave and forsake this wickedness, being in the Lord s sight so great an offence and abomination. Infinite places al ost might be brought out of the Scriptures of

[c] Josaphat, and Josias] J saphat, Josias 1563 A. [d] first chapter of the book of Numbers, *and in the margin* Numb. i] *so i all.* [e] Numbers, and by] Numbers, by 1563 A. [f] strow] straw *from* 1582. [g] flee] fly 15 3 A.

the Old Testament concerning this matter, but these few at this time shall serve for all.

You will say peradventure, these things pertain to the Jews, what have we to do with them? Indeed they pertain no less to us Christians than to them. For, if we be the people of God, how can the word and law of God not appertain to us? St. Paul, alleging one text out of the Old Testament, concludeth generally for other Scriptures of the Old Testament as well as that, saying, *Whatsoever is written before*, meaning in the Old Testament, (Rom. xv, [4.]) *is written for our instruction:* which sentence is most specially true of such writings of the Old Testament as contain the immutable law and ordinances of God, in no age or time to be altered, nor of any persons of any nations or age to be disobeyed, such as the above rehearsed places be. Notwithstanding, for your further satisfying herein, according to my promise, I will, out of the Scriptures of the New Testament or Gospel of our Saviour Christ likewise, make a confirmation of the said doctrine against idols or images and of our duty concerning the same.

First, the Scriptures of the New Testament do in sundry places make mention with rejoicing, as for a most excellent benefit and gift of God, that they which received the faith of Christ were *turned from their dumb* and dead *images unto the true and living God, who is* to be *blessed for ever*[λ]; namely, in these places; the fourteenth and seventeenth of the Acts of the Apostles; the eleventh to the Romans; the first Epistle to the Corinthians, the twelfth chapter; to the Galathians, the fourth; and the first to the Thessalonians, the first chapter.

λ [Rom. i, 25.] [Acts xiv, 15; xvii, 30: Rom. xi, 30: 1 Cor. xii, 2,3: Gal. iv, 8, 9: 1 Thess. i, 4-9.]

And in like wise the said idols or[h] images, and worshipping of them, are in the Scriptures of the New Testament by the Spirit of God much abhorred and detested, and earnestly forbidden: as appeareth both in the forenamed places, and also many others[i] besides; as in the seventh and fifteenth of the Acts of the Apostles; [Acts vii, 41, 42; xv, 20, 29.] the first to the Romans, where is set forth the horrible plague of idolaters, given over by God *into a reprobate sense* [Rom. i, 23-32.] to work all wickedness and abominations not to be spoken, as usually spiritual and carnal fornication go together. In the first Epistle to the Corinthians, the fifth chapter, [1 Cor. v, 11.] we are forbidden once *to keep company*, or *to eat* and drink, *with such as be called brethren* or Christians *that do worship images*. In the fifth to the Galathians, the worshipping of [Gal. v, 20.]

h idols or] or idols 1623. i others] other *from* 1582.

images is numbered amongst *the works of the flesh:* and, the [1 Cor. x. 20–22.] first[k] to the Corinthians, the tenth, it is called the service of devils, and that such as use it shall be destroyed. And in the [1 Cor. vi, 9, 10: Gal. v, 20, 21.] sixth chapter of the said Epistle, and the fifth to the Galathians, is denounced, that such *image worshippers shall never come into the inheritance of the kingdom of heaven.* And in sundry other places is threatened[μ] [Eph. v, 5, 6: Col. iii, 5, 6: Rev. xxi, 8.], that the *wrath of God shall come upon all such.* And therefore St. John in his Epistle exhorteth us, as his *dear children,* to *beware of images.* [1 John v, [21.]] And St. Paul warneth us to *flee from the worshipping of them, if we be wise,* [1 Cor. x, [14, 15, 21.]] that is to say, if we care for health and fear destruction, if we regard the kingdom of God and life everlasting, and dread the wrath of God and everlasting damnation: for it is not possible that we should be worshippers of images and the true servants of God also; as St. Paul teacheth, the[l] second to the Corinthians, the sixth [2 Cor. vi, 14–16.] chapter, affirming expressly that *there can be no more consent or agreement between the temple of God,* which all true Christians be, *and images, than between righteousness and unrighteousness, between light and darkness, between the faithful and the unfaithful, or between Christ and the devil.* Which place enforceth, both that we should not worship images, and that we should not have images in the temple, for fear and occasion of worshipping them, though they be of themselves things indifferent; for the Christian is the holy[m] temple and lively image of God, as the place well declareth to such as will read and weigh it.

And, whereas all godly men did ever abhor that any kneeling and worshipping or offering should be used to themselves when they were alive, for that it was the honour due to God only, as appeareth in the Acts of the Apostles by St. Peter forbidding it [Acts x, [25, 26;] xiv, 14–18.] to Cornelius and by St. Paul and Barnabas forbidding the same to the citizens in Lystra, yet we like mad men fall down before the dead idols or images of Peter and Paul, and give that honour to stocks and stones which they thought abominable to be given to themselves being alive. And the good angel of God, as appeareth in the book of St. John's Revelation [Rev. xix[n], [10; xxii, 8, 9.]], refused to be kneeled unto, when that honour was offered him of John. *Beware,* saith the angel, *that thou do it not; for I am thy fellow-servant.* But the evil angel Satan desireth nothing so much as to be kneeled unto, and thereby at once both to rob God of his

[k] and, the first] and in the first *from* 1571. *See note* l. [l] teacheth, the] teacheth in the *from* 1582. [m] Which place—is the holy] Which place both inforceth, that neither the material church or temple ought to have any images in it (for of it is taken the ground of the argument), neither that any true Christian ought to have any ado with filthy and dead images, for that he is the holy 1563 A 1. [n] Rev. xix] *omitted after* 1563 A 1, *the leaf in* 1563 A *being a cancel.*

due honour and work[o] the damnation of such as make him so low courtesy, as in the story of the Gospel appeareth in sundry places. Yea, and he offered our Saviour Christ all earthly goods on the condition that he would kneel down and worship him. But our Saviour repelleth Satan by the Scriptures, saying, *It is written, Thou shalt worship thy Lord God, and him alone shalt thou serve.* But we, by not worshipping and serving God alone, as the Scriptures teacheth[p] us, and by worshipping of images contrary to the Scriptures, pluck Satan to us, and are ready without reward to follow his desire; yea, rather than fail, we will offer him gifts and oblations to receive our service. But let us, brethren, rather follow the counsel of the good angel of God than the suggestion of subtile Satan, that wicked angel and old serpent; who, according to the pride whereby he first fell, attempteth alway by such sacrilege to deprive God (whom he envieth) of his due honour, and, because his own face is horrible and ugly, to convey it to himself by the mediation of gilt stocks and stones, and withal to make us the enemies of God and his own suppliants and slaves, and in the end to procure us for a reward everlasting destruction and damnation. Therefore above all things, if we take ourselves to be Christians indeed, as we be named, let us credit the word, obey the law, and follow the doctrine and example of our Saviour and Master Christ, repelling Satan's suggestion to idolatry and worshipping of images, according to the truth alleged and taught out of the Testament and Gospel of our said heavenly Doctor and Schoolmaster Jesus Christ, *who*[v] *is God,* to be *blessed for ever.* Amen.

Matt. iv, [10:] Luke iv, [8.]

[v] [Rom. ix, 5.]

[o] and work] and to work *from* 1571. [p] teacheth] teach 1623.

THE SECOND PART OF THE HOMILY

AGAINST PERIL OF IDOLATRY[a].

YOU have heard, well beloved, in the first part of this Homily, the doctrine of the word of God against idols and images, against idolatry and worshipping of images, taken out of the Scriptures of the Old Testament and the New, and confirmed by the examples as well of the Apostles as of our Saviour Christ himself. Now, although our Saviour Christ *taketh not* or needeth not *any testimony of men*, and that which is once confirmed by the certainty of his eternal truth hath no more need of the confirmation of man's doctrine and writings, than the bright sun at noon tide hath need of the light of a little candle to put away darkness and to encrease his light; yet, for your further contentation, it shall in this second part be declared (as in the beginning of the first part was promised) that this truth and doctrine concerning the forbidding of images and worshipping of them, taken out of the holy Scriptures as well of the Old Testament as the New, was believed and taught of the old holy fathers and most ancient learned doctors, and received in the old primitive Church, which was most uncorrupt and pure. And this declaration shall be made out of the said holy doctors' own writings and out of the ancient histories ecclesiastical to the same belonging.

John v, [34.]

Lib. contra coronandi morem.

Tertullian, a most ancient writer and doctor of the Church, who lived about one hundred and threescore years after the death of our Saviour Christ, both in sundry other places of his works, and specially in his book written against the manner of Crowning, and in another little treatise entitled, Of the Soldier's Crown or Garland[1], doth most sharply and vehemently

[a] THE HOMILY AGAINST PERIL OF IDOLATRY] THIS HOMILY 1563 A.

1 The Homilist took the quotation which follows, together with many other quotations and topics in this Second Part, from the first book of Bullinger's work *De Origine Erroris*, printed at Zurich in 1539, where (*cap.* 29, *fol.* 142 a) it is cited from Tertullian's treatise "*De Corona Militis*"; and it is likely that, finding mention made somewhere else of a book written by Tertullian "*contra coronandi morem*", against the fashion of wearing garlands, he thought they were distinct treatises instead of being one and the same. *De Corona Militis* is the title of the treatise in all the earlier editions of Tertullian: but Rigault on the authority of the most ancient MS, and more recently Oehler, have justly

write and inveigh against images or idols; and upon St. John's words, the first Epistle and fifth chapter, saith thus. "St. John," saith he[2], "deeply considering the matter, saith, *My little children, keep yourselves from* images or *idols*. He saith not now, Keep yourselves from idolatry, as it were from the service and worshipping of them; but from the images or idols themselves, that is, from the very shape and likeness of them. For it were an unworthy thing, that the image of the living God should become the image of a dead idol." Do not, think you,[b] those persons which place images or idols in[c] churches and temples, yea, shrine them even over the Lord's table, even as it were of purpose to the worshipping and honouring of them, take good heed to either St.[d] John's counsel or Tertullian's? For so to place images and idols, is it to keep themselves from them, or else to receive and embrace them?

1 John v, [21.]

Clemens in his book to James, brother of the Lord, saith[3]: "What can be so wicked or so unthankful, as to receive a benefit of God, and to give thanks therefore unto stocks and stones? Wherefore awake ye, and understand your health. For God hath need of no man, nor requireth any thing, nor can be hurt in any thing: but we be they which are either holpen or hurt, in that we be thankful to God or unthankful."[e]

Lib. v ad Jacob. Domini.

Origenes in his book against Celsus saith thus[4]: "Christian men and Jews, when they hear these words of the Law[a], *Thou shalt fear the Lord thy God*, and *shalt not make any image*, do not only abhor the temples, altars, and images of the gods, but,

a [Deut. vi, 13: Exod. xx, 4.]

b Do not, think you,] Do not you think 1570–1574, Do you not think *from* 1582. c or idols in] and idols in *from* 1570. d either St.] either of St. *from* 1574. e Clemens—or unthankful.] *omitted* 1623.

shortened it to *De Corona;* because, although the treatise may have been occasioned by the act of an individual soldier, its object was to dissuade Christians of every station and profession from the practice of wearing garlands, as pertaining to idolatry.

2 Altius Johannes, *Filioli*, inquit, *custodite vos ab idolis;* non jam ab idololatria quasi officio [quasi ab officio *edd. vett.*], sed ab idolis, id est, ab ipsa effigie eorum. Indignum enim ut imago Dei vivi imago idoli et mortui fias [fiat *edd. vett.*] *Tertull. De Coron.* 10; *Opp.* I, 441.

3 Quid certe tam impium, tam ingratum, quam a Deo beneficium consequi, et reddere lignis ac lapidibus gratiam? Propter quod expergiscimini et intelligite salutem vestram. Deus enim nullius indiget, neque aliquid requirit, neque in aliquo laeditur: sed nos sumus qui aut juvamur aut laedimur, in eo quo grati aut ingrati sumus. *Recognitt. S. Clement.* V, 26, *vol.* I, 552.

4 Χριστιανοὶ δὲ καὶ Ἰουδαῖοι διὰ τὸ, **Κύριον τὸν Θεόν σου φοβηθήσῃ καὶ αὐτῷ μόνῳ λατρεύσεις**, καὶ διὰ τὸ, **Οὐκ ἔσονταί σοι θεοὶ ἕτεροι πλὴν ἐμοῦ**, καὶ, **Οὐ ποιήσεις σεαυτῷ εἴδωλον**, ... οὐ μόνον ἐκτρέπονται νεὼς καὶ βωμοὺς καὶ ἀγάλματα, ἀλλὰ καὶ ἐπὶ τὸ ἀποθνήσκειν, ὅτε δεῖ, ἑτοίμως ἔρχονται ὑπὲρ τοῦ μὴ μολῦναι τὴν περὶ τοῦ Θεοῦ τῶν ὅλων ὑπόληψιν διά τινος τοιούτου παρανομήματος. Orig. cont. Cels. VII, 64; Opp. I, 740 A.

if need be, will rather die than they should defile themselves with any impiety." And shortly after[f] he saith[5]: "In the commonwealth of the Jews the carver of idols and image maker was cast far off and forbidden, lest they should have any occasion to make images, which might pluck certain foolish persons from God, and turn the eyes of their souls to the contemplation of earthly things." And in another place of the same book[6]: "It is not only," saith he, "a mad and frantic part to worship images, but also once to dissemble or wink at it." And, "A man may know God and his only Son, and those which have had such honour given them by God that they be called *gods*[β]; but it is not possible that any should by worshipping of images get any knowledge of God."

β [Exod. xxii, 28: Ps. lxxxii, 1, 6: John x, 34, 35.]

Athanasius in his book against the Gentiles hath these words[7]. "Let them tell, I pray you, how God may be known by an image. If it be by the matter of the image[g], then there needeth no shape or form, seeing that God hath appeared in all material creatures, which do testify his glory. Now if they say he is known by the form or fashion, is he not better to be known by the living things themselves, whose fashions the images express? For of surety the glory of God should be more evidently known, if it were declared by reasonable and living creatures rather than by dead and unmoveable images. Therefore, when ye do carve[h]

f shortly after] *so in all.* g of the image] of an image *from* 1567. h carve] grave *from* 1571.

5 Οὔτε γὰρ ζωγράφος οὔτ' ἀγαλματοποιὸς ἐν τῇ πολιτείᾳ αὐτῶν ἦν, ἐκβάλλοντος πάντας τοὺς τοιούτους ἀπ' αὐτῆς τοῦ νόμου· ἵνα μηδεμία πρόφασις ᾖ τῆς τῶν ἀγαλμάτων κατασκευῆς, τοὺς ἀνοήτους τῶν ἀνθρώπων ἐπισπωμένης, καὶ καθελκούσης ἀπὸ τοῦ Θεοῦ εἰς γῆν τοὺς ὀφθαλμοὺς τῆς ψυχῆς. Ibid. IV, 31, p. 524 E.

6 Ἐπεὶ δὲ καὶ τὴν Ἡρακλείτου παρέθετο λέξιν . . ., ἠλίθιον εἶναι τὸ τοῖς ἀγάλμασιν εὔχεσθαι, ἐὰν μὴ γιγνώσκῃ τις θεοὺς καὶ ἥρωας, οἵτινές εἰσι· λεκτέον ὅτι γιγνώσκειν μέν ἐστι Θεὸν καὶ τὸν Μονογενῆ αὐτοῦ, καὶ τοὺς τετιμημένους ὑπὸ Θεοῦ τῇ **θεὸς** προσηγορίᾳ καὶ μετέχοντας τῆς θεότητος αὐτοῦ, ἑτέρους ὄντας παρὰ πάντας τοὺς θεοὺς τῶν ἐθνῶν, οἵτινές εἰσι δαιμόνια· οὐ μὴν δυνατόν ἐστι καὶ γιγνώσκειν τὸν Θεὸν καὶ τοῖς ἀγάλμασιν εὔχεσθαι. καὶ οὐ μόνον τὸ εὔχεσθαι τοῖς ἀγάλμασιν ἠλίθιόν ἐστιν, ἀλλὰ γὰρ καὶ τὸ συμπεριφερόμενον τοῖς πολλοῖς προσποιεῖσθαι τοῖς ἀγάλμασιν εὔχεσθαι. Ibid. VII, 65, 66, p. 740 E, p. 741 A.

7 Εἴποι γὰρ ἄν τις πρὸς αὐτοὺς παρελθὼν ἐπ' ἀληθείᾳ κρινούσῃ, Πῶς ἀποκρίνεται ἢ γνωρίζεται Θεὸς διὰ τούτων; πότερον διὰ τὴν περικειμένην αὐτοῖς ὕλην, ἢ διὰ τὴν ἐν αὐτοῖς μορφήν; Εἰ μὲν γὰρ διὰ τὴν ὕλην, τίς ἡ χρεία τῆς μορφῆς, καὶ μή, πρὶν πλασθῆναι ταῦτα, διὰ πάσης ἁπλῶς ὕλης ἐπιφαίνεσθαι τὸν Θεόν; μάτην δὲ καὶ τοὺς ναοὺς οὗτοι περιετείχισαν συγκλείοντες ἕνα λίθον ἢ ξύλον ἢ χρυσοῦ μέρος, πάσης τῆς γῆς πεπληρωμένης τῆς τούτων οὐσίας. Εἰ δὲ ἡ ἐπικειμένη μορφὴ αἰτία γίνεται τῆς θείας ἐπιφανείας, τίς ἡ χρεία τῆς ὕλης τοῦ χρυσοῦ καὶ τῶν ἄλλων, καὶ μὴ μᾶλλον δι' αὐτῶν τῶν φύσει ζώων, ὧν εἰσι μορφαὶ τὰ γλύμματα, τὸν Θεὸν ἐπιφαίνεσθαι; καλλίων γὰρ ἂν ἡ περὶ τοῦ Θεοῦ δόξα κατὰ τὸν αὐτὸν λόγον ἐγεγόνει, εἰ διὰ ζώων ἐμψύχων λογικῶν τε καὶ ἀλόγων ἐπεφαίνετο, καὶ μὴ ἐν ἀψύχοις καὶ ἀκινήτοις προσεδοκᾶτο. ἐφ' οἷς μάλιστα καθ' ἑαυτῶν ἀσέβειαν ἐργάζονται. Athanas. Orat. c. Gentes, § 20; Opp. I, 19 E, ed. Paris. 1698.

or paint images, to the end to know God thereby, surely ye do an unworthy and unfit thing." And in another place of the same book he saith[8]: "The invention of images came of no good, but of evil; and whatsoever hath an evil beginning can never in any thing be judged good, seeing it is altogether naught." Thus far Athanasius, a very ancient, holy, and learned bishop and doctor, who judgeth both the first beginning and the end and all together of images or idols to be naught.

Lactantius likewise, an old and learned writer, in his book of the Origin of Error hath these words[9]. "God is above man, and is not placed beneath, but is to be sought in the highest region. Wherefore there is no doubt, but that no religion is in that place wheresoever any image is. For, if religion stand in godly things, and there is no godliness but in heavenly things, then be images without religion." These be Lactantius' words, Lib. ii, cap. 16.
who was above thirteen hundred years ago, and within three hundred years after our Saviour Christ.

Cyrillus, an old and holy doctor, upon the Gospel of St. John hath these words[10]. "Many have left the Creator, and have worshipped the creature; neither have they been abashed to say unto a stock, Thou art my father; and unto a stone, Thou begottest me. For many, yea, almost all, alas for sorrow, are fallen unto such folly, that they have given the glory of deity" (or godhead) "to things without sense or feeling."

Epiphanius, Bishop of Salamine in Cyprus, a very holy and learned man, who lived in Theodosius the Emperor's time, about three hundred and ninety years after our Saviour Christ's ascension, writeth thus[i] to John, Patriarch of Jerusalem. "I entered," saith Epiphanius[11], "into a certain church to pray: I found

[i] thus] this *from* 1570.

8 Πῶς δὲ καὶ εἰς τὴν τῶν εἰδώλων μανίαν καταβεβήκασιν, ἤδη λέγειν ἀναγκαῖον· ἵνα γινώσκῃς, ὅτι ὅλως ἡ τῶν εἰδώλων εὕρεσις οὐκ ἀπὸ ἀγαθοῦ ἀλλ' ἀπὸ κακίας γέγονε. τὸ δὲ τὴν ἀρχὴν ἔχον κακὴν ἐν οὐδενί ποτε καλὸν κριθείη, ὅλον ὂν φαῦλον. Ibid. § 7, p. 7 D.

9 Deus autem major est homine: supra ergo, non infra est; nec in ima potius, sed in summa regione quaerendus est. Quare non est dubium quin religio nulla sit ubicumque simulacrum est. Nam si religio ex divinis rebus est, divini autem nihil est nisi in coelestibus rebus, carent ergo religione simulacra, quia nihil potest esse coeleste in ea re quae fit ex terra. *Lactant. Divin. Institutt. Lib.* II *De Orig. Error. c.* 19.

10 Λελατρεύκασι γάρ τινες τῇ κτίσει παρὰ τὸν Κτίσαντα, καὶ τῷ ξύλῳ τετολμήκασιν εἰπεῖν, Πατήρ μου εἶ σύ, καὶ τῷ λίθῳ, Σύ με ἐγέννησας. Πρὸς γὰρ δὴ τοσοῦτον οἱ δείλαιοι κατώλισθον ἀμαθίας μέτρον, ὡς καὶ ταῖς αἰσθήσεως ἀμοιρούσαις ὕλαις τὴν θείαν ἁπλῶς ἐπωνυμίαν χαρίσασθαι καὶ τῆς τὰ πάντα ὑπερκειμένης οὐσίας τὴν ἄρρητον περιθεῖναι δόξαν. Cyril. Alexandr. Comment. in Joan. Evang. XI, 5; Opp. IV, 952 B, ed. Paris. 1638.

11 Praeterea audivi [Praeterea quod audivi *Petav.*] quosdam murmurare contra me, quia quando simul pergebamus

there a linen cloth hanging in the church door, painted, and having in it the image of Christ, as it were, or of some other Saint (for I remember not well whose image it was): therefore when I did see[k] the image of a man hanging in the church of Christ contrary to the authority of the Scriptures, I did tear it, and gave counsel to the keepers of that[l] church, that they should wind a poor man that was dead in the said cloth, and so bury him." And afterwards the same Epiphanius, sending another unpainted cloth, for that painted one which he had torn, to the said Patriarch, writeth thus. "I pray you, will the elders of that place to receive this cloth, which I have sent by this bearer, and command them that from henceforth no such painted cloths, contrary to our religion, be hanged in the church of Christ. For it becometh your goodness rather to have this care, that you take away such scrupulosity; which is unfitting for the church of Christ, and offensive to the people committed to your charge."

And this epistle, as worthy to be read of many, did St. Jerome himself translate into the Latin tongue. And, that ye may know that St. Jerome had this holy and learned Bishop Epiphanius in most high estimation, and therefore did translate this epistle as a writing of authority, hear what a testimony the said St. Jerome giveth him in another place, in his treaty against the errors of John, Bishop of Jerusalem, where he hath

k did see] do see 1574–1595. l of that] of the *from* 1567.

ad sanctum locum qui vocatur Bethel, ut ibi collectam tecum ex more ecclesiastico facerem, et venissem ad villam quae dicitur Anablatha, vidissemque ibi praeteriens lucernam ardentem, et interrogassem quis locus esset, didicissemque esse ecclesiam, et intrassem ut orarem, inveni ibi velum pendens in foribus ejusdem ecclesiae tinctum atque depictum et habens imaginem, quasi Christi, vel Sancti cujusdam, (non enim satis memini cujus imago fuerit;) cum ergo hoc vidissem, et detestatus essem in ecclesia [vidissem, in ecclesia *Petav.*] Christi contra auctoritatem Scripturarum hominis pendere imaginem, scidi illud, et magis dedi consilium custodibus ejusdem loci, ut pauperem mortuum eo obvolverent et efferrent. Illique contra murmurantes dixerunt, Si scindere voluerat, justum erat ut aliud daret velum atque mutaret. Quod cum audissem, me daturum esse pollicitus sum, et illico esse missurum. Paululum autem morarum fuit in medio .... Nunc autem misi quod potui reperire, et precor ut jubeas presbytero [presbyteros *Petav.*] ejusdem loci suscipere velum a Lectore [latore *Petav.*] quod a nobis missum est, et deinceps praecipere, in ecclesia Christi istiusmodi [ejusmodi *Petav.*] vela, quae contra religionem nostram veniunt, non appendi. Decet enim honestatem tuam hanc magis habere solicitudinem, ut scrupulositatem tollat, quae indigna [*the Ambrosian MS. of Jerome has* et scrupulositatem, quae digna] est Ecclesia Christi et populis qui tibi crediti [qui crediti *Petav.*] sunt. *Epiphan. Epist. ad Joan. Episc. Hieros. a S. Hieron. Latine reddita, Epiphan. Opp.* II, 317, *ed. Petav. Paris.* 1622; *Hieron. Opp.* I, 251 C.

these words. "Thou hast," saith St. Jerome[12], "pope Epiphanius, which doth openly in his letters call thee an heretic. Surely thou art not to be preferred before him, neither for age, nor learning, nor godliness of life, nor by the testimony of the whole world." And shortly after in the same treaty saith St. Jerome: "Bishop Epiphanius was ever of so great veneration and estimation, that Valens the Emperor," who was a great persecutor, "did not once touch him. For heretics, being princes, thought it their shame, if they should persecute such a notable man." And in the Tripartite Ecclesiastical History, the ninth book and forty-eighth chapter, is testified, that Epiphanius, being yet alive, did work miracles; and that, after his death, devils being expelled at his grave or tomb did roar[13]. Thus you see what authority St. Jerome and that most ancient History give unto the holy and learned Bishop Epiphanius: whose judgment of images in churches and temples, then beginning by stealth to creep in, is worthy to be noted.

All notable bishops were then called popes.

Lib. ix, cap. 48.

First, he judged it contrary to Christian religion and the authority of the Scriptures to have any images in Christ's church. Secondly, he rejected not only carved, graven, and molten images, but also painted images, out of Christ's church. Thirdly, that he regarded not whether it were the image of Christ or of any other Saint, but, being an image, would not suffer it in the church. Fourthly, that he did not only remove it out of the church, but with a vehement zeal tare it asunder[m], and exhorted that a corse should be wrapped and buried in it, judging it meet for nothing but to rot in the earth; following herein the example of the good King Ezechias[y], who brake the brazen serpent to pieces, and burned it to ashes, for that idolatry was committed to it. Last of all, that Epiphanius thinketh it the duty of vigilant bishops to be careful that no images be permitted in the church, for that they be occasion of scruple and offence to the people committed to their charge.

y [2 Kings xviii, 4.]

Now, whereas neither St. Jerome, who did translate the said[n]

m asunder] in sunder 1582, 1623. n said] same *from* 1582.

12 Habes papam Epiphanium, qui te aperte missis literis haereticum vocat. Certe nec aetate, nec scientia, nec vitae merito, nec totius orbis testimonio, major illo es. . . . . Ille vel Presbyter monasterii ab Eutychio audiebatur, vel postea Episcopus Cypri a Valente non tangebatur. Tantae enim venerationis semper fuit, ut regnantes haeretici ignominiam suam putarent, si talem virum persequerentur. *Hieron. contra Ioan. Ierosol.* § 4, *Opp.* II, 411 B, D.

13 Eo quoque tempore fuit Epiphanius, Cypriorum Episcopus, ad cujus sepulcrum hactenus daemones expelluntur, &c. *Cassiodor. Hist. Eccles. Tripart.* IX, 48, from *Sozom.* VII, 27.

epistle, nor the authors of that most ancient History Ecclesiastical Tripartite, who do most highly commend Epiphanius (as is aforesaid), nor no[o] other godly or learned bishop at that time or shortly after, have written any thing against Epiphanius' judgment concerning images, it is an evident proof that in those days, which were about four hundred years after our Saviour Christ, there were no images publicly used and received in the Church of Christ, which was then much less corrupt and more pure than now it is. And, whereas images began at that time secretly and by stealth to creep out of private men's houses into the churches, and that first in painted cloths and walls, such bishops as were godly and vigilant, when they espied[p] them, removed them away as unlawful and contrary to Christian religion, as did here Epiphanius: to whose judgment you have not only St. Jerome, the translator of his epistle, and the writer of the History Tripartite, but also all the learned and godly bishops and[q] clerks, yea, and the whole Church of that age, and so upward to our Saviour Christ's time by the space of about four hundred years, consenting and agreeing.

This is written the more largely of Epiphanius, for that our image maintainers now a days, seeing themselves so pressed with this most plain and earnest act and writing of Epiphanius, a bishop and doctor of such antiquity, holiness[r], and authority, labour by all means (but in vain against the truth) either to prove that this epistle was neither of Epiphanius' writing nor St. Jerome's translation, either, if it be, say they, it is of no great force; for this Epiphanius, say they, was a Jew, and, being converted to the Christian faith and made a bishop, retained the hatred which Jews have to images still in his mind, and so did and wrote against them as a Jew, rather than as a Christian[14]. O Jewish impudency and malice of such devisers! It would be proved, and not said only, that Epiphanius was a Jew. Furthermore, concerning the reason they make, I would admit it gladly. For, if Epiphanius' judgment against images is not to be admitted, for that he was of[s] a Jew (an enemy to images, which be God's enemies) converted to Christ's religion, then likewise followeth it, that no sentence in the old doctors and fathers sounding for images ought to be of any authority,

[o] nor no] nor any 1623. [p] espied] spied *from* 1582. [q] bishops and] *omitted* 1623. [r] holiness] *omitted after* 1574. [s] was of] *so in the text of* 1563 A, *but* was born of *in the correction of* "*Faultes escaped*" *at the end of that volume, and in all editions since. See p.* 187, *lines* 3 *and* 15.

14 See *Jewel, Defence of Apology, Part* v, *Chap.* iii, *Div.* 3.

for that in the primitive Church the most part of learned writers, as Tertullian, Cyprian, Ambrose, Austin, and infinite others, were[t] of Gentiles (which be favourers and worshippers of images) converted to the Christian faith, and so let somewhat slip out of their pens sounding for images, rather as Gentiles than Christians; as Eusebius in his History Ecclesiastical and St. Jerome saith plainly, that images came first from the Gentiles to us Christians[15]. And much more doth it follow, that the opinion of all the rabblement of the popish church, maintaining images, ought to be esteemed of small or no authority; for that it is no marvel that they, which have from their childhood been brought up amongst images and idols, and have drunk in idolatry almost with their mother's milk, hold with images and idols, and speak and write for them. But indeed it would not be so much marked, whether he were of a Jew or a Gentile converted to Christ's[u] religion that writeth, as how agreeably[x] or contrarily[y] to God's word he doth write, and so to credit or discredit him. Now, what God's word saith of idols and images and the worshipping of them, you heard at large in the first part of this Homily.

St. Ambrose in his treaty of the death of Theodosius the Emperor saith[16]: "Helene found the cross and the title on it: she worshipped the King, and not the wood surely, for that is an ethnish[z] error and the vanity of the wicked, but she worshipped him that hanged on the cross, and whose name was written in the title:" and so forth. See both the godly Empress' fact, and St. Ambrose' judgment at once. They thought it had been an heathenish error and vanity of the wicked to have worshipped the cross itself, which was embrued with our Saviour Christ's own precious blood: and we fall down before every cross piece of timber, which is but an image of that cross.

St. Augustine, the best learned of all ancient doctors, in his forty-fourth Epistle to Maximus saith[17]: "Know thou, that

t others, were] others more, were *from* 1582. u to Christ's] unto Christ's *from* 1574. x agreeably] agreeable *from* 1574. y contrarily] contrary *from* 1582. z ethnish] heathenish 1595, 1623.

15 See the passages cited from *Eusebius* and *Jerome* in notes 23 and 24 below, p. 190.

16 Invenit ergo titulum; Regem adoravit; non lignum utique, quia hic gentilis est error et vanitas impiorum; sed adoravit illum qui pependit in ligno, scriptus in titulo. *Ambros. de Obitu Theodosii* § 46, *Opp.* II, 1211 A.

17 Ad summam tamen, ne te hoc lateat et in sacrilega convitia imprudentem trahat, scias a Christianis catholicis, quorum in vestro oppido etiam Ecclesia constituta est, nullum coli mortuorum,

none of the dead, nor any thing that is made of God, is worshipped as God of the catholic Christians, of whom there is a Church also in your town." Note that by St. Augustine such as worshipped the dead or creatures be no[a] catholic Christians. The same St. Augustine teacheth, in the twenty-second[b] book of the City of God, the tenth chapter, that[18] neither temples or churches ought to be builded or made for Martyrs or Saints, but to God alone; and that there ought no priests to be appointed for Martyr or Saint, but to God only. The same St. Augustine in his book of the Manners of the Catholic Church hath these words[19]: "I know that many be worshippers of tombs and pictures; I know that there be many that banquet most riotously over the graves of the dead, and, giving meat to dead carcases, do bury themselves upon the buried, and attribute their gluttony and drunkenness to religion." See, he esteemeth worshipping of Saints' tombs and pictures[c] as good religion as gluttony and drunkenness, and no better at all. St. Augustine greatly alloweth Marcus Varro[20] affirming that religion is most pure without images. And saith himself[21]:

Lib. IV de Civ. Dei, cap. 31.

[a] be no] be not *from* 1574. [b] twenty-second] xii. 1623. [c] Saints' tombs and pictures] Saints, Tombs, and Pictures *till* 1582.

nihil denique ut numen adorari quod sit factum et conditum a Deo, sed unum ipsum Deum, qui fecit et condidit omnia. *Augustin. Epist.* XVII (*al.* XLIV) *ad Max. Madaur.* § 5; *Opp.* II, 22 F.

18 Illi talibus diis suis et templa aedificaverunt, et statuerunt aras, et sacerdotes instituerunt, et sacrificia fecerunt. Nos autem Martyribus nostris non templa sicut diis, sed memorias sicut hominibus mortuis quorum apud Deum vivunt spiritus, fabricamus; nec ibi erigimus altaria, in quibus sacrificemus Martyribus, sed uni Deo et Martyrum et nostro; ad quod sacrificium, sicut homines Dei qui mundum in ejus confessione vicerunt, suo loco et ordine nominantur, non tamen a sacerdote qui sacrificat invocantur. Deo quippe, non ipsis, sacrificat, quamvis in memoria sacrificet eorum; quia Dei sacerdos est, non illorum. *Augustin. de Civ. Dei,* XXII, 10; *Opp.* VII, 673 F. The word Memoria in this passage signifies a memorial Church or Chapel, in which sense it is often used by Christian writers. In Augustine's tract *De Cura Gerenda pro Mortuis* the expressions Memoria Martyris and Basilica Martyris are used interchangeably; *Opp.* VI, 515 A, B, 519 B, G. Compare *Augustin. Serm. ad Pop.* 273 (al. *de Divers.* 101), *cap.* 7; *Opp.* V, 1107 G, 1108 A: and see *Bingham, Orig. Eccles.* VIII, i, 8. See also note 84 on the Third Part of this Homily.

19 Novi multos esse sepulcrorum et picturarum adoratores: novi multos esse, qui luxuriosissime super mortuos bibant, et epulas cadaveribus exhibentes super sepultos seipsos sepeliant, et voracitates ebrietatesque suas deputent religioni. *Augustin. de Mor. Eccles. Cathol.* § 75; *Opp.* I, 713 E.

20 Quapropter, cum solos dicit [*sc.* Varro] animadvertisse quid esset Deus qui eum crederent animam mundum gubernantem, castiusque existimat sine simulacris observari religionem, quis non videat quantum propinquaverit veritati? *Augustin. de Civ. Dei,* IV, 31; *Opp.* VII, 112 A.

21 Plus enim valent simulacra ad curvandam infelicem animam quod *os habent,* .... quam ad corrigendam quod *non loquentur* .... *Augustin. Enarrat.* II *in Psalm.* cxiii, § 6; *Opp.* IV, 1262 G.

"Images be of more force to crooken an unhappy soul than to teach and instruct it." And saith further[22]: "Every child, yea, every beast knoweth that it is not God that they see. Wherefore then doth the Holy Ghost so often monish us of that which all men know?" Whereunto St. Augustine himself answereth thus: "For," saith he, "when images are placed in temples, and set in honourable sublimity, and begin once to be worshipped, forthwith breedeth the most vile affection of error." This is St. Augustine's judgment of images in churches, that by and by they breed error and idolatry.

In Psalm. xxxvi et cxiii.

It would be too[d] tedious to rehearse all other places which might be brought out of the ancient doctors against images and idolatry: wherefore we shall hold ourself[e] contented with these few at this present.

Now as concerning Histories Ecclesiastical touching this matter, that you[f] may know why and when and by whom images were first used privately, and afterwards not only received into the Christians' churches and temples, but in conclusion worshipped also, and how the same was gainsaid, resisted, and forbidden, as well by godly bishops and learned doctors, as also by sundry Christian princes, I will briefly collect into a compendious history that which is at large and in sundry places written by divers ancient writers and historiographers concerning this matter.

As the Jews, having most plain and express commandment of

d too] *omitted after* 1574. e ourself] ourselves *from* 1574. f you] ye *from* 1571.

22 The Homilist has here blended two passages from St. Augustine.

Quanto ergo melius mures atque serpentes et id genus animantium cetera de simulacris gentium, si ita dicendum est, quodammodo judicant, in quibus quia non sentiunt humanam vitam non curant humanam figuram .... Quis puer interrogatus non hoc certum esse respondeat, quod *simulacra gentium os habent, et non loquentur*, ...? Cur ergo tantopere Spiritus Sanctus curat Scripturarum plurimis locis haec insinuare atque inculcare velut inscientibus, quasi non omnibus apertissima atque notissima; nisi quia species membrorum, quam naturaliter in animantibus viventem videre atque in nobismetipsis sentire consuevimus, quamquam, ut illi asserunt, in signum aliquod fabrefacta atque eminenti collocata suggestu, cum adorari atque honorari a multitudine coeperit, parit in unoquoque sordidissimum erroris affectum? *Enarrat.* II *in Psalm.* cxiii, §§ 2, 3; *Opp.* IV, 1261 A, C.

Et idola quidem omni sensu carere quis dubitet? Verumtamen cum his locantur sedibus honorabili sublimitate, ut a precantibus atque immolantibus adtendantur, ipsa similitudine animatorum membrorum atque sensuum, quamvis insensata et exanima, afficiunt infirmos animos, ut vivere ac spirare videantur, accedente praesertim veneratione multitudinis, qua tantus eis cultus impenditur. *Epist.* CII (*al.* XLIX), *Quaest.* iii, § 18; *Opp.* II, 279 F.

In his exposition of Psalm xxxvi, cited in the margin, Augustine says nothing about images. Perhaps the passage intended is *Enarrat. in Psalm.* xcvi, § 11; *Opp.* IV, 1047 D, E.

God that they should neither make nor worship any image (as it is at large before declared), did notwithstanding, by the example of the Gentiles or heathen people that dwelt about them, fall to the making of images and worshipping of them, and so to the committing of most abominable idolatry; for the which God by his holy Prophets doth most sharply reprove and threaten them, and afterward did accomplish his said threatenings by extreme punishing of them (as is also above specified); even so some of the Christians in old time, which were converted from worshipping of idols and false gods unto the true living God and to our Saviour Jesus Christ, did of a certain blind zeal, and as[g] men long accustomed to images, paint or carve images of our Saviour Christ, his mother Mary, and of the Apostles, thinking that this was a point of gratitude and kindness towards those by whom they had received the true knowledge of God and the doctrine of the Gospel. But these pictures or images came not yet into churches, nor were not worshipped[h] of a long time after.

And, lest you should think that I do say this of mine own head only without authority, I allege for me Eusebius, Bishop of Cesarea and the most ancient author of the Ecclesiastical History, (who lived about the three hundred and thirtieth year of our Lord, in Constantinus Magnus' days, and his son Constantius, Emperors,) in the seventh book of his History Ecclesiastical, the fourteenth[i] chapter, and St. Jerome upon the tenth chapter of the Prophet Jeremy; who both expressly say, that the "error"[k] of images (for so St. Jerome[23] calleth it) "hath" come in and "passed" to the Christians from the Gentiles "by an heathenish use" and custom. The cause and means Eusebius sheweth, saying[24], "It is no marvel if they which being Gentiles before and

[g] zeal, and as] zeal, as 1623. [h] not worshipped] not yet worshipped 1623. [i] fourteenth] *so in all*. [k] error] errors *in all*. *See p.* 191, *l.* 15, *and the citation from Jerome in note* 23.

23 *Argento et auro decoravit illud*, ut fulgore utriusque materiae decipiat simplices. Qui quidem error ad nos usque transivit, ut religionem in divitiis arbitremur. *Hieron. in Jerem.* x, 4; *Opp.* IV, 911 B. See more of the context cited in note 100 on the Third Part of this Homily.

24 Τοῦτον τὸν ἀνδριάντα εἰκόνα τοῦ Ἰησοῦ φέρειν ἔλεγον. . . . Καὶ θαυμαστὸν οὐδὲν τοὺς πάλαι ἐξ ἐθνῶν εὐεργετηθέντας πρὸς τοῦ Σωτῆρος ἡμῶν ταῦτα πεποιηκέναι, ὅτε καὶ τῶν Ἀποστόλων αὐτοῦ τὰς εἰκόνας Παύλου καὶ Πέτρου καὶ αὐτοῦ δὴ τοῦ Χριστοῦ διὰ χρωμάτων ἐν γραφαῖς σωζομένας ἱστορήσαμεν· ὡς εἰκὸς τῶν παλαιῶν ἀπαραφυλάκτως [al. ἀπαραλλάκτως] οἷα σωτῆρας ἐθνικῇ συνηθείᾳ παρ' ἑαυτοῖς τοῦτον τιμᾷν εἰωθότων τὸν τρόπον. Euseb. Hist. Eccles. VII, xviii, 3.

But the writer of the Homily used the version of Rufinus. Et nihil mirum si hi qui ex gentilibus crediderant, pro beneficiis quae a Salvatore fuerant consecúti, hujusmodi velut munus videbantur offerre, cum videamus etiam nunc

did[l] believe seemed to offer this as a gift unto[m] our Saviour for the benefits which they had received of him. Yea, and we do see now that images of Peter and Paul and our[n] Saviour himself be made, and tables to be painted: which me think to have been observed and kept indifferently by an heathenish custom; for the heathen are wont so to honour them whom they judged honour worthy. For that some tokens of old men should be kept for the remembrance of posterity is a token of their honour that were before, and the love of those that come after." Thus far I have rehearsed Eusebius' words. Where note ye, that both St. Jerome and he agree[o] herein, that these images came in amongst Christian men by such as were Gentiles and accustomed to idols, and, being converted to the faith of Christ, retained yet some remnants of Gentility not throughly purged; for St. Jerome calleth it an "error" manifestly. And the like example we see, in the Acts of the Apostles, of the Jews: who, when they were converted to Christ, would have brought in their circumcision (whereunto they were so long accustomed) with them into Christ's religion; with whom the Apostles, namely St. Paul, had much ado for the staying of that matter. But of circumcision was less marvel, for that it came first in by God's ordinance and commandment. A man may most justly wonder of images, so directly against God's holy word and strait commandment, how they should enter in. But images were not yet worshipped in Eusebius' time, nor publicly set up in churches and temples; and they who privately had them did err of a certain zeal, and not by malice: but afterwards they crept out of private houses into churches, and so bred first superstition and last of all idolatry amongst Christians, as hereafter shall appear.

Acts xv.

In the time of Theodosius and Martian, Emperors, who reigned about the year of our Lord 460, and eleven hundred[p] years ago, when the people of the city of Nola once a year did celebrate the birthday of St. Felix in the temple, and used to banquet there sumptuously, Pontius Paulinus, Bishop of Nola,

[l] and did] *so in all.* [m] unto] to 1623. [n] and our] and of our *from* 1571. [o] agree] agreeth *from* 1563 B. [p] eleven hundred] 1100 *till* 1582, 1117 *from* 1582.

Apostolorum Petri et Pauli et ipsius Salvatoris imagines designari tabulasque depingi. Sed et antiquas ipsorum imagines a quibusdam conservatas nos vidimus: quod mihi videtur ex gentili consuetudine indifferenter observatum, quod ita soleant honorare quos honore dignos duxerint. Insignia etenim veterum reservari ad posteriorum memoriam, illorum honoris, horum vero amoris, indicium est. *Euseb. Caes. Eccles. Hist.* VII, 14, *Ruf. Interpr., ed. Basil.* 1528, *p.* 166 A.

caused the walls of the temple to be painted with stories taken out of the Old Testament, that the people, beholding and considering those pictures, might the better abstain from too much surfeiting and riot.[25] And about the same time Aurelius Prudentius, a very learned and Christian poet, declareth how he did see painted in a church the history of the passion of St. Cassian, a schoolmaster and martyr, whom his own scholars, at the commandment of the tyrant, tormented with the pricking or stabbing in of their pointels or brazen pens into his body, and so by a thousand wounds and mo (as saith Prudentius [26]) most cruelly slew him. And these were the first paintings in churches that were notable of antiquity. And so by this example came in painting, and afterward images of timber and stone and other matter, into the churches of Christians.

Now, and ye[27] will[q] consider this beginning, men are not so ready to worship a picture on a wall or in a window, as an embossed and gilt image, set with pearl and stone. And a process of a story painted with the gestures and actions of many persons, and commonly the sum of the story written withal, hath another use in it than one dumb idol or image standing by itself. But from learning by painted stories it came by little and little to idolatry. Which when godly men, as well emperors and learned bishops as others, perceived, they commanded that such pictures, images, or idols should be used no more. And I will, for a declaration thereof, begin with the decree of the ancient Christian Emperors Valens and Theodosius the Second, who reigned about four hundred years after our Saviour Christ's

q ye will] ye well 1623.

25 See *Paulin. Poem.* XXIV, *De S. Felice Natal. Carm.* IX, 511–595.

26 Stratus humi tumulo advolvebar, quem sacer ornat
  Martyr dicato Cassianus corpore.
Dum lacrimans mecum reputo mea vulnera et omnes
  Vitae labores ac dolorum acumina,
Erexi ad coelum faciem: stetit obvia contra
  Fucis colorum picta imago Martyris,
Plagas mille gerens, totos lacerata per artus,
  Ruptam minutis praeferens punctis cutem.
Innumeri circum pueri, miserabile visu,
  Confossa parvis membra figebant stilis.
* * * * * * * *
Aedituus consultus ait: Quod prospicis, hospes,
  Non est inanis aut anilis fabula.
Historiam pictura refert, quae tradita libris
  Veram vetusti temporis monstrat fidem.
Praefuerat studiis puerilibus, &c.

Prudent. Περιστεφ. IX, 5–21.

27 and ye: an ye, if ye.

ascension, who forbad that any images should be made or painted privately; for certain it is that there was none in temples publicly in their time. These Emperors did write unto the Captain of the Army attending on the Emperors after this sort. "Valens and Theodosius, Emperors, unto the Captain of the Army. Whereas we have a diligent care to maintain the religion of God above in all things, we will grant to no man to set forth, grave, carve, or paint the image of our Saviour Christ in colours, stone, or any other matter; but, in what place soever it shall be found, we command that it be taken away, and that all such as shall attempt anything contrary to our decrees or commandment herein shall be most sharply punished." This decree is written in the books named Libri Augustales, the Imperial Books, gathered by Tribonianus [r], Basilides, Theophilus, Dioscorus, and Satira, men of great authority and learning, at the commandment of the emperor Justinian; and is alleged by Petrus Crinitus [s], a notable learned man, in the ninth book and ninth chapter of his work entitled De Honesta Disciplina, that is to say, Of Honest Learning [28]. Here you see what Christian

r Tribonianus] Tribunianus *till* 1623. s Crinitus] Erinilus, Erinius, *or* Erimus *till* 1623.

28 Impp. Theod. et Valentin. AA. Eudoxio P.P. Cum sit nobis cura diligens per omnia Superni Numinis religionem tueri, signum Salvatoris Christi nemini licere vel in solo vel in silice vel in marmoribus humi positis insculpere vel pingere, sed quodcunque reperitur tolli, gravissima poena multando eo qui contrarium statutis nostris tentaverit, specialiter imperamus. Dat. XII Kalend. Jun. Hierio et Ardaburio Coss. *Cod. Justin.* I, viii.

The date of this decree is A.D. 427. The error in the name of the Emperor Valentinian, which appears in the Homily, is due to Crinitus (or Riccio) himself, whose words are these: Sed libitum est verba ex libris Augustalibus referre..., quoniam et Valens et Theodosius Augusti Imperatores Praefecto Praetorio ad hunc modum scripserunt: Cum sit nobis &c. After the decree he adds this sentence: In quo si quis autorem desiderat, is Imperatorum decreta et edicta legat, quae a viris doctissimis Triboniano, Basilide, Theophilo, Dioscoroque et caeteris per Satyram collecta sunt, imperante hoc maxime Augusto Justiniano. *Petr. Crinit. de Honest. Discipl.* IX, 9.

But none of Justinian's commissioners bore any name like Satyra. The writer of the Homily mistook the words "per Satyram," which even Crinitus did not use quite rightly. Per satyram, or more properly Per saturam, was a figurative expression, bearing some resemblance to our phrase "in hotchpot." In Justinian's own Prooemium to the Pandects the phrase "quasi per satyram collectum" is applied to a most unsystematic compilation, which used to be the first work put into the hands of students of law at that time, and which was the very reverse of the orderly method of the Digest. If, instead of saying that the commissioners collected the laws per saturam, Crinitus had said that Justinian reenacted them per saturam, in the lump and not piecemeal, his language would have been more nearly accurate. For Satura Lex, as Gratian defines it, is one quae de pluribus simul rebus loquitur, dicta quidem a copia rerum et quasi a saturitate. *Decret.* I, ii, 7, *Satyra.* See *Hotman, Antiqq. Roman.* I, i, "Satyra lex."

Concerning the imperial decree itself it is right to add that jurists put quite another interpretation upon it. They

princes of most ancient times decreed against images, which then began to creep in amongst the Christians. For it is certain that by the space of three hundred years and more after the death of our Saviour Christ, and before these godly Emperors' reign[t], there were no images publicly in churches or temples. How would the idolaters glory, if they had so much antiquity and authority for them, as is here against them!

Now shortly after these days the Goths, Vandals, Huns, and other barbarous and wicked nations burst into Italy and all parts of the West countries of Europe with huge and mighty armies, spoiled all places, destroyed cities, and burned libraries; so that learning and true religion went to wrack, and decayed incredibly. And so the bishops of those latter days being of less learning, and in the middle[u] of wars[x] taking less heed also than did the bishops afore, by ignorance of God's word and negligence of bishops, and specially barbarous princes not rightly instructed in true religion bearing the rule, images came into the Church of Christ in the said West parts, where these barbarous people ruled, not now in painted cloths only, but embossed in stone, timber, metal, and other like matter; and were not only set up, but began to be worshipped also. And therefore Serenus, Bishop of Massile, the head town of Gallia Narbonensis (now called the Province), a godly and learned man, who was about six hundred years after our Saviour Christ, seeing the people by occasion of images fall to most abominable idolatry, brake to pieces all the images of Christ and Saints which were in that city; and was therefore complained upon to Gregory, the first of that name Bishop of Rome, who was the first learned bishop that did allow the open having of images in churches, that can be known by any writing or history of antiquity.

And upon this Gregory do all image worshippers at this day ground their defence. But, as all things that be amiss have

[t] reign] reigned *from* 1582. [u] middle] middest *from* 1571. [x] of wars] of the wars *from* 1582.

say that "signum Salvatoris Christi" is the figure of the cross, and that the decree forbids the placing of that figure anywhere on the ground, ne pedibus conculcetur, for fear it should be trampled on or trodden under foot; and they illustrate this by the seventy-third canon of the Concilium in Trullo or Quinisextum, which sat A.D. 691. Τοῦ ζωοποιοῦ σταυροῦ δείξαντος ἡμῖν τὸ σωτήριον, πᾶσαν σπουδὴν ἡμᾶς τιθέναι χρὴ τοῦ τιμὴν τὴν ἀξίαν ἀποδιδόναι τῷ δι' οὗ σεσώσμεθα τοῦ παλαίου πτώματος. ὅθεν καὶ νῷ καὶ λόγῳ καὶ αἰσθήσει τὴν προσκύνησιν αὐτῷ ἀπονέμοντες τοὺς ἐν τῷ ἐδάφει τοῦ σταυροῦ τύπους ὑπό τινων κατασκευαζομένους ἐξαφανίζεσθαι παντοίως προστάττομεν, ὡς ἂν μὴ τῇ τῶν βαδιζόντων καταπατήσει τὸ τῆς νίκης ἡμῖν τρόπαιον ἐξυβρίζοιτο. τοὺς οὖν ἀπὸ τοῦ νῦν σταυροῦ τύπον ἐπὶ τῷ ἐδάφει κατασκευάζοντας ὁρίζομεν ἀφορίζεσθαι. Concil. Labbe VI, 1175, Mansi XI, 976.

from a tolerable beginning grown worse and worse, till they at the last became untolerable, so did this matter of images. First men used privately stories painted in tables, cloths, and walls; afterwards gross and embossed images privately in their own houses. Then afterwards pictures first, and after them embossed images, began to creep into churches, learned and godly men ever speaking against them. Then by use it was openly maintained that they might be in churches, but yet forbidden that they should be worshipped. Of which opinion was Gregory, as by the said Gregory's Epistle to the forenamed Serenus, Bishop of Massile, plainly appeareth; which Epistle is to be found in the book of the Epistles[y] of Gregory, or Register, in the tenth part of the fourth Epistle[29], where he hath these words[30]: "That thou didst forbid images to be worshipped, we praise altogether; but that thou didst break them, we blame. For it is one thing to worship the picture, and another thing by the picture of the story to learn what is to be worshipped. For, that which Scripture is to them that read, the same doth picture perform unto idiots" (or the unlearned) "beholding:" and so forth. And after a few words: "Therefore it should not have been broken, which was set up, not to be worshipped in churches, but only to instruct the minds of the ignorant." And a little after: "Thus thou shouldest have said, If you will have images in the church for that instruction wherefore they were made in old time, I do permit that they may be made, and that you may have them. And shew them that not the sight of the story which is opened by the picture, but that worshipping which was inconveniently given to the pictures, did mislike you. And if any would make images, not to forbid them, but avoid by all

y of the Epistles] of Epistles *from* 1574.

29 Bullinger, from whom this is taken (*cap.* xxiv, *fol.* 117 b), says, *In Registro sive epistol. libro, Parte* 10. *epistol.* 4, meaning the fourth Epistle in the tenth Part of the Register or book of Epistles.

30 Et quidem, quia eas adorari vetuisses, omnino laudavimus; fregisse vero reprehendimus.... Aliud est enim picturam adorare, aliud per picturae historiam quid sit adorandum addiscere. Nam, quod legentibus scriptura, hoc idiotis praestat pictura cernentibus; quia in ipsa etiam ignorantes vident quid sequi debeant, in ipsa legunt qui literas nesciunt. .... Frangi ergo non debuit, quod non ad adorandum in ecclesiis sed ad instruendas solummodo mentes fuit nescientium collocatum.... Atque eis dicendum, Si ad hanc instructionem ad quam imagines antiquitus factae sunt habere vultis in ecclesia, eas modis omnibus et fieri et haberi permitto. Atque indica quod non tibi ipsa visio historiae, quae pictura teste pandebatur, displicuerit, sed illa adoratio quae picturis fuerat incompetenter exhibita..... Et, si quis imagines facere voluerit, minime prohibe; adorari vero imagines modis omnibus veta. *Gregor. I Epist.* XI, 13 (*al.* IX, 9); *Opp.* II, 1100 B, C, 1101 A, *ed. Paris.* 1705.

means to worship any image." By these sentences taken here and there out of Gregory's Epistle to Serenus, (for it were too long to rehearse the whole,) ye may understand whereunto the matter was now come, six hundred years after Christ; that the having of images or pictures in the churches were then maintained[z] in the West part of the world (for they were not so froward[a] yet in the East Church), but the worshipping of them was utterly forbidden. And you may withal note, that seeing there is no ground for worshipping of images in Gregory's writing, but a plain condemnation thereof, that such as do worship images do unjustly allege Gregory for them. And further, if images in the Church do not teach men, according to Gregory's mind, but rather blind them, it followeth that images should not be in the church by his sentence, who only would they should be placed there to the end that they might teach the ignorant. Wherefore, if it be declared that images have been and be worshipped, and also that they teach nothing but errors and lies, (which shall by God's grace hereafter be done[31],) I trust that then by Gregory's own determination all images and image-worshippers shall be overthrown.

But in the mean season Gregory's authority was so great in all the West Church, that by his encouragement men set up images in all places: but their judgment was not so good to consider why he would have them set up, but they fell all on heaps to manifest idolatry by worshipping of them, which Bishop Serenus (not without just cause) feared would come to pass. Now, if Serenus his judgment, thinking it meet that images whereunto idolatry was committed should be destroyed, had taken place, idolatry had been overthrown; for to that which is not no man committeth idolatry. But of Gregory's opinion, thinking that images might be suffered in churches, so it were taught that they should not be worshipped, what ruin of religion and what mischief ensued afterward to all Christendom, experience hath to our great hurt and sorrow proved: first, by the schism rising between the East and the West Church about the said images; next, by the division of the Empire into two parts by the same occasion of images, to the great weakening of all Christendom; whereby, last of all, hath followed the utter overthrow of the Christian religion and noble Empire in Greece and all the East parts of the world, and the encrease of Mahomet's

[z] were then maintained] *so in all.* [a] froward] forward 1587, 1595, 1623.

31 See below, pp. 217, 223–239.

false religion, and the cruel dominion and tyranny of the Saracens and Turks; who do now hang over our necks also that dwell in the West parts of the world, ready at all occasions to overrun us. And all this do we owe unto our idols and images and our idolatry in worshipping of them.

But now give you ear a little to the process of the history. Wherein I do much follow the Histories of Paulus Diaconus and others joined with Eutropius, an old writer[32]: for, though some of the authors were favourers of images, yet do they most plainly and at large prosecute the histories of those times: whom Baptist Platina also in his History of Popes, as in the Lives of Constantine and Gregory the Second, Bishops of Rome, and other places where he entreateth of this matter, doth chiefly follow. After Gregory's time, Constantine, Bishop of Rome, assembled a Council of bishops in the West Church, and did condemn Philippicus, then Emperor, and John, Bishop of Constantinople, of the heresy of the Monothelites, not without a cause indeed, but very justly. When he had so done, by the consent of the learned about him, the said Constantine, Bishop of Rome, caused the images of the ancient fathers, which had been at those six Councils which were allowed and received of all men, to be painted in the entry of St. Peter's church at Rome[33]. When the Greeks had knowledge hereof, they began to dispute and reason the matter of images with the Latins, and held this opinion, that images could have no place in Christ's Church; and the Latins held the contrary, and took part with the images. So the East and West Churches, which agreed evil before, upon this contention about images fell to utter enmity, which was never well reconciled yet. But in the mean season Philippicus and Arthemius or Anastasius, Emperors, commanded images and pictures to be pulled down and rased out in every place of their dominion. After them came Theodosius the Third: he commanded the defaced images to be painted again in their places[34]. But this Theodosius reigned but one year. Leo, the third of that name, succeeded him; who was a Syrian born, a very wise, godly, merciful, and valiant prince. This Leo by proclamation commanded, that all images set up in churches to

Eutrop. Lib. de Rebus Rom. xxiii.

Platina in Vitis Constantini et Greg. II.

32 This is the collection which is now commonly known by the title of *Historia Miscella*. But the writer of the Homily is really following *Bullinger*, *cap.* 25; and Bullinger's statements are not all vouched by the *Historia Miscella*, nor does he himself cite it till he comes to Constantine the Fifth, nor *lib.* XXIII of it till he speaks of the second Nicene Council.

33 *Platina de Vit. Constantini.*

34 *Ibid.*

be worshipped should be plucked down and defaced, and required specially the Bishop of Rome that he should do the same; and himself in the mean season caused all images that were in the imperial city Constantinople to be gathered on an heap into the middle[b] of the city, and there publicly burned them to ashes, and whited over and rased out all pictures painted upon the walls of the temples, and punished sharply divers maintainers of images[35]. And, when some did herefore[c] report him to be a tyrant, he answered, that such of all other were most justly punished, which neither worshipped God aright, nor regarded the imperial majesty and authority, but maliciously rebelled against wholesome and profitable laws. When Gregorius, the third of that name Bishop of Rome, heard of the Emperor's doings in Greece concerning images[d], he assembled a Council of Italian bishops against him; and there made decrees for images, and that more reverence and honour should yet be given to them than was before; and stirred up the Italians against the Emperor, first at Ravenna, and moved them to rebellion. And, as Auspurgensis[e] and Anthonius[f] Bishop of Florence testify in their Chronicles, he caused Rome and all Italy at the last[g] to refuse their obedience and the payment of any more tribute to the Emperor[36], and so by treason and rebellion maintained their idolatry. Which example other bishops of Rome have continually followed and gone through withal most stoutly.

Treason and rebellion for the defence of images.

After this Leo, which[h] reigned thirty four[i] years[37], succeeded his son Constantine the Fifth; who, after his father's example, kept images out of the temples. And, being moved with the Council which Gregory had assembled in Italy for images against his father, he also assembled a Council of all the learned men and bishops of Asia and Greece; although some writers place this Council in Leo Isauricus his father's latter days. In

b into the middle] in the middest *from* 1567. c herefore] therefore *from* 1570. d concerning images] concerning the images *from* 1582. e Auspergensis] Aspurgensis 1570–1595, Uspergensis 1623. f Anthonius] *so in all.* g last] least *from* 1582. h which] who 1623. i thirty four] *so in all.*

35 *Platina de Vit. Greg. II.*

36 *Hist. Miscell.* XXI: *Platina de Vit. Greg. III: Chron. Abbat. Ursperg.* (*Conrad von Lichtenau*) *an.* 731: *Antonin. Chron. Tit.* XIV, *cap.* i. But part of what is here related of Gregory III is ascribed by some of these authorities to his predecessor Gregory II.

37 Leo Isaurus died after a reign of little more than twenty four years. The error is Bullinger's, *cap.* 25, *fol.* 119 a. Near the end of *Hist. Miscell.* XXI there are two consecutive sentences which state the periods of the reigns of Leo and of his son; and Bullinger's eye seems to have passed hastily from the first to the second of them.

A Council against images.

this great assemble[k] they sat in Council from the fourth of the Idus of February to the sixth of the Idus of August[38], and made concerning the use of images this decree: "It is not lawful for them that believe in God through Jesus Christ to have any images, neither of the Creator nor of any creatures, set up in temples to be worshipped; but rather that all images[l], by the law of God and for the avoiding of offence, ought to be taken out of churches[m 39]." And this decree was executed in all places where any images were found in Asia or Greece. And the Emperor sent the determination of this Council holden at Constantinople to Paul then Bishop of Rome[40], and commanded him to cast all images out of the churches: which he, trusting in the friendship of Pipine[n], a mighty prince, refused to do. And both he and his successor Stephanus the Third, who assembled another Council in Italy for images[41], condemned the Emperor and the Council of Constantinople of heresy; and made a decree, that "the holy images" (for so they called them) of Christ, the blessed Virgin, and other Saints were indeed worthy honour and worshipping[42]. When Constantine was dead, Leo the

[k] assemble] assembly *from* 1574. [l] all images] all things 1623. [m] of churches] of the churches *from* 1567. [n] Pipine] *so in all, from the Latin Pipinus.*

38 *Hist. Miscell.* XXII, *an. Constant.* 13; where the number of bishops who were at the Council is set down as 38 instead of 338. It sat A.D. 754.

39 "It is not lawful—out of churches." This is an exact translation of Bullinger's words in his edition of 1539, fol. 119 a: De usu imaginum tandem sic decrevere, Non licere Deo per Jesum Christum fidentibus ulla neque Creatoris neque creaturarum simulachra in templis habere ad cultum, quin potius illa omnia secundum legem Dei et ob scandalum vitandum tollenda esse e templis. Bullinger might seem to have taken this from the *Historia Miscella* (or *Eutropius* as he calls it), but it is not there, neither does it occur totidem verbis in any collection of the *Concilia.*

But in his last edition, published in 1568, at fol. 67 b, he cites some account of the Council as published "a Joanne Sagittario Burdegalensi" in a book called *Canones Conciliorum,* and gives as the "Definitio" or "Decretum" a passage which corresponds with the following. Ἐκ τούτων οὖν τῶν θεοπνεύστων καὶ μακαρίων γραφῶν τε καὶ πατέρων βεβαίως οἰκοδομηθέντες . . . ὁμοφώνως ὁρίζομεν, ἀπόβλητον εἶναι καὶ ἀλλοτρίαν καὶ ἐβδελυγμένην ἐκ τῆς τῶν Χριστιανῶν ἐκκλησίας πᾶσαν εἰκόνα ἐκ παντοίας ὕλης καὶ χρωματουργικῆς τῶν ζωγράφων κακοτεχνίας πεποιημένην· μηκέτι τολμᾷν ἄνθρωπον τὸν οἱονδήποτε ἐπιτηδεύειν τὸ τοιοῦτον ἀσεβὲς καὶ ἀνόσιον ἐπιτήδευμα. ὁ δὲ τολμῶν ἀπὸ τοῦ παρόντος κατασκευάσαι εἰκόνα, ἢ προσκυνῆσαι, ἢ στῆσαι ἐν ἐκκλησίᾳ ἢ ἐν ἰδιωτικῷ οἴκῳ, ἢ κρύψαι, εἰ μὲν ἐπίσκοπος ἢ πρεσβύτερος ἢ διάκονος εἶεν, καθαιρείσθω· εἰ δὲ μονάζων ἢ λαϊκὸς, ἀναθεματιζέσθω, καὶ τοῖς βασιλικοῖς νόμοις ὑπεύθυνος ἔστω, ὡς ἐναντίος τῶν τοῦ Θεοῦ προσταγμάτων καὶ ἐχθρὸς τῶν πατρικῶν δογμάτων. Concil. Labbe VII, 504 E, 508 C; Mansi XIII, 324 D, 328 B.

40 Paul I became Pope in succession to Stephen II May 29, 757, and died June 28, 767.

41 *Platina de Vit. Steph. III.* This Council met at Rome A.D. 769.

42 Si quis sanctas imagines Domini nostri Jesu Christi et ejus Genitricis atque omnium Sanctorum secundum sanctorum patrum statuta venerari noluerit, anathema sit. *Concil. Labbe* VI, 1723 C, *Mansi* XII, 720 D.

Fourth his son reigned after him; who married a woman of the city of Athens, named Theodora, who also was called Hirene[43], by whom he had a son, named Constantine the Sixth; and, dying whilst his son was yet young, left the regiment of the empire and governance of his young son to his wife Hirene. These things were done in the Church about the year of our Lord 760[44].

Or Eirene.

Note here, I pray you, in this process of the story, that in the churches of Asia and Greece there were no images publicly by the space of almost seven hundred years. And there is no doubt but the primitive Church next the Apostles' times[o] was most pure. Note also, that when the contention began about images, how of six Christian Emperors, who were the chief magistrates by God's law to be obeyed, only one, which was Theodosius (who reigned but one year), held with images. All the other Emperors, and all the learned men and bishops of the east Church, and that in assembled Councils, condemned them; besides the two Emperors before mentioned, Valens[45] and Theodosius the Second, who were long before these times, who straitly forbad that any images should be made. And universally after this time all the Emperors of Greece, only Theodosius excepted, destroyed continually all images. Now on the contrary part note ye, that the Bishops of Rome, being no ordinary magistrates appointed of God out of their diocese, but usurpers of princes' authority contrary to God's word, were the maintainers of images against God's word, and stirrers up of sedition and rebellion and workers of continual treason against their sovereign lords, contrary to God's law and the ordinances of all human laws, being not only enemies to God, but also rebels and traitors against their princes. These be the first bringers in of images openly into churches; these be the maintainers of them in the churches; and these be the means whereby they have maintained them, to wit, conspiracy, treason, and rebellion against God and their princes.

Now to proceed in the history most worthy to be known. In the nonage of Constantine the Sixth, the Empress Hirene his

o times] time *from* 1570.

43 In saying that Irene had also the name of Theodora the writer of the Homily follows Bullinger, who seems to have mistaken some words of Sabellicus cited below in note 47.

44 Leo IV became sole Emperor on the death of his father September 14, 775, and died September 8, 780. His son Constantine VI was born January 14, 771.

45 See before, p. 193, n. 28.

mother, in whose hands the regiment of the empire remained, was governed much by the advice of Theodore, Bishop, and Tharasius, Patriarch of Constantinople, who practised and held with the Bishop of Rome in maintaining of images most earnestly. By whose counsel and entreaty the Empress first most wickedly digged up the body of her father in law Constantine the Fifth, and commanded it to be openly burned, and the ashes to be thrown into the sea. Which example (as the constant report goeth) had like to have been put in practice with princes' corses in our days, had the authority of the holy father continued but a little longer[46]. The cause why the Empress Hirene thus used her father in law was, for that he, when he was alive, had destroyed images, and had taken away the sumptuous ornaments of churches, saying that Christ, whose temples they were, allowed poverty and not pearls and precious stones[47]. Afterward the

46 "The common talk was, that if he had not so suddenly ended his life, he would have opened and revealed the purpose of the chief of the clergy (meaning the Cardinal), which was to have taken up King Henry's body at Windsor and to have burned it." *Foxe, Acts and Monuments*, VIII, 637, *ed.* 1849, speaking of Hugh Weston, late Dean of Windsor, who had been "put from all his spiritual livings" by Cardinal Pole in Queen Mary's reign for adultery, and died immediately after the accession of Elizabeth.

47 Bullinger, *cap.* XXV, *fol.* 119 b, *ed.* 1539, has this sentence: Haec illa Hiraene est quae, Theodori antistitis papisantis precibus expugnata, Constantini Imperatoris soceris [*sic*] sui cadaver impie refossum publice cremari jussit cineremque jactari in mare, ideo quod vivus contrivisset idola et templi ornamenta sustulisset, dicens Christum, cujus templa essent, pauperiem non gemmas probasse. He evidently took this from two sentences in *Sabellic. Rhaps. Hist. Ennead.* VIII, *Lib.* viii, (*Tom.* II, *col.* 592 A, *ed.* 1560,) but carelessly threw them into one. Theodora, sive Hirene illa fuit potius, ejus [*sc.* Constantini] nurus, mulier pientissima, Theodori antistitis hortatu cadaver refossum publice cremari jussit, cineremque jactavit in mare. Leo, qui hujus [*sc.* Constantini] fuit filius, paternae impietati, cujus non minus quam imperii haeres fuit, sacrilegium adjecit: nam, quum insano flagraret gemmarum amore, nec ex profano conquisitis expleri posset, ex Sophiae sacrario abstulit, cavillo usus, Christum, cujus templum illud esset, pauperiem non gemmas probasse.

But the exhumation of Constantine Copronymus is ascribed by the ancient authorities, not to Irene, nor even to Theodora, but to Michael III. See for example among the Byzantine Historians *Leo Grammaticus*, or that *Continuator of Theophanes* who wrote an account of the reign of Michael III, *p.* 371 E, *ed. Venet.* 1729, not far from the end of his History; and *Cedrenus*, *p.* 370 B, at the end of his account of the reign of Copronymus. See also *Nicetas David* in his *Life of Ignatius Patriarch of Constantinople*, *Concil. Labbe* VIII, 1208 E, *Mansi* XVI, 241 A. The Emperor Michael III, born in 836, succeeded his father Theophilus January 20, 842, under the guardianship of his mother Theodora. Her influence ceased and she left the court in 857. His uncle Bardas, to whose instigation Cedrenus refers the outrage, was declared Caesar in 856, and was killed in 866. Michael died September 24, 867.

Among the many Theodores of history it is difficult to say who is meant by the "Theodorus antistes" mentioned by Sabellicus. Perhaps he intended Theodorus Graptus, who with his brother Theophanes was so cruelly treated by the Emperor Theophilus, but who never was a bishop, and who did not

said Hirene, at the persuasion of Adrian, Bishop of Rome, and Paul the Patriarch of Constantinople, and his successor Tharasius, assembled a Council of the bishops of Asia and Greece at the city Nicea[48]; where, the Bishop of Rome's legates being presidents of the Council, and ordering all things as they listed, the Council which was[p] assembled before under the Emperor Constantine the Fifth, and had decreed that all images should be destroyed, was condemned as an heretical Council and assemble[q], and a decree was made, that images should be set[r] up in all the churches of Greece, and that honour and worship also should be given unto the said images[49]. And so the Empress, sparing no diligence in setting up of images nor cost in decking them in all churches, made Constantinople within a short time altogether like Rome itself. And now you may see that cummen[s] to pass which Bishop Serenus feared, and Gregory the First forbad in vain, to wit, that images should in no wise be worshipped. For now not only the simple and unwise, unto whom images (as the Scriptures teach) be specially a snare, but the bishops and learned men also, fall to idolatry by occasion of images, yea, and make decrees and laws also for[t] the maintenance of the same. So hard is it, and indeed impossible, any long time to have images publicly in churches and temples without idolatry; as by the space of little more than one hundred years betwixt Gregory the First forbidding most straitly the worshipping of images, and Gregory the Third, Paul, and Leo the Third, Bishops of Rome, with this Council, commanding and decreeing that images should be worshipped, most evidently appeareth.

A decree that images should be worshipped.

Now, when Constantine the young Emperor came to the age of twenty years, he was daily in less and less estimation. For such as were about his mother persuaded her, that it was God's

p which was] which were *from* 1582. q assemble] assembly *from* 1574. r set] put *from* 1582. s cummen] come *from* 1582. t laws also for] laws for *from* 1574.

live to return from exile, although both these things have been said of him by some writers. See *Pagi on Baron. an.* 842, XVI, XVII. If Theodora had any thing to do with the exhumation, she may have been urged to it by Theophanes Graptus, who did return from exile, was present at the grand restoration of images at Constantinople by Theodora in 842, and was afterwards made bishop of Nicea by her.

48 *Hist. Miscell.* XXIII, *ann. Iren. et Constant.* 4, 8. The Council sat A. D. 787.

49 Τούτων οὕτως ἐχόντων . . . ὁρίζομεν . . . ἀνατίθεσθαι τὰς σεπτὰς καὶ ἁγίας εἰκόνας . . . ἐν ταῖς ἁγίαις τοῦ Θεοῦ ἐκκλησίαις . . . καὶ ταύταις ἀσπασμὸν καὶ τιμητικὴν προσκύνησιν ἀπονέμειν . . . καὶ θυμιαμάτων καὶ φώτων προσαγωγὴν πρὸς τὴν τούτων τιμὴν ποιεῖσθαι, καθὼς καὶ τοῖς ἀρχαίοις εὐσεβῶς εἴθισται. ἡ γὰρ τῆς εἰκόνος τιμὴ ἐπὶ τὸ πρωτότυπον διαβαίνει, καὶ ὁ προσκυνῶν τὴν εἰκόνα προσκυνεῖ ἐν αὐτῇ τοῦ ἐγγραφομένου τὴν ὑπόστασιν. Concil. Labbe VIII, 556 C–E, Mansi XIII, 377 C–E.

determination that she should reign alone, and not her son with her. The ambitious woman, believing the same, deprived her son of all imperial dignity; and compelled all the men of war with their captains to swear to her, that they would not suffer her son Constantine to reign during her life. With which indignity the young prince being moved recovered the regiment of the empire unto himself by force; and being brought up in true religion in his father's time, seeing the superstition of his mother Hirene and the idolatry committed by images, cast down, brake, and burned all the idols and images that his mother had set up. But, within a few years after, Hirene the Empress, taken again into her son's favour, after she had persuaded him to put out Nicephorus his uncle's eyes, and to cut out the tongues of his four other uncles, and to forsake his wife, and by such means to bring him in hatred[u] with all his subjects, now further to declare that she was no changeling, but the same woman that had before digged up and burned her father in law's body, and that she would be as natural a mother as she had been kind[x] daughter, seeing the images which she loved so well, and had with so great cost set up, daily destroyed by her son the Emperor, by the help of certain good companions deprived her son of the empire; and first, like a kind and loving mother, put out both his eyes, and laid him in prison; where, after long and many torments, she at the last most cruelly slew him[50]. In this History joined to Eutropius it is written, that the sun was darkened by the space of seventeen days most strangely and dreadfully, and that all men said, that for the horribleness of that cruel and unnatural fact of Hirene, and the putting out of the Emperor's eyes, the sun had lost his light. But indeed God would signify by the darkness of the sun, into what darkness and blindness of ignorance and idolatry all[y] Christendom should fall by the occasion of images, the bright sun of his eternal truth, and light of his holy word, by the mists and black clouds of men's traditions being blemished and darkened: as by sundry most terrible earthquakes happening[z] about the same time[51] God signified, that the quiet state[a] of true religion should by such idolatry be most horribly tossed and turmoiled.

[u] in hatred] into hatred *from* 1582. [x] been kind] been a kind 1623. [y] all] of 1582, *omitted* 1623. [z] happening] that happened *from* 1563 B. [a] quiet state] quieter state 1570, quiet estate *from* 1571.

50 Crudeliter et insanabiliter oculos ejus evellunt, ita ut hunc mors subsequens confestim extingueret, consilio matris suae. *Hist. Miscell.* XXIII, *an. Constant.* 7.

51 *Ibid. an. Constant.* 6.

And here may you see what a gracious and virtuous lady this Hirene was, how loving a niece to her husband's uncles, how kind a mother in law to her son's wife, how loving a daughter to her father in law, how natural a mother to her own son, and what a stout and valiant captain the bishops of Rome had of her for the setting up and maintenance of their idols or images. Surely they could not have found a meeter patron for the maintenance of such a matter than this Hirene; whose ambition and desire of rule was insatiable, whose treason, continually studied and wrought, was most abominable, whose wicked and unnatural cruelty passed Medea and Progne, whose detestable parricides have ministered matter to poets to write their horrible tragedies. And yet certain historiographers, who do put in writing all these her horrible wickedness[b], for love they had to images, which she maintained, do praise her as a godly Empress and as sent from God[52]. Such is the blindness of false superstition, if it once take possession in a man's mind, that it will both declare the vices of wicked princes, and also commend them. But, not long after, the said Hirene, being suspected to the princes and lords of Greece of treason in alienating the empire to Charles king of the Francons and for practising a secret marriage between herself and the said king, and being convicted of the same, was by the said lords deposed and deprived again of the empire, and carried into exile into the island Lesbos, where she ended her lewd life[53].

Another Council against images.

Whiles[c] these tragedies about images were thus in working[d] in Greece, the same question of the use of images in churches began to be moved in Spain also. And at Elibery, a noble[e] city now called Granate, was a Council of Spanish bishops and other learned men assembled[54]; and there, after long deliberation and debating of the matter, it was concluded at length of the whole[f] Council after this sort in the thirty-sixth article[55]:

b wickedness] wickednesses 1587, 1595, 1623. c whiles] while 1587, 1595, 1623. d thus in working] thus working *from* 1582. e noble] notable 1595, 1623. f of the whole] by the whole 1623.

52 Pia Imperatrix : Piissima : Deo dilecta Eirene. *Ibid. ann.* 4, 5, 6.

53 *Ibid. ann. Iren.* 5, 6; and XXIV, *an. Niceph.* 1: *Sabellic. Rhaps. Hist. Ennead.* VIII, *Lib.* ix.

54 The Concilium Eliberitanum or Illiberitanum sat at Illiberis, by some called Elvira, from the ruins of which the Moorish city of Granada arose in the tenth century. Various dates within the third and fourth centuries have been assigned to it: the best chronologers place it about A. D. 300. See note 58 below.

55 Placuit picturas in ecclesia esse non debere, ne quod colitur et adoratur in parietibus depingatur. *Concil. Labbe* I, 974, *Mansi* II, 11.

Decrees[g] of the Council against images.

"We think that pictures ought not to be in churches, lest that which is honoured or worshipped be painted on walls." And in the forty-first canon of that Council it is thus written[56]: "We thought good to admonish the faithful, that, as much as in them lieth, they suffer no images to be in their houses: but, if they fear any violence of their servants, at the least let them keep themselves clean and pure from images; if they do not so, let them be accounted as none of the Church." Note here, I pray you, how a whole and great country in the West and South parts of Europe, nearer to Rome a great[h] deal than to Greece in situation of place, do agree with the Greeks against images, and do not only forbid them in churches, but also in private houses, and do excommunicate them that do the contrary. And another Council of the learned men of all Spain also, called Concilium Toletanum Duodecimum, decreed and determined likewise against images and image worshippers[57].

Yet another Council against images.

But, when these decrees of the Spanish Council at Elibery came to the knowledge of the Bishop of Rome and his adherents, they, fearing[i] lest all Germany also would decree against images and forsake them, thought to prevent the matter, and by the consent and help of the prince of Francons (whose power was then most great in the West parts of the world) assembled a Council of Germans at Frankford, and there procured the Spanish Council against images aforementioned to be condemned by the name of the Felician heresy, (for that Felix, Bishop of Aquitania, was chief in that Council,) and obtained that the acts of the second Nicene Council assembled by Hirene (the holy empress whom ye heard of before) and the sentence of the bishop of Rome for images might be received[58]. For much

g Decrees] Doctors *from* 1574. h a great] a greater *from* 1582. i fearing] feared 1563 B—1570.

56 Admoneri placuit fideles, ut in quantum possint prohibeant, ne idola in domibus suis habeant: si vero vim metuunt servorum, vel seipsos puros conservent; si non fecerint, alieni ab Ecclesia habeantur. *Labbe* I, 975, *Mansi* II, 12.

57 Praecepta haec Domini [sc. *Exod.* xx, 4, 5; xxii. 20; *Deut.* xvii, 2–5] apponentes..., cultores idolorum, veneratores lapidum, accensores facularum, et excolentes sacra fontium vel arborum admonemus, ut agnoscant quod ipsi se spontaneae morti subjiciunt qui diabolo sacrificare videntur. *Concil. Tolet.* XII *cap.* XI; *Concil. Labbe* VI, 1234, *Mansi* XI, 1037. This Council sat A.D. 681.

58 In these mistakes concerning the Councils of Illiberis and Frankfort and the Felician heresy the writer of the Homily followed Bullinger, cap. xxv, who in his edition of 1568 thus acknowledged them. Videntur in hac expositione Platina in Vita Adriani et Nauclerus Generat. 27 una cum aliquot neotericis scriptoribus aberrasse. Quos et ego secutus (ne quid dissimulem) in priore hujus operis mei editione existimavi

after this sort do the papists report the[k] history of the Council of Frankford[59]. Notwithstanding, the book of Carolus Magnus his own writing (as the title sheweth[60]), which is now put in print and commonly in men's hands, sheweth the judgment of that prince, and of the whole Council of Frankford also, to be against images and against the second Council of Nice assembled by Hirene for images, and calleth it an arrogant, foolish, and ungodly Council, and declareth the assemble[l] of the Council of Frankford to have been directly made and gathered against that Nicene Council and the errors of the same[61]. So that it

[k] report the] report of the *from* 1567. [l] assemble] assembly 1587, 1595, 1623.

in Francfordiensi Synodo damnatam esse Felicianam haeresim de tollendis imaginibus. Sed et perperam putavi Eliberi coactam esse Synodum in Hispania quae authore Felice hoc damnaverit usum imaginum in templis. Dicam postea de Eliberana Synodo. Ex historiis autem probatioribus constat, Felicem non ob imagines, sed aliam ob causam..., esse damnatum, deinde reprobatam in Francfordiensi Synodo separatim Nicenam Synodum. *Fol.* 69 a. In cap. xxx he speaks again of the Council of Illiberis, placing it about A. D. 320, and citing the same two canons, 36 and 41.

59 Several of the "Neoterici Scriptores" to whom Bullinger refers (in the passage cited in note 58) as having led him into his mistake about the Council of Frankfort, are enumerated by Goldast at p. 64 of his collection of *Imperialia Decreta de Cultu Imaginum.* Binius also in his third note on the title of the Council of Frankfort maintained that that Council decided in favour of the worship of images, and not against it, although both Bellarmine and Baronius had already admitted the contrary. *Concil. Labbe* VII, 1069, *Mansi* XIII, 914.

60 Opus Inlustrissimi et Excellentissimi seu Spectabilis Viri, Caroli, nutu Domini, Regis Francorum, Gallias, Germaniam, Italiamque, sive harum finitimas provincias, Domino opitulante Regentis, contra Synodum, quae in partibus Graeciae pro adorandis imaginibus stolide sive arroganter gesta est. Besides this title, there are places also in the body of the work which shew that it was put forth in the name of Charlemagne; but the person whom he employed to write it was probably Alcuin. See Heumann's Preface to the edition of it which he published at Hanover in 1731, §§ 26–29. The work was first printed at Paris, but without name of place, in 1549.

61 Nos denique Propheticis, Evangelicis, et Apostolicis Scripturis contenti, et sanctorum orthodoxorum Patrum... institutis imbuti, et sanctas et universales sex Synodos... suscipientes, omnes novitates vocum et stultiloquas adinventiones abjicimus; et non solum non suscipimus, verum etiam tanquam purgamenta despicimus; sicut et eam quae propter adorandarum imaginum impudentissimam traditionem in Bithyniae partibus gesta est Synodum. Cujus scripturae textus... ad nos usque pervenit: contra cujus errores... scribere compulsi sumus..... Quod opus aggressi sumus cum conniventia sacerdotum in regno a Deo nobis concesso catholicis gregibus praelatorum. *Carol. Magn. de Imp. Imagg. Cult. Praefat. pp.* 10, 11.

Charlemagne's judgment however was not entirely "against images," but against all worship of them. Nos denique, he says,... imagines in ornamentis ecclesiarum et memoria rerum gestarum habentes, et solum Deum adorantes, et ejus Sanctis opportunam venerationem exhibentes, nec cum illis [*sc.* Iconoclastis] frangimus, nec cum istis [*sc.* Graecis in Conc. Nic. II] adoramus. *Praefat. p.* 12.

The Council of Frankfort sat A. D. 794. The beginning of its Acts, including the first two canons, is as follows.

Convenientibus, Deo favente, aposto-

must needs follow, that either there were in one prince's time two Councils assembled at Frankford, one contrary to another[m], which by no history doth appear, or else that, after their custom, the popes and papists have most shamefully corrupted that Council[n], as their manner is to handle, not only Councils, but also all Histories and writings of the old doctors, falsifying and corrupting them for the maintenance of their wicked and ungodly purposes, as hath in times of late come to light, and doth in our days more and more continually appear most evidently. Let the forged gift of Constantine[62], and the notable attempt to falsify the first Nicene Council for the pope's supremacy, practised by popes in St. Augustine's time, be a witness hereof; which practice indeed had then taken effect, had not the diligence and wisdom of St. Augustine and other learned and godly bishops in Afrike by their great labour and charges also resisted and stopped the same[63].

The forged gift of Constantine, &c. Nicene Council like to be falsified.

m another] the other 1623. n that Council] the Council 1623.

lica auctoritate, atque piissimi domni nostri Caroli Regis jussione, anno XXVI principatus sui, cunctis regni Francorum, seu Italiae, Aquitaniae, Provinciae, episcopis ac sacerdotibus synodali concilio; inter quos ipse mitissimus sancto interfuit conventui:

1. Ubi in primordio capitulorum exortum est de impia ac nefanda haeresi Elipandi Toletanae sedis Episcopi et Felicis Orgellitanae eorumque sequacibus, qui male sentientes in Dei Filio asserebant adoptionem. Quam omnes qui supra sanctissimi patres et respuentes una voce contradixerunt, atque hanc haeresim funditus a sancta Ecclesia eradicandam statuerunt.

2. Allata est in medium quaestio de nova Graecorum Synodo, quam de adorandis imaginibus Constantinopoli fecerunt, in qua scriptum habebatur, ut qui imaginibus Sanctorum, ita ut Deificae Trinitati, servitium aut adorationem non impenderent anathema judicarentur. Qui supra sanctissimi patres nostri omnimodis adorationem et servitutem renuentes contempserunt atque consentientes condemnaverunt. *Concil. Labbe* VII, 1057, *Mansi* XIII, 909. Constantinople is here named as the place where the Council sat, because it was originally summoned to meet there.

62 Jewel in his *Defence of the Apology, Part* V, *Ch.* vi, *Div.* 10, on "Constantine's Donation," has this passage. "The fable hereof is so peevish, that the wisest and best learned of your very friends, Platina, Cardinal Cusanus, Marsilius Patavinus, Laurentius Valla, Antoninus Florentinus, Otho Frisingensis, Hieronymus Paulus Catalanus, Volaterranus, Nauclerus, Capnion, Molinaeus, and others, have openly reproved it unto the world, and have written against it, and are much ashamed of your follies. And, to allege one instead of many, Cardinal Cusanus hereof hath written thus: Donationem Constantini diligenter expendens reperi ex ipsamet scriptura manifesta argumenta confictionis et falsitatis: 'Advisedly weighing this donation or grant of Constantine' (whereby the pope claimeth all his temporal power) 'even in the penning thereof I find manifest tokens of falsehood and forgery.' *Nic. Cusan. de Concord. Cath. Lib.* III, *cap.* ii." The most effective of the works to which Jewel refers was Valla's *De falso Credita et Ementita Constantini Donatione Declamatio,* written about 1440, which seems to have been first published in 1517 by Ulrich Hutten with a dedication to Pope Leo X. See *Milman's History of Latin Christianity, Book* I, *ch.* ii, *note* a.

63 Pope Zosimus in the year 418 tried

Now to come towards an end of this history, and to shew you the principal point that came to pass by the maintenance of images. Whereas, from Constantinus Magnus' time until that day[o], all authority imperial and princely dominion of the Empire of Rome remained continually in the right and possession of the Emperors, who had their continuance and seat imperial at Constantinople, the city royal, Leo the Third, then Bishop of Rome, seeing the Greek Emperors so bent against his *gods of gold and silver, timber and stone*[8], and having the king of the Francons or Frenchmen, named Charles, whose power was exceeding great in the West countries, very appliable to his mind for causes hereafter appearing, under the pretence that they of Constantinople were for that matter of images under the Pope's ban and curse, and therefore unworthy to be Emperors or to bear rule, and for that the Emperors of Greece, being far off, were not ready at a beck to defend the Pope against the Lombards his enemies and others[p] with whom he had variance, this Leo the Third, I say, attempted a thing exceeding strange and unheard of before and of incredible[q] boldness and presumption: for he by his papal authority doth translate the government of the Empire and the crown and name imperial from the Greeks, and giveth it unto Charles the Great, king of the Francons[64]; not without the consent of the forenamed Hirene, Empress of Greece, who also sought to be joined in marriage with the said Charles. For the which cause the said Hirene was by the lords of Greece deposed and banished, as one that had betrayed the Empire, as ye before have heard. And the said princes of Greece did, after the deprivation of the said Hirene, by common consent elect and create (as they always had done) an Emperor, named Nicephorus: whom the Bishop of Rome and they of the West would not acknowledge for their Emperor, for they had already created them another. And so there became two Emperors[65]: and the Empire, which was before one, was divided into two parts upon occasion of idols and images and the wor-

8 [Dan. v, 4, 23.]

These things were done about the 803 year of our Lord.

o that day] this day *from* 1582. p others] other *from* 1570. q incredible] uncredible *from* 1582.

to establish his right to receive appeals from the judgments of bishops in Africa by citing a canon made by the Synod of Sardica in 347 as having been made by the great Council of Nicea in 325, and the attempt was continued by his two immediate successors, Boniface I and Celestine I. For an account of the case see *Jewel's Reply to Harding's Answer, Art.* IV. *Div.* vi, "The Pope a Forger," or *Milman's History of Latin Christianity, Book* II, *ch.* iv.

64 *Platina de Vit. Leon. III.*

65 *Sabellic. Rhaps. Hist. Ennead.* VIII, *Lib.* ix.

shipping of them; even as the kingdom of the Israelites was in old time for the like cause of idolatry divided in king Roboam his time. And so the Bishop of Rome, having the favour of Charles the Great by this means assured to him, was wondrously enhanced in power and authority, and did in all the West Church, specially[r] in Italy, what he lust; where images were set up, garnished, and worshipped of all sorts of men. But images were not so fast set up and so much honoured in Italy and the West, but Nicephorus, Emperor of Constantinople, and his successors Scauratius, the two Michaels, Leo, Theophilus[66], and other Emperors their successors in the Empire of Greece, continually pulled them down, brake them, burned them, and destroyed them as fast. And, when Theodorus Emperor would at the Council of Lyons have agreed with the Bishop of Rome, and have set up images, he was by the nobles of the Empire of Greece deprived, and another chosen in his place[67]. And so rose a jealousy, suspicion, grudge, hatred, and enmity between the Christians and Empires of the East countries and West, which could never be quenched nor pacified. So that, when the Saracens first, and afterward the Turks, invaded the Christians, the one part of Christendom would not help the other. By reason whereof at the last the noble Empire of Greece, and the city imperial Constantinople, was lost, and is come into the hands of the infidels; who now have overrun almost all Christendom, and possessing past the middle of Hungary, which is part of the

Or Stauratius.

[r] specially] especially 1623.

66 The Emperors here enumerated were not all Iconoclasts, and upon the death of Theophilus in the year 842 image worship, at least the worship of Icons or pictures, if not of *graven* images, was finally established in the East by his widow Theodora.

The authorities cited in most of the preceding notes are those which the writer of the Homily seems to have followed. The reader may be further referred to Milman's *History of Latin Christianity, Book* IV, *chapters* vii *and* viii, for an account of image worship and of iconoclasm in the East, and to the following chapters of the same book for a history of the immediate consequence of the latter in the West.

67 It was the Emperor Michael Palaeologus, the usurping successor of Theodore Lascaris II, who, in order to maintain himself in secure possession of Constantinople, which he had recovered in 1261 from Baldwin II the last of the Latin Emperors, solemnly acknowledged the absolute supremacy of the see of Rome at the great Council of Lyons under Pope Gregory X in 1274, and afterwards endangered his throne, and actually forfeited the privilege of Christian burial, by attempting to force his clergy to make the same acknowledgment at the bidding of Pope Nicholas III. But the worship of images was not then in question. *Pachymeres, Mich.* I, II, V, VI; *Andron.* I, 11; VI, 2: *Concil. Labbe* XI, 957–967, *Mansi* XXIV, 64–73: *Gibbon,* LXI, LXII: *Milman's History of Latin Christianity,* XI, iv.

West Empire, do hang over all our heads to the utter danger of all Christendom.

Thus we see what a sea of mischiefs the maintenance of images hath brought with it; what an horrible schism between the East and the West Church; what an hatred between one Christian and another; Councils against Councils, Church against Church, Christians against Christians, princes against princes; rebellions, treasons, unnatural and most cruel murders; the daughter digging up and burning her father the emperor his[s] body; the mother, for love of idols, most abominably murdering her own son, being an emperor; at the last, the tearing in sunder of Christendom and the Empire into two pieces, till the Infidels, Saracens, and Turks, common enemies to both parts, have most cruelly vanquished, destroyed, and subdued the one part, the whole Empire of Greece, Asia the Less, Thracia, Macedonia, Epirus, and many other great and goodly countries and provinces, and have won a great piece of the other Empire, and put the whole in dreadful fear and most horrible danger[68]. For it is (not without a just and great cause) to be dread, lest, as the Empire of Rome was even for the like cause of images and the worshipping of them torn in pieces and divided, as was for idolatry the kingdom of Israel in old time divided, so like punishment as for the like offence fell upon the Jews will also light upon us; that is, lest the cruel tyrant and enemy of our common wealth and religion, the Turk, by God's just vengeance, in like wise partly murder and partly lead away into captivity us Christians, as did the Assyrian and Babylonian kings murder and lead away the Israelites; and lest the Empire of Rome and Christian religion be so utterly brought under foot, as was then the kingdom of Israel and true religion of God. Whereunto the matter already, as I have declared, shrewdly inclineth on our part; the greater part of Christendom, within less than three hundred years' space, being

[s] emperor his] emperor's (*but without the comma*) *from* 1567.

68 Among the occasional Forms of Prayer which were set forth by authority in the reign of Queen Elizabeth, two, in 1565 and 1566, were specially appointed "to excite all godly people to pray unto God for the delivery of those Christians that are now invaded by the Turk," and a third in 1572 contains allusions to the same danger. See the volume of *Liturgical Services temp. Eliz.* edited for the Parker Society in 1847 by the Rev. W. K. Clay, *pp.* 460, 461, 519, 527, 540–547. The alarm caused by the progress of the Turks is again shewn in the Second Part of the Homily of the Place and Time of Prayer.

brought in[t] captivity and most miserable thraldom under the Turks[u], and the noble Empire of Greece clean everted: whereas, if the Christians, divided by these image matters, had holden together, no infidels and miscreants[69] could thus have prevailed against Christendom. And all this mischief and misery which we have hitherto fallen into do we owe to our mighty *gods of gold and silver, stock and stone*[ε]; in whose help and defence, where they cannot help themselves, we have trusted so long, until our enemies the infidels have overcome and overrun us almost altogether: a just reward for those that have left the mighty living God, the Lord of hosts, and have stooped and given the honour due to him to dead blocks and stocks, who *have*[ζ] *eyes and see not, ears and hear not*[x], *feet and cannot go*, and so forth, and are *cursed* of God, *and all they that make them, and that put their trust in them.*

[ε] [Dan. v, 4, 23.]

[ζ] [Ps. cxv, 5-8; xcvii, 7: Deut. xxvii, 15: Is. xlii, 17; xlv, 16: Wisd. xiv, 8.]

Thus you understand, well beloved in our Saviour Christ, by the judgment of the old learned and godly doctors of the Church and by ancient Histories Ecclesiastical, agreeing to the verity of God's word alleged out of the Old Testament and the New, that images and image worshipping were in the primitive Church, which was most pure and uncorrupt, abhorred and detested as abominable and contrary to true Christian religion; and that, when images began to creep into the Church, they were not only spoken and written against by godly and learned bishops, doctors, and clerks, but also condemned by whole Councils of bishops and learned men assembled together; yea, the said images by many Christian emperors and bishops were defaced, broken, and destroyed, and that above seven hundred and eight hundred years ago; and that therefore it is not of late days, as some would bear you in hand[70], that images and image worshipping have been spoken and written against. Finally, you have heard what mischief and misery hath, by the occasion of the said images, fallen upon whole Christendom, besides the loss of infinite souls, which is most horrible of all. Wherefore let us beseech God, that we, being warned by his holy word forbidding all idolatry, and by the writings[y] of old

[t] brought in] brought into *from* 1567. [u] Turks] Turk *from* 1570. [x] ears and hear not] *omitted after* 1574. [y] writings] writing *from* 1582.

69 miscreants: misbelievers, *mécréants.*

70 bear you in hand: lead you on in belief; sometimes, in expectation.

How you were borne in hand, how crossed. *Shakespeare, Macb.* III, 1.

See before, p. 103, n. 13. Jewel renders fingunt "they bear us in hand" in his *Treatise of the Sacraments, p.* 1129, *ed.* Park. Soc.

godly doctors and Ecclesiastical Histories, written and preserved by God's ordinance for our admonition and warning, may flee from all idolatry, and so escape the horrible punishment and plagues, as well worldly as everlasting, threatened for the same. Which God our heavenly Father grant us for our only Saviour and Mediator Jesus Christ's sake. Amen.

THE THIRD PART OF THE HOMILY

AGAINST IMAGES AND THE WORSHIPPING OF THEM,

CONTAINING THE CONFUTATION OF THE PRINCIPAL ARGUMENTS WHICH ARE USED TO BE MADE FOR THE MAINTENANCE OF IMAGES: WHICH PART MAY SERVE TO INSTRUCT THE CURATES THEMSELVES, OR MEN OF[a] GOOD UNDERSTANDING.

NOW ye have heard how plainly, how vehemently, and that in many places, the word of God speaketh against not only idolatry and worshipping of images, but also against idols and images themselves: (I mean always thus herein, in that we be stirred and provoked by them to worship them, and not as though they were simply forbidden by the New Testament without such occasion and danger[b].) And ye have[c] heard likewise out of Histories Ecclesiastical the beginning, proceeding, and success of idolatry by images, and the great contention in the Church of Christ about them to the great trouble and decay of Christendom. And withal ye have heard the sentences of old ancient fathers and godly learned doctors and bishops against images and idolatry, taken out of their own writings. It remaineth that such reasons as be made for the maintenance of images, and excessive painting, gilding, and decking, as well of them as of temples[d] or churches, also be answered and confuted, partly by application of some places before alleged to their reasons, and partly by otherwise answering the same. Which part hath the last place in this treatise, for that it cannot well be[e] understanded[f] of the meaner sort, nor the arguments of image maintainers can without prolixity too much tedious be answered, without the knowledge of the treatise going before. And, although divers things before mentioned be here rehearsed again, yet this repetition is not superfluous, but in a manner necessary; for that the simple sort cannot else understand how the foresaid places are to be applied to the

[a] OR MEN OF] OR TO BE READ IN SUCH AUDITORIES AS BE OF 1563 A 1. [b] (I mean——and danger.)] *not in* 1563 A 1. [c] And ye have] and have 1563 A 1. [d] of temples] of the temples *from* 1563 B. [e] well be] be well *from* 1571. [f] understanded] understood 1623.

arguments of such as do maintain images, wherewith otherwise they might be abused.

First, it is alleged by them that maintain images, that all laws, prohibitions, and curses noted by us out of the holy Scripture, and sentences of the doctors also by us alleged, against images and the worshipping of them, appertain to the idols of the Gentiles or Pagans, as the idol of Jupiter, Mars, Mercury, &c., and not to our images of God, of Christ, and his Saints. But it shall be declared both by God's word and the sentences of the ancient doctors and judgment of the primitive Church, that all images, as well ours as the idols of the Gentiles, be forbidden and unlawful, namely, in churches and temples.

And first this is to be replied out of God's word, that the images of God the Father, the Son, and the Holy Ghost, either severally, or the images of the Trinity, which we had in every church, be by the Scriptures expressly and directly forbidden and condemned, as appeareth by these places.

Deut. iv, [12, 16.]

The Lord spake unto you out of the middle of fire: you heard the voice or sound *of his words, but you did see no form* or shape *at all. Lest peradventure you, being deceived, should make to yourself any graven image or likeness:* and so forth, as is at large rehearsed in the first part of this treaty[g] against images. And therefore in the old Law the middle of the propitiatory, which represented[h] God's seat, was empty; lest any should take occasion to make any similitude or likeness of him. Esay, after he hath set forth the incomprehensible Majesty of God, he asketh,

Is. xl, [18–21.]

To whom then will ye make God like? or what similitude will ye set up unto him? Shall the carver make him a carven[i] *image? And shall the goldsmith cover him with gold, or cast him into a form of silver plates? And for the poor man shall the image maker frame an image of timber, that he may have somewhat to set up also?* And after this he crieth out, O wretches, *heard ye never of this? Hath it not been preached to you sith*[k] *the beginning,* how by the creation of the world and the greatness of the work they might understand the Majesty of God, the Maker and Creator of all, to be greater than that it could be expressed or set forth in any image or bodily similitude? Thus far the Prophet Esay; who from the forty-fourth chapter to the forty-ninth intreateth in a manner of no other thing. And St. Paul in the

[g] treaty] treatise *from* 1582. [h] represented] presented *from* 1571. [i] carven] carved *from* 1582. [k] sith] since *from* 1571.

Acts of the Apostles evidently teacheth the same, that no similitude can be made unto God in *gold, silver, stone,* or any other matter. By these and many other places of Scripture it is evident, that no image either ought or can be made unto God. For how can *God*[α], *a* most pure *Spirit,* whom *man never saw,* be expressed by a gross, bodily, and visible similitude? How can the infinite Majesty and greatness of God, incomprehensible to man's mind[β], much more not able to be compassed with the sense, be expressed in a finite[1] and little image? How can a dead and *dumb image* express *the living God*[γ]? What can an image, which when it is fallen cannot rise up again, which can neither help his friends nor hurt his enemies, express of the most puissant and mighty God, who alone is able to reward his friends and to destroy his enemies everlastingly? A man might justly cry with the prophet Habacuc[1], *Shall such images* instruct or *teach* any thing right of God? or shall they become doctors? Wherefore men that have made an image of God, whereby to honour him, have thereby dishonoured him most highly, diminished his Majesty, blemished his glory, and falsified his truth. And therefore St. Paul saith that such as have framed any similitude or image of God like a mortal man or any other likeness, in timber, stone, or other matter, *have changed his truth into a lie.* For both they thought it to be no longer that which it was, a stock or a stone, and took it to be that which it was not, as God, or an image of God. Wherefore an image of God is not only a lie, but a double lie also. But *the devil is a liar, and the father of lies:* wherefore the lying images which be made of God, to his great dishonour and horrible danger of his people, came from the devil. Wherefore they be convict of foolishness and wickedness in making of images of God or the Trinity: for that no image of God ought or can be made, as by the Scriptures and good reason evidently appeareth; yea, and once to desire an image of God cometh of infidelity, thinking not God to be present except they might see some sign or image of him, as appeareth by the Hebrews in the wilderness willing Aaron to make them gods[δ] whom they might see go before them.

Acts xvii, [29.]

α [John i, 18; iv, 24: 1 Tim. vi, 16: 1 John iv, 12, 20.]

β [Job xi, 7.]

γ [2 Kings xix, 4: Acts xiv, 15: 1 Cor. xii, 2: 2 Cor. vi, 16: 1 Thess. i, 9.]

Hab. ii, [19.]

Rom. i, [25.]

John viii, [44.]

δ [Exod. xxxii, 1.]

Where they object, that seeing in Esaias and Daniel be certain descriptions of God, as sitting on a high seat, &c., why may not

[Is. vi, 1: Dan. vii, 9, 10.]

[1] a finite] an infinite 1570–1574, a small *from* 1582.

1 Vae qui dicit ligno, Expergiscere: Surge, lapidi tacenti. Numquid ipse docere poterit? *Vulg.*

a painter likewise set him forth in colours to be seen, as it were a judge sitting in a throne, as well as he is described in writing of the Prophets[m], seeing that scripture or writing, and picture, differ but a little? first it is to be answered, that things forbidden by God's word, as painting of images of God, and things permitted of God, as such descriptions used of the Prophets, be not all one; neither ought nor can man's reason (although it shew never so goodly) prevail any thing against God's express word and plain statute law, as I may well term it. Furthermore the Scripture, although it have certain descriptions of God, yet, if you read on forth, it expoundeth itself, declaring[e] that *God is a* pure *Spirit*, infinite, who *replenisheth heaven and earth:* which the picture doth not, nor expoundeth not itself[n], but rather, when it hath set God forth in a bodily similitude, leaveth a man there, and will easily bring one into the heresy of the Anthropomorphites, thinking God to have hands and feet and to sit as a man doth; which they that do, saith St. Augustine in his book De Fide et Symbolo, cap. VII[2], fall "into that sacrilege which the Apostle detesteth in those who *have changed the glory of the incorruptible God into the similitude of a corruptible man.* For it is wickedness for a Christian to erect such an image to God in a temple; and much more wickedness to erect such a one in his heart" by believing of it.

e [John iv, 24: 1 Kings viii, 27: Acts xvii, 24, 25: Jer. xxiii, 24.]

[Rom. i, 23.]

But to this they reply, that, this reason notwithstanding, images of Christ may be made, for that he took upon him flesh, and became man. It were well that they would first grant that they have hitherto done most wickedly in making and maintaining of images of God and of the Trinity in every place, whereof they are by force of God's word and good reason convicted, and then to descend to the trial for other images.

Now concerning their objection, that an image of Christ may be made, the answer is easy: for in God's word and religion it is not only inquired[o] whether a thing may be done or no, but

m of the Prophets] by the Prophets 1623.

n expoundeth not itself] expoundeth itself *from* 1582.

o inquired] required *from* 1570.

2 Credimus etiam, quod SEDET AD DEXTERAM PATRIS. Nec ideo tamen quasi humana forma circumscriptum esse Deum Patrem arbitrandum est, ut de illo cogitantibus dextrum aut sinistrum latus animo occurrat, aut idipsum quod sedere Pater dicitur flexis poplitibus fieri putandum est; ne in illud incidamus sacrilegium in quo execratur Apostolus eos qui *commutaverunt gloriam incorruptibilis Dei in similitudinem corruptibilis hominis.* Tale enim simulacrum Deo nefas est Christiano in templo collocare; multo magis in corde nefarium est, ubi vere est templum Dei si a terrena cupiditate atque errore mundetur. *Augustin. de Fide et Symb.* § 14, *Opp.* VI, 157 C.

also whether it be lawful and agreeable to God's word to be done or no. For all wickedness may be and is daily done which yet ought not to be done. And the words of the reasons above alleged out of the Scriptures are, that images neither ought nor can be made unto God. Wherefore to reply that images of Christ may be made, except withal it be proved that it is lawful for them to be made, is, rather than to hold one's peace, to say somewhat, but nothing to the purpose.

And yet it appeareth that no image can be made of Christ but a lying image, as the Scripture peculiarly calleth images *lies*[ς]. For Christ is God and man: seeing therefore that of the Godhead[p], which is the most excellent part, no image[q] can be made, it is falsely called the image of Christ: wherefore images of Christ be not only defects, but also lies. Which reason serveth also for the images of Saints, whose souls, the more[r] excellent parts of them, can by no images be represented[s] and expressed: wherefore they be no images of Saints, whose souls reign in joy with God, but of the bodies of Saints, which as yet lie putrified in the graves. Furthermore, no true image can be made of Christ's body, for it is unknown now of what form and countenance he was. And there be in Greece and at Rome and in other places divers images of Christ, and none of them like to another[t], and yet every of them affirmeth that theirs is the true and lively image of Christ, which cannot possibly[u] be. Wherefore, as soon as an image of Christ is made, by and by is a lie made of him, which by God's word is forbidden. Which also is true of the images of any Saints of antiquity, for that it is unknown of what form and countenance they were. Wherefore, seeing that religion ought to be grounded upon truth, images, which cannot be without lies, ought not to be made or put to any use of religion, or to be placed in churches and temples, places peculiarly appointed to true religion and service of God. And thus much, that no true image of God, our Saviour Christ, or his Saints can be made: wherewithal is also confuted that their allegation, that images be the laymen's books. For it is evident of that[x] which is afore rehearsed, that they teach no things of God, of our Saviour Christ, and of his Saints but lies and errors. Wherefore either they be no books, or, if they be, they be false and lying books, the teachers of all error.

ς [Jer. x, 14; li, 17:] Rom. i, [25.]

p of the Godhead] for the Godhead *from* 1567. q image] images *from* 1563 G. r more] most *from* 1582. s represented] presented *from* 1582. t another] other *from* 1567. u possibly] possiblie 1563 A, possible *from* 1563 B. x of that] by that 1623.

And now, if it should be admitted and granted that an image of Christ could truly be made, yet is it[y] unlawful that it should be made, yea, or that the image of any Saint should be made, specially to be set up in temples to the great and unavoidable danger of idolatry, as hereafter shall be proved. And first concerning the image of Christ, that, though it might be had truly, yet it were unlawful to have it in churches publicly, is a notable

Lib. i, cap. 24.

place in Ireneus; who reproved the heretics called Gnostici[3], for that they carried about the image of Christ, made truly after his own proportion in Pilate's time, as they said, and therefore more to be esteemed than those lying images of him which we now have. The which Gnostici also used to set garlands upon the head of the said image, to shew their affection to it. But to go to God's word. Be not, I pray you, the words of the

ς Lev. xxvi, [1:] Deut. v, [8.] *Sculptile, Fusile, Similitudo.* Deut. [iv, 15–18;] xxvii, [15.]

Scripture plain[ς]? *Beware lest thou, being deceived, make to thyself,* to say, to any use of religion, *any graven image, or any similitude of any thing,* &c. And, *Cursed be the man that maketh a graven or molten image, abomination before the Lord,* &c. Be not our images such? Be not our images of Christ and his Saints either carved, or molten and cast[z], or similitudes of men and women? It is happy that we have not followed the Gentiles in making of images of beasts, fishes, and vermins also. Notwithstanding, the image of an horse, as also the image of the ass that Christ rode on[4], have in divers places been brought into the church and temple of God. And is not that which is written in the beginning of the Lord's most holy law, and daily read

Exod. xx, [4, 5.]

unto you, most evident also? *Thou shalt not make any likeness of any thing in heaven above, in earth beneath, or in the water under the earth,* &c. Could any more be forbidden and said than this, either of the kinds of images, which be either *carved, molten,* or otherwise *similitudes,* or of things whereof images are forbidden to be made? Are not all things either *in heaven, earth, or water*

y is it] it is *from* 1582.

z and cast] or cast *from* 1570.

3 Gnosticos se autem vocant. Et imagines, quasdam quidem depictas, quasdam autem et de reliqua materia fabricatas, habent, dicentes formam Christi factam a Pilato illo in tempore quo fuit Jesus cum hominibus. Et has coronant, et proponunt eas cum imaginibus mundi philosophorum, . . . et reliquam observationem circa eas, similiter ut gentes, faciunt. *Iren. contra Haeres.* I, xxv (*al.* xxiv), 6; *Opp.* I. 105, *ed. Venet.* 1734.

4 See the description of the procession on Palm Sunday with a wooden ass upon wheels and an image of Christ upon it, in *Naogeorgi* (*Th. Kirchmaier's*) *Regnum Papisticum, Lib.* IV, *pp.* 146–148 *ed.* 1559, or in *Barnabe Googe's* translation of the poem, *fol.* 50 *ed.* 1570. Both are quoted in *Brand's Popular Antiquities*, "*Palm Sunday,*" *vol.* I, *pp.* 68, 73, *ed. Ellis* 1841.

under the earth? And be not our images of Christ and his Saints *likenesses of things in heaven, earth, or in the water?*

If they continue in their former answer, that these prohibitions concern the idols of the Gentiles and not our images, first, that answer is already confuted concerning the images of God and the Trinity at large, and concerning the images of Christ also by Ireneus. And that the law of God is likewise to be understanded[a] against all our images, as well of Christ as his Saints, in temples and churches, appeareth further by the judgment of the old doctors and the primitive Church. Epiphanius renting a painted cloth, wherein was the picture of Christ or of some Saint, affirming it to be against our religion that any such image should be had in the temple or church (as is afore[b] at large declared[5]), judged, that not only idols of the Gentiles, but that all images of Christ and his Saints also, were forbidden by God's word and our religion. Lactantius, affirming it to be certain that no true religion can be where an image[c] or picture is (as is before declared[6]), judged, that as well all images and pictures, as the idols of the Gentiles, were forbidden; else would he not so generally have spoken and pronounced of them. And St. Augustine (as is before alleged[7]) greatly alloweth M. Varro affirming that religion is most pure without images; and saith himself, "Images be of more force to crook an unhappy soul than to teach and instruct it." And he saith further: "Every child, yea, every beast knoweth that it is not God that they see. Wherefore then doth the Holy Ghost so often[d] monish us of that which all men know?" Whereunto St. Augustine answereth thus: "For," saith he, "when images are placed in temples, and set in honourable sublimity, and begin once to be worshipped, forthwith breedeth the most vile affection of error." This is St. Augustine's judgment of images in churches, that by and by they breed error and idolatry. The Christian emperors, the learned bishops, all the learned men of Asia, Greece, and Spain, assembled in Councils at Constantinople and in Spain, seven and eight hundred years ago and more, condemning and destroying all images, as well of Christ as of the Saints, set up by the Christians, (as is before at large declared[8],) testify that they understood God's word so, that it forbad our images as well as

Lib. iv, cap. 31, de Civ. Dei.

In Psalm. xxxvi, et cxiii.

[a] understanded] understood 1587, 1595, 1623. [b] afore] before *from* 1567. [c] an image] any image *from* 1582. [d] often] oft 1563 B–1574.

[5] See p. 183, n. 11.
[6] See p. 183, n. 9.
[7] See pp. 188, 189, nn. 20, 21, 22.
[8] See pp. 192–209.

the idols of the Gentles. And, as it is written (Sap. xiv) that [Wisd. xiv, [13.]] *images were not from the beginning, neither shall they continue to the end,* so were they not in the beginning in the primitive Church: God grant they may in the end be destroyed! For [Orig. contr. Cels. Lib. iv et viii. Cypr. contr. Demetr.] all Christians in the primitive Church, as Origen against Celsus, Cyprian also, and Arnobius do testify[9], were sore charged and complained on, that they had no altars nor images. Wherefore did they not, I pray you, conform themselves to the Gentiles in making of images, but for lack of them sustained their heavy displeasure, if they had taken it to be lawful by God's word to have images? It is evident therefore that they took all images to be unlawful in the church or temple of God, and therefore had none, though the Gentiles therefore were most highly displeased, following this rule, [Acts v, [29.]] *We must obey God rather than men.* And Zephyrus[e] in his notes upon the Apology of Tertullian gathereth, that all his vehement persuasion[10] "should be but cold, except we know this once for all, that Christian men in his time did most hate images with their ornaments." And Ireneus (as is above declared[11]) reproveth the heretics called Gnostici, for that they carried about the image of Christ. And therefore the primitive Church, which is specially to be followed as most incorrupt and pure, had publicly in churches neither idols of the Gentiles nor any other images, as things directly forbidden by God's word.

And thus it is declared by God's word, the sentences of the doctors, and the judgment of the primitive Church, which was most pure and sincere, that all images, as well ours as the idols of the Gentiles, be by God's word forbidden, and therefore unlawful, specially in temples and churches.

Now if they, as their custom is, flee to this answer, that God's word forbiddeth not absolutely all images to be made, but that

e Zephyrus] Zephyrius *till* 1582.

9 See *Orig. c. Cels.* VII, 62, and VIII, 17; *Opp.* I, 738, 754: and *Arnob. Disputatt. adv. Gentes* VI, 1, *p.* 202 *ed. Orell.* 1816. Cyprian's *Liber ad Demetrianum*, cited in the margin, states that the Christians were complained of for not worshipping the gods of the Gentiles, quod dii vestri a nobis non colantur, not specifically for having "no altars nor images."

10 Qui locus persuadendi frigeret penitus hoc tempore, quanquam ex abundantia haec ad plebem dicta sunt, nisi perpetuo illud teneamus, Christianos tunc temporis odisse maxime statuas cum suis ornamentis, et in fundendis precibus quemlibet sibi angulum ut in coelum suspicerent satis esse putasse. *Zephyrus in Tertull. Apolog. p.* 867, *ed. Basil.* 1562; *vol.* II, *p.* 674, *ed. Paris.* 1566, 8vo; *p.* 145, *ed. Colon.* 1622. This sentence, which is the last but one of the Comment or Paraphrase on cap. 29, coming in between "expilantur." and "Praeterea", is tacitly omitted in all the editions of Tertullian by Pamelius.

11 See p. 218, n. 3.

they should not be made to be worshipped; and that therefore we may have images, so we worship them not, for that they be things indifferent, which may be abused, or well used: (which seemeth also to be the judgment of Damascene[12], and Gregory the First as is before[f] declared[13]; and this is one of their chief allegations for the maintenance of images, which hath[g] been alleged sith[h] Gregory the First's[i] time:) well, then we be come to their second allegation, which in part we would not stick to grant them. For we are not so superstitious or scrupulous, that we do abhor either flowers wrought in carpets, hangings, and other arras, either the images[j] of princes printed or stamped in their coins, which when Christ did see in a Roman coin, we read not that he reprehended it; neither do we condemn the arts of painting and image making, as wicked of themselves. But we would admit and grant them, that images used for no religion, or superstition rather, we mean images of none worshipped, nor in danger to be worshipped of any, may be suffered. But images placed publicly in temples cannot possibly be without danger of worshipping and idolatry: wherefore they are not publicly to be had or suffered in temples and churches.

Damasc. Lib. iv de Fide Orth. cap. 17. Gregor. in Epist. ad Seren. Massil.

The Jews, to whom this law was first given, (and yet, being a moral commandment, and not ceremonial, as all doctors interpret it, bindeth us as well as them;) the Jews, I say, who should have the true sense and meaning of God's law, so peculiarly given unto them, neither had in the beginning any images publicly in their temple (as Origenes[14] and Josephus[15] at large declareth), neither after the restitution of the temple would by any means consent to Herod, Pilate, or Petronius, that images should be placed only in the temple at Hierusalem, although no worshipping of images was required at their hands, but rather

Orig. contr. Cels. Lib. iv. Joseph. Ant. Lib. xvii, cap. 8; Lib. xviii, cap. 5; Lib. xviii, cap. 15.

[f] as is before] as is above *from* 1567. [g] hath] have *from* 1570. [h] sith] since *from* 1571. [i] First's] First his *from* 1563 B. [j] either the images] either images 1623.

12 Ἐπεὶ δὲ οὐ πάντες ἴσασι γράμματα, οὐδὲ τῇ ἀναγνώσει σχολάζουσιν, οἱ πατέρες συνεῖδον ὥσπερ τινὰς ἀριστείας ἐν εἰκόσι ταῦτα γράφεσθαι εἰς ὑπόμνησιν σύντομον. ἀμέλει πολλάκις μὴ κατὰ νοῦν ἔχοντες τὸ τοῦ Κυρίου πάθος, τὴν εἰκόνα τῆς Χριστοῦ σταυρώσεως ἰδόντες, τοῦ σωτηρίου πάθους εἰς ὑπόμνησιν ἐλθόντες, πεσόντες προσκυνοῦμεν, οὐ τῇ ὕλῃ, ἀλλὰ τῷ εἰκονιζομένῳ· ὥσπερ οὐδὲ τῇ ὕλῃ τοῦ εὐαγγελίου, οὐδὲ τῇ τοῦ σταυροῦ ὕλῃ προσκυνοῦμεν, ἀλλὰ τῷ ἐκτυπώματι· τί γὰρ διαφέρει σταυρὸς μὴ ἔχων τὸ τοῦ Κυρίου ἐκτύπωμα τοῦ ἔχοντος; ὡσαύτως καὶ ἐπὶ τῆς θεομήτορος· ἡ γὰρ εἰς αὐτὴν τιμὴ εἰς τὸν ἐξ αὐτῆς σαρκωθέντα ἀνάγεται. ὁμοίως δὲ καὶ τὰ τῶν ἁγίων ἀνδρῶν ἀνδραγαθήματα, ἐπαλείφοντα ἡμᾶς πρὸς ἀνδρείαν καὶ ζῆλον καὶ μίμησιν τῆς αὐτῶν ἀρετῆς καὶ δόξαν Θεοῦ. ὡς γὰρ ἔφημεν, ἡ πρὸς τοὺς εὐγνώμονας τῶν ὁμοδούλων τιμὴ ἀπόδειξιν ἔχει τῆς πρὸς τὸν κοινὸν Δεσπότην εὐνοίας· καὶ ἡ τῆς εἰκόνος τιμὴ πρὸς τὸ πρωτότυπον διαβαίνει. Joan. Damascen. de Fide Orthod. IV, 16 (17 *edd. vett.*); Opp. I, 281 A, ed. Lequien 1712.

13 See p. 195, n. 30.

14 See before, p. 181, n. 4.

15 *Joseph. Antiqq.* XVII, vi (*al.* viii), 2, 3; XVIII, iii (*al.* iv), 1; viii, 2, 3 (*al.* xi).

offered themselves to the death than to assent that images should once be placed in the temple of God. Neither would they suffer any image maker among them: and Origen addeth[k] this cause[16], lest their minds should be plucked from God to the contemplation of earthly things. And they are much commended for this earnest zeal in maintaining of God's honour and true religion. And truth it is that the Jews and Turks, who abhor images and idols as directly forbidden by God's word, will never come to the truth of our religion, whiles these[l] stumblingblocks of images remain amongst us, and lie in their way. If they object yet the brazen serpent which Moses did set up, or the images of the cherubins[m], or any other images which the Jews had in their temple, the answer is easy. We must in religion obey God's general law, which bindeth all men, and not follow examples of particular dispensation, which be no warrants for us; else we may by the same reason resume circumcision and sacrificing of beasts and other rites permitted to the Jews. Neither can those images of cherubin[n], set in secret where no man might come nor behold, be any example for our public setting up of images in churches and temples.

But to let the Jews go. Where they say that images, so they be not worshipped, as things indifferent may be tolerated[o] in temples and churches; we infer and say for the adversative, that all our images of God, our Saviour Christ, and his Saints, publicly set up in churches and temples[p], places peculiarly appointed to the true worshipping of God, be not things indifferent nor tolerable, but against God's law and commandment, taking their own interpretation and exposition of it. First, for that all images so set up publicly have been worshipped of the unlearned and simple sort shortly after they have been publicly so set up, and, in conclusion, of the wise and learned also. Secondly, for that they are worshipped in sundry places now in our time also. And thirdly, for that it is impossible that images of God, Christ, or his Saints, can be suffered, specially[q] in temples and churches, any while or space without worshipping of them; and that idolatry, which is most abominable before God, cannot possibly[r] be escaped and avoided without the abolishing and destruction of images and pictures in temples and churches; for that idolatry is to images, specially in temples and churches,

[k] addeth] added 1623. [l] these] the *from* 1574. [m] cherubins] cherubims *from* 1571. [n] cherubin] cherubim *from* 1571. [o] tolerated] tolerable *from* 1574. [p] churches and temples] temples and churches 1623. [q] specially] especially 1623. [r] possibly] possiblie 1563 A, possible 1563 B–1567.

16 See before, p. 182, n. 5.

an inseparable accident (as they term it); so that images in churches and idolatry go always both together, and that therefore the one cannot be avoided except the other, specially in all public places, be destroyed. Wherefore, to make images and publicly to set them up in temples[s] and churches, places appointed peculiarly to the service of God, is to make images to the use of religion, and not only against this precept, *Thou shalt make no manner of image*[t], but against this also, *Thou shalt not bow down to them, nor worship them*: for they being so set[u] up have been, be, and ever will be worshipped.

[Exod. xx, 4, 5.]

And the full proof of that which in the beginning of the first part of this treaty was touched is here to be made and performed, to wit, that our images and idols of the Gentiles be all one, as well in the things themselves, as also in that our images have been before, be now, and ever will be worshipped in like form and manner as the idols of the Gentiles were worshipped, so long as they be suffered in churches and temples. Whereupon it followeth, that our images in churches have been, be, and ever will be none other but abominable idols, and be therefore no things indifferent. And every of these parts shall be proved in order, as hereafter followeth.

And first, that our images and the idols of the Gentiles be all one concerning themselves is most evident, the matter of them being *gold, silver*, or other metal, stone, wood, clay, or plaster, as were *the idols of the Gentiles*; and so, being either *molten* or cast, either *carved, graven*, hewed[x], or otherwise formed and fashioned, after the similitude and *likeness of man or woman*, be dead and dumb *works of man's hands*, having *mouth*[y] *and speak not, eyes and see not, hands and feel not, feet and go not*; and so, as well in form as matter, be altogether like the idols of the Gentiles: insomuch that all the titles which be given to the idols in the Scriptures may be verified of our images. Wherefore no doubt but the like curses which are mentioned in the Scriptures will light upon the makers and worshippers of them both.

Simulacra gentium, argentum et aurum. Fusile. Sculptile. Similitudo. Simulacrum. Opera manuum hominum. [Ps. cxiii (*al.* cxv), 4, 5, 7; Deut. iv, 16; xxvii, 15.]

Secondly, that they have been and be worshipped in our time in like form and manner as were the idols of the Gentiles is now to be proved. And, for that idolatry standeth chiefly in the mind, it shall in this part first be proved, that our image-maintainers have had and have the same opinions and judgment

[s] up in temples] up in the temples 1623. [t] image] images *from* 1582. [u] being so set] being set *from* 1563 G. [x] hewed] hewen 1623. [y] mouth] mouths 1623.

of Saints, whose images they have made and worshipped, as the Gentiles idolaters had of their gods. And afterward [z] shall be declared, that our image maintainers and worshippers have used and use the same outward rites and manner of honouring and worshipping their images as the Gentiles did use before their idols, and that therefore they commit idolatry as well inwardly and outwardly as did the wicked Gentiles idolaters.

And concerning the first part, of the idolatrious [a] opinions of our image maintainers. What, I pray you, be such Saints with us to whom we attribute the defence of certain countries, spoiling God of his due honour herein, but Dii Tutelares of the Gentiles idolaters; such as were Belus to the Babylonians and Assyrians, Osiris and Isis to the Egyptians, Vulcan to the Lemnians [b], and such [c] other? What be such Saints to whom the safeguard of certain cities are appointed, but Dii Praesides with the Gentiles idolaters; such as were at Delphos Apollo, at Athens Minerva, at Carthage Juno, at Rome Quirinus, &c.? What be such Saints to whom, contrary to the use of the primitive Church, temples and churches be builded and altars erected, but Dii Patroni of the Gentiles idolaters; such as were in the Capitol Jupiter, in Paphus' temple Venus, in Ephesus' temple Diana, and such like? Alas, we seem in thus thinking and doing to have learned our religion, not out of God's word, but out of the pagan poets; who say,[17]

Dii Tutelares.

Dii Praesides.

Dii Patroni.

> Excessere omnes adytis arisque relictis
> Dî quibus imperium hoc steterat, &c.,

that is to say, "All the gods by whose defence this empire stood are gone out of the temples, and have forsaken their altars."

And where one Saint hath images in divers places, the same Saint hath divers names thereof, most like to the Gentiles. When you hear of our Lady of Walsingham [18], our Lady of

[z] afterward] afterwards 1623. [a] idolatrious] idolatrous *from* 1582. [b] Lemnians] Lennians *till* 1570. [c] and such] and to such *from* 1582.

17 *Virgil. Aen.* II, 351.

18 "The people in speaking of our lady: Of al our Ladies, saith one, I love best our Lady of Walsingam. And I, saith the other, our Lady of Ippiswitch. In whiche woordes what meneth she but her love and her affeccion to the stocke that standeth in the chapel of Walsingam or Ippiswiche? What say you whan the people speke of this fashion in theyr paines and perils: Helpe, holy cross of Bradman; Helpe, our dere lady of Walsingam? Doth it not plainly appeare that either thei trust in the images in Christes stede and our Ladies, letting Christ and oure Lady go, or take at the lest wise those ymages that thei wene thei wer verely the one Christ, the other our Lady her self." *Sir Thomas More's Dialogue concerning Heresies,* I, 17, *Works,* p. 140 C, quoted (in part) in *Wordsworth's Ecclesiastical Biography, vol.* I, *p.* 160, *n.* 8, *ed.* 1810. Pilgrimages "to Wyllesdon" are mentioned in the

Ipswich, our Lady of Wilsdon, and such other, what is it but an imitation of the Gentiles idolaters' Diana Agrotera, Diana Coryphea, Diana Ephesia, &c., Venus Cypria, Venus Paphia, Venus Gnidia? Whereby is evidently meant, that the Saint for the image sake should in those places, yea, in the images themselves, have a dwelling: which is the ground of their idolatry; for where no images be they have no such means[d]. Terentius Varro sheweth that there were three hundred Jupiters in his time[19]: there were no fewer Veneres and Dianae: we had no fewer Christophers, Ladies, and Mary Magdalenes, and other Saints. Oenomaus and Hesiodus shew that in their time there were thirty thousand gods[20]: I think we had no fewer Saints, to whom we gave the honour due to God.

And they have not only spoiled the true living God of his due honour in temples, cities, countries, and lands by such devices and inventions, as the Gentiles idolaters have done before them, but the sea and waters have as well special Saints with them as they had gods with the Gentiles, Neptune, Triton, Nereus, Castor and Pollux, Venus, and such other; in whose places be come St. Christopher, St. Clement, and divers other, and specially our Lady, to whom shipmen sing, Ave, maris stella[21]. Neither hath the fire scaped their[e] idolatrious[f] inventions: for instead of Vulcan and Vesta, the Gentiles' gods of the fire, our men have placed St. Agatha, and make letters on her day for to quench fire with[22]. Every artificer and profession hath his spe-

[d] means] *so in all. But did not the author write* names? [e] scaped their] scaped the 1623.
[f] idolatrious] idolatrous *from* 1574.

same chapter of the *Dialogue*. It is a village in Middlesex, a little to the westward of Hampstead.

19 Romanus Cynicus Varro trecentos Joves, sive Jupitros dicendos, sine capitibus introducit. *Tertull. Apolog.* XIV, *Opp.* I, 170. The passage in Varro is not extant.

20 Τρὶς γὰρ μύριοί εἰσιν ἐπὶ χθονὶ πουλυβοτείρῃ
ἀθάνατοι Ζηνὸς, φύλακες θνητῶν ἀνθρώπων. Hes. Opera et Dies, 250.

Θύουσι γὰρ αἱ πόλεις . . . ἄλλοις παμπόλλοις Ἡσιοδείοις θεοῖς. Τρὶς γὰρ ὡς ἀληθῶς μύριοί εἰσιν ἐπὶ χθονὶ πουλυβοτείρῃ, οὐκ ἀθάνατοι, ἀλλὰ λίθινοι καὶ ξύλινοι, δεσπόται ἀνθρώπων. From the Γοήτων φωρὰ of Oenomaus, preserved in Euseb. Praepar. Evang. v, 36.

21 The hymn beginning, Ave, maris stella, is to be found in most editions of the Breviary. It contains the famous stanza in which the Virgin is desired to shew that she still has maternal authority over our Blessed Lord:

Monstra te esse matrem:
Sumat per te preces
Qui pro nobis natus
Tulit esse tuus.

22 On St. Agatha's letters see before, p. 62, n. 20.

cial Saint, as a peculiar god: as, for example, scholars[23] have St. Nicholas and St. Gregory, painters St. Luke; neither lack soldiers their Mars nor lovers their Venus amongst Christians. All diseases have their special Saints, as gods, the curers of them; the pocks St. Roch, the falling evil St. Cornelis[24], the toothache St. Appoline[25], &c. Neither do beasts and cattle lack their gods with us: for St. Loy[26] is the horseleach, and St. Anthony the swineherd, &c.

23 Gregorius curat pueros, elementaque tradit
Prima, deinde etiam studiorum instillat amorem.
Naogeorg. (or *Kirchmaier*) *Regn. Papist. Lib.* III, *p.* 115, *ed.* 1559.

Thus rendered by *Barnabe Googe, fol.* 38 b:

Saint Gregorie lookes to little boyes, to teache their a, b, c,
And makes them for to love their bookes, and schollers good to be.

24 St. Cornelis was the name commonly used in England for St. Cornelius, Bishop of Rome, contemporary with St. Cyprian. He is the patron of those who suffer from epilepsy or the falling sickness.

25 Appoline was the usual name in England, as Apolline is in France, for Apollonia, a martyr at Alexandria, who, among other tortures, is said to have had all her teeth beaten out.

Culta putres sanat Diva Appollonia dentes. *Neogeorg. ibid. p.* 114.

Saint Appolin the rotten teeth doth help when sore they ache.
Barnabe Googe, ibid. f. 38 a.

In the *Horae beatae Mariae Virginis ad usum Sarum* the following anthem or short hymn occurs:

Virgo Christi egregia,
Pro nobis, Apollonia,
Funde preces ad Dominum,
Ut tollat omne noxium;
Ne pro reatu criminum
Morbo vexemur dentium
Vel capitis torquentium.

26 "Saint Loy we make our horseleche, and must let our horse rather renne unshod and marre his hoofe, than to shooe him on his daye." *Sir Thomas More's Dialogue concerning Heresies,* II, 10, *Works, p.* 194 F. To which More in his own character answers, "And peradventure, sith saint Loy was a ferrour, it is no great faute to praye to him for the helpe of our horse:" adding however, "Me seemeth the devocion to ronne somwhat to far, if the smithes will not for any necessite set on a show upon saint Loyes day, and yet lefull ynough to praye for the helpe of a pore mans horse." *Ibid. chap.* II, *p.* 197 D, F.

Loye or Loy is the English name for Eloy, Eligius, Bishop of Noyon in the seventh century. He was well skilled in the goldsmith's craft, and is therefore usually represented with a hammer as well as a crosier; whence later legends have made him a blacksmith and (as Sir Thomas More says) a farrier. His chief day is the first of December: but the Feast of his Translation is kept on the twenty-fifth of June, and it is on this day that the Company of Smiths at Newcastle on Tyne hold their annual meeting in pursuance of an ordinance made in 1677, which enjoins them to choose their officers yearly on St. Loy Day.

Bullinger, it is true, cap. 34, assigns the patronage of horses and of smiths to a St. Eulogius; and for this reason among others it has been questioned whether St. Loy and St. Eligius are one and the same. See *Sir Henry Ellis* on *Brand's Popular Antiquities,* I, 203, *note* f, *ed.* 1841. But Kirchmaier, although he uses the name Eulogius, (perhaps taking it from Bullinger,) yet gives the description which belongs to Eligius:

Where is God's providence and due honour in the mean season? who saith[η], *The heavens be mine, and the earth is mine, the whole world and all that in it is: I do give victory, and I put to flight: Of me be all counsels and help*, &c.: *Except I keep the city, in vain doth he watch that keepeth it: Thou, Lord, shalt save both men and beasts.* But we have left him neither heaven, nor earth, nor water, nor country, nor city, peace ne[g] war, to rule and govern, neither men, nor beasts, nor their diseases to cure; that a godly man might justly for zealous indignation cry out, O heaven, O earth and seas, what madness and wickedness against God are men fallen into! what dishonour do the creatures to their Creator and Maker! And, if we remember God sometime, yet, because we doubt of his ability or will to help, we join to him another helper, as he were a noun adjective, using these sayings: such as learn, God and St. Nicholas be my speed; such as neese[27], God help and St. John; to the horse, God and St. Loy save thee[28]. Thus are we become *like horses*[θ] *and moyles*[h], *which have no understanding.* For is there not one God only, who by his power and wisdom made all things, and by his providence governeth the same, and by his goodness maintaineth and saveth them? Be not *all things of him*[ι], by him, *and through him?* Why dost thou turn from the Creator to the creatures? This is the manner of the Gentiles idolaters: but thou art a Christian, and therefore *by Christ*[κ] alone hast *access to* God *the Father*, and help of him only.

η [Ps. lxxxix, 11; l, 12; cxliv, 10; xxi, 12; lxxiv, 12 *al.* 13; cxxvii, 1; xxxvi, 6.]

θ [Ps. xxxii, 9.]

ι [Rom. xi, 36.]

κ [Eph. ii, 18: 1 Tim. ii, 5.]

These things are not written to any reproach of the Saints themselves, who were the true servants of God, and did give all honour to him, taking none unto themselves, and are blessed souls with God; but against our foolishness and wickedness, making of the true servants of God false gods by attributing to them the power and honour which is God's, and due to him only. And, for that we have such opinions of the power and

g ne] nor 1623. h moyles] mules *from* 1582.

Curat equos faber Eulógius, tutatur et omnes
Fabros, seu ferrum tractent, seu pulchrius aurum. *Naogeorg. ibid. p.* 116.

And Caxton in his translation of the *Legenda Aurea, ff.* 189, 190, *ed.* 1483, uniformly renders Eligius by "Saint Loye."

27 neese: now written *sneeze.* "The child neesed seven times." 2 *Kings* IV, 35, where however *sneezed* is now printed. "By his neesings a light doth shine." *Job* XLI, 18, of Leviathan. Sternutatio ejus splendor ignis. *Vulg.*

28 In Chaucer a carter says to his toiling horse,

I pray God save thy body and Seint Loy. *The Freres Tale, v.* 7146.

ready help of Saints, all our Legends, Hymns, Sequences[29], and Masses did contain stories, lauds, and praises of them, and prayers to them, yea, and sermons also altogether of them and to their praises, God's word being clean laid aside. And this we do altogether agreeable to the Saints as did the Gentiles idolaters to their false gods. For these opinions which men have had of mortal persons, were they never so holy, the old most godly and learned Christians have written against the feigned[i] gods of the Gentiles; and Christian princes have destroyed their images: who, if they were now living, would doubtless likewise both write against our false opinions of Saints, and also destroy their images. For it is evident that our image maintainers have the same opinion of Saints which the Gentiles had of their false gods, and thereby are moved to make them images, as the Gentiles did.

Medioximi Dii.

If answer be made, that they make Saints but intercessors to God, and means for such things as they would obtain of God; that is even, after the Gentiles' idolatrious[k] usage, to make them, of Saints, gods called Dii Medioximi, to be mean[30] intercessors and helpers to God, as though he did not hear, or should be weary if he did all alone. So did the Gentiles teach that there was one chief power working by other as means; and so they made all gods subject to fate or destiny: as Lucian in his Dialogues feigneth that Neptune made suit to Mercury, that he might speak with Jupiter[31]. And therefore in this also it is most evident that our image maintainers be all one in opinion with the Gentiles idolaters.

Now remaineth the third[l] part, that their rites and ceremo-

[i] against the feigned] *so in all. But did not the author write* against of the feigned? [k] idolatrious] idolatrous *from* 1582. [l] third] *so in all. But did not the author write* other *or* second? *See p.* 223, *l.* 38—*p.* 224, *l.* 9, "And, for that idolatry——of our image maintainers."

29 Sequences are short anthems of praise or jubilation chanted in the service of the Mass immediately before the Gospel. In the preface to an *Expositio Sequentiarum secundum usum Sarum*, printed in 8vo. at Paris in February $150\frac{2}{3}$, they are described as Dei Sanctorumque ejus laudationes, quas alii Sequentias, alii Prosas vocant. Dr. Rock in his *Church of our Fathers, Vol.* III, *Part* ii, *p.* 21, says that in early times it was usual, in singing "Alleluia" at that part of the service, to dwell on the last syllable of the word even for several minutes together; and that the name Sequentia, originally given to that wordless prolongation of the chant, was continued to the anthems which were substituted for it, and of which he thinks Alcuin was the inventor. The name Prosa seems to signify the absence of metre, by which such anthems were for the most part distinguished from hymns.

30 mean: intermediate. In our ancient feodal tenures a *mesne* lord was one who held all his land of the king, but had tenants under himself.

31 *Lucian. Deor. Dialog.* IX.

nies in honouring or worshipping of the images or Saints[m] be all one with the rites which the Gentiles idolaters used in honouring their idols.

First, what meaneth it, that Christians, after the example of the Gentiles idolaters, go on pilgrimage to visit images, where they have the like at home, but that they have a more opinion of holiness and virtue in some images than other some, like as the Gentiles idolaters had? Which is the readiest way to bring them to idolatry by worshipping of them, and directly against God's word, who saith, *Seek me, and ye shall live; and do not seek Bethel, neither enter*[n] *not into Gilgal, neither go to Bersaba.* Amos v, [4, 5.] And against such as had any superstition in the holiness[o] of the place, as though they should be heard for the place sake[p], saying, *Our fathers worshipped in this mountain, and ye say that at Hierusalem is the place where men should worship,* John iv, [20–23.] our Saviour Christ pronounceth: *Believe me, the hour cometh, when you shall worship the Father neither in this mountain nor at Hierusalem, but true worshippers shall worship the Father in spirit and truth.* But it is too well known, that by such pilgrimage going Lady Venus and her son Cupid were rather worshipped wantonly in the flesh, than God the Father and our Saviour Christ his Son truly worshipped in the spirit. And it was very agreeable (as St. Paul teacheth) that they which fell to idolatry, which Rom. i, [23–29.] is spiritual fornication, should also fall into carnal fornication and all uncleanliness[q] by the just judgments of God delivering them over to abominable concupiscences.

What meaneth it, that Christian men, after the use of the Gentiles idolaters, cap and kneel before images? Which, if they had any sense and gratitude, would kneel before men, carpenters, masons, plasterers, founders, and goldsmiths, their makers and framers, by whose means they have attained this honour, which else should have been evil favoured and rude lumps of clay or plaster, pieces of timber, stone, or metal, without shape or fashion, and so without all estimation and honour; as that idol in the pagan poet confesseth, saying[32], "I was once Horatius. a vile block, but now I am become a god," &c. What a fond

m images or Saints] *so in all. But did not the author write* images of Saints? n Bethel, neither enter] Bethel, enter *from* 1582. o in the holiness] in holiness 1623. p place sake] place's sake *from* 1570. q uncleanliness] uncleanness *from* 1571.

32 Olim truncus eram ficulnus, inutile lignum,
Quum faber, incertus scamnum faceretne Priapum,
Maluit esse Deum. Deus inde ego. *Horat. Sat.* I, viii, 1.

thing is it for man, who hath life and reason, to bow himself to a dead and unsensible image, the work of his own hand! Is not this stooping and kneeling before them *adoration* of them, which is forbidden so earnestly by God's word? Let such as so fall down before images of Saints know and confess that they exhibit that honour to dead stocks and stones which the Saints themselves[λ], Peter, Paul, and Barnabas, would not to be given them being alive, which the angel of God forbiddeth to be given to him.

Adorare. Gen. xxiii, [7, 12;] and xxxiii, [3:] 1 Kings i, [16, 23.][33]

λ Acts x, [25, 26;] and xiv, [13–18:] Rev. xix, [10; xxii, 8, 9.][34]

And, if they say they exhibit such honour not to the image, but to the Saint whom it representeth, they are convicted of folly, to believe that they please Saints with that honour which they abhor as a spoil of God's honour: for they be no changelings, but now both, having greater understanding and more fervent love of God, do more abhor to deprive him of his due honour, and, being now like unto the angels of God, do with angels flee to take unto them by sacrilege the honour due to God. And herewithal is confuted their lewd distinction of Latria and Dulia[35]: where it is evident that the Saints of God cannot abide that as much as any outward worshipping be done or exhibited to them. But Satan, God's enemy, desiring to rob God of his honour, desireth[μ] exceedingly that such honour might be given to him. Wherefore those which give the honour due to the Creator to any creature do service acceptable to no Saints, who be the friends of God, but unto Satan, God's[r] and man's mortal and sworn enemy. And to attribute such desire of divine honour to Saints is to blot them with a most odious and devilish ignominy and villany, and indeed of Saints to make them Satans and very devils, whose property is to challenge to themselves the honour which is due to God only.

μ Matt. iv, [9.]

And furthermore, in that they say that they do not worship the images, as the Gentiles did their idols, but God and the Saints, whom the images do represent, and therefore that their doings before images be not like the idolatry of the Gentiles before their idols, St. Augustine, Lactantius, and Clemens do prove evidently that by this their answer they be all one with

r God's] God *from* 1582.

33 In these passages the verb *Adorare* is used in the Vulgate of the bowing down of Abraham before the children of Heth, of Jacob before Esau, of Bathsheba and Nathan before David.

34 In *Acts* x, 25, *Rev.* xix, 10, and xxii, 8, *Adorare* is used in the Vulgate of the worship tendered by Cornelius to Peter and by John to the angel.

35 See *Jewel's Reply to Harding, Art.* xiv *"Of Adoration of Images," Div.* xii *"Latria, Doulia."*

the Gentiles idolaters. "The Gentiles," saith St. Augustine[36], "which seem to be of the purer religion say, We worship not the images, but by the corporal image we do behold the signs of the things which we ought to worship." [Augustine Psal. cxiii.] And Lactantius saith[37]: "The Gentiles say, We fear not the images, but them after whose likeness the images be made, and to whose names they be consecrate[s]." [Lactantius Lib. ii Instit.] Thus far Lactantius. And Clemens saith[38]: "That serpent the devil uttereth these words by the mouth of certain men, We to the honour of the invisible God worship visible images: which surely is most false." [Lib. v ad Jacobum Domini Fratrem.] See how, in using the same excuses which the Gentiles idolaters pretended, they shew themselves to be all one[t] with them in idolatry. For, notwithstanding this excuse, St. Augustine[39], Clemens, and Lactantius prove them idolaters. And Clemens saith[40] that the serpent, the devil, putteth such excuses in the mouth of idolaters. And the Scriptures saith[u] they worshipped[x] the stocks and stones[v], notwithstanding this excuse, even as our image maintainers do. And Ezechiel[y] therefore calleth the gods of the Assyrians *stocks and stones*[ξ] [41], although they were but images of their gods. So are our images of God and the Saints named by the names of God and his Saints, after the use of the Gentiles. And the same Clemens saith thus in the same book[42]: "They dare not give the name of the Emperor to any other, for he punisheth his offender and traitor by and by; but they dare give the name of God to other, because he for repentance suffereth his offenders." And even

[v [Deut. iv, 28; xxviii, 36: Ezek. xx, 32.] ξ [2 Kings xix, 18.]]

s consecrate] consecrated 1623. t be all one] join 1623. u Scriptures saith] Scriptures say *from* 1582. x worshipped] worship *from* 1563 G. y Ezechiel] *so in all. See note* 41.

36 Videntur autem sibi purgatioris esse religionis qui dicunt, Nec simulacrum nec daemonium colo, sed effigiem corporalem ejus rei signum intueor quam colere debeo. *Augustin. Enarr. in Psalm.* CXIII, §4; *Opp.* IV, 1261 F.

37 Non ipsa, inquiunt, timemus, sed eos ad quorum imaginem ficta et quorum nominibus consecrata sunt. *Lactant. Divin. Institutt.* II, 2.

38 Per alios item serpens ille proferre verba hujuscemodi solet: Nos ad honorem invisibilis Dei imagines visibiles adoramus: quod certissime falsum est. *Recognitt. S. Clement.* V, 23, *vol.* I, 552. See more of the context cited below in note 108.

39 *Augustin. ibid.* § 5, *col.* 1262.

40 Intelligite ergo quia latentis intrinsecus serpentis est ista suggestio, quae persuadet pios vos videri posse, cum insensibilia colitis. *Recognitt. ibid.*

41 The Homilist mistook Hezekiah for Ezekiel in the passage which he is here translating from Bullinger: Et cum hanc ob rem constaret idola aliud jam non esse quam lignum, lapidem, vel metallum, Ezechias deos Assyriorum *lapides et ligna* appellat, et Scriptura non semel dicit Gentes ipsas ligna et lapides adorare ac colere. *Cap.* 29, *fol.* 145 a *ed.* 1539, *fol.* 80 a *ed.* 1568. It was Bullinger's mistake to say that Hezekiah was speaking of "the gods of the Assyrians."

42 Sed Caesaris quidem nomen nulli alii audetis imponere, quia reum suum statim punit; Dei vero audetis, quia reum suum punire propter poenitentiam differt. *Recognitt. ibid. c.* 22.

so do our image worshippers give both names of God and the Saints, and also the honour due to God, to their images, even as did the Gentiles idolaters to their idols.

What should it mean, that they, according as did the Gentiles idolaters, light candles at noon time[z] or at midnight before them, but therewith to honour them? For other use is there none in so doing. For in the day it needeth not, but was ever a proverb of foolishness, to light a candle at noon time[a]; and in the night it availeth not to light a candle before the blind; and God hath neither use nor honour thereof. And concerning this candle lighting, it is notable that Lactantius above a thousand years ago hath written after this manner[43]: "If they would behold the heavenly light of the sun, then should they perceive that God hath[b] no need of their candles, who for the use of man hath made so goodly a light. And whereas in so little a circle of the sun, which for the great distance seemeth to be no greater than a man's head, there is so great brightness, that the sight of man's eye is not able to behold it, but, if one steadfastly look upon it a while, his eyes will be dulled and blinded with darkness; how great light, how great clearness, may we think to be with God, with whom is no night nor darkness?" and so forth. And by and by he saith: "Seemeth he therefore to be in his right mind, which offereth[c] up to the Giver of all light[d] the light of a wax candle for a gift? He requireth another light of us, which is not smoky, but bright and clear, even the light of the mind and understanding." And shortly after he saith: "But their gods, because they be earthly, have need of light,

Lib. vi Instit. cap. 2.

[z], [a] noon time] none time *till* 1567. [b] hath] had *till* 1563 G. [c] which offereth] who offereth 1623. [d] of all light] of light *from* 1567.

43 Vel si coeleste lumen, quod dicimus solem, contemplari velint, jam sentient quam non indigeat lucernis eorum Deus, qui ipse in usum hominis tam claram, tam candidam, lucem dedit. Et tamen cum in tam parvo circulo, qui propter longinquitatem non amplius quam humani capitis videtur habere mensuram, tantum sit fulgoris, ut eum mortalium luminum acies non queat contueri, et si paulisper intenderis hebetatos oculos caligo ac tenebrae consequantur; quid tandem luminis, quid claritatis, apud ipsum Deum, penes quem nulla nox est, esse arbitremur?.... Num igitur mentis suae compos putandus est, qui Autori et Datori luminis candelarum ac cerarum lumen offert pro munere? Aliud vero ille a nobis exigit lumen, et quidem non fumidum, sed (ut ait poeta [sc. *Lucret.* v, 282]) liquidum atque clarum, mentis scilicet.... Illorum autem dii, quia terreni sunt, egent luminibus, ne in tenebris sint. Quorum cultores, quia coeleste nihil sapiunt, etiam religiones quibus deserviunt ad terram revocant. In ea enim lumine opus est, quia ratio ejus et natura tenebrosa est. Itaque diis non coelestem sensum, sed humanum potius attribuunt: ideoque illis necessaria et grata credunt esse, quae nobis; quibus aut esurientibus opus est cibo, aut sitientibus potu, aut veste algentibus, aut, cum sol decesserit, lumine, ut videre possimus. *Lactant. Divin. Institutt.* VI, 2.

lest they remain in darkness. Whose worshippers, because they understand no heavenly thing, do draw the religion[e] which they use down to the earth; in the which, being dark of nature, is need of light. Wherefore they give to their gods no heavenly, but the earthly understanding of mortal men. And therefore they believe those things to be necessary and pleasant unto them which are so to us; who have need either of meat when we be hungry, or drink when we be thirsty, or clothing when we be acold, or, when the sun is set, candle light, that we may see." Thus far Lactantius, and much more, too long here to write, of candle lighting in temples before images and idols for religion: whereby appeareth both the foolishness thereof, and also that in opinion and act we do agree altogether in our candle religion with the Gentiles idolaters.

What meaneth it, that they, after the example of the Gentiles idolaters, burn incense, offer up gold to images, hang up crutches, chains, and ships, legs, arms, and whole men and women of wax before images, as though by them or Saints (as they say) they were delivered from lameness, sickness, captivity, or shipwrack? Is not this *Colere imagines, to worship images*, so earnestly forbidden in God's word? If they deny it, let them read the eleventh chapter of Daniel the Prophet; who saith of Antichrist, *He shall worship god whom his fathers knew not with gold, silver, and with precious stone, and other things of pleasure:* in which place the Latin word is *Colet*. And in the second of Paralipomenon, the twenty-ninth chapter, all the outward rites and ceremonies, as burning of incense and such other, wherewith God in the temple was honoured, is called *Cultus*, to say *worshipping;* which is forbidden straitly by God's word to be given to images. Do not all stories ecclesiastical declare, that our holy Martyrs, rather than they would bow and kneel or offer up one crumb of incense before an image or idol, have suffered a thousand kinds of most horrible and dreadful death? And, what excuse[f] soever they make, yet, that all this running on pilgrimage, burning of incense and candles, hanging up of crutches, chains, ships, arms, legs, and whole men and women of wax, kneeling, and holding up of hands, is done to the images, appeareth by this, that where no images be, or where they have been and be taken away, they do no such things at all; but the[g] places frequented when the images were there, now they

Colere.

[Dan. xi, 38.]

[2 Chron. xxix, 11, 35.]

Cultus.

[e] draw the religion] draw religion *from* 1563 B. [f] excuse] excuses *from* 1582. [g] but the] but all the *from* 1574.

be taken away, be forsaken and left desert; nay, now they hate and abhor the place deadly: which is an evident proof, that that which they did before was done in respect of the images.

Wherefore, when we see men and women on heaps to go on pilgrimage to images, kneel before them, hold up their hands before them, set up candles, burn incense before them, offer up gold and silver unto them, hang up ships, crutches, chains, men and women of wax before them, attributing health and safeguard, the gifts of God, to them or the Saints whom they represent (as they rather would have it); who, I say, who can doubt, but that our image maintainers, agreeing in all idolatrious[h] opinions, outward rites and ceremonies, with the Gentiles idolaters, agree also with them in committing most abominable idolatry?

And, to increase this madness, wicked men, which have the keeping of such images, for their more lucre and advantage, after the example of the Gentiles idolaters, have reported and spread abroad, as well by lying tales as written fables, divers miracles of images: as that such an image miraculously was sent from heaven, even like Palladium or *Magna Diana Ephesiorum*[o]; such another was as miraculously found in the earth, as the man's head was in Capitol[44] or the horse head in Capua[45]. Such an image was brought by angels; such an one came itself far from the East to the West, as dame Fortune flit[i] to Rome[46]. Such an image of our Lady was painted by St. Luke, whom of a physician they have made a painter for that purpose. Such an one a hundred[k] yokes of oxen could not move; like Bona Dea, whom the ship could not carry[47]; or Jupiter Olympius, which laughed the artificers to scorn that went about to remove him to Rome. Some images, though they were hard and stony, yet for tender heart and pity wept. Some, like Castor and Pollux[49], helping their friends in battle, sweat, as marble pillars do in dankish weather. Some spake more monstruously[l] than ever did Balaam's ass, who had life and breath in him. Such a creple[m] came and saluted this Saint of oak, and by and

o [Acts xix, 28, 34, 35.]

h idolatrious] idolatrous *from* 1582. i flit] fled 1623. k a hundred] an hundred *from* 1582. l monstruously] monsterously 1587, 1595; monstrously 1623. m creple] criple *or* cripple *from* 1582.

44 See *Varro de Ling. Lat.* v, 41, *ed. Müller: Liv.* I, 55.

45 Perhaps the Homilist should have written "Carthage" instead of "Capua." See *Virg. Aen.* I, 443–445.

46 Perhaps the writer had in his mind Plutarch's figurative description of Fortune's passage to Rome. *De Fortuna Romanorum, Opp.* II, 317 E, 318 A, *ed.* 1599.

47 See *Ov. Fast.* IV, 300–328: *Sueton. Tiber.* 2: *Lactant. Divin. Institutt.* II, 8.

49 See *Val. Max.* I, viii, I.

by he was made whole; and lo, here hangeth his crutch. Such an one in a tempest vowed to St. Christopher, and scaped; and behold, here is his ship of wax. Such an one by St. Leonard's help brake out of prison; and see where his fetters hang. And infinite thousands mo miracles by like or more shameless lies were reported. Thus do our image maintainers in earnest apply to their images all such miracles as the Gentiles have feigned of their idols. And, if it were to be admitted that some miraculous acts were by illusion of the devil done where images be, (for it is evident that the most part were feigned lies and crafty jugglings of men,) yet followeth it not therefore, that such images are either to be honoured, or suffered to remain; no more than Ezechias left the brazen serpent undestroyed[π] when it was worshipped, although it were both set up by God's commandment, and also approved by a great and true miracle, for as many as beheld it were by and by healed: neither ought miracles to persuade[n] us to do contrary to God's word. For the Scriptures have, for a warning hereof, foreshewed[ρ] that the kingdom of Antichrist shall be mighty in miracles and wonders to the strong illusion of all the reprobate.

π [2 Kings xviii, 4: Numb. xxi, 8, 9.]

ρ [Matt. xxiv, 24: 2 Thess. ii, 9–12: Rev. xiii, 13, 14.]

But in this they pass the folly and wickedness of the Gentiles, that they honour and worship the reliques and bones of our Saints, which prove that they be mortal men and dead, and therefore no gods to be worshipped; which the Gentiles would never confess of their gods for very shame. But the reliques we must kiss and offer unto, specially on Relique Sunday[50]. And while we offer, that we should not be weary or repent us of our cost, the music and minstrelsy goeth merrily all the offertory time with praising and calling upon those Saints whose reliques be then in presence. Yea, and the water also wherein those reliques have been dipped must with great reverence be reserved, as very holy and effectuous[o]. Is this agreeable to St. Chrysostom, who writeth thus of reliques[51]? "Do not regard

Homilia de septem Macchabaeis.

n miracles to persuade] miracles persuade *from* 1582. o effectuous] effectual 1623.

50 The Festum Reliquiarum was not, and perhaps still is not, kept on the same day every where. From the Calendar and from the rubric before the office of the day in an edition of the *Salisbury Breviary* printed in 1516 it appears that in England at that time it was celebrated on the first Sunday after the feast of the Translation of "St. Thomas the Martyr," that is, after July 7, but that at some previous time it had been kept on the octave of the Nativity of the Virgin, that is, on September 15. The first Lection there appointed for the day begins thus: Hodie, dilectissimi, omnium Sanctorum quorum reliquiae in hac continentur ecclesia sub una solennitatis laetitia celebramus festivitatem.

51 Μὴ γάρ μοι τὴν κόνιν εἴπῃς, μηδὲ

the ashes of the Saints' bodies, nor the reliques of their flesh and bones, consumed with time; but open the eyes of thy faith, and behold them clothed with heavenly virtue and the grace of the Holy Ghost, and shining with the brightness of the heavenly light." But our idolaters found too much vantage of reliques and relique water to follow St. Chrysostom's counsel. And, because reliques were so gainful, few places were there but they had reliques provided for them. And, for more plenty of reliques, some one Saint had many heads, one in one place, and another in another place. Some had six arms and twenty six[p] fingers. And, where our Lord bare his cross alone, if all the pieces of the reliques thereof were gathered together, the greatest ship in England would scarcely bear them: and yet the greatest part of it, they say, doth yet remain in the hands of the infidels; for the which they pray in their beads' bidding, that they may get it also into their hands for such godly use and purpose[52]. And not only the bones of the Saints, but every thing appertaining to them was an holy relique. In some place they offer a sword, in some the scabbard, in some a shoe, in some a saddle that had been set upon some holy horse, in some the coals wherewith St. Laurence was roasted, in some place the tail of the ass which our Lord Jesus Christ sat on, to be kissed and offered to[q] for a relique. For, rather than they would lack a relique, they would offer you a horse bone instead of a virgin's arm, or the tail of the ass, to be kissed and offered unto for reliques. O wicked, impudent, and most shameless men, the devisers of these things! O seely[53], foolish, and dastardly daws[54], and more beastly[55] than the ass whose tail they kissed, that believe such things. Now

p twenty six] xxvi *in all*. q offered to] offered unto *from* 1563 H, *except* 1574.

τὴν τέφραν λογίζου, μηδὲ τὰ χρόνῳ δαπανηθέντα ὀστᾶ· ἀλλ' ἄνοιξον τῆς πίστεως τοὺς ὀφθαλμοὺς, καὶ βλέπε παρακαθημένην αὐτοῖς τοῦ Θεοῦ τὴν δύναμιν, περιβεβλημένην αὐτοῖς τοῦ Πνεύματος τὴν χάριν, περιστέλλουσαν αὐτοὺς τοῦ οὐρανίου φωτὸς τὴν δόξαν. Chrysost. in Maccab. Hom. I, Opp. II, 622 B.

52 "Also ye shal pray for the holy lande, and for the holy crosse that Jhesu Crist deyed on for redempcion of mannys sowle, that it may come into the power of cristen men, the more to be honoured for our prayers." *Liber Festivalis, ed. Caxton*, 1483, "*The bedes on the Sonday.*" This is printed in *Coxe's Forms of Bidding Prayer, p.* 29; and other examples occur at *pp.* 11, 40, and 54 of the same volume.

53 seely: simple, artless, unsuspicious. Spenser uses also the modern form of the word, *silly*, in the same sense. In 2 Tim. iii, 6, "silly women" is the rendering of *γυναικάρια*, mulierculae.

54 daws: stupid birds.

"SERV. Where dwellest thou?
COR. I' the city of kites and crows.
SERV. I' the city of kites and crows?—
What an ass it is!—Then thou dwellest with daws too?"
Shakespeare, Coriol. IV, 5.

Dullard is given as a synonyme for "das-

God be merciful to such miserable and seely Christians, who by the fraud and falsehood of those which should have taught them the way of truth and life have been made, not only more wicked than the Gentiles idolaters, but also no wiser than asses, *horses, and mules*[r], *which have no understanding!* [Ps. xxxii, 9.]

Of these things already rehearsed it is evident, that our image maintainers have not only made images and set them up in temples, as did the Gentiles idolaters their idols, but also that they have had the same idolatrious[s] opinions of the Saints, to whom they have made images, which the Gentiles idolaters had of their false gods; and have not only worshipped their images with the same rites, ceremonies, superstition, and all circumstances, as did the Gentiles idolaters their idols, but in many points also have far exceeded them in all wickedness, foolishness, and madness. And, if this be not sufficient to prove them image worshippers, that is to say, idolaters, lo, you shall hear their own open confession. I mean not only the decrees of the second Nicene Council under Hirene, the Roman Council under Gregory the Third; in the which, as they teach that images are to be honoured and worshipped (as is before declared[56]), so yet do they it warily and fearfully, in comparison to the blasphemous bold blazing of manifest idolatry to be done to images set forth of late, even in these our days, the light of God's truth so shining that, above other their abominable[t] doings and writings, a man would marvel most at their impudent, shameless, and most shameful blustering boldness, who would not at the least have chosen them a time of more darkness as meeter to utter their horrible blasphemies in, but have now taken an harlot's face, not purposed to blush, in setting abroad the furniture of their spiritual wheredom. And here the plain blasphemy of the reverend father in God, James Naclantus, Bishop of Clugium, written in his exposition of St. Paul's Epistle to the Romans, and the first chapter, and put in print now of late at Venice, may stand instead of all: whose words of image worshipping be these in Latin, as he did write them, not one syllable altered[57].

Ergo non solum fatendum est, fideles in Ecclesia adorare co-

r mules] moyles 1563 B–1574. s idolatrious] idolatrous *from* 1582. t other their abominable] other abominable *from* 1571.

tard" in the *Promptorium Parvulorum* edited by Mr. Albert Way for the Camden Society.

55 beastly: brutish, irrational. Compare *bête* and *bêtise* in French.

56 See p. 198, l. 15, and p. 202, n. 49.

57 *Naclant. Enarratt. in Epist. ad Rom. cap.* 1, *fol.* 42 a, *ed.* 1557; *Opp.* 1, 204, *ed.* 1567. The author was Episcopus Clugiensis, Bishop of Chiozza or Chioggia near Venice, anciently Fossa Clodia, afterwards Clugia.

ram imagine, ut nonnulli ad cautelam forte loquuntur, sed et adorare imaginem, sine quo volueris scrupulo: quin et eo illam venerantur cultu, quo et prototypon ejus. Propter quod, si illud habet adorari latria, et illa latria; si dulia vel hyperdulia, et illa pariter ejusmodi cultu adoranda est.

The sense whereof in English is this: "Therefore it is not only to be confessed, that the faithful in the Church do worship before an image, (as some peradventure do warily speak,) but also do[u] worship the image itself, without any scruple or doubt at all: yea, and they worship the image with the same kind of worship wherewith they worship the copy of the image" (or the thing whereafter the image is made). "Wherefore, if the copy itself is to be worshipped with divine honour," (as is God the Father, Christ, and the Holy Ghost,) "the image of them is also to be worshipped with divine honour; if the copy ought to be worshipped with inferior honour or higher worship, the image also is to be worshipped with the same honour or worship."

Thus far hath Naclantus: whose blasphemies let Pope Gregorius the First confute, and by his authority damn them to hell, as his successors have horribly thundered. For, although Gregory permitteth images to be had, yet he forbiddeth them by any means to be worshipped, and praiseth much Bishop Serenus for the forbidding the worship[v] of them, and willeth him to teach the people to avoid by all means to worship any image[58].

Gregor. Epist. ad Seren. Massil.

But Naclantus bloweth forth his blasphemous idolatry, willing images to be worshipped with the highest kind of adoration and worship. And, lest such wholesome doctrine should lack authority, he groundeth it upon Aristotle in his book De Somno et Vigilia, that is, Of Sleeping and Waking, as by his printed book, noted so in[w] the margent[x], is to be seen[59]. Whose impudent

[u] also do] also to *till* 1571. [v] the worship] the worshipping *from* 1582. [w] noted so in] noted in 1623. [x] margent] margin 1623.

58 See before, p. 195, n. 30.

59 The sentence in Naclantus next before the passage quoted by our Homilist is this: Tradunt [*sc.* philosophi] unum eundemque motum ad imaginem et ad rem cujus imago est terminari: eo quod et unum ratio est alteri, ut unus integerque constituatur terminus; a quo et unus denominatur motus. And it has the reference, *Aristo. de Som. et Vig.*, set against it in the margin. But this proposition, thus stated, is not to be found either in that treatise or any where else in Aristotle. No doubt the passage intended is one in his next preceding treatise, De Memoria et Reminiscentia, I, 15, 16, Οἷον γὰρ τὸ ἐν τῷ πίνακι κ.τ.λ. It is to that treatise that Aquinas, who repeatedly uses the proposition in proof of the same conclusion, refers for it in Sum. Th. III, xxv, 3; from which place indeed, and from Cardinal Caietan's (or some similar) commentary upon it, Naclantus appears to have taken his argument.

wickedness and idolatrious[y] judgment I have therefore more largely set forth, that ye may (as Virgil speaketh of Sinon[z]) "of one know all[60]" these image worshippers and idolaters, and understand to what point in conclusion the public having of images in temples and churches hath brought us, comparing the times and writings of Gregory the First with our days and the[a] blasphemies of such idolaters as this beast[b] of Belial, named Naclantus, is.

Of image worshipping.

Wherefore, now it is by the testimony of the old godly fathers and doctors, by the open confession of bishops assembled in Councils, by most evident signs and arguments, opinions, idolatrious acts[c], deeds, and worshipping done to our[d] images, and by their own open confession and doctrine set forth in their books, declared and shewed that our[e] images have been and be commonly worshipped, yea, and that they ought so to be; I will out of God's word make this general argument against all such makers, setters up, and maintainers of images in public places. And first of all I will begin with the words of our Saviour Christ: *Woe be to that man by whom an offence is given. Woe be to him that offendeth one of these little ones,* or weak ones. *Better were it for him that a millstone were hanged about his neck, and he cast into the middle of the sea and drowned, than he should offend one of these little ones,* or weak ones. And in Deuteronomy God himself denounceth him *accursed that maketh the blind to wander in his way.* And in Leviticus: *Thou shalt not lay a stumbling-block,* or stone, *before the blind.* But images in churches and temples have been, and be, and (as afterward shall be proved) ever will be offences or stumblingblocks[f], specially to the weak, simple, and blind common people, deceiving their hearts by the cunning of the artificer, as the Scripture expressly in sundry places doth testify[σ], and so bringing them to idolatry. Therefore woe be to the erecter, setter up, and maintainer of images in churches and temples; for a greater penalty remaineth for him than the death of the body.

Matt. xviii, [6, 7: Luke xvii, 1, 2.]

Deut. xxvii, [18.]

Lev. xix, [14.]

σ Wisd. xiii, [10;] xiv, [18–21.]

If answer be yet made, that this offence may be taken away by diligent and sincere doctrine and preaching of God's word, as by other means; and that images in churches and temples therefore be not things absolutely evil to all men, although dan-

y idolatrious] idolatrous *from* 1582. z Sinon] Simon *in all.* a days and the] days the 1623. b beast] instrument 1623. c idolatrious acts] idolatrous acts *from* 1574. d to our] to their 1623. e that our] that their 1623. f or stumblingblocks] and stumblingblocks *from* 1567.

60 Crimine ab uno
Disce omnes. *Virg. Aen.* II, 65.

gerous to some; and therefore that it were to be holden, that the public having of them in churches and temples is not expedient, as a thing perilous, rather than unlawful, as[g] a thing utterly wicked; then followeth the third article to be proved, which is this, that it is not possible, if images be suffered in churches and temples, either by preaching of God's word, or by any other means, to keep the people from worshipping of them, and so to avoid idolatry.

And first concerning preaching. If it should be admitted, that, although images were suffered in churches, yet might idolatry by diligent and sincere preaching of God's word be avoided; it should follow of necessity, that sincere doctrine might always be had and continue as well as images, and so, that, wheresoever to offence were erected an image, there also of reason a godly and sincere preacher should and might be continually maintained. For it is reason, that the warning be as common as the stumblingblock, the remedy as large as is the offence, the medicine as general as the poison. But that is not possible, as both reason and experience teacheth. Wherefore preaching cannot stay idolatry, images being publicly suffered.

For an image, which will last for many hundred years, may for a little be bought; but a good preacher cannot be with much[h] continually maintained.

Item, if the prince will suffer it, there will be by and by many, yea, infinite images; but sincere preachers were, and ever shall be, but a few in respect of the multitude to be taught.

[Matt. ix, 37.] For our Saviour Christ saith, *The harvest is plentiful, but the workmen be but a few:* which[i] hath been hitherto continually true, and will be to the world's end; and in our time and here in our country so true, that every shire should scarcely have one good preacher, if they were divided.

Now images will continually to the beholders preach their doctrine, that is, the worshipping of images and idolatry; to the which preaching mankind is exceeding prone and enclined to give ear and credit, as experience of all nations and ages doth too much prove. But a true preacher, to stay this mischief, is in very many places scarcely heard once in an whole[j] year, and somewheres[k] not once in seven years, as is evident to be proved. And that evil opinion which hath been long rooted in men's hearts cannot suddenly by one sermon be rooted out clean[l].

[g] unlawful, as] unlawful, and 1623. [h] be with much] without much be *from* 1582. [i] but a few: which] but few: which *from* 1582. [j] an whole] a whole *from* 1563 B. [k] somewheres] somewhere *from* 1574. [l] clean] clear *till* 1571.

And as few are inclined to credit sound doctrine, as many, and almost all, be prone to superstition and idolatry. So that herein appeareth not only a difficulty, but also an impossibility, of the remedy.

Further, it appeareth not by any story of credit that true and sincere preaching hath endured in any one place above one hundred years; but it is evident that images, superstition, and worshipping of images and idolatry have continued many hundred years. For all writings and experience do testify, that good things do by little and little ever decay, until they be clean banished[m], and contrariwise evil things do more and more encrease, till they come to a full perfection of wickedness[n]. Neither need we to seek examples far off for a proof hereof: our present matter is an example. For preaching of God's word, most sincere in the beginning, by process of time waxed less and less pure, and after corrupt, and last of all altogether laid[o] down and left off, and other inventions of men crept in place[p] of it. And, on the other part, images among Christian men were first painted, and that in whole stories together, which had some signification in them; afterwards they were embossed, and made of timber, stone, plaster, and metal. And first they were only kept privately in private men's houses; and then after they crept into churches and temples, but first by painting, and after by embossing; and yet were they nowhere at the first worshipped. But shortly after they began[q] to be worshipped of the ignorant sort of men, as appeareth by the Epistle that Gregory, the first of that name Bishop of Rome, did write to Serenus, Bishop of Marcelles[r].[61] Of the which two bishops, Serenus, for idolatry committed to images, brake them and burned them; Gregory, although he thought it tolerable to let them stand, yet he judged it abominable that they should be worshipped, and thought, as is now alleged, that the worshipping of them might be stayed by teaching of God's word, according as he exhorteth Serenus to teach the people, as in the same Epistle appeareth. But whether Gregory's opinion or Serenus' judgment were better herein consider ye, I pray you; for experience by and by confuteth Gregory's opinion. For, notwithstanding Gregory's writing and the preaching of others, images being once publicly set up in temples and churches, simple men and women

[m] banished] *so in all. Did the author write* vanished? [n] of wickedness] and wickedness *from* 1582. [o] laid] *so in all.* [p] crept in place] *so in all.* [q] began] begonne 1563 A. [r] Marcelles] *so in all.*

61 See before, p. 195, n. 30.

shortly after fell on heaps to worshipping of them; and at the last the learned also were carried away with the public error, as with a violent stream or flood; and at the second Council Nicene the bishops and clergy decreed, that images should be worshipped[62]: and so, by occasion of these stumblingblocks, not only the unlearned and simple, but the learned and wise, not the people only, but the bishops, not the sheep, but also the shepherds themselves, (who should have been guides in the right way, and light to shine in darkness), being blinded by the bewitching of images, as blind guides of the blind, fell both into the pit of damnable idolatry. In the which all the world, as it were drowned, continued until our age, by the space of about[s] eight hundred years, unspoken against in a manner. And this success had Gregory's order: which mischief had never come to pass had Bishop Serenus' way been taken, and all idols and images been utterly destroyed and abolished; for no man worshippeth that that is not. And thus you see how, from having of images privately, it came to public setting of them up in churches and temples, although without harm at the first, as was then of some wise and learned men judged; and, from simple having them there, it came at last[t] to worshipping of them; first by the rude people, who specially (as the Scriptures[u] teachen[v] [r]) are in danger of superstition and idolatry, and afterwards by the bishops, the learned, and by the whole[w] clergy. So that laity and clergy, learned and unlearned, all ages, sects, and degrees of men, women, and children of whole Christendom (an horrible and most dreadful thing to think) have been at once drowned in abominable idolatry, of all other vices most detested of God and most damnable to man, and that by the space of eight hundred years and more. And to this end is come that beginning of setting up of images in churches, then judged harmless, in experience proved not only harmful, but exitious and pestilent and to the destruction and subversion of all good religion universally. So that I conclude, as it may be possible in some one city or little country to have images set up in temples and churches, and yet idolatry, by earnest and continual preaching of God's true word and the sincere Gospel of our Saviour Christ, may be kept away for a short time; so is it impossible that, images once set up and suffered in temples and

r Wisd. xiii and xiv.

s about] above *from* 1567. t at last] at the last *from* 1567. u Scriptures] Scripture 1623. v teachen] teacheth *from* 1563 B. w by the whole] by the holy 1563 A *by error for* hole, *as* whole *was then commonly written.*

62 See before, p. 202, n. 49.

churches, any great countries, much less [x] the whole world, can any long time be kept from idolatry. And the godly will respect not only their own city, country, and time, and the health of men of their age, but be careful for all places and times and the salvation of men of all ages: at the least they will not lay such stumblingblocks and snares for the feet of other countrymen and ages which experience hath already proved to have been the ruin of the world.

Wherefore I make a general conclusion of all that I have hitherto said. If the stumblingblocks and poisons of men's souls by setting up of images will be many, yea, infinite, if they be suffered, and the warnings of the said [y] stumblingblocks and remedies for the said poisons by preaching but few, as is already declared; if the stumblingblocks be easy to be laid, the poisons soon provided, and the warnings and remedies hard to know or come by; if the stumblingblocks lie continually in the way, and poison be ready at hand everywhere, and warnings and remedies but seldom given; and if all men be more ready of themselves to stumble and be offended than to be warned, all men more ready to drink of the poison than to taste of the remedy, (as is before partly, and shall hereafter more fully be, declared); and so, in fine, the poison continually and deeply drunk of many, the remedy seldom and faintly tasted of a few; how can it be but infinite [z] of the weak and infirm shall be offended, infinite by ruin shall break their necks, infinite by deadly venom be poisoned in their souls? And how is the charity of God or love of our neighbour in our hearts then, if, when we may remove such dangerous stumblingblocks, such pestilent poisons, we will not remove them? What shall I say of them which will lay stumblingblocks where before was [a] none, and set snares for the feet, nay, for the souls of weak and simple ones, and work the danger of their eternal ruin [b], for whom our Saviour Christ shed his precious [c] blood? Where better it were that the arts of painting, plastering, carving, graving, and founding had never been found nor used, than one of them whose souls in the sight of God are so precious should by occasion of image or picture perish and be lost.

And thus is it declared, that preaching cannot possibly stay idolatry, if images be set up publicly in temples and churches. And as true is it that no other remedy, as writing against idola-

[x] less] *sic in all.* [y] of the said] of the same *from* 1571; *but the Bodleian copy of* 1574 *has* said *here, and* same *for* said *in the next line.* [z] but infinite] but that infinite 1623. [a] before was] before there was *from* 1582. [b] eternal ruin] everlasting destruction *from* 1582. [c] his precious] his most precious *from* 1582.

try, councils assembled, decrees made against it, severe laws likewise and proclamations of princes and emperors, neither extreme punishments and penalties, nor any other remedy, could or can be possibly[d] devised for the avoiding of idolatry, if images be publicly set up and suffered.

For, concerning writing against images and idolatry to them committed, there hath been alleged unto you, in the second part of this treatise, a great many of places[e] out of Tertullian, Origen, Lactantius, St. Augustine, Epiphanius, St. Ambrose, Clemens, and divers other learned and holy bishops and doctors of the Church. And, besides these, all Histories Ecclesiastical and books of other godly and learned bishops and doctors are full of notable examples and sentences against images and the worshipping of them. And, as they have most earnestly written, so did they sincerely and most diligently in their time teach and preach according to their writings and examples. For they were then preaching bishops, and more often seen in pulpits than in princes' palaces; more often occupied in his legacy who said, *Go ye into the whole world, and preach the gospel to all men,* than in embassages and affairs of princes of this world. And, as they were most zealous and diligent, so were they of excellent learning and godliness of life, and by both of great authority and credit with the people, and so of more force and likelihood to persuade the people, and the people more like to believe and follow their doctrine. But, if their preachings could not help, much less could their writings; which do but come to the knowledge of a few that be learned, in comparison to continual preaching, whereof the whole multitude is partaker.

[Mark xvi, 15.]

Neither did the old fathers, bishops, and doctors, severally only by preaching and writing, but also together, great numbers of them assembled in synods and councils, make decrees and ecclesiastical laws against images and the worshipping of them; neither did they so once or twice, but divers times and in divers ages and countries, assemble[f] synods and councils, and made severe decrees against images and worshipping of them; as hath been at large in the second part of this Homily before declared. But all their writing, preaching, assembling in councils, decreeing, and making of laws ecclesiastical, could nothing help, either to pull down images to whom idolatry was committed, or against idolatry whilst images stood. For those blind books and dumb

[d] possibly] possible 1623. [e] many of places] many places *from* 1582. [f] assemble] assembled *from* 1582.

schoolmasters, I mean images and idols (for they call them laymen's books and schoolmasters), by their carved and painted writings, teaching and preaching idolatry, prevailed against all their written books and preaching with lively voice, as they call it.

Well, if preaching and writing could not keep men from worshipping of images and idolatry, if pens[g] and words could not do it, you would think that penalty and swords[h] might do it, I mean, that princes by severe laws and punishments might stay this unbridled affection of all men to idolatry, though images were set up and suffered. But experience proveth that this can no more help against idolatry than writing and preaching. For Christian Emperors, whose authority ought of reason and by God's law to be greatest, above eight in number, and six of them successively reigning one after another (as is in the histories before rehearsed[63]), making most severe laws and proclamations against idols and idolatry, images and the worshipping of images, and executing most grievous punishments, yea, the penalty of death upon the maintainers of images and upon idolaters and image worshippers, could not bring to pass, that either images once set up might throughly be destroyed, or that men should refrain from the worshipping of them being set up. And what think you then will come to pass, if men of learning should teach the people to make them, and should maintain the setting up of them, as things necessary in religion?

To conclude: it appeareth evidently by all stories and writing[i] and experience of times[k] past, that neither preaching, neither writing, neither the consent of the learned, nor authority of the godly, nor the decrees of councils, neither the laws of princes, nor extreme punishments of the offenders in that behalf, nor no[l] other remedy or means, can help against idolatry, if images be suffered publicly. And it is truly said, that times past are schoolmasters of wisdom to us that follow and live after. Therefore, if in times past the virtuest[m] and best learned, the most diligent also, and in number almost infinite, ancient fathers, bishops, and doctors, with their writing, preaching, industry, earnestness, authority, assembles[n], and councils, could do nothing against images and idolatry to images once set up; what can we, neither in learning, nor holiness of life, neither in

[g] pens] pen *from* 1582. [h] swords] sword *from* 1582. [i] and writing] and writings *from* 1570. [k] of times] in times *from* 1582. [l] no] any *from* 1582. [m] virtuest] most virtuous 1623. [n] assembles] assemblies 1587, 1595, 1623.

63 See pp. 197–200; p. 203, l. 10; p. 210, n. 66.

diligence, neither authority, to be compared with them, but men in contempt, and of no estimation (as the world goeth now), a few also in number, in so great a multitude and malice of men; what can we do, I say, or bring to pass, to the stay of idolatry or worshipping of images, if they be allowed to stand publicly in temples and churches? And, if so many, so mighty emperors, by so severe laws and proclamations, so rigorous and extreme punishments and executions, could not stay the people from setting up and worshipping of images, what will ensue, think you, when men shall commend them as necessary books of the laymen? Let us therefore of these latter days learn this lesson of the experience of the ancient[o] antiquity, that idolatry cannot possibly[p] be separated from images any long time; but that, as an unseparable accident, or as a shadow followeth the body when the sun shineth, so idolatry followeth and cleaveth to the public having of images in temples and churches; and finally, as idolatry is to be abhorred and avoided, so are images, which cannot be long without idolatry, to be put away and destroyed.

Besides the which experiments and proofs[q] of times before, the very nature and origin of images themselves draweth to idolatry most violently, and man's[r] nature and inclination also is bent to idolatry so vehemently, that it is not possible to sever or part images, nor to keep men, from idolatry, if images be suffered publicly.

That I speak of the nature and origin of images is this. Even as the first invention of them is naught, and no good can come of that which had an evil beginning, for they be altogether naught, as Athanasius, in his book against the Gentiles, declareth[64]; and St. Hierome also upon the Prophet Hieremy, the sixth[s] chapter, and Eusebius, the seventh book of his Ecclesiastical History, the eighteenth chapter, testify[t], that they[u] first came from the Gentiles, which were idolaters and worshippers of images, unto us[65]; and as *the invention of them was the beginning of spiritual fornication*, as the word of God testifieth, Sap. xiv; so will they, naturally as it were and of[x] necessity, turn to their origin from whence they came, and draw us with them most violently to idolatry, abominable to God and all godly

[Wisd. xiv, 12.]

[o] of the ancient] of ancient *from* 1574. [p] possibly] possible *till* 1571. *See before, p.* 217, u, *p.* 222, r. [q] proofs] proof *from* 1582. [r] man's] men's *from* 1582. [s] sixth] *so in all.* [t] testify] testifieth *from* 1563 B. [u] that they] that as they *in all.* [x] were and of] were of 1623.

64 See before, p. 183, n. 8.

65 See before, p. 190, nn. 23, 24.

men. For, if the origin of images and worshipping of them, as it is recorded[v] in the eighth[y] chapter of the Book of Wisdom, began of a blind love of a fond father, framing for his comfort an image of his son being dead, and so at the last men fell to the worshipping of the image of him whom they did know to be dead; how much more will men and women fall to the worshipping of the images of God, our Saviour Christ, and his Saints, if they be suffered to stand in churches and temples publicly! For, the greater the opinion is of the majesty and holiness of the person to whom an image is made, the sooner will the people fall to the worshipping of the said images[z]. Wherefore the images of God, our Saviour Christ, the blessed Virgin Mary, the Apostles, Martyrs, and other of notable holiness, are of all other images most dangerous for the peril of idolatry; and therefore greatest heed to be taken[a] that none of them be suffered to stand publicly in churches and temples. For there is no great dread lest any should fall to the worshipping of the images of Annas, Cayphas, Pilate, or Judas the traitor, if they were set up. But to the other, it is already at full proved, that idolatry hath been, is, and is most like continually to be committed.

[v] [Wisd. xiv, 15.]

Now, as was before touched, and is here more[b] largely to be declared, the nature of man is none otherwise bent to worshipping of images, if he may have them and see them, than it is bent to whoredom and adultery in the company of harlots. And, as unto a man given to the lust of the flesh, seeing a wanton harlot, sitting by her, and embracing her, it profiteth little for one to say[φ], *Beware of fornication; God will condemn fornicators and adulterers;* (for neither will he, being overcome with greater enticements of the strumpet, give ear or take heed to such godly admonitions; and, when he is left afterwards alone with the harlot, nothing can follow but wickedness;) even so, suffer images to be in sight[c] in churches[d] and temples, ye shall in vain bid them[χ] *beware of images* (as St. John doth) and *flee idolatry* (as all the Scriptures warn us); ye shall in vain preach and teach them against idolatry. For a number will notwithstanding fall headlongs[e] unto it, what by the nature of images, and by[f] the inclination of their own corrupt nature. Wherefore, as a[g] man given to lust to sit down by a strumpet is to tempt God, so is it likewise, to erect an idol in this prone-

[φ] 1 Cor. vi, [18:] 1 Thess. iv, [3:] Heb. xiii, [4.]

[χ] 1 John v, [21: 1 Cor. x, 14.]

[y] eighth] viii, 8, *or* eight *in all.* [z] images] image *from* 1582. [a] be taken] the taken 1563 A. [b] more] most *from* 1582. [c] be in sight] be sight 1571, be set *from* 1574. [d] in churches] in the churches *from* 1582. [e] headlongs] headlong *from* 1582. [f] and by] and what by 1623. [g] as a] as for a 1623.

ness of man's nature to idolatry, nothing but a tempting. Now, if any will say that this similitude proveth nothing, yet, I pray them, let the word of God, out of the which the similitude is taken, prove something. Doth not the word of God call idolatry spiritual *fornication*[ψ]? Doth it not call a gilt or painted idol or image a strumpet with a painted face[ω]? Be not the spiritual wickedness[h] of an idol's enticing like the flatteries of a wanton harlot? Be not men and women as prone to spiritual fornication, I mean idolatry, as to carnal fornication? If this be denied, let all nations upon the earth, which have been idolaters (as by all stories appeareth), prove it true. Let the Jews and the people of God, which were so often and so earnestly warned, so dreadfully threatened, concerning images and idolatry, and so extremely punished therefore, and yet fell unto it, prove it to be true; as in almost all the books of the Old Testament, namely, the Kings and the Chronicles and the Prophets, it appeareth most evidently. Let all ages and times, and men of all ages and times, of all degrees and conditions, wise men, learned men, princes, idiots, unlearned, and commonalty, prove it to be true. If you require examples: for wise men, ye have the Egyptians and the Indian Gymnosophists, the wisest men of the world; you have Salomon, the wisest of all other; for learned men, the Greeks, and namely the Athenians, exceeding all other nations in superstition and idolatry, as in the history of the Acts of the Apostles[α] St. Paul chargeth them; for princes and governors, you have the Romans[β], the rulers of the roast (as they say); you have the same forenamed king Salomon, and all the kings of Israel and Juda after him, saving David, Ezechias, and Josias, and one or two more. All these, I say, and infinite others, wise, learned, princes and governors, being all idolaters, have you for examples and a proof of men's inclination to idolatry. That I may pass over with silence, in the mean time, infinite multitudes and millions of idiots and unlearned, the ignorant and gross people, *like*[γ] *unto horses and moyles*[i], *in whom is no understanding*, whose peril and danger to fall on heaps to idolatry by occasion of images the Scriptures specially foreshew[δ] and give warning of. And indeed how should the unlearned, simple, and foolish scape the nets and snares of idols and images, in the which the wisest and best[k] learned have been so entangled, trapped, and wrapped? Where-

ψ Lev. xvii, [7;] xx, [5:] Numb. xxv, [1, 2:] Deut. xxxi, [16.]

ω Bar. vi, [9–11, *or* 8–10 *in Vulg.*]

α Acts xvii, [16, 22.]

β Rom. i, [23.]

γ Ps. xxxi [xxxii, 9.]

δ Wisd. xiii, xiv, &c.

h wickedness] wickednesses *from* 1582. i moyles] mules *from* 1582. k and best] and the best *from* 1582.

fore the argument holdeth this ground sure, that men be as inclined of their corrupt nature to spiritual fornication as to carnal: which the wisdom of God foreseeing, to the general prohibition, that[ε] *none should make to themselves any image or similitude*, addeth a cause depending of man's corrupt nature: *Lest*, saith God, *thou, being deceived with error, honour and worship them*[66].

[ε Deut. iv, [15–19.]]

And of this ground of man's corrupt inclination, as well to spiritual fornication as to carnal, it must needs follow, that, as it is the duty of the godly magistrate, loving honesty and hating whoredom, to remove all strumpets and harlots, specially out of places notoriously suspected or resorted unto of naughty packs[67], for the avoiding of carnal fornication; so is it[l] the duty of the same godly magistrate, after the examples of the godly kings Ezechias and Josias, to drive away all spiritual harlots, I mean idols and images, specially[m] out of suspected places, churches and temples, dangerous for idolatry to be committed to images placed there, as it were in the appointed place and height of honour and worship (as St. Augustine saith[68]), where the living God only, and not dead stones nor stocks[n], is to be worshipped: it is, I say, the office of godly magistrates likewise to avoid images and idols out of churches and temples, as spiritual harlots out of suspected places, for the avoiding of idolatry, which is spiritual fornication.

[August. in Psal. xxxvi et cxiii; et Lib. iv, cap. 3, de Civ. Dei.]

And, as he were the enemy of all honesty that would[o] bring strumpets and harlots out of their secret corners into the public market place, there freely to dwell and occupy[p] their filthy merchandise, so is he the[q] enemy of the true worshipping of God that bringeth idols and images into the temple and church, the house of God, there openly to be worshipped, and to spoil[r] the *zealous*[s] *God*[69] of his honour, who *will*[ζ] *not give it to any*

[ζ [Is. xlii, 8.]]

[l] so is it] so it is *from* 1570. [m] specially] especially 1623. [n] nor stocks] and stocks *from* 1567. [o] would] should *from* 1582. [p] occupy] practise 1623. [q] is he the] is the 1623. [r] spoil] rob 1623. [s] zealous] jealous 1587, 1595.

66 Custodite igitur solicite animas vestras . . ., ne forte decepti faciatis vobis sculptam similitudinem aut imaginem . . . ; ne forte elevatis oculis ad coelum videas solem et lunam et omnia astra coeli, et errore deceptus adores ea et colas, quae creavit Dominus Deus tuus in ministerium cunctis gentibus quae sub coelo sunt. *Vulg.*

67 naughty packs. "Call her a naughty pack, with that one word thou hast taken all from her and left her bare and foul." *Vives* cited by *Richardson* on "Pack." See also *Nares' Glossary*, "Naughty-pack."

68 See *Augustin. Epist.* CII cited before, p. 189, n. 22. The references in the margin are repeated, needlessly and with error, from pp. 188 and 189.

69 Ego sum Dominus Deus tuus fortis zelotes. *Exod.* xx, 5. Dominus zelotes nomen ejus, Deus est aemulator. *Ibid.* xxxiv, 14. *Vulg.*

other, nor his glory to carven[t] *images;* who is as much forsaken, and the bond of love between man and him as much broken, by idolatry, which is spiritual fornication, as is the knot and bond of marriage broken by carnal fornication. Let all this be taken as a lie, if the word of God enforce it not to be true. *Cursed be the man,* saith God in Deuteronomium[u], *that maketh a carven*[x] *or molten image, and placeth it in a secret corner: and all the people shall say, Amen.* Thus saith God: for at that time no man durst have or worship images openly, but in corners only; and, the whole world being the great temple of God, he that in any corner thereof robbeth God of his glory, and giveth it to stocks and stones, is pronounced by God's word accursed. Now he that will bring these spiritual harlots out of their lurking corners into public churches and temples, that spiritual fornication may there openly of all men and women without shame be committed with them, no doubt that person is cursed of God, and twice cursed, and all good and godly men and women will say, *Amen,* and their *Amen* will take effect also.

Deut. xxvii, [15.]

Yea, and furthermore the madness of all men professing the religion of Christ, now by the space of a sort of hundred years, and yet even in our time, in so great light of the Gospel, very many running on heaps by sea and land, to the great loss of their time, expense and waste of their goods, destitution of their wives, children, and families, and danger of their own bodies and lives, to Compostle[y], Rome, Jerusalem, and other far countries[70], to visit dumb and dead stocks and stones, doth sufficiently prove the proneness of man's corrupt nature to the seeking of idols once set up and the worshipping of them.

And thus, as well by the origin and nature of idols and images themselves, as by the proneness and inclination of man's corrupt nature to idolatry, it is evident, that neither images, if they be publicly set up, can be separated, nor men, if they see

t, x carven] carved 1623. u Deuteronomium] Deuteronomy 1623. y Compostle] Compostile 1563 B–1574, Compostella *from* 1582.

70 "A short pilgrimage is not worth a pin: neither is an image in so much honour and respect in that countrey where it is, as in farre countries. For example, the Italians, yea, those that dwell neare Rome, will mocke and scoffe at our English and other pilgrims that go to Rome to see the Pope's Holiness and St. Peter's chaire; and yet they themselves will runne to see the Reliques of Saint James of Compostella in the kingdome of Gallicia in Spaine, which is above twelve hundred English miles." *Weever's Funeral Monuments, Discourse, chap.* XVII, *p.* 172, *ed.* 1631, quoted in *Wordsworth's Ecclesiastical Biography, vol.* 1, *p.* 11, *n.* 1, *ed.* 1810.

images in temples and churches, can be stayed and kept, from idolatry.

Now, whereas they yet allege, that howsoever the people, princes, learned, and wise of old time have fallen into idolatry by occasion of images, that yet in our time the most part, specially the learned, wise, and of any authority, take no hurt nor offence by idols and images, neither do run into far countries to them and worship them; and that they know well what an idol or image is, and how to be used; and that therefore it followeth, images in churches and temples to be an indifferent thing, as the which of some is not abused; and that therefore they may justly hold (as was in the beginning of this part by them alleged) that it is not unlawful or wicked absolutely to have images in churches and temples, though it may, for the danger of the simpler[z] sort, seem to be not altogether expedient: whereunto[a] may be well replied, that Salomon also, the wisest of all men, did well know what an idol or image was, and neither took any harm thereof a great while himself, and also with his godly writings[η] armed others against the danger of them; but yet afterward the same Salomon, suffering his wanton paramours to bring their idols into his court and palace, was by carnal harlots persuaded and brought at the last to the committing of spiritual fornication with idols, and, of the wisest and godliest prince, became the most foolishest and wickedest also. Wherefore it is better even for the wisest to regard this warning[θ], *He that loveth danger shall perish therein*, and[ι], *Let him that standeth beware he fall not*[b], rather than wittingly and willingly to lay such a stumblingblock for his own feet and others that may perhaps bring at last to breakneck[c].

η Wisd. xiii, xiv.

θ Ecclus. iii, [26;] and xiii, [1.]

ι 1 Cor. x, [12.]

The good king Ezechias did know well enough that the brazen serpent was but a dead image, and therefore he took no hurt himself thereby through idolatry to it. Did he therefore let it stand, because himself took no hurt thereof? No, not so; but being a good king, and therefore regarding the health of his seely subjects deceived by that image and committing idolatry thereto, he did not only take it down, but also brake it to pieces[κ]. And this he did to that image that was set up by the commandment of God[λ], in the presence whereof great miracles were wrought, as that which was a figure of our Saviour Christ to come, who should deliver us from the mortal sting of the old

κ 2 Kings xviii, [4.]

λ [Numb. xxi, 8, 9: John iii, 14, 15.]

z simpler] simple *from* 1563 B. a whereunto] *so in all.* b he fall not] lest he fall *from* 1567. c breakneck] break neck *from* 1574.

serpent Satan. Neither did he spare it in respect of the ancientness or antiquity of it, which had continued about[d] seven hundred years; nor for[e] that it had been suffered and preserved by so many godly kings before his time. How, think you, would that godly prince, if he were now living, handle our idols, set up against God's commandment directly, and being figures of nothing but folly, and for fools to gaze on, till they become as wise as the blocks themselves which they stare on, and so fall[f] down as dared larks[71] in that gaze, and, being themselves alive, worship a dead stock or stone, gold or silver, and so become idolaters, abominable and cursed before the living God, giving the honour due unto him which made them when they were nothing, and to our Saviour Christ, who redeemed them being lost, to the dead and dumb idol, *the work of man's hand*[μ], which never did nor can do any thing for them, no, is not able to stir, nor once to move, and therefore worse than a vile worm, which can move and creep? The excellent king Josias also did take himself no hurt of images and idols, for he did know well what they were. Did he therefore, because of his own knowledge, let idols and images stand? Much less did he set any up. Or rather did he not, by his knowledge and authority also, succour the ignorance of such as did not know what they were by utter taking away of all such stumblingblocks as might be occasion of ruin to his people and subjects?

μ [Deut. iv, 28: Is. xlvi, 7.]

Will they, because a few took no hurt by images or idols, break the general law of God, *Thou shalt make to thee no similitude*, &c.? They might as well, because Moyses was not seduced by Jethro's daughter, nor Boos by Ruth, being strangers, reason that all the Jews might break the general law of God, forbidding[ν] his people to join their children in marriage with strangers, lest they seduce their children that they should not follow God. Wherefore they which thus reason, Though it be not expedient, yet is it[g] lawful, to have images publicly, and do

[Exod. xx, 4.]

ν [Exod. xxxiv, 16: Deut. vii, 3, 4.]

[d] about] above *from* 1570. [e] nor for] not for 1563 A. [f] fall] fell *till* 1563 H. [g] yet is it] yet it is *from* 1567.

71 dared: lying still from terror at some object presented to their eyes, as the flashing of light reflected from a mirror, the fluttering of a piece of scarlet cloth, the hovering of a hawk, till the fowler could at last get near enough to throw a net over them. See *Nares' Glossary*.

> And, running straight where as she heard his voice,
> Enclosed the bush about, and there him tooke
> Like darred larke, not daring up to looke
> On her whose sight before so much he sought.
>
> *Spenser, Faerie Queene, Canto* VI *Of Mutabilitie*, 47.

prove that lawfulness by a few picked and chosen men; if they object that indifferently to all men which a very few can have without hurt and offence, they seem to take the multitude for "vile souls" (as he saith in Virgil[72]), of whose loss or[h] safeguard no reputation is to be had, for whom yet Christ paid as dearly as for the mightiest princes[i] or the wisest and best learned in the earth. And they that will have it generally to be taken for indifferent, for that[j] a very few take no hurt of it, though infinite multitudes besides[k] perish thereby, shew that they put little difference between the multitude of Christians and brute beasts, whose danger they do so little esteem.

Besides this, if they be bishops or parsons, or otherwise having charge of men's consciences, that thus reason, It is lawful to have images publicly, though it be not expedient, what manner of pastors shew they themselves to be to their flock, which thrust unto them that which they themselves confess not to be expedient for them, but to the utter ruin of the souls committed to their charge, for whom they shall give a strait account before *the Prince of pastors*[g][73] at the last day? For indeed to object to the weak and ready to fall of themselves such stumbling-blocks is a thing, not only not expedient, but unlawful, yea, and most wicked also. Wherefore it is to be wondered how they can call images set up in churches and temples, to no profit or benefit of any, and to so great peril and danger, yea, hurt and destruction of many or rather infinite, things indifferent. Is not the public setting up of them rather a snare for all men and the tempting of God? I beseech these reasoners to call to mind their own accustomed ordinance and decree whereby they determined that the Scripture, though by God himself commanded[o] to be known of all men, women, and children, should not be read of the simple, nor had in the vulgar tongue, for that (as they said) it was dangerous by bringing the simple people into errors. And will they not forbid images to be set up in churches and temples, which are not commanded but forbidden most straitly by God, but let them still be there, yea, and maintain them also, seeing the people are brought not in danger only

g [1 Pet. v, 4.]

o Deut. xxxi, [10–13.]

h loss or] loss and *from* 1570. i princes] prince *from* 1570. j indifferent, for that] indifferent, that *from* 1582. k besides] beside *from* 1570.

72 Scilicet, ut Turno contingat regia conjunx,
Nos, animae viles, inhumata infletaque turba,
Sternamur campis. *Aen.* XI, 371.

73 Princeps pastorum. *Vulg.*

but indeed into most abominable error[l] and detestable idolatry thereby? Shall God's word, by God commanded to be read unto all and known of all, for danger of heresy (as they say) be shut up? and idols and images, notwithstanding they be forbidden by God, and notwithstanding the danger of idolatry by them, shall they yet be set up, suffered, and maintained in churches and temples? O worldly and fleshly wisdom, ever bent[m] to maintain the inventions and traditions of men by carnal reason, and by the same to disannul or deface the holy ordinances, laws, and honour of the eternal God, who is to be honoured and praised for ever. Amen.

NOW it remaineth, for the conclusion of this treaty, to declare as well the abuse of churches and temples by too costly and sumptuous decking and adorning of them, as also[n] the lewd painting, gilding, and clothing of idols and images, and so to conclude the whole treaty.

Tertull. Apol. cap. 39.

In Tertullian's time, an hundred and threescore years after Christ, Christians had none other temples but common houses, whither they for the most part secretly resorted[74]. And so far off was it that they had before his time any goodly or gorgeous-decked temples, that laws were made in Antoninus[o] Verus and Commodus the Emperors' times, that no Christians should dwell in houses, come in public baths, or be seen in streets or any where abroad[75]; and that, if they were once accused to be

Euseb. Lib. v Eccles. Hist.

[l] error] errors *from* 1582. [m] ever bent] even bent *from* 1582. [n] as also] and also 1563 B–H. [o] Antoninus] Antonius *from* 1563 EF.

74 The writer of the Homily took his assertion in the text and his reference in the margin from the following passage in *Bullinger, cap.* 21, *fol.* 100 a *ed.* 1539, which Bullinger himself took bodily from *Joachim Vadianus* or *Von Watte, Epitome Trium Terrae Partium, "Ionia," p.* 234 *ed.* 1534. Ipse Tertullianus, vetus author et qui sub Imperatore Pertinace multo tempore Romae fuit, palam innuit ne suo quidem tempore alia templa Christianis fuisse quam simplices domos, in quibus statis diebus fideles congregabantur, convivia etiam et Coenam illam Sacram pro veteri more celebrantes, aliaque id genus quae publicae disciplinae erant exercentes. De qua re ipse XXXIX cap. Apologetici disseruit.

What Tertullian there says may be thus given. Corpus sumus de conscientia religionis et disciplinae unitate et spei foedere. Coimus in coetum et congregationem, ut ad Deum quasi manu facta precationibus ambiamus orantes .... Coimus ad litterarum divinarum commemorationem .... Ibidem etiam exhortationes, castigationes, et censura divina .... Praesident probati quique seniores .... *Apolog.* XXXIX, *Opp.* I, 254–257.

Concerning the early use of churches, that is, buildings set apart for divine worship, see *Bingham, Orig. Eccles.* VIII, i, 13–17, especially § 15, in which other treatises of Tertullian are quoted.

75 Παντὶ γὰρ σθένει ἐνέσκηψεν ὁ ἀντικείμενος, ... ὥστε μὴ μόνον οἰκιῶν καὶ βαλανείων καὶ ἀγορᾶς εἴργεσθαι, ἀλλὰ καὶ τὸ καθόλου φαίνεσθαι ἡμῶν τινὰ αὐτοῖς

Christians, they should by no means be suffered to escape. As was practised in[p] Apollonius a noble senator of Rome, who, being accused of his own bondman and slave that he was a Christian, could neither by his defence and apology, learnedly and eloquently written and read publicly in the senate, nor in respect that he was a citizen, nor for the dignity of his order, nor for the vileness and unlawfulness of his accuser, being his own slave, by likelihood of malice moved to forge lies against his lord, nor for no other respect or help, could be delivered from death[76]. So that Christians were then driven to dwell in caves and dens: so far off was it that they had any public temples adorned and decked as they now be. Which is here rehearsed to the confutation of those impudent shameless liars[q], which report such glorious glosed fables of the goodly[r] and gorgeous temples[s] that St. Peter, Linus, Cletus, and those thirty bishops their successors had at Rome until the time of the Emperor Constantine, and which St. Polycarp should have in Asia, or Ireneus in France; by such lies, contrary to all true histories, to maintain the superfluous gilding and decking of temples now a days, wherein they put almost the whole sum and pith of our religion. But in those times the world was won to Christendom, not by gorgeous, gilted[t], and painted temples of Christians, which had scarcely houses to dwell in, but by the godly and as it were golden minds[77] and firm faith of such as in all adversity and persecution professed the truth of our religion.

Hieronymus.

And, after these times, in Maximian[u] and Constantius the Emperors' proclamation the places where Christians resorted to public prayer were called "Conventicles".[78] And in Galerius

Euseb. Lib. viii, cap. 19; et Lib. ix, cap. 9.

[p] practised in] practised on *from* 1582. [q] impudent shameless liars] *omitted* 1623. [r] goodly] godly 1563. [s] gorgeous temples] gorgeous temple *from* 1567. [t] gilted] gilded 1623. [u] Maximian] Maximinian 1623.

ἀπειρῆσθαι ἐν ὁποίῳ δήποτε τόπῳ. Epist. Eccless. Vienn. et Lugd. ap. Euseb. Hist. Eccles. v, i, 3. Rufinus rendered the latter part thus: ita ut primo nobis domorum prohiberetur habitatio, tum deinde usus balnearum, post etiam processus ad publicum, ad ultimum ne omnino in quolibet loco domi forisque publico privatoque videremur. *Pag.* 100 A, *ed. Basil.* 1528.

76 Apollonius, Romanae urbis senator, sub Commodo Principe a servo Severo proditus quod Christianus esset, impetrato ut rationem fidei suae redderet, insigne volumen composuit, quod in senatu legit; et nihilominus sententia senatus pro Christo capite truncatus est, veteri apud eos obtinente lege, absque negatione non dimitti Christianos, qui semel ad eorum judicium pertracti essent. *Hieron. De Viris Illustr.* sive *De Scriptor. Eccles. cap.* 42, *Opp.* II, 869.

77 See note 91 below.

78 Προθυμότατα καὶ ἐν τούτῳ τὴν συγχώρησιν τὴν ἡμετέραν ἐπεκτεῖναι δεῖν ἐνομίσαμεν, ἵνα αὖθις ὦσι Χριστιανοί, καὶ τοὺς οἴκους ἐν οἷς συνήγοντο συνθῶσιν. Euseb. Hist. Eccles. VIII, xvii, 6. The version of Rufinus is this: Libenter etiam erga hos indulgentiam nostram credidimus porrigendam, ut rursus sint Christiani, et conventicula in quibus orare consue-

Maximinus the Emperor's Epistle they are called Oratories and Dominica[x], to say, places dedicate to the service of the Lord[79]. (And here by the way it is to be noted, that at that time there were no churches or temples erected unto any Saint, but to God only; as St. Augustine also recordeth, saying, "We build no temples unto our Martyrs[80].") And Eusebius himself calleth churches "houses of prayer[81];" and sheweth that in Constantine the Emperor's time all men rejoiced, seeing, "instead of low conventicles," which tyrants had destroyed, "high temples to be builded[82]." Lo, until[y] the time of Constantine, by the space of above three hundred years after our Saviour Christ, when Christian religion was most pure and indeed golden, Christians had but low and poor conventicles and simple oratories, yea, caves under the ground called Cryptae, where they for fear of persecution assembled secretly together; a figure whereof remaineth in the vaults which yet are builded under great churches, to put us in remembrance of the old state of the primitive Church before Constantine: whereas in Constantine's time and after him were builded great and goodly temples for Christians, called Basilicae, either for that the Greeks used to

De Civitate. Lib.viii,cap.1.

Cryptae.

Basilicae.

x Dominica] Dominicae 1623. y until] unto *from* 1563 EF.

verunt exstruant et reaedificent. *Lib.* VIII, *cap.* xix, *p.* 199 B. The genuine words of the edict, preserved by Lactantius, *De Morte Persecutt. c.* 34, are as follow. Promptissimam in his quoque indulgentiam nostram credidimus porrigendam, ut denuo sint Christiani, et conventicula sua componant.

This edict was issued A.D. 311, shortly before the death of Galerius. In Rufinus it runs in the names of Galerius Maximianus and Flavius Valerius Constantius. In the Greek text Galerius is called Maximinus, the second Emperor is rightly named Constantinus, and the name of a third, Licinius, is added.

79 Καὶ τὰ κυριακὰ δὲ τὰ οἰκεῖα ὅπως κατασκευάζοιεν συγκεχώρηται. Euseb. Hist. Eccles. IX, x, 8. Sed et orationum domos, id est, dominica sua, ut instaurent pro voluntate sua permittimus. *Rufin. Interpr.* IX, ix, *p.* 210 B. Rufinus sets the name of Galerius Maximinus at the head of this edict. It was issued A.D. 313 by Caius Valerius Maximinus Jovius, nephew to Galerius.

80 See *Augustin. de Civ. Dei* XXII, 10, cited before, p. 188, n. 18.

81 Συντετέλεσται δῆτα καθ' ἡμᾶς ἅπαντα, ὁπηνίκα τῶν μὲν προσευκτηρίων τοὺς οἴκους ἐξ ὕψους εἰς ἔδαφος αὐτοῖς θεμελίοις καταρριπτουμένους .... ἐπείδομεν. Euseb. Hist. Eccles. VIII, ii, 1. Summa namque malorum nobis affuit omnium tunc cum domus orationis et ecclesiae Dei vivi ad solum deductae sunt atque ab ipsis subversae sunt fundamentis. *Rufin. Interpr.* VIII, i, *p.* 183 B.

82 Ἡμῖν .... ἄλεκτος παρῆν εὐφροσύνη, καί τις ἔνθεος ἅπασιν ἐπήνθει χαρὰ, πάντα τόπον τὸν πρὸ μικροῦ ταῖς τῶν τυράννων δυσσεβείαις ἠρειπωμένον ὥσπερ ἐκ μακρᾶς καὶ θανατηφόρου λύμης ἀναβιώσκοντα θεωμένοις, νεὼς τε αὖθις ἐκ βάθρων εἰς ὕψος ἄπειρον ἐγειρομένους καὶ πολὺ κρείττονα τὴν ἀγλαΐαν τῶν πάλαι πεπολιορκημένων ἀπολαμβάνοντας. Euseb. Hist. Eccles. X, ii, 1. Ex quo aderat cunctis velut divino munere infusa laetitia, maxime videntibus ea loca quae paulo ante impiis tyrannorum machinis fuerant destructa rediviva constructione clariora et celsiora consurgere, templaque excelsa pro humilibus conventiculis elevari. *Rufin. Interpr.* IX, x, *p.* 212 B.

call all great and goodly places Basilicas, or for that the high and everlasting King, God and our Saviour Christ, was served in them[83]. But, although Constantine and other princes, of good zeal to our religion, did sumptuously deck and adorn Christians' temples, yet did they dedicate at that time all churches or temples[z] to God or our Saviour Christ, and to no Saint[84]; for that abuse began long after in Justinian's time[85]. Nov. Const. 3 et 67.

And that gorgeousness then used, as it was borne with as rising of a good zeal, so was it signified of the godly learned even at that time, that such cost might otherwise have been better bestowed. Let St. Hierome, although otherwise too great a liker and allower of external and outward things, be a proof hereof, who hath these words in his Epistle to Demetriades[a]. "Let other," saith St. Hierome[86], "build churches, cover walls with tables of marble, carry together huge pillars, and gild their tops or heads, which do not feel or understand their precious decking and adorning; let them deck the doors with ivory and silver, and set the golden altars with precious stones. I blame it not. Let every man abound in his own sense: and better is it so to do than carefully to keep their riches laid up in store. But thou hast another way appointed thee, to clothe Christ in the poor[π], to visit him in the sick, feed him in the hungry, lodge him in those who do lack harbour, and *specially*[b] *such*[ρ] *as be of the household of faith.*" And the same St. Hierome toucheth

π [Matt. xxv, 40.]
ρ [Gal. vi, 10.]

z or temples] and temples *from* 1570. a Demetriades] *so in all.* b specially] especially 1582, 1623.

83 See *Euseb. de Vit. Constantin.* III, 31, 32. See also *Bingham, Orig. Eccles.* VIII, 1, 5.

84 See *Hooker, Eccles. Polit.* v, xiii; and *Bingham, Orig. Eccles.* VIII, ix, 8, 9; shewing that a church was not therefore dedicated to a Saint because it bore his name as a memorial of him.

85 *Bullinger, cap.* 21, *fol.* 101 b, says that the practice began a little before Justinian's time, and quotes the first of the two Constitutions here cited in the margin to prove it. That Constitution speaks of "venerabilis domus sanctae gloriosaeque Virginis et Dei genetricis Mariae" built "a piae memoriae Verina," of "veneranda domus sancti Martyris Theodori a Sphoratio [*al.* Porcatio] gloriosae memoriae dedicata," and of "venerabilis domus sanctae Helenae," churches at Constantinople. *Authent. Collat.* I, iii, *Novell.* 3, *cap.* i. The other Constitution, *Authent. Collat.* v, xxii, *Novell.* 67, says nothing at all about the dedication of churches; and *Bullinger*, from whom no doubt the Homilist took the reference, cited it (*fol.* 102 a) for a different purpose.

86 Alii aedificent ecclesias; vestiant parietes marmorum crustis; columnarum moles advehant, earumque deaurent capita, preciosum ornatum non sentientia; ebore argentoque valvas, et gemmis aurata distinguant altaria. Non reprehendo, non abnuo. Unusquisque in sensu suo abundet. Meliusque est hoc facere, quam repositis opibus incubare. Sed tibi aliud propositum est, Christum vestire in pauperibus, visitare in languentibus, pascere in esurientibus, suscipere in his qui tecto indigent, et *maxime in domesticis fidei.* Hieron. Epist. LXXX ad Demetriadem Virginem § 14, Opp. I, 985 A.

the same matter somewhat more freely in his Treaty of the Life of Clerks to Nepotian, saying thus [87]: "Many build walls, and erect pillars of churches; the smooth marbles do glister, the roof shineth with gold, the altar is set with precious stone[c]; but of the ministers of Christ there is no election or choice. Neither let any man object and allege against me the rich temple that was in Jewry, the table, candlesticks, incense-ships [88], platters, cups, mortars, and other things all of gold. Then were these things allowed of the Lord, when the priests offered sacrifices, and the blood of beasts was accounted the redemption of sins. Howbeit *all these things*[σ] went before *in figure, and they were written for us, upon whom the end of the world is come.* And now, when that our Lord being poor hath dedicate the poverty of his house, let us remember his cross, and we shall esteem riches as mire or dung[d]. What do we marvel at that which Christ calleth[τ] *wicked mammon?* Whereto do we so highly esteem and love that which St. Peter[υ] doth for a glory testify that he had not?" Hitherto St. Hierome. Thus ye[e] see how St. Hierome teacheth the sumptuousness amongst the Jews to be a figure to signify, and not an example to follow, and that those outward things were suffered for a time, until Christ our Lord came, who turned all those outward things into spirit, faith, and truth. And the same St. Hierome upon the seventh chapter of Jeremy saith [89]: "God commanded both the Jews at

σ [1 Cor. x, 11.]
τ [Luke xvi, 11.]
υ [Acts iii, 6.]

c stone] stones *from* 1582. d or dung] and dung *from* 1582. e Thus ye] Thus you *from* 1567.

87 Multi aedificant parietes, et columnas ecclesiae substruunt; marmora nitent, auro splendent laquearia, gemmis altare distinguitur; et ministrorum Christi nulla electio est. Neque vero mihi aliquis opponat dives in Judaea templum, mensam, lucernas, thuribula, patellas, scyphos, mortariola, et caetera ex auro fabrefacta. Tunc haec probabantur a Domino, quando sacerdotes hostias immolabant, et sanguis pecudum erat redemtio peccatorum. Quamquam *haec omnia* praecesserint *in figura: scripta sunt autem propter nos, in quos fines seculorum devenerunt.* Nunc vero, quum paupertatem domus suae pauper Dominus dedicarit, cogitemus crucem ejus, et divitias lutum putabimus. Quid miramur quod Christus vocat *iniquum mammona?* Quid suspicimus et amamus quod Petrus se non habere gloriose testatur? *Hieron. Epist.* LII *ad Nepotianum de Vita Clericorum* § 10, *Opp.* I, 262 D.

88 The word *thuribula* is not quite rightly rendered by *incense-ships. Thuribulum* was a vessel in which incense was burnt, a *censer:* the *incense-ship* or (as we should now say) *incense-boat,* having its name from its shape, was called in Latin *navicula* or *navis,* and was used for supplying the censer with incense. See *Du Cange* on the words. "The massmonger . . . hath also . . . censers, ship, frankincense, . . . and many other suchlike ornaments, more meet for the priesthood of Aharon than for the ministery of the new testament." *Becon, Comparison between the Lord's Supper and the Pope's Mass,* 12. "A paire of Senssours" and "a Shippe for frankensence with a spone," are two items in the Inventory of the Duke of Richmond's Goods taken July 25, 1526, edited by John Gough Nichols, Esq., in Vol. III of the *Camden Miscellany.*

89 Praecepit autem et tunc populo

that time, and now us who are placed in the Church, that we have no trust in the goodliness of building and gilt roofs and in walls covered with tables of marble, and say, *The temple of the Lord, The temple of the Lord, The temple of the Lord*[f]. For that is the temple of the Lord wherein dwelleth true faith, godly conversation, and the company of all virtues." And upon the prophet Agge he describeth the true and right decking or ornaments of the temple after this sort. "I," saith St. Hierome[90], "do think the silver, wherewith the house of God is decked, to be the doctrine of the Scriptures, of the which it is spoken[φ], φ [Ps. xii, 6.] *The doctrine of the Lord is a pure doctrine, silver tried in fire*[h], *purged from dross, purified seven times.* And I do take gold to be that which remaineth in the hid sense of the saints and the secret of the heart, and shineth with the true light of God. Which is evident that the Apostle[χ] also meant of the saints that χ [1 Cor. iii, 12.] *build upon the foundation of Christ*, some *silver*, some *gold*, some *precious stones*; that by the gold the hid sense, by silver godly utterance, by precious stones works which please God, might be signified. With these metals the Church of our Saviour is made more goodly and gorgeous than was the Synagogue in old time: with these lively stones is the Church and house of Christ builded, and peace is given to it for ever." All these be St. Hierome's sayings.

No more did the old godly bishops and doctors of the Church allow the outrageous[i] furniture of temples and churches with plate, vessels of gold, silver, and precious vestures[k]. St. Chrysostom saith, in the ministry of the holy Sacraments there is no need of golden vessels, but of golden minds[91]. And St. Am-

[f] The temple of the Lord] *twice only from* 1582. [h] in fire] in the fire 1623. [i] outrageous] oversumptuous 1623. [k] vestures] vestments 1623.

Judaeorum, et hodie nobis qui videmur in Ecclesia constituti, ne fiduciam habeamus in aedificiorum splendore auratisque laquearibus et vestitis parietibus marmorum crustis, et dicamus, *Templum Domini, Templum Domini, Templum Domini est.* Illud enim Templum Domini est, in quo habitat vera fides, sancta conversatio, omniumque virtutum chorus. *Hieron. in Jerem.* VII, 4; *Opp.* IV, 891 C.

90 Sed ego argentum, quo domus Dei ornatur, existimo eloquia Scripturarum, de quibus dicitur, *Eloquia Domini eloquia casta, argentum igne examinatum, probatum terrae, purgatum septuplum*; et aurum, quod in occulto sanctorum sensu et in cordis versatur arcano, et splendet vero lumine Dei. Quod et Apostolum de sanctis qui *super fundamentum Christi aedificant* sensisse perspicuum est: *Aurum, argentum, lapides pretiosos*: ut in auro sensus occultus sit, in argento sermo decens, in lapide pretioso opera Deo placentia. His metallis illustrior fit Ecclesia Salvatoris, quam quondam Synagoga fuerat: his lapidibus vivis aedificatur domus Christi, et pax ei praebetur aeterna. *Hieron. in Aggae.* II, 1–9; *Opp.* VI, 758 A.

91 Φύγωμεν τοίνυν τοῦτο τὸ βάραθρον, μηδὲ νομίζωμεν ἀρκεῖν ἡμῖν εἰς σωτηρίαν,

ii Offic. cap. 28.

brose saith[92]: "Christ sent his Apostles without gold, and gathered his Church without gold. The Church hath gold, not to keep it, but to bestow it on the necessities of the poor." "The Sacraments look for no gold, neither do they please God for the commendation of gold, which are not bought for gold. The adorning and decking of the Sacraments is the redemption of captives." Thus much St.[l] Ambrose. St. Hierome commendeth Exuperius, Bishop of Tolose, that he carried the Sacrament of the Lord's Body in a wicker basket and the Sacrament of his Blood in a glass, and so cast covetousness out of the church[93]. And Bonifacius, Bishop and Martyr, as it is recorded in the Decrees, testifieth that in old time the ministers used treen[m], and not golden, vessels[94]. And Zephyrinus, the sixteenth bishop of Rome, made a decree that they should use vessels of glass[95]. Likewise were the vestures used in the Church in old time very plain and single and nothing costly. And Rabanus at large declareth, that this costly and manifold furniture of vestments of late used in the Church was fet[96] from the Jewish usage, and agreeth with Aaron's apparelling almost altogether[97]. For the maintenance of the which, Innocentius the pope pronounceth boldly that all the customs of the old Law be not abolished, that we might, in such apparel, of Christians the more willingly become Jewish[98].

Tit. de Consecr. Can. Triburien.

Lib. i Instit. cap. 14.

l much St.] much saith St. *from* 1582. m treen] wooden 1623.

εἰ χήρας καὶ ὀρφανοὺς ἀποδύσαντες ποτήριον χρυσοῦν καὶ λιθοκόλλητον προσενέγκωμεν τῇ τραπέζῃ. εἰ γὰρ βούλει τιμῆσαι τὴν θυσίαν, τὴν ψυχὴν προσένεγκε, δι' ἣν καὶ ἐτύθη· ταύτην χρυσῆν ποίησον. Chrysost. in Matth. Hom. L (*al.* LI); Opp. VII, 518 A.

92 Qui enim sine auro misit Apostolos Ecclesias sine auro congregavit. Aurum Ecclesia habet, non ut servet, sed ut eroget, et subveniat in necessitatibus .... Aurum Sacramenta non quaerunt, neque auro placent, quae auro non emuntur. Ornatus Sacramentorum redemptio captivorum est. *Ambros. de Offic. Ministr.* II, xxviii, 137, 138; *Opp.* II, 103 B, D.

93 Sanctus Exuperius Tolosae Episcopus, viduae Sareptensis imitator, esuriens pascit alios .... Nihil illo ditius; qui Corpus Domini canistro vimineo, Sanguinem portat in vitro; qui avaritiam ejecit e templo; qui absque funiculo et increpatione *cathedras vendentium columbas*, id est, dona Sancti Spiritus, *mensasque subvertit* mammonae, et *nummulariorum aera* dispertit, ut *domus Dei domus vocetur orationis, et non latronum spelunca.* (Matth. XXI, 12, 13: Joan. II, 14, 15.) *Hieron. Epist.* CXXV (*al.* 4) *ad Rusticum Monachum,* § 20; *Opp.* I, 941 D, E.

94 *Decret.* III, *De Consecr.*, i, 44, *Vasa in quibus*; being can. 18 of the Council of Trebur, A.D. 895, *Concil. Mansi* XVIII, 142.

95 *Ibid.*

96 fet: fetched. In the Authorised Version of the Bible the old form was kept in these places, 2 Sam. IX, 5, XI, 27, 1 Kings VII, 13, IX, 28, 2 Kings XI, 4, 2 Chron. XII, 11, Jer. XXVI, 23, Acts XXVIII, 13; but *fetched* has long been printed for it.

97 *Rab. Maur. de Instit. Cler. Lib.* I, *cc.* 4, 14, 15.

98 Sed ipsi [*sc.* Graeci] rursum opponunt quia, cum veritas venit, figura

This is noted, not against churches and temples, which are most necessary and ought to have their due use and honour (as is in another Homily for their purpose[n] declared[99]), nor against the convenient cleanliness[o] and ornaments thereof, but against the sumptuousness and abuses of temples[p] and churches. For it is a church or temple also that glistereth[q] with no marble, shineth with no gold nor silver; glittereth[r] with no pearls nor precious stones, but, with plainness and frugality, signifieth no proud doctrine nor people, but humble, frugal, and nothing esteeming earthly and outward things, but gloriously decked with inward ornaments, according as the Prophet declareth, saying[ψ], *The King's daughter is altogether glorious inwardly.* ψ [Ps. xlv, 13.]

Now concerning outrageous[s] decking of images and idols with painting, gilding, adorning with precious vestures, pearl, and stone, what is it else but, for the further provocation and enticement to spiritual fornication, to deck spiritual harlots most costly and wantonly? Which the idolatrious[t] Church understandeth well enough. For she, being indeed not only an harlot (as the Scriptures[u] calleth her) but also a foul, filthy, old, withered harlot, (for she is indeed of ancient years,) and understanding her lack of natural[x] and true beauty, and great loathsomeness which of herself she hath, doth (after the custom of such harlots) paint herself, and deck and tire herself with gold, pearl, stone, and all kind of precious jewels; that she, shining with the outward beauty and glory of them, may please the foolish fantasy of fond lovers, and so entice them to spiritual fornication with her: who, if they saw her, I will not say naked, but in simple apparel, would abhor her as the foulest and filthiest harlot that ever was seen; according as appeareth by the description of the garnishing of *the great strumpet* of all strumpets, *the mother of whoredom*, set forth by St. John in his Revelation, Rev. xvii. xviii.

n their purpose] that purpose *from* 1574. o cleanliness] cleanness *from* 1582. p of temples] of the temples *from* 1582. q glistereth] glittereth *from* 1582. r glittereth] glistereth *from* 1582. s outrageous] excessive 1623. t idolatrious] idolatrous *from* 1582. u Scriptures] Scripture 1623. x natural] nature *from* 1582.

cessavit . . . Quum ergo ad verum Pascha perventum est, quae praecesserant in typico cessaverunt . . . Et ideo Christus, sicut verum Pascha confecit sine lactucis agrestibus, sic et absque panibus azymis, ne veterem ritum in novo sacrificio retineret, ac per hoc nos Judaizare doceret. Nam utrumque pariter erat in Lege praescriptum [*sc.* Exod. XII, 8.]

Sciendum ergo quod non omnes antiquae Legis consuetudines abjecit Ecclesia . . . Adhuc enim faciem plenae lunae considerat, ne Pascha celebret in defectu. Adhuc . . . habet candelabrum et lucernas et vestes et vasa et pontifices et Levitas . . . . Legales ergo consuetudines non penitus sunt abolitae. *Innoc. III Myster. Miss.* IV, 4.

99 See the first Homily in this Second Book.

who by her glory provoked the princes of the earth to commit whoredom with her. Whereas, on the contrary part, the true Church of God, as a chaste matron, *espoused* (as the Scripture teacheth[w]) *to one husband, our Saviour Jesus Christ*, whom alone she is content only to please and serve, and looketh not to delight the eyes or phantasies of any other strange lovers or wooers, is content with her natural ornaments, not doubting by such sincere simplicity best to please him, which can[y] well skill of the difference between a painted visage and true natural beauty.

w [2 Cor. xi, 2.]

And concerning such glorious gilding and decking of images, both God's word written in the tenth chapter of the Prophet Jeremy[z], and St. Hierome's commentaries upon the same, are most worthy to be noted. First, the words of the Scriptures be these: *The workman with his axe hewed the timber out of the wood with the work of his hands: he decked it with gold and silver: he joined it with nails and pins and the stroke of an*[a] *hammer, that it might hold together. They be made smooth as the palm, and they cannot speak: if they be borne, they remove, for they cannot go. Fear ye them not, for they can neither do evil nor good.* Thus saith the Prophet. Upon which text St. Hierome hath these words[100]: "This is the description of idols, which the Gentiles worship. Their matter is vile and corruptible. And, whereas the artificer is mortal, the things he maketh must needs be corruptible. *He decketh it with silver and gold,* that with the glittering or shining of both metals he may deceive the simple. Which error indeed hath passed over from the Gentiles, that we should judge religion to stand in riches." And by and by after he saith: "They have the beauty of metals,

Jer. x, [3-5.]

y which can] who can 1623. z Jeremy] Hierome 1563 A–G, 1567–1571. a stroke of an] stroke an 1582, 1623.

100 Descriptio idolorum quae venerantur gentes. *Lignum,* inquit, *de saltu praecidit:* materia ergo idolorum vilis atque corruptibilis. *Opus manuum artificis:* quum artifex mortalis sit, mortalia ergo et illa quae fabricatur. *Argento et auro decoravit illud:* ut fulgore utriusque materiae decipiat simplices. Qui quidem error ad nos usque transivit, ut religionem in divitiis arbitremur... *In similitudinem palmae fabricata:* habent pulchritudinem metallorum, et picturae arte decorata sunt; sed utilitatem non possident, qua praebeant aliquos fructus artifici....

Quicquid de idolis diximus ad omnia dogmata quae sunt contraria veritati referri potest. Et ipsi enim ingentia pollicentur, et simulacrum vani cultus de suo corde confingunt. Jactant grandia, et ad decipiendos simplices quosque quasi aureis sensibus et eloquiis argenti splendore fulgentibus imperitorum obstringunt aciem, et a suis inventoribus sublimantur: in quibus nulla est utilitas, et quorum cultura proprie gentium est et eorum qui ignorant Deum. *Hieron. in Jerem.* X, 3–5; *Opp.* IV, 911.

and be beautified by the art of painting; but good or profit is there none in them." And shortly after again: "They make great promises, and devise an image of vain worshipping of their own phantasies: they make great brags to deceive every simple body: they dull and amaze the understanding of the unlearned, as it were with golden senses[b], and eloquence shining with the brightness of silver. And of their own devisers and makers are these images advanced and magnified: in the which is no utility nor profit at all, and the worshipping of the which properly pertaineth to the Gentiles and heathen and such as know not God." Thus far of St. Hierome's words. Whereupon you may note as well his judgment of images themselves, as also of the painting, gilding, and decking of them; that it is an error which came from the Gentiles; that it persuadeth religion to remain in riches; that it amazeth and deceiveth the simple and unlearned with golden senses[c] and silver-shining eloquence; and that it appertaineth properly to the Gentiles and heathens and such as know not God. Wherefore the having, painting, gilding, and decking of images, by St. Hierome's judgment, is erroneous, seducing and bringing into error (specially the simple and unlearned), heathenish, and void of the knowledge of God. Surely the Prophet Daniel, in the eleventh chapter, declareth such sumptuous decking of images with gold, silver, and precious stones to be a token of Antichrist's kingdom, who, as the Prophet foresheweth[a], shall worship God with such gorgeous things. a [Dan. xi, 38.]

Now usually such outrageous[d] adorning and decking of images hath risen and been maintained, either of offerings provoked by superstition and given in idolatry, or of spoils, robberies, usury, or goods otherwise unjustly gotten, whereof wicked men have given part to the images or Saints (as they call them), that they might be pardoned of the whole; as of divers writings and old monuments concerning the cause and end of certain great gifts may well appear. And indeed such money, so wickedly gotten, is most meet to be put to so wicked an use[e]. And that which they take to be amends for the whole before God is more abominable in his sight than both the wicked getting and the more wicked spending of all the rest. For how the Lord alloweth such gifts he declareth evidently in the Prophet Esay, saying, *I* (saith the Lord) *do love judgment, and I hate spoil and raveny* Is. lxi, [8.]
offered in sacrifice. Which the very Gentiles understood: for

b, c senses] sentences 1587, 1595, 1623. d outrageous] excessive 1623. e an use] a use *from* 1567.

Dialogo de Legibus x.

Plato sheweth[101] that such men as suppose that God doth pardon wicked men, if they give part of their spoils and ravine[f] to him, take him to be like a dog, that would be entreated and hired with part of the prey to suffer the wolves to werry[g] the sheep.

Lib. ii Instit. cap. 4.

And in case the goods wherewith images be decked were justly gotten, yet is it[h] extreme madness so foolishly and wickedly to bestow goods purchased by wisdom and truth. Of such lewdness Lactantius writeth thus[102]: "Men do in vain deck images of the gods with gold, ivory, and precious stone, as though they could take any pleasure of these[i] things. For what use have they of precious gifts, which understand nor feel nothing? Even the same that dead men have. For with like reason do they bury dead bodies farced[103] with spices and odours and clothed with precious vestures, and deck images, which neither felt or knew when they were made, nor understand when they be honoured, for they get no sense and understanding by their consecration." Thus far Lactantius, and much more, too long here to rehearse, declaring that, as little girls play with little puppets, so be these decked images great puppets for old fools to play with. And, that we may know what, not only men of our religion, but ethnics also judge of such decking of dead images, it is not unprofitable to hear what Seneca, a wise and excellent learned senator of Rome and philosopher, saith concerning the foolishness of ancient and grave men, used in his time in worshipping and decking of images[104]. "'We,' saith

[f] ravine] rapine 1623. [g] werry] weery 1567–1574; weary 1582, 1587, 1623; worry 1595. [h] yet is it] yet it is *from* 1582. [i] of these] of those 1582–1595, in those 1623.

101 Τοῦτον δὴ τὸν λόγον ἀναγκαῖον λέγειν τὸν λέγοντα, ὡς εἰσὶ συγγνώμονες ἀεὶ θεοὶ τοῖς τῶν ἀνθρώπων ἀδίκοις καὶ ἀδικοῦσιν, ἂν αὐτοῖς τῶν ἀδικημάτων τις ἀπονέμῃ, καθάπερ κυσὶ εἰ λύκοι τῶν ἁρπασμάτων σμικρὰ ἀπονέμοιεν, οἱ δὲ ἡμερούμενοι τοῖς δώροις συγχωροῖεν τὰ ποίμνια διαρπάζειν. ἆρ' οὐχ οὗτος ὁ λόγος ὁ τῶν φασκόντων παραιτητοὺς εἶναι θεούς; Plat. Legg. x, p. 906 c.

102 Frustra igitur homines auro, ebore, gemmis deos excolunt et exornant; quasi vero ex his rebus ullam possint capere voluptatem. Quis usus est pretiosorum munerum nihil sentientibus? An ille, qui mortuis? Pari enim ratione defunctorum corpora odoribus ac pretiosis vestibus illita et convoluta humi condunt, qua deos honorant, qui neque, cum fierent, sentiebant, neque, cum coluntur, sciunt; nec enim sensum consecratione sumpserunt. *Lactant. Divin. Institutt.* II, 4; *Opp.* I, 125, *ed. Paris.* 1748.

103 farced: stuffed.

104 Non videbat [sc. *Persius*, *Sat.* II, 70] simulacra ipsa et effigies deorum ... nihil aliud esse quam grandes pupas, non a virginibus, quarum lusibus venia dari potest, sed a barbatis hominibus consecratas. Merito igitur etiam senum stultitiam Seneca deridet. Non, inquit, bis pueri sumus, ut vulgo dicitur, sed semper: verum hoc interest, quod majora [*al.* majores] nos ludimus. Ergo his ludicris et ornatis et grandibus pupis et unguenta et thura et odores inferunt: his opimas et pingues hostias immolant, quibus est quidem os, sed carens officio

Seneca, 'be not twice children, as the common saying is, but always children: but this is the difference, that we being elder play the children.' And in these plays they bring in before great and well decked puppets," for so he calleth images, "ointments, incense, and odours. To these puppets they offer up sacrifice, which have a mouth, but not the use of teeth. Upon these they put attiring and precious apparel, which have no use of clothes. To these they give gold and silver, which they who receive it," meaning the images, "lack as well as they that have given it from them." And Seneca much commendeth Dionysius, king of Sicily, for his merry robbing of such decked and jewelled puppets.

But you will ask, What doth this appertain to our images, which is written against the idols of the Gentiles? Altogether surely. For what use or pleasure have our images of their decking and precious ornaments? Did our images understand when they were made? or know when they be so trimmed and decked? Be not these things bestowed upon them as much in vain as upon dead men which have no sense? Wherefore it followeth, that there is like foolishness and lewdness in decking of our images as great puppets for old fools, like children, to play the wicked play of idolatry before, as was amongst[k] the ethnics and Gentiles. Our churches stand full of such great puppets, wondrously decked and adorned; garlands and coronets be set on their heads, precious pearls hanging about their necks; their fingers shine with rings set with precious stone[l]; their dead and stiff bodies are clothed with garments stiff with gold. You would believe that the images of our men Saints were some princes of Persy[m] land with their proud apparel, and the idols of our women Saints were nice and well trimmed harlots, tempting their paramours to wantonness: whereby the Saints of God are not honoured, but most dishonoured, and their godliness, soberness, chastity, contempt of riches and of the vanity of the world, defaced and brought in doubt by such monstruous[n] decking, most differing from their sober and godly lives. And, be-

[k] amongst] among *from* 1570. [l] stone] stones *from* 1563 B. [m] Persy] Persia 1587, 1595, 1623. [n] monstruous] monstrous *from* 1570.

dentium; his peplos et indumenta pretiosa, quibus usus velaminis nullus est; his aurum et argentum consecrant, quae tam non habent qui accipiunt, quam qui illa donarunt. Nec immerito Dionysius Siciliae tyrannus &c. *Lactant. ibid.* pp. 126, 127. The fragment of Seneca here preserved ends with the word "ludimus." And Lactantius seems to have taken what he says of Dionysius from *Valerius Maximus*, I, i, *Extern.* 3, who himself probably took it from *Cicero De Nat. Deor.* III, 34.

cause the whole pageant must throughly be played, it is not enough thus to deck idols, but at the last come in the priests themselves likewise decked with gold and pearl, that they may be meet servants for such lords and ladies, and fit worshippers of such gods and goddesses. And with a solemn pace they pass forth before these golden puppets, and down[o] to the ground on their marrowbones before these honourable idols, and then, rising up again, offer up odours and incense unto them, to give the people an example of double idolatry by worshipping not only the idol, but the gold also and riches wherewith it is garnished. Which things the most part of our old Martyrs rather than they would do, or once kneel or offer up one crumb of incense before an image, suffered most cruel and terrible deaths, as the histories of them at large do declare.

Gregor. Epist. ad Seren. Massil. Damasc. de Fide Orthod. Lib. iv, cap. 17.

And here again their allegation out of Gregory the First and Damascene, that images be the laymen's books, and that picture is[p] the scripture of idiots and simple persons[105], is worthy to be considered. For, as it hath been touched in divers places before how they be books teaching nothing but lies, as by St. Paul in the first chapter to the Romans evidently appeareth of the images of God, so, what manner of books and scripture these painted and gilt images of Saints be unto the common people, note well, I pray you. For, after that our preachers shall have instructed and exhorted the people to the following of the virtues of the Saints, as, contempt of this world, poverty, soberness, chastity, and such like virtues, which undoubtedly were in the Saints; think you, as soon as they turn their faces from the preacher, and look upon the graven books and painted scripture of the glorious gilt images and idols, all shining and glittering with metal and stone and covered with precious vestures, or else, with Chaerea in Terence, behold "a painted table"[106], wherein is set forth by the art of the painter an image with a nice and wanton apparel and countenance, more like to Venus or Flora than Mary Magdalene, or, if like to Mary Magdalene, it is when she played the harlot rather than when she wept for her sins; when, I say, they turn about from the preacher to

[Rom. i, 25.]

[o] and down] and fall down *from* 1582. [p] picture is] pictures are *from* 1582.

105 See *Gregory* cited before, p. 195, n. 30; and *Damascene* at p. 221, n. 12.

106 Dum apparatur, virgo in conclavi sedet
Suspectans tabulam quandam pictam. . . .
* * * * * * * * *
Egomet quoque id spectare coepi &c.
Terent. Eunuch. III, v, 35–43.

these books and schoolmasters and painted scriptures, shall they not find them lying books, teaching other manner of lessons, of esteeming of riches, of pride and vanity in apparel, of niceness and wantonness, and peradventure of whoredom, as Chaerea of like pictures was taught, and in Lucian one learned of Venus Gnidia[107] a lesson too abominable here to be remembered? Be not these, think you, pretty books and scriptures for simple people, and specially[q] for wives and young maidens, to look in, read on, and learn such lessons of? What will they think either of the preacher[r], who taught them contrary lessons of the Saints, and therefore by these carven[s] doctors are[t] charged with a lie, or of the Saints themselves, if they believe these graven books and painted scriptures of them, who make the Saints now reigning in heaven with God, to their great dishonour, schoolmasters of such vanity, which they in their lifetime most abhorred? For what lessons of contempt of riches and vanity of this world can such books, so besmeared with gold, set with stone[u], covered with silks, teach? What lessons of soberness and chastity can our women learn of these pictured scriptures with their nice apparel and wanton looks?

But away, for shame, with these coloured cloaks of idolatry, of the books[x] and scriptures of images and pictures to teach idiots, nay, to make idiots and stark fools and beasts of Christians. Do men, I pray you, when they have the same books at home with them, run on pilgrimage to seek like books at Rome, Compostella, or Hierusalem, to be taught by them, when they have the like to learn of at[y] home? Do men reverence some books, and despise and set light by other of the same sort? Do men kneel before their books, light candles at noon time[z], burn incense, offer up gold and silver and other gifts, to their books? Do men either feign or believe miracles to be wrought by their books? I am sure that the New Testament of our Saviour Jesus Christ, containing the word of life, is a more lively, express, and true image of our Saviour, than all carved, graved[a], molten, and painted images in the world be; and yet none of all these things be done to that book or scripture of the Gospel of our Saviour, which be done to images and pictures, the books and scriptures of laymen and idiots, as they

[q] specially] especially 1623. [r], [t] preacher *and* are] *so in all.* [s] carven] carved 1623. [u] with stone] with precious stones 1582, 1623. [x] of the books] *so in all.* [y] learn of at] learn at *from* 1582. [z] noon time] none time *till* 1567. [a] graved] graven *from* 1563 B.

107 *Lucian. Imagg. c.* IV: *Pseudo-Lucian. Amorr. cc.* XV, XVI.

call them. Wherefore, call them what they list, it is most evident by their deeds, that they make of them none other[b] books nor scriptures[c] than such as teach most filthy and horrible idolatry, as the users of such books daily prove by continual practising of the[d] same. O books and scriptures, in the which the devilish schoolmaster Satan hath penned the lewd lessons of wicked idolatry for his dastardly disciples and scholars to behold, read, and learn, to God's most high dishonour and their most horrible damnation! Have not we been much bound, think you, to those which should have taught us the truth out of God's book and his holy Scripture, that they have shut up that book and Scripture from us, (and none of us so bold as once to open it or read on it,) and, instead thereof, to spread us abroad these goodly carven and gilted[e] books and painted scriptures, to teach us such good and godly lessons? Have not they done well, after they ceased to stand in pulpits themselves and to teach the people committed to their instruction, keeping silence of God's word and become *dumb dogs* (as the Prophet calleth them), to set up in their stead, on every pillar and corner of the church, such goodly doctors, as dumb, but more wicked than themselves be? We need not to complain of the lack of one dumb parson, having so many dumb devilish vicars, I mean these idols and painted puppets, to teach in their stead.

[Is. lvi, 10.]

Now in the mean season, whilst the dumb and dead idols stand thus decked and clothed, contrary to God's law and commandment, the poor Christian people, the lively images of God, commended to us so tenderly by our Saviour Christ as most dear to him, stand naked, shivering for cold, and their teeth chattering in their heads, and no man covereth them; are pined with hunger and thirst, and no man giveth them a penny to refresh them; whereas pounds be ready at all times, contrary to God's word and[f] will, to deck and trim dead stocks and stones, which neither feel cold, hunger, ne[g] thirst. Clemens hath a notable sentence concerning this matter, saying thus[108]:

Lib. v ad Jacobum Domini.

[b] none other] no other *from* 1567. [c] scriptures] scripture *from* 1574. [d] practising of the] practising the *from* 1571. [e] gilted] gilten *from* 1574. [f] word and] *omitted after* 1574. [g] ne] nor 1623.

108 Per alios item serpens ille proferre verba hujuscemodi solet: Nos ad honorem invisibilis Dei imagines visibiles adoramus: quod certissime falsum est. Si enim vere velitis Dei imaginem colere, homini benefacientes veram in eo Dei imaginem coleretis. In omni enim homine est imago Dei; non in omnibus vero similitudo, sed ubi benigna anima est et mens pura. Si ergo vere vultis honorare imaginem Dei, nos vobis quod verum est aperimus; ut homini, *qui ad*

"That serpent the devil doth by the mouth of certain men utter these words, We for the honour of the invisible God do worship visible images: which doubtless is most false. For, if you will truly honour the image of God, you should, by doing well to man, honour the true image of God in him. For the image of God is in every man: but the likeness of God is not in every one, but in those only which have a godly heart and pure mind. If you will therefore truly honour the image of God, we do declare to you the truth, that ye do well to man, who is *made after the image of God*[β], that you give honour and reverence to him, and refresh the hungry with meat, the thirsty with drink, the naked with clothes, the sick with attendance, the stranger harbourless with lodging, the prisoners with necessaries: and this shall be accounted as truly bestowed upon God. And these things are so directly appertaining to God's honour, that whosoever doeth not this shall seem to have reproached and done villany to the image of God. For what honour of God is this, to run to images of stock and stone and to honour vain and dead figures as God[h], and to despise man, in whom is the true image of God?" And by and by after he saith: "Understand ye therefore that this is the suggestion of the serpent Satan lurking within you, which persuadeth you that you are godly, when you honour insensible and dead images, and that you be not ungodly, when you hurt or leave unsuccoured the lively and reasonable creatures." All these be the words of Clemens. Note, I pray you, how this most ancient and learned doctor, within one hundred years of our Saviour Christ's time, most plainly teacheth, that no service of God or religion acceptable to him can be in honouring of dead images, but in succouring of the poor, the lively images of God; according to St. James, who saith, *This is the pure and true religion before God the Father, to succour fatherless and motherless*

β [James iii, 9.]

[James i, 27.]

h as God] of God *from* 1567.

imaginem Dei factus est, benefaciatis, honorem et reverentiam deferatis, esurienti cibum, sitienti poculum, nudo indumentum, aegro ministerium, peregrino hospitium, et in carcere posito necessaria ministretis: et hoc est quod vere Deo delatum reputabitur. Haec autem in tantum ad honorem Dei imaginis cedunt, ut qui ista non fecerit contumeliam imagini Divinae intulisse credatur. Quis ergo iste honor Dei est, per lapideas et ligneas formas discurrere et inanes atque exanimes figuras tanquam numina venerari, et hominem, in quo vere imago Dei est, spernere? . . . Intelligite ergo quia latentis intrinsecus serpentis est ista suggestio, quae persuadet pios vos videri posse, cum insensibilia colitis, et non videri impios, cum sensibiles et rationabiles laeditis. *Recognitt. S. Clement.* v, 23; *vol.* 1, 552.

children and widows in their affliction, and to keep himself undefiled from this world.

True religion then and pleasing of God standeth not in making, setting up, painting, gilding, clothing, and decking of dumb and dead images, which be but great puppets and maumentsⁱ[109] for old fools in dotage and wicked idolatry to dally and play with; nor in kissing of them, capping, kneeling, offering to them, in censing[k] of them, setting up of candles, hanging up of legs, arms, or whole bodies of wax before them, or praying and asking of them or of Saints things belonging only to God to give: but all these things be vain and abominable and most damnable before God. Wherefore all such do not only bestow their money and labour in vain, but with their pains and cost purchase to themselves God's wrath and utter indignation and everlasting damnation both of body and soul. For ye have heard it evidently proved in these Homilies against Idolatry, by God's word, the doctors of the Church, Ecclesiastical Histories, reason, and experience, that images have been and be worshipped, and so idolatry committed to them, by infinite multitudes, to the great offence of God's Majesty and danger of infinite souls; and that idolatry cannot possibly be separated from images set up in churches and temples, gilded and decked gorgeously[l]; and that therefore our images be indeed very idols, and so all the prohibitions, laws, curses, threatenings of horrible plagues, as well temporal as eternal, contained in the holy Scripture concerning idols and the makers, maintainers[m], and worshippers of them, appertain also to our images set up in churches and temples, to[n] the makers, maintainers, and worshippers of them. And all those names of abomination which God's word in the holy Scripture[o] giveth to the idols of the Gentiles appertain to our images, being idols like to them, and having like idolatry committed unto them: and God's own mouth in the holy Scriptures calleth them

[i] maumenta] mawmets *or* maumets 1571–1587, mammets 1595, babies 1623. [k] censing] sensing *from* 1563 B. [l] gorgeously] gloriously 1623. [m] makers, maintainers] makers and maintainers 1623. [n] temples, to] temples, and to *from* 1582. [o] Scripture] Scriptures *from* 1563 B.

109 maumenta: great dolls, nearly the same as puppets. See the passage last cited from *Lactantius*, p. 264, n. 104. But in its earlier signification the word means a real idol or image. "Mawment: Ydolum, Simulacrum." "Mawmentrye: Ydolatria" (*sic*). *Promptorium Parvulorum, ed. Alb. Way,* where see his note. And yet it is an abbreviation of the name of Mahomet, the foe to all idolatry; and its more correct form is maumet or mawmet. See *Trench on the Study of Words, Lect.* III, *p.* 85, *ed.* 1856. The form maumenta may perhaps be compared with Mahound and Mahoune, used for Mahomet by the Romance writers, and by Spenser after them.

vanities[γ], *lies*[δ], *deceits*[ε][110], *uncleanliness*[p][ζ], filthiness, dung, mischief, and *abomination before the Lord*[κ]. Wherefore God's horrible wrath and our most dreadful danger cannot be avoided without the destruction and utter abolishing of all such images and idols out of the church and temple of God: which to accomplish, God put in the minds of all Christian princes!

γ [Deut. xxxii, 21.]
δ [Jer. xvi, 19.]
ε [Amos ii, 4.]
ζ [2 Chron. xxix, 5.]
κ [Deut. xxvii, 15.]

And in the mean time let us take heed and be wise, O ye beloved of the Lord, and let us have no strange gods, but one only God, who made us when we were nothing, the Father of our Lord Jesus Christ, who redeemed us when we were lost, and with his Holy Spirit, who doth[q] sanctify us. For[λ] *this is life everlasting, to know him to be the only true God, and Jesus Christ, whom he hath sent*. Let us honour and worship for religion sake[r] none but him: and him let us worship and honour as he will himself, and hath declared by his word that he will be honoured and worshipped; not in nor by images or idols, which he hath most straitly forbidden, neither in kneeling, lighting of candles, burning of incense, offering up of gifts unto images and idols, to believe that we shall please him; for all these be abomination before God; but let us honour and worship God *in spirit and truth*[μ], fearing and loving him above all things, trusting in him only, calling upon him and praying to him only, praising and lauding of him only, and all other in him and for him. For *such worshippers* doth our heavenly Father love, who is the most purest[s] Spirit, and therefore will be worshipped *in spirit and truth*. And such worshippers were Abraham, Moses, David, Helias, Peter, Paul, John, and all other the holy Patriarchs, Prophets, Apostles, Martyrs, and all true Saints of God; who all, as the true friends of God, were enemies and destroyers of images and idols, as the enemies of God and his true religion.

λ John xvii, [3.]
μ John iv, [23, 24.]

Wherefore take heed and be wise, O ye beloved of the Lord; and that which others, contrary to God's word, bestow wickedly, and to their damnation, upon dead stocks and stones, (no images, but enemies, of God and his Saints,) that bestow ye, as the faithful servants of God, according to God's word, mercifully upon poor men and women, fatherless children, widows, sick persons, strangers, prisoners, and such others that be in any necessity; that ye may, at that great day of the Lord, hear

p uncleanliness] uncleanness 1595, 1623. q Spirit, who doth] *so in all*. r religion sake] religion's sake *from* 1571. s the most purest] a most pure 1623.

110 Deceperunt enim eos idola sua. *Amos* II, 4, *Vulg.*

that most blessed and comfortable saying of our Saviour Christ: [Matt. xxv, 34-40.] *Come, ye blessed, into the kingdom of my Father, prepared for you before the beginning of the world. For I was hungry, and ye gave me meat; thirsty, and ye gave me drink; naked, and ye clothed me; harbourless, and ye lodged me; in prison, and ye visited me; sick, and ye comforted me. For, whatsoever ye have done for the poor and needy in my name and for my sake, that have ye done for me.* To the which his heavenly kingdom God *the Father of mercies*[v] bring us for Jesus Christ's sake, our only Saviour, Mediator, and Advocate: to whom with the Holy Ghost, one immortal, invisible, and most glorious God, be all honour and thanksgiving and glory world without end. Amen.

v [2 Cor. i, 3.]

AN HOMILY

FOR REPAIRING AND KEEPING CLEAN AND COMELY ADORNING OF CHURCHES.

IT is a common custom used of all men, when they intend to have their friends or neighbours to come to their houses to eat or drink with them, or to have any solemn assembly to treat and talk of any matter, they will have their houses, which they keep in continual reparations, to be clean and fine, lest they should be counted sluttish, or little to regard their friends and neighbours. How much more then ought the house of God, which we commonly call the church, to be sufficiently repaired in all places, and to be honourably adorned and garnished, and to be kept clean and sweet, to the comfort of the people that shall resort thereto[a]!

It appeareth in the holy Scripture, how God's house, which was called his holy temple, and was the mother church of all Jewry, fell sometimes into decay, and was oftentimes profaned and defiled, through the negligence and ungodliness of such as had charge[b] thereof. But when godly kings and governors were in place, then commandment was given forthwith, that the church and temple of God should be repaired, and the devotion of the people to be gathered for the reparation of the same. We read in the fourth Book of the Kings[α], how that king Joas, being a godly prince, gave commandment to the priests to convert certain offerings of the people towards the reparation and amendment of God's temple. Like commandment gave that most godly king Josias[β] concerning the reparation and reedification of God's temple, which in his time he found in sore decay. It hath pleased Almighty God, that these histories touching the reedifying and repairing of his holy temple should be written at large, to the end we should be taught thereby, first, that God is well pleased that his people should have a convenient place to resort unto and to come together to praise and magnify God's holy Name. And, secondly, he is highly pleased with all those which diligently and zealously go about to amend and restore

α 2 Kings xii, [4, 5.]

β 2 Kings xxii, [3–6.]

[a] thereto] thereunto 1623.   [b] had charge] had the charge *from* 1582.

such places as are appointed for the congregation of God's people to resort unto, and wherein they humbly and jointly render thanks to God for his benefits, and with one heart and voice praise his holy Name. Thirdly, God was sore displeased with his people, because they builded, decked, and trimmed up their own houses, and suffered God's house to be in ruin and decay, to lie uncomely and fulsomely. Wherefore God was sore grieved with them, and plagued them, as appeareth in the Prophet Haggeus: *Thus saith the Lord, Is it time for you to dwell in your seeled*[c] *houses, and the Lord's house not regarded? Ye have sowed much, and gathered in but little; your meat and your clothes have neither filled you nor made you warm; and he that had his wages put it in a bottomless purse.* By these plagues, which God laid upon his people for neglecting of his temple, it may evidently appear that God will have his temple, his church, the place where his congregation shall resort to magnify him, well edified, well repaired, and well maintained.

Hag. i, [2, 4, 6.]

Some, neither regarding godliness nor the place of godly exercise, will say the temple in the old law was commanded to be built and repaired by God himself, because it had great promises annexed unto it, and because it was a figure, a sacrament, or a signification of Christ, and also of his Church. To this may be easily answered, first, that our churches are not destitute of promises, forasmuch as our Saviour Christ saith, *Where two or three are gathered in*[d] *my name, there am I in the middes*[e] *among them.* A great number therefore coming to church together in the name of Christ have there, that is to say, in the church, their God and Saviour Christ Jesus presently[f] among the congregation of his faithful people by his grace, by his favour and godly assistance, according to his most assured and comfortable promises. Why then ought not Christian people to build them temples and churches, having as great promises of the presence of God as ever had Salomon for the material temple which he did build? As touching the other point, that Salomon's temple was a figure of Christ, we know that now, in the time of the clear light of Christ Jesus the Son of God, all shadows, figures, and significations are utterly gone, all vain and unprofitable ceremonies, both Jewish and heathenish, fully abolished; and therefore our churches are not set up for figures and significations of Messias and Christ to come, but for other godly and

[Matt. xviii, 20.]

[c] seeled] *so in all. See Richardson on "Ceil."* [d] gathered in] gathered together in 1623.
[e] middes] middest *from* 1571. [f] presently] present 1623.

necessary purposes, that is to say, that, like as every man hath his own house to abide in, to refresh himself in, to rest in, with such like commodities, so Almighty God will have his house and palace[g], whither the whole parish and congregation shall resort. Which is called the church and temple of God, for that the Church, which is the company of God's people, doth there assemble and come together to serve him; not meaning hereby that the Lord, *whom the heaven of heavens is not able to hold*[γ] or comprise, doth dwell in the church of lime and stone, made with man's hands, as wholly and only contained there within and no where else; for so he never dwelt in Salomon's temple. Moreover, the church or temple is counted and called holy, yet not of itself, but because God's people resorting thereunto are holy, and exercise themselves in holy and heavenly things.

γ [2 Chron. ii, 6.]

And, to the intent ye may understand further why churches were built among Christian people, this was the greatest consideration: that God might have his place, and that God might have his time, duly to be honoured and served of the whole multitude in the parish; first, there to hear and learn the blessed word and will of the everlasting God; secondly, that there the blessed Sacraments which our Lord and Saviour Christ Jesus hath ordained and appointed should be duly, reverently, and honourably[h] ministered; thirdly, that there the whole multitude of God's people in the parish should with one voice and heart call upon the Name of God, magnify and praise the Name of God, render earnest and hearty thanks to our heavenly Father for his heap of benefits daily and plentifully poured upon us, not forgetting to bestow our alms upon God's poverty[i], to the intent God may bless us the more richly.

Thus ye may well perceive and understand wherefore churches were built and set up amongst Christian people, and dedicated and appointed to these godly uses, and utterly[k] exempted from all filthy, profane, and worldly uses. Wherefore all they that have little mind or devotion to repair and build God's temple are to be counted people of much ungodliness, spurning against good order in Christ's Church, despising the true honour of God, with evil example offending and hindering their neighbours, otherwise well and godly disposed. The world thinketh but[l] a trifle to see their church in ruin and decay; but, whoso doth not lay to their helping hands, they sin against God and his

g palace] place *from* 1582. h honourably] decently 1623. i poverty] poor 1623. k utterly] wholly 1623. l thinketh but] thinketh it but *from* 1582.

holy congregation. For, if it had not been sin to neglect and pass little upon[m] the reedifying and building up again of his temple, God would not have been so much grieved, and so soon[n] have plagued his people, because they builded and decked their own houses so gorgeously, and despised the house of God their Lord. It is sin and shame to see so many churches so ruinous, and so foully decayed, almost in every corner. If a man's private house, wherein he dwelleth, be decayed, he will never cease till it be restored up again. Yea, if his barn, where he keepeth his corn, be out of reparations, what diligence useth he to make it in perfect state again! If his stable for his horse, yea, the sty for his swine, be not able to hold out water and wind, how careful is he to do cost thereon! And shall we be so mindful of our common base houses, deputed to so low occupying[o]? and be forgetful toward that house of God, wherein be ministered[p] the words of our eternal salvation, wherein be intreated[q] the Sacraments and mysteries of our redemption? The fountain of our regeneration is there presented to[r] us; the partaking of the Body and Blood of our Saviour Christ is there offered unto us; and shall we not esteem the place where so heavenly things[s] be handled? Wherefore, if ye have any reverence to the service of God, if ye have any common honesty, if ye have any conscience in keeping of necessary and godly ordinances, keep your churches in good repair; whereby ye shall not only please God, and deserve his manifold blessings, but also deserve the good report of all godly people.

The second point which appertaineth to the maintenance of God's house is to have it well adorned and comely and clean kept: which things may be the more easily performed[t], when the church is well repaired. For, like as men are well refreshed and comforted when they find their houses having all things in good order and all corners clean and sweet, so, when God's house, the church, is well adorned with places convenient to sit in, with the pulpit for the preacher, with the Lord's table for the ministration of his Holy Supper, with the font to Christen in, and also is kept clean, comely, and sweetly, the people is the more[u] desirous and the more comforted to resort thither, and to tarry there the whole time appointed them.

[m] pass little upon] slightly regard 1623. [n] soon] sone 1563 A, soone *from* 1563 B. *Did the author write* sore? *See before, p 274, l. 7.* [o] low occupying] vile employment 1623. [p] ministered] intreated 1623. [q] intreated] ministered 1623. [r] presented to] presented unto *from* 1582. [s] things be] things are 1623. [t] performed] reformed *from* 1582. [u] is the more] is more 1582–1595, are more 1623.

With what earnestness, with what vehement zeal did our Saviour Christ[8] drive the buyers and sellers out of the temple of God, and hurled down the tables of the changers of money and the seats of the dove sellers, and could not abide[c] that any man should[x] carry a vessel through the temple! He told them that they had made his Father's house *a den of thieves*, partly through their superstition, hypocrisy, false worship, false doctrine, and insatiable covetousness, and partly through contempt, abusing that place with walking and talking, with worldly matters, without all fear of God and due reverence to that place. What dens of thieves the churches of England have been made by the blasphemous buying and selling the most precious Body and Blood of Christ in the mass, as the world was made to believe, at diriges[1], at month's minds[2], in trentals[y][3], in abbeys and chantries, beside other horrible abuses, God's holy name be blessed for ever, we[z] now see and understand. All these abominations they that supply the room of Christ have cleansed and purged the churches of England of, taking away all such fulsomeness and filthiness as through blind devotion and ignorance hath crept into the Church this[a] many hundred years.

8 Matt. xxi, [12, 13: John ii, 14, 15.]

c [Mark xi, 16.]

Wherefore, O ye good Christian people, ye dearly beloved in Christ Jesu, ye that glory not in worldly and vain religion, in fantastical adorning and decking, but rejoice in heart to see the glory of God truly set forth, and the churches restored to their ancient and godly use, render your most hearty[b] thanks to the goodness of Almighty God, who hath in our days stirred up the hearts, not only of his godly preachers and ministers, but also of

x that any man should] any man to *from* 1582. y in trentals] at trentals *from* 1582. z ever, we] ever, which we *from* 1582. a this] these *from* 1582. b your most hearty] your hearty *from* 1582.

1 The whole Office of the Dead was often called the Dirige, as in each of the *Three Primers put forth in the Reign of Henry VIII* which have been reprinted at the University Press. But the name belongs especially to the Matins or second part of the Office, which begins with this anthem, taken from *Psal.* v, 9: *Dirige, Domine Deus meus, in conspectu tuo viam meam.* The Evensong or first part of the Office was in like manner known by the name of Placebo from the anthem with which it opens, *Placebo Domino in regione vivorum*, being *Psal.* CXIV (*Hebr.* CXVI), 9.

2 month's minds: services of remembrance, performed a month after death or interment. "CHRIS. The custom in times past was that there should be monthminds and yearminds kept for the dead. EPAPH. To what end? CHRIS. That the dead might be remembered and prayed for." *Becon's Sick Man's Salve, p.* 126 *ed. Park. Soc.* The Office of the Dead was used on these occasions, and the rubrics in it direct certain variations to be made "in die trecennali," others "in anniversariis," others again "in trigintalibus" (trentals). The services were often very costly. See *Brand's Popular Antiquities,* II, 192, *ed. Ellis* 1841.

3 On "trentals" see before, p. 60, note 16.

his faithful and most Christian magistrates and governors, to bring such godly things to pass. And, forasmuch as your churches are scoured and swept from the sinful and superstitious filthiness wherewith they were defiled and disfigured, do ye your parts, good people, to keep your churches comely and clean: suffer them not to be defiled with rain and weather, with dung of doves and owls, stares[4] and choughs, and other filthiness, as it is foul and lamentable to behold in many places of this country. It is the house of prayer, not the house of talking, of walking, of brawling, of minstrelsy, of hawks, of dogs. Provoke not the displeasure and plagues of God for despising and abusing his holy house, as the wicked Jews did. But have God in your heart: be obedient to his blessed will: bind yourselves, every man and woman to their[c] power, toward the reparations and clean keeping of your church[d]; to the intent ye[e] may be partakers of God's manifold blessings, and that ye may the better be[f] encouraged to resort to your parish church, there to learn your duties toward[g] God and your neighbour, there to be present and partakers of Christ's holy Sacraments, there to render thanks to your heavenly Father for the manifold benefits which he daily poureth upon you, there to pray together and to call upon God's holy Name. Which be blessed world without end. Amen.[h]

[c] their] your 1623. [d] your church] the church *from* 1574. [e] intent ye] intent that ye 1623. [f] the better be] be the better *from* 1571. [g] duties toward] duty towards *from* 1574. [h] Amen.] *omitted till* 1582.

4 stares: starlings.

AN HOMILY

OF GOOD WORKS: AND FIRST OF FASTING.

THE life which we live in this world, good Christian people, is of the free benefit of God lent us, yet not to use it at our pleasure after our own fleshly will, but to trade over the same in those works which are beseeming them that are become new creatures in Christ. These works the Apostle calleth *good works*, saying, *We are God's workmanship, created in Christ Jesu* (Eph. ii, [10.]) *to good works, which God hath ordained, that we should walk in them.* And yet his meaning is not by these words to induce us to have any affiance, or to put any confidence, in our works, as by the merit and deserving of them to purchase to ourselves and others remission of sin, and so consequently everlasting life. For that were mere blasphemy against God's mercy, and great derogation to the bloodshedding of our Saviour Jesus Christ. For it is of the free grace and mercy of God, by the mediation of the blood of his Son Jesus Christ, without merit or deserving on our part, that our sins are forgiven us, that we are reconciled and brought again into his favour, and are made heirs of his heavenly kingdom. "Grace," saith St. Augustine[1], "belongeth[a] to God, (August. de Diver. Quaest. ad Simplic. Lib. 1, Qu. 28.) who doth call us: and then hath he good works, whosoever received grace. Good works then bring not forth grace, but are brought forth by grace. The wheel," saith he, "turneth round, not to the end that it may be made round; but, because it is first made round, therefore it turneth round. So no man doeth good works, to receive grace by his good works; but, because he hath first received grace, therefore consequently he doeth good works." And in another place he saith[2]: "Good works go not before (August. de Fide et Operibus, cap. 4.) in him which shall afterward be justified; but good works do follow after, when a man is first justified." St. Paul therefore

[a] belongeth] belonging *from* 1582.

1 Vocantis est ergo gratia: percipientis vero gratiam consequenter sunt opera bona, non quae gratiam pariant, sed quae gratia pariantur. Non enim ut ferveat calefacit ignis, sed quia fervet: nec ideo bene currit rota, ut rotunda sit, sed quia rotunda est. Sic nemo propterea bene operatur, ut accipiat gratiam, sed quia accepit. *Augustin. ad Simplic. Lib.* I, *Quaest.* II, § 3; *Opp.* VI, 90 C.

2 Sequuntur enim justificatum, non praecedunt justificandum. *Augustin. de Fide et Operibus*, § 21; *Opp.* VI, 177 C.

teacheth that we must do good works for divers respects: first, to shew ourselves obedient children unto our heavenly Father, who *hath ordained them, that we should walk in them;* secondly, for that they are good declarations and testimonies of our justification; thirdly, that others, *seeing our good works*[a], *may* the rather by them be stirred up and excited to *glorify our Father which is in heaven.* Let us not therefore be slack to do good works, seeing it is the will of God that we should walk in them, assuring ourselves that at the last day every man shall receive of God, for his labour done in true faith, a greater reward than his works have deserved. And, because somewhat shall now be spoken of one particular good work, whose commendation is both in the Law and in the Gospel, thus much is said in the beginning generally of all good works; first, to remove out of the way of the simple and unlearned this dangerous stumblingblock, that any man should go about to purchase or buy heaven with his works; secondly, to take away (so nigh[b] as may be) from envious minds and slanderous tongues all just occasion of slanderous speaking, as though good works were rejected.

[a] [Matt. v, 16.]

This good work which shall now[c] be entreated of is fasting, which is found in the Scriptures to be of two sorts; the one outward, pertaining to the body; the other inward, in the heart and mind. This outward fast is an abstinence from meat, drink, and all natural food, yea, from all delicious pleasures and delectations worldly. When this outward fast pertaineth to one particular man or to a few, and not to the[d] whole number of the people, for causes which hereafter shall be declared, then it is called a private fast. But, when the whole multitude of men, women, and children in a township or city, yea, through[e] a whole country, do fast, it is called a public fast. Such was that fast which the whole multitude of the children of Israel were commanded to keep the tenth day of the seventh month, because Almighty God appointed that day to be a cleansing day, a day of an[f] atonement, a time of reconciliation, a day wherein the people were cleansed from their sins. The order and manner how it was done is written in the sixteenth and twenty-third chapter[g] of Leviticus. That day the people did lament, mourn, weep, and bewail their former sins. And, whosoever upon that day did not humble his soul, bewailing his sins, as is said, abstaining from all bodily food until the evening, *that soul,* saith

Lev. xvi, [29–34;] xxiii, [27–32.]

[Lev. xxiii, 29.]

[b] nigh] much 1623. [c] which shall now] which now shall *from* 1563 B. [d] not to the] not the 1623. [e] through] *so* WHITGIFT, though *every edition of the Homilies entire.* [f] an] *omitted* 1623. [g] chapter] chapters *from* 1582.

Almighty[h] God, *should be destroyed from among his people.* We do not read that Moses ordained by order of law any days of public fast throughout the whole year, more than that one day. The Jews, notwithstanding, had more times of common fasting, which the prophet Zachary reciteth to be *the fast of the fourth, the fast of the fifth, the fast of the seventh, and the fast of the tenth month.* [Zech. viii, [19.]] But, for that it appeareth not in the Levitical[i] law when they were instituted, it is to be judged that those other times of fasting, more than the fast of the seventh month, were ordained among the Jews by the appointment of their governors, rather of devotion, than by any open[j] commandment given from God.

Upon the ordinance of this general fast good men took occasion to appoint to themselves private fasts, at such times as they did either earnestly lament and bewail their sinful lives, or did addict themselves to more fervent prayer, that it might please God to turn his wrath from them, when either they were admonished and brought to the consideration thereof by the preaching of the Prophets, or otherwise when they saw present danger to hang over their heads. This sorrowfulness of heart, joined with fasting, they uttered sometime by their outward behaviour and gesture of body, putting on sackcloth, sprinkling themselves with ashes and dust, and sitting or lying upon the earth. For, when good men feel in themselves the heavy burden of sin, see damnation to be the reward of it, and behold with the eye of their mind the horror of hell, they tremble, they quake, and are inwardly touched with sorrowfulness of heart for their offences, and cannot but accuse themselves, and open this their grief unto Almighty God, and call unto him for mercy. This being done seriously, their mind is so occupied, partly with sorrow and heaviness, partly with an earnest desire to be delivered from this danger of hell and damnation, that all lust[k] of meat and drink is laid apart, and loathsomeness of all worldly things and pleasures cometh in place; so that nothing then liketh them more, than to weep, to lament, to mourn, and both with words and behaviour[l] of body to shew themselves weary of this life. Thus did David fast[β], when he made intercession to Almighty God for the child's life, begotten in adultery of Bethsabe, Ury's wife. [β [2 Sam. xii, 16–23.]] King Achab fasted after this sort[γ], when it repented him of murdering of Naboth, and bewailed[m] his own sinful doings. [γ [1 Kings xxi, 27–29.]] Such

[h] saith Almighty] saith the Almighty *from* 1582. [i] Levitical] *omitted after* 1574. [j] open] express 1623. [k] lust] desire 1623. [l] behaviour] behaviour *from* 1563 B. [m] Naboth, and bewailed] Naboth, and bewailing 1567, 1570; Naboth, bewailing *from* 1571.

was[n] the Ninivites' fast[δ], brought to repentance by Jonas' preaching. When forty thousand of the Israelites were slain in battle against the Benjamites, the Scripture saith[ε], *all the children of Israel and the whole multitude of people went out to*[o] *Bethel, and sat there weeping before the Lord, and fasted all that day until*[p] *night.* So did[ζ] Daniel, Hester, Nehemias, and many others in the Old Testament fast.

[δ] [Jonah iii, 5–10.]

[ε] Judg. xx, [21–26.]

[ζ] [Dan. ix, 3; x, 2, 3: Esth. iv, 16: Neh. i, 4.]

But, if any man will say, It is true, so they fasted indeed; but we are not now under that yoke of the Law, we are set at liberty by the freedom of the Gospel; therefore those rites and customs of the old Law bind not us, except it can be shewed by the Scriptures of the New Testament, or by examples out of the same, that fasting now under the Gospel is a restraint of meat, drink, and all bodily food and pleasures from the body, as before: first, that we ought to fast is a truth more manifest than that it should here need to be proved; the Scriptures which teach the same are evident. The doubt therefore that is, is whether, when we fast, we ought to withhold from our bodies all meat and drink during the time of our fast, or no. That we ought so to do may be well gathered upon a question moved by the Pharisees to Christ, and by his answer again to the same. *Why*, say they, *do John's disciples fast often, and pray, and we likewise, but thy disciples eat and drink*, and fast not at all? In this smooth question they couch up subtilly this argument or reason. Whoso fasteth not, that man is not of God. For fasting and prayer are works both commended and commanded of God in his Scriptures; and all good men from Moses till this time, as well the Prophets as others, have exercised themselves in these works. John also and his disciples at this day do fast oft, and pray much; and so do we the Pharisees in like manner. But thy disciples fast not at all: which if thou wilt deny, we can easily prove it. For whosoever eateth and drinketh fasteth not: thy disciples eat and drink: therefore they fast not. Of this we conclude, say they, necessarily, that neither art thou, nor yet thy disciples, of God. Christ maketh answer, saying, *Can ye make that the children of the wedding shall fast while the bridegroom is with them? The days shall come when the bridegroom shall be taken from them: in those days shall they fast.* Our Saviour Christ, like a good Master, defendeth the innocency of his disciples against the malice of the arrogant Pharisees, and

[Luke v, [33–35.]]

[n] Such was] Such were *from* 1582. [o] of people went out to] of the people went to *from* 1582. [p] until] till 1623.

proveth that his disciples are not guilty of transgressing any jot of God's law, although as then they fasted not; and[q] in his answer reproveth the Pharisees of superstition and ignorance. Superstition, because they put a religion in their doings, and ascribed holiness to the outward work wrought, not regarding to what end fasting is ordained. Of ignorance, for that they could not discern between time and time: they knew not that there is a time[r] of rejoicing and mirth, and a time again of lamentation and mourning; which both he teacheth in his answer, as shall be touched more largely hereafter, when we shall shew what time is most fit to fast in[3]. But here, beloved, let us note, that our Saviour Christ, in making his answer to their question, denied not, but confessed, that his disciples fasted not, and therefore agreeth to the Pharisees in this, as unto a manifest truth, that whoso eateth and drinketh fasteth not. Fasting then, even by Christ's assent, is a withholding of meat, drink, and all natural food from the body for the determined time of fasting.

[r] [Eccles. iii, 4.]

And that it was used in the primitive Church appeareth most evidently by the Chalcedon Council, one of the four first general Councils. The fathers assembled there, to the number of six hundred and thirty, considering with themselves how acceptable a thing fasting is to God, when it is used according to his word; again, having before their eyes also the great abuses of the same crept into the Church at those days, through the negligence of them which should have taught the people the right use thereof, and by vain gloses devised of men; to reform the said abuses, and to restore this so good and godly a work to the true use thereof, decreed in that Council, that every person, as well in his private as public fast, should continue all the day without meat and drink till after the Evening Prayer, and whosoever did eat or drink before the Evening Prayer was ended should be accounted and reputed not to consider the purity of his fast.[4] This canon teacheth so evidently how fasting was used in the

[q] they fasted not; and] they fasted, and *from* 1582.

3 See p. 293.

4 Solent plures, qui se jejunare putant, mox ut signum audiunt ad nonam, manducare: qui nullatenus jejunare credendi sunt, si ante manducaverint quam vespertinum celebretur officium. *Theodulfi Aurelianensis Episcopi Capitulare, cap.* 39; *Sirmondi Opp.* II, 941, or *Concil. Mansi* XIII, 1005. Gratian, following earlier compilers, cites the passage as "ex Concilio Cabilonensi" in *Decret.* III *De Consecr.*, i, 50. Aquinas, in his *Secunda Secundae,* CXLVII, vii, 3, made the further mistake of ascribing it to the Council of Chalcedon; and Dr. Corrie thinks he is the earliest writer who has done so.

primitive Church, as by words it cannot be more plainly expressed. Fasting then, by the decree of those six hundred and thirty fathers, grounding their determination in this matter upon the sacred Scriptures, and long continued usage or practice, both of the Prophets and other godly persons before the coming of Christ, and also of the Apostles and other devout men in the New Testament, is a withholding of meat, drink, and all natural food from the body for the determined time of fasting.

Thus much is spoken hitherto to make plain unto you what fasting is. Now hereafter shall be shewed the true and right use of fasting.

Good works are not all of one sort. For some are of themselves, and of their own proper nature, always good; as, to love God above all things, to love my[r] neighbour as myself[s], to honour father[t] and mother, to honour the higher powers, to give to every man that which is his due, and such like. Other works there be, which, considered in themselves without further respect, are of their own nature mere[u] indifferent, that is, neither good nor evil, but take their denomination of the use or end whereunto they serve. Which works, having a good end, are called good works, and are so indeed; but yet that cometh not of themselves, but of the good end whereunto they are referred. On the other side, if the end that they serve unto be evil, it cannot then otherwise be but that they must needs be evil also. Of this sort of works is fasting, which of itself is a thing merely indifferent, but is[x] made better or worse by the end that it serveth unto. For, when it respecteth a good end, it is a good work; but, the end being evil, the work itself is also evil.

To fast then with this persuasion of mind, that our fasting and other[y] good works can make us good, perfect[z], and just men, and finally bring us to heaven, this is a devilish persuasion, and that fast so[a] far off from pleasing God[b], that it refuseth his mercy, and is altogether derogatory to the merits of Christ's death and his precious bloodshedding. This doth the parable of

Luke xviii, [10–13.]

the Pharisee and the Publican teach. *Two men,* saith Christ, *went up together to the temple*[c] *to pray, the one a Pharisee, the other a publican. The Pharisee stood and prayed thus within*[d] *himself: I thank thee, O God, that I am not as other men are, extortioners, unjust, adulterers, and as this publican is: I fast*

[r] my] thy 1623. [s] myself] thyself 1623. [t] honour father] honour thy father 1623. [u] mere] merely 1623. [x] but is] but it is *from* 1582. [y] and other] and our *from* 1570. [z] us good, perfect] us perfect *from* 1567. [a] fast so] fast is so *from* 1582. [b] pleasing God] pleasing of God *from* 1582. [c] to the temple] into the temple *from* 1567. [d] within] with 1623.

twice in the week, I give tithes of all that I possess. The publican stood afar off, and would not lift up his eyes to heaven; but smote his breast, and said, God, be merciful to me a sinner. In the person of this Pharisee our Saviour Christ setteth out to the eye and to the judgment of the world a perfect, just, and righteous man, such one[e] as is not spotted with those vices that men commonly are infected with, extortion, bribery, polling and pilling their neighbours[f], robbers and spoilers of commonweals, crafty and subtile in chopping and changing, using false weights and detestable perjury in their buying and selling, fornicators, adulterers, and vicious livers. This[g] Pharisee was no such man, neither faulty in any such like notorious crime; but, where other transgressed by leaving things undone which yet the law required, this man did more than was requisite by law[h], for he fasted twice[i] in the week and gave tithes of all that he had. What could the world then justly blame in this man? yea, what outward thing more could be desired to be in him, to make him a more perfect and a more just man? Truly, nothing by man's judgment: and yet our Saviour Christ preferreth the poor Publican without fasting before him with his fast. The cause why he doth so is manifest. For the Publican, having no good works at all to trust unto, yielded up himself unto God, confessing his sins, and hoped certainly to be saved by God's free mercy only. The Pharisee gloried and trusted so much to his works, that he thought himself sure enough without mercy, and that he should come to heaven by his fasting and other deeds. To this end serveth that parable; for it is spoken to them *that trusted in themselves that they were righteous, and despised other.* [Luke xviii, 9.] Now, because the Pharisee directed[k] his works to[l] an evil end, seeking by them justification, which indeed is the proper work of God without our merits, his fasting twice in the week and all his other works, though they were never so many and seemed to the world never so good and holy, yet in very deed before God they are altogether evil and abominable.

The mark also that the hypocrites shoot at with their fast is to appear holy in the eye of the world, and so to win commendation and praise of men. But our Saviour Christ saith of them[θ], *They have their reward,* that is, they have praise and commendation of men, but of God they have none at all. For whatsoever tendeth to an evil end is itself by that evil end made evil also.

θ Matt. vi, [16.]

e such one] such a one 1587, 1595, 1623. f neighbours] neighbour *from* 1570. g This] The *from* 1563 G. h by law] by the law 1623. i twice] thrice 1623. k directed] directeth 1623. l works to] work to *from* 1570.

Again, so long as we keep ungodliness in our hearts, and suffer wicked thoughts to tarry there, though we fast as oft as did either St. Paul or John Baptist, and keep it as straitly as did the Ninivites, yet shall it be not only unprofitable to us, but also a thing that greatly displeaseth Almighty God. For he saith[ι] that *his soul abhorreth and hateth such fastings, yea, they are a burden unto him, and he is weary of bearing them.* And therefore he inveigheth[m] most sharply against them, saying by the mouth of the Prophet Esay, *Behold, when ye[n] fast, your lust remaineth still, for ye do[o] no less violence to your debtors. Lo, ye fast to strife and debate, and to smite with the fist of wickedness. Now ye shall not fast thus, that you may make your voice to be heard above. Think ye this fast pleaseth me, that a man should chasten himself for a day? Should that be called a fasting, or a day that pleaseth the Lord?*

ι Is. i, [13, 14.]

Is. lviii, [3, 4, 5.]

Now, dearly beloved, seeing that Almighty God alloweth not our fast for the work sake[p], but chiefly respecteth our heart, how it is affected, and then esteemeth our fast either good or evil by the end that it serveth for, it is our part to *rent our hearts, and not our garments,* as we are advertised by the Prophet Joel; that is, our sorrow and mourning must be inward in the heart[q], and not in outward shew only; yea, it is requisite that first, before all things, we cleanse our hearts from sin, and then to direct our fast to such an end as God will allow to be good. There be three ends, whereunto if our fast be directed, it is then a work profitable to us and accepted of God. The first is, to chastise the flesh, that it be not too wanton, but tamed and brought in subjection to the spirit. This respect had St. Paul in his fast when he said, *I chastise my body, and bring it into subjection, lest by any means it cometh to pass that, when I have preached to other, I myself be found a castaway.* The second, that the spirit may be more fervent and earnest[r] in prayer[s]. To this end fasted the prophets and teachers that were at Antioch[κ], before they sent forth Paul and Barnabas to preach the Gospel. The same two Apostles fasted for the like purpose[λ], when they commended to God by their earnest prayers the congregations that were at Antioch, Pisidia[t], Iconium, and Lystra[u]; as we read in the Acts of the Apostles. The third, that our fast be a testimony and witness with us

Joel ii, [13.]

1 Cor. ix, [27.]

κ Acts xiii, [1–3.]

λ Acts xiv, [23.]

m inveigheth] envieth 1563 A. n when ye] when you *from* 1570. o ye do] do ye 1623. p work sake] work's sake *from* 1563 B. q in the heart] in heart *from* 1567. r fervent and earnest] earnest and fervent *from* 1582. s in prayer] to prayer *from* 1567. t Antioch, Pisidia] *so in all.* u Lystra] Listris *till* 1574.

before God of our humble submission to his high Majesty, when we confess and acknowledge our sins unto him, and are inwardly touched with sorrowfulness of heart, bewailing the same in the affliction of our bodies. These are the three ends or right uses of fasting. The first belongeth most properly to private fast; the other two are common as well to public fast as to private. And thus much for the use of fasting.

Lord, have mercy[x] upon us, and give us grace, that, while we live in this miserable world, we may through thy help bring forth this and such other fruits of the Spirit, commended and commanded in thy holy word, to the glory of thy Name and to our comforts, that after the race of this wretched life we may live everlastingly with thee in thy heavenly kingdom; not for the merits and worthiness of our works, but for thy mercies' sake, and the merits of thy dear Son Jesus Christ: to whom with thee and the Holy Ghost be all laud, honour, and glory for ever and ever. Amen.

[x] Lord have mercy] *See below, p.* 293, *note* o.

THE SECOND PART OF THE HOMILY

OF FASTING.

IN the former Homily, beloved, was shewed, that, among the people of the Jews, fasting, as it was commanded them from God by Moyses, was to abstain the whole day, from morrow[a] till night, from meat, drink, and all manner of food that nourisheth the body; and that whoso tasted aught before the evening on the day appointed to fasting was accounted among them a breaker of his fast. Which order, though it seemeth strange to some in these our days, because it hath not been so used generally[b] in this realm of many years past, yet that it was so among God's people (I mean the Jews, whom, before the coming of our Saviour Christ, God did vouchsafe to choose unto himself a peculiar people above all other nations of the earth), and that our Saviour Christ so understood it, and the Apostles after Christ's ascension did so use it, was there sufficiently proved by the testimonies and examples of the holy Scriptures, as well of the New Testament as of the Old. The true use of fasting was there also shewed. In this second part of this Homily shall be shewed, that no constitution or law made by man, for things which of their own proper nature be mere indifferent, can bind the conscience of Christian men to a perpetual observation and keeping thereof; but that the higher powers hath[c] full liberty to alter and change every such law and ordinance, either ecclesiastical or political, when time and place shall require.

But first an answer shall be made to a question that some may make, demanding what judgment we ought to have of such abstinences as are appointed by public order and laws made by princes and by the authority of the magistrates, upon policy, not respecting any religion at all in the same; as when any realm, in consideration of the maintaining of fisher towns bordering upon the seas, and for the encrease of fishermen, of whom do spring mariners to go upon the sea, to the furnishing of the navy of the realm, whereby not only the commodities[d] of other

[a] morrow] morning 1623. [b] used generally] generally used *from* 1582. [c] hath] have *from* 1582. [d] only the commodities] only commodities *from* 1582.

countries may be transported, but also may be a necessary defence to resist the invasion of the adversary.[e]

For the better understanding of this question it is necessary that we make a difference between the policies of princes, made for the ordering of their commonweals, in provision of things serving to the more sure[f] defence of their subjects and countries, and between ecclesiastical policies in prescribing such works by which, as by secondary means, God's wrath may be pacified and his mercy purchased. Positive laws made by princes for conservation of their policy, not repugnant unto God's law, ought of all Christian subjects with reverence of the magistrate to be obeyed, not only for fear of punishment, *but also*, as the Apostle saith, *for conscience sake;* conscience, I say, not of the thing, which of the own[g] nature is indifferent, but of our obedience, which by the law of God we owe unto the magistrate, as unto *God's minister*. By which positive laws though we subjects, for certain times and days appointed, be restrained from some kinds of meats and drink, which God by his holy word hath left free to be taken and used of all men *with thanksgiving*[α] in all places and at all times; yet, for that such laws of princes and other magistrates are not made to put holiness in one kind of meat and drink more than another, to make one day more holy than another, but are grounded merely upon policy, all subjects are bound in conscience to keep them by God's commandment, who by the Apostle[β] willeth all, without exception, to submit themselves unto the authority of *the higher powers*.

[Rom. xiii, 4, 5.]

α [1 Tim. iv, 3, 4.]

β [Rom. xiii, 1.]

And in this point concerning our duties which be here dwelling in England, environed with the sea as we be, we have great occasion in reason to take the commodities of the water, which Almighty God by his divine providence hath laid so nigh unto us, whereby the encrease of victuals upon the land may the better be spared and cherished, to the sooner reducing of victuals to a more moderate price, to the better sustenance of the poor. And doubtless he seemeth to be too dainty an Englishman, which[h], considering the great commodities which may ensue, will not forbear some piece of his licentious appetite upon the ordinance of his Prince with the consent of the wise of the realm[1]. What good English heart would not wish the[i] old

e as when any realm——of the adversary] *thus imperfect in all.* f more sure] most sure *from* 1582. g the own] it own *from* 1582. h Englishman, which] Englishman, who 1623. i wish the] wish that the *from* 1582.

1 The Parliament which sat from January 12 to April 10, 1563 N. S., during which time was also sitting that Convocation which agreed to the Second

ancient glory should return to the realm, wherein it hath with great commendations excelled before our days, in the furniture of the navy of the same? What will more daunt the hearts of the adversary[k] than to see us as well[l] fenced and armed on the sea as we be reported to be on the land? If the Prince requested our obedience to forbear one day from flesh more than we do, and to be contented with one meal in the same day, should not our own commodity thereby persuade us to subjection? But now that two meals be permitted on that day to be used, which sometime our elders in very great numbers in the realm did use with one only spare meal, and that in fish only, shall we think it so great a burden that is prescribed? Furthermore, consider the decay of the towns nigh the seas, which should be most ready by the number of the people there to repulse the enemy; and we which dwell further off upon the land, having them as our buckler to defend us, should be the more in surety[m]. If they be our neighbours, why should we not wish them to prosper? If they be our defence, as nighest at hand to repel the enemy, to keep out the rage of the seas, which else would break upon our fair pastures, why should we not cherish them?

Neither do we urge that in the ecclesiastical policy prescrib-

[k] adversary] adversaries *from* 1582. [l] us as well] us well 1582, 1623. [m] surety] safety 1623.

Book of Homilies, passed "An Act touching certain politic constitutions made for the maintenance of the Navy," enacting (among other things) that every Wednesday, except in Christmas week and Easter week, should be observed "as a fish day," and that no person should eat flesh on any fish day without a proper licence, except that on Wednesdays any person who should have three dishes of sea fish at his table might also have one dish of flesh at the same meal. This was done "for the benefit and commodities of this realm to grow as well in maintenance of the Navy as in sparing and increase of flesh victual;" and the statute contains this special clause: "And because no manner of person shall misjudge of the intent of this statute, limiting orders to eat fish and to forbear eating of flesh, but that the same is purposely intended and meant politicly for the increase of fishermen and mariners and repairing of port towns and navigation, and not for any superstition to be maintained in the choice of meats; be it enacted, that whosoever shall by preaching, teaching, writing, or open speech, notify that any eating of fish and forbearing of flesh mentioned in this statute is of any necessity for the saving of the soul of man, or that it is the service of God, or otherwise than as other politic laws are and be, that then such person shall be punished as spreaders of false news are or ought to be." *Stat.* 5 *Eliz. c.* 5, §§ 11, 12, 22, 23. The Act 2 *and* 3 *Edw. VI c.* 19, ordering every Friday and Saturday and certain other days to be observed as fish days, and forbidding the eating of flesh on them, was partly based on similar considerations: as was also the previous Proclamation of King Edward VI on the same subject; one passage of which, where this realm is described as "environed with the seas," was manifestly in the mind of the person who wrote this portion of the Homily. See *Cardwell's Documentary Annals, No.* VI, *vol.* I, *p.* 32, 7–24, *ed.* 1839. See also *No.* LXXXV *ibid. p.* 370.

ing a form of fasting to humble ourselves in the sight of Almighty God, that that order which was used among the Jews, and practised by Christ's Apostles after his ascension, is of such force and necessity, that that only ought to be used among Christians, and none other: for that were to bind God's people unto the yoke and burden of Moyses' policy; yea, it were the very way to bring us, which are set at liberty by the freedom of Christ's Gospel, into the bondage of the Law again, which God forbid that any man should attempt or purpose. But to this end it serveth, to shew how far the order of fasting now used in the Church at this day differeth from that which then was used. God's Church ought not neither may it be so tied to that or any other order now made or hereafter to be made and devised by the authority of man, but that it may lawfully for just causes alter, change, or mitigate those ecclesiastical decrees and orders, yea, recede wholly from them, and break them, when they tend either to superstition or to impiety, when they draw the people from God rather than work any edification in them.

This authority Christ himself used, and left it unto his[n] Church. He used it, I say; for the order or decree made by the elders for washing ofttimes, which was diligently observed of the Jews, yet tending to superstition, our Saviour Christ altered and changed the same in his Church into a profitable Sacrament, the Sacrament of our regeneration or new birth.

This authority to mitigate laws and decrees ecclesiastical the Apostles practised, when they, writing from Hierusalem unto the congregation that was at Antioch, signified unto them that they would *not lay any further burden upon them, but these necessaries*, that is, *that they should abstain from things offered unto idols, from blood, from that which is strangled, and from fornication*, notwithstanding that Moyses' law required many other observances. Acts xv, [28, 29.]

This authority to change the orders, decrees, and constitutions of the Church was after the Apostles' time used of the fathers about the manner of fasting, as it appeareth in the Tripartite History, where it is thus written[2]. "Touching fasting, we find that it was diversely used in divers places by divers Tripart. Hist. Lib. ix, cap. 38.

[n] unto his] to his *from* 1582.

2 Nam in ipsis jejuniis aliter apud alios invenimus observari. Romani enim tres [*al.* sex] ante Pascha septimanas, praeter Sabbatum et Dominicam, sub continuatione jejunant. Illyrici vero, et tota Hellas, Alexandria quo-

men. For they at Rome fast three weeks together before Easter, saving upon the Saturdays and Sundays, which fast they call Lent." And after a few lines in the same place it followeth: "They have not all one uniform order in fasting. For some do fast and abstain both from fish and flesh. Some, when they fast, eat nothing but fish. Others there are which, when they fast, eat of all water fowls as well as of fish, grounding themselves upon Moyses, that such fowls have their substance of the water, as the fishes have. Some others, when they fast, will neither eat herbs nor eggs. Some fasters there are, that eat nothing but dry bread. Others, when they fast, eat nothing at all, no, not so much as dry bread. Some fast from all manner of food till night, and then eat without making any choice or difference of meats. And a thousand such like divers kinds of fasting may be found in divers places of the world, of divers men diversely used." And, for all this great diversity in fasting, yet charity, the very true bond of Christian peace, was not broken, neither did the diversity of fasting break at any time their agreement and concord in faith[3]. "To abstain sometime from certain meats, not because the meats are evil, but because they are not necessary, this abstinence," saith St. Augustine[4], "is not evil. And to restrain the use of meats when necessity and time shall require, this," saith he, "doth properly pertain to Christian men."

Euseb. Lib. v, cap. 24.

Dogm. Ecclesiast. cap. 66.

Thus ye have heard, good people, first, that Christian subjects are bound even in conscience to obey princes' laws, which are not repugnant to the laws of God. Ye have also heard that Christ's Church is not so bound to observe any order, law, or decree made by man to prescribe a form in religion, but that

que, ante sex septimanas jejunant: eaque jejunia Quadragesimam vocant. Alii vero &c.

Sed etiam ciborum abstinentiam non similem habent. Nam alii omnino ab animatis abstinent: alii ex animantibus pisces solummodo comedunt. Quidam cum piscibus vescuntur et volatilibus, dicentes haec secundum Moysen ex aqua habere substantiam. Alii vero etiam caulibus et ovis abstinere noscuntur. Quidam sicco tantummodo pane vescuntur: alii neque hoc. Alii usque ad nonam jejunantes horam sine discretione ciborum reficiuntur. Et innumerae consuetudines apud diversos inveniuntur. *Cassidor. Hist. Eccles. Tripart.* IX, 38, from *Socr.* V, 22.

3 Καὶ οὐδὲν ἔλαττον πάντες οὗτοι εἰρήνευσάν τε καὶ εἰρηνεύομεν πρὸς ἀλλήλους, καὶ ἡ διαφωνία τῆς νηστείας τὴν ὁμόνοιαν τῆς πίστεως συνίστησι. Iren. Epist. ap. Euseb. Hist. Eccles. V, xxiv, 10.

4 Abstinere autem ab aliquibus, non quasi malis, sed quasi non necessariis, non est malum. Moderari vero eorum [*MSS.* carnium] usum pro necessitate et tempore proprie Christianorum est. *Gennadius de Ecclesiasticis Dogmatibus*, c. XXXIII (*al.* LXVI), *Augustin. Opp.* VIII, *Append.* 79 B.

the Church hath full power and authority from God to change and alter the same, when need shall require; which hath been shewed you by the example of our Saviour Christ, by the practice of the Apostles, and of the fathers since that time.[o]

Now shall be shewed briefly what time is meet for fasting: for all times serve not for all things; but, as the Wise Man saith, *all things have their times. There is a time to weep, and a time again to laugh; a time to mourn, and a time to rejoice,* &c. (Eccles. iii, [1, 4.]) Our Saviour Christ excused his disciples, and reproved the Pharisees, because they neither regarded the use of fasting, nor considered what time was meet for the same. Which both he teacheth in his answer, saying[γ], *The children of the marriage cannot mourn while the bridegroom is with them.* Their question was of fasting, his answer is of mourning, signifying unto them plainly, that the outward fast of the body is no fast before God except it be accompanied with the inward fast, which is a mourning and a lamentation in the[p] heart, as is before declared. Concerning the time of fasting, he saith[δ], *The days will come when the bridegroom shall be taken from them: in those days they shall fast.* By this it is manifest, that it is no time of fasting while the marriage lasteth and the bridegroom is there present; but, when the marriage is ended and the bridegroom gone, then is it a meet time to fast.

γ Matt. ix, [15.]

δ Matt. ix, [15:] Luke. v, [35.]

Now to make plain unto you what is the sense and meaning of these words, We are at the marriage, and again, The bridegroom is taken from us. Ye shall note, that so long as God revealeth his mercy unto us, and giveth us of his benefits, either spiritual or corporal, we are said to be with the bridegroom at the marriage. So was that good old father Jacob at the marriage, when he understood that his son Joseph was alive[ε] and ruled all Egypt under king Pharao. So was David in the marriage with the bridegroom, when he had gotten the victory of great Goliah[ζ], and had smitten off his head. Judith and all the people of Bethulia were the children of the wedding, and had the bridegroom with them, when God had by the hand of a woman slain Holofernes[η], the grand captain of the Assyrians' host, and discomfited all their enemies. Thus were the Apostles the children of the marriage, while Christ was corporally present with them, and defended them from all dangers, both spiritual and corporal. But the marriage is said then to be

ε [Gen. xlv, 26–28.]

ζ [1 Sam. xvii, 49–58.]

η [Judith xiii–xvi.]

o Lord, have mercy (*p.* 287, *l.* 8) —— since that time.] *not in* 1563 A 1, *the Homily not being then divided into two Parts.* p in the] of the 1623.

ended, and the bridegroom to be gone, when Almighty God smiteth us with affliction, and seemeth to leave us in the midst of a number of adversities. So God sometime striketh private men privately with sundry adversities, as trouble of mind, loss of friends, loss of goods, long and dangerous sicknesses, &c. Then is it a fit time for that man to humble himself to Almighty God by fasting, and to mourn and bewail[q] his sins with a sorrowful heart, and to pray unfeignedly, saying with the prophet David, *Turn away thy face, O Lord, from my sins, and blot out of thy remembrance all mine offences.* Again, when God shall afflict a whole region or country with wars, with famine, with pestilence, with strange diseases and unknown sicknesses, and other such like calamities, then is it time for all states and sorts of people, high and low, men, women, and children, to humble themselves by fasting, and bewail their sinful living before God, and pray with one common voice, saying thus, or some other such like prayer: Be favourable, O Lord, be favourable unto thy people, which turneth unto thee in weeping, fasting, and praying: spare thy people, whom thou hast redeemed with thy precious blood, and suffer not thine enheritance to be destroyed and brought to confusion.

Ps. li, [9.]

Fasting thus used with prayer is of great efficacy, and weigheth much with God. So the angel Raphael told Tobias. It also appeareth by that which our Saviour Christ answered to his disciples, demanding of him why they could not cast forth the evil spirit out of him that was brought unto them. *This kind*, saith he[θ], *is not cast out but by fasting and prayer.* How available fast[r] is, how much it weigheth with God, and what it is able to obtain at his hand, cannot better be set forth than by opening unto you and laying before you some of those notable things that have been brought to pass by it.

Tob. xii, [8.]

θ [Matt. xvii, 21.]

Fasting was one of the means whereby Almighty God was occasioned to alter the thing which he had purposed concerning Ahab for murdering the innocent man Naboth to possess his vineyard. *God spake unto Elia, saying, Go thy way, and say unto Ahab, Hast thou killed, and also gotten possession? Thus saith the Lord, In the place where dogs licked the blood of Naboth shall dogs even lick thy blood also. Behold, I will bring evil upon thee, and will take away thy posterity: yea, the dogs shall eat him of Ahab's stock that dieth in the city, and him that dieth*

1 Kings xxi, [17–29.]

q and bewail] and to bewail *from* 1582.

r fast] fasting *from* 1567, *but* fast WHITGIFT.

in the fields[s] *shall the fowls of the air eat.* This punishment had Almighty God determined for Ahab in this world, and to destroy all the male kind that was begotten of Ahab's body, besides that punishment which should have happened unto him in the world to come. *When Ahab heard this, he rent his clothes, and put sackcloth upon him, and fasted, and lay in sackcloth, and went barefooted. Then the word of the Lord came to Elia, saying, Seest thou how Ahab is humbled before me? Because he submitteth himself before me, I will not bring that evil in his days; but in his son's days will I bring it upon his house.* Although Ahab, through the wicked counsel of Jezabel his wife, had committed shameful murder, and against all right disherited[t] and dispossessed for ever Naboth's stock of that vineyard; yet upon his humble submission in heart unto God, which he declared outwardly by putting on sackcloth and fasting, God changed his sentence, so that the punishment which he had determined fell not upon Ahab's house in his time, but was differred[u] unto the days of Joram his son. Here we may see of what force our outward fast is, when it is accompanied with the inward[w] fast of the mind, which is (as is said) a sorrowfulness of heart, detesting and bewailing our sinful doings.

The like is to be seen in the Ninivites. For when God had determined to destroy the whole city of Ninive, and the time which he had appointed was even now at hand, he sent the Prophet Jonas to say unto them, *Yet forty days, and Ninive shall be overthrown. The people by and by believed God, and gave themselves to fasting: yea, the king, by the advice of his council, caused to be proclaimed, saying, Let neither man nor beast, bullock nor sheep, taste any thing, neither feed nor drink water; but let man and beast put on sackcloth, and cry mightily unto God; yea, let every man turn from his evil way and from the wickedness that is in their hands. Who can tell if God will turn and repent, and turn away from his fierce wrath, that we perish not?* And upon this their hearty repentance, thus declared outwardly with fasting, renting of their clothes, putting on sackcloth, and sprinkling themselves with dust and ashes, the Scripture saith, *God saw their works, that they turned from their evil ways, and God repented of the evil that he had said that he would do unto them, and he did it not.*

Jonah iii, [4-10.]

Now, beloved, ye have heard, first, what fasting is, as well

[s] fields] field *from* 1571. [t] disherited] disinherited 1623. [u] differred] deferred *from* 1563 H. [w] inward] outward 1563 A.

that which is outward in the body, as that which is inward in the heart. Ye have heard also, that there are three ends or purposes, whereunto if our outward fast be directed, it is a good work that God is pleased with. Thirdly, hath been declared, what time is most meet for to fast, either privately or publicly. Last of all, what things fasting hath obtained of God, by the examples of Ahab and the Ninivites. Let us therefore, dearly beloved, seeing there are many more causes of fasting and mourning in these our days than hath been of many years heretofore in any one age, endeavour ourselves, both inwardly in our hearts and also outwardly with our bodies, diligently to exercise this godly exercise of fasting in such sort and manner as the holy Prophets, the Apostles, and divers other devout persons for their time used the same. God is now the same God that was[x] then; God that *loveth*[ι] *righteousness, and* that *hateth iniquity;* God which *willeth not*[κ] *the death of a sinner, but rather that he turn from his wickedness and live;* God that hath promised[λ] to turn to us, if we refuse not to turn unto him[y]. Yea, if we *turn our evil works*[μ] *from before his eyes, cease to do evil, learn to do well, seek to do right, relieve the oppressed, be a right judge to the fatherless, defend the widow, break our bread to the hungry, bring the poor that wander into our house, clothe the naked, and despise not our brother which is our own flesh; then shalt thou call,* saith the Prophet, *and the Lord shall answer; thou shalt cry, and he shall say, Here I am*[z]. Yea, God which heard Ahab and the Ninivites, and spared them, will also hear our prayers, and spare us, so that we, after their example, will unfeignedly turn unto him: yea, he will bless us with his heavenly benedictions the time that we have to tarry in this world, and after the race of this mortal life he will bring us to his heavenly kingdom, where we shall reign in everlasting blessedness with our Saviour Christ. To whom with the Father and the Holy Ghost be all honour and glory for ever and ever. Amen.

ι [Ps. xlv, 7.]
κ [Ezek. xxxiii, 11.]
λ [Zech. i, 3: Mal. iii, 7.]
μ [Is. i, 16, 17; lviii, 7, 9.]

x that was] that he was *from* 1582.
y unto him] to him *from* 1567.
z Here I am] Here am I *from* 1567.

AN HOMILY

AGAINST GLUTTONY AND DRUNKENNESS.

YE have heard in the former Sermon, well beloved, the description and the virtue of fasting, with the true use of the same. Now ye shall hear how foul a thing gluttony and drunkenness is before God, the rather to move you to use fasting the more diligently. Understand ye therefore, that Almighty God, to the end that we might *keep*[α] *ourselves undefiled* and *serve him in holiness and righteousness* according to his word, hath charged in his Scriptures so many as *look*[β] *for the glorious appearing of our Saviour Christ to lead their lives in all sobriety, modesty, and temperance*[a]. Whereby we may learn how necessary it is for every Christian, that will not be found unready at the coming of our Saviour Christ, to *live soberminded in this present world:* forasmuch as otherwise being unready he cannot enter with Christ into glory; and, being unarmed in this behalf, he must needs be in continual danger of that cruel *adversary*, the *roaring lion*, against whom the Apostle Peter warneth us to prepare ourselves in continual sobriety, that we may *resist, being steadfast in faith.* To the entent therefore that this soberness may be used in all our behaviour, it shall be expedient for us to declare unto you how much all kind of excess offendeth the Majesty of Almighty God, and how grievously he punisheth the immoderate abuse of those his creatures which he ordained[b] to the maintenance of this our needy life, as meats, drinks, and apparel, and again to shew the noisome diseases and great mischiefs that commonly do follow them that inordinately give up themselves to be carried headlong with such pleasures as are joined either with dainty and overlarge fare or else with costly and sumptuous apparel.

α [James i, 27: Luke i, 74, 75.]

β Tit. ii, [12, 13.]

1 Pet. v, [8, 9.]

And first, that ye may perceive how detestable and hateful all excess in eating and drinking is before the face of Almighty God, ye shall call to mind what is written by St. Paul to the Galathians, where he numbereth gluttony and drunkenness among those horrible crimes with the which (as he saith) *no man shall enherit the kingdom of heaven.* He reckoneth them

Gal. v, [19–21.]

[a] temperance] temperancy *from* 1567. [b] ordained] ordaineth *from* 1570.

among *the deeds of the flesh*, and coupleth them with idolatry, whoredom, and murder, which are the greatest offences that can be named among men. For the first spoileth God of his honour; the second defileth his holy temple, that is to wit, our own bodies; the third maketh us companions of Cain in the slaughter of our brethren; and whoso committeth them, as St. Paul saith, *cannot enherit the kingdom of God.* Certainly that sin is very odious and lothsome before the face of God which causeth him to turn his favourable countenance so far from us, that he should clean bar us out of the doors and disherit us of his heavenly kingdom. But he so much abhorreth all beastly banqueting, that, by his Son our Saviour Christ in the Gospel, he declareth his terrible indignation against all belly
Luke vi, [25.] gods, in that he pronounceth them accursed, saying, *Woe be to you that are full, for ye shall hunger.* And by the Prophet Esay
Is. v, [11, 12, 22.] he crieth out, *Woe be to you that rise up early, to give yourselves to drunkenness, and set all your minds so on drinking, that ye*[c] *sit sweating*[d] *thereat until it be night.*[1] *The harp, the lute, the shalm, and plenty of wine are at your feasts: but the works of the Lord ye do not behold, neither consider the works of his hands. Woe be unto you that are strong to drink wine, and are mighty to avaunce*[e] *drunkenness.* Here the Prophet plainly teacheth that feasting[f] and banqueting maketh men forgetful of their duty towards God, when they give themselves to all kinds of pleasure[g], not considering nor regarding *the works of the Lord,*
1 Tim. iv, [3.] who *hath created meats* and drinks, as St. Paul saith, *to be received thankfully of them that believe and know the truth.* So that the very beholding of these creatures, being the handywork of Almighty God, might teach us to use them thankfully, as God hath ordained. Therefore they are without excuse before God which either filthily feed themselves, not respecting the
[Ibid. 5.] sanctification which is *by the word of God and prayer,* or else unthankfully abuse the good creatures of God by surfeiting and drunkenness: forasmuch as God's ordinance[h] in his creatures plainly forbiddeth[i] it.

They that give themselves therefore to bibbing and banqueting, being altogether without[k] consideration of God's judg-

[c] that ye] that you 1623. [d] sweating] swearing 1563 B—1595, swilling 1623. [e] avaunce] advaunce *or* advance *from* 1563 B. [f] feasting] fasting 1582, 1623. [g] pleasure] pleasures *from* 1563 G. [h] ordinance] ordinances *from* 1567. [i] forbiddeth] forbid 1623. [k] altogether without] without all *from* 1582.

[1] Vae, qui consurgitis mane ad ebrietatem sectandam et potandum usque ad vesperam, ut vino aestuetis. *Vulg.*

ments, are suddenly oppressed in the day of vengeance. And thereof our Saviour Christ warneth his disciples, saying[l], *Take heed to yourselves, lest at any time your hearts be overcome with surfeiting and drunkenness and cares of this world, and so that day come on you unwares.* Luke xxi, [34.] Whosoever then will take warning at Christ, let him take heed to himself, lest, his heart being overwhelmed by surfeiting and drowned in drunkenness, he be taken unwares with that unthrifty *servant* which, thinking not on his master's coming, began to smite his fellow servants, *and to eat and drink*[m], *and to be drunken*, and, being suddenly taken, hath his just reward *with unbelieving* hypocrites. Ibid. xii, [45, 46.] They that use to drink deeply and to feed at full, wallowing themselves in all kind of wickedness, are brought asleep in that slumbering forgetfulness of God's holy will and commandments. Therefore Almighty God crieth by the Prophet Joel, *Awake, ye drunkards; weep and howl, all ye drinkers of wine; because the new wine shall be pulled from your mouth.* Joel i, [5.] Here the Lord terribly threateneth to withdraw his benefits from such as abuse them, and to pull the cup from the mouth of drunkards. Here we may learn not to sleep in drunkenness and surfeiting, lest God deprive us of the use of his creatures, when we unkindly abuse them. For certainly the Lord our God will not only take away his benefits when they are unthankfully abused, but also, in his wrath and heavy displeasure, take vengeance on such as immoderately abuse them.

If our first parents[y], Adam and Eve, had not obeyed their greedy appetite in eating the forbidden fruit, neither had they lost the fruition of God's benefits which they then enjoyed in Paradise, neither had they brought so many mischiefs both to themselves and to all their posterity. But, when they passed the bonds that God had appointed them, as unworthy of God's benefits, they are expelled and driven out of Paradise, they may no longer eat the fruits of that garden which by excess they had so much abused; as transgressors of God's commandment, they and their posterity are brought to a perpetual shame and confusion; and, as accursed of God, they must now sweat for their living which before had abundance at their pleasure. Even so, if we in eating and drinking exceed when God of his large liberality sendeth plenty, he will soon change plenty into scarceness; and, whereas we gloried in fulness, he will make us

[y] Gen. iii.

[l] And thereof our Saviour Christ warneth his disciples, saying] And therefore our Saviour Christ warneth his disciples, saying 1570–1574; Therefore Christ saith to his disciples *from* 1582. [m] and drink] and to drink 1623.

empty, and confound us with penury; yea, we shall be compelled to labour and travail with pains in seeking for that which we sometime enjoyed at ease. Thus the Lord will not leave them unpunished which, not[n] regarding his works, follow the lust and appetite[o] of their own hearts.

Noah. [2 Pet. ii, 5.]

δ Gen. [ix, 20–23.]

The patriarch Noah, whom the Apostle calleth the *preacher of righteousness*, a man exceedingly in God's favour, is in holy Scripture made an example[δ] whereby we may learn to avoid drunkenness. For, when he had poured in wine more than was convenient, in filthy manner he lay naked in his tent, his privities discovered. And, whereas sometime he was much[p] esteemed, he is now become a laughingstock to his wicked son Cham, no small grief to Sem and Japheth, his other two sons, which were ashamed of their father's beastly behaviour. Here we may note that drunkenness bringeth with it shame and derision, so that it never escapeth unpunished.

Lot.

ε Gen. [xix, 30–38.]

Epist. 84.¶

Lot in like manner, being overcome[ε] with wine, committeth[q] abominable incest with his own daughters. So will Almighty God give over drunkards to the shameful lusts of their lewd[r] hearts. Here is Lot by drinking fallen so far beside himself, that he knoweth not his own daughters. Who would have thought that an old man in that heavy case, having lost his wife and all that he had, which had seen even now God's vengeance in fearful manner declared on the five cities for their vicious living, should be so far past the remembrance of his duty? But men overcome with drink are altogether mad, as Seneca saith[2]. He was deceived by his daughters: but now many deceive themselves, never thinking that God by his horrible[s] punishments will be avenged on them that offend by excess. It is no small plague that Lot purchased by his drunkenness. For he had copulation most filthy[t] with his own daughters, which conceived thereby; so that the matter is brought to light, it can no longer be hid. Two incestuous children are born, Ammon and Moab; of whom came two nations, the Ammonites and Moabites, abhorred of God, and cruel adversaries to his people the Israelites. Lo, Lot hath gotten to himself by drinking sorrow and care with perpetual infamy and reproach unto the

[n] which, not] who, not 1623. [o] lust and appetite] lusts and appetites *from* 1570. [p] was much] was so much *from* 1571. [q] committeth] committed *from* 1574. [r] lewd] own *from* 1567. [s] horrible] terrible *from* 1563 G. [t] filthy] filthily *from* 1570.

2 Dic .... nihil aliud esse ebrietatem quam voluntariam insaniam. Extende in plures dies illum ebrii habitum, numquid de furore dubitabis? Nunc quoque non est minor, sed brevior. *Senec. Epist. Moral.* LXXXIII, § 17.

world's end. If God spared not his servant Lot, being otherwise a godly man, nephew unto Abraham, one that entertained[ζ] the angels of God, what will he do to these beastly bellyslaves, which, void of all godliness or virtuous behaviour, not once, but continually day and night, give themselves wholly to bibbing and banqueting?

ζ [Gen. xix, 1–3.]

But let us yet further behold the terrible examples of God's indignation against such as greedily follow their unsatiable lusts. Amnon[u] the son of David[η], feasting himself with his brother Absalon, is cruelly murdered of his own brother. Holofernes[θ], a valiant and mighty captain, being overwhelmed with wine, had his head stricken from his shoulders by that seely woman Judith. Simon the high priest[ι], and his two sons Mattathias and Judas, being entertained by[y] Ptolemy the son of Abobus, who had before married Simon's daughter, after much eating and drinking were traitorously murdered of their own kinsman. If the Israelites had not given themselves to belly cheer, they had never so often fallen to idolatry. Neither would we at this day be so addict to superstition, were it not that we so much esteemed the filling of our bellies. The Israelites[κ], when they served idols, *sat down to eat and drink, and rose again to play,* as the Scripture reporteth: therefore, seeking to serve their bellies, they forsook the service of the Lord their God. So are we drawn to consent unto wickedness when our hearts are overwhelmed by drunkenness and feasting. So Herod[λ], setting his mind on banqueting, was content to grant that the holy man of God, John the Baptist[z], should be beheaded at the request of his whore's daughter. Had not the rich glutton[μ] been so greedily given to the pampering of his belly, he would never have been so unmerciful to the poor Lazarus, neither had he felt the torments of unquenchable[a] fire. What was the cause that God so horribly punished Sodom and Gomorra? was it not their *proud banqueting and continual idleness*[ν], which caused them to be so lewd of life and so unmerciful towards the poor? What shall we now think of the horrible excess, whereby so many have perished and been brought to destruction?

Amnon.[x]
η 2 Sam. xiii, [23–29.]
θ Judith xiii, [2–8.]
ι [1 Mac. xvi, 11–16.]
κ Exod. xxxii, [6:] 1 Cor. x, [7.]
λ Matt. xiv, [6–11.]
μ Luke xvi, [19–25.]
ν Ezek. xvi, [49, 50.]

The great Alexander, after that he had conquered the whole world, was himself overcome by drunkenness; insomuch that, being drunken, he slew his faithful friend Clitus; whereof, when he was sober, he was so much ashamed that for anguish

Alexander.

u, x Amnon] Ammon *till* 1623. y entertained by] entertained of *from* 1567. z John the Baptist] John Baptist *from* 1563 B. a of unquenchable] of the unquenchable *from* 1571.

of heart he wished death. Yet, notwithstanding, after this he left not his banqueting, but in one night swilled in so much wine that he fell into a fever; and, when as by no means he would abstain from wine, within few days after in miserable sort he ended his life[3]. The conqueror of the whole world is made a slave by excess, and becometh so mad, that he murdereth his dear friend: he is plagued with sorrow, shame, and grief of heart for his intemperancy, yet can he not leave it; he is kept in captivity; and he, which sometime had subdued many, is become a subject to the vile belly. So are drunkards and gluttons altogether without power of themselves, and the more they drink, the drier they wax[4]; one banquet provoketh another; they study to fill their greedy stomachs. Therefore it is commonly said, A drunken man is always dry, and, A glutton's gut is never filled.

Unsatiable truly are the affections and lusts of man's heart; and therefore we must learn to bridle them with the fear of God, so that we yield not to our own lusts, lest we kindle God's indignation against ourselves, when we seek to satisfy our 1 Cor. x, [31.] beastly appetite. St. Paul teacheth us, *whether we eat or drink, or whatsoever we do, to do all to the glory of God.* Where he appointeth, as it were by a measure, how much a man may eat and drink; that is to wit, so much that the mind be not made sluggish by cramming in meat and pouring in drink, so that it cannot lift up itself to the praise and glory[b] of God. Whatsoever he be then that by eating and drinking makes[c] himself unlusty[d] to serve God, let him not think to escape unpunished.

Ye have heard how much Almighty God detesteth the abuse of his creatures, as he himself declareth, as well by his holy word, as also by the fearful examples of his just judgments[e]. Now, if neither the word of God can restrain our raging lusts and greedy appetites, neither the manifest examples of God's vengeance fear us from riotous and excessive eating and drinking, let us yet consider the manifold mischiefs that proceed

[b] praise and glory] glory and praise *from* 1571. [c] makes] maketh 1623. [d] unlusty] unfit 1623. [e] judgments] judgment *from* 1570.

3 This story of Alexander is a translation from *Peter Martyr, De Vino et Ebrietate, In Libr. Judic. Comment. cap.* IX; and the preceding narratives of Noah, Lot, Amnon, Holofernes, and Simon, together with much of what follows in the Homily, are taken in like manner from the same place.

4 A few sentences in this and the next page are taken, with very little alteration, from *Bishop Pilkington's Exposition upon Haggai* i, 5, 6; *Works, pp.* 51–53, *ed. Parker Society.*

thereof; so shall we know the tree by the fruits. It hurteth the body; it infecteth the mind; it wasteth the substance; and is noyful[f] to the neighbours. But who is able to express the manifold dangers and inconveniences that follow of intemperate diet?

Oft cometh sudden death by banqueting: sometime the members are dissolved, and so the whole body is brought into a miserable state. He that eateth and drinketh unmeasurably kindleth ofttimes such an unnatural heat in his body, that his appetite is provoked thereby to desire more than it should; or else it overcometh his stomach, and filleth all the body full of sluggishness; makes it unlusty[g] and unfit to serve either God or man, not nourishing the body, but hurting it; and last of all bringeth[h] many kinds of incurable diseases, whereof ensueth sometimes desperate death. But what should I need to say any more in this behalf? For, except God bless our meats and give them strength to feed us; again, except God give strength to nature to digest, so that we may take profit by them; either shall we filthily vomit them up again, or else shall they lie stinking in our bodies, as in a lothsome sink or canell[i][5], and so diversely infect the whole body. And surely the blessing of God is so far from such as use riotous banqueting, that in their faces be sometimes seen the express tokens of this intemperancy, as Salomon noteth in his Proverbs. *To whom is woe?* Prov. xxiii, [29-35.] saith he; *to whom is sorrow? to whom is strife? to whom is brawling? to whom are wounds without cause? and for whom is the redness of eyes? Even to them that tarry long at the wine.* Mark, I beseech you, the terrible tokens of God's indignation. *Woe* and *sorrow, strife* and *brawling, wounds without cause,* disfigured face, and *redness of eyes* are to be looked for when men set themselves to excess and gourmandise[j], devising all means to encrease their greedy appetites by tempering the wine and saucing it in such sort that it may be more delectable and pleasant unto them. It were expedient that such delicate persons should be ruled by Salomon, who, in consideration of the foresaid[k] inconveniences, forbiddeth the very sight of wine. *Look not upon the wine,* saith he, *when it is red, and when it sheweth his colour in the cup, or goeth down pleasantly. For in the end*

[f] noyful] noisome 1623. [g] unlusty] unable 1623. [h] bringeth] bring 1563 G-1595. [i] canell] chanell *from* 1571. [j] gourmandise] gurmandise *in all.* [k] foresaid] aforesaid *from* 1567, *except* 1582 *and* 1587.

[5] canell, now written channel: a gutter. Pilkington says, "as in a sink or kennel," which is another form of the same word.

thereof it will bite like a serpent, and hurt like a cockatrice. Thine eyes shall look upon strange women, and thine heart shall speak lewd things. And thou shalt be as one that sleepeth in the middes[l] *of the sea, and as he that sleepeth in the top of the mast. They have stricken me, shalt thou*[m] *say, but I was not sick; they have beaten me, but I felt it not; therefore will I seek it yet still.* Certainly that must needs be very hurtful which biteth and infecteth like a poisoned serpent, whereby men are brought to filthy fornication, which causeth the heart to devise mischief. He doubtless is in great danger that sleepeth in the midst of the sea, for soon is he[n] overwhelmed with waves. He is like to fall suddenly that sleepeth in the top of the mast. And surely he hath lost his senses that cannot feel when he is stricken, that knoweth not when he is beaten. So surfeiting and drunkenness bites by the belly, and causeth continual gnawing in the stomach, brings men to whoredom and lewdness of heart, with dangers unspeakable, so that men are bereaved and robbed of their senses, and are altogether without power of themselves. Who seeth not now the miserable estate whereinto men are brought by these foul filthy monsters, gluttony and drunkenness? The body is so much disquieted by them, that, as Jesus the son of Sirach affirmeth, the unsatiable feeder never sleepeth quietly, such an unmeasurable heat is kindled, whereof ensueth continual ache and pain to the whole body.

Ecclus. xxxi, [20.]

And no less truly is the mind[o] also annoyed by surfeiting banquets. For sometimes men are stricken with phrensy of mind, and are brought in manner[p] to mere[q] madness; some wax so brutish and blockish, that they become altogether void of understanding[6]. It is an horrible thing that any man should maim himself in any member; but for a man of his own accord to bereave himself of his wits is a mischief intolerable. The Prophet Osee, in the fourth chapter, saith that *wine and drunkenness taketh away the heart.* Alas then, that any man should yield unto that whereby he might bereave himself of the possession of his own heart. *Wine*[ξ] *and women lead wise men out of the way, and bring men of understanding to reproof and*

Hos. iv, [11.]

ξ Ecclus. xix, [2.]

l middes] *so in all.* m shalt thou] thou shalt *from* 1571. n is he] he is *from* 1567. o is the mind] the mind is *from* 1567. p in manner] in like manner 1623. q mere] nere 1563 A–G; neere 1563 H; neare 1567, 1570; meare 1571; mere *or* meere *from* 1574. *See note* 6 *below, and note* 2 *before.*

6 Percutiuntur ebrii plerumque spiritu stuporis, et in furorem quodammodo vertuntur: brutescunt, ita ut nihil intelligentiae videatur in eis reliquum. *P. Martyr, ibid.*

shame[7], saith Jesus the son of Sirach. Yea, he asketh[o], *What is the life of man that is overcome with drunkenness?*[8] *Wine drunken with excess maketh bitterness of mind, and causeth brawling and strife.* In magistrates it causeth cruelty instead of justice, as that wise philosopher Plato perceived right well, when he affirmed, that "a drunken man hath a tyrannous heart," and therefore will rule all at[r] his pleasure, contrary to right and reason[9]. And certainly drunkenness maketh men forget both law and equity: which caused king Salomon so straitly to charge that no wine should be given unto rulers, *lest peradventure by drinking they forget what the law appointeth them, and so change the judgment of all the children of the poor.* Therefore among all sorts of men excessive drinking is most intolerable in a magistrate or man of authority, as Plato saith. For a drunkard knoweth not where he is himself: if then a man of authority should be a drunkard, alas, how might he be a guide unto other men, standing in need of a governor himself[10]? Besides this, a drunken man can keep nothing secret; many fond, foolish, and filthy words are spoken when men are at their banquets. "Drunkenness," as Seneca affirmeth, "discovereth all wickedness, and bringeth it to light; it removeth all shamefastness, and encreaseth all mischief. The proud man, being drunken, uttereth his pride, the cruel man his cruelty, and the envious man his envy, so that no vice can lie hid in a drunkard. Moreover, in that he knoweth not himself, fumbleth[s] and stammereth in his speech, staggereth to and fro in his going, beholdeth[t] nothing steadfastly with his staring eyes, believeth that the house runneth round about him[11]," it is evi-

[o] Ecclus. xxxi, [27, 29.]

Prov. xxxi, [4, 5.]

De Republ. Lib. iii.

[r] rule all at] rule at *from* 1582. [s] himself, fumbleth] himself, he fumbleth *from* 1574. [t] beholdeth] beholding 1623.

7 Vinum et mulieres apostatare faciunt sapientes, et arguent sensatos. *Vulg.*

8 Quae vita est quae minuitur vino? *Ecclus.* XXXI, 33 *Vulg.*, 27 Auth. Vers.

9 Οὐκοῦν, ὦ φίλε, εἶπον, καὶ μεθυσθεὶς ἀνὴρ τυραννικόν τι φρόνημα ἴσχει; Ἴσχει γάρ. Plat. Republ. IX, p. 573 B. But the quotation is taken from Peter Martyr, as cited in note 3: Unde Plato in 6 [*leg.* 9] Dialogo de Justo [*sive* Republ.] ab initio, Ebrium, inquit, habere animum tyrannicum, quod omnibus pro libidine, non ex ulla ratione seu lege, velit imperare.

10 Μέθης μὲν δὴ εἴπομεν ὅτι ἀφεκτέον αὐτοῖς· παντὶ γάρ που μᾶλλον ἐγχωρεῖ ἢ φύλακι μεθυσθέντι μὴ εἰδέναι ὅπη γῆς ἐστι. Γελοῖον γάρ, ἦ δ' ὅς, τόν γε φύλακα φύλακος δεῖσθαι. Ibid. III, p. 403 E.

11 Certe eruit omne vitium ebrietas et incendit et detegit: obstantem malis conatibus verecundiam removet.... Ubi possedit animum nimia vis vini, quicquid mali latebat emergit.... Crescit insolenti superbia, crudelitas saevo, malignitas livido: omne vitium laxatur et prodit. Adjice illam ignorationem sui, dubia et parum explanata verba, incertos oculos, gradum errantem, vertiginem capitis, tecta ipsa mobilia velut aliquo turbine circumagente totam domum. *Senec. Epist. Moral.* LXXXIII, §§ 18–20.

dent that the mind is brought clean out of frame by excessive (Prov. xx, [1.]) drinking: so that *whosoever is deceived by wine or strong drink* becometh, as Salomon saith, *a mocker or a mad man, so that he can never be wise.* If any man think that he may drink much wine, and yet be well in his wits, he may as well suppose, as Seneca saith, "that when he hath drunken poison he shall not die[12]." For, wheresoever excessive drinking is, there must needs follow perturbation of mind; and, where the belly is stuffed with dainty fare, there the mind is oppressed with slothful sluggishness. "A full belly maketh a gross understanding," (Ad Sororem, Serm. 24.) saith St. Bernard[13], and much meat maketh a weary mind.

But, alas, now a days men pass little either for body or mind: so they have worldly wealth and riches abundant to satisfy their unmeasurable lusts, they care not what they do. They are not ashamed to shew their drunken faces, and to play the mad men[u] openly. They think themselves in good case, and that all is well with them, if they be not pinched by lack and poverty. Lest any of us therefore might take occasion to flatter himself in this beastly kind of excess by the abundance of riches, let us call to mind what Salomon writeth in the twenty-first of his (Prov. xxi, [17.]) Proverbs. *He that loveth wine and fat fare shall never be rich,* saith he. And in the twenty-third chapter he maketh a vehe- (Prov. xxiii, [20, 21.]) ment exhortation on this wise: *Keep not company with drunkards and gluttons, for the glutton and drunkard shall come to poverty.* He that draweth his patrimony through his throat, and eateth and drinketh more in one hour or in one day than he is able to earn in a whole week, must needs be an unthrift, and come to beggary.

But some will say, What need any to find fault with this? he hurteth no man but himself, he is no man's foe but his own. Indeed I know this is commonly spoken in defence of these beastly belly gods: but it is easy to see how hurtful they are, not only to themselves, but also to the commonwealth by their

[u] mad men] mad man 1623.

[12] Nam, si illud argumentaberis, sapientem multo vino inebriari, et retinere rectum tenorem, etiam si temulentus sit; licet colligas, nec veneno poto moriturum, nec sopore sumpto dormiturum. *Senec. ibid.* § 25. But the quotation is taken from Peter Martyr: Sed quoniam aliqui sunt qui jactant se posse multo etiam hausto vino esse compotes mentis et integri judicii, rogo eos ut audiant Senecam, Epistola jam adducta, qui ait, Dicant etiam tales veneno hausto se non morituros, &c.

[13] Pinguis venter non gignit subtilem sensum. *Ad Sororem de Modo bene Vivendi*, c. XXIV, *ad calc. Bernard. Opp.* II, 863 B. Perhaps the Homilist had in mind the following passage also: Sed ex vilissimis cibis vitanda satietas est. Nihil enim ita obruit animum ut plenus venter et exaestuans. *Hieron. adv. Jovin.* II, 12; *Opp.* II, 342 B.

example. Every one that meeteth them is troubled with brawling and contentious language; and ofttimes, raging in beastly lusts, *like fed*[x] *horses, they neigh on their neighbours' wives,* as [Jer. v, 8.] Jeremy saith, and defile their children and daughters. Their example is evil to them among whom they dwell; they are an occasion of offence to many; and, whiles they waste their substance in banqueting, their own household is not provided of things necessary, their wives and their children are evil entreated, they have not wherewith to relieve their poor neighbours in time of necessity, as they might have if they lived soberly. They are unprofitable to the commonwealth; for a drunkard is neither fit to rule, nor to be ruled. They are a slander to the Church or congregation of Christ; and therefore St. Paul doth excommunicate them among whoremongers, ido- [1 Cor. v, [11.]] laters, covetous persons, and extortioners, forbidding Christians to eat with any such.

Let us therefore, good people, eschew, every one of us, all intemperancy; let us love sobriety and moderate diet, oft give ourselves to abstinence[y] and fasting, whereby the mind of man is more lift up to God, more ready to all godly exercises, as prayer, hearing and reading of God's word, to his spiritual comfort. Finally, whosoever regardeth the health and safety of his own body, or wisheth always to be well in his wits, or desireth quietness of mind, and abhorreth fury and madness; he that would be rich and escape poverty; he that is willing to live without the hurt of his neighbour, a profitable member of the commonwealth, a Christian without slander of Christ and his Church; let him avoid all riotous and excessive banqueting; let him learn to keep such measure as behoveth him that professeth true godliness; let him follow St. Paul's rule[π], and so *eat and drink to the glory* and praise *of God,* who *hath created*[ρ] *all things to be* soberly *used with thanksgiving.* To whom be all honour and glory for ever. Amen.

π [1 Cor. x, 31.]
ρ [1 Tim. iv, 3, 4.]

x fed] high fed 1623.   y abstinence] abstinency *from* 1582.

AN HOMILY

AGAINST EXCESS OF APPAREL.

WHERE ye have heretofore been excited and stirred to use temperance of meats and drinks, and to avoid the excess thereof, many ways hurtful to the state of the commonwealth, and also[a] odious before Almighty God, being the Author and Giver of such creatures, to comfort and stablish our frail nature with thanks unto him, and not by abusing of them to provoke his liberality to severe punishing of that disorder; in like manner it is convenient that ye be admonished of another foul and chargeable excess, I mean of apparel, at these days so outrageous[b], that neither Almighty God by his word can stay our proud curiosity in the same, neither yet godly and necessary laws, made of our Princes and oft repeated with the penalties[1], can bridle this detestable abuse; whereby both God is openly contemned, and the Prince's laws manifestly disobeyed, to the great peril of the realm. Wherefore, that sobriety also in this excess may be espied among us, I shall declare unto you both the moderate use of apparel approved by God in his holy word, and also the abuses thereof, which he forbiddeth and disalloweth, as it may appear by the inconveniences which daily encrease by the just judgment of God where that measure is not kept which he himself hath appointed.

If we consider the end and purpose whereunto Almighty God hath ordained his creatures, we shall easily perceive that he alloweth us apparel, not only for necessity's sake, but also for an honest comeliness. Even as in herbs, trees, and sundry fruits we have, not only divers necessary uses, but also the pleasant sight and sweet smell to delight us withal; wherein we may behold the singular love of God towards mankind, in that he hath provided both to relieve our necessities and also to refresh our senses with an honest and moderate recreation. Therefore David in the hundred and fourth Psalm, confessing God's careful pro-

Ps. civ, [14, 15.]

[a] and also] and so *from* 1582. [b] outrageous] gorgeous 1623.

[1] See *Stat.* 37 *Edw. III, cc.* 8–15 (repealed in the next year, 38 *Edw. III, st.* 1, *c.* 2); 3 *Edw. IV, c.* 5; 22 *Edw. IV, c.* 1; 1 *Hen. VIII, c.* 14, repeated in 6 *Hen. VIII, c.* 1, and in 7 *Hen. VIII, c.* 6; 24 *Hen. VIII, c.* 13.

vidence, sheweth that God not only provideth things necessary for men, as herbs and other meats, but also such things as may rejoice and comfort, as *wine to make glad the heart, oils and ointments to make the face to shine.* So that they are altogether past the limits of humanity which, yielding[c] only to necessity, forbid the lawful fruition of God's benefits. With whose traditions we may not be led, if we give ear to St. Paul, who[d], writing to the Colossians, willeth[e] them not to hearken unto such men as shall say, *Touch not, Taste not, Handle not,* superstitiously (Col. ii, [21.]) bereaving them of the fruition of God's creatures.

And no less truly ought we to beware, lest, under pretence of Christian liberty, we take licence to do what we list, avauncing[f] ourselves in sumptuous apparel, and despising other, preparing ourselves in fine bravery to wanton, lewd, and unchaste behaviour. To the avoiding whereof, it behoveth us to be mindful of four lessons taught in holy Scripture, whereby we shall learn (Four lessons.) to temper ourselves, and to restrain our immoderate affections, to that measure which God hath appointed. The first is, that (1.) *we make not provision for the flesh, to accomplish the lusts thereof,* (Rom. xiii, [14.]) with costly apparel; as that harlot did of whom Salomon speaketh, Proverbs the seventh, which *perfumed her bed, and decked* (Prov. vii, [16, 17.]) *it with costly ornaments of Egypt,* to the fulfilling of her lewd lust: but rather ought we by moderate temperance to cut off all occasions whereby the flesh might get the victory. The se- (2.) cond is written by St. Paul in the seventh chapter of his first Epistle to the Corinthes, where he teacheth us to *use this world* (1 Cor. vii, [31.]) *as though we used it not*[2]*:* whereby he cutteth away, not only all ambition, pride, and vain pomp in apparel, but also all inordinate care and affection, which withdraweth us from the contemplation of heavenly things and consideration of our duty towards God. They that are much occupied in caring for things pertaining to the body are most commonly negligent and careless in matters concerning the soul. Therefore our Saviour Christ willeth us *not to take thought what we shall eat, or what* (Matt. vi, [31, 33.]) *we shall drink, or wherewith we shall be clothed, but rather to seek the kingdom of God and the righteousness thereof*[3]. Whereby we may learn to beware, lest we use those things to our hinder-

[c] which yielding] who yielding 1623. [d] who] *omitted* 1623. [e] willeth] willing *from* 1582
[f] avauncing] advauncing *or* advancing *from* 1571.

2 Οἱ χρώμενοι τῷ κόσμῳ τούτῳ, ὡς μὴ καταχρώμενοι. Qui utuntur hoc mundo, tanquam non utantur. *Vulg.*

3 Ζητεῖτε δὲ πρῶτον τὴν βασιλείαν τοῦ Θεοῦ καὶ τὴν δικαιοσύνην αὐτοῦ. Quaerite ergo primum regnum Dei et justitiam ejus. *Vulg.*

ance which God hath ordained for our comfort and furtherance
3. towards his kingdom. The third is, that we take in good part
our estate and condition, and content ourselves with that which
God sendeth, whether it be much or little. He that is ashamed
of base and simple attire will be proud of gorgeous apparel, if
Phil. iv, [12.] he may get it. We must learn therefore of the Apostle St. Paul
both *to use plenty and also to suffer penury*, remembering that
we must yield accounts of those things which we have received
unto him who abhorreth all excess, pride, ostentation, and vanity; who also utterly condemneth and disalloweth whatsoever
draweth us from our duty towards God[g], or diminisheth our
charity towards our neighbours and brethren[h], whom we ought
4. to love as ourselves. The fourth and last rule is, that every
man behold and consider his own vocation, inasmuch as God
hath appointed every man his degree and office, within the limits
whereof it behoveth him to keep himself. Therefore all may
not look to wear like apparel[4], but every one according to his
degree[5], as God hath placed him. Which if it were observed,
many one doubtless should be compelled to wear a russet[6] coat,
which now ruffleth in silks and velvets, spending more by the
year in sumptuous apparel than their fathers received for the
whole revenue of their lands. But, alas, now a days how many
may we behold occupied wholly in pampering the flesh, taking
no care at all but only how to deck themselves, setting their
affection altogether on worldly bravery, abusing God's goodness (when he sendeth plenty, to satisfy their wanton lusts,
having no regard to the degree wherein God hath placed them!

[g] towards God] toward God 1623. [h] brethren] children *from* 1582.

4 All the statutes cited in note 1 regulate apparel according to rank and property.

5 A few sentences in this and the next two pages are taken, with very little alteration, from *Bishop Pilkington's Exposition upon Haggai* i, 5, 6; *Works, pp.* 55–57, *ed. Parker Society.*

6 "Russet," like blanket, first denoted colour. The statute 37 Edw. III c. 14 ordains "that carters, ploughmen, . . . and all other people that have not forty shillings of goods nor of chattels, shall not take nor wear no manner of cloth" (*Fr.* "drap", broadcloth), "but blanket and russet wool of twelve pence" (*Fr.* "blanket et russet laune de xii d"); meaning apparently a woollen stuff of coarse texture, which might be had either white or brown. And it is likely that these colours were not artificial, but merely the natural tinctures of the wool from which the yarn was spun. In *Fabyan's Chronicle, an.* 1501–2, cited by Richardson, we read, "Also aboute thys tyme the Gray Fryers were compelled to take theyr old habit russet, as the shepe doth dye it." It is probable also that it was this difference of colour which determined men's choice of the blanket for their covering by night, and left the russet for the clothes in which the rough work of day was to be done.

The Israelites were contented with such apparel as God gave them, although it were base and simple; and God so blessed them, that their shoes[α] and clothes lasted them forty years: yea, and (α Deut. xxix, [5.]) those clothes which their fathers had worn the children[i] were content[j] to use afterward. But we are never contented, and therefore we prosper not; so that most commonly he that ruffleth in his sables, in his fine furred gown, corked slippers, trim buskins, and warm mittons[k], is more ready to chill for cold than the poor labouring man, which can abide in the field all the day long, when the north wind blows, with a few beggarly clouts about him. We are loth to wear such as our fathers hath left[l] us; we think not that sufficient or good enough for us. We must have one gown for the day, another for the night; one long, another short; one for winter, another for summer; one through furred, another but faced; one for the workingday, another for the holy day; one of this colour, another of that colour; one of cloth, another of silk or damask: we must have change of apparel, one afore dinner, another[m] after; one of the Spanish fashion, another Turkey[7]: and, to be brief, never content with sufficient. Our Saviour Christ bad his disciples they should not have[β] two coats: but the most men, far unlike to (β Matt. x, [10.]) his scholars, have their presses so full of apparel, that many knoweth[n] not how many sorts they have. Which thing caused St. James to pronounce this terrible curse against such wealthy worldlings: *Go to, ye rich men, weep and howl on your wretchedness that shall come upon you: your riches are corrupt, and your garments are motheaten: ye have lived in pleasure on the earth, and in wantonness; ye have nourished your hearts as in the day of slaughter.* (James v, [1, 2, 5.]) Mark, I beseech you, St. James calleth them miserable, notwithstanding their riches and plenty of apparel, forasmuch as they pamper their bodies to their own destruction. What was the rich glutton[γ] the better for his fine fare and (γ Luke xvi, [19–25.]) costly apparel? Did not he nourish himself to be tormented in hell fire? Let us learn therefore to *content ourselves, having food and raiment,* as St. Paul teacheth; (1 Tim. vi, [8, 9.]) lest, *desiring to be en-*

[i] the children] their children *from* 1570. [j] content] contented *from* 1582. [k] mittons] *so in all.* [l] hath left] have left *from* 1571. [m] dinner, another] dinner, and another 1623. [n] knoweth] know *from* 1582.

7 "Their [Englishmen's] coat must be made after the Italian fashion, their cloak after the use of the Spaniards, their gown after the manner of the Turks, their cap must be of the French fashion," &c. *Becon, Jewel of Joy, p.* 438 *ed. Parker Society.* In the conference at Hampton Court the Puritan divines "appeared before His Majesty in Turky gownes, not in their scholastical habits, suiting to their degrees." *Cardwell's History of Conferences, p.* 180, *l.* 10.

riched with abundance, we *fall into temptations, snares, and many noisome lusts, which drown men in perdition and destruction.*

Certainly such as delight in gorgeous apparel are commonly puffed up with pride and filled with divers vanities. So were *the daughters of Sion* and people of Jerusalem, whom Esay the Prophet threateneth, because they *walked with stretched out necks and wandering eyes, mincing as they went, and nicely treading with their feet*, that Almighty *God should*[o] *make their heads bald, and discover their secret shame. In that day*, saith he, *shall the Lord take away the ornament of the slippers, and the cauls, and the round attires, and the sweet balls, and the bracelets, and the attires of the head, and the slops*[8], *and the headbands, and the tablets, and the earrings, the rings, and the mufflers, the costly apparel, and the veils, and wimples, and the crisping pin*[p], *and the glasses, and the fine linen, and the hoods, and the lawns.* So that Almighty God would not suffer his benefits to be vainly and wantonly abused, no, not of that people whom he most tenderly loved, and had chosen to himself before all other.

Isai. iii, [16-23.]

No less truly is the vanity that is used amongst[q] us in these days. For the proud and haughty stomachs of the daughters of England are so maintained with divers disguised sorts of costly apparel, that (as Tertullian, an ancient father, saith) "there is left no difference in apparel between an honest matron and a common strumpet[9]." Yea, many men are become so effeminate, that they care not what they spend in disguising themselves, ever desiring new toys and inventing new fashions. Therefore a certain man that would picture every countryman in his accustomed apparel, when he had painted other nations, he pictured the Englishman all naked, and gave him cloth under his arm, and bad him make it himself as he thought best, for he changed his fashion so often, that he knew not how to make it[10]. Thus

Apol. con. Gentes, cap. vi.

[o] should] would *from* 1574. [p] pin] *so in all.* [q] amongst] among *from* 1582.

[8] slops: loose trowsers. So too the Geneva Bible of 1562, and the Bishops' Bible in 1568. The Vulgate has *periscelidas;* our Authorised Version *the ornaments of the legs.* Gesenius explains the original word to mean a sort of chain which eastern ladies wore to fetter their legs and keep them from striding as they walked, in fact, to make them *mince* or take short steps *as they went.* The Homilist has omitted one article of dress after *the bracelets,* which in the Vulgate is called *mitras,* in the Geneva Bible *bonnets,* in the Bishops' Bible and in our own *mufflers.*

[9] Video et inter matronas atque prostibulas nullum de habitu discrimen relictum. *Tertull. Apolog.* VI; *Opp.* I, 134.

[10] See the first chapter of "The fyrst boke of the Introduction of knowledge,

with our phantastical devices we make ourselves laughingstocks to other nations; while one spendeth his patrimony upon pounces and cuts [11], and other[r] bestoweth more on a dancing shirt than might suffice to buy him honest and comely apparel for his whole body. Some hang their revenues about their necks, ruffling in their ruffs; and many a one jeopardeth his best joint, to maintain himself in sumptuous raiment. And every man, nothing considering his estate and condition, seeketh to excel other in costly attire. Whereby it cometh to pass that, in abundance and plenty of all things, we yet complain of want and penury, while one man spendeth that which might serve a multitude, and no man distributeth of the abundance which he hath received, and all men excessively waste that which should serve to supply the necessities of other.

The cause of dearth.

There hath been very good provision made against such abuses by divers good and wholesome laws [12]; which if they were practised as they ought to be of all true subjects, they might in some part serve to diminish this raging and riotous excess in apparel. But, alas, there appeareth amongst us little fear and obedience either of God or man. Therefore must we needs look for God's fearful vengeance from heaven, to overthrow our presumption and pride, as he overthrew Herod [8], who in his royal apparel, forgetting God, was smitten of an angel, and eaten up of worms. By which terrible example God hath taught us that we are but worms' meat, although we pamper ourselves never so much in gorgeous apparel. Here we may learn that which Jesus the son of Sirach teacheth, *not to be proud of clothing and rai-*

8 Acts xii, [21–23.]

Ecclus. xi, [4.]

r and other] another *from* 1563 D.

the which doth teache a man to speake parte of all maner of Languages, and to knowe the usage and fashion of al maner of countreys ....: made by Andrew Borde, of Phisicke Doctor." The Dedication bears the date of 3 May 1542. The book, a thin volume in quarto, was "imprented at London" without date by "Wyllyam Copland." It was reprinted by Messrs. R. and A. Taylor in 1814.

11 "Pounces" were holes pierced or punched out, no doubt in some ornamental pattern and worked round with the needle: "cuts" were made with shears from the outer edge into the piece so as to leave loose ends, and were also finished with needle work. "Ther is also the costlewe furring in hir gounes, so moche pounsoning of chesel to maken holes, so moche dagging of sheres." *Chaucer, Canterbury Tales, The Persones Tale,* "De Superbia," *vol.* II, *p.* 314, *ed. Oxf.* 1798, where "dagging" is an old word for jagging or cutting into slips. See *Richardson.* "The lorde mayer had iiij. footemen all in whyte sylke, cutte, ruffed, and pounced." *Hall's Chronicle, Hen. VIII, an.* 31, *fol.* 235 b, cited by *Richardson* on "Ruff." There is an amusing story of a gown "made as full of cuts as" the tailors "sheeres" could "make it," in *Camden's Remains, pp.* 198, 199, *ed.* 1614. See also Petruchio's interview with the tailor in *The Taming of the Shrew,* IV, 3; and the *Old Play* cited by *Steevens on Shakespeare, vol.* IX, *p.* 151, *ed.* 1803.

12 See note 1.

ment, neither to exalt ourselves in the day of honour, because the works of the Lord are wonderful and glorious, secret and unknown, teaching us with humbleness of mind every one to be mindful of the vocation whereunto God hath called him.

Let Christians therefore endeavour themselves to quench the care of pleasing the flesh. Let us use the benefits of God in this world in such wise that we be not too much occupied in providing for the body. Let us content ourselves quietly with that which God sendeth, be it never so little. And, if it please him to send plenty, let us not wax proud thereof, but let us use it moderately, as well to our own comfort, as to the relief of such as stand in necessity. He that in abundance and plenty of apparel hideth his face from him that is naked *despiseth his own flesh,* as Esay the Prophet saith[13]. Let us learn to know ourselves, and not to despise other. Let us remember that we stand all before the Majesty of Almighty God, who shall judge us by his holy word, wherein he forbiddeth excess, not only to men, but also to women: so that none can excuse themselves, of what estate or condition soever they be. Let us therefore present ourselves before his throne, as Tertullian exhorteth, with the ornaments which the Apostle speaketh of, Ephesians the sixth chapter, *having our loins girt about with the verity, having the breastplate of righteousness, and shod with shoes prepared by the Gospel of peace.* Let us take unto us simplicity, chastity, and comeliness, submitting our necks to the sweet yoke[e] of Christ. Let women be subject to their husbands, and they are sufficiently attired, saith Tertullian[14]. The wife of one Philo an heathen philosopher, being demanded why she ware no gold, she answered, that she thought her husband's virtues sufficient ornaments[15]. How much more ought Christian women, instructed by the word of God, content[s] themselves in their husbands! Yea, how much more ought every Christian to content himself in our Saviour Christ, thinking himself sufficiently garnished with his heavenly virtues!

Isai. lviii, [7.]

Eph. vi, [14, 15.]

e Matt. xi, [30.]

s God, content] God, to content *from* 1571.

13 Cum videris nudum, operi eum, et carnem tuam ne despexeris. *Vulg.*

14 Prodite vos jam medicamentis et ornamentis exstructae Prophetarum et Apostolorum, sumentes de simplicitate candorem, de pudicitia ruborem, depictae oculos verecundia et os taciturnitate, inserentes in aures sermones Dei, adnectentes cervicibus jugum Christi. Caput maritis subjicite, et satis ornatae eritis. *Tertull. de Cult. Fem.* II, 13; *Opp.* I, 734.

15 Ἡ Φίλωνος γυνὴ ἐρωτηθεῖσα διὰ τί μόνη τῶν ἄλλων ἐν συνόδῳ οὐ φορεῖ χρυσοῦν κόσμον ἔφη, Ὅτι αὐτάρκης κόσμος μοι ἐστὶν ἡ τοῦ ἀνδρὸς ἀρετή. Stob. Florileg. LXXIV (*al.* LXXII), 54.

But it will be here objected and said of some nice and vain women, that all which we do in painting our faces, in dyeing our hair, in embalming our bodies, in decking us with gay apparel, is to please our husbands, to delight his eyes, and to retain his love toward[t] us. O vain excuse, and most shameful answer, to the reproach of thy husband. What couldest thou more say to set out his foolishness, than to charge him to be pleased and delighted with the devil's tire? Who can paint her face, and curl her hair, and change it into an unnatural colour, but therein doth work reproof to her Maker, who made her, as though she could make herself more comely than God hath appointed the measure of her beauty? What do these women but go about to reform that which God hath made, not knowing that all things natural is the work[u] of God, and things disguised and unnatural be the works of the devil; and as though a wise and a Christian[x] husband should delight to see his wife in such painted and flourished visions[y], which common harlots mostly[z] do use, to train therewith their lovers to naughtiness; or as though an honest woman could delight to be like an harlot for pleasing of her husband?

Nay, nay, these be but the vain[a] excuses of such as go about to please rather others than their husbands. And such attires be but to provoke her to shew herself abroad to entice others: a worthy matter. She must keep debate with her husband to maintain such apparel, whereby she is the worse housewife, the seldomer at home to see to her charge, and so to neglect[b] his thrift by giving great provocation to her household to waste and wantonness, while she must wander abroad to shew her own vanity and her husband's foolishness. By which her pride she stirreth up much envy of others, which be so vainly[c] delighted as she is. She doth but deserve mocks and scorns, to set out all her commendation in Jewish and ethnic apparel, and yet brag of her Christianity. She doth but waste superfluously her husband's stock by such sumptuousness, and sometime[d] is[e] the cause of much bribery, extortion, and deceit in her husband's occupying[f], that she may be the more gorgeously set out to the sight of the vain world, to please the devil's eyes, and not God's, who giveth to every creature sufficient and moderate comeliness,

[t] toward] towards *from* 1567. [u] is the work] are the work 1623. [x] and a Christian] and Christian *from* 1567. [y] visions] visages 1623. [z] mostly] most 1623. [a] but the vain] but vain *from* 1570. [b] so to neglect] so neglect *from* 1582. [c] so vainly] as vainly 1623. [d] sometime] sometimes *from* 1563 B. [e] sometime is] sometimes she is 1623. [f] occupying] dealings 1623.

wherewith we should be contented, if we were of God. What other thing doest thou by those means but provokest others[g] to tempt thee, to deceive thy soul, by the bait of thy pomp and pride? What else doest thou but settest out thy pride, and makest of thy undecent[h] apparel of thy body the devil's net, to catch the souls of them which behold thee? O thou woman, not a Christian, but worse than a paynim, thou minister of the devil, why pamperest thou that[i] carrion[j] flesh so high, which sometime doth stink and rot on the earth as thou goest? Howsoever thou perfumest thyself, yet cannot thy beastliness be hidden or overcome with thy smells and savours, which do rather deform and misshape thee than beautify thee. What meant Salomon to say of such trimming of vain women, when he said, [Prov. xi, 22.] *A fair woman without good manners and conditions is like a sow which hath a ring of gold upon her snout*, but that the more thou garnish thyself with these outward blazings, the less thou carest for the inward garnishing of thy mind, and so dost but defoul[k] thyself by such array, and not beautify thyself?

[1 Pet. iii, 3–5.] Hear, hear, what Christ's holy Apostles do write. *Let not the outward apparel of women*, saith St. Peter, *be decked with the braiding of hair, with wrapping on of gold, or goodly clothing: but let the mind and the conscience, which is not seen with the eyes, be pure and clean: that is*, saith he, *an acceptable and an excellent thing before God. For so the old ancient holy women attired themselves, and were obedient to their husbands.* And [1 Tim. ii, 9, 10.] St. Paul saith, that *women should apparel themselves with shamefastness and soberness, and not with braids of their hair, or gold, or pearl, or precious clothes, but as women should do which will express godliness by their good outward works*[16].

If we[l] will not keep the Apostles' precepts, at the least let us hear what pagans, which were ignorant of Christ, have said in this matter. Democrates[m] saith, "The ornament of a woman standeth in scarcity of speech and apparel[17]." Sophocles saith of such apparel thus: "It is not an ornament, O thou fool, but

[g] others] other *from* 1571. [h] thy undecent] the undecent *from* 1582. [i] pamperest thou that] pamperest that 1563 A. [j] carrion] carreyn, carreine, *or* carren *in all.* [k] defoul] deform 1623. [l] If we] If ye *from* 1567. [m] Democrates] *so in all.*

16 Τὰς γυναῖκας ἐν καταστολῇ κοσμίῳ μετὰ αἰδοῦς καὶ σωφροσύνης κοσμεῖν ἑαυτὰς, μὴ ἐν πλέγμασιν ἢ χρυσῷ ἢ μαργαρίταις ἢ ἱματισμῷ πολυτελεῖ, ἀλλ', ὃ πρέπει γυναιξὶν ἐπαγγελλομέναις θεοσέβειαν, δι' ἔργων ἀγαθῶν. Mulieres in habitu ornato; cum verecundia et sobrietate ornantes se, non in tortis crinibus aut auro aut margaritis vel veste pretiosa, sed quod decet mulieres promittentes pietatem per opera bona. *Vulg.*

17 Δημοκρίτου. Κόσμος ὀλιγομυθίη γυναικί· καλὸν δὲ καὶ κόσμου λιτότης. Stob. Florileg. LXXIV (*al.* LXXII), 38.

a shame, and a manifest shew of thy folly[18]." Socrates[n] saith that "that is a garnishing to a woman which declareth out her honesty[18]." The Grecians use it in a proverb, "It is not gold or pearl which is a beauty to a woman, but good conditions[18]." And Aristotle biddeth that "a woman should use less apparel than the law doth suffer; for it is not the goodliness of apparel, nor the excellency of beauty, nor the abundance of gold, that maketh a woman to be esteemed, but modesty and diligence to live honestly in all things[19]." This outrageous vanity is now grown so far, that there is no shame taken of it. We read in histories that, when king Dionysius sent to the women of Lacedemon rich robes, they answered and said that "they shall do us more shame than honour," and therefore refused them[18]. The women in Rome in old time abhorred that gay apparel which king Pyrrhus sent to them, and none were so greedy and vain to accept them[20]. And a law was openly made of the senate, and a long time observed, "that no woman should wear over half an ounce of gold, nor should wear clothes of divers colours[21]."

[n] Socrates] *so in all.*

18 *Ταῖς Λυσάνδρου θυγατράσιν ὁ τύραννος ὁ Σικελικὸς ἱμάτια καὶ πλόκια τῶν πολυτελῶν ἔπεμψεν· ὁ δὲ Λύσανδρος οὐκ ἔλαβεν, εἰπών, Ταῦτα τὰ κόσμια καταισχυνεῖ μου μᾶλλον ἢ κοσμήσει τὰς θυγατέρας. πρότερος δὲ Λυσάνδρου Σοφοκλῆς τοῦτο εἶπεν·*

Οὐ κόσμος, οὐκ, ὦ τλῆμον, ἀλλ' ἀκοσμία
φαίνοιτ' ἂν εἶναι σῶν τε μαργότης φρενῶν.

κόσμος γάρ ἐστιν, ὡς ἔλεγε Κράτης, τὸ κοσμοῦν· κοσμεῖ δὲ τὸ κοσμιωτέραν γυναῖκα ποιοῦν· ποιεῖ δὲ ταύτην [*al.* *τοιαύτην*] *οὐ χρυσὸς οὔτε σμάραγδος οὔτε κόκκος, ἀλλ' ὅσα σεμνότητος, εὐταξίας, αἰδοῦς ἔμφασιν περιτίθησιν.* Plutarch. Conjug. Praecept. XXVI, p. 141 D. In Stob. Florileg. LXXIV (*al.* LXXII), 48, where the words of Crates are given, the Latin version of *κοσμεῖ δὲ τὸ κοσμιωτέραν γυναῖκα ποιοῦν* in Conrad Gesner's edition, published at Zurich in 1543, is Ornat autem quod honestiorem mulierem facit.

19 Sumptu autem et vestitu et apparatu minori etiam utatur quam leges permiserint civitatis, considerans quod nec vestimentorum nitor nec excellentia formae nec auri magnitudo tantum valet ad mulieris laudem quantum modestia in rebus ac studium honeste decoreque vivendi. *Aristot. Oeconom. Aretino interprete* II, i, 4, *ed. Paris.* 1526, *fol.* 141 a. Leonardo Bruni of Arezzo, known by the name of Aretinus, addressed to Cosmo de' Medici his translation of the Economics of Aristotle, dividing the work into two Books. Of his second Book no Greek text has ever been found, and Bruni's Latin was annexed to Book I (as capp. vii and viii) by later editors, who published the true Book II. But Bekker omits it altogether, and modern critics have no doubt that it was composed by Bruni himself. See *Goettling, Praefat. ad Aristot. Oeconom. ed. Jenae* 1830, *p.* XIX, *not.*

20 Patrum nostrorum memoria per legatum Cineam Pyrrhus non virorum modo sed etiam mulierum animos donis tentavit. Nondum lex Oppia ad coercendam luxuriam muliebrem lata erat: tamen nulla accepit. *Oratio M. Porc. Catonis ap. Liv.* XXXIV, 4.

21 Tulerat eam [*sc.* legem] C. Oppius . . . in medio ardore Punici belli, ne qua mulier plus semuncia auri haberet, neu vestimento versicolori uteretur. *Liv.* XXXIV, 1. Anno vigesimo post abrogata est quam lata. *Ibid.* 8.

But perchance some dainty dame will say and answer me, that they must do something to shew their birth and blood, to shew their husband's riches: as though nobility were chiefly seen by these things, which be common to those which be most vile; as though thy husband's riches were not better bestowed than in such superfluities; as though, when thou were[o] Christened, thou didst not renounce the pride of the world[p] and the pomp of the flesh. I speak not against convenient apparel for every state agreeable, but against the superfluity, against the vain delight to covet such vanities, to devise new fashions to feed thy pride with, to spend so much upon thy carcase, that thou and thy husband are compelled to rob the poor to maintain thy costliness. Hear how that noble holy woman, Queen Hester, setteth out these goodly ornaments (as they be called), when, in respect of saving God's people, she was compelled to put on such glorious apparel, knowing that it was a fit stale[q] [22] to blind the
[Esth. xiv, 16.] eyes of carnal fools. Thus she prayed: *Thou knowest, O Lord, the necessity which I am driven to, to put on this apparel, and that I abhor this sign of pride and of this glory which I bear on my head, and that I defy it as a filthy cloth, and that I wear it*
ς [Judith x, 3, 4, 23; xii, 15; xvi, 8, 9.] *not when I am alone.* Again, by what means was Holofernes[ς] deceived but by[r] the glittering shew of apparel? which that holy woman Judith did put on her, not as delighting in them, nor seeking vain voluptuous pleasure by them; but she ware it of pure necessity by God's dispensation, using this vanity to overcome the vain eyes of God's enemy. Such desire was in those holy noble[s] women, being very loth and unwilling otherwise to wear such sumptuous apparel, by the which others should be caused to forget themselves. These be commended in Scripture for abhorring such vanities, which by constraint and great necessity, against their hearts' desire, were[t] compelled to wear them for a time. And shall such women be worthy commendations, which neither be comparable with these women aforesaid in nobility, nor comparable to them in their good zeals[u] to God and his people, whose daily delight and seeking is to flourish in such gay shifts and changes, never satisfied, nor regarding who

[o] were] wast 1623. [p] the world] this world *from* 1571. [q] stale] stable *from* 1582. [r] deceived but by] deceived by 1623. [s] those holy noble] those noble *from* 1567. [t] desire, were] desire, they were 1623. [u] zeals] zeal *from* 1582.

22 stale: lure, decoy. In obedience to Prospero's command,

> "The trumpery in my house, go bring it hither
> For stale to catch these thieves,"

Ariel returns "loaden with glistering apparel." *Shakespeare, Tempest,* IV, 1.

smarteth for their apparel so they may come by it? O vain men, which be subjects to their wives in these inordinate affections. O vain women, to procure so much hurt to themselves, by the which they come the sooner to misery in this world, and in the mean time be abhorred of God, hated and scorned of wise men, and in the end like to be joined with such who in hell, too late repenting themselves, shall openly complain with these words[η]; *What hath our pride profited us? or what profit hath the pomp of riches brought us? All those[w] things are passed away like a shadow. As for virtue, we did never shew any sign thereof; and thus are we[x] consumed in our wickedness.*

η [Wisd. v, 8, 9, 13.]

If thou sayest that the custom is to be followed, and the use of the world doth compel thee to such curiosity; then I ask of thee, whose custom should be followed? wise folks' manners, or fools'? If thou sayest, the wise; then I say, follow them, for fools' customs who should follow but fools? Consider that the consent of wise men ought to be alleged for a custom. Now, if any lewd custom be used, be thou the first to break it; labour to diminish it and lay it down; and more laud afore[y] God and more commendation shalt thou win by it than by all the glory of such superfluity.

Thus ye have heard declared unto you, what God requireth by his word concerning the moderate use of his creatures. Let us learn to use them moderately, as he hath appointed. Almighty God hath taught us to what end and purpose we should use our apparel. Let us therefore learn so to behave ourselves in the use thereof, as it becometh[z] Christians, always shewing ourselves thankful to our heavenly Father for his great and merciful benefits; who giveth unto us *our daily bread*, that is to say, all things necessary for this our needy life; unto whom we shall render accounts for all his benefits at *the glorious appearing of our Saviour Christ*[θ]. To whom with the Father and the Holy Ghost be all honour, praise, and glory for ever and ever. Amen.

θ [Tit. ii, 13.]

w All those] All these *from* 1582. x are we] we are *from* 1563 B. y afore] before *from* 1582. z as it becometh] as becometh *from* 1563 B.

AN HOMILY OR SERMON

CONCERNING PRAYER.

THERE is nothing in all man's life, well beloved in our Saviour Christ, so needful to be spoken of, and daily to be called upon, as hearty, zealous, and devout prayer; the necessity whereof is so great, that without it nothing may be well obtained at God's hand. [James i, [17.]] For, as the Apostle James saith, *every good and perfect gift cometh from above, and proceedeth from the Father of lights:* [α Rom. x, [12.]] who is also said to be *rich*[α] *and liberal towards all them that call upon him,* not because he either will not or cannot give without asking, but because he hath appointed prayer as an ordinary means between him and us.

There is no doubt but he always *knoweth what we have need of*[β] [β Matt. vi, [8.]], and is always most ready to give abundance of those things that we lack. Yet, to the intent we might acknowledge him to be the Giver of all good things, and behave ourselves thankfully towards him in that behalf, loving, fearing, and worshipping him sincerely and truly, as we ought to do, he hath profitably and wisely ordained that in time of necessity we should humble ourselves in his sight, pour out the secrets of our heart before him, and crave help at his hands, with continual, earnest, and devout prayer. By the mouth of his holy Prophet David he saith on this wise: [[Ps. l, 15.]] *Call upon me in the days of thy trouble, and I will deliver thee.* Likewise in the Gospel, by the mouth of his well beloved Son Christ, he saith, [Matt. vii, [7, 8.]] *Ask, and it shall be given you; knock, and it shall be opened: for whosoever asketh receiveth; whosoever seeketh findeth; and to him that knocketh it shall be opened.* St. Paul also, most agreeably consenting hereunto, [1 Tim. ii, [8:] Phil. iv, [6:] Col. iv, [2.]] *willeth men to pray every where*[1], *and to continue therein with thanksgiving.* Neither doth the blessed Apostle St. James in this point any thing dissent, but, earnestly exhorting all men to diligent prayer, saith, [James i, [5.]] *If any man lack wisdom, let him ask it of God, which giveth liberally to all men, and reproacheth no man.* Also in another place: [James v, [16.]] *Pray one for another,* saith he, *that ye may be healed; for the righteous man's prayer availeth much, if*

[1] Βούλομαι οὖν προσεύχεσθαι τοὺς ἄνδρας ἐν παντὶ τόπῳ. 1 Tim. ii, 8.

it be fervent. What other thing are we taught by these and such other places, but only this, that Almighty God, notwithstanding his heavenly wisdom and foreknowledge, will be prayed unto, that he will be called upon, that he will have us no less willing on our part to ask than he on his part is willing to give?

Therefore most fond and foolish is the opinion and reason of those men, which therefore think all prayer to be superfluous and vain, because God *searcheth*[γ] *the heart and the reins*, and knoweth[δ] the meaning of the spirit before we ask. For, if this fleshly and carnal reason were sufficient to disannul prayer, then why did our Saviour Christ so often cry to his disciples[ε], *Watch and pray?* why did he prescribe them a form of prayer, saying[ϛ], *When ye pray, pray after this sort, Our Father, which art in heaven,* &c.? why did he pray so often and so earnestly himself[ζ] before his passion? finally, why did the Apostles, immediately after his ascension, gather themselves[η] together into one several place, and there continue a long time in prayer? Either they must condemn Christ and his Apostles of extreme folly, or else they must needs grant, that prayer is a thing most necessary for all men at all times and in all places.

γ [Ps. vii, 9.]
δ Rom. viii, [27: Matt. vi, 8.]
ε Matt. [xxvi, 41: Mark xiii, 33: Luke xxi, 36.]
ϛ [Matt. vi, 9: Luke xi, 2.]
ζ Luke xxii, 41–44.]
η Acts i, [13, 14.]

Sure it is, that there is nothing more expedient or needful for mankind in all the world than prayer. *Pray always,* saith St. Paul[θ], *with all manner of prayer*[a] *and supplication, and watch thereto*[b] *with all diligence.* Also in another place[ι] he willeth us to *pray* continually *without any intermission* or ceasing, meaning thereby that we ought never to slack nor[c] faint in prayer, but to continue therein to our lives' end. A number of other such places might here be alleged of like effect, I mean, to declare the great necessity and use of prayer: but what need many proofs in a plain matter, seeing there is no man so ignorant but he knoweth, no man so blind but he seeth, that prayer is a thing most needful in all estates and degrees of men? For only by the help hereof we attain to those heavenly and everlasting treasures which God our heavenly Father hath reserved and laid up for us his[d] children in his dear and well beloved Son Jesus Christ, with this covenant and promise[κ] most assuredly confirmed and sealed unto us, that, if we ask, we shall receive.

θ Eph. vi, [18.]
ι 1 Thess. v, [17.]
κ John xvi, [23–27.]

Now, the great necessity of prayer being sufficiently known, that our minds and hearts may be the more provoked and stirred

[a] manner of prayer] manner prayer *from* 1563 B. [b] thereto] therefore 1623. [c] nor] or *from* 1571. [d] for us his] for his *from* 1571.

thereunto, let us briefly consider what wonderful strength and power it hath to bring strange and mighty things to pass. We read in the Book of Exodus[λ] that Josua, fighting against the Amalekites, did conquer and overcome them, not so much by virtue of his own strength, as by the earnest and continual prayer of Moyses; who as long as he held up his hands to God, so long did Israel prevail; but, when he fainted and let his hands down, then did Amalek and his people prevail; insomuch that Aaron and Hur, being in the mount with him, were fain to stay up his hands until the going down of the sun, otherwise had the people of God that day been utterly discomfited and put to flight. Also we read in another place[μ] of Josua himself, how he at the besieging of Gibeon, making his humble petition to Almighty God, caused the sun and the moon to stay their course, and to stand still in the midst of heaven for the space of a whole day, until such time the[e] people were sufficiently avenged upon their enemies. And was not Jehosaphat's prayer[ν] of great force and strength, when God at his request caused his enemies to fall out among themselves and wilfully to destroy one another? Who can marvel enough at the effect and virtue of Elia's prayer? *He, being*[ξ] *a man subject to affections as we are, prayed to the Lord that it might not rain, and there fell no rain upon the earth for the space of three years and six months. Again he prayed that it might rain, and there fell great plenty, so that the earth brought forth her encrease most abundantly.* It were too long to tell of Judith[o], Esther, Susanna, and of divers other godly men and women, how greatly they prevailed in all their doings by giving their minds earnestly and devoutly to prayer. Let it be sufficient at this time to conclude with the sayings of Augustine and Chrysostom, whereof the one calleth prayer "the key of heaven[2]," the other plainly affirmeth that "there is nothing in all the world more strong than a man that giveth himself to fervent prayer[3]."

λ Exod. xvii, [10–13.]

μ Joshua x, [12, 13.]

ν 2 Chron. xx, [1–24.]

ξ [James v, 17, 18:] 1 Kings [xvii, 1;] xviii, [42–45: Luke iv, 25.]

o [Judith ix; xii, 8; xiii, 4–9: Esth. iv, 16; xiv: Susanna 42–44.]

Aug. Serm. 226 de Tempore. Chrys. sup. Matt. xxii.

Now then, dearly beloved, seeing prayer is so needful a thing, and of so great strength before God, let us, according as we are taught by the example of Christ and his Apostles, be earnest and diligent in calling on the Name of the Lord. Let us never faint, never slack, never give over; but let us daily and hourly,

e time the] time as the 1623.

2 Oratio justi clavis est coeli. *Augustin. Opp.* v *Append. Serm.* XLVII (*olim* De Tempore 226) *col.* 90 F.

3 Οὐδὲν γὰρ ἀνθρώπου γνησίως εὐχομένου δυνατώτερον. Chrysost. in Matth. Hom. LVII (*al.* LVIII); Opp. VII, 581 C.

early and late, in season and out of season, be occupied in godly meditations and prayers. What if we obtain not our petition[f] at the first? yet let us not be discouraged, but let us continually cry and call upon God: he will surely hear us at length, if for no other cause, yet for very importunity's sake. Remember the parable of the unrighteous judge and the poor widow[ϖ], how she by her importunate means caused him to do her justice against her adversary, although otherwise he feared neither God nor man. *Shall not God much more avenge his elect,* saith our Saviour Christ, *which cry unto him day and night?* Thus he taught his disciples, and in them all other true Christian men, *to pray always, and never to faint* or shrink. Remember also the example of the woman of Chanaan[g][ρ], how she was rejected of Christ, and called dog, as one most unworthy of any benefit at his hands; yet she gave not over, but followed him still, crying and calling upon him to be good and merciful unto her daughter; and at length, by very importunity, she obtained her request. O let us learn by these examples to be earnest and fervent in prayer; assuring ourselves[σ] that, *whatsoever we ask* of God the Father in the name of his Son Christ and *according to his will,* he will undoubtedly grant it. He is truth itself; and, as truly as he hath promised it, so truly will he perform it. God, for his great mercy's sake, so work in our hearts by his Holy Spirit, that we may always make our humble prayers unto him, as we ought to do, and always obtain the thing which we ask, through Jesus Christ our Lord. To whom with the Father and the Holy Ghost be all honour and glory world without end. Amen.

ϖ Luke xviii, [1–7.]

ρ Matt. xv, [22–28.]

σ John xvi, [23: 1 John v. 14, 15.]

f petition] petitions *from* 1563 G.

g Chanaan] Canaan *from* 1563 D.

THE SECOND PART OF THE HOMILY

CONCERNING PRAYER.

IN the first part of this Sermon ye heard the great necessity, and also the great force, of devout and earnest prayer declared and proved unto you, both by divers weighty testimonies, and also by sundry good examples of holy Scripture. Now shall you learn whom you ought to call upon, and to whom ye[a] ought always to direct your prayers.

We are evidently taught in God's holy Testament, that Almighty God is the only fountain and wellspring of all goodness, and that, whatsoever we have in this world, we receive it only at his hands. James i, [17.] To this effect serveth the place of St. James. *Every good and perfect gift,* saith he, *cometh from above, and proceedeth from the Father of lights.* To this effect also serveth the testimony of Paul in divers places of his Epistles[α], witnessing that *the spirit of wisdom,* the spirit of knowledge *and revelation,* yea, every good and heavenly gift, as faith, hope, charity, *grace, and peace,* cometh only and solely of God. In consideration whereof he bursteth out into a sudden passion, and saith[β], *O man, what thing hast thou which thou hast not received?* Therefore, whensoever we need or lack anything pertaining either to the body or the[b] soul, it behoveth us to run only unto God, who is the only giver of all good things. Our Saviour Christ in the Gospel, teaching his disciples how they should pray, sendeth[c] them to the Father in his name, saying[γ], *Verily, verily, I say unto you, Whatsoever ye ask the Father in my name, he will give it unto you.* And in another place[δ]: *When ye pray, pray after this sort, Our Father, which art in heaven,* &c. And doth not God himself, by the mouth of his Prophet David[ε], will and command us to call upon him? The Apostle wisheth[ζ] *grace and peace to all them that call on the Name* of the Lord and *of his Son Jesus Christ:* as doth also the Prophet Joel, saying, *And it shall come to pass, that whosoever shall call on the Name of the Lord shall be saved.* Joel ii, [32:] Acts ii, [21.]

Thus then it is plain by the infallible word of truth and life,

α [Rom. i, 7; v, 1–5: 1 Cor. xii, 8: Eph. i, 17; ii, 8: 1 Thess. iii, 12.]
β 1 Cor. iv, [7.]
γ John xvi, [23.]
δ Matt. vi, [9:] Luke xi, [2.]
ε Ps. l, [15.]
ζ [1 Cor. i, 2, 3.]

[a] to whom ye] to whom you *from* 1582. [b] or the] or to the *from* 1563 EF. [c] sendeth] sending 1623.

that in all our necessities we must flee unto God, direct our prayers unto him, call upon his holy Name, desire help at his hands, and at no[d] other's. Whereof if ye[e] will yet have a further reason, mark that which followeth. There are certain conditions most requisite to be found in every such a one that must be called upon, which if they be not found in him unto whom we pray, then doth our prayer avail us nothing, but is altogether in vain. The first is this, that he to whom we make our prayers be able to help us. The second is, that he will help us. The third is, that he be such a one as may hear our prayers. The fourth is, that he understand better than we ourselves what we lack and how far we have need of help. If these things be to be found in any other saving only God, then may we lawfully call upon some other besides God. But what man is so gross but he well understandeth that these things are only proper to him which is omnipotent and *knoweth all things*, even *the very secrets of the heart*, that is to say, only and to God alone? [1 John iii, 20: Ps. xliv, 21.] Whereof it followeth, that we must call neither upon angel nor yet upon saint, but only and solely upon God. As St. Paul doth write: *How shall men call upon him in whom they have not believed?* [Rom. x, [14.]] So that invocation or prayer may not be made without faith in him on whom we call[f], but that we must first believe in him, before we can make our prayers[g] unto him: whereupon we must only and solely pray unto God. For to say that we should believe either in angel or saint or in any other living creature were most[h] horrible blasphemy against God and his holy word; neither ought this fancy enter[i] into the heart of any Christian man, because we are expressly taught in the word of the Lord only to repose our faith in the blessed Trinity, in whose only Name we are also baptized according to the express commandment of our Saviour Jesus Christ in the last of Matthew[j]. [Matt. xxviii, [19.]]

But, that the truth hereof may the better appear, even to them that be most simple and unlearned, let us consider what prayer is. St. Augustine calleth it "a lifting up of the mind to God, that is to say, an humble and lowly pouring out of the heart to God[1]." [De Spir. et Lit. cap. 50.] Isidorus saith, that "it is an affection of the [De Summo Bono, cap. viii, Lib. iii.]

[d] no] none *from* 1582. [e] if ye] if we 1623. [f] we call] they call *from* 1563 EF. [g] prayers] prayer *from* 1582. [h] were most] were more 1567–1574, were mere *from* 1582. [i] fancy enter] fancy to enter *from* 1563 B. *See before, p.* 314, *note* s. [j] of Matthew] of St. Matthew *from* 1582.

[1] Oratio est mentis devotio, id est, conversio in Deum per pium et humilem affectum. Affectus est spontanea quaedam ac dulcis ipsius animi ad Deum inclinatio. *Scriptor Incertus de Spiritu et Anima, cap.* L; *Augustin. Opp.* VI *Ap-*

heart, and not a labour of the lips[2]." So that, by these places, true prayer doth consist, not so much in the outward sound and voice of words, as in the inward groaning and crying of the heart to God. Now then, is there any angel, any virgin, any patriarch or prophet among the dead, that can understand or know the meaning of the heart? The Scripture saith *it is God that searcheth the heart and reins*[k], and that *he only knoweth the hearts of the children of men.* As for the Saints, they have so little knowledge of the secrets of the heart, that many of the ancient fathers greatly doubt whether they know anything at all that is commonly done on earth. And, albeit some think they do, yet St. Augustine, a doctor of great authority and also antiquity, hath this opinion of them, that they know no more what we do on earth, than we know what they do in heaven. For proof whereof he allegeth the words of Esay the Prophet, where it is said, *Abraham is ignorant of us, and Israel knoweth us not*[3]. His mind therefore is this, not that we should put any religion in worshipping them[l] or praying unto them, but that we should honour them by following their virtuous and godly life[4]. For, as he witnesseth in another place, the Martyrs and holy men in times past were wont after their death to be remembered and named of the priest at Divine Service, but never to be invocated or called upon. And why so? "Because the priest," saith he[5], "is God's priest, and not theirs:" whereby he is bound to call upon God, and not upon them.

Ps. vii, [9:] Rev. ii, [23:] Jer. xvii, [10:] 2 Chron. vi, [30.]

Lib. de Cura pro Mort. agenda, c. 13. [Is. lxiii, 16.]

De vera Relig. cap. 55.

Lib. xxii de Civ. Dei, cap. 10.

Thus you see, that the authority both of Scripture[m] and also of Augustine doth not permit that we should pray unto them. O that all men would studiously read and *seach the Scriptures!* then should they not be drowned in ignorance, but should easily perceive the truth, as well of this point of doctrine, as of all the rest. For there doth the Holy Ghost plainly teach us,

John v, [39.]

k and reins] and the reins 1623. l worshipping them] worshipping of them *from* 1582. m of Scripture] of the Scripture 1623.

pend. 55 D, cited again at the beginning of the Homily of Common Prayer and Sacraments.

2 Oratio cordis est, non labiorum. *Isid. Hispal. Sentent.* III, 7; *Opp. p.* 460 A, *ed. Colon.* 1617.

3 Isaias Propheta dicit, *Tu es enim Pater noster, quia Abraham nescivit nos, et Israel non cognovit nos.* Si tanti Patriarchae quid erga populum ex his procreatum ageretur ignoraverunt, quibus Deo credentibus populus ipse de illorum stirpe promissus est, quomodo mortui vivorum rebus atque actibus cognoscendis adjuvandisque miscentur? *Augustin. de Cura pro Mortuis gerenda,* § 16; *Opp.* VI, 526 D.

4 Non sit nobis religio cultus hominum mortuorum. . . . Honorandi ergo sunt propter imitationem, non adorandi propter religionem. *Augustin. de Vera Religione,* § 108; *Opp.* I, 786 B.

5 See *Augustin. de Civ. Dei,* XXII, 10, cited before, p. 188, n. 18.

that Christ is our only mediator and intercessor with God, and that we must seek and run to no other[n]. *If any man sinneth,* saith St. John, *we have an advocate with the Father, Jesus Christ the righteous; and he is the propitiation for our sins.* (1 John ii, [1, 2.]) St. Paul also saith, *There is one God, and one mediator between God and man, even the man Jesus Christ.* (1 Tim. ii, [5.]) Whereunto agreeth the testimony of our Saviour himself, witnessing[η] that *no man cometh to the Father, but only by him,* who is *the way, the truth, the life,* (η John xiv, [6.]) yea, and *the* only *door*[θ] whereby we must enter into the kingdom of heaven, (θ John x, [9.]) because God is pleased[ι] in no other but in him. (ι Matt. xvii, [5.]) For which cause also he crieth and calleth unto us, that we should come unto him, saying[κ], *Come unto me, all ye that labour and be heavy laden, and I shall refresh you.* (κ Matt. xi, [28.]) Would Christ have us so necessarily come unto him? and shall we most unthankfully leave him, and run unto other? This is even that which God so greatly complaineth of by his Prophet Jeremy, saying, *My people have committed two great offences; they have forsaken me the fountain of the waters of life, and have digged to themselves broken pits, that can hold no water.* ([Jer. ii, 13.]) Is not that man, think you, unwise that will run for water to a little brook, when he may as well go to the head spring? Even so may his wisdom be justly suspected that will flee unto Saints in time of necessity, when he may boldly and without fear declare his grief and direct his prayer unto the Lord himself.

If God were strange, or dangerous to be talked withal, then might we justly draw back, and seek to some other. But *the Lord*[λ] *is nigh unto them*[o] *that call upon him in* faith and *truth:* (λ Ps. cxliv [cxlv, 18.]) and *the prayer*[μ] *of the humble and meek hath always pleased him*[6]. (μ Judith ix.) What if we be sinners? shall we not therefore pray unto God? or shall we despair to obtain any thing at his hands? Why did Christ then teach us to ask forgiveness of our sins, saying, *And forgive us our trespasses, as we forgive them that trespass against us?* ([Matt. vi, 12.]) Shall we think that the Saints are more merciful in hearing sinners than God? David saith, that *the Lord is full of compassion and mercy, slow to anger, and of great kindness.* (Ps. ciii, [8.]) St. Paul saith, that *he is rich in mercy towards*[p] *all them that call upon him.* (Ephes. ii, [4: Rom. x, 12.]) And he himself by the mouth of his Prophet Esay saith, *For a little while have I forsaken thee, but* (Is. liv, [7, 8.])

[n] must seek and run to no other] must seek and run to another 1582, must not seek and run to another 1587, 1595, 1623. [o] unto them] unto all them *from* 1582. [p] towards] toward *from* 1582.

6 Humilium et mansuetorum semper tibi placuit deprecatio. *Judith* IX, 16, *Vulg.*

with great compassion will I gather thee: for a moment in mine anger I have hid my face from thee, but with everlasting mercy have I had[q] *compassion upon thee.* Therefore the sins of any man ought not to withhold him from praying unto the Lord his God; but, if he be truly penitent and steadfast in faith, let him assure himself that the Lord will be merciful unto him and hear his prayers.

O but I dare not (will some man say) trouble God at all times with my prayers: we see that in kings' houses, and courts of princes, men cannot be admitted, unless they first use the help and mean of some special nobleman, to come unto the speech of the king, and to obtain the thing that they would have. To this reason doth St. Ambrose answer very well, writing upon the first chapter to the Romans. "Therefore," saith he[7], "we use to go unto the king by officers and noblemen, because the king is a mortal man, and knoweth not to whom he may commit the government of the commonwealth. But to have God our friend, from whom nothing is hid, we need not any helper that should further us with his good word, but only a devout and godly mind." And, if it be so, that we need one to intreat for us, why may we not content ourselves with that *one Mediator*[v], *which is at the right hand of God* the Father, and there *liveth for ever to make intercession for us?* As the blood of Christ did redeem us on the cross, and cleanse us from our sins, even so it is now *able to save all them that come unto God* by it. For Christ, sitting in heaven, *hath*[ξ] *an everlasting priesthood*, and always prayeth to his Father for them that be penitent, obtaining by virtue of his wounds, which are evermore in the sight of God, not only perfect remission of our sins, but also all other necessaries that we lack in this world: so that his only[r] mediation[s] is sufficient in heaven, and needeth no other's to help him.

Ambros. super cap. i. Rom.

v [1 Tim. ii, 5; Rom. viii, 34:] Heb. vii, [25.]

ξ [Heb. vii, 24; ix, 12, 24; x, 12.]

Why then do we pray one for another in this life? some man perchance will here demand. Forsooth we are willed so to do by the express commandment[o] both of Christ and his disciples, to declare therein, as well the faith that we have in

o Matt. [v, 44;] vi, [9–13:] James v, [16:] Col. iii, [3:] 1 Tim. ii, [1, 2.]

q have I had] I have had 1623. r his only] this only *from* 1582. s mediation] mediator *from* 1563 B.

7 Nam et ideo ad regem per tribunos aut comites itur, quia homo utique est rex, et nescit quibus debeat rempublicam credere. Ad Deum autem, quem utique nihil latet, (omnium enim merita novit,) promerendum suffragatore non opus est, sed mente devota. *Hilar. Diac. Comment. in Epist. ad Rom.* 1, 22; *Ambros. Opp.* II *Append.* 33 A.

Christ towards God, as also the mutual charity that we bear one towards another, in that we pity our brother's case, and make our humble petition to God for him. But, that we should pray unto Saints, neither have we any commandment in all the Scripture, nor yet example which we may safely follow. So that, being done without authority of God's word, it lacketh the ground of faith, and therefore[π] cannot be acceptable before God. *For*[ρ] *whatsoever is not of faith is sin:* and the Apostle saith[σ], that *faith cometh by hearing, and hearing by the word of God.*

[π] Heb. xi, [6.] [ρ] Rom. xiv, [23.] [σ] Rom. x, [17.]

Yet thou wilt object further, that the Saints in heaven do pray for us, and that their prayer proceedeth of an earnest charity that they have towards their brethren on earth. Whereto it may be well answered, first, that no man knoweth whether they do pray for us, or no. And, if any will go about to prove it by the nature of charity, concluding that, because they did pray for men on earth, therefore they do much more the same now in heaven; then may it be said by the same reason, that as oft as we do weep on earth they do also weep in heaven, because while they lived in this world it is most certain and sure they did so. As for[t] that place which is written in the Apocalypse[τ], namely, that the angel did offer up the prayers of the saints upon the golden altar, it is properly meant, and ought properly to be understood, of those saints that are yet living on earth, and not of them that are dead; otherwise what need were it that the angel should offer up their prayers, being now in heaven before the face of Almighty God? But, admit the Saints do pray for us, yet do we not know how, whether specially for them which call upon them, or else generally for all men, wishing well to every man alike. If they pray specially for them which call upon them, then it is like they hear our prayers, and also know our hearts' desire. Which thing to be false, it is already proved, both by the Scriptures, and also by the authority of Augustine.

[τ] [Rev. viii, 3, 4.]

Let us not therefore put our trust or confidence in the Saints or Martyrs that be dead. Let us not call upon them, nor desire help at their hands: but let us always lift up our hearts to God in the name of his dear Son Christ; for whose sake as God hath promised to hear our prayers, so[u] he will truly perform it. Invocation is a thing proper unto God: which if we attribute unto the Saints, it soundeth to their reproach, neither can they well

[t] As for] And for *from* 1563 C, *except* 1563 E. [u] prayers, so] prayer, so *from* 1563 B.

bear it at our hands. When Paul had healed a certain lame man, which was impotent in his feet, at Lystra[υ], the people would have done sacrifice to him and Barnabas; who, renting their clothes, refused it, and exhorted them to worship the true God. Likewise in the Revelation[φ], when St. John fell before the angel's feet to worship him, the angel would not permit him to do it, but commanded him that he should *worship God.* Which examples declare unto us, that the saints and angels in heaven will not have us do[x] any honour unto them that is due and proper unto God. He only is our Father; he only is omnipotent; he only knoweth and understandeth all things; he only can help us at all times and in all places; *he suffereth*[χ] *the sun to shine upon the good and the bad; he feedeth the young ravens that cry unto him; he saveth both man and beast; he will not that any one hair of our head shall perish,* but is always ready to help and preserve all them that put their trust in him, according as he hath promised, saying[ψ], *Before they call, I will answer; and whiles they speak, I will hear.* Let us not therefore any thing mistrust his goodness; let us not fear to come before the throne of his mercy; let us not seek the aid and help of Saints; but *let us come boldly*[ω] ourselves, nothing doubting but God for Christ's sake, *in whom he is well pleased*[α], will hear us without a spokesman, and accomplish our desire in all such things as shall be agreeable to his most holy will. So saith Chrysostom[8], an ancient doctor of the Church; and so must we steadfastly believe, not because he saith it, but much more because it is the doctrine of our Saviour Christ himself, who hath promised[β], that if we pray to the Father in his name we shall certainly be heard, both to the relief of our necessities, and also to the salvation of our souls, which he hath purchased unto us, *not with gold or silver, but with his precious blood*[γ] shed once for all upon the cross.

To him therefore with the Father and the Holy Ghost, three Persons and one God, be all honour, praise, and glory for ever and ever. Amen.

υ Acts xiv, [8–18.]
φ Rev. xix, [10; xxii, 8, 9.]
χ [Matt. v, 45: Ps. cxlvii, 9; xxxvi, 6: Luke xii, 7; xxi, 18.]
ψ Isai. lxv, [24.]
ω [Heb. iv, 16; x, 19–23.]
α [Matt. xvii, 5.]
Chrysost. vi Hom. de Profect. Evang.
β [John xiv, 13, 14; xv, 16; xvi, 23–27.]
γ [1 Pet. i, 18, 19.]

x us do] us to do *from* 1563 B.

8 Οὐ χρεία σοι μεσιτῶν ἐπὶ τοῦ Θεοῦ, οὐδὲ πολλῆς τῆς περιδρομῆς καὶ τοῦ κολακεῦσαι ἑτέρους· ἀλλὰ κἂν ἔρημος ᾖς, κἂν ἀπροστάτευτος, αὐτὸς διὰ σαυτοῦ παρακαλέσας τὸν Θεὸν ἐπιτεύξῃ πάντως. Chrysost. Hom. de Prof. Evang., Opp. III, 309 A.

THE THIRD PART OF THE HOMILY

OF PRAYER.[a]

YE were taught in the other part of this Sermon, unto whom ye ought to direct your prayers in time of need and necessity, that is to wit, not unto angels or saints, but unto the eternal and everliving God: who, because he is merciful, is always ready to hear us, when we call upon him in true and perfect faith; and, because he is omnipotent, he can easily perform and bring to pass the thing that we request to have at his hands. To doubt of his power, it were a plain point of infidelity, and clean against the doctrine of the Holy Ghost, which teacheth that he is all in all. And as touching his goodwill in this behalf, we have express testimonies in the Scripture[b], how that he will help us, and also *deliver*[α] us, if we *call upon him in time of trouble.* So that in both these respects we ought rather to call upon him than upon any other. Neither ought any man therefore to doubt to come boldly unto God, because he is a sinner. For *the Lord*, as the Prophet David saith[β], *is gracious and merciful; yea, his mercy and goodness endureth for ever.* He that sent his own Son into the world *to save sinners*[γ], will he not also hear sinners, if with a true penitent heart and a steadfast faith they pray unto him? Yes, *if*[δ] *we acknowledge our sins, God is faithful and just to forgive us our sins, and to cleanse us from all unrighteousness;* as we are plainly taught by the examples[ε] of David, Peter, Mary Magdalene, the Publican, and divers other. And, whereas we must needs use the help of some mediator and intercessor, let us content ourselves with him that is the true and only *Mediator of the New Testament*[ζ], namely, the Lord and Saviour Jesus Christ. For, as St. John saith, *if any man sin, we have an advocate with the Father, Jesus Christ the righteous, who is the propitiation for our sins.* And St. Paul in his first Epistle to Timothy saith, *There is one God, and one mediator between God and man, even the man Jesus Christ; who gave himself a ransom for all men, to be a testimony in due time.*

α Ps. l, [15.]
β Ps. [ciii, 8; cvii, 1.]
γ 1 Tim. i, [16: John iii, 17.]
δ 1 John i, [9.]
ε [2 Sam. xii, 13: Mark xvi, 7, 9: Luke xviii, 14: John xxi, 15–19.]
ζ [Heb. xii, 24.]
1 John ii, [1, 2.]
1 Tim. ii, [5, 6.]

Now, after this doctrine established, you shall be instructed

a OF PRAYER] CONCERNING PRAYER *from* 1567. b in the Scripture] in Scripture *from* 1563 B.

for what kind of things and what kind of persons ye ought to make your prayers unto God. It greatly behoveth all men, when they pray, to consider well and diligently with themselves what they ask and require at God's hands, lest, if they desire the thing[c] which they ought not, their petitions be made void and of none effect. There came on a time unto Agesilaus the king a certain importunate suitor, who requested him in a matter earnestly, saying, "Sir, and it please your grace, you did once promise me." "Truth," quoth the king, "if it be just that thou requirest, then I promised thee; otherwise I did only speak it, and not promise it." The man would not so be[d] answered at the king's hand, but, still urging him more and more, said, "It becometh a king to perform the least word he hath spoken, yea, if he should only beck with his head." "No more," saith the king, "than it behoveth one that cometh to a king to speak and ask those things which are rightful and honest." Thus the king cast off this unreasonable and importunate suitor.[1] Now, if so great consideration be to be had when we kneel before an earthly king, how much more ought to be had when we kneel before the heavenly King, who is only delighted with justice and equity, neither will admit any vain, foolish, or unjust petition! Therefore it shall be good and profitable throughly to consider and determine with ourselves, what things we may lawfully ask of God without fear of repulse, and also what kind of persons we are bound to commend unto God in our daily prayers.

Two things are chiefly to be respected in every good and godly man's prayer, his own necessity, and the glory of Almighty God. Necessity belongeth either outwardly to the body, or else inwardly to the soul. Which part of man, because it is much more precious and excellent than the other, therefore we ought first of all to crave such things as properly belong to the salvation thereof; as, the gift of repentance, the gift of faith, the gift of charity and good works, remission and forgiveness of sins, patience in adversity, lowliness in prosperity, and such other like *fruits of the Spirit*[ζ], as, *hope, love, joy, peace, long-suffering, gentleness, goodness, meekness, and temperancy;* which things God requireth of all them that profess themselves to be his children, saying unto them on this[e] wise[η], *Let your light so shine before men, that they may see your good works, and glorify*

ζ Gal. v, [22, 23: Rom. xv, 13.]

η Matt. v, [16.]

c the thing] that thing 1587, 1595, 1623. d so be] be so *from* 1582. e on this] in this *from* 1570.

1 See *Plutarch. Apophthegm. Lacon., Agesil. Magn.* IV, *p.* 208 C.

your Father which is in heaven. And in another place he also[f] saith[e], *Seek first the kingdom of God and his righteousness, and then all other things shall be given unto you.* Wherein he putteth us in mind, that our chief and greatest care ought to be for those things which pertain to the health and safeguard of the soul, because *we have here,* as the Apostle saith, *no continuing city, but do seek after another in the world to come.*

[e] Matt. vi, [33.] — Heb. xiii, [14.]

Now, when we have sufficiently prayed for things belonging to the soul, then may we lawfully, and with safe conscience, pray also for our bodily necessities, as meat, drink, clothing, health of body, deliverance out of prison, good luck in our daily affairs, and so forth, according as we shall have need. Whereof what better example can we desire to have than of Christ himself, who taught his disciples and all other Christian men first to pray for heavenly things, and afterward for earthly things, as is to be seen in that prayer[t] which he left unto his Church, commonly called the Lord's Prayer? In the third book of Kings and third chapter it is written, that *God appeared by night in a dream unto Salomon the king, saying, Ask of me whatsoever thou wilt, and I will give thee*[g]. Salomon made his humble prayer, and asked a wise and prudent heart, that might judge and understand what were good and what were ill, what were godly and what were ungodly, what were righteous and what were unrighteous in the sight of the Lord. *It pleased God wondrously that he had asked this thing. And God said unto him, Because thou hast requested this word, and hast not desired many days and long years upon the earth, neither abundance of riches and goods, nor yet the life of thine enemies which hate thee, but hast desired wisdom to sit in judgment, behold, I have done unto thee according to thy words; I have given thee a wise heart, full of knowledge and understanding, so that there was never none*[h] *like thee beforetime, neither shall be in time to come. Moreover, I have besides this given thee that which thou hast not required, namely, worldly wealth and riches, princely honour and glory, so that thou shalt therein also pass all kings that ever were.* Note in this[i] example how Salomon, being put to his choice to ask of God whatsoever he would, requested not vain and transitory things, but the high and heavenly treasures of wisdom; and that in so doing he obtaineth, as it were in recompense, both riches and honour. Wherein is given us to understand, that in

[t] Matt. vi, [9–13:] Luke xi, [2–4.] — [1 Kings iii, 5–13.]

[f] he also] also he *from* 1582. [g] give thee] give it thee *from* 1582. [h] never none] never any 1623. [i] Note in this] Note this *from* 1567.

our daily prayers we should chiefly and principally ask those things which concern the kingdom of God and the salvation of our own souls, nothing doubting but all other things shall, according to the promise of Christ, be given unto us.

But here we must take heed that we forget not that other end whereof mention was made before, namely, the glory of God. Which unless we mind and set before our eyes in making our prayers, we may not look to be heard or to receive any thing of the Lord. [Matt. xx, 20–23.] In the twentieth chapter of Matthew *the mother of the two sons of Zebedee came unto Jesus, worshipping him, and saying, Grant that my two sons may sit in thy kingdom, the one at thy*[k] *right hand, and the other at thy left hand.* In this petition she did not respect the glory of God, but plainly declared the ambition and vainglory of her own mind; for which cause she was also most worthily repelled and rebuked at the Lord's hand. In like manner we read in the Acts of one Simon Magus, [Acts viii, [18–20.]] a sorcerer, how that *he, perceiving that through laying on of the Apostles' hands the Holy Ghost was given, offered them money, saying, Give me also this power, that, on whomsoever I lay my hands, he may receive the Holy Ghost.* In making this request he sought not the honour and glory of God, but his own private gain and lucre, thinking to get great store of money by this feat; and therefore it was justly said unto him, *Thy money perish with thee, because thou thinkest that the gift of God may be obtained with money.* By these and such other examples we are taught, whensoever we make our prayers unto God, chiefly to respect the honour and glory of his Name. Whereof we have this general precept in the Apostle Paul: [1 Cor. x, [31:] Col. iii, [17.]] *Whether ye eat or drink, or whatsoever you*[l] *do, look that you*[m] *do it to the glory of God.* Which thing we shall best of all do, if we follow the example of our Saviour Christ, who, praying[κ] that the bitter cup of death might pass from him, would not therein have his own will fulfilled, but referred the whole matter to the good will and pleasure of his Father.

[κ Matt. xxvi, [39: Mark xiv, 36:] Luke xxii, [42.]]

And hitherto concerning those things that we may lawfully and boldly ask of God.

Now it followeth that we declare what kind of persons we are bound in conscience to pray for. St. Paul, writing to Timothy, exhorteth him to make [1 Tim. ii, [1, 2.]] *prayers and supplications for all men,* exempting none, of what degree or state soever they be. In

[k] one at thy] one on the 1582, one on thy 1623.
[l] whatsoever you] whatsoever ye *from* 1574.
[m] that you] that ye *from* 1582.

which place he maketh mention by name of *kings and rulers which are in authority*, putting us thereby to knowledge how greatly it concerneth the profit of the commonwealth to pray diligently for the higher powers. Neither is it without good cause, that he doth so often[λ] in all his Epistles crave the prayers of God's people for himself. For in so doing he declareth to the world how expedient and needful it is daily to call upon God for the ministers of his holy word and sacraments, that they *may have the door of utterance opened* unto them, that they may truly understand the Scriptures, that they may effectually preach the same unto the people, and bring forth the true fruits thereof to the example of all other. After this sort did the congregation continually pray[μ] for Peter at Hierusalem, and for Paul among the Gentiles, to the great encrease and furtherance of Christ's Gospel. And if we, following their good example herein, will study to do the like, doubtless it cannot be expressed how greatly we shall both help ourselves, and also please God.

[λ] Col. iv, [3, 4:] Rom. xv, [30–32:] 2 Thess. iii, [1, 2:] Eph. vi, [19, 20.]

[μ] Acts xii, [5: 2 Cor. i, 11: Phil. i, 19: Philem. 22.]

To discourse and run through all degrees of persons it were too long: therefore ye shall briefly take this one conclusion for all. Whomsoever we are bound by express commandment to love, for those also we are[n] bound in conscience to pray: but we are bound by express commandment to love all men as ourselves: therefore we are also bound to pray for all men even as well as if it were for ourselves, notwithstanding we know them to be our extreme and deadly enemies; for so doth our Saviour Christ plainly teach us in his holy Gospel[o], saying, *Love your enemies, bless them that curse you, do good to them that hate you, pray for them that persecute you, that ye may be the children of your Father which is in heaven.* And, as he taught his disciples, so did he practise himself in his lifetime, praying for his enemies upon the cross, and desiring his Father[ν] to forgive them, because they knew not what they did: as did also that holy and blessed Martyr Stephen[ξ], when he was cruelly stoned to death of the stubborn and stiffnecked Jews, to the example of all them that will truly and unfeignedly follow their Lord and Master Christ in this miserable and mortal life.

Matt. v, [44, 45.]

[ν] Luke xxiii, [34.]

[ξ] Acts vii, [60.]

Now to entreat of that question, whether we ought to pray for them that are departed out of this world, or no. Wherein if we will cleave only unto the word of God, then must we needs grant, that we have no commandment so to do. For the Scripture doth acknowledge but two places after this life, the one

[n] also we are] also are we *from* 1563 B.

[o] his holy Gospel] his Gospel *from* 1567.

proper to the elect and blessed of God, the other to the reprobate and damned souls; as may be well gathered by the parable of Lazarus[o] and the rich man. Which place St. Augustine expounding saith on this[p] wise[2]: "That which Abraham speaketh unto the rich man in Luke's Gospel, namely, that the just cannot go into those places where the wicked are tormented, what other things doth it signify but only this, that the just, by reason of God's judgment, which may not be revoked, can shew no deed of mercy in helping them which after this life are cast into prison *until they pay the uttermost farthing?*" These words, as they confound the opinion of helping the dead by prayer, so they do clean confute and take away the vain error of purgatory, which is grounded upon this saying[q] of the Gospel: *Thou shalt not depart thence, until thou hast paid the uttermost farthing.* Now doth St. Augustine say, that those men which are cast into prison after this life on that condition may in no wise be holpen, though we would help them never so much. And why? Because the sentence of God is unchangeable, and cannot be revoked again. Therefore let us not deceive ourselves, thinking that either we may help other, or other may help us by their good and charitable prayers in time to come. For, as the Preacher saith, *when the tree falleth, whether it be toward the south, or toward the north, in what place soever the tree falleth, there it lieth;* meaning thereby, that every mortal man dieth either in the state of salvation or damnation, according as the words of the Evangelist John do also plainly import, saying, *He that believeth on the Son of God hath eternal life; but he that believeth not on the Son shall never see life, but the wrath of God abideth upon him.* Where is then the third place, which they call purgatory? or where shall our prayers help and profit the dead? St. Augustine doth only acknowledge two places after this life, heaven and hell. As for the third place, he doth plainly deny that there is any such to be found in all Scripture[3].

[Margin: o Luke xvi, [19–26.] — Lib. ii Evang. Quaest. cap. 38. — [Matt. v, 26.] — Eccles. xi, [3.] — John iii, [36.] — Lib. v Hypognost.]

p on this] in this *from* 1570. q this saying] the saying 1623.

2 Quod autem dicit, ad ea loca in quibus torquentur impii justos, etiam si velint, non posse transire, quid aliud significat nisi post hanc vitam ita receptis in carcere ut non inde exeant *donec reddant novissimum quadrantem*, per incommutabilitatem divinae sententiae, nullum auxilium misericordiae posse praeberi a justis, etiam si eam velint praebere? *Augustin. Quaest. Evangel.* II, xxxviii, 3; *Opp.* III, *Par.* II, 265 A.

3 Primum enim locum fides catholicorum divina auctoritate *regnum* credit esse *coelorum*, unde, ut dixi, non baptizatus excipitur; secundum *gehennam*, ubi omnis apostata vel a Christi fide alienus aeterna supplicia experietur: tertium penitus ignoramus, imo nec esse

Chrysostom likewise is of this mind, that, unless we wash away our sins in this present world, we shall find no comfort afterward[4]. And St. Cyprian saith, that after death[5] "repentance and sorrow of pain shall be without fruit; weeping also shall be in vain, and prayer shall be to no purpose." Therefore he counselleth all men to make provision for themselves while they may, because, "when they are once departed out of this life, there is no place for repentance, nor yet for satisfaction." Let these and such other places be sufficient to take away the gross error of purgatory out of our heads; neither let us dream any more that the souls of the dead are anything at all holpen by our prayers: but, as the Scripture teacheth us, let us think that the soul of man, passing out of the body, goeth straightways either to heaven or else to hell, whereof the one needeth no prayer, and the other is without redemption.

Chrysost. in Heb. ii, Homil. iv.

Cyprian. contra Demetrianum.

The only purgatory wherein we must trust to be saved is the death and blood of Christ; which if we apprehend with a true and steadfast faith, it purgeth and cleanseth us from all our sins, even as well as if he were now hanging upon the cross. *The blood of Christ,* saith St. John, *hath cleansed us from all sin. The blood of Christ,* saith St. Paul[π], *hath purged our consciences from dead works to serve the living God.* Also in another place he saith[ρ], *We be sanctified* and made holy *by the offering up of the body of Jesus Christ,* done *once for all*[6]. Yea, he addeth more, saying[σ], *With* the *one oblation* of his blessed body and precious blood *he hath made perfect for ever and ever all them that are sanctified.* This then is that purgatory wherein all Christian men must put[r] their whole trust and confidence[s], nothing doubt-

1 John i, [7: Rev. i, 5.]

π Heb. ix, [14.]

ρ Heb. x, [10.]

σ Ibid. [14.]

r men must put] men put *from* 1582. s confidence] confidences *till* 1567.

in Scripturis sanctis inveniemus. *Incert. Auctor. Hypognost.* v, 5, *Augustin. Opp.* x *Append.* 40 B.

4 Οὐδὲ γὰρ οἷόν τε λοιπὸν εὑρεῖν τινα παραμυθίαν ἐκεῖ τὸν μὴ ἐν τῷ παρόντι βίῳ ἀπονιψάμενον τὰ ἡμαρτημένα. Chrysost. in Genes. Hom. v, Opp. IV, 33 D. The Homily cited in the margin contains nothing on this subject. Probably the passage intended is *In Epist. ad Hebr. Hom.* VII, *Opp.* XII, 75 B, C, 76 A, where Chrysostom distinguishes between "the throne of grace" (Heb. iv, 16) and the throne of judgment.

5 Erit tunc sine fructu poenitentia, dolor poenae [Erit tunc sine fructu poenitentiae dolor poenae *ed. Paris.* 1726], inanis ploratio, et inefficax deprecatio. In aeternam poenam sero credent qui in vitam aeternam credere noluerunt. Securitati igitur et vitae, dum licet, providete.... Quando istinc excessum fuerit, nullus jam poenitentiae locus est, nullus satisfactionis effectus. Hic vita aut amittitur aut tenetur: hic saluti aeternae cultu Dei et fructu fidei providetur. *Cyprian. ad Demetrian. pp.* 195, 196, *ed. Oxon., p.* 224 *ed. Paris.*

6 Ἐν ᾧ θελήματι ἡγιασμένοι ἐσμὲν οἱ διὰ τῆς προσφορᾶς τοῦ σώματος τοῦ Ἰησοῦ Χριστοῦ ἐφάπαξ. In qua voluntate sanctificati sumus per oblationem corporis Jesu Christi semel. *Vulg.*

ing but, if they truly repent them of their sins, and die in perfect faith, that then they shall forthwith pass from death to life. If this kind of purgation will not serve them, let them never hope to be released by other men's prayers, though they should continue therein unto the world's end. He that cannot be saved by faith in Christ's blood, how shall he look to be delivered by man's intercessions? Hath God more respect to man on earth, than he hath to Christ in heaven? *If any man sin*, saith St. John, *we have an advocate with the Father, even Jesus Christ the righteous, and he is the propitiation for our sins.* But we must take heed that we call upon this Advocate while we have space given us in this life, lest, when we are once dead, there be no hope of salvation left unto us. For, as every man sleepeth with his own cause, so every man shall rise again with his own cause.[7] And look, in what state he dieth, in the same state he shall be also judged[8], whether it be to salvation or damnation.

1 John ii, [1, 2.]

Let us not therefore dream either of purgatory, or of prayer for the souls of them that be dead; but let us earnestly and diligently pray for them which are expressly commanded in holy Scripture, namely, for kings and rulers, for ministers of God's holy word and sacraments, for the saints of this world, otherwise called the faithful, to be short, for all men living, be they never so great enemies to God and his people, as Jews, Turks, pagans, infidels, heretics, &c. Then shall we truly fulfil the commandment of God in that behalf, and plainly declare ourselves to be the true *children of our heavenly Father, which suffereth*[t] *the sun to shine upon the good and the bad, and the rain to fall upon the just and the unjust.* For which and all other benefits most abundantly bestowed upon mankind from the beginning let us give him hearty thanks, as we are most bound, and praise his Name for ever and ever. Amen.

[Matt. v, 45.]

[t] which suffereth] who suffereth 1623.

7 Unusquisque hominum cum causa sua dormit, cum causa sua surgit. *Augustin. in Joan. Evang.* XI, 11, *Tractat.* XLIX, § 9; *Opp.* III, 623 B.

8 In quo enim quemque invenerit suus novissimus dies, in hoc eum comprehendet mundi novissimus dies: quoniam, qualis in die isto quisque moritur, talis in die illo judicabitur. *Augustin. ad Hesych. Epist.* CXCIX (*al.* 80), § 2; *Opp.* II, 743 B.]

AN HOMILY

OF THE PLACE AND TIME OF PRAYER.

GOD, through his almighty power, wisdom, and goodness, created in the beginning heaven and earth, the sun, the moon, the stars, the fowls of the air, the beasts of the earth, the fishes in the sea, and all other creatures, for the use and commodity of man; whom also he had created to his own image and likeness, and given him the use and government over them all, to the end he should use them in such sort as he had given him in charge and commandment, and also that he should declare himself thankful and kind for all those benefits so liberally and so graciously bestowed upon him, utterly without any deserving on his behalf. And, although we ought at all times and in all places to have in remembrance and to be thankful to our gracious Lord, according as it is written, *I will magnify the Lord at all times*, and again, *Wheresoever the Lord beareth rule, O my soul, praise the Lord;* Ps. xxxiii [xxxiv, 1;] cii [ciii, 22.] yet it appeareth to be God's good will and pleasure, that we should at special times and in special places gather ourselves together, to the intent his name might be renowmed [a] and his glory set forth in the congregation and the assembly [b] of his saints.

As concerning the time which Almighty God hath appointed his people to assemble together solemnly, it doth appear by the Fourth Commandment of God. *Remember*, saith God, *that thou keep holy the Sabbath day.* [Exod. xx, 8.] Upon the which day, as is plain in the Acts of the Apostles, the people accustomably resorted together, and heard diligently the Law and the Prophets read among them. Acts xiii, [14, 15, 42.] And, albeit this Commandment of God doth not bind Christian people so straitly to observe and keep the utter ceremonies of the Sabbath day as it was given unto the Jews, as touching the forbearing of work and labour in time of great necessity, and as touching the precise keeping of the seventh day after the manner of the Jews; (for we keep now the first day, which is our Sunday, and make that our Sabbath, that is, our day of rest, in the honour of our Saviour Christ, who as

[a] renowmed] renowned 1582. [b] and the assembly] and assembly *from* 1567.

upon that day rose from death, conquering the same most triumphantly;) yet, notwithstanding, whatsoever is found in the Commandment appertaining to the law of nature, as a thing most godly, most just, and needful for the setting forth of God's glory, it ought to be retained and kept of all good Christian people. And therefore by this Commandment we ought to have a time, as one day in a week[c], wherein we ought to rest, yea, from our lawful and needful works. For, like as it appeareth by this Commandment, that no man in the six days ought to be slothful or idle, but diligently to labour in that state wherein God hath set him, even so God hath given express charge to all men[a], that upon the Sabbath day, which is now our Sunday, they should cease from all weekly and workday labour; to the intent that, like as God himself wrought six days, and rested the seventh, and blessed and sanctified it, and consecrated it to quietness and rest from labour, even so God's obedient people should use the Sunday holily, and rest from their common and daily business, and also give themselves wholly to heavenly exercises of God's true religion and service. So that God doth not only command the observation of this holy day, but also by his own example doth stir and provoke us to diligent[d] keeping of the same. Good natural children will not only become obedient to the commandment of their parents, but also have a diligent eye to their doings, and gladly follow the same. So, if we will be the children of our heavenly Father, we must be careful to keep the Christian Sabbath day, which is the Sunday; not only for that it is God's express commandment, but also to[e] declare ourselves to be loving children in following the example of our gracious Lord and Father. Thus it may plainly appear, that God's will and commandment was to have a solemn time and standing day in the week, wherein the people should come together and have in remembrance his wonderful benefits, and to render him thanks for them, as appertaineth to loving, kind, and obedient people.

a [Gen. ii, 2, 3: Exod. xvi, 22-30; xx, 11.]

This example and commandment of God the godly Christian people began to follow immediately after the ascension of our Lord Christ, and began to choose them a standing day in the week[f] to come together in; yet not the seventh day, which the Jews kept, but the Lord's day, the day of the Lord's resurrection, the day after the seventh day, which is the first of[g] the

c in a week] in the week *from* 1574. d to diligent] to the diligent *from* 1571. e but also to] but to 1563 A. f in the week] of the week *from* 1563 EF. g first of] first day of 1623.

week. Of the which day mention is made by St. Paul on this wise: *In the first day of the sabbath*[1] *let every man lay up what he thinketh good,* meaning for the poor. By *the first day of the sabbath* is meant our Sunday, which is the first day after the Jews' seventh day. And in the Apocalypse it is more plain, where as St. John saith, *I was in the Spirit upon the Sunday*[h][2]. Sithence which time God's people hath always in all ages without any gainsaying used to come together upon the Sunday, to celebrate and honour the Lord's blessed Name, and carefully to keep that day in holy rest and quietness, both men, women[i], child, servant, and stranger. For the transgression and breach of which day God hath declared himself much to be grieved, as it may appear[β] by him who for gathering of sticks on the Sabbath day was stoned to death.

1 Cor. xvi, [2.]

Rev. i, [10.]

β Numb. xv, [32-36.]

But, alas, all these notwithstanding, it is lamentable to see the wicked boldness of those that will be counted God's people, who pass nothing at all of keeping and hallowing the Sunday. And these people are of two sorts. The one sort, if they have any business to do, though there be no extreme need, they must not spare for the Sunday; they must ride and journey on the Sunday; they must drive and carry on the Sunday; they must row and ferry on the Sunday; they must buy and sell on the Sunday; they must keep markets and fairs on the Sunday: finally, they use all days alike; workdays and holy days are all[k] one. The other sort yet is[l] worse. For, although they will not travail nor labour on the Sunday as they do on the week day, yet they will not rest in holiness, as God commandeth; but they rest in ungodliness and in filthiness[m], prancing in their pride, pranking and pricking, pointing and painting themselves, to be gorgeous and gay; they rest in excess and superfluity, in gluttony and drunkenness, like rats and swine; they rest in brawling and railing, in quarrelling and fighting; they rest in wantonness, in toyish talking, in filthy fleshliness; so that it doth too evidently appear that God is more dishonoured and the devil better served on the Sunday than upon all the days in the week beside[n]. And, I assure you, the beasts, which are commanded to rest on the Sunday, honour God better than this

h upon the Sunday] upon the Lord's day 1623. i men, women] man, woman *from* 1567. k are all] all are *from* 1567. l sort yet is] sort is *from* 1567. m and in filthiness] and filthiness *from* 1567. n beside] besides *from* 1582.

1 Κατὰ μίαν σαββάτων. Per unam sabbathi. *Vulg.*

2 Ἐν τῇ Κυριακῇ ἡμέρᾳ. In Dominica die. *Vulg.*

kind of people; for they offend not God, they break not their holy day[o]. Wherefore, O ye people of God, lay your hands upon your hearts; repent and amend this grievous and dangerous wickedness; stand in awe of the commandment of God; gladly follow the example of God himself; be not disobedient to the godly order of Christ's Church, used and kept from the Apostles' time until this day; fear the displeasure and just plagues of Almighty God, if ye be negligent and forbear not labouring and travailing on the Sabbath day or Sunday, and do not resort together to celebrate and magnify God's blessed Name in quiet holiness and godly reverence.

Now concerning the place where the people of God ought to resort together, and where especially they ought to celebrate and sanctify the Sabbath day, that is, the Sunday, the day of holy rest. That place is called God's temple or the church, because the company and congregation of God's people, which is properly called the Church, doth there assemble themselves on the days appointed for such assemblies and meetings. And, forasmuch as Almighty God hath appointed a special time to be honoured in, it is very meet, godly, and also necessary, that there should be a place appointed where these people should meet and resort to serve their gracious God and merciful Father.

γ [Exod. xxv–xxxi, xxxv–xl.]

Truth it is, the holy Patriarchs for a great number of years had neither temple nor church to resort unto. The cause was, they were not stayed in any place, but were in a continual peregrination and wandering, that they could not conveniently build any church. But so soon as God had delivered his people from their enemies, and set them in some liberty in the wilderness, he set them up[γ] a costly and a curious tabernacle, which was as it were the parish church, a place to resort unto of the whole multitude, a place to have his sacrifices made in, and other observances and rites to be used in. Furthermore, after that God, according to the truth of his promise, had placed and quietly settled his people in the land of Canaan, now called Jewry, he commanded[δ] a great and a magnificent[p] temple to be builded by king Salomon, as seldom the like hath been seen; a temple so decked and adorned, so gorgeously garnished, as was meet and expedient for people of that time, which would be allured and stirred with nothing so much as with such outward goodly gay things. This was now the temple of God, indued also with

δ [1 Chron. xxii.]

o holy day] holy days 1623.

p and a magnificent] and magnificent 1582, 1623

many gifts and sundry promises: this was the parish church[q], and the mother church of all Jewry: here was God honoured and served: hither was the whole realm of all the Israelites bound to come at three[ε] solemn feasts in the year, to serve their Lord God here. But let us proceed further. In the time of Christ and his Apostles there was[r] yet no temples nor churches for Christian men; for why[3] they were always for the most part in persecution, vexation, and trouble, so that there could be no liberty nor license obtained for that purpose. Yet God delighted much that they should often resort together in a place, and therefore after his ascension[ζ] they remained together in an upper chamber. Sometime[η] they entered into the temple, sometime into the synagogues; sometime they were[s] in prisons, sometime[t] in their houses, sometime in the[u] fields, &c. And this continued so long till the faith of Christ Jesu[x] began to multiply in a great part of the world. Now, when divers realms were established in God's true religion, and God had given them peace and quietness, then began kings, noblemen, and the people also, stirred up with a godly zeal and ferventness, to build up temples and churches, whither the people might resort, the better to do their duty towards God, and to keep holy their Sabbath day, the day of rest. And to these temples have the Christians customably used to resort from time to time, as unto meet places where they might with common consent praise and magnify God's Name, yielding him thanks for the benefits that he daily poureth upon them both mercifully and abundantly; where they might also hear his holy word read, expounded, and preached sincerely, and receive his holy sacraments ministered unto them duly and purely.

ε [Exod. xxiii, 14–17: Deut. xvi, 1–17: 2 Chron. viii, 12, 13.]

ζ [Acts i, 13, 14.]

η [Acts ii, 46; xii, 12; xiii, 5, 14; xvi, 13, 25; xxi, 5.]

True it is, that the chief and special temples of God, wherein he hath greatest pleasure, and most delighteth[y] to dwell in, are[z] the bodies and minds of true Christians and the chosen people of God, according to the doctrine of holy Scriptures declared by St. Paul. *Know ye not*, saith he, *that ye be the temple of God, and that the Spirit of God doth dwell in you? The temple of God is holy, which ye are.* And again in the same Epistle: *Know*

1 Cor. iii, [16, 17.]

1 Cor. vi, [19.]

q was the parish church] was the public church 1623. r there was] there were 1623. s sometime they were] sometimes they were 1623. t prisons, sometime] prison, sometimes *from* 1563 B. u sometime in the] sometimes in the *from* 1563 G. x Jesu] Jesus *from* 1567. y delighteth] delight *till* 1567. *See before, p.* 154, *l.* 5. z dwell in, are] dwell, are *from* 1563 EF.

3 for why: because, for. "Forwhy: Quoniam, Quia, Nam." *Promptuarium Parvulorum Clericorum, ed. Wynkyn de Worde* 1516. "This word *enim* . . . signifieth *cause thus, forwhi.*" *Prologue to Wycliffite Version of the Bible, Vol.* 1, *p.* 60.

ye not that your body is the temple of the Holy Ghost dwelling in you, whom you have given you of God, and that ye be not your own? Yet, this notwithstanding, God doth allow the material temple made of[a] lime and stone (so oft as his people do come[b] together into it to praise his holy Name) to be his house, and the place where he hath promised to be present, and where he will hear the prayers of them that call upon him. The which thing both Christ and his Apostles, with all the rest of holy[c] fathers, do sufficiently declare by this; that, albeit they certainly knew that their prayers were heard in what place soever they made them, though it were in caves, in woods, and in deserts, yet, so oft as they could conveniently, they resorted to the material temples, there with the rest of the congregation to join in prayer and true worship.

Wherefore, dearly beloved, you that profess yourselves to be Christians, and glory in that name, disdain not to follow the example of your Master Christ, whose scholars (you say) ye be[d]; shew you to be like them whose schoolmates you take upon you to be, that is, the Apostles and disciples of Christ. Lift up[θ] *pure hands*[4] with clean hearts in all places and at all times. But do the same in the temples and churches upon the Sabbath days also. Our godly predecessors, and the ancient fathers of the primitive Church, spared not their goods to build churches; no, they spared not to venture[e] their lives in time of persecution, and to hazard their blood, that they might assemble themselves together in churches. And shall we spare a little labour to come unto churches[f]? Shall neither their example, nor our duty, nor the commodities that thereby should come unto us, move us? If we will declare ourselves to have the fear of God, if we will shew ourselves true Christians, if we will be the followers of Christ our Master, and of those godly fathers that have lived before us and now have received the reward of true and faithful Christians, we must both willingly, earnestly, and reverently come unto the material churches and temples to pray, as unto fit places appointed for that use; and that upon the Sabbath day, as at most convenient time for God's people to cease from bodily and worldly business, to give themselves to holy rest and godly contemplation, pertaining to the service of

θ [1 Tim. ii, 8: Heb. x, 22.]

[a] made of] made with *from* 1567. [b] people do come] people come *from* 1567. [c] of holy] of the holy *from* 1563 B. [d] ye be] you be *from* 1582. [e] to venture] *omitted after* 1563. [f] unto churches] to churches *from* 1567.

4 'Επαίροντας ὁσίους χεῖρας. 1 Tim. II, 8. Levantes puras manus. *Vulg.*

Almighty God: whereby we may reconcile ourselves to God, be partakers of his reverent[g] Sacraments, and be devout hearers of his holy word; so to be established in faith to Godward, in hope against all adversity, and in charity toward our neighbours; and thus, running our course as good Christian people, we may at the last attain the reward of everlasting glory through[h] the merits of our Saviour Jesus Christ. To whom with the Father and the Holy Ghost be all honour and glory. Amen.

[g] reverent] holy 1623.

[h] through] thorough 1563 A.

THE SECOND PART OF THE HOMILY

OF THE PLACE AND TIME OF PRAYER.

IT hath been declared unto you, good Christian people, in the former Sermon read unto you, at what time and into what place ye shall come together to praise God. Now I entend to set before your eyes, first, how zealous and desirous ye ought to be to come to your church, secondly, how sore God is grieved with them that do despise or little regard to come to the church upon the holy restful day.

It may well appear by the Scriptures[α], that many of the godly Israelites, being now in captivity for their sins among the Babylonians, full often wished and desired to be again at Hierusalem. And at their return through God's goodness, though many of the people were negligent, yet the fathers[β] were marvellous devout to build up the temple, that God's people might repair thither to honour him. And King David, when he was a banished man out of his country, out of Hierusalem the holy city, from the sanctuary, from the holy place, and from the tabernacle of God, what desire, what ferventness was in him towards[a] that holy place! what wishings and prayers made he to God to be a dweller in the house of the Lord! *One thing*, saith he[γ], *have I asked of the Lord, and this will I still crave, that I may resort and have my dwelling in the house of the Lord so long as I live.* Again[δ], *O how I joyed when I heard those[b] words, We shall go into the Lord's house.* And in other places of the Psalms he declareth for what entent and purpose he hath such a fervent desire to enter into the temple and church of the Lord. *I will fall down*, saith he[ε], *and worship in the holy temple of the Lord.* Again[ζ], *I have appeared in thy holy place, that I might behold thy might and power, that I might behold thy glory and magnificence*[1]. Finally he saith[η], *I will shew forth thy Name to my brethren, I will praise thee in the middes[c] of the congregation.* Why then had David such an earn-

α [Ps. cxxxvii: Dan. ix.]
β [Ezra i, iii, v, vi: Hagg. i.]
γ Ps. xxvi [xxvii, 4.]
δ Ps. cxxi [cxxii, 1.]
ε Ps. cxxxvii, [cxxxviii, 2.]
ζ Ps. lxiii, [2.]
η Ps. xxi [xxii, 22.]

a towards] toward *from* 1582. b those] these *from* 1563 G. c middes] middest *from* 1582.

1 Sic in sancto apparui tibi, ut viderem virtutem tuam et gloriam tuam. *Ps.* LXII, 3, *Vulg.*

est desire to the house of God? First, because there he would worship and honour God. Secondly, there he would have a contemplation and a sight of the power and glory of God. Thirdly, there he would praise the Name of God with all the congregation and company of the people. These considerations of this blessed Prophet of God ought to stir up and kindle in us the like earnest desire to resort to the church, especially upon the holy restful days; there to do our duties and to serve God; there to call to remembrance how God, even of his mere mercy and for the glory of his Name sake, worketh mightily to conserve us in health and wealth[d] and godliness, and mightily preserveth us from the assaults and rages of our fierce and cruel enemies; and there joyfully in the number of his faithful people to praise and magnify the Lord's holy Name. Set before your eyes also that ancient father Simeon, of whom the Scripture speaketh thus, to his great commendation and an encouragement for us to do the like. *There was a man at Hierusalem,* Luke ii, [25-38.] *named Simeon, a just man, fearing God: he came by the Spirit of God into the temple, and was told by the same Spirit, that he should not die before he saw the Anointed of the Lord.* In the temple his promise was fulfilled; in the temple he saw Christ, and *took him in his arms;* in the temple he brast[e] out into the mighty praise of God his Lord. *Anna also, a*[f] *prophetess,* Anna. *an old widow, departed not out*[g] *of the temple, giving herself to prayer and fasting day and night: and she, coming about the same time,* was likewise inspired, and *confessed, and spake of the Lord to all them who*[h] *looked for the redemption of Israel.* This blessed man and this blessed woman were not disappointed of wonderful fruit, commodity, and comfort, which God sent them by their diligent resorting to God's holy temple.

Now ye shall hear how grievously God hath been offended with his people, for that they passed so little upon his holy temple, and foully either despised or abused the same. Which thing may plainly appear by the notable plagues and punishments which God hath laid upon his people, especially in this, that he stirred up their adversaries horribly to beat down, and utterly to destroy, his holy temple with a perpetual desolation. Alas, how many churches, countries, and kingdoms of Christian people have of late years been plucked down, overrun[i], and left waste, with grievous and intolerable tyranny and

[d] health and wealth] health, wealth *from* 1563 D. [e] brast] brake 1623. [f] Anna also, a] Anna, a *from* 1563 D. [g] departed not out] departed out 1623. [h] them who] them that *from* 1571. [i] down, overrun] down and overrun 1623.

cruelty of the enemy of our Lord Christ, the great Turk, who hath so universally scourged the Christians, that never the like was heard or read[j] of! Above thirty years past the great Turk had overrun, conquered, and brought into his dominion and subjection twenty Christian kingdoms, turning away the people from the faith of Christ, poisoning them with the devilish religion of wicked Mahomet, and either destroying their churches utterly, or filthily abusing them with their[k] wicked and detestable errors. And now this great Turk, this bitter and sharp scourge of God's vengeance, is even at hand in this part of Christendom, in Europe, at the borders of Italy, at the borders of Germany, greedily gaping to devour us, to overrun our country, to destroy our churches also, unless we repent our sinful life, and resort more diligently to the church to honour God, to learn his blessed will, and to fulfil the same[2].

The Jews in their time provoked justly the vengeance of God, for that partly they abused his holy temple with the detestable idolatry of the heathen, and superstitious vanities of their own inventions, contrary to God's commandment; partly they resorted unto it as hypocrites, spotted, imbrued, and foully defiled with all kind of wickedness and sinful life; partly many of them passed little upon the holy temple, and forced[l] not[3] whether they came thither or no. And have not the Christians of late days, and even in our days also, in like manner provoked the displeasure and indignation of Almighty God, partly, because they have profaned and defiled their churches with heathenish and Jewish abuses, with images and idols, with numbers of altars too too[m][4] superstitiously and intolerably abused, with gross abusing and filthy corrupting of the Lord's holy Supper, the blessed Sacrament of his Body and Blood, with an infinite number of toys and trifles of their own devices, to make a goodly[n] outward shew, and to deface the homely[o], simple, and sincere religion of Christ Jesus? Partly, they resort to the church like hypocrites, full of all iniquity and sinful life, having a vain and a dangerous[p] fancy and persuasion, that if they

[j] heard or read] heard and read *till* 1574. [k] with their] *so in all.* [l] forced] cared 1623. [m] too too] toto 1563 A–E; to to 1563 G *and* H, 1567. [n] a goodly] a godly 1563 EF–1574. [o] homely] plain 1623. [p] and a dangerous] and dangerous *from* 1567.

2 On the alarm caused by the progress of the Turks, see before, p. 210, n. 68.

3 forced not: thought it of no force or importance. See before, p. 163, n. 4.

4 too too: a reduplication for the sake of emphasis, which was still used in the latter part of the seventeenth century. See *Todd on Spenser, Faerie Queene*, III, iv, 26.

come to the church, besprinkle them with holy water, hear a mass, and be blessed with the chalice[5], though they understand not one word of the whole service, nor feel one motion of repentance in their hearts, all is well, all is sure. Fie upon such mocking and blaspheming of God's holy ordinance. Churches were made for another purpose, that is, to resort thither and to serve God truly, there to learn his blessed will, there to call upon his mighty Name, there to use the holy Sacraments, there to travail how to be in charity with thy neighbour, there to have thy poor and needy neighbour in remembrance, from thence to depart better and more godly than thou camest thither. Finally, God's vengeance hath been and is daily provoked, because much wicked people pass nothing to resort to the church, either for that they are so sore blinded, that they understand nothing of God and godliness, and care not with devilish example to offend their neighbours; or else for that they see the church altogether scoured of such gay gazing sights as their gross fantasy was greatly delighted with, because they see the false religion abandoned and the true restored, which seemeth an unsavoury thing to their unsavoury taste; as may appear by this, that a woman said to her neighbour, Alas, gossip, what shall we now do at church, since all the saints are taken away, since all the goodly sights we were wont to have are gone, since we cannot hear the like piping, singing, chanting, and playing upon the organs, that we could before? But, dearly beloved, we ought greatly to rejoice and give God thanks, that our churches are delivered of[q] all

q delivered of] delivered out of 1623.

5 In England, on those more solemn festivals when the form, "Ite, missa est," was used at the end of the service of the mass, the priest used to hold up the chalice in his right hand while he gave his benediction to the people and made the sign of the cross over them. The custom is mentioned in *Tyndale's Obedience of a Christian Man, p.* 225; *Bradford's Hurt of Hearing Mass, p.* 316; *Pilkington's Exposition upon Haggai* I, 9, *p.* 82; *edd. Park. Soc.;* and in *Becon's Reliques of Rome, Works* III, 342 a, *ed.* 1563. And in *Pat.* 25 *Henr. VI, p.* 2, *m.* 17, printed in *Monast. Anglic.* II, 372 (VI, 614, *new edit.*), it is stated that the Vicars of Folketon used to go every year on the Feast of St. Andrew to the Chapel of a certain Hospital, "et Missam tunc (falsely printed *hanc*) ibidem solempniter cum Benedictione Calicis celebrare;" a passage cited by Du Cange under "Benedictio Calicis," but with no explanation of the words. The more correct name, "Benedictio cum Calice," is found in the rubric prefixed to the form of the Benediction in the York Missal, from which it has been printed by *Dr. Rock* in his *Church of our Fathers, vol.* III, *part* II, *p.* 168. In the Missal itself it occurs just before the Sequentiae Communes, not far from the end, falling in the second column of sign. "&" 8 b of the folio edition printed at York in 1516. The same (or nearly the same) form is given from an Evreux Missal by *Martene De Antiq. Eccles. Rit.* I, iv, 12, *Ord.* XXIV.

those things which displeased God so sore, and filthily defiled his holy house and his place of prayer; for the which he hath justly destroyed many nations, according to the saying of St. Paul, *If any man defile the temple of God, God will him destroy*[6]. And this ought we greatly to praise God for, that such superstitious and idolatrious[r] manners as were utterly naught and defaced God's glory are utterly abolished, as they most justly deserved, and yet those things that either God was honoured with or his people edified are decently retained, and in our churches comely practised.

1 Cor. iii, [17.]

But now, forasmuch as ye perceive it is God's determinate pleasure ye should resort unto your churches upon the day of holy rest; seeing ye hear what displeasure God conceiveth, what plagues he poureth upon his disobedient people; seeing ye understand what blessings of God are given, what heavenly commodities come, to such people as desirously and zealously use to resort unto their churches; seeing also ye are now friendly bidden and jointly called, beware that ye slack not your duty; take heed that you suffer nothing to let you hereafter to come to the church at such times as you are orderly[s] appointed and commanded. Our Saviour Christ telleth in a parable[θ], that *a great supper* was prepared, guests were bidden, many excused themselves, and would not come: *I tell you*, saith Christ, *none of them that were called shall taste of my supper*. This *great supper* is the true religion of Almighty God, wherewith he will be worshipped in the due receiving of his Sacraments, and sincere preaching and hearing his[t] holy word, and practising[u] the same by godly conversation. This feast is now prepared in God's banqueting house, the church; you are thereunto called and jointly bidden; if you refuse to come, and make your excuses, the same will be answered to you that was unto them. Now come therefore, dearly beloved, without delay, and cheerfully enter into God's feastinghouse, and become partakers of the benefits provided and prepared for you. But see that ye come thither with your holyday garment, not like hypocrites, not of a custom and for manner[x] sake, not with lothsomeness,

θ Luke xiv, [16–24.]

[r] idolatrious] idolatrous *from* 1582. [s] orderly] ordinarily *from* 1567. *Compare* "at times by common order appointed," *p.* 154, *l.* 36. [t] hearing his] hearing of his *from* 1582. [u] word, and practising] word, practising *till* 1567. [x] manner] manner's (*but of course without the mark of elision*) 1595, 1623.

[6] Οὐκ οἴδατε ὅτι ναὸς Θεοῦ ἐστε, καὶ τὸ πνεῦμα τοῦ Θεοῦ οἰκεῖ ἐν ὑμῖν; εἴ τις τὸν ναὸν τοῦ Θεοῦ φθείρει, φθερεῖ τοῦτον ὁ Θεός· ὁ γὰρ ναὸς τοῦ Θεοῦ ἅγιός ἐστιν, οἵτινές ἐστε ὑμεῖς. 1 Cor. III, 16, 17.

as though ye had rather not come than come, if ye were at your liberty. For God hateth and punisheth such counterfeit hypocrites, as appeareth by Christ's former parable. *My friend,* saith God[t], *how camest thou in without a wedding garment?* and therefore *commanded his servants to bind him hand and foot, and to cast him into the utter*[y] *darkness, where shall be weeping and wailing and gnashing of teeth.* To the intent ye[z] may avoid the like danger at God's hand, come to the church on the holyday, and come in your holyday garment; that is to say, come with a cheerful and a godly mind; come to seek God's glory, and to be thankful unto him; come to be at one[a] with thy neighbour, and to enter in friendship and charity with him. Consider that all thy doings stink before the face of God, if thou be not in charity with thy neighbour. Come with an heart sifted and cleansed from worldly and carnal affections and desires. Shake off all vain thoughts which may hinder thee from God's true service. The bird, when she will flee[b], shaketh her wings: shake and prepare thyself to flee[c] higher than all the birds in the air; that, after thy duty duly done in this earthly temple and church, thou mayest flee[d] up, and be received into the glorious temple of God in heaven, through Christ Jesus our Lord. To whom with the Father and the Holy Ghost be all glory and honour. Amen.

t [Matt. xxii. 12, 13.]

y into the utter] into utter *from* 1567. z intent ye] intent that ye 1623. a at one] attone 1563 A—F, atone 1563 G. b c d flee] fly 1563 B—F, 1595.

AN HOMILY WHEREIN IS DECLARED

THAT COMMON PRAYER AND SACRAMENTS OUGHT TO BE MINISTERED IN A TONGUE THAT IS UNDERSTANDED[a] OF THE HEARERS.

AMONG the manifold exercises of God's people, dear Christians, there is none more necessary for all estates and at all times than is Public Prayer and the due use of Sacraments. For in the first we beg at God's hand[b] all such things as otherwise we cannot obtain; and in the other he embraceth us, and offereth himself to be embraced of us. Knowing therefore that these two exercises are so necessary for us, let us not think it unmeet to consider, first, what Prayer is, and what a Sacrament is; and then, how many sorts of Prayer[c] there be, and how many Sacraments: so shall we the better understand how to use them aright.

Augustin. de Spiritu et Anima.

Augustin. Lib. ii contr. Advers. Leg. et Proph.

Augustin. ad Bonifacium.

To know what they be St. Augustine teacheth us. In his book entituled, Of the Spirit and the Soul, he saith this[d] of Prayer: "Prayer is," saith he, "the devotion of the mind, that is to say, the returning to God through a godly and humble affection; which affection is a certain willing and sweet enclining of the mind itself towards God[1]." And in the second book against the Adversary of the Law and Prophets[e] he calleth Sacraments "holy signs[2]." And writing to Bonifacius of the baptism of infants he saith[3]: "If Sacraments had not a certain similitude of those things whereof they be Sacraments, they should be no Sacraments at all. And of this similitude they do for the most part receive the names of the self things they signify." By

[a] understanded] understood 1623. [b] hand] hands *from* 1582. [c] sorts of Prayer] sorts of Prayers 1563 G *and* H, *and from* 1571. *See page* 353, *lines* 11, 13, 37. [d] saith this] saith thus *from* 1582. [e] and Prophets] and the Prophets *from* 1567.

1 *Scriptor Incertus de Spiritu et Anima, cap.* L, cited before in the Second Part of the Homily concerning Prayer, p. 325, n. 1.

2 Sacramenta, id est, sacra signa. *Augustin. contra Adversar. Legis et Proph.* II, § 33; *Opp.* VIII, 599 C.

3 Si enim Sacramenta quamdam similitudinem earum rerum quarum Sacramenta sunt non haberent, omnino Sacramenta non essent. Ex hac autem similitudine plerumque etiam ipsarum rerum nomina accipiunt. *Augustin. Epist.* XCVIII, § 9; *Opp.* II, 267 F.

these words of St. Augustine it appeareth, that he alloweth the common description of a Sacrament, which is, that it is a visible sign of an invisible grace, that is to say, that setteth out to the eyes and other outward senses the inward working of God's free mercy, and doth, as it were, seal in our hearts the promises of God. And so was Circumcision a Sacrament, which preached unto the outward senses the inward cutting away of the foreskin of the heart, and sealed and made sure in the hearts of the circumcised the promise of God touching the promised seed that they looked for.

Now let us see how many sorts of Prayer and how many Sacraments there be. In the Scriptures we read of three sorts of Prayer, whereof two are private, and the third is common. The first is that which St. Paul speaketh of in his Epistle to Timothy, saying, *I will that men pray in every place*[4], *lifting up pure hands, without wrath and striving*[f]; and it is the devout lifting up of the mind to God without the uttering of the heart's grief or desire by open voice. Of this Prayer we have example in the first Book of the Kings in Anna the mother of Samuel, when in the heaviness of her heart she prayed in the temple, desiring to be made fruitful. *She prayed in her heart,* saith the text, *but there was no voice heard.* After this sort must all Christians pray, not once in a week or once in a day only, but, as St. Paul writeth to the Thessalonians, *without ceasing:* and, as St. James writeth, *the continual prayer of a just man is of much force*[5]. The second sort of Prayer is spoken of in the Gospel of Matthew where it is said, *When thou prayest, enter into thy secret closet, and, when thou hast shut the door to thee, pray unto thy Father in secret; and thy Father, which seeth in secret, shall reward thee.* Of this sort of Prayer there be sundry examples in the Scriptures; but it shall suffice to rehearse one, which is written in the Acts of the Apostles. Cornelius, *a devout man, a captain of the Italian army,* saith to Peter, that, *being in his house in prayer at the ninth hour, there appeared unto him one in a white garment,* &c. This man prayed unto God in secret, and was rewarded openly. These be the two private sorts of Prayer; the one mental, that is to say, the devout lifting up of the mind to God; and the other vocal, that

1 Tim. ii, [8.]

1 Sam. i, [13.]

1 Thess. v, [17.]

James v, [16.]

Matt. vi, [6.]

Acts x, [1, 2, 30.]

[f] and striving] or striving *from* 1582.

4 Βούλομαι οὖν προσεύχεσθαι τοὺς ἄνδρας ἐν παντὶ τόπῳ.

5 Πολὺ ἰσχύει δέησις δικαίου ἐνεργουμένη. Multum enim valet deprecatio justi assidua. *Vulg.*

is to say, the secret uttering of the griefs and desires of the heart with words, but yet in a secret closet or some solitary place.

The third sort of Prayer is Public or Common. Of this Prayer speaketh our Saviour Christ when he saith, *If two of you shall agree upon earth upon any thing, whatsoever ye shall ask, my Father which is in heaven shall do it for you: for, wheresoever two or three be gathered together in my name, there am I in the midst of them.* Although God have promised[g] to hear us when we pray privately, so it be done faithfully and devoutly; (for he saith[α], *Call upon me in the day of thy trouble, and I will hear thee;* and *Helias, being but a mortal man,* saith St. James, *prayed, and heaven was shut three years and six months; and again he prayed, and the heaven gave rain;*) yet by the histories of the Bible it appeareth that Public and Common Prayer is most available before God; and therefore it is[h] much to be lamented that it is no better esteemed among us, which profess to be but one body in Christ. When the city Ninive[i] was threatened[β] to be destroyed within forty days, the prince and people[j] joined themselves together in public prayer and fasting, and were preserved. In the prophet Joel God commandeth[k] a fasting to be proclaimed, and the people to be gathered together, young and old, man and woman, and are taught to say with one voice, *Spare us, O Lord, spare thy people, and let not thine enheritance be brought to confusion.* When the Jews should have been destroyed all in one day through the malice of Haman[γ], at the commandment of Hester they fasted and prayed, and were preserved. When Holofernes besieged Bethulia[δ], by the advice of Judith they fasted and prayed, and were delivered. When Peter was in prison[ε], the congregation joined themselves together in prayer, and Peter was wonderfully delivered. By these histories it appeareth that Common or Public Prayer is of great force to obtain mercy and deliverance at our heavenly Father's hand. *Therefore*[ζ]*, brethren, I beseech you,* even *for the tender mercies of God,* let us no longer be negligent in this behalf; but, as a people[l] willing to receive at God's hand such good things as in the Common Prayer of the Church are craved, let us join ourselves together in the place of Common Prayer, and with one voice and one heart beg of[m] our heavenly Father all those things which he knoweth to be necessary for us. I forbid you

Matt. xviii, [19, 20.]

α Ps. l, [15.]

James v, [17, 18.]

β Jonah iii, [4–10.]

Joel ii, [15–17.]

γ Esth. iv, [16.]

δ Judith viii, [17–27.]

ε Acts xii, [5–12.]

ζ [Rom. xii, 1.]

g have promised] hath promised *from* 1563 B. h therefore it is] therefore is *from* 1563 D. i city Ninive] city of Ninive *from* 1563 B. j and people] and the people 1623. k commandeth] commanded *from* 1571. l a people] the people *from* 1570. m beg of] beg at *from* 1563 B.

not private prayer, but I exhort you to esteem Common Prayer as it is worthy. And before all things be sure that, in all these three sorts of Prayer, your minds be devoutly lifted up to God; else are your prayers to no purpose, and this saying shall be verified in you, *This people honoureth me with their lips, but their heart is far from me.* Is. xxix, [13:] Matt. xv, [8.]

Thus much for the three sorts of Prayer whereof we read in the Scriptures.

Now with like or rather more brevity you shall hear how many Sacraments there be that were instituted by our Saviour Christ, and are to be continued and received of every Christian in due time and order, and for such purpose as our Saviour Christ willed them to be received. And as for the number of them, if they should be considered according to the exact signification of a Sacrament, namely, for visible[n] signs expressly commanded in the New Testament, whereunto is annexed the promise of free forgiveness of our sin and of our holiness and joining in Christ, there be but two, namely, Baptism, and the Supper of the Lord. For, although Absolution hath the promise of forgiveness of sin, yet by the express word of the New Testament it hath not this promise annexed and tied to the visible sign, which is imposition of hands. For this visible sign, I mean laying on of hands, is not expressly commanded in the New Testament to be used in Absolution, as the visible signs in Baptism and the Lord's Supper are; and therefore Absolution is no such Sacrament as Baptism and the Communion are. And, though the Ordering of Ministers hath his visible sign and promise, yet it lacks the promise of remission of sin, as all other Sacraments besides do[o]. Therefore neither it nor any other Sacrament else be such Sacraments as Baptism and the Communion are. But in a general acception[p] the name of a Sacrament may be attributed to any thing whereby an holy thing is signified. In which understanding of the word the ancient writers have given this name, not only to the other five commonly of late years taken and used for supplying the number of the seven Sacraments, but also to divers and sundry other ceremonies, as to oil, washing of feet, and such like; not meaning thereby to repute them as Sacraments in the same signification

Dionysius. Bern. de Coen. Dom. et Ablut. Pedum.

[n] for visible] for the visible *from* 1567.

[o] besides do] besides the two above named do 1623.

[p] And as for the number——acception] And as for the number of them, if they should be considered according to the exact signification, as fully so expressed and commended by Christ in the New Testament, there be two, namely, Baptism and the Supper of the Lord: but in a general acception 1563 A 1.

that the two forenamed Sacraments are[6]. And therefore St. Augustine weighing the true signification and exact meaning of the word, writing to Januarius, and also in the third book of Christian Doctrine, affirmeth that the Sacraments of the Christians, as they are "most excellent in signification", so are they "most few in number"; and in both places maketh mention expressedly[q] of two, the Sacrament of Baptism, and the Supper of the Lord[7]. And, although there are retained by the order of the Church of England, besides these two, certain other rites and ceremonies about the Institution of Ministers in the Church, Matrimony, Confirmation of children[r] by examining them of their knowledge in the Articles of the Faith and joining thereto the prayers of the Church for them, and likewise for Visitation[s] of the Sick; yet no man ought to take these for Sacraments in such signification and meaning as the Sacrament of Baptism and the Lord's Supper are, but either for godly states of life, necessary in Christ's Church, and therefore worthy to be set forth by public action and solemnity by the ministry of the Church, or else judged to be such ordinances as may make for the instruction, comfort, and edification of Christ's Church.

[q] expressedly] expressly *from* 1582. [r] of children] of the children 1623. [s] for Visitation] for the Visitation *from* 1567.

[6] The writer who passes under the name of Dionysius calls the Holy Communion τελετῶν τελετή (rendered sacramentorum consummatio in the old translation), and says that other τελεταὶ are imperfect without it. *Pseudo-Dionys. Areop. de Eccles. Hierarch.* III, i. He also calls Unction μύρου τελετή. *Ibid.* IV, i.

Sacramentum dicitur sacrum signum sive sacrum secretum. Multa siquidem fiunt propter se tantum; alia vero propter alia designanda, et ipsa dicuntur signa, et sunt. Ut enim de usualibus sumamus exemplum, datur annulus absolute propter annulum, et nulla est significatio: datur ad investiendum de haereditate aliqua, et signum est; ita ut jam dicere possit qui accipit, Annulus non valet quicquam, sed haereditas est quam quaerebam. In hunc itaque modum appropinquans passioni Dominus de gratia sua investire curavit suos, ut invisibilis gratia signo aliquo visibili praestaretur. Ad hoc instituta sunt omnia Sacramenta, ad hoc Eucharistiae Participatio, ad hoc Pedum Ablutio, ad hoc denique ipse Baptismus, initium Sacramentorum, in quo *complantamur similitudini mortis ejus.* (Rom. vi, 5.) *Bernard. Serm. in Coena Dom.* § 2; *Opp.* I, 897 C.

[7] Primo itaque tenere te volo, quod est hujus disputationis caput, Dominum nostrum Jesum Christum, sicut ipse in Evangelio [*sc.* Matth. xi, 29, 30] loquitur, *leni jugo suo* nos subdidisse *et sarcinae levi:* unde Sacramentis numero paucissimis, observatione facillimis, significatione praestantissimis, societatem novi populi colligavit; sicuti est Baptismus Trinitatis nomine consecratus, Communicatio Corporis et Sanguinis ipsius, et si quid aliud in Scripturis canonicis commendatur; exceptis iis quae servitutem populi veteris pro congruentia cordis illorum et prophetici temporis onerabant, quae et in quinque libris Moysi leguntur. *Augustin. Epist.* LIV *ad Januar.* § 1; *Opp.* II, 124 A.

Quaedam pauca pro multis, eademque factu facillima et intellectu augustissima et observatione castissima, ipse Dominus et Apostolica tradidit disciplina; sicuti est Baptismi Sacramentum et Celebratio Corporis et Sanguinis Domini. *De Doctrin. Christ.* III, § 13; *Opp.* III, 49 B.

Now, understanding sufficiently what Prayer is, and what a Sacrament is also, and how many sorts of prayers there be, and how many Sacraments of our Saviour Christ's institution, let us see whether the Scriptures and the example[t] of the primitive Church will allow any vocal prayer, that is, when the mouth uttereth the petitions with voice, or any manner of Sacrament, or other public and common[u] rite or action pertaining to the profit and edifying of the poor congregation[x], to be ministered in a tongue unknown or not understand[y] of the minister or people; yea, and whether any person may privately use any vocal prayer in a language that he himself understandeth not. To this question we must answer, No.

And first of Common Prayer and administration of Sacraments. Although reason, if it might rule, would soon persuade us to have our Common Prayer and administration of Sacraments in[z] a known tongue, both for that to pray commonly is for a multitude to ask one and the self thing with one voice and one consent of mind, and to administer a Sacrament is by the outward word and element to preach to the receiver the inward and invisible grace of God[a]; and also for that both these exercises were first instituted, and are still continued, to the end that the congregation of Christ might from time to time be put in remembrance of their unity in Christ, and that, as members all of one body, they ought, both in prayers and otherwise, to seek and desire one another's commodity, and not their own without other's; yet we shall[b] not need to fly[c] to reason's proofs[d] in this matter, sith we have both the plain and manifest words of the Scripture, and also the consent of the most learned and ancient writers, to commend the prayers of the congregation in a known tongue.

First, Paul to the Corinthians saith, *Let all things be done to edifying*. Which cannot be, unless common prayers and administration of Sacraments be in a tongue known to the people. For, where the prayers spoken by the minister, and the words in the administration of the Sacraments, be not understanded[e] of them that be present, they cannot thereby be edified. For as[η], when the trumpet that is blown in the field giveth an uncertain sound, no man is thereby stirred up to prepare himself

1 Cor. xiv, [26.]

η [Ibid. 7, 8.]

[t] and the example] and the examples 1563 B—1574, and examples *from* 1582. [u] and common] or common 1623. [x] poor congregation] unlearned 1623. [y] understand] understood 1587, 1595, 1623. [z] of Sacraments in] of the Sacraments in *from* 1582. [a] of God] *not in* 1563 A. [b] yet we shall] yet shall we *from* 1563 D. [c] fly] flee *from* 1563 G. [d] reason's proofs] reasons and proofs *from* 1582. [e] understanded] understood 1623.

to the fight; and as, when an instrument of music maketh no distinct sound, no man can tell what is piped; even so, when prayers or administration of Sacraments shall be in a tongue unknown to the hearers, which of them shall be thereby stirred up to lift up his mind to God, and to beg with the minister at God's hand those things which in the words of his prayers the minister asketh? or who shall in the ministration of the Sacraments understand what invisible grace is to be craved of the hearer, to be wrought in the inward man? Truly no man at all. For, saith St. Paul[θ], *he that speaketh in a tongue unknown shall be unto*[f] *the hearer an alient*[g]*:* which in a Christian congregation is a great absurdity. For we are *not strangers*[ι] one to another, *but* we are *the citizens of the saints, and of the household of God, yea, and members all of*[h] *one body.* And therefore, whiles our minister is in rehearsing the prayer that is made in the name of us all, we must give diligent ear[i] to the words spoken by him, and in heart beg at God's hand those things that he beggeth in words. And, to signify that we so do[k], we say, Amen, at the end of the prayer that he maketh in the name of us all. And this thing can we not do for edification, unless we understand what is spoken. Therefore it is required of necessity, that the Common Prayer be had in a tongue that the hearers do understand. If ever it had been tolerable to use strange tongues in the congregation[l], the same might have been in the time of Paul and the other Apostles, when they were miraculously endued with the gift[m] of tongues. For it might then have persuaded some to embrace the Gospel, when they had heard men that were Hebrews born, and unlearned, speak the Greek, the Latin, and other languages. But Paul thought it not tolerable then; and shall we use it now, when no man cometh by the knowledge[n] of tongues otherwise than by diligent and earnest study? God forbid: for we should by that means bring all our Church exercises to frivolous superstition, and make them altogether unfruitful.

θ [Ibid. 2, 11.]

ι Eph. ii, [19:] 1 Cor. x, [17;] and xii, [12–27.]

Luke writeth that, when Peter and John were discharged by the princes and high priests of Jerusalem, *they came to their fellows and told them all that the princes of the priests and elders had spoken unto them*[o]. *Which when they heard, they lifted up their voice together to God with one assent, and said, Lord, thou*

Acts iv, [23, 24.]

[f] be unto] be to *from* 1582. [g] alient] aliant *from* 1574. [h] members all of] members of *from* 1563 D. [i] ear] ears 1623. [k] so do] do so 1623. [l] the congregation] the congregations *from* 1563 D. [m] with the gift] with gift 1582, with gifts 1623. [n] the knowledge] that knowledge *from* 1574. [o] unto them] to them 1623.

art he that hast made heaven and earth, the sea, and all things that are in them, &c. Thus could they not have done if they had prayed in a strange tongue that they had not understand[p]. And no doubt of it, they did not all speak with several voices[q], but some one of them spake in the name of them all, and the rest, giving diligent ear to his words, consented thereunto; and therefore it is said, that *they lifted up their voice together*. St. Luke saith not, *their voices*, as many, but, *their voice*, as one. That one voice therefore was in such language as they all understood, otherwise they could not have lifted it up with the consent of their hearts; for no man can give consent to[r] the thing he[s] knoweth not.

As touching the times before the coming of Christ, there was never man yet that would affirm, that either the people of God or other had their prayers or administrations of Sacraments[t] or sacrifices in a tongue that they themselves understood not. As for the time since Christ, till that usurped power of Rome began to spread itself, and to enforce all the nations of Europe to have the Romish language in admiration, it appeareth, by the consent of the most ancient and learned writers, that there was no strange or unknown tongue used in the congregations[u] of Christians.

Justinus Martyr, who lived about one hundred and sixty years after Christ, saith thus of the administration of the Lord's Supper in his time[8]. "Upon the Sunday assembles[w] are made, both of them that dwell in cities, and of them that dwell in the country also: amongst whom, as much as may be, the writings of the Apostles and Prophets are read. Afterwards, when the reader doth cease, the chief minister maketh an exhortation, exhorting them to follow so[x] honest things. After this we rise all together, and offer prayers: which being ended, as we have said, bread and wine and water are brought forth; then the head minister offereth prayers and thanksgiving with all his

Justin. Apol. 2.

[p] understand] understood 1587, 1595, 1623. [q] several voices] several voice 1623. [r] consent to] consent of *from* 1563 E F. [s] thing he] thing that he 1623. [t] of Sacraments] of the Sacraments 1623. [u] congregations] congregation *from* 1582. [w] assembles] assemblies *from* 1582. [x] so] *omitted after* 1574.

8 Τῇ τοῦ ἡλίου λεγομένῃ ἡμέρᾳ πάντων κατὰ πόλεις ἢ ἀγροὺς μενόντων ἐπὶ τὸ αὐτὸ συνέλευσις γίνεται, καὶ τὰ ἀπομνημονεύματα τῶν Ἀποστόλων ἢ τὰ συγγράμματα τῶν Προφητῶν ἀναγινώσκεται μέχρις ἐγχωρεῖ. εἶτα, παυσαμένου τοῦ ἀναγινώσκοντος, ὁ προεστὼς διὰ λόγου τὴν νουθεσίαν καὶ πρόκλησιν τῆς τῶν καλῶν τούτων μιμήσεως ποιεῖται. ἔπειτα ἀνιστάμεθα κοινῇ πάντες, καὶ εὐχὰς πέμπομεν· καὶ, ὡς προέφημεν, παυσαμένων ἡμῶν τῆς εὐχῆς, ἄρτος προσφέρεται καὶ οἶνος καὶ ὕδωρ, καὶ ὁ προεστὼς εὐχὰς ὁμοίως καὶ εὐχαριστίας, ὅση δύναμις αὐτῷ, ἀναπέμπει, καὶ ὁ λαὸς ἐπευφημεῖ λέγων τὸ ἀμήν. Justin. Mart. Apol. I, § 67.

power, and the people answer, Amen." These words with their circumstances, being duly considered, do declare plainly, that not only the Scriptures were read in a known tongue, but also that prayer was made in the same, in the congregations of Justin's time.

Basilius Magnus and Johannes Chrysostomus did in their time prescribe public orders of public administration, which they call Liturgies [9]; and in them they appointed the people to answer to the prayers of the minister sometime, Amen, sometime, Lord have mercy upon us, sometime, And with thy spirit, and, We have our hearts lifted up to [y] the Lord, &c.; which answers the people could not have made in due time, if the prayers had not been made [z] in a tongue that they understood.

Epist. 63.

The same Basil, writing to the clergy of Neocaesarea, saith thus of his usage in Common Prayer [10]: "Appointing one to begin the song, the rest follow; and so with divers songs and prayers passing over the night, at the dawning of the day all together, even as it were with one mouth and one heart, they sing unto the Lord a song of confession, every man framing unto himself

Basil. Hom. 4.

meet words of repentance." In another place he saith [11]: "If the sea be fair, how is not the assemble [a] of the congregation much more fair, in which a joined sound of men, women, and children, as it were of the waves beating on the shore, is sent forth in our prayers unto our God?" Mark his words: "a joined sound," saith he, "of men, women, and children;" which cannot be, unless they all understand the tongue wherein the

k 1 Cor. xiv, [16.]

prayer is had [b]. And Chrysostom upon the words of Paul [k]

y up to] up unto *from* 1563 B. z been made in] been in *from* 1567. a assemble] assembly 1623. b is had] is said *from* 1567.

9 Liturgies attributed to Basil and Chrysostom are printed in many Collections of Liturgies. Concerning them see the second and third Sections of *Palmer's Dissertation on Primitive Liturgies* in the first volume of his *Origines Liturgicae*.

10 Ἐκ νυκτὸς γὰρ ὀρθρίζει παρ' ἡμῖν ὁ λαὸς ἐπὶ τὸν οἶκον τῆς προσευχῆς, καὶ ἐν πόνῳ καὶ θλίψει καὶ συνοχῇ δακρύων ἐξομολογούμενοι τῷ Θεῷ, τελευταῖον, ἐξαναστάντες τῶν προσευχῶν, εἰς τὴν ψαλμῳδίαν καθίστανται. καὶ νῦν μὲν διχῇ διανεμηθέντες ἀντιψάλλουσιν ἀλλήλοις, ὁμοῦ μὲν τὴν μελέτην τῶν λογίων ἐντεῦθεν κρατύνοντες, ὁμοῦ δὲ καὶ τὴν προσοχὴν καὶ τὸ ἀμετεώριστον τῶν καρδιῶν ἑαυτοῖς διοικούμενοι· ἔπειτα πάλιν ἐπιτρέψαντες ἑνὶ κατάρχειν τοῦ μέλους οἱ λοιποὶ ὑπηχοῦσι· καὶ οὕτως ἐν τῇ ποικιλίᾳ τῆς ψαλμῳδίας τὴν νύκτα διενεγκόντες, μεταξὺ προσευχόμενοι, ἡμέρας ἤδη ὑπολαμπούσης, πάντες κοινῇ, ὡς ἐξ ἑνὸς στόματος καὶ μιᾶς καρδίας, τὸν τῆς ἐξομολογήσεως ψαλμὸν ἀναφέρουσι τῷ Κυρίῳ, ἴδια ἑαυτῶν ἕκαστος τὰ ῥήματα τῆς μετανοίας ποιούμενοι. Basil. Epist. CCVII (*al.* LXIII) ad Cler. Neocaes. § 3; Opp. III, 311 B.

11 Εἰ δὲ θάλασσα καλὴ καὶ ἐπαινετὴ τῷ Θεῷ, πῶς οὐχὶ καλλίων ἐκκλησίας τοιαύτης σύλλογος, ἐν ᾗ συμμιγὴς ἦχος, οἷόν τινος κύματος ἠϊόνι προσφερομένου, ἀνδρῶν καὶ γυναικῶν καὶ νηπίων, κατὰ τὰς πρὸς τὸν Θεὸν ἡμῶν δεήσεις ἐκπέμπεται; Basil. in Hexaem. Hom. IV, § 7; Opp. I, 39 D.

saith, so soon as the people hear these words, World without end, they all do forthwith answer, Amen. This could they not do, unless they understood the word spoken by the priest[c] [12].

Dionysius saith, that hymns were said of the whole multitude of people in the administration of the Communion [13]. Dionysius.

Cyprian saith [14]: "The priest doth prepare the minds of the brethren with a preface before the prayer, saying, Lift up your hearts, that, whiles the people doth answer, We have our hearts lifted up to the Lord, they may be[d] admonished that they ought to think on none other thing than the Lord." Cyprian. Serm. 6 de Orat. Dom.

St. Ambrose writing upon the words of St. Paul[λ] saith [15]: "This is it that he saith, because he which speaketh in an unknown tongue speaketh to God, for he knoweth all things; but men know not, and therefore there is no profit of this thing." And again upon these words[μ]: *If thou bless, or give thanks, with the spirit, how shall he that occupieth the room of the unlearned say, Amen, at thy giving of thanks, seeing he understandeth not what thou sayest?* "That[e] is," saith Ambrose [16], "if thou speak the praise of God in a tongue unknown to the hearers. For the unlearned, hearing that which he understandeth not, knoweth not the end of the prayer, and answereth not, Amen, which word is as much to say as, Truth, that the blessing or thanksgiving may be confirmed. For the confirmation of the prayer is fulfilled by them that do answer, Amen, that all things

λ 1 Cor. xiv, [2.]

μ [Ibid. 16.]

[c] by the priest] *not in* 1563 A. [d] they may be] they be *from* 1563 EF. [e] That] This *from* 1582.

12 Ἂν εὐλογήσῃς τῇ τῶν βαρβάρων φωνῇ, οὐκ εἰδὼς τί λέγεις, οὐδὲ ἑρμηνεῦσαι δυνάμενος, οὐ δύναται ὑποφωνῆσαι τὸ ἀμὴν ὁ λαϊκός· οὐ γὰρ ἀκούων τὸ **εἰς τοὺς αἰῶνας τῶν αἰώνων**, ὅπερ ἐστὶ τέλος, οὐ λέγει τὸ **ἀμήν**. Chrysost. in Epist. I ad Cor. Hom. XXXV; Opp. X, 325 E.

13 Οἱ δὲ τῆς λειτουργικῆς διακοσμήσεως ἔκκριτοι σὺν τοῖς ἱερεῦσιν ἐπὶ τοῦ θείου θυσιαστηρίου προτιθέασι τὸν ἱερὸν ἄρτον καὶ **τὸ τῆς εὐλογίας ποτήριον** (I Cor. X, 16), προομολογηθείσης ὑπὸ παντὸς τοῦ τῆς ἐκκλησίας πληρώματος τῆς καθολικῆς ὑμνολογίας. Pseudo-Dionys. Areop. de Eccles. Hierarch. III, ii.

14 Ideo et sacerdos ante orationem praefatione praemissa parat fratrum mentes dicendo, Sursum corda, ut, dum respondet plebs, Habemus ad Dominum, admoneatur nihil aliud se quam Dominum cogitare debere. *Cyprian. de Orat. Dom. p.* 152 *ed. Oxon., p.* 213 *ed. Paris.*

15 *Nam qui loquitur lingua non hominibus loquitur, sed Deo; nemo enim audit: spiritu autem loquitur mysteria.* Hoc est quod dicit, quia qui loquitur incognita lingua Deo loquitur, quia ipse omnia novit; homines vero nesciunt, ideoque nullus est ex hac re profectus: *spiritu autem loquitur mysteria,* non sensu, quia ignorat quod dicit. *Hilar. Diac. Comment. in Epist.* I *ad Cor.* XIV, 2; *Ambros. Opp.* II *Append.* 156 B.

16 Hoc est, si laudem Dei lingua loquaris ignota audientibus. Imperitus enim, audiens quod non intelligit, nescit finem orationis, et non respondet, Amen, id est, Verum, ut confirmetur benedictio. Per hos enim impletur confirmatio precis qui respondent, Amen, ut omnia dicta veri testimonio in audientium mentibus confirmentur. *Ibid. in v.* 16, *col.* 157 C.

spoken might be confirmed in the minds of the hearers through the testimony of the truth." And after many weighty words to the same end he saith[17]: "The conclusion is this, that nothing should be done in the Church in vain; and that this thing ought chiefly to be laboured for, that the unlearned also might take profit, lest any part of the body should be dark through ignorance." And, lest any man should think all this to be meant of preaching, and not of prayer, he taketh occasion of (ν [Ibid. 28.]) these words of St. Paul[ν], *If there be not an interpreter, let him keep silence in the Church*, to say as followeth[18]: "Let him pray secretly, or speak to God, who heareth all things that be dumb: for in the Church must he speak that may profit all persons."

(ξ [Ibid. 16.]) St. Hierome writing upon these words of St. Paul[ξ], *How shall he that supplieth the place of the unlearned* &c., saith[19]: "It is the layman whom Paul understandeth here to be in the place of the ignorant man, which hath no ecclesiastical office. How shall he answer, Amen, to the prayer that[f] he understandeth not?" (o [Ibid. 14.]) And a little after[g], upon these[h] words of St. Paul[o], *For if I should pray in a tongue* &c., he saith thus[20]: "This is Paul's meaning: if any man speak in strange and unknown tongues, his mind is made unfruitful, not to himself, but to the hearer; for, whatsoever is spoken, he knoweth it not."

(Ps. xviii.) St. Augustine, writing upon the eighteenth Psalm, saith[21]: "What this should be we ought to understand, that we may sing with reason of man, not[i] with chattering of birds. For ousels[22] and popinjays[23] and ravens and pies[k] and other such

f prayer that] prayer of that *from* 1574. g a little after] *so in all.* h these] the *from* 1563 G. i man, not] man, and not *from* 1567. k ousels and popinjays and ravens and pies] owls, popinjays, ravens, pies *from* 1567.

17 *Omnia ad aedificationem fiant.* Conclusio haec est, ut nihil incassum in Ecclesia geratur, hocque elaborandum magis, ut et imperiti proficiant, ne quid sit corporis per imperitiam tenebrosum. *Ibid. in v.* 26, *col.* 158 E.

18 Hoc est, intra se tacite oret, aut loquatur Deo, qui audit muta omnia. In Ecclesia enim ille debet loqui qui omnibus prosit. *Ibid. in v.* 28.

19 Laicum significat, qui nullo gradu ecclesiastico fungitur. Then the writer of the Homily seems to have taken words of St. Paul, which are the lemma for the next Comment, as part of the Comment itself. *Quomodo dicet, Amen, super tuam benedictionem, quoniam quid dicas nescit?* On these the Exposition is, Quomodo tuae perhibet benedictioni testimonium vel consensum. *Scriptor. Incert. Comment. in Epist.* I *ad Cor., Hieron. Opp.* XI, 939 F.

20 Hoc dicit: quoniam, si quis incognitis aliis linguis loquatur, mens ejus non ipsi efficitur sine fructu, sed audienti; quicquid enim dicitur ignorat. *Ibid.* 939 D.

21 Quid hoc sit intelligere debemus, ut humana ratione, non quasi avium voce, cantemus. Nam et meruli et psittaci et corvi et picae et hujusmodi volucres saepe ab hominibus docentur sonare quod nesciunt: scienter autem cantare naturae hominis divina voluntate concessum est. *Augustin. Enarr.* II *in Psal.* XVIII, § 1; *Opp.* IV, 81 E.

22 ousels: perhaps blackbirds. Some writers call them so, while others more

like birds are taught by men to prate they know not what; but to sing with understanding is given by God's holy will to the nature of man." Again, the same Augustine saith[24]: "There needeth no speech when we pray, saving perhaps as the priests do for to declare their meaning, not that God, but that men may hear them, and so being put in remembrance by consenting with the priest they may hang upon God." De Magist.

Thus are we taught both by the Scriptures[l] and ancient doctors, that in the administration of Common Prayer and Sacraments no tongue unknown to the hearers ought to be used. So that for the satisfying of a Christian man's conscience we need to spend no more time in this matter. But yet to stop the mouths of the adversaries, which stay themselves much upon general decrees, it shall be good to add to these testimonies of Scriptures and doctors one Constitution made by Justinian the Emperor, who lived five hundred and twenty[m] and seven years after Christ, and was Emperor of Rome. The Constitution is this[25]. "We command that all bishops and priests do celebrate the holy oblation and the prayers used in holy Baptism, not speaking low, but with a clear or loud voice, which may be heard of the people, that thereby the mind of the hearers may be stirred up with great devotion in uttering the praises[n] of the Nov. Const. 123.

[l] Scriptures] Scripture *from* 1582. [m] hundred and twenty] hundred twenty *from* 1582. [n] praises] prayers *from* 1563 EF.

correctly use the two names for different birds. The Ring Ousel nearly resembles the Blackbird: both belong to the family of Merulidae.

23 popinjays: parrots.

24 Quare non opus est locutione cum oramus, id est, sonantibus verbis, nisi forte sicut sacerdotes faciunt significandae mentis suae causa, non ut Deus, sed ut homines audiant, et consensione quadam per commemorationem suspendantur in Deum. *Augustin. de Magistro*, § 2; *Opp.* I, 542 B.

25 Ad haec jubemus omnes episcopos et presbyteros non in secreto, sed cum ea voce quae a fidelissimo populo exaudiatur, divinam oblationem et precationem quae fit in sancto baptismate facere; ut inde audientium animi in majorem devotionem et Dei laudationem et benedictionem efferantur. Sic enim et divinus Apostolus docet, dicens in priore ad Corinthios Epistola: *Caeterum*, inquit, *si solum benedicis spiritu, is qui idiotae locum implet quomodo tuae gratiarum actioni subjiciet* Deo sanctum illud *Amen, siquidem quid dicas non novit? Tu autem pulchre gratias agis, sed alius non aedificatur.* Et rursus in ea quae est ad Romanos sic dicit: *Corde quidem creditur ad justitiam, ore autem confessio fit ad salutem.* Idcirco igitur convenit, ut ea precatio quae in sancta allatione dicitur et aliae orationes cum voce a sanctissimis episcopis et presbyteris proferantur Domino nostro Jesu Christo, Deo nostro cum Patre et Spiritu Sancto; scituris religiosissimis sacerdotibus quod, si quid horum contempserint, et horrendo *Dei et Salvatoris nostri Jesu Christi* judicio rationem reddituri sunt, et nos ista cognoscentes non relinquemus quieta et inulta. *Authent. Collat.* IX, XX, 6; *Nov. Const.* 137, *c.* 6. In the Greek text of this law it is one and the same word, προσκομιδή, which is here rendered Oblatio in one place and Allatio in another.

Lord God. For so the holy Apostle teacheth in his first Epistle [1 Cor. xiv, 16, 17.] to the Corinthians, saying, *Truly, if thou only bless*, or give thanks, *in spirit, how doth he which*[o] *occupieth the place of the unlearned say, Amen, at thy*[p] *giving of thanks*[q] *unto God? for he understandeth not what thou sayest. Thou verily givest thanks well, but the other is not edified.* And again, in the Epistle to [Rom. x, 10.] the Romans, he saith: *With the heart a man believeth unto righteousness, and with the mouth confession is made unto salvation.* Therefore for these causes it is convenient, that, among other prayers, those things also which are spoken in the holy oblation be uttered and spoken of the most religious bishops and priests unto our Lord Jesus Christ, our God with the Father and the Holy Ghost, with a loud voice. And let the most religious priests know this, that if they neglect any of these things, that they shall give an account for them in the dreadful judgment *of* π [Tit. ii, 13.] *the great God and our Saviour Jesus Christ*[π]; neither will we, when we know it, rest and leave it unrevenged." This Emperor, as Sabellicus writeth[26], favoured the bishop of Rome; and yet we see how plain a decree he maketh for the praying[r] and administering of Sacraments in a known tongue, that the devotion of the hearers might be stirred up by knowledge, contrary to the judgment of them that would have ignorance to make devotion. He maketh it also a matter of damnation to do these things in a tongue that the hearers understand not. Let us therefore conclude, with God and all good men's assent, that no Common Prayer or Sacraments ought to be ministered in a tongue that is not understanded[s] of the hearers.

Now a word or two of private prayer in an unknown tongue. We took in hand, where we began to speak of this matter, not only to prove that no Common Prayer or administration of Sacraments ought to be in a tongue unknown to the hearers, but also that no person ought to pray privately in that tongue that he himself understandeth not. Which thing shall not be hard[t] to prove, if we forget not what prayer is. For, if prayer be that devotion of the mind which enforceth the heart to lift up itself to God, how should it be said that that person prayeth that understandeth not the words that his tongue speaketh in prayer? Yea, how can it be said that he speaketh? For to speak is by

[o] he which] he that 1623. [p] at thy] at that thy 1623. [q] giving of thanks] giving thanks 1623. [r] for the praying] for praying *from* 1582. [s] understanded] understood 1623. [t] hard] heard 1623.

26 *Sabellic. Rhaps. Hist. Ennead.* VIII, *Lib.* ii, *sub fin.*

voice to utter the thought of the mind; and the voice that a man uttereth in speaking is nothing else but the messenger of the mind, to bring abroad the knowledge of that which otherwise lieth secret in the heart, and cannot be known, according to that which St. Paul writeth: *What man*, saith he, *knoweth the things that appertain to man, saving only the spirit of man, which is in man?* (1 Cor. ii, [11.]) He therefore that doth not understand the voices that his tongue doth utter cannot properly be said to speak, but rather to counterfeit, as parrots and such other birds use to counterfeit men's voices. No man therefore that feareth to provoke the wrath of God against himself will be so bold to speak to[u] God unadvisedly, without regard of reverent understanding, in his presence; but he will prepare his heart before he presume to speak unto God. And therefore in our Common Prayer the minister doth oftentimes say, Let us pray, meaning thereby to admonish the people, that they should prepare their ears to hear what he shall[x] crave at God's hand, and their hearts[y] to consent to the same, and their tongues to say, Amen, at the end thereof. On this sort did the Prophet David prepare his heart, when he said, *My heart is ready, O God, my heart is ready, I will sing and declare a psalm.* (Ps. lvii, [7.]) The Jews also, when in the time of Judith[ρ] they did with all their heart pray God to visit his people of Israel, had so prepared their hearts before they began to pray. (ρ [Judith iv, 9–15.]) After this sort had Manasses prepared his heart before he prayed and said, *And now, O Lord, do I bow the knees of mine*[z] *heart, asking of thee part of thy merciful kindness.* (2 Paral. xxxvi [Prayer of Manasses.]) When the heart is thus prepared, the voice uttered from the heart is harmonious in the ears of God[a]. Otherwise he regardeth it not, to accept it; but, forasmuch as the person that so babbleth his words without sense in the presence of God sheweth himself not to regard the Majesty of him that he speaketh to, he taketh him as a contemner of his Almighty Majesty, and giveth him his reward among hypocrites, which make an outward shew of holiness, but their hearts are full of abominable thoughts even in the time of their prayers. For it is *the heart* that *the Lord looketh upon*, as it is written in the history of Kings. (1 Sam. xvi, [7.]) If we therefore will that our prayers be not abominable before God, let us so prepare our hearts before we pray, and so understand the things that we ask when we pray, that both

[u] speak to] speak of *from* 1563 EF. [x] he shall] he should *from* 1563 B. [y] and their hearts] and the hearts *till* 1571. [z] mine] my *from* 1582. [a] ears of God] ears God 1563 A.

our hearts and voices may together sound in the ears of God's Majesty, and then we shall not fail to receive at his hand the things that we ask; as good men which have been before us did, and so have from time to time received that which for their souls' health they did at any time desire.

De Catechizandis Rudibus.

St. Augustine seemeth to bear in this matter: for he saith thus of them which, being brought up in grammar and rhetoric, are converted to Christ, and so must be instructed in Christian religion. "Let them know also," saith he [27], "that it is not the voice, but the affection of the mind, that cometh to the ears of God. And so shall it come to pass, that, if haply[b] they shall mark that some bishops or ministers in the Church do call upon God either with barbarous words, or with words disordered, or that they understand not, or do disorderly divide the words that they pronounce, they shall not laugh them to scorn." Hitherto he seemeth to bear with praying in an unknown tongue; but in the next sentence he openeth his mind thus: "Not for that these things ought not to be amended, that the people might say[c], Amen, to that which they do plainly understand. But yet these things must be godly borne[d] withal of these catechists, or instructors of the faith, that they may learn, that, as in the common place where matters are pleaded the goodness of an oration consisteth in sound, so in the Church it consisteth in devotion." So that he alloweth not the praying in a tongue not understand[e] of him that prayeth, but he instructeth the skilful orator to bear with the rude tongue of the devout simple minister.

To conclude. If the lack of understanding the words that are spoken in the congregation do make them unfruitful to the hearers, how should not the same make the words read unfruitful to the reader? The merciful goodness of God grant us his grace to call upon him as we ought to do, to his glory and our endless felicity; which we shall do, if we humble ourselves in

[b] haply] happily *from* 1582. [c] might say] may say *from* 1563 G. *See before, page* 362, *lines* 1, 5. [d] these things must be godly borne] these godly things must be borne *from* 1587. [e] understand] understood 1587, 1595, 1623.

27 Noverint etiam non esse vocem ad aures Domini nisi animi affectum: ita enim non irridebunt, si aliquos antistites et ministros Ecclesiae forte animadverterint vel cum barbarismis et soloecismis Deum invocare, vel eadem verba quae pronuntiant non intelligere, perturbateque distinguere. Non quia ista minime corrigenda sunt, ut populus ad id quod plane intelligit dicat, Amen; sed tamen pie toleranda sunt ab eis qui didicerint, ut sono in foro, sic voto in Ecclesia bene dici. *Augustin. de Catechiz. Rud.* § 13, *Opp.* VI, 272 C.

his sight, and in all our prayers, both common and private, have our minds fully fixed upon him. *For the prayer of them that humble themselves shall pierce through the clouds; and till it draw nigh unto God, it will not be answered; and till the Most High do regard it, it will not depart. And the Lord will not be slack, but he will deliver the just, and execute judgment.* To him therefore be all honour and glory for ever and ever. Amen.

Ecclus. xxxv, [17, 18.]

AN INFORMATION

FOR THEM WHICH TAKE OFFENCE

AT CERTAIN PLACES OF THE HOLY SCRIPTURE.

THE FIRST PART.[a]

THE great utility and profit that Christian men and women may take, if they will, by hearing and reading the holy Scriptures, dearly beloved, no heart can sufficiently conceive, much less is any[b] tongue able with words to express. Wherefore Satan, our old[c] enemy, seeing the Scriptures to be the very mean and right way to bring the people to the true knowledge of God, and that Christian religion is greatly furthered by diligent hearing and reading of them, he also perceiving what an hindrance and let they be to him and his kingdom, doeth what he can to drive the reading of them out of God's Church. And for that end he hath always stirred up, in one place or other, cruel tyrants, sharp persecutors, and extreme enemies unto God and his infallible truth, to pull with violence the holy Bibles out of the people's hands, and have[d] most spitefully destroyed and consumed the same to ashes in the fire, pretending most untruly, that the much hearing and reading of God's word is an occasion of heresy, carnal[e] liberty, and the overthrow of all good order in all well ordered commonweals.

If to know God aright be an occasion of evil, then must we[f] needs grant, that the hearing and reading of the holy Scriptures is the cause of heresy, carnal liberty, and the subversion of all good orders. But the knowledge of God and of ourselves is so far off from[g] being an occasion of evil, that it is the readiest, yea, the only mean to bridle carnal liberty, and to kill all our fleshly affections. And the ordinary way to attain this knowledge is with diligence to hear and read the holy Scriptures.

2 Tim. iii, [16.]

For *the whole Scriptures*, saith St. Paul, *were given by the inspiration of God:* and shall we Christian men think to learn the knowledge of God and of ourselves in any earthly man's work

[a] THE FIRST PART.] *not in* 1563 A. [b] is any] is my *from* 1567. [c] old] *omitted after* 1567. [d] and have] and hath 1563 F. [e] heresy, carnal] heresy and carnal *from* 1563 B. *See below, line* 25. [f] must we] we must 1623. [g] far off from] far from *from* 1567.

or writing[h] sooner or better than in the holy Scriptures written by the inspiration of the Holy Ghost? *The Scriptures were not brought unto us by the will of man; but holy men of God,* as witnesseth St. Peter, *spake as they were moved by the holy Spirit of God.* 2 Pet. i, [21.] The Holy Ghost is the Schoolmaster of truth, which leadeth his scholars, as our Saviour Christ saith of him, *into all truth.* John xvi, [13.] And whoso is not led and taught by this[i] Schoolmaster cannot but fall into deep error, how goodly[k] soever his pretence is, what knowledge and learning soever he hath of all other works and writings, or how fair soever a shew or face of truth he hath in the estimation and judgment of the world.

If some man will say, I would have a true pattern and a perfect description of an upright life approved in the sight of God, can we find, think ye, any better, or any such again, as Christ Jesus is, and his doctrine? whose virtuous conversation and godly life the Scripture so lively painteth and setteth forth before our eyes, that we, beholding that pattern, might shape and frame our lives, as nigh as may be, agreeable to the perfection of the same. *Follow you me,* saith St. Paul, *as I follow Christ.* 1 Cor. xi, [1.] And St. John in his Epistle saith, *Whoso abideth in Christ must walk even so as he walked*[l] *before him.* 1 John ii, [6.] And where shall we learn the order of Christ's life but in the Scripture?

Another would have a medicine to heal all diseases and maladies of the mind. Can this be found or gotten otherwheres[m] than out of God's own book, his sacred Scriptures? Christ taught so much, when he said to the obstinate Jews, *Search the Scriptures, for in them ye think to have eternal life.* John v, [39.] If the Scriptures contain in them everlasting life, it must needs follow, that they have also present remedy against all that is an hinderance and let unto eternal life.

If we desire[1] the knowledge of heavenly wisdom, why had we rather learn the same of man than of God himself, who, as St. James saith, is the Giver of wisdom? James i, [5.] Yea, why will we not learn it at Christ's own mouth, who, promising[a] to be present with his Church till the world's end, doth perform his promise, in that he is not only with us by his grace and tender pity, but also in this, that he speaketh presently unto us in the holy Scriptures, to the great and endless comfort of all them that

a Matt. xxviii, [20.]

h work or writing] work of writing *from* 1582. i by this] by his *from* 1582. k goodly] godly *from* 1563 B. l he walked] he hath walked 1623. m otherwheres] otherwhere *from* 1563 B.

1 This and the next two paragraphs are translated, with a little change of order, from the latter part of a short tract of *Erasmus, "Paraclesis, id est Adhortatio, ad Christianae Philosophiae Studium," Opp.* v, 120, 121, *ed.* 1540.

have any feeling of God at all in them? Yea, he speaketh now in the Scriptures more profitably to us, than he did by word[n] of mouth to the carnal Jews, when he lived with them here upon earth. For they, I mean the Jews, could nother[o] hear nor see those things which we may now both hear and see, if we will bring with us those ears and eyes that Christ is heard and seen with, that is, diligence to hear and read his holy Scriptures, and true faith to believe his most comfortable promises.

If one could shew but the print of Christ's foot, a great number, I think, would fall down and worship it: but to the holy Scriptures, where we may see daily, if we will, I will not say the print of his feet only, but the whole shape and lively image of him, alas, we give little reverence, or none at all. If any could let us see Christ's coat, a sort of us would make hard shift, except we mought[p] come nigh to gaze upon it, yea, and kiss it too: and yet all the clothes that ever he did wear can nothing so truly nor so lively express him unto us, as do the Scriptures. Christ's image[q], made in wood, stone, or metal, some men, for the love they bear to Christ, do garnish and beautify the same with pearl, gold, and precious stone: and should we not, good brethren, much rather embrace and reverence God's holy books, the sacred Bible, which do represent Christ unto us more truly than can any image? The image can but express the form or shape of his body, if it can do so much: but the Scripture[r] doth in such sort set forth Christ, that we may see him both[s] God and man; we may see him, I say, speaking unto us, healing our infirmities, dying for our sins, rising from death for our justification. And, to be short, we may in the Scriptures so perfectly see whole Christ with the eye of faith, as we, lacking faith, could not with these bodily eyes see him, though he stood now present here before us.

Let every man, woman, and child therefore with all their heart thirst and desire God's holy Scriptures, love them, embrace them, have their delight and pleasure in hearing and reading them; so as at length we may be transformed and changed into them. For the Holy Scriptures are God's treasure house, wherein are found all things needful for us to see, to hear, to learn, and to believe, necessary for the attaining of eternal life.

Thus much is spoken, only to give you a taste of some of the

[n] by word] by the word *from* 1582. [o] nother] neither *from* 1563 G. [p] mought] might *from* 1582. [q] Christ's image] Christ's images *from* 1563 G. [r] Scripture] Scriptures *from* 1574. [s] see him both] see both *from* 1571.

commodities which ye may take by hearing and reading the holy Scriptures; for, as I said in the beginning, no tongue is able to declare and utter all. And, although it is more clear than the noon day that to be ignorant of the Scriptures is the cause of error, as Christ saith to the Sadducees, *Ye err, not knowing the Scriptures;* (Matt. xxii, [29.]) and that error doth[t] hold back and pluck men away from the knowledge of God; and, as St. Hierome saith, "not to know the Scriptures is to be ignorant of Christ[2];" yet, this notwithstanding, some there be that think it not meet for all sorts of men to read the Scriptures, because they are, as they think, in sundry places stumblingblocks to the unlearned; first, for that the phrase of the Scripture[u] is sometime so homely[x], gross, and plain, that it offendeth the fine and delicate wits of some courtiers; furthermore, for that the Scripture also reporteth, even of them that have their commendation to be the children of God, that they did divers acts, whereof some are contrary to the law of nature, some repugnant to the law written, and other some seem to fight manifestly against public honesty; all which things, say they, are unto the simple an occasion of great offence, and cause many to think evil of the Scriptures, and to discredit their authority. Some are offended at the hearing and reading of the diversity of the rites and ceremonies of the sacrifices and oblations of the Law. And some worldly witted men think it a great decay to the quiet and prudent governing of their commonwealths[y] to give ear to the simple and plain rules and precepts of our Saviour Christ in his Gospel; as being offended that a man should be ready to turn his right ear[β] to him that strake him on the left, and to him which would take away his coat, to offer him also his cloak, with such other sayings of perfection in Christ's meaning: for carnal reason, being alway an enemy[γ] to God, and not perceiving the things of God's Spirit, doth abhor such precepts; which yet, rightly understanded[z], infringeth no judicial policies nor Christian men's governments. And some there be which, hearing the Scriptures to bid[a] us to live without carefulness[δ], without study or forecasting, do deride the simplicity[b] of them. Therefore, to remove and put away occasions of

β [Matt. v, 39, 40.]
γ [Rom. viii, 7: 1 Cor. ii, 14.]
δ [Matt. vi, 25-34.]

t error doth] error do 1563 A. u of the Scripture] of the Scriptures 1563 B–1574. x homely] simple 1623. y commonwealths] commonweals *from* 1563 G. z understanded] understood 1623. a to bid] do bid 1563 C–1570. b simplicity] simplicities *from* 1563 C.

2 Ignoratio Scripturarum ignoratio Christi est. *Hieron. Prolog. ad Isaiam, Opp.* IV, 1.

offence so much as may be, I will answer orderly to these objections.

First, I shall rehearse some of those places that men are offended at for the homeliness[c] and grossness of speech, and will shew the meaning of them.

Deut. xxv, [5–10.] In the book of Deuteronomy it is written, that Almighty God made a law, if a man died without issue, his brother or next kinsman should marry his widow, and the child that were[d] first born between them should be called his child that was dead, that the dead man's name mought[e] not be put out in Israel; and, if the brother or next kinsman would not marry the widow, then she before the magistrates of the city should pull off his shoe and spit in his face, saying, *So be it done to that man that will not build his brother's house.* Here, dearly beloved, the pulling off his shoe and spitting in his face were ceremonies, to signify unto all the people of that city, that the woman was not now in fault that God's law in that point was broken, but the whole shame and blame thereof did now redound to that man which openly before the magistrates refused to marry her: and it was not a reproach to him alone, but to all his posterity also; for they were called ever after, *The house of him whose shoe is pulled off.*

Ps. lxxv, [10.] Another place out of the Psalms. *I will break*, saith David, *the horns of the ungodly, and the horns of the righteous shall be exalted.* By *an horn* in the Scripture is understand[f] power, might, strength, and sometime rule and government. The Prophet then saying, *I will break the horns of the ungodly,* meaneth, that all the power, strength, and might of God's enemies[g] shall not only be weakened and made feeble, but shall at length also be clean broken and destroyed; though for a time, for the better trial of his people, God suffereth the enemies to prevail and have the upper hand. In the hundred and thirty second Psalm Ps. cxxxii, [17.] it is said, *I will make David's horn to flourish.* Here *David's horn* signifieth his kingdom. Almighty God therefore by this manner of speaking promiseth to give David victory over all his enemies, and to stablish him in his kingdom spite of all his enemies.

[Ps lx, 8.] And in the threescore[h] Psalm it is written, *Moab is my washpot, and over Edom will I cast out my*[i] *shoe,* &c. In that place the Prophet sheweth how graciously God hath dealt with his

[c] homeliness] simplicity 1623. [d] that were] that was *from* 1582. [e] mought] might *from* 1563 G. [f] understand] understood 1587, 1595, 1623. [g] God's enemies] God's enemy *from* 1570. [h] threescore] lx. *till* 1563 G. [i] cast out my] cast my 1582, 1623.

people, the children of Israel, giving them great victories upon their enemies on every side. For, the Moabites and Idumeans being two great nations, proud people, stout and mighty, God brought them under and made them servants to the Israelites; servants, I say, to stoop down to pull off their shoes and wash their feet. Then, *Moab is my washpot, and over Edom will I cast out my shoe,* is as if he had said, The Moabites and the Idumeans, for all their stoutness against us in the wilderness, are now made our subjects, our servants, yea, underlings to pull off our shoes and wash our feet. Now, I pray you, what uncomely manner of speech is this, so used in common phrase among the Hebrews? It is a shame that Christian men should be so light headed, to toy as ruffians do of[k] such manner speeches, uttered in good grave signification by the Holy Ghost. More reasonable it were for vain man[l] to learn and reverence[m] the form of God's words, than to gaud[n] at them to his[o] damnation.

Some again are offended to hear that the godly fathers had many wives and concubines, although after the phrase of the Scripture a concubine is an honest name; for every concubine is a lawful wife, but every wife is not a concubine. And, that ye may the better understand this to be true, ye shall note that it was permitted to the fathers of the Old Testament to have at one time mo wives than one: for what purpose ye shall afterward hear. Of which wives, some were free women born, some were bond women and servants. She that was free born had a prerogative above those that were servants and bond women. The free born woman was by marriage made the ruler of the house under her husband, and is called the mother of the household, the mistress[p] or the dame of the house after our manner of speaking, and had by her marriage an interest, a right, and an ownership in his[q] goods unto whom she was married. Other servants and bond women were given by the owners of them, as the manner was then, I will not say always, but for the most part, unto their daughters at the[r] day of their marriage, to be handmaidens unto them. After such a sort did Pharao king of Egypt give unto Sara, Abraham's wife, Agar the Egyptian to be her maid. So did Laban give[e] unto his daughter Lia, at the day of her marriage, Zilpha to be her handmaid;

[e] Gen. xxix, [24, 29.]

[k] do of] do with 1623. [l] man] men *from* 1563 C. [m] learn and reverence] learn reverence 1570, learn to reverence *from* 1571. [n] gaud] sport 1623. [o] to his] to their *from* 1582. [p] mistress] mastres 1563 A; maistres, maistresse, *or* maystresse 1563 B–1582; mistris 1587, mistres 1595; masters 1623. [q] in his] of his *from* 1563 EF. [r] daughters at the] daughters at that *from* 1571.

and to his other daughter Rahel he gave another bondmaid, named Bilha[s]. And the wives, that were the owners of their handmaids[t], gave them in marriage to their husbands upon divers occasions. Sara gave[ζ] her maid Agar in marriage to Abraham. Lia gave[η] in like manner her maid Zilpha to her husband Jacob. So did Rahel, his other wife, give him Bilha[s] her maid, saying unto him, *Go in unto her, and she shall bear upon my knees:* which is as if she had said, Take her to wife, and the children that she shall bear will I take upon my lap, and make of them as if they were mine own. These handmaidens or bond women, although by marriage they were made wives, yet they had not this prerogative, to rule in the house, but were still underlings, and in subjection[u] to their mistress[x], and were never called mothers of the household, mistresses or dames of the house, but are called sometime wives[y], sometime concubines. The plurality of wives was by a special prerogative suffered to the fathers of the Old Testament, not for satisfying their carnal and fleshly lusts, but to have many children; because every one of them hoped, and begged ofttimes of God in their prayers, that that blessed seed which God promised should come into the world to break the serpent's head mought[z] come and be born of his stock and kinred.

ζ Gen. xvi, [3.]

η Gen. xxx, [9; and 3, 4.]

Now of those which take occasion of carnality and evil life by hearing and reading in God's book what God hath suffered[a], even in those men whose commendation is praised in the Scripture. As that Noe, whom St. Peter calleth the eighth *preacher of righteousness*[3], was so drunk with wine[θ], that in his sleep he uncovered his own privities. The just man Lot was in like manner drunken[ι], and in his drunkenness lay with his own daughters, contrary to the law of nature. Abraham, whose faith was so great, that for the same he deserved to be called of God's own mouth[κ] *a father of many nations, the father of all believers,* besides with Sara his wife, had also[λ] carnal company with Agar, Sara's handmaid. The Patriarch Jacob[μ] had to his wives two sisters at one time. The Prophet David[ν], and King Salomon his son, had many wives and concubines, &c. Which things we

2 Pet. ii, [5.]

θ Gen. ix, [21.]

ι Gen. xix, [30–36.]

κ Gen. xvii, [4, 5:] Rom. iv, [11–18.]

λ Gen. xvi, [4.]

μ Gen. xxix, [23–30.]

ν [2 Sam. iii, 2–5; v. 13: 1 Kings xi, 1–3.]

[s] Bilha] Bilham *or* Bylham *till* 1574. [t] handmaids] handmaidens 1623. [u] in subjection] in such subjection 1623. [x] mistress] mastres 1563 A *and* B; masters *or* maisters *from* 1563 C; *but* mistrisses 1587, mistresses 1595. *See note* p *above. See also the note of Steevens, citing Waldron, on the passage*, For affection, Mistress of passion, sways it to the mood Of what it likes or loathes, *in Merchant of Venice*, IV, 1; *Shakespeare's Plays*, VII, 346, 347, *ed.* 1803. [y] sometime wives] sometimes wives *from* 1563 C. [z] mought] might *from* 1563 G. [a] hath suffered] had suffered *from* 1574.

3 Ἀλλ' ὄγδοον Νῶε δικαιοσύνης κήρυκα ἐφύλαξε. In Tyndale's Bible, and in Cranmer's, the rendering is the same as in the Homily.

see plainly to be forboden[b] us by the law of God, and are now repugnant to all public honesty. These and such like in God's book, good people, are not written that we should or may do the like, following their examples, or that we ought to think that God did allow every of these things in those men: but we ought rather to believe and to judge, that Noe in his drunkenness offended God highly, Lot lying with his daughters committed horrible incest. We ought then to learn by them this profitable lesson, that, if so godly men as they were, which otherwise felt inwardly God's Holy Spirit inflaming their[c] hearts with the fear and love of God, could not by their own strength keep themselves from committing horrible sin, but did so grievously fall that without God's great mercy they had perished everlastingly, how much more ought we then, miserable wretches, which have no feeling of God within us at all, continually to fear, not only that we may fall as they did, but also be overcome and drowned in sin, which they were not; and so, by considering their fall, take the better occasion to acknowledge our own infirmity and weakness, and therefore more earnestly to call unto Almighty God with hearty prayer incessantly for his grace, to strengthen us, and to defend us from all evil. And, though through infirmity we chance at any time to fall, yet we may, by hearty repentance and true faith, speedily rise again, and not sleep and continue in sin, as the wicked doth.

Thus, good people, should we understand such matters expressed in the divine Scriptures, that this holy *table*[g] of God's word be not turned to us to be *a snare, a trap, and a stumbling-stone*[4], to take hurt by the abuse of our understanding: but let us esteem them in such a[d] reverent humility, that we may find our necessary food therein, to strengthen us, to comfort us, to instruct us, as God of his great mercy hath appointed them, in all necessary works; so that we may be perfect before him in the whole course of our life. Which he grant us who hath redeemed us, our Lord and Saviour Jesus Christ: to whom with the Father and the Holy Ghost be all honour and glory for evermore. Amen.

g [Ps. lxix, 22.]

b forboden] forbidden *from* 1563 EF. c inflaming their] inflaming in their *from* 1571. d in such a] in a 1623.

4 Fiat mensa eorum coram ipsis in laqueum et in retributionem [*al.* retributiones] et in scandalum. *Vulg.*

THE SECOND PART OF THE INFORMATION

FOR THEM WHICH TAKE OFFENCE

AT CERTAIN PLACES OF THE HOLY SCRIPTURE.

YE have heard, good people, in the Homily last read unto you, the great commodity of holy Scriptures: ye have heard how ignorant men, void of godly understanding, seek quarrels to discredit them: some of their reasons have ye heard answered. Now we will proceed, and speak of such politic wise men which be offended, for that Christ's precepts should seem to destroy all order in governance, as they do allege for example[a] such as these be. *If any man*[α] *strike thee on the right cheek, turn the other unto him also. If any will*[b] *contend to take thy coat from thee, let him have cloak and all. Let not*[β] *thy left hand know what thy right hand doeth. If thine eye*[γ]*, thine hand, thy*[c] *foot offend thee, pull out thine eye, cut off thy hand*[d]*, thy foot, and cast it from thee. If thine enemy,* saith St. Paul[δ], *be an hungered, give him meat; if he thirst*[e]*, give him drink: so doing, thou shalt heap hot burning coals upon his head.* These sentences, good people, unto a natural man seem mere absurdities, contrary to all reason. *For a natural man,* as St. Paul saith[ε], *understandeth not the things that belong to God, neither can he* so long as old Adam dwelleth in him. Christ therefore meaneth, that he would have his faithful servants[f] so far from vengeance and resisting wrong, that he would rather have him[f] ready to suffer another wrong, than by resisting to break charity, and to be out of patience. He would have our good deeds so far from carnal[g] respects, that he would not have our nighest friends know of our well doing, to win a vain[h] glory. And, though our friends and kinsfolks be as dear as our right eyes and our right hands, yet, if they would pluck us from God, we ought to renounce them and forsake them.

α [Matt. v, 39, 40.]
β Matt. vi, [3.]
γ Matt. xviii, [8, 9.]
δ Rom. xii, [20.]
ε 1 Cor. ii, [14.]

Thus, if ye will be profitable hearers and readers of the holy Scriptures, you must first[i] deny yourselves, and keep under your carnal senses, taken by the outward words, and search the

a example] examples 1563 D—1570. b any will] any man will *from* 1563 G. c hand, thy] hand, or thy *from* 1567. d thy hand] thine hand *from* 1563 EF. e he thirst] he be thirst 1563 C, he be thirsty *from* 1563 D. f servants *and* him] *so in all.* g from carnal] from all carnal *from* 1563 C. h win a vain] win vain 1623. i you must first] ye must first *from* 1571.

inward meaning; reason must give place to God's Holy Spirit; you must submit your worldly wisdom and judgment unto his divine wisdom and judgment. Consider that the Scripture, in what strange form soever it be pronounced, is the word of the living God. Let that always come to your remembrance which is so oft repeated of the Prophet Esay. *The mouth*[ζ] *of the Lord*, saith he, *hath spoken it*. The almighty[j] and everlasting *God*[η], *who* with his only word *created heaven and earth*, hath decreed it. *The Lord*[θ] *of hosts, whose ways are in the seas, whose paths are in the deep waters*, that Lord and God by whose word all things in heaven and in earth are created, governed, and preserved, hath so provided it. *The God of gods*[ι] *and Lord of all lords*, yea, God that is *God alone*, incomprehensible, almighty, and everlasting, he hath spoken it: it is his word. It cannot therefore be but truth, which proceedeth from the God of all truth; it cannot be but wisely and prudently commanded, what Almighty God hath devised; how vainly soever, through want of grace, we miserable wretches do imagine and judge of his most holy word.

ζ [Is. i. 20; xl, 5; lviii, 14.]
η [Is. xlii, 5; xliv, 24; xlv, 18.]
θ [Ps. lxxvii, 19: Is. xliii, 16; li, 15; liv, 5: 2 Pet. iii, 5, 7.]
ι [Deut. x, 17: Ps. lxxxvi, 10.]

The Prophet David, describing an happy man, saith, *Blessed is the man that hath not walked after the counsel of the ungodly, nor stand*[k] *in the way of sinners, nor sit*[k] *in the seat of the scornful*. There are three sorts of people, whose company the Prophet would have him to flee and avoid which shall be an happy man and partaker of God's blessing. First, he may not *walk after the counsel of the ungodly*. Secondly, he may not *stand in the way of sinners*. Thirdly, he must not *sit in the seat of the scornful*. By these three sorts of people, *ungodly men, sinners*, and *scorners*, all impiety is signified and fully expressed. By *the ungodly* he understandeth those which have no regard of Almighty God, being void of all faith, whose hearts and minds are so set upon the world, that they study only how to accomplish their worldly practices, their carnal imaginations, their filthy lust and desire, without any fear of God. The second sort he calleth *sinners*: not such as do fall through ignorance or of frailness; for then who should be found free? what man ever lived upon earth, Christ only excepted, but he hath sinned? *The just man falleth seven times, and riseth again*. Though the godly do fall, yet they walk not on purposedly[l] in sin; they stand not still to continue and tarry in sin; they sit not down like

Ps. i, [1.]
Prov. xxiv, [16.]

j The almighty] the almighty 1563 G—1571, and almighty *from* 1574. k stand *and* sit] *so in all*. l purposedly] purposely *from* 1563 G.

careless men, without all fear of God's just punishment for sin; but defying sin, through God's great grace and infinite mercy, they rise again, and fight against sin. The Prophet then calleth them *sinners* whose hearts are clean turned from God, and whose whole conversation of life is nothing but sin: they delight so much in the same, that they choose continually to abide and dwell in sin. The third sort he calleth *scorners,* that is, a sort of men, whose hearts are so stuffed with malice, that they are not contented to dwell in sin, and to lead their lives in all kind of wickedness, but also they do contemn and scorn in other all godliness, true religion, all honesty and virtue.

Of the two first sorts of men, I will not say but they may take repentance, and be converted unto God. Of the third sort, I think I may, without danger of God's judgment, pronounce, that never any yet converted unto God by repentance, but continued on still[m] in their abominable wickedness, heaping up to themselves damnation, against the day of God's inevitable judgment. Examples of such scorners we read of in[n] the second
2 Chron. xxx, [1–10.]
book of Chronicles. When the good king Ezechias in the beginning of his reign had destroyed idolatry, purged the temple, and reformed religion in his realm, he sent messengers into every city, to gather the people unto Hierusalem, to solemnize the feast of Easter in such sort as God had appointed it[o]. *The posts went from city to city through the land of Ephraim and Manasses even unto Zabulon.* And what did the people, think ye? Did they laud and praise the name of the Lord, which had given them so good a king, so zealous a prince to abolish idolatry, and to restore again God's true religion? No, no. The Scripture saith, the people *laughed them to scorn, and mocked*
[2 Chron. xxxvi, 15–20.]
the king's messengers. And in the last chapter of the same book it is written, that Almighty *God, having compassion upon his people, sent his messengers the Prophets unto them*, to call them from their abominable idolatry and wicked kind of living. *But they mocked his messengers, they despised his words, and misused his Prophets, until the wrath of the Lord arose against his people, and till there was no remedy:* for he gave them up into the hands of their enemies, even unto Nabuchodonozor king of Babylon, who spoiled them of their goods, brent[p] their city, and led them, their wives, and their children, captives unto Babylon.
[k][Gen. vi, vii: Luke xvii, 27.]
The wicked people that were in the days of Noe[k] made but a

[m] continued on still] continued still *from* 1582. [n] read of in] read in *from* 1563 C. [o] appointed it.] appointed. *from* 1567. [p] brent] burnt 1587, 1595, 1623.

mock at the word of God, when Noe told them that God would take vengeance upon them for their sins. The flood therefore came suddenly upon them, and drowned them, with the whole world. Lot preached to the Sodomites[λ], that, except they repented, both they and their city should be destroyed. They thought his sayings impossible to be true, they mocked and scorned[q] his admonition, and reputed him as an old doating fool. But, when God by his holy angels had taken Lot, his wife, and two daughters from among them, he rained down fire and brimstone from heaven, and brent[r] up those scorners and mockers of his holy word. And what estimation had Christ's doctrine among the Scribes and Pharisees? what reward had he among them? The Gospel reporteth thus: *The Pharisees, which were covetous, did scorn him in his doctrine.* O then ye see that worldly rich men scorn[s] the doctrine of their salvation. The worldly wise men scorn the doctrine of Christ, as foolishness[μ] to their understanding. These scorners have ever been, and ever shall be till[t] the world's end. For St. Peter prophesied, that such scorners should be in the world before the latter day. Take heed therefore, my brethren, take heed. Be not ye[u] scorners of God's most holy word. Provoke him not to pour out his wrath now upon you, as he did then upon those gibers and mockers. Be not wilful murderers of your own souls. Turn unto God while there is yet time of mercy: ye shall else repent it in the world to come, when it shall be too late; for there shall be *judgment without mercy*[ν].

λ [Gen. xix: Luke xvii, 28, 29.]
[Luke xvi, 14.]
μ [1 Cor. i, 18–23; ii, 14.]
2 Pet. iii, [3, 4.]
ν [James ii, 13.]

This mought[x] suffice to admonish us, and cause us henceforth to reverence God's holy Scriptures: but *all men have not faith*[ξ]. This therefore shall not satisfy and content all men's minds; but, as some are carnal, so they will still continue, and abuse the Scripture carnally[y] to their greater damnation. *The unlearned and unstable,* saith St. Peter, *pervert the holy Scriptures to their own destruction.* Jesus Christ, as St. Paul saith, is *to the Jews an offence, to the Gentiles foolishness; but to God's children, as well of the Jews as of the Gentiles, he is the power and wisdom of God.* The holy man Simeon saith[o], *that he is set forth for the fall and rising again of many in Israel.* As Christ Jesus is a fall to the reprobate, which yet perish through their own default, so is his word, yea, the whole book of God, a cause

ξ [2 Thess. iii, 2.]
2 Pet. iii, [16.]
1 Cor. i, [23, 24.]
o Luke ii, [34.]

[q] mocked and scorned] scorned and mocked *from* 1563 D. [r] brent] burnt 1587, 1595, 1623. [s] rich men scorn] rich men scorneth 1563 A. [t] be till] be to *from* 1571. [u] Be not ye] Be ye not *from* 1563 D. [x] mought] might *from* 1563 G. [y] Scripture carnally] Scriptures carnally *from* 1563 G.

of damnation unto them through their incredulity. And, as he is a rising up to none other than those which are God's children by adoption, so is his word, yea, the whole Scripture, *the power*[π] *of God to salvation to them* only *that do believe it.* Christ himself, the Prophets before him, the Apostles after him, all the true ministers of God's holy word, yea, every word in God's book, is unto the reprobate *the savour*[ρ] *of death unto death.* Christ Jesus, the Prophets, the Apostles, and all the true ministers of his word, yea, every jot and tittle in the holy Scripture, have[z] been, is[z], and shall be for evermore *the savour of life unto* eternal *life* unto all those whose hearts God hath purified by true faith. Let us earnestly take heed that we make no jesting-stock of the books of holy Scriptures. The more obscure and dark the sayings be to our understanding, the further let us think ourselves to be from God and his Holy Spirit, who was the Author of them. Let us with more reverence endeavour ourselves to search out the wisdom hidden in the outward bark of the Scripture. If we cannot understand the sense and the reason of the saying, yet let us not be scorners, jesters, and deriders; for that is the uttermost token and shew of a reprobate, of a plain enemy to God and[a] his wisdom. They be not idle fables to jest at, which God doth seriously pronounce; and for serious matters let us esteem them.

π [Rom. i, 16.]

ρ [2 Cor. ii, 16.]

And, though in sundry places of the Scriptures be set out divers rites and ceremonies, oblations and sacrifices, let us not think strange of them, but refer them to the times and people for whom they served; although yet to learned men they be not unprofitable to be considered, but to be expounded as figures and shadows of things and persons afterward openly revealed in the New Testament. Though the rehearsal of the genealogies and pedigrees[b] of the fathers be not to much edification of the plain ignorant people, yet is there nothing so impertinently uttered in all the whole book of the Bible, but may serve to spiritual purpose in some respect to all such as will bestow their labours to search out the meanings. These may not be condemned because they serve not to our understanding, nor make not to[c] our edification. But let us turn our labour to understand, and to carry away, such sentences and stories as be more fit for our capacity and instruction.

And, whereas we read in divers Psalms[σ] how David did wish

σ [Ps. xxxv, 4, 8, 26; lxviii, 30; cix, 13.]

[z] have *and* is] *so in all.* [a] and his wisdom] in his wisdom *till* 1563 G. [b] pedigrees] petegrues 1563 A—F, petegrees 1563 G—1574, pedegrees *from* 1582. [c] make not to] make to *from* 1582.

to the adversaries of God sometime shame[d], rebuke, and confusion, sometime the decay of their offspring and issue, sometime that they might perish and come suddenly to destruction, (as he did wish to the captains of the Philistians[e], *Cast forth*, saith he[r], *thy lightning, and tear them; shoot out thine arrows, and consume them;*) with such other manner of imprecations; yet ought we not to be offended at such prayers of David, being a Prophet as he was, singularly beloved of God, and rapt in spirit, with an ardent zeal to God's glory. He spake them not[f] as of[g] a private hatred and in a stomach against their persons, but wished spiritually the destruction of such corrupt errors and vices which reigned in all devilish persons set against God. He was of like mind as St. Paul was, when he did deliver Hymeneus and Alexander with the notorious fornicator to Satan to their temporal confusion, *that their spirit might be saved against the day of the Lord*. And, when David did profess in some places that he hated[v] the wicked, yet in other places of his Psalms he professeth that he hated them *with a perfect hate*, not with a malicious hate to the hurt of the soul. Which perfection of spirit, because it cannot be performed in us, so corrupted in affections as we be, we ought not to use in our private causes the like words in form, for that we cannot fulfil the like words in sense. Let us not therefore be offended, but search out the reason of such words before we be offended; that we may the more reverently judge of such sayings, though strange to our carnal understandings, yet, to them that be spiritually minded, judged to be zealously and godly pronounced.

[r] Ps. cxliv, [6.]

[1 Tim. i, 20: 1 Cor. v, 5.]

[v] [Ps. xxvi, 5; xxxi, 6; cxxxix, 21, 22.]

God therefore, for his mercy's sake, vouchsafe to purify our minds through faith in his Son Jesus Christ, and to instil the heavenly drops of his grace into our hard stony hearts, to supple the same; that we be not contemners and deriders of his infallible word, but that with all humbleness of mind and Christian reverence we may endeavour ourselves to hear and to read his sacred Scriptures, and inwardly so to digest them, as shall be to the comfort of our souls and sanctification[h] of his holy Name. To whom with the Son and the Holy Ghost, three Persons and one living God, be all laud, honour, and praise for ever and ever. Amen.

[d] sometime shame] sometimes shame *from* 1563 G. [e] Philistians] Philistines *from* 1574. [f] spake them not] spake not 1623. [g] not as of] not of *from* 1563 D. [h] souls and sanctification] souls sanctification *from* 1582.

AN HOMILY

OF ALMSDEEDS AND MERCIFULNESS

TOWARD THE POOR AND NEEDY.

AMONGST the manifold duties that Almighty God requireth of his faithful servants the true Christians, by the which he would that both his Name should be glorified, and the certainty of their vocation declared, there is none that is either more acceptable unto him or more profitable for them, than are the works of mercy and pity shewed upon the poor which be afflicted with any kind of misery. And yet, this notwithstanding, such is the slothful sluggishness of our dull nature to that which is good and godly, that we are almost in nothing more negligent and less careful than we are therein. It is therefore a very necessary thing, that God's people should awake their sleepy minds, and consider their duty on this behalf. And meet it is that all true Christians should desirously seek and learn what God by his holy word doth herein require of them; that, first knowing their duty, whereof many by their slackness seem to be very ignorant, they may afterwards diligently endeavour to perform the same. By the which both the godly charitable persons may be encouraged to go forwards and continue in their merciful deeds of giving alms[a] to the poor, and also such as hitherto have either neglected or contemned it may yet now at the length[b], when they shall hear how much it appertaineth to them, advisedly consider it, and virtuously apply themselves thereunto.

And, to the intent that every one of you may the better understand that which is taught, and also easilier bear away, and so take more fruit of, that shall be said, when several matters are severally handled; I mind particularly, and in this order, to speak and entreat of these points.

First, I will shew how earnestly Almighty God in his holy word doth exact the doing of almsdeeds of us, and how acceptable they be unto him.

Secondly, how profitable it is for us to use them, and what commodity and fruit they will bring unto us.

[a] giving alms] almsgiving *from* 1567. [b] at the length] at length *from* 1574.

Thirdly and last[c], I will shew out of God's word, that whoso is liberal to the poor, and relieveth them plenteously, shall notwithstanding have sufficient for himself, and evermore be without danger of penury and scarcity.

Concerning the first, which is the acceptation and dignity or price of almsdeeds before God, know this, that to help and succour the poor in their need and misery pleaseth God so much, that, as the holy Scripture in sundry places recordeth, nothing can be more thankfully taken or accepted of God. For first we read, that Almighty God doth account that to be given and to be bestowed upon himself that is bestowed upon the poor. For so doth the Holy Ghost testify unto us by the Wise Man, saying, *He that hath pity upon the poor lendeth unto the Lord* himself. Prov. xix, [17.] And Christ in the Gospel advoucheth[d], and as a most certain truth bindeth it with an oath, that the alms bestowed upon the poor was bestowed upon him, and so shall be reckoned at the last day. For thus he saith to the charitable almsgivers, when he sitteth as Judge in the doom to give sentence of every man according to his deserts: *Verily I say unto you, Whatsoever* good and merciful deed *you did upon any of the least of these my brethren, ye did the same unto me.* Matt. xxv, [35–40.] In relieving their hunger, *ye relieved mine;* in quenching their thirst, *ye quenched mine;* in clothing them, *ye clothed me;* and, when ye harboured them, *ye lodged me* also; when ye visited them, *being sick or in*[e] *prison, ye visited me.* For, as he that receiveth[f] a prince's ambassadors, and entertaineth them well, doth honour the prince from whom those ambassadors do come, so he that receiveth the poor and needy, and helpeth them in their affliction and distress, doth thereby receive and honour Christ their Master: who, as he was poor and needy himself whilst he lived here amongst us to work the mystery of our salvation, so at[g] his departure hence he promised in his stead to send unto us those that were poor[a], by whose means his absence should be supplied; and therefore that we would do unto him we must do unto them.

a [Matt. xxvi, 11.]

And for this cause doth Almighty[h] God say unto Moyses, *The land wherein you dwell shall never be without poor men,* Deut. xv, [11.] because he would have continual trial of his people, whether they loved him or no; that, in shewing themselves obedient unto his will, they might certainly assure themselves of his love and favour towards them, and nothing doubt but

c last] lastly 1623. d advoucheth] avoucheth 1595, 1623. e sick or in] sick in *from* 1582. f receiveth] hath received *from* 1574. g salvation, so at] salvation, at 1623. h doth Almighty] doth the Almighty 1623.

that, as his law and ordinances[i], wherein he commanded them that they should *open their hand unto their brethren that were poor and needy in the land,* were accepted of them and willingly performed, so he would on his part lovingly accept them, and truly perform his promises that he had made unto them.

The holy Apostles and disciples of Christ, who, by reason of his daily conversation, saw by his deeds, and heard in his doctrine, how much he tendered the poor; the godly fathers also that were both before and since Christ, indued without doubt with the Holy Ghost, and most certainly certified of God's holy will; they both do most earnestly exhort us, and in all their writings almost continually admonish us, that we would remember the poor, and bestow our charitable alms upon them. St. Paul crieth unto us after this sort[β]: *Comfort the feeble minded, lift up the weak, and be charitable toward*[k] *all men*[1]. And again[γ]: *To do good to the poor, and to distribute alms gladly, see that thou do not forget; for with such sacrifices is God*[l] *pleased.* Esay the Prophet teacheth on this wise: *Deal thy bread to the hungry, and bring the poor wandering home to thy house. When thou seest the naked, see thou clothe him, and hide not thy face from thy poor neighbour, neither despise thou thine own flesh.* And the holy father Toby giveth this counsel. *Give alms,* saith he, *of thine own goods, and turn never thy face from the poor. Eat thy bread with the hungry, and cover the naked with thy clothes.* And the learned and godly doctor Chrysostom giveth this admonition: "Let merciful alms be always with us as a garment[2];" that is, as mindful as we will be to put our garments upon us, to cover our nakedness, to defend us from the cold, and to shew ourselves comely, so mindful let us be at all times and seasons, that we give alms to the poor, and shew ourselves merciful towards them. But what mean these often admonitions and earnest exhortations of the Prophets, Apostles, fathers, and holy doctors? Surely, as they were faithful to Godward, and therefore discharged their duty truly in telling us what was God's will, so, of a singular love to usward, they laboured not only to inform us, but also to persuade with us, that to give alms, and to succour the poor and needy, was a

β 1 Thess. v, [14.]

γ Heb. xiii, [16.]

Is. lviii, [7.]

Tob. iv, [7, 16.]

Ad Pop. Antioch. Hom. 35.

i ordinances] ordinance *from* 1582. k toward] towards *from* 1582. l is God] God is *from* 1571.

1 Μακροθυμεῖτε πρὸς πάντας.

2 Οὐ γὰρ εἶπεν (Col. III, 12), Ἐλεήσατε, ἁπλῶς, ἀλλ', Ἐνδύσασθε· ἵνα, ὥσπερ τὸ ἱμάτιον ἀεὶ μεθ' ἡμῶν ἐστιν, οὕτω καὶ ἡ ἐλεημοσύνη. Chrysost. in Epist. ad Rom. Hom. XIV, Opp. IX, 588 C: Ad Pop. Ant. Hom. XXXV Lat., Opp. ed. Basil. 1530 Tom. IV, p. 498.

very acceptable thing and an high sacrifice to God, wherein he greatly delighted and had a singular pleasure. For so doth the wise man the son of Sirach teach us, saying, *Whoso is merciful and giveth alms, he offereth the right thank offering.* And he addeth thereunto, *The right thank offering maketh the altar fat, and a sweet smell is it*[m] *before the Highest; it is acceptable before God, and shall never be forgotten.* Ecclus. xxxv, [2, 6, 7.]

And the truth of this doctrine is verified by the examples[n] of those holy and charitable fathers of whom we read in the Scriptures, that they were given to merciful compassion towards the poor, and charitable relieving of their necessities. Such a one was Abraham, in whom God had so great pleasure, that he vouchsafed to come unto him[δ] in form of an angel, and to be entertained of him at his house. Such was his kinsman Lot, whom God so favoured for receiving[ε] his messengers into his house, which otherwise should have lain[o] in the street, that he saved him with his whole family from the destruction of Sodom and Gomorra. Such were the holy fathers Job and Toby, with many others, who felt most sensible proofs of God's especial[p] love towards them. And, as all these by their mercifulness and tender compassion, which they shewed to the miserable afflicted members of Christ in the relieving, helping, and succouring them with their temporal goods in this life, obtained God's favour, and were dear, acceptable, and pleasant in his sight; so now they themselves take pleasure in the fruition of God, in the pleasant joys of heaven, and are also in God's eternal word set before us, as perfect examples ever before our eyes, both how we shall please God in this our mortal[q] life, and also how we may come to live in joy with them in everlasting pleasure and felicity. For most true is that saying which St.[r] Augustine hath, that the giving of alms and relieving of the poor is the right way to heaven. Via coeli pauper est[3]: "The poor man," saith he, "is the way to heaven." They used in times past to set in highways' sides the picture of Mercury pointing with his finger which was the right way to the town[4]. And we use in cross-

δ [Gen. xviii.]
ε [Gen. xix.]

m smell is it] smell it is *from* 1563 D. n the examples] the example 1623. o lain] lien 1623. p especial] special *from* 1582. q this our mortal] this mortal *from* 1567. r St.] *omitted after* 1574.

3 Via coeli est pauper, per quam venitur ad Patrem. *Augustin. Serm.* 367, al. *de Verb. Dom.* 25; *Opp.* v, 1453 B.

4 The notion that statues (not pictures) of Mercury used to be set in highways as hand-posts, "ad semitas monstrandas," seems to have been drawn by lexicographers (as Constantine and Stephens) and other writers from the words ὅδιος and ἐνόδιος applied as epithets to Hermes: but it is not confirmed by any passage that has been

ways to set up a wooden or stone cross, to admonish the travelling man which way he must turn, when he cometh thither, to direct his journey aright. But God's word, as St. Augustine saith, hath set in the way to heaven the poor man and his house; so that whoso will go aright thither, and not turn out of the way, must go by the poor. The poor man is that Mercury that shall set us the ready way; and, if we look well to this mark, we shall not wander much out of the right path.

The manner of wise worldly men among[s] us is, that, if they know a man of meaner[t] estate than themselves to be in favour with the prince or any other nobleman, whom they either fear or love, such a one they will be glad to benefit and pleasure, that, when they have need, he may[u] become their spokesman, either to help with his good word[x] to obtain a commodity or to escape a displeasure. Now surely it ought to be a shame to us, that worldly men for temporal things, that last but for a season, should be more wise and provident in procuring them, than we in heavenly. Our Saviour Christ testifieth of poor men, that they are dear unto him, and that he loveth them especially: for he calleth them his *little ones*[ς], by a name of tender love; he saith they be his *brethren*. And St. James saith, that God hath chosen them to be heirs[y] of his kingdom. *Hath not God*, saith he, *chosen the poor of this world to himself, to make them hereafter the rich heirs of that kingdom which he hath promised to them that love him?* And we know that the prayer which they make for us shall be acceptable and regarded of God. Their complaint shall be heard also. Thereof doth Jesus the son of Sirach certainly assure us, saying, *If the poor complain of thee in the bitterness of his soul, his prayer shall be heard; even he that made him shall hear him. Be courteous therefore unto the poor*[5]. We know also, that he who acknow-

ς [Matt. x, 42; xxv, 40.]

James ii, [5.]

Ecclus. iv, [6, 7.]

s among] amongst *from* 1567. t of meaner] of a meaner 1623. u he may] they may *from* 1570. x to help with his good word] *omitted after* 1570. y be heirs] be the heirs *from* 1571.

quoted from ancient authors; for *Theocr. Idyll.* XXV, 3–6, which is cited by Constantine, is not sufficient for the purpose. The *Epigr. Incert. Auct.* 235 in *Anthol. Gr.* belongs to a statue of Hermes placed in a field, not to shew the path to travellers at a loss, but to warn trespassers to keep it. Such statues however were set up as distance posts, as by Hipparchus midway between Athens and the several townships (δῆμοι) about it. See *Pseudo-Plat. Hipparch.* p. 228 D, cited by *Böckh, Inscr. Gr.* 12. See also *Epigr. Incert. Auct.* 234 in *Anthol. Gr.*, on a heap of stones thrown by travellers at the base (as it would seem) of such a statue, a heap called "acervus Mercurii" in *Prov.* XXVI, 8, *Vulg.*

5 Maledicentis enim tibi in amaritudine animae exaudietur deprecatio illius: exaudiet autem eum qui fecit illum. Congregationi pauperum affabilem te facito. *Vulg.*

ledgeth himself to be their Master and Patron, and refuseth not to take them for his servants, is both able to pleasure and displeasure us, and that we stand every hour in need of his help. Why should we then be either negligent or unwilling to procure their friendship and favour, by the which also we may be assured to get his favour, that is both able and willing to do us all pleasures that are for our commodity and wealth? Christ doth declare by this, how much he accepteth our charitable affection toward the poor, in that he promiseth a reward[y] unto them that give but a cup of cold water in his name to them that have need thereof; and that reward is the kingdom of heaven. No doubt is it therefore but that[z] God regardeth highly that which he rewardeth so liberally. For he that promiseth a princely recompence for a beggarly benevolence declareth that he is more delighted with the giving than with the gift, and that he as much esteemeth the doing of the thing as the fruit and commodity that cometh of it.

[y] [Matt. x, 42: Mark ix, 41.]

Whoso therefore hath hitherto neglected to give alms, let him know that God now requireth it of him; and he that hath been liberal to the poor, let him know that his godly doings are accepted and thankfully taken at God's hands, which he will requite with double and treble. For so saith the Wise Man: *He which sheweth mercy to the poor doth lay his money in bank to the Lord for a large interest and gain;* the gain being chiefly the possession of the life everlasting thorough[a] the merits of our Saviour Jesus Christ. To whom with the Father and the Holy Ghost be all honour and glory for ever. Amen.

[Prov. xix, 17.]

[z] therefore but that] therefore that *from* 1571. [a] thorough] through *from* 1563 B.

THE SECOND PART OF THE SERMON

OF ALMSDEEDS.

YE have heard before, dearly beloved, that to give alms unto the poor, and to help them in time of necessity, is so acceptable unto our Saviour Christ, that he counteth that to be done to himself that we do for his sake unto them. Ye have heard also how earnestly both the Apostles, Prophets, holy fathers, and doctors, do exhort us unto the same. And ye see how well-beloved and dear unto God they were whom the Scriptures report unto us to have been good almsmen. Wherefore, if either their good examples, or the wholesome counsel of godly fathers, or the love of Christ, whose especial favour we may be assured by this means to obtain, may move us or do any thing at all with us, let us provide that[a] from henceforth we shew unto Godward this thankful service, to be mindful and ready to help them that be poor and in misery.

Now will I, this second time that I entreat of almsdeeds, shew unto you how profitable it is for us to exercise them, and what fruit thereby shall rise[b] unto us, if we do them faithfully. Our Saviour Christ in the Gospel[a] teacheth us, that it profiteth a man nothing to have in possession all the riches of the whole world and the wealth or glory thereof, if in the mean season he lose his soul, or do that thing whereby it should become captive unto death, sin, and hell fire. By the which saying he not only instructeth us how much the soul health[c] is to be preferred before worldly commodities, but also[d] serveth to stir up our minds, and to prick us forwards, to seek diligently and learn by what means we may preserve and keep our souls ever in safety; that is, how we may recover their health[e], if it be lost or empaired, and how it may be defended and maintained, if we once[f] have it. Yea, he teacheth us also thereby to esteem that as a precious medicine and an inestimable jewel, that hath such strength and virtue in it, that can either procure or preserve so incomparable a treasure. For, if we greatly regard that medicine or salve

a Matt. xvi, [26.]

[a] provide that] provide us that *from* 1582. [b] rise] arise *from* 1571. [c] soul health] soul's health 1623. [d] but also] but it also 1623. [e] their health] our health *from* 1567. [f] we once] once we *from* 1582.

that is able to heal sundry and grievous diseases of the body, much more will we esteem that which hath like power over the soul. And, because we might be the better[g] assured both to know and have[h] in readiness that so profitable a remedy, he, as a most faithful and loving teacher, sheweth himself both what it is, and where we may find it, and how we may use and apply it. For, when both he and his disciples were grievously accused of the Pharisees to have defiled their souls in breaking the constitutions of the elders, because they went to meat, and washed not their hands before, according to the custom of the Jews; Christ, answering their superstitious complaint, teacheth them an especial remedy how to keep clean their souls, notwithstanding the breach of such superstitious orders: *Give alms,* saith he, *and, behold, all things are clean unto you.* (Luke xi, [41.]) He teacheth them, that to be merciful and charitable in helping the poor is the means to keep the soul pure and clean in the sight of God. We are taught therefore by this, that merciful almsdealing is profitable to purge the soul from the infection and filthy spots of sin. The same lesson doth the Holy Ghost also teach in sundry places of the Scripture, saying[β], *Mercifulness and almsgiving purgeth from all sins, and delivereth from death, and suffereth not the soul to come into darkness. A great confidence may they have before the high God that shew mercy and compassion to them that are afflicted*[1]. The wise Preacher the son of Sirach confirmeth the same, when he saith that, *as water quencheth burning fire, even so mercy and alms resisteth and reconcileth sins.* (Ecclus. iii, [30.]) And sure it is that mercifulness quaileth the heat of sin so much, that they shall not take hold upon man to hurt him; or, if he[i] have by any infirmity and weakness[k] been touched and annoyed with them, straightways shall mercifulness wipe and wash them away[l], as salves and remedies to heal their sores and grievous diseases. And thereupon that holy father Cyprian taketh good occasion[2] to exhort earnestly to the merciful work of giving alms and helping the poor; and there he admonisheth to consider how

β Tob. iv, [10, 11: Prov. xvi, 6.]

g be the better] be better *from* 1563 B. h and have] and to have 1623. i if he] if ye *from* 1570. k and weakness] or weakness *from* 1574. l wash them away] wash away 1623.

1 Eleemosyna ab omni peccato et a morte liberat, et non patietur animam ire in tenebras. Fiducia magna erit coram Summo Deo eleemosyna omnibus facientibus eam. *Tob.* IV, 11, 12, *Vulg.*

2 See the opening of Cyprian's treatise *De Opere et Eleemosynis*, ending with this sentence: Agnoscamus itaque, fratres carissimi, divinae indulgentiae munus salubre; et emundandis purgandisque peccatis nostris, qui sine aliquo conscientiae vulnere esse non possumus, medelis spiritalibus vulnera nostra curemus. *Cyprian. Opp. p.* 198 *ed. Oxon., p.* 237 *ed. Paris.*

wholesome and profitable it is to relieve the needy and help the afflicted, by the which we may purge our sins and heal our wounded souls.

But here[m] some will say unto me, If almsgiving and our charitable works towards the poor be able to wash away sins, to reconcile us to God, to deliver us from the peril of damnation, and make us the sons and heirs of God's kingdom, then is[n] Christ's merit[o] defaced, and his blood shed in vain; then are we justified by works, and by our deeds may we merit heaven; then do we in vain believe that *Christ died for to put away our sins, and that he rose for our justification,* as St. Paul teacheth. [Tit. ii, 14: Rom. iv, 25.] But ye shall understand, dearly beloved, that neither those places of Scripture[p] before alleged, neither the doctrine of the blessed Martyr Cyprian, neither any other godly and learned man, when they, in extolling the dignity, profit, fruit, and effect of virtuous and liberal alms, do say that it washeth away sins and bringeth us to the favour of God, do mean that our work and charitable deed is the original cause of our acceptation[q] before God, or that for the dignity or worthiness thereof our sins be[r] washed away, and we purged and cleansed of all the spots of our iniquity; for that were indeed to deface Christ, and to defraud him of his glory. But they mean this, and this is the understanding of those and such like sayings: that God, of his mercy and especial[s] favour towards them whom he hath appointed to everlasting salvation, hath so offered his grace effectually[t], and they have so received it fruitfully, that, although by reason of their sinful living outwardly they seemed before to have been the children of wrath and perdition, yet now, the Spirit of God mightily working in them unto obedience to God's will and commandments, they declare by their outward deeds and life, in shewing[u] of mercy and charity, which cannot come but of the Spirit of God and his especial grace, that they are the undoubted children of God, appointed to everlasting life: and so, as by their wickedness and ungodly living they shewed themselves, according to the judgment of men, (which follow *the outward appearance*[y]), to be reprobates and castaways, so now by their obedience unto God's holy will, and by their mercifulness and tender pity, (wherein they shew themselves to be like unto God, who is the fountain and spring of all mercy,)

Sam. xvi,

[m] here] yet *from* 1582. [n] then is] then are 1623. [o] merit] merits *from* 1567. [p] of Scripture] of the Scripture 1623. [q] acceptation] acception *from* 1563 G. [r] sins be] sins may be *from* 1567. [s] and especial] and special 1623. [t] effectually] especially *from* 1563 G. [u] in shewing] in the shewing *from* 1563 B.

they declare openly and manifestly unto the sight of men, that they are the sons of God, and elect of him unto salvation.

For, as the good fruit is not the cause that the tree is good, but the tree must first be good before it can bring forth good fruit; so the good deeds of man are not the cause that maketh man[x] good, but he is first made good by the Spirit and grace of God, that effectually worketh in him, and afterward he bringeth forth good fruits. And then, as the good fruit doth argue the goodness of the tree, so doth the good and merciful deed of the man argue and certainly prove the goodness of him that doeth it, according to Christ's saying[y], *Ye shall know them by their fruits.* [Matt. vii, 16.] And, if any man will object, that evil and naughty men do sometime[z] by their deeds appear to be very godly and virtuous, I will answer, that so[a] doth the crab and choke-pear[3] seem outwardly to have sometime as fair a red and as mellow a colour as the fruit which[b] is good indeed, but he that will bite and take a taste shall easily judge betwixt the sour bitterness of the one and the sweet savouriness of the other. And, as the true Christian man, in thankfulness of his heart for the redemption of his soul purchased by Christ's death, sheweth kindly[4] by the fruit of his faith his obedience to God, so the other, as a merchant with God, doeth all for his own gain, thinking to win heaven by the merit of his works, and so defaceth and obscureth the price of Christ's blood, who only wrought our purgation.

The meaning then of these sayings in the Scriptures and other holy writings[5], *Almsdeeds do wash away our sins*, and, *Mercy to the poor doth blot out our offences*, is, that we, doing these things according to God's will and our duty, have our sins

5 [Tob. xii, 9: Prov. xvi, 6: Dan. iv, 27.]

x maketh man] make the man *till* 1563 D, maketh men 1623. y saying] sayings *from* 1563 G. z do sometime] do sometimes *from* 1563 G. a answer, that so] answer, so *from* 1570. b fruit which] fruit that *from* 1582.

3 In *Gerard's Herball*, III, 94, "Of the wilde Peare tree," (but III, 100, in *Johnson's* enlarged edition,) the first two kinds are "Pyrum strangulatorium maius" and "P. s. minus," "The great," and "The small, Choke Peare;" and in his General Description he says some of the wild pears are "of such a choking taste, that they are not to be eaten of hogs and wilde beasts, much lesse of men."

"This Bosbury-tree" [a pear yielding excellent perry,] "and such generally that bear the most lasting liquor and winy, is of such unsufferable taste that hungry swine will not smell to it, or, if hunger tempt them to taste, at first crush they shake it out of their mouths; ... and the clowns call other pears, of best liquor, Choak-pears, and will offer money to such as dare adventure to taste them, for their sport." *Beale's Aphorisms concerning Cider*, in *Pomona, the Appendix to Evelyn's Sylva, Aph.* 45.

4 kindly: perhaps "after his kind." *Gen.* I, 11. See *Matt.* V, 45; *John* VIII, 39, 42. So we pray in the Litany for "the kindly fruits of the earth."

indeed washed away and our offences blotted out, not for the worthiness of them, but by the grace of God *which worketh all in all*[e]; and that for the promise that God hath made to them that are obedient unto his commandment, that he which is the Truth might be justified in performing the truth due to his true promise. Almsdeeds do wash away our sins, because God doth vouchsafe then to repute us as clean and pure, when we do them for his sake, and not because they deserve or merit our purging, or for that they have any such strength and virtue in themselves.

e [1 Cor. xii, 6.]

I know that some men, too much addict to the advancing of their good works[c], will not be contented with this answer; and no marvel, for such men can no answer content nor[d] suffice. Wherefore, leaving them to their own wilful sense, we will rather have regard of[e] the reasonable and godly; who, as they most certainly know and persuade themselves that all goodness, all bounty, all mercy, all benefits, all forgiveness of sins, and whatsoever can be named good and profitable either for the body or for the soul, do come only of God's mercy and mere favour, and not of themselves, so, though they do never so many and so excellent good deeds, yet are they never puffed up with the vain confidence of them. And, though they hear and read in God's word and otherwhere in godly men's works, that almsdeeds, mercy, and charitableness doth wash away sin and blot out iniquity, yet do they not arrogantly and proudly stick or trust[f] unto them, or brag themselves of them, as the proud Pharisee[f] did, lest with the Pharisee they should be condemned; but rather, with the humble and poor Publican, confess themselves sinful wretches and unworthy[g] to look up to heaven, calling and craving for mercy, that with the Publican they may be pronounced of Christ to be justified. The godly do learn, that, when the Scriptures say that by good and merciful works we are reconciled to God's favour, we are taught then to know what Christ by his intercession and mediation obtaineth for us of his Father when we be obedient to his will; yea, they learn in such manners[h] of speaking a comfortable argument of God's singular favour and love, that attributeth that unto us and to our doings, that he by his Spirit worketh in us, and through his grace procureth for us. And yet, this notwithstanding, they cry out with St. Paul, *O wretches that we*

f [Luke xviii, 10–14.]

[Rom. vii, 24.]

c their good works] their works 1623. d nor] or *from* 1582. e regard of] regard to *from* 1563 B. f or trust] and trust *from* 1571. g wretches and unworthy] wretches, unworthy *from* 1567. h manners] manner *from* 1574.

are; and acknowledge, as Christ teacheth, that, *when they have* [Luke xvii, 10.] *all done, they are but unprofitable servants;* and with the blessed king David, in respect of the just judgments of God, they do tremble, and say, *Who shall be able to abide it, Lord, if* [Ps. cxxx, 3.] *thou wilt give sentence according to our deserts?* Thus they humble themselves, and are exalted of God; they count themselves vile, and of God are counted pure and clean; they condemn themselves, and are justified of God; they think themselves unworthy of the earth, and of God are thought worthy of heaven. Thus of[i] God's word are they truly taught how to think rightly of merciful dealing of alms, and of God's especial mercy and goodness are made partakers of those fruits that his word hath promised.

Let us then follow their examples, and both shew obediently in our life those works of mercy that we are commanded, and have that right opinion and judgment of them that we are taught; and we shall, in like manner as they, be made partakers and feel the fruits and rewards that follow such godly living. So shall we know by proof what profit and commodity doth come of giving alms[k] and succouring of the poor.

[i] Thus of] Thus by 1623. [k] giving alms] giving of alms *from* 1570.

THE THIRD PART OF THE HOMILY

OF ALMSDEEDS.

YE have already heard two parts of this Treatise of Almsdeeds: the first, how pleasant and acceptable before God the doing of them is; the second, how much it behoveth us, and how profitable it is, to apply ourselves unto them. Now in this[a] third part will I take away that let that hindereth many from doing of them[b].

There be many that, when they hear how acceptable a thing in the sight of God the giving of alms is, and how much God extendeth his favour towards them that are merciful, and what fruits and commodities doth come to them by it, they wish very gladly with themselves that they also might obtain these benefits, and be counted such of God as whom he would love or do for. But yet these men are with greedy covetousness so pulled back, that they will not bestow one halfpenny or one shive[c][1] of bread, that they might be thought worthy of God's benefits, and so to come into his favour. For they are evermore fearful and doubting lest by often giving, although it were but a little at a time, they should consume their goods, and so impoverish themselves, that even themselves at the length should not be able to live, but should be driven to beg and live of other men's alms. And thus they seek excuses to withhold themselves from the favour of God, and choose with pinching covetousness rather to lean unto the devil, than by charitable mercifulness either to come unto Christ, or to suffer Christ to come unto them. O that we had some cunning and skilful physician, that were able to purge them of this so pestilent an humour, that so sore infecteth, not their bodies, but their minds, and so by corrupting their souls bringeth their bodies and souls into danger of hell fire.

Now, lest there be any such among us, dearly beloved, let us diligently search for that physician, which is Jesus Christ, and

[a] in this] in the *from* 1567. [b] doing of them] doing them *from* 1563 G. [c] shive] piece 1623.

[1] shive : slice.

earnestly labour that of his mercy he will truly instruct us, and give us a present medicine[d] against so perilous a disease.

Hearken then, whosoever thou art that fearest lest by giving to the poor thou shouldest bring thyself to beggary. That which thou takest from thyself to bestow upon Christ can never be consumed and wasted away. Wherein thou shalt not believe me; but, if thou have faith and be a true Christian, believe the Holy Ghost, give credit to the authority of God's word, that thus teacheth. For thus saith the Holy Ghost by Salomon: *He that giveth unto the poor shall never want.* [Prov. xxviii, [27.]] Men suppose that by hoarding and laying up still they shall at the length be[e] rich, and that by distributing and laying out, although it be for most necessary and godly uses, they shall be brought to poverty. But the Holy Ghost, which knoweth all truth, teacheth us another lesson, contrary to this. He teacheth us[α] that there is a kind of dispending that shall never diminish the stock, and a kind of saving that shall bring a man to extreme poverty. For, where he saith that the good almsman shall never have scarcity, he addeth[β], *But he that turneth away his eyes from such as be in necessity shall suffer great poverty himself.* How far different then is the judgment of man from the judgment of the Holy Ghost!

[α] [Prov. xi, 24.]
[β] [Prov. xxviii, 27.]

The holy Apostle Paul, a man full of the Holy Ghost, and made privy even of the secret will of God, teacheth that the liberal almsgiver shall not thereby be impoverished. *He that ministereth*, saith he, *seed unto the sower will minister also bread unto you for food; yea, he will multiply your seed, and encrease the fruits of your righteousness*[2]. [2 Cor. ix, [10.]] He is not content here[f] to advertise them that they shall not lack, but he sheweth them also after what[g] sort God will provide for them. Even as he provideth[h] seed for the sower in multiplying it and giving great increase, so will he[i] multiply their goods and encrease them, that there shall be great abundance.

And, lest we should think his sayings to be but words, and not truth, we have an example thereof in the third book of Kings, which doth confirm and seal it up as a most certain truth. The poor widow[γ] that received the banished Prophet of

[γ] [1 Kings xvii, 8–16.]

[d] medicine] remedy *from* 1563 D. [e] at the length be] at length be *from* 1571. [f] here] *omitted after* 1574. [g] after what] in what *from* 1582. [h] provideth] provided *from* 1574. [i] will he] he will *from* 1571.

2 This is cited from Cyprian. *Qui administrat, inquit, semen seminanti, et panem ad edendum praestabit, et multiplicabit seminationem vestram, et augebit incrementa frugum justitiae vestrae, ut in omnibus locupletemini.* De Opere et Eleemosynis, Opp. p. 201 ed. Oxon., p. 240 ed. Paris.

God, Elias, when as she had but an[k] handful of meal in a vessel and a little oil in a cruse, whereof she would make a cake for herself and her son, that after they had eaten that they might die, because in that great famine there was no more food to be gotten; yet, when she gave part thereof unto[l] Elias, and defrauded her own hungry belly, mercifully to relieve him, she was so blessed of God, that neither the meal nor the oil was consumed all[m] the time while that famine did last, but thereof both the Prophet Elias, she, and her son were sufficiently nourished and had enough.

O consider this example, ye unbelieving and faithless covetous persons, who discredit God's word, and think his power diminished. This poor woman, in the time of an extreme and long dearth, had but one handful of meal and a little cruse of oil; her only son was ready to perish before her face for hunger, and she herself like to pine away: and yet, when the poor Prophet came and asked part, she was so mindful of mercifulness that she forgat her own misery; and, rather than she would omit the occasion given to give alms and work a work of righteousness, she was content presently to hazard her own and her son's life. And you, who have great plenty of meats and drinks, great store of motheaten apparel, yea, many of you great heaps of gold and silver, and he that hath least hath more than sufficient, now in this time, when, thanks be to God, no great famine doth oppress you, your children being well clothed and well fed, and no danger of death for famine to be feared, will rather cast doubts and perils of unlikely penury, than you will part with any piece of your superfluities, to help feed and[n] succour the poor, hungry, and naked Christ, that cometh to your doors a begging[3]. This poor and seely widow never cast doubts in all her misery what want[o] she herself should have; she never distrusted the promise that God had made[p] to her by the Prophet; but straightway went about to relieve the hungry Prophet of God, yea, preferring his necessity before her own. But we, like unbelieving wretches, before we will give one mite, we will cast a thousand doubts of danger, whether that will stand us in any stead that we give to the poor, whether we

[k] but an] but a *from* 1582. [l] unto] to *from* 1582. [m] consumed all] consumed of all 1563 A. [n] help feed and] help to feed and 1571, 1574; help and *from* 1582. [o] want] wants 1623. [p] God had made] God made *from* 1567.

[3] Auro parietes, auro laquearia, auro fulgent capita columnarum, et nudus atque esuriens ante fores nostras Christus in paupere moritur. *Hieron. Epist. ad Gaudentium* 128 (al. 12); *Opp.* 1, 959 C.

should not have need of it at any other time, and whether here it would not have been more profitably bestowed. So that it is not more[q] hard to wrench a strong nail, as the proverb saith, out of a post, than to wring a farthing out of our fingers. There is neither the fear nor the love of God before our eyes; we will more esteem a mite, than we either desire God's kingdom, or fear the devil's dungeon. Hearken, therefore, ye merciless misers, what will be the end of this your unmerciful dealing. As certainly as God nourished this poor widow in the time of famine, and encreased her little store, so that she had enough and felt no penury when other pined away, so certainly shall God plague you with poverty in the middes[r] of plenty. Then, when other have abundance and be fed to the full[s], you shall utterly waste and consume away yourselves; your store shall be destroyed, your goods plucked from you; all your glory and wealth shall perish; and that which when you had you might have enjoyed yourself in peace, and might have bestowed upon other most godly, ye shall seek with sorrow and sighs, and no where shall find it. For your unmercifulness towards other ye shall find no man that will shew mercy towards you. You that had stony hearts towards other shall find all the creatures of God to youwards[t] as hard as brass and iron.

Alas, what fury and madness doth possess our minds, that in a matter of truth and certainty we will not give credit to the truth, testifying unto that which is most certain. Christ saith[δ] δ [Matt. vi, 33.]
that, if we will first seek the kingdom of God, and do the works of righteousness thereof[4], we shall not be left destitute, all other things shall be given to us plenteously. Nay, say we, I will first look that I be able to live myself, and be sure that I have enough for me and mine; and, if I have any thing over, I will bestow it to get God's favour, and the poor shall then have part with me. See, I pray you, the perverse judgment of men. We have more care to nourish the carcase, than we have fear to see our soul perish. And, as Cyprian saith[5], "whilst we stand in Serm. de Eleemosyna.

q is not more] *so* WHITGIFT, is more *every edition of the Homilies entire.* r middes] middest *from* 1563 G. s to the full] at full *from* 1563 G. t youwards] youward *from* 1567.

4 Ζητεῖτε δὲ πρῶτον τὴν βασιλείαν τοῦ Θεοῦ καὶ τὴν δικαιοσύνην αὐτοῦ. Quaerite ergo primum regnum Dei et justitiam ejus. *Vulg.*

5 Metuis ne patrimonium tuum forte deficiat, si operari ex eo largiter coeperis; et nescis miser quia, dum times ne res familiaris deficiat, vita ipsa et salus deficit; et, dum ne quid de rebus tuis minuatur attendis, non respicis quod ipse minuaris, amator magis mammonae quam animae tuae; ut, dum times ne pro te patrimonium tuum perdas, ipse pro patrimonio tuo pereas. *Cyprian. De Opere et Eleemosynis, Opp. p.* 201 *ed. Oxon., p.* 240 *ed. Paris.*

doubt lest our goods fail in being over liberal, we put it out of doubt that our life and health faileth in not being liberal at all. Whilst we are careful for diminishing of our stock, we are altogether careless to diminish ourselves. We love mammon, and lose our souls. We fear lest our patrimony should perish from us, but we fear not lest we should perish for it." Thus do we perversely love that we[u] should hate, and hate that we should love; we be negligent where we should be careful, and careful where we need not.

This vain[x] fear to lack ourselves, if we give to the poor, is much like the fear of children and fools, which when they see the bright glimpsing[y] of a glass, they do imagine straightway that it is the lightning, and yet the brightness of a glass never was the lightning. Even so, when we imagine that by spending upon the poor a man may come to poverty, we are cast into a vain fear; for we never heard nor[z] knew, that by that means any man came to misery, and was left destitute, and not considered of God. Nay, we read to the contrary in the Scripture, as I have before shewed, and as by infinite testimonies and examples may be proved, that, whosoever serveth God faithfully and unfeignedly in any vocation, God will not suffer him to decay, much less to perish. The Holy Ghost teacheth us by

Prov. x, [3.]

Salomon, that *the Lord will not suffer the soul of the righteous to perish for hunger*. And therefore David saith unto all them that

[Ps. xxxiv, 9, 10.]

are merciful, *O fear the Lord, ye that be his saints; for they that fear him lack nothing. The lions do lack and suffer hunger; but they which seek the Lord shall want no manner of thing that is*

[e] 1 Kings xvii, [2-6.]

good. When Elias[e] was in the desert, God fed him by the ministry of a raven, that evening and morning brought him sufficient victuals. When Daniel was shut up in the lions' den,

[ς] [Bel and the Dragon, 30-39.]

God prepared meat[ς] for him, and sent it thither to him. And there was the saying of David fulfilled: *The lions do lack and suffer hunger; but they which seek the Lord shall want no good thing.* For, while the lions, which should have been fed with his flesh, roared for hunger and desire of their prey, whereof they had no power, although it were present before them, he in the meantime was fresh fed from God, that should with his flesh have filled the lions. So mightily doth God work to preserve and maintain those whom he loveth; so careful is he also to feed them who in any state or vocation do unfeignedly serve

[u] love that we] love that which we 1623. [x] This vain] Thus vain *from* 1574. [y] glimpsing] glymsing 1563 A, glimering 1563 B—F, *then* glimmering. [z] nor] or *from* 1567.

him. And shall we now think that he will be unmindful of us, if we be obedient to his word, and according to his will have pity upon[a] the poor? He gives[b] us all wealth before we do any service for it; and will he see us to lack[c] necessaries when we do him true service? Can a man think that he that feedeth Christ can be forsaken of Christ and left without food? or will Christ deny earthly things unto them whom he promiseth heavenly things for his true service[6]?

It cannot be therefore, dear brethren, that by giving of alms we should at any time want ourselves; or that we, which relieve other men's need, should ourselves be oppressed with penury. It is contrary to God's word; it repugneth with his promise; it is against Christ's property and nature to suffer it; it is the crafty surmise of the devil to persuade us it. Wherefore stick not to give alms freely, and trust notwithstanding, that God's goodness will minister unto us sufficiency and plenty, so long as we shall live in this transitory life, and, after our days here well spent in his service and the love of our brethren, we shall be crowned with everlasting glory, to reign with Christ our Saviour in heaven. To whom with the Father and the Holy Ghost be all honour and glory for ever. Amen.

[a] upon] on *from* 1582. [b] gives] giveth *from* 1563 EF. [c] us to lack] us lack *from* 1563 G.

6 Quando enim factum est ut justo possent deesse subsidia vitae, cum scriptum sit, *Non occidet fame Dominus animam justam?* Helias in solitudine corvis ministrantibus pascitur, et Danieli in lacu ad leonum praedam jussu regis incluso prandium divinitus apparatur; et tu metuis ne operanti tibi et Dominum promerenti desit alimentum? ... Tu Christiano, tu Dei servo, tu operibus bonis dedito, tu Domino suo caro aliquid existimas defuturum? Nisi si putas quia qui Christum pascit a Christo ipse non pascitur, aut eis terrena deerunt quibus coelestia et divina tribuuntur. *Cyprian. ibid. pp.* 201, 202, *ed. Oxon.; pp.* 240, 241, *ed. Paris.*

AN HOMILY OR SERMON

CONCERNING THE NATIVITY AND BIRTH OF OUR SAVIOUR JESUS CHRIST.

AMONG all the creatures that God made in the beginning of the world most excellent and wonderful in their kind, there was none, as Scripture[a] beareth witness, to be compared almost in any point unto man; who, as well in body and in[b] soul, exceeded all other no less than the sun in brightness and light exceedeth every small and little star in the firmament. He was made according to the image[α] and similitude of God; he was indued with all kind of heavenly gifts; he had no spot of uncleanness in him; he was sound and perfect in all parts, both outwardly and inwardly; his reason was uncorrupt; his understanding was pure and good; his will was obedient and godly; he was made altogether like unto God in righteousness, in holiness, in wisdom, in truth, to be short, in all kind of perfection. When he was thus created and made, Almighty God, in token of his great love towards him, chose out a special place of the earth for him, namely, Paradise; where he lived in all tranquillity and pleasure, having great abundance of worldly goods, and lacking[c] nothing that he might justly require or desire to have. For, as it is said, *God made him lord and ruler over all the works of his hands, that he should have under his feet all sheep and oxen, all beasts of the field, all fowls of the air, all fishes of the sea,* and use them always[d] at his own pleasure, according as he should have need. Was not this a mirror of perfection? Was not this a full, perfect, and blessed estate? Could any thing else be well added hereunto? or greater felicity desired in this world?

α [Gen. i, 26, 27; v, 1; ix, 6: James iii, 9.]

Ps. viii, [6-8.]

But, as the common nature of all men is in time of prosperity and wealth to forget not only themselves but also God, even so did this first man Adam: who, having but one commandment at God's hand, namely, that he should not eat of the fruit of knowledge of good and ill, did notwithstanding most unmindfully, or rather most wilfully, break it, in forgetting the strait

[a] as Scripture] as the Scripture *from* 1563 G. [b] and in soul] and soul 1623. [c] lacking] lackynge 1563 A–C, lacke 1563 D, lackte *or* lackt 1563 E—1574. [d] always] alway 1563 D—1574.

charge of his Maker, and giving ear to the crafty suggestion of that wicked serpent the devil. Whereby it came to pass, that, as before he was blessed, so now he was accursed; as before he was loved, so now he was abhorred; as before he was most beautiful and precious, so now he was most vile and wretched, in the sight of his Lord and Maker. Instead of the image of God, he was become now[e] the image of the devil; instead of the citizen of heaven, he was become the bondslave of hell; having in himself no one part of his former purity and cleanness, but being altogether spotted and defiled; insomuch that now he seemed to be nothing else but a lump of sin, and therefore by the just judgment of God was condemned to everlasting death.

This so great and miserable a plague, if it had only rested on Adam, who first offended, it had been so much the easier, and might the better have been borne. But it fell not only on him, but also on his posterity and children for ever; so that the whole brood of Adam's flesh should sustain the selfsame fall and punishment which their forefather by his offence most justly had deserved. St. Paul in the fifth chapter to the Romans saith, *By the offence of only Adam the fault came upon all men to condemnation, and by one man's disobedience many were made sinners.* [Rom. v, 18, 19.] By which words we are taught, that, as in Adam all men universally sinned, so in Adam all men universally received the reward of sin, that is to say, became mortal and subject unto death, having in themselves nothing but everlasting damnation both of body and soul. *They became*, as David saith, *corrupt and abominable; they went all out of the way; there was none that did good, no not one.* [Ps. xiv, 1, 3.] O what a miserable and woful state was this, that the sin of one man should destroy and condemn all men, that nothing in all the world might be looked for but only pangs of death and pains of hell! Had it been any marvel if mankind had been utterly driven to desperation, being thus fallen from life to death, from salvation to destruction, from heaven to hell?

But behold the great goodness and tender mercy of God in this[f] behalf. Albeit man's wickedness and sinful behaviour was such that it deserved not in any part to be forgiven, yet, to the intent he might not be clean destitute of all hope and comfort in time to come, he ordained a new covenant, and made a sure promise thereof, namely, that he would send a Messias or Me-

[e] become now] now become *from* 1563 E.

[f] in this] in his *from* 1582.

diator into the world, which should make intercession, and put himself as a stay between both parties, to pacify the wrath and indignation conceived against sin, and to deliver man out of the miserable curse and cursed misery whereinto he was fallen headlong by disobeying the will and commandment of his only[g] Lord and Maker. This covenant and promise was first made unto Adam himself immediately after his fall, as we read in the third of Genesis, where God said to the serpent on this wise: *I* [Gen. iii, 15.] *will put enmity between thee and the woman, between thy seed and her seed: he shall break thine head, and thou shalt bruise his heel.* Afterward the selfsame covenant was also more amply and plainly renewed unto Abraham, where God promised him, that Gen. xii, [3; xxii, 18.] *in his seed all nations and families of the earth should be blessed.* Again, it was continued and confirmed unto Isaac[β] (β Gen. xxvi, [4.]) in the same form of words as it was before unto his father. And, to the intent that mankind might not despair, but always live in hope, Almighty God never ceased to publish, repeat, confirm, and continue the same by divers and sundry testimonies of his Prophets; who, for the better persuasion of the thing, prophesied the time, the place, the manner, and circumstance of his birth, the afflictions[h] of his life, the kind of his death, the glory of his resurrection, the receiving of his kingdom, the deliverance of his people, with all other circumstances belonging thereunto. [Isa. vii, 14: Matt. i, 23.] Esay prophesied that he should be born of a virgin, and called Emmanuel. [Mic. v, 2: Matt. ii, 6.] Micheas prophesied that he should be born in Bethleem, a place of Jewry. [Ezek. xxxiv, 23, 24.] Ezechiel prophesied that he should come of the stock and lineage of David. [Dan. vii, 14.] Daniel prophesied *that all nations and languages should serve him.* [Zech. ix, 9: Matt. xxi, 5.] Zachary prophesied that he should come *in poverty, riding upon an ass*[1]. [Mal. iv, 5: Matt. xi, 14; xvii, 12.] Malachi prophesied that he should send Elias before him, which was John the Baptist. [Zech. xi, 12, 13.] Jeremy[k] prophesied that he should be sold for thirty pieces of silver, &c. And all this was done, that the promise and covenant of God, made unto Abraham and his posterity concerning the redemption of the world, might be credited and fully believed.

[Gal. iv, 4, 5.] Now, as the Apostle Paul saith, *when the fulness of time was come*, that is, the perfection and course of years appointed from the beginning, then *God*, according to his former covenant and promise, *sent* a Messias, otherwise called a Mediator, into[l] the

g his only] the only *from* 1570. h afflictions] affliction *from* 1570. k Jeremy] *so, or* Hieremy, *in all. See Matt.* xxvii, 9. l Mediator, into] Mediator, unto *from* 1570.

1 Pauper, et ascendens super asinum. *Vulg.*

world; not such a one as Moyses was, not such a one as Josua, Saul, or David was, but such a one as should deliver mankind from the bitter curse of the law, and make perfect satisfaction by his death for the sins of all people; namely, he sent *his* dear and only *Son* Jesus Christ, *made*, as the Apostle saith, *of a woman, and made under the law, that he might redeem them that were in bondage of the law, and make them the children of God by adoption.* Was not this a wonderful great love towards us that were his professed and open enemies? towards us that were *by nature the children of wrath* and firebrands of hell fire? [Eph. ii, 3.] *In this*, saith St. John, *appeared the great love of God, that he sent his only begotten Son into the world to save us*, when we were his extreme enemies. [1 John iv, 9, 10.] *Herein is love, not that we loved him, but that he loved us, and sent his Son to be a reconciliation for our sins.* St. Paul also saith: *Christ, when we were yet of no strength, died for us being ungodly. Doubtless a man will scarce die for a righteous man. Peradventure some one durst die for him of whom he hath*[m] *received good. But God setteth out his love towards us, in that he sent Christ to die for us, when we were yet void of all goodness.* Rom. v, [6, 7, 8.] This and such other comparisons doth the Apostle use, to amplify and set forth the tender mercy and great goodness of God, declared towards mankind, in sending down *a Saviour* from heaven, even *Christ the Lord.* [Luke ii, 11.] Which one benefit among all other is so great and wonderful, that neither tongue can well express it, neither heart think it, much less give sufficient thanks to God for it.

But here is a great controversy between us and the Jews, whether the same Jesus which was born of the Virgin Mary be the true Messias and true Saviour of the world, so long promised and prophesied of before. They, as they are, and have been always, proud and *stiffnecked*, would never acknowledge him until this day, but have looked and gaped[n] for another to come. [Acts vii, 51, 52.] They have this fond imagination in their heads, that Messias[o] shall come, not, as Christ did, like a poor pilgrim and simple[p] soul, riding upon an ass, but like a valiant and mighty king, in great royalty and honour; not, as Christ did, with a few fishermen and men of a small[q] estimation in the world, but with a great army of strong men, with a great train of wise and noble men, as knights, lords, earls, dukes, princes, and so forth. Neither do they think that their Messias shall slanderously suffer

[m] he hath] they have *from* 1567. [n] gaped] waited 1623. [o] that Messias] that the Messias 1623. [p] simple] meek 1623. [q] of a small] of small *from* 1571.

death, as Christ did, but that he shall stoutly conquer and manfully subdue all his enemies, and finally obtain such a kingdom on earth as never was seen from the beginning. While they feign unto themselves after this sort a Messias of their own brain, they deceive themselves, and account Christ as an abject [1 Cor. i, 23.] and fool[r] of the world. Therefore *Christ crucified,* as St. Paul saith, is *unto the Jews a stumblingblock and to the Gentiles foolishness;* because they think it an absurd thing, and contrary to all reason, that a Redeemer and Saviour of the whole world should be handled after such sort[s] as he was, namely, scorned, reviled, scourged, condemned, and last of all cruelly hanged. This, I say, seemed in their eyes strange and most absurd; and therefore neither they would at that time, neither will they as yet, acknowledge Christ to be their Messias and Saviour. But we, dearly beloved, that hope and look to be saved, must both steadfastly believe and also boldly confess, that the same Jesus which was born of the Virgin Mary was the true Messias and Mediator between God and man, promised and prophesied of so Rom. x, [10, 11.] long before. For, as the Apostle writeth, *with the heart man believeth unto righteousness, and with the mouth confession is made unto salvation.* Again in the same place: *Whosoever believeth in him shall never be ashamed nor confounded.* Whereto agreeth also the testimony of St. John, written in the fourth chapter of [1 John iv, 15.] his first general Epistle, on this wise: *Whosoever confesseth that Jesus is the Son of God, he dwelleth in God, and God in him.*

There is no doubt but in this point all Christian men are fully and perfectly persuaded. Yet shall it not be a lost labour to instruct and furnish you with a few places concerning this matter, that ye may be able to stop the blasphemous mouths of all them that most Jewishly, or rather devilishly, shall at any time go about to teach or maintain the contrary. First, ye have the γ [Luke i, 11–20, 26–37.] witness and testimony of the angel Gabriel[γ], declared as well to Zachary the high priest as also to the blessed Virgin. Secondly, ye have the witness and testimony of John the Baptist, pointing [John i, 29.] unto Christ, and saying, *Behold the Lamb of God, that taketh away the sins of the world.* Thirdly, ye have the witness and testimony of God the Father, who thundered from heaven, and [Matt. xvii, 5.] said, *This is my dearly beloved Son, in whom I am well pleased; hear him.* Fourthly, ye have the witness and testimony of the δ [Matt. iii, 16.] Holy Ghost[δ], which came down from heaven in manner of a white[t] dove, and lighted upon him in time of his baptism. To

[r] fool] scorn 1623. [s] such sort] such a sort *from* 1563 EF. [t] white] *omitted* 1623.

these might be added a great number more, namely[ε], the witness and testimony of the wise men that came to Herod, the witness and testimony of Simeon and Anna, the witness and testimony of Andrew and Philip, Nathanael and Peter, Nicodemus and Martha, with divers other: but it were too long to repeat all, and a few places are sufficient in so plain a matter, specially among them that are already persuaded. Therefore, if the privy imps of Antichrist and crafty instruments of the devil shall attempt or go about to withdraw you from this true Messias, and persuade you to look for another that is not yet come, let them not in any case seduce you, but confirm yourselves with these and such other testimonies of holy Scripture, which are so sure and certain, that all the devils in hell shall never be able to withstand them. For, as truly as God liveth, so truly was Jesus Christ the true Messias and Saviour of the world, even the same Jesus which, as this day, was born of the Virgin Mary, without all help of man, only by the power and operation of the Holy Ghost.

ε [Matt. ii, 1–11: Luke ii, 25–38: John i, 40–49; iii, 2; vi, 69; xi, 27.]

Concerning whose nature and substance, because divers and sundry heresies are risen in these our days through the motion and suggestion of Satan, therefore it shall be needful and profitable for your instruction to speak a word or two also of this part. We are evidently taught in the Scripture, that our Lord and Saviour Christ consisteth of two several natures; of his manhood, being thereby perfect man; and of his Godhood[u], being thereby perfect God[x]. It is written: *The Word*[ζ], that is to say, the second person in Trinity, *became flesh. God*[η] *sending his own Son in the similitude of sinful flesh, fulfilled those things which the law could not. Christ*[θ], *being in form of God, took on him the form of a servant, and was made like unto man, being found in shape as a man. God*[ι] *was shewed in flesh, justified in spirit, seen of angels, preached to the Gentiles, believed on in the world, and received up in glory.* Also in another place[κ]: *There is one God, and one Mediator between God and man, even the man Jesus Christ.* These be plain places for the proof and declaration of both natures united and knit together in one Christ. Let us diligently consider and weigh the works that he did whiles he lived on earth, and we shall thereby also perceive the selfsame thing to be most true. In that he did hunger and

ζ John i, [14.]

η Rom. viii, [3.]

θ Phil. ii, [6, 7, 8.]

ι 1 Tim. iii, [16.]

κ [1 Tim. ii, 5.]

u Godhood] Godhead *from* 1563 G. x consisteth of——perfect God] consisted of two several natures, being, as touching his outward flesh, perfect man, as touching his inward spirit, perfect God 1563 A 1.

thirst, eat and drink, sleep and wake; in that he preached his Gospel to the people; in that he wept and sorrowed for Jerusalem; in that he paid tribute for himself and Peter; in that he died and suffered death; what other thing did he else declare but only this, that he was perfect man as we are? For which cause he is called in holy Scripture sometime *the son of David*, sometime *the Son of man*, sometime *the son of Mary*, sometime *the son of Joseph*, and so forth. Now in that he forgave sins; in that he wrought miracles; in that he did cast out devils; in that he healed men with his only word; in that he knew the thoughts of men's hearts; in that he had the seas at his commandment; in that he walked on the water; in that he rose from death to life; in that he ascended into heaven, and so forth; what other thing did he shew therein but only that he was perfect God, coequal with his Father[y] as touching his Deity? Therefore he saith[λ], *The Father and I are all one:* which is to be understood of his Godhead; for, as touching his manhood, he saith[μ], *The Father is greater than I am.*

[Matt. i, 1; xvi, 13: Mark vi, 3: John vi, 42.]

λ [John x, 30.]

μ [John xiv, 28.]

Where are now those Marcionites, that deny Christ to have been born in flesh[z], or to have been perfect man? Where are now those Arians, which deny Christ to have been perfect God, of equal substance with the Father? If there be any such, ye may[a] easily reprove them with these testimonies of God's word, and such other: whereunto I am most sure they shall never be able to answer. For the necessity of our salvation did require such a Mediator and Saviour, as under one person should be a partaker of both natures. It was requisite he should be man: it was also requisite he should be God. For, as the transgression came by man, so was it meet the satisfaction should be made by man. And, because *death*, according to St. Paul[ν], *is the* just *stipend* and reward *of sin*[2], therefore, to appease the wrath of God, and to satisfy his justice, it was expedient[ξ] that our Mediator should be such a one as might take upon him the sins of mankind, and sustain the due punishment thereof, namely, death. Moreover, he came in flesh, and in the selfsame flesh ascended into heaven, to declare and testify unto us, that all faithful people which steadfastly believe in him shall likewise come unto the same mansion place whereunto he[o], being our

ν [Rom. vi, 23.]

ξ [Heb. ii, 14–17.]

o [Heb. vi, 19, 20.]

y his Father] the Father *from* 1563 G. z born in flesh] born in the flesh *from* 1567. a ye may] he may 1574–1595, we may 1623.

2 Stipendia enim peccati mors. *Vulg.*

chief captain, is gone before. Last of all, he became man, that we thereby might receive the greater comfort, as well in our prayers as also in our adversity; considering with ourselves, that we have a Mediator that is true man as we are, *who also is* [Heb. iv, 15.] *touched with our infirmities, and was tempted even in like sort as we are.* For these and sundry other causes it was most needful he should come, as he did, in the flesh. But, because no creature, in that he is only a creature, hath or may have power to destroy death and give life, to overcome hell and purchase heaven, to remit sins and give righteousness, therefore it was needful that our Messias, whose proper duty and office that was, should be not only full and perfect man, but also full and perfect God, to the entent he might more fully and perfectly make satisfaction for mankind. God saith, *This is my wellbeloved* Matt. iii, [17.] *Son, in whom I am well pleased.* By which place we learn that Christ appeased and quenched the wrath of his Father, not in that he was only the Son of man, but much more in that he was the Son of God.

Thus ye have heard declared out of the Scriptures, that Jesus Christ was the true Messias and Saviour of the world, that he was by nature and substance perfect God and perfect man, and for what causes[b] it was expedient he should be so.

Now, that we may be the more mindful and thankful unto God in this behalf, let us briefly consider and call to mind the manifold and great benefits that we have received by the nativity and birth of this our Messias and Saviour. Before Christ's coming into the world, all men universally were[c] nothing else but[π] *a wicked and crooked generation*[3], rotten and *corrupt trees, stony ground, full of brambles and briers, lost sheep, prodigal sons,* naughty and *unprofitable*[d] *servants, unrighteous stewards, workers of iniquity, the brood of adders, blind guides, sitting in darkness and in the shadow of death,* to be short, nothing else but children of perdition and inheritors of hell fire. To this doth St. Paul bear witness in divers places of his Epistles[e], and Christ also himself in sundry places of his Gospel. But after he was once come down from heaven, and had taken our frail nature upon him, he made[ρ] *all them that would receive him*[f] truly, and believe his word, *good trees,* and *good ground, fruitful*

π [Deut. xxxii, 5: Matt. vii, 17: Mark iv, 5, 16: Heb vi, 8: Jer. l, 6: Luke xv, 6, 13; xvii, 10: Matt. xxiv, 48; xxv, 26: Luke xvi, 8; xiii, 27: Matt. xii, 34; xxiii, 24: Luke ii, 79: Rom. v, 12: 1 Cor. xv, 22.]

ρ [John i, 12: Matt. vii, 17;

[b] causes] cause *from* 1567. [c] universally were] universally in Adam were *from* 1571. [d] naughty and unprofitable] naughty unprofitable 1623. [e] Epistles] Epistle *from* 1582. [f] receive him] receive them 1563 A *and* B *and* D–F.

3 Generatio prava atque perversa. *Deut.* xxxii, 5, *Vulg.*

xiii, 8, 23: John xv, 2: Is. lx, 21: John xii, 36: Phil. iii, 20: John x, 16: Eph. v, 30: James ii, 5: John xv, 14: Rom. viii, 29: 1 Cor. v, 7.] [1 Pet. ii, 24, 25, and 9.]

and pleasant *branches, children of light, citizens of heaven, sheep of his fold, members of his body, heirs of his kingdom, his* true *friends* and *brethren*, sweet and lively bread, the elect and chosen *people of God.* For, as St. Peter saith in his first Epistle and second chapter, *he bare our sins in his body upon the cross; he healed us and made us whole by his stripes; and, whereas before we were sheep going astray, he by his coming brought us home again to the true Shepherd and Bishop of our souls;* making us *a chosen generation, a royal priesthood, an holy nation, a peculiar*[g] *people* of God, in that[σ] *he died for our offences, and rose again for*[h] *our justification.* St. Paul to Timothy[i], the third chapter: *We were,* saith he[τ], *in times past unwise, disobedient, deceived, serving divers lusts and pleasures, living in hatred, envy, maliciousness,* and so forth. *But after the lovingkindness of God our Saviour appeared towards mankind, not according to the righteousness that we had done, but according to his great mercy, he saved us by the fountain of the new birth and by the renewing of the Holy Ghost; which he poured upon us abundantly thorough*[k] *Jesus Christ our Saviour, that we, being once justified by his grace, should be heirs of eternal life through hope* and faith in his blood. In these and such other places is set out before our eyes, as it were in a glass, the abundant grace of God received in Christ Jesu; which is so much the more wonderful, because it came not of any desert of ours, but of his mere and tender mercy, even then when we were his extreme enemies.

σ [Rom. iv, 25.]

τ [Tit. iii, 3-7.]

Matt. [i, 21;] v, [17:] John xviii, [37:] Luke iv, [17-21, 43:] John viii, [12:] Matt. ix, [13;] xi, [28:] John xii, [31:] Col. i, [21, 22:] Heb. x, [10: 1 John iii, 8:] Rom. iii, [25: 1 John ii, 2.]

But, for the better understanding and consideration of this thing, let us behold the end of his coming: so shall we perceive what great commodity and profit his nativity hath brought unto us miserable and sinful creatures. The end of his coming was *to save* and deliver *his people, to fulfil the law* for us, *to bear witness unto the truth, to* teach and *preach the words of his Father, to give light unto the world, to call sinners to repentance, to refresh them that labour and be heavy laden, to cast out the prince of this world, to reconcile us in the body of his flesh, to dissolve the works of the devil*[4], last of all, to become *a propitiation for our sins, and not for ours only, but also for the sins of the whole world.* These were the chief ends wherefore Christ became man, not for any profit that should come to himself thereby,

g peculiar] particular *from* 1582. h rose again for] rose for 1623. i Timothy] *so in all.*
k thorough] through *from* 1563 G.

4 Ut dissolvat opera diaboli. 1 *Joh.* iii, 8, *Vulg.*

but only for our sakes; that we might understand the will of God, be partakers of his heavenly light, be delivered out of the devil's claws, released from the burden of sin, justified through faith in his blood, and finally received up into everlasting glory, there to reign with him for ever. Was not this a great and singular love of Christ towards mankind, that, *being the express* and lively *image of God,* he would notwithstanding *humble himself, and take upon him the form of a servant,* and that only to save and redeem us? [Heb. i, 3: Phil. ii, 7, 8.] O how much are we bound to the goodness of God in this behalf! How many thanks and praises do we owe unto him for this our salvation, wrought by his dear and only Son Christ: who became a pilgrim in earth, to make us citizens in heaven; who became the Son of man, to make us the sons of God; who became obedient to the law, to *deliver us from the curse of the law;* who *became poor, to make us rich;* [Gal. iii, 13; iv, 4, 5: 2 Cor. viii, 9.] vile, to make us precious; subject to death, to make us live for ever. What greater love could we seely creatures desire or wish to have at God's hands?

Therefore, dearly beloved, let us not forget this exceeding love of our Lord and Saviour; let us not shew ourselves unmindful or unthankful towards[1] him: but let us love him, fear him, obey him, and serve him. Let us confess him with our mouths, praise him with our tongues, believe on him with our hearts, and glorify him with our good works. Christ is *the light*[v]: let us receive the light. Christ is *the truth:* let us believe the truth. Christ is *the way:* let us follow the way. And, because he is our *only Master*[φ], our only Teacher, our *only Shepherd,* and Chief Captain, therefore let us become his servants, his scholars, his sheep, and his soldiers. As for sin, the flesh, the world, and the devil, whose servants and bondslaves we were before Christ's coming, let us utterly cast them off, and defy them, as the chief and only enemies of our soul. And, seeing we are once delivered from their cruel tyranny by Christ, let us never fall into their hands again, lest we chance to be in worse[m] case than ever we were before. *Happy*[χ] *are they,* saith Scripture[n], *that continue to the end. Be faithful*[ψ], saith God, *until death, and I will give thee a crown of life.* Again he saith in another place[ω]: *He that putteth his hand unto the plough, and looketh back, is not meet for the kingdom of God.* Therefore let us be strong, *steadfast*[a], *and unmoveable, abounding always in*

[v] [John xii, 46; xiv, 6.]
[φ] [Matt. xxiii, 8, 10: John vi, 68; x, 16.]
[χ] [Dan. xii, 12: Matt. x, 22.]
[ψ] [Rev. ii, 10.]
[ω] [Luke ix, 62.]
[a] [1 Cor. xv, 58.]

[1] towards] toward *from* 1582. [m] in worse] in a worse *from* 1571. [n] saith Scripture] saith the Scripture *from* 1563 G.

the works of the Lord. Let us receive Christ, not for a time, but for ever; let us believe his word, not for a time, but for ever; let us become his servants, not for a time, but for ever; in consideration that he hath redeemed and saved us, not for a time, but for ever; and will receive us into his heavenly kingdom, there to reign with him, not for a time, but for ever. To him therefore with the Father and the Holy Ghost be all honour, praise, and glory for ever and ever. Amen.

AN HOMILY FOR GOOD FRIDAY,

CONCERNING THE DEATH AND PASSION

OF OUR SAVIOUR JESUS CHRIST.

IT should not become us, well beloved in Christ[a], being that people which be[b] redeemed from the devil, from sin and death, and from everlasting damnation by Christ, to suffer this time to pass forth without any meditation and remembrance of that excellent work of our redemption, wrought as about this time, thorough[c] the great mercy and charity of our Saviour Jesu[d] Christ, for us wretched sinners and his mortal enemies. For, if a mortal man's deed done to the behoof of the commonwealth be had in remembrance of us, with thanks for the benefit and profit which we receive thereby, how much more readily should we have in memory this excellent act and benefit of Christ's death; whereby he hath purchased for us the undoubted pardon and forgiveness of our sins; whereby he made at one the Father of heaven with us, in such wise that he taketh us now for his loving children, and for the true *inheritors with Christ*, his natural Son, of the kingdom of heaven! [Rom. viii, 17.]

And verily so much more doth Christ's kindness appear unto us, in that it pleased him to deliver himself[α] of all his godly[e] honour, which he was equally in with his Father in heaven, and to come down into this vale of misery, to be made mortal man, and to be in the state of a most low servant, serving us for our wealth and profit, us, I say, which were his sworn enemies, which had renounced his holy law and commandments, and followed the lusts and sinful pleasures of our corrupt nature; and yet, I say, did Christ put himself between God's deserved wrath and our sin, and rent that *obligation*[β][1] wherein we were in danger to God, and paid our debt. Our debt was a great deal too great for us to have paid; and without payment God the Father could never be at one with us: neither was it possible to be loosed

α Phil. ii, [6, 7.]

β Col. ii, [14.]

[a] in Christ] brothers and sisters TAV. [b] which be] which he *from* 1563 D, *except* 1563 H. [c] thorough] through *from* 1563 G. [d] Jesu] Jesus *from* 1563 G. [e] godly] goodly 1623.

[1] Χειρόγραφον.

from this debt by our own ability. It pleased therefore him[f] to be the payer thereof, and to discharge us quite.

Who can now consider the grievous debt of sin which could none otherwise be paid but by the death of an innocent, and will not hate sin in his heart? If God hateth sin so much, that he would allow neither man nor angel for the redemption thereof, but only the death of his only and wellbeloved Son, who will not stand in fear thereof? If we, my friends, consider this, that for our sins this most innocent Lamb was driven to death, we shall have much more cause to bewail ourselves, that we were the cause of his death, than to cry out of the malice and cruelty of the Jews, which pursued him to his death. We did the deeds wherefore he was thus stricken and wounded: they were only the ministers of our wickedness.

It is meet then we should step low down into our hearts, and bewail our own wretchedness and sinful living. Let us know for a certainty, that, if the most dearly beloved Son of God was thus punished and stricken for the sin which he had not done himself, how much more ought we sore to be stricken for our daily and manifold sins which we commit against God, if we earnestly repent us not, and be not sorry for them. No man can love sin, which God hateth so much, and be in his favour. No man can say that he loveth Christ truly, and have his great enemy (sin, I mean, the author of his death) familiar and in friendship with him. So much do we love God and Christ, as we hate sin. We ought therefore to take great heed that we be not favourers thereof, lest we be found enemies to God and traitors to Christ. For not only they which nailed Christ upon the cross

[γ Heb. vi, [6.]] are his tormentors and crucifiers, but all they, saith St. Paul[γ], *crucify again the Son of God*, as much as is in them, which do[g] commit vice and sin, which brought him to his death.

[δ Rom. vi, [23.]] [ε Rom. viii, [13.]] If *the wages*[δ] *of sin be death*, and death everlasting, surely it is no small danger to be in service thereof. *If we live*[ε] *after the flesh* and after the sinful lusts thereof, St. Paul threateneth, yea Almighty God in St. Paul threateneth, that *we shall* surely *die*.

[ζ [Rom. vi, 11.]] [η Rom. viii, [10, 11.]] We can none otherwise[ζ] live to God but by dying to sin. *If Christ*[η] *be in us, then is sin dead in us: and, if the Spirit of God be in us, which raised Christ from death to life, so shall the same Spirit raise us to the resurrection of everlasting life.* But, if sin rule and reign in us, then is God, which is the fountain of all grace and virtue, departed from us; then hath the devil and his

[f] therefore him] him therefore *from* 1571.

[g] which do] who do 1623.

ungracious spirit rule and dominion in us. And surely, if in such miserable state we die, we shall not rise to life, but fall down to death and damnation, and that without end.

Christ hath not so re-deemed[h] us from sin, that we should live in sin.

For Christ hath not so redeemed us from sin, that we may safely return thereto again; but he hath redeemed us[θ], that we should forsake the motions thereof, and live to righteousness. Yea, we be therefore washed in our baptism from the filthiness of sin, that we should live afterward in the pureness of life. In baptism we promised to renounce the devil and his suggestions, we promised to be, *as obedient children*[ι], always following God's will and pleasure. Then, if he be our Father[κ] indeed, let us give him his due honour. If we be his children, let us shew him our obedience, like as Christ openly declared his obedience to his Father, which, as St. Paul writeth, was *obedient even to the very death, the death of the cross.*

θ [Tit. ii, 14.]
ι [1 Pet. i, 14.]
κ Mal. i, [6.]
Phil. ii, [8.]

And this he did for us all that believe in him. For himself he was not punished; for he was pure and undefiled of all manner of sin. *He was wounded,* saith Esay, *for our wickedness, and striped*[i] *for our sins:* he suffered the penalty of them himself, to deliver us from danger. *He bare,* saith Esay, *all our sores and infirmities upon his own back:* no pain did he refuse to suffer in his own body, that he might deliver us from pain everlasting. His pleasure it was thus to do for us: we deserved it not. Wherefore, the more we see ourselves bound unto him, the more he ought to be thanked of us; yea, and the more hope may we take, that we shall receive all other good things of his hand, in that we have received the gift of his only Son through his liberality. For, *if God,* saith St. Paul, *hath not spared his own Son* from pain and punishment, *but delivered him for us all* unto the death, *how should he not give us all other things with him?* If we want any thing either for body or soul, we may lawfully and boldly approach to God as to our merciful Father, to ask that we desire, and we shall obtain it. For such power is given to us[λ], *to be the children of God, so many as believe in Christ's name.* In his name whatsoever we ask[μ], we shall have it granted us. For so well pleased is the Father, Almighty God, with Christ his Son, that for his sake he favoureth us, and will deny us nothing. So pleasant was this sacrifice and oblation of his Son's death, which he so obediently and innocently suffered, that he would[k] take it for the only and full amends

Isa. liii, [4, 5.]
Rom. viii, [32.]
λ John i, [12.]
μ Matt. xxi, [22: John xvi, 23–27.]

[h] not so redeemed (*in the margin*)] not redeemed *from* 1563 D. [i] striped] stripped *from* 1582. [k] that he would] that we should *from* 1582.

for all the sins of the world. And such favour did he purchase by his death of his heavenly Father for us, that for the merit thereof, (if we be true Christians indeed, and not in word only,) we be now fully in God's grace again, and clearly discharged from our sin.

No tongue surely is able to express the worthiness of this so precious a death. For in this standeth the continual pardon of our daily offences, in this resteth our justification, in this we be allowed, in this is purchased the everlasting health of all our souls; yea, *there is none other thing that can be named under heaven to save our souls*, but this only work of Christ's precious offering of his body upon the altar of the cross. Certes there can be no work of any mortal man, be he never so holy, that shall be coupled in merits with Christ's most holy act. For no doubt all our thoughts and deeds were of no value, if they were not allowed in the merits of Christ's death. All our righteousness is[l] far unperfect, if it be compared with Christ's righteousness. For in his acts and deeds there was no spot of sin or of any unperfectness; (and for this cause they were the more able to be the true amends of our unrighteousness[m];) where our acts and deeds be full of imperfection and infirmities, and therefore nothing worthy of themselves to stir God to any favour, much less to challenge the glory that[n] is due to Christ's act and merit: for *not to us*, saith David, *not to us, but to thy Name give the glory, O Lord.*

Acts iv, [12.]

Our deeds be full of imperfection.

Ps. cxiii [cxv, 1.]

Let us therefore, good friends, with all reverence glorify his Name; let us magnify and praise him for ever. For he hath dealt with us according to his great mercy; by himself hath he purchased our redemption. He thought it not enough to spare himself and to send his angel to do this deed; but he would do it himself[v], that he might do it the better, and make it the more perfect redemption. He was nothing moved with the intolerable[o] pains that he suffered in the whole course of his long passion, to repent him thus to do good to his enemies; but he opened his heart for us, and bestowed himself wholly for the ransoming of us. Let us therefore now open our hearts again to him, and study in our lives to be thankful to such a Lord, and evermore to be mindful of so great a benefit.

v Heb. i, [3.]

Yea, let us take up our cross with Christ, and follow him.

[l] righteousness is] unrighteousness is 1563 A—F. [m] our unrighteousness] our righteousness *from* 1582. [n] the glory that] that glory that 1623. [o] intolerable] unsufferable TAV., *but* unspeakable *in other copies.*

His passion is not only the ransom and whole amends for our sin, but it is also a most perfect example of all patience and sufferance. For, if[ξ] *it behoved Christ thus to suffer, and to enter into* the *glory* of his Father, how should[p] it not become us to bear patiently our small crosses of adversity and the troubles of this world? For surely, as saith St. Peter[ο], *Christ therefore suffered, to leave us an example to follow his steps.* And[π], *if we suffer with him, we shall be sure also to reign with him* in heaven. *Not that*[ρ] *the sufferance of this transitory life should be worthy of that glory to come;* but gladly should we be content[q] to suffer[σ], to be like Christ in our life, that so by our works we may *glorify our Father which is in heaven.* And, as it is painful and grievous to bear the cross of Christ in the griefs and displeasures of this life, so it bringeth forth[τ] the joyful fruit of hope in all them that be exercised therewith. Let us not so much[υ] behold the pain, as the reward that shall follow that labour.

ξ Acts xvii, [3: Luke xxiv, 26, 46.]
ο 1 Pet. ii, [21.]
π 2 Tim. ii, [12.]
ρ Rom. viii, [18.]
σ Matt. v, [10–12, 16.]
τ Heb. xii, [11.]
υ [Ibid. 1, 2.]

Nay, let us rather endeavour ourselves in our sufferance to endure innocently and guiltless, as our Saviour Christ did. For, if we suffer for our deservings, then hath not *patience*[φ] *his perfect work* in us: *but, if*[χ] *undeservingly*[r] *we suffer* loss of goods and life, if we suffer to be evil spoken of, for the love of Christ, *this is thankful afore God;* for so did Christ suffer. *He never did sin, neither was there*[s] *any guile found in his mouth. Yea, when he was reviled with taunts, he reviled not again; when he was wrongfully dealt with, he threatened not again,* nor revenged his quarrel, *but delivered his cause to him that judgeth rightly.* Perfect patience careth not what or how[t] much it suffereth, nor of whom it suffereth, whether of friend or foe; but studieth to suffer innocently and without deserving. Yea, he in whom perfect charity is careth so little to revenge, that he rather studieth to *do good for evil*[ψ], *to bless and say well of them that curse him, to pray for them that pursue him,* according to the example of our Saviour Christ, who is the most perfect example and pattern of all meekness and sufferance. Which, hanging upon his cross in most fervent anguish, bleeding in every part of his blessed body, being set in the middes[u] of his enemies and crucifiers, and, notwithstanding[x] the intolerable pains which they saw him in[y], being of them mocked and

φ James i, [4.]
χ 1 Pet. ii, 19–23.]
The patience of Christ.
Perfect patience.
ψ Matt. v, [44.]
The meekness of Christ.

p how should] why should *from* 1582. q content] contented *from* 1570. r undeservingly] undeservedly 1623. s there] *omitted after* 1574. t or how] nor how *from* 1563 G. u middes] middest 1587, 1595, 1623. x and, notwithstanding] And he, notwithstanding *from* 1563 B. y him in] in him 1563 G—1574.

scorned despitefully without all favour and compassion, had yet towards them such compassion in heart, that he prayed to his Father of heaven for them, and said [ω], *O Father, forgive them, for they wote not what they do.* What patience was it also which he shewed when one of his own Apostles and servants, which was put in trust of him, came to betray him unto his enemies to the death! He said nothing worse to him but [a], *Friend, wherefore art thou come?*

ω Luke xxiii, [34.]
a Matt. xxvi, [50.]

Thus, good people, should we call to mind the great examples of charity which Christ shewed in his passion, if we will fruitfully remember his passion. Such charity and love should we bear one to another, if we will be the true servants of Christ. *For, if we love but them which love* and say well by *us, what great thing is it that we do?* saith Christ: *do not* the paynims and *open sinners so?* We must be more perfect in our charity than thus, *even as our Father in heaven is perfect; which maketh the light of his sun to rise upon the good and the bad, and sendeth his rain upon the kind and unkind.* After this manner should we shew our charity indifferently, as well to one as to another, as well to friend as foe, *like obedient children* [β], after the example of our good Father [z] in heaven. For, if Christ was *obedient* [γ] to his Father *even to the death,* and that the most shameful death (as the Jews esteemed it), *the death of the cross,* why should not we [a] be obedient to God in lower points of charity and patience?

Matt. v, [45–48.]
β [1 Pet. i, 14.]
γ [Phil. ii, 8.]

Let us forgive then our neighbours their small faults, *as God* [δ] *for Christ's sake hath forgiven us* our great. It is not meet [ε] that we should crave forgiveness of our great offences at God's hands, and yet will not forgive the small trespasses of our neighbours against us. We do call for mercy in vain, if we will not shew mercy to our neighbours. For, if we will not put wrath [b] and displeasure forth of our hearts to our Christian brother, no more will God forgive the displeasure and wrath that our sins have deserved afore him. For under this condition [ζ] doth God forgive us, if we forgive other. It becometh not Christian men to be hard one to another, nor yet to think their neighbour unworthy to be forgiven. For, howsoever unworthy he is, yet is Christ worthy to have thee do thus much for his sake: he hath deserved it of thee, that thou shouldest forgive thy neighbour. And God is also to be obeyed, which

δ [Eph. iv, 32.]
ε Ecclus. xxviii, [1–5:] Matt. xviii, [35.]
ζ [Matt. vi, 14, 15.]

[z] our good Father] our Father *from* 1582. [a] not we] we not *from* 1563 EF. [b] put wrath] put out wrath TAV.

command[c] us to forgive, if we will have any part of the pardon which our Saviour Christ purchased once of God the Father by shedding of his precious blood. Nothing becometh Christ's servants so much as mercy and compassion.

Let us then be favourable one to another: *and pray*[η] *we one for another, that we may be healed* from all frailties of our life, the less to offend one the other; and that we may be *of one mind*[θ] *and one*[d] *spirit,* agreeing together in brotherly love and concord, even *like the dear children of God.* By these means shall we move God to be merciful to our sins[e]. Yea, and we shall be hereby the more ready to receive our Saviour and Maker in his blessed Sacrament to our everlasting comfort and health of soul. Christ delighteth to enter and to dwell[f] in that soul where love and charity ruleth, and where peace and concord is seen. For thus writeth St. John[ι]: *God is charity; he that abideth in charity abideth in God, and God in him. And by this,* saith he[κ], *we shall know that we be of God, if we love our brothers*[g]. Yea, and *by this shall we know that we be shifted*[h] *from death to life, if we love one another. But he which hateth his brother,* saith the same Apostle, *abideth in death,* even in the danger of everlasting death; and is moreover the child of damnation and of the devil, cursed of God, and hated (so long as he so remain[i]) of God and of all[k] his heavenly company. For, as peace and charity make us the blessed children of Almighty God, so doth hatred and envy make us the cursed children of the devil.

η James v, [16.]
θ [Phil. i, 27; ii, 2:] Eph. v, [1, 2.]
ι 1 John iv, [16.]
κ 1 John iii, [19; 14, 15;] ii, [11.]

God give us all grace to follow Christ's example[l] in peace and in charity, in patience and sufferance; that we now may have him our guest to enter and dwell within us, so as we may be in full surety, having such a pledge of our salvation. If we have him and his favour, we may be sure that we have the favour of God by his means. For he sitteth on the right hand[λ] of his[m] Father, as our proctor and attorney, pleading and suing for us in all our needs and necessities. Wherefore, if we want any gift of godly wisdom, we may ask it of God for Christ's sake, and we shall have it.

λ Rom. viii, [34.]

Let us consider and examine ourself[n], in what want we be concerning this virtue of charity and patience. If we see that

[c] command] commandeth *from* 1563 B. [d] and one] and of one TAV. [e] to our sins] unto our sins 1623. [f] and to dwell] and dwell *from* 1563 G. [g] brothers] brethren *from* 1563 G. [h] shifted] delivered 1623. [i] remain] remaineth *from* 1563 EF. [k] and of all] and all *from* 1563 EF. [l] example] examples *from* 1574. [m] of his] of God his *from* 1582. [n] examine ourself] examine ourselves *from* 1582.

our hearts be nothing inclined thereunto in forgiving them that have offended against us, then let us knowledge our want, and wish of[o] God to have it. But, if we want it and see in ourself[p] no desire thereunto, verily we be in a dangerous case afore[q] God, and have need to make much earnest prayer to God, that we may have such an heart changed, to the graffing[r] in of a new. For, unless we forgive other, we shall never be forgiven of God. No, not all the prayers and merits[s] of other can pacify God unto us, unless we be at peace and at one with our neighbour: nor all our deeds and good works can move God to forgive us our debts to him, except we forgive to other. He setteth more[μ] by mercy than by sacrifice. Mercy moved our Saviour Christ to suffer for his enemies: it becometh us then to follow his example. For it shall little avail us to have in meditation the fruits and price of his passion, to magnify them, and to delight or trust to[t] them, except we have in mind his examples in passion, to follow them. If we thus therefore consider Christ's death, and will stick thereto with fast faith for the merit and deserving thereof, and will also frame ourself[u] in such wise to bestow ourselves and all that we have by charity to the behoof of our neighbour, as Christ spent himself wholly for our profit, then do we truly remember Christ's death; and, being thus followers of Christ's steps, we shall be sure to follow him thither where he sitteth now with the Father and the Holy Ghost. To whom be all honour and glory. Amen.

μ [Hos. vi, 6: Mic. vi. 6–8: Matt. ix, 13.]

[o] wish of] wish to *from* 1570. [p] in ourself] in ourselves *from* 1582. [q] afore] before *from* 1570. [r] graffing] grafting TAV., *and* 1623. [s] merits] good works 1623. [t] trust to] trust in *from* 1582. [u] frame ourself] frame ourselves 1623.

THE SECOND HOMILY

CONCERNING THE DEATH AND PASSION OF OUR SAVIOUR CHRIST.

THAT we may the better conceive the great mercy and goodness of our Saviour Christ in suffering death universally for all men, it behoveth us to descend into the bottom of our conscience, and deeply to consider the first and principal cause wherefore he was compelled so to do.

When our great-grandfather Adam had broken[α] God's commandment in eating the apple forbidden him in Paradise at the motion and suggestion of his wife, he purchased thereby, not only to himself, but also to his posterity for ever, the just wrath and indignation of God; who, according to his former sentence pronounced at the giving of the commandment, condemned both him and all his to everlasting death, both of body and soul. For it was said unto him: *Thou shalt eat freely of every tree in the garden: but as touching the tree of knowledge of good and ill, thou shalt in no wise eat of it; for in what hour soever thou eatest thereof thou shalt die the death.* Now, as the Lord had spoken, so it came to pass. Adam took upon him to eat thereof, and in so doing he died the death; that is to say, he became mortal, he lost the favour of God, he was cast out of Paradise, he was no longer a citizen of heaven, but a firebrand of hell and a bondslave to the devil. To this doth our Saviour bear witness in the Gospel, calling us[β] *lost sheep*, which have *gone astray* and wandered from *the* true *Shepherd*[γ] *of our souls.* To this also doth St. Paul bear witness, saying, that *by the offence of only Adam death came upon all men to condemnation.* So that now neither he nor any[a] of his had any right or interest at all in the kingdom of heaven, but were become plain reprobates and castaways, being perpetually damned to the everlasting pains of hell fire.

α Gen. iii, [17–19.]
Gen. ii, [16, 17.]
β Luke xv, [4.]
γ [1 Pet. ii, 25.]
Rom. v, [12, 18.]

In this so great misery and wretchedness, if mankind could have recovered himself again, and obtained forgiveness at God's hands, then had his case been somewhat tolerable; because he

[a] nor any] or any *from* 1582.

might have attempted some way how to deliver himself from eternal death. But there was no way left unto him; he could do nothing that might please[b][1] God's wrath; he was altogether unprofitable in that behalf; *there was none*[c] *that did good, no, not one.* [Ps. liii, [3: Rom. iii, 12.]] And how then could he work his own salvation? Should he go about to pacify God's heavy displeasure by offering up [8] brent[d] sacrifices, according as it was ordained in the old Law? [8 Heb. ix, [9, 12.]] by offering up the blood of oxen, the blood of calves, the blood of goats, the blood of lambs, and so forth? O these things were of no force nor strength to take away sins; they could not put away the anger of God; they could not cool the heat of his wrath, nor yet bring mankind into favour again: they were but only figures and shadows of things to come, and nothing else. Read the Epistle to the Hebrews, [Heb. x, [1-4, 11.]] there shall you find this matter largely discussed: there shall you learn in most plain words, that the bloody sacrifice of the old Law was unperfect, and not able to deliver man from the state of damnation by any means; so that mankind in trusting thereunto should trust to a broken staff, and in the end deceive himself. What should he then do? Should he go about to observe[e] and keep the law of God divided into two tables, and so purchase to himself eternal life? Indeed, if Adam and his posterity had been able to satisfy and fulfil the law perfectly in loving God above all things and their neighbour as themselves, then should they have easily quenched the Lord's wrath, and escaped the terrible sentence of eternal death pronounced against them by the mouth of Almighty God. For it is written, *Do this*[f], *and thou shalt live*; [Luke x, [28.]] that is to say, Fulfil my commandments, keep thyself upright and perfect in them according to my will; then shalt thou live and not die. Here is eternal life promised with this condition, so[g] that they keep and observe the law. But such was the frailty of mankind after his fall, such was his weakness and imbecility, that he could not walk uprightly in God's commandments, though he would never

[b] please] pacify *from* 1567. [c] none] not one 1623. [d] brent] burnt *from* 1582. [e] observe] serve *from* 1582. [f] Do this] Do thus *from* 1582. [g] condition, so] condition, and so 1623.

[1] Although Wycliffe uses forms and inflections of the verb *to please* in the sense of *appease* or *pacify* (as in *Gen.* XLIII, 14, *Ps.* XLVIII, 8, LXXVII, 38, *Is.* LX, 7, 1 *Macc.* I, 47), yet for the most part they are replaced by some other word in Purvey's recension of his translation. And it seems very likely that in this place the Homilist did not write *please*, but *pease*, the old form of *appease*, of which Richardson gives several instances under "Peace," and which occurs five times in the short section headed "Prayer peaseth God's wrath" in *Marshall's Primer*, the first of the *Three Primers put forth in the Reign of Henry VIII*, which have been reprinted at the University Press, *p.* 231.

so fain; but daily and hourly fell from his bounden duty, offending the Lord his God divers ways to the great increase of his condemnation, insomuch that the Prophet David crieth out on this wise: *All have gone astray, all are become unprofitable;* [Ps. liii, [3.]] *there is none that doeth good, no, not one.* In this case what profit could he have by the law? None at all. For, as St. James saith, *he that shall observe the whole law, and yet faileth* [James ii, [10.]] *in one point, is become guilty of all.* And in the book of Deuteronomy it is written: *Cursed be he,* saith God, *which abideth* [Deut. xxvii, [26: Gal. iii, 10.]] *not in all things that are written in the book of the law, to do them.* Behold the law bringeth a curse with it, and maketh us[h] guilty, not because [ε] it is of itself naught or unholy, (God forbid [ε [Rom. vii, 12–23.]] we should so think,) but because the frailty of our sinful flesh is such that we can never fulfil it according to the perfection that the Lord requireth. Could Adam then, think you, hope or trust to be saved by the law? No, he could not: but, the more he looked on the law, the more he saw his own damnation set before his eyes, as it were in a most clear[i] glass. So that now of himself he was most wretched and miserable, destitute of all hope, and never able to pacify God's heavy displeasure, nor yet to escape the terrible judgment of God, whereinto[j] he and all his posterity were fallen by disobeying the strait commandment of the Lord their God.

But O [ζ] the abundant riches of God's great mercy! O the [ζ Rom. xi, [33.]] unspeakable goodness of his heavenly wisdom! When all hope of righteousness was past on our part; when we had nothing in ourselves whereby we might quench his burning wrath, and work the salvation of our own souls, and rise out of the miserable estate wherein we lay; then, even then, did Christ the Son of God, by the appointment of his Father, come down from heaven, to be wounded for our sakes, to be *reputed with the* [[Isa. liii, 12.]] *wicked,* to be condemned unto death, to take upon him the reward of our sins, and to give his body to be broken on the cross for our offences. *He,* saith the Prophet Esay, meaning Christ, [Isa. liii, [4, 5.]] *hath borne our infirmities, and hath carried our sorrows; the chastisement of our peace was upon him, and by his stripes are we*[k] *made whole.* St. Paul likewise saith: *God made him a* [2 Cor. v, [21.]] *sacrifice for our sins which knew not sin, that we should be made the righteousness of God by him.* And St. Peter most agreeably writing in this behalf saith: *Christ hath once died and suffered* [1 Pet. iii, [18.]]

h maketh us] maketh it 1623. i a most clear] a clear 1623. j whereinto] whereunto 1623. k are we] we were 1623.

for our sins, the just for the unjust, &c. To these might be added an infinite number of other places to the same effect; but these few shall be sufficient for this time.

Now then, as it was said at the beginning, let us ponder and weigh the cause of his death, that thereby we may be the more moved to glorify him in our whole life. Which if you will have comprehended briefly in one word, it was nothing else on our part but only the transgression and sin of mankind. When the
Matt. i, [20, 21.]
angel came to warn Joseph that he should not fear to take Mary to his wife, did he not therefore will the child's name to be called *Jesus*, because he should *save his people from their sins?* When John the Baptist preached Christ, and shewed him unto the[l]
John i, [29.]
people with his finger, did he not plainly say unto them, *Behold the Lamb of God, which taketh away the sins of the world?* When the woman of Cananie[m] besought Christ to help her daughter, which was possessed with a devil, did he not openly confess that
Matt. xv, [22, 24.]
he was *sent to save the lost sheep of the house of Israel* by giving his life for their sins? It was sin then, O man, even thy sin, that caused Christ, the only Son of God, to be crucified in the flesh, and to suffer the most vile and slanderous death of the cross. If thou haddest kept thyself upright, if thou haddest observed the commandments, if thou haddest not presumed to
η Rom. v, [12–19.] θ [Phil. ii, 6, 7: John vi, 32, 35; iv, 10; vii, 37: Rev. xxi, 6: John xi, 25.]
transgress[η] the will of God in thy first father Adam, then Christ[θ], *being in form of God*, needed not *to have taken upon him the shape of a servant*; being immortal in heaven, he needed not to become mortal on earth; being *the true bread* of the soul, he needed not to hunger; being *the* healthful *water of life*, he needed not to thirst; being *life* itself, he needed not to have suffered death. But to these and many other such extremities was he driven by thy sin, which was so manifold and great, that God could be only pleased in him and no[n] other.

Canst thou think of this, O sinful man, and not tremble within thyself? Canst thou hear it quietly, without remorse of conscience and sorrow of heart? Did Christ suffer his passion for thee, and wilt thou shew no compassion towards him? While Christ was yet hanging on the cross and yielding up the ghost,
Matt. xxvii, [51, 52.]
the Scripture witnesseth that *the veil of the temple did rent in twain*, that *the earth*[o] *did quake*, that *the stones clave asunder*, that *the graves did open, and the dead bodies rise;* and shall the heart of man be nothing moved to remember how grievously

[l] unto the] to the *from* 1570. [m] Cananie] Canane 1563 G—1570, Canaan *from* 1571. [n] and no] and none *from* 1563 G. [o] that the earth] and the earth *from* 1563 G.

and cruelly he was handled of the Jews for our sins? shall man shew himself to be more hardhearted than stones? to have less compassion than dead bodies? Call to mind, O sinful creature, and set before thine eyes, Christ crucified; think thou seest his body stretched out in length upon the cross, his head crowned with sharp thorn, his[p] hands and his feet pierced with nails, his heart opened with a long spear, his flesh rent and torn with whips, his brows sweating water and blood; think thou hearest him now crying in an intolerable agony to his Father, and saying, *My God, my God, why hast thou forsaken me?* [Matt. xxvii, 46.] Couldest thou behold this woful sight or hear this mournful voice without tears, considering that he suffered all this, not for any desert of his own, but only for the grievousness of thy sins? O that mankind should put the everlasting Son of God to such pains! O that we should be the occasion of his death, and the only cause of his condemnation! May we not justly cry, Woe worth[2] the time that ever we sinned?

O my brethren, let this image of Christ crucified be always printed in our hearts; let it stir us up to the hatred of sin, and provoke our minds to the earnest love of Almighty God. For why[3], is not sin, think you, a grievous thing in his sight, seeing for the transgressing of God's precept in eating of one apple he condemned all the world to perpetual death, and would not be pacified but only with the blood of his own Son? True, yea, most true is that saying of David: *Thou, O Lord, hatest all them that work iniquity; neither shall the wicked and evil man dwell with thee.* Ps. v, [4.] By the mouth of his Prophet[q] Esay he crieth mainly out against sinners, and saith: *Woe be unto you that draw iniquity with cords of vanity, and sin as it were with cart ropes.* Is. v, [18.] Did not God give[r] a plain token how greatly he hated and abhorred sin, when he drowned[ι] all the world save only eight persons? when he destroyed[κ] Sodom and Gomorre with fire and brimstone? when in three days' space he killed[λ] with pestilence threescore and ten thousand for David's offence? when he drowned[μ] Pharao and all his host in the Red Sea? when he turned[ν] Nabuchodonozor the king into the form of a brute beast, creeping upon all four? when he suffered[ξ] Achitophel

ι Gen. vii. κ Gen. xix, [24.] λ 2 Sam. xxiv, [13, 15.] μ Exod. xiv, [28.] ν Dan. iv, [33.] ξ 2 Sam. xvii, [23:] Acts i, [18:] Matth. xxvii, 5.]

p thorn, his] thorns, his 1587, 1595; thorns, and his 1623. q his Prophet] his holy Prophet 1623. r Did not God give] Did not give 1582; Did he not give 1587, 1595; Did not he give 1623.

2 Woe worth: Woe be unto; from the Anglo-Saxon *weorthan*, to be or to become. The phrase was very common when the Homilies were written, and remains in *Ezek.* xxx, 2.

3 For why: see before, p. 343, n. 3.

and Judas to hang themselves upon the remorse of sin, which was so terrible to their eyes? A thousand such examples are to be found in Scripture, if a man would stand to seek them out. But what need we? This one example which we have now in hand is of more force, and ought more to move us, than all the rest. Christ, being the Son of God and perfect God himself, who never committed sin, was compelled to come down from heaven, and to[s] give his body to be bruised and broken on the cross for our sins. Was not this a manifest token of God's great wrath and displeasure towards sin, that he could be pacified by no other means but only by the sweet and precious blood of his dear Son? O sin, sin, that ever thou shouldest drive Christ to such extremity! Woe worth the time that ever thou camest into the world. But what booteth it now to bewail? Sin is come, and so come that it cannot be avoided. There is no man living, no, not the justest man on the earth, but he *falleth seven times a day*[4], as Salomon saith. (Prov. xxiv, [16.]) And our Saviour Christ, although he hath delivered us from sin, yet not so that we shall be free from committing sin, but so that it shall not be imputed[o] (o [Rom. viii, 1,]) to our condemnation. He hath taken upon him *the just reward*[π] *of sin*, which was *death*, (π Rom. vi, [23.]) and by death hath overthrown death, that we believing in him might live for ever and not die. Ought not this to engender extreme hatred of sin in us, to consider that it did violently, as it were, pluck God out of heaven, and make[t] him feel the horrors and pains of death? O that we would sometimes consider this in the midst of our pomps and pleasures: it would bridle the outrageousness of the flesh; it would abate and assuage our carnal affects[u]; it would restrain our fleshly appetites, that we should not run at randon[5], as we commonly do. To commit sin wilfully and desperately, without fear of God, is nothing else but to crucify Christ anew, as we are expressly taught in the Epistle to the Hebrews. (Heb. vi, [6.]) Which thing if it were deeply printed in all men's hearts, then should not sin reign every where so much as it doth, to the great grief and torment of Christ now sitting in heaven.

Let us therefore remember and always bear in mind Christ crucified, that thereby we may be inwardly moved both to abhor sin throughly, and also with an earnest and zealous heart to

s heaven, and to] heaven, to *from* 1582. t and make] to make *from* 1563 G. u affects] affections 1623.

4 Septies enim cadet [*al.* enim in die cadet] justus. *Vulg.*

5 randon: an old French or perhaps Anglo-Norman word, now written random. See *Todd on Spenser, Shepheards Calender, May*, 46.

love God. For this is another fruit which the memorial of Christ's death ought to work in us, an earnest and unfeigned love towards God. *So God loved the world,* saith St. John, *that he gave his only begotten Son, that whosoever believed*[x] *in him should not perish, but have life everlasting.* John iii, [16.] If God declared so great love towards us his seely creatures, how can we of right but love him again? Was not this a sure pledge of his love, to give us his own Son from heaven? He might have given us an angel if he would, or some other creature, and yet should his love have been far above our deserts. Now he gave us, not an angel, but his Son. And what Son? His only Son, his natural Son, his wellbeloved Son, even that Son whom he had made Lord and Ruler over[y] all things. Was not this a singular token of great love? But to whom did he give him? He gave him to the whole world, that is to say, to Adam and all that should come after him. O Lord, what had Adam or any other man deserved at God's hands, that he should give us his own Son? We were[z] all miserable persons, sinful persons, damnable persons, justly driven out of paradise, justly excluded from heaven, justly condemned to hell fire: and yet (see a wonderful token of God's love) he gave us his only begotten Son, us, I say, that were his extreme and deadly enemies; that we, by virtue of his blood shed upon the cross, might be clean purged from our sins, and made righteous again in his sight. Who can choose but marvel, to hear that God should shew such unspeakable love towards us, that were his deadly enemies? Indeed, O mortal man, thou oughtest of right to marvel at it, and to acknowledge therein God's great goodness and mercy towards mankind; which is so wonderful, that no flesh, be it never so worldly wise, may well conceive it or express it. For, as St. Paul testifieth, *God* greatly *commendeth* and setteth out *his love towards us, in that he sent his Son Christ to die for us, when we were yet sinners* Rom. v, [8.] and open enemies of his Name. If we had in any manner of wise deserved it at his hands, then had it been no marvel at all; but there was no desert on our part, wherefore he should do it. Therefore, thou sinful creature, when thou hearest that God gave his Son to die for the sins of the world, think not he did it for any desert or goodness that was in thee, for thou wast then the bondslave of the devil; but fall down upon thy knees, and cry with the Prophet David, *O Lord, what is man, that thou art so mindful of him? or the son of man, that thou so regardest him?* Ps. viii, [4.]

[x] believed] believeth *from* 1582. [y] over] of *from* 1571. [z] We were] We are *from* 1571.

And, seeing he hath so greatly loved thee, endeavour thyself to [Luke x, 27.] love him again *with all thy heart, with all thy soul, and with all thy strength,* that therein thou mayest appear not to be unworthy of his love. I report me to thy own[a] conscience, whether thou wouldest not think thy love ill bestowed upon him that could not find in his heart to love thee again? If this be true, as it is most true, then think how greatly it belongeth[b] to thy duty[c] to love God, which hath so greatly loved thee, that he hath not spared his own only Son from so cruel and shameful a death for thy sake.

And hitherto concerning the cause of Christ's death and passion, which as it was on our part most horrible and grievous sin, so on the other side it was the free gift of God, proceeding of his mere and tender love towards mankind, without any merit or desert of our part. The Lord for his mercies' sake grant that we never forget this great benefit of our salvation in Christ Jesu, but that we always shew ourselves thankful for it, abhorring all kind of wickedness and sin, and applying our minds wholly to the service of God and the diligent keeping of his commandments.

Now resteth to[d] shew unto you how to apply Christ's death and passion to our comfort, as a medicine to our wounds, so that it may work the same effect in us wherefore it was given, namely, the health and salvation of our souls. For, as it profiteth a man nothing to have salve, unless it be well applied to the part affected[e], so the death of Christ shall stand us in no force, unless we apply it to ourselves in such sort as God hath appointed. Almighty God commonly worketh by means, and in this thing he hath also ordained a certain mean whereby we may take fruit and profit to our souls' health. What mean is that? Forsooth it is faith; not an unconstant or wavering faith, but a [John iii, [16.]] sure, steadfast, grounded, and unfeigned faith. *God sent his Son into the world*, saith St. John. To what end? *That whosoever believed*[f] *in him should not perish, but have life everlasting.* Mark these words, *That whosoever believed*[g] *in him.* Here is the mean whereby we must apply the fruits of Christ's death unto our deadly wound; here is the mean whereby we must obtain eternal [Rom. x, [10.]] life; namely, faith. *For*, as St. Paul teacheth in his Epistle to the Romans, *with the heart man believeth unto righteousness, and*

a thy own] thine own *from* 1563 EF, *except* 1595. b belongeth] behoveth *from* 1563 G. c to thy duty] thee in duty 1623. d Now resteth to] Now it remaineth that I 1623. e affected] infected *from* 1574. f believed (*line* 34)] believeth 1563 F *and all from* 1567. g believed (*line* 35)] believeth *from* 1563 B.

with the mouth confession is made unto salvation. Paul, being demanded of the keeper of the prison *what he should do to be saved,* (Acts xvi, [30, 31.]) made this answer: *Believe in the Lord Jesus; so shalt thou and thine house be both*[h] *saved.* After the Evangelist had described and set forth unto us at large the life and the death of the Lord Jesus, in the end he concludeth with these words: *These things are written, that we may believe Jesus Christ to be the Son of God, and through faith obtain eternal life.* (John xx, [31.]) To conclude with the words of St. Paul, which are these: *Christ is the end of the law unto salvation for every one that doth believe*[5]. (Rom. x, [4.]) By this then you may well perceive that the only mean and instrument of salvation required of our parts is faith, that is to say, a sure trust and confidence in the mercies of God, whereby we persuade ourselves, that God both hath and will forgive our sins, that he hath accepted us again into his favour, that he hath released us from the bonds of damnation, and received us again into the number of his elect people, not for our merits or deserts, but only and solely for the merits of Christ's death and passion, who became man for our sakes, and humbled himself to sustain the reproach of the cross, that we thereby might be saved, and made inheritors of the kingdom of heaven. This faith is required at our hands; and this if we keep steadfastly in our[i] hearts, there is no doubt but we shall obtain salvation at God's hands, as did Abraham, Isaac, and Jacob, of whom the Scripture saith, that *they believed, and it was imputed unto them for righteousness.* (Gen. xv, [6:] Rom. iv, [3, 9, 22, 24.]) Was it imputed unto them?[k] and shall it not be imputed unto us?[l] Yes, *if we have* the same *faith* as they had, *it shall be* as truly *imputed unto us* for righteousness, as it was unto them. For it is one faith that must save both us and them, even a sure and steadfast faith in Christ Jesu[m]; who, as ye have heard, came into the world for this end, *that whosoever believed*[n] *in him should not perish, but have life everlasting.* (John iii, [16.])

But here we must take heed that we do not halt with God through an unconstant and wavering faith, but that it be strong and steadfast to our lives' end. *He that wavereth,* saith St. James, *is like a wave of the sea; neither let that man think that he shall obtain any thing at God's hands.* (James i, [6, 7.]) Peter coming to Christ upon the water[p], because he fainted in faith, was in danger of drowning. (p Matt. xiv, [28–31.]) So we, if we begin to waver or doubt, it is to be

h be both] both be *from* 1570. i in our] at our 1623. k them?] them only? *from* 1563 B.
l us?] us also? *from* 1563 B. m Jesu] Jesus 1623. n believed] believe *from* 1567.

5 Τέλος γὰρ νόμου Χριστὸς εἰς δικαιοσύνην παντὶ τῷ πιστεύοντι.

feared lest we shall sink as Peter did, not into the water, but into the bottomless pit of hell fire. Therefore I say unto you, that we must apprehend the merits of Christ's death and passion by faith; and that with a strong and steadfast faith, nothing doubting but that Christ[σ], by his one[o] oblation and once offering of himself upon the cross, hath taken away our sins, and hath restored us again into God's favour, so fully and perfectly that no other sacrifice for sin shall hereafter be requisite or needful in all the world.

σ [Heb. x, 10–18.]

Thus have ye heard[p] in few words the mean whereby we must apply the fruits and merits of Christ's death unto us, so that it may work the salvation of our souls, namely, a sure, steadfast, perfect, and grounded faith. For, as all they which beheld steadfastly[τ] the brasen serpent were healed and delivered, at the very sight thereof, from their corporal diseases and bodily stings, even so all they which behold Christ crucified with a true and lively faith shall undoubtedly be delivered from the grievous wounds[q] of the soul, be they never so deadly or many in number. Therefore, dearly beloved, if we chance at any time, through frailty of the flesh, to fall into sin, as it cannot be chosen but we must needs fall often; and if we feel the heavy burden thereof to press our souls, tormenting us with the fear of death, hell, and damnation; let us then use that mean which God hath appointed in his word, to wit, the mean of faith, which is the only instrument of salvation now left unto us. Let us steadfastly behold Christ crucified with the eyes of our heart. Let us only trust to be saved by his death and passion, and to have our sins clean washed away through his most precious blood; that in the end of the world, when he shall come again to judge both the quick and the dead, he may receive us into his heavenly kingdom, and place us in the number of his elect and chosen people, there to be partakers of that immortal and everlasting life which he hath purchased unto us by virtue of his bloody wounds. To him therefore with the Father and the Holy Ghost be all honour and glory world without end. Amen.

τ Numb. xxi, [9:] John iii, [14, 15.]

o his one] his own *from* 1570. p ye] you *from* 1582. q wounds] wound 1623.

AN HOMILY

OF THE RESURRECTION

OF OUR SAVIOUR JESUS CHRIST.

FOR EASTER DAY.

IF ever at any time the greatness or excellency of any matter, spiritual or temporal, hath stirred up your minds to give diligent ear, good Christian people, and wellbeloved in our Lord and Saviour Jesu[a] Christ, I doubt not but that I shall have you now at this present season most diligent and ready hearers of the matter which I have at this time to open unto you. For I come to declare that great and most comfortable article of our Christian religion and faith, the resurrection of our Lord Jesus.

So great surely is the matter of[b] this article, and of so great weight and importance, that it was thought worthy to keep our said Saviour still on earth forty days[c], after he was risen from death to life, to the confirmation and stablishment[d] thereof in the hearts of his disciples. So that, as Luke clearly testifieth in the first chapter of the Acts of the Apostles, he was conversant with his disciples by the space of forty days continually [Acts i, 3.] together, to the intent he would in his person, being[e] now glorified, teach and instruct them, which should be the teachers of other, fully and in most absolute and perfect wise the truth of this most Christian article, which is the ground and foundation of our whole religion, before he would ascend up to his Father into the heavens, there to receive the glory of his most triumphant conquest and victory.

Assuredly, so highly comfortable is this article to our consciences, that it is even the very lock and key of all our Christian religion and faith. *If it were not true*, saith the holy[f] Apostle [1 Cor. xv, [14–22.]] Paul, *that Christ rose again, then our preaching were in vain, your faith which ye have*[g] *received were but void, ye were yet in* the danger of *your sins*. *If Christ be not risen again*, saith the

[a] Jesu] Jesus *from* 1567. [b] the matter of] *not in* TAV. [c] forty days] *not in* TAV. [d] stablishment] establishment 1623. [e] being] *not in* TAV. [f] the holy] this holy TAV. (*his text being Rom.* iv, 25), *and* 1563 A–F. [g] ye have] you have *from* 1563 B.

Apostle, *then are they* in very evil case, and utterly *perished, that be entered their sleep in Christ; then are we the most miserable of all men, which have our hope fixed in Christ,* if he be yet under the power of death, and as yet not restored to his bliss again. *But now is he*[h] *risen again from death,* saith the Apostle Paul, *to be the firstfruits of them that be asleep,* to the intent to raise them to everlasting life again. Yea, if it were not true that Christ is risen again, then were it neither true that he is ascended up to heaven; nor that he sent down from heaven unto us the Holy Ghost; nor that he sitteth on the right hand of his heavenly Father, having the rule of heaven and earth, reigning (as the Prophet saith[α]) *from sea to sea;* nor that he should after this world be the judge as well of the living as of the dead, to give reward to the good and judgment to the evil.

[α] Ps. lxxi [lxxii, 8.]

That these links therefore of our faith should all hang together in steadfast establishment and confirmation, it pleased our Saviour not straightway to withdraw himself from the bodily presence and sight of his disciples; but he chose out forty days wherein he would declare unto them by manifold and most strong arguments and tokens, that he had conquered death, and that he was also truly risen again to life. *He began,* saith Luke, *at Moses and all the Prophets, and expounded*[i] *unto them the prophecies that were written in all the Scriptures of him,* to the intent to confirm the truth of his resurrection, long before spoken of; which he verified indeed, as it is declared very apparently and manifestly, by his oft appearance to sundry persons at sundry times. First, he sent his angels[β] to the sepulchre, which did[k] shew unto certain women the[l] empty grave, saving that the burial linen remained therein; and by these signs were these women fully instructed that he was risen again, and so did they testify it openly. After this Jesus himself[γ] appeared to Mary Magdalene, and after that to other certain[m] women; and straight afterward he appeared to Peter, then to the two disciples which were going to Emmaus. He appeared to the disciples[δ] also, as *they were gathered together, for fear of the Jews, the doors*[n] *shut.* At another time he was seen at the sea of Tiberias[ε] of Peter and Thomas and of other disciples, when they were fishing. He was seen of more[ς] than five hundred brethren in the mount of Galilee, where Jesus appointed

Luke xxiv, [27.]

[β] Matt. xxviii, [1–8: Luke xxiv, 1–12.]

[γ] John xx, [14–18: Matt. xxviii, 9, 10:] 1 Cor. xv, [5:] Luke xxiv, [13–34.]

[δ] [John xx, 19.]

[ε] John xxi, [1–14.]

[ς] 1 Cor. xv, [6.]

[h] is he] he is 1623. [i] expounded] expowned TAV. [k] which did] who did *from* 1567. [l] women the] women that the stone of the grave was removed from the entrance thereof, and shewed them the TAV. [m] other certain] certain other *from* 1567. [n] doors] door *from* 1582.

them to be by his angel, when he said, *Behold, he shall go before you into Galilee; there shall ye see him, as he hath said unto you.* [Mark xvi, 7: Matt. xxviii, 7, 10.] After this[η] he appeared unto James; and last of all he was visibly seen of all the Apostles at such time as he was taken up into heaven. [η [1 Cor. xv, 7:] Acts i, [4-11.]] Thus at sundry times he shewed himself after he was risen again, to confirm and stablish this article. And in these revelations[θ] sometime he shewed them his hands, his feet, and his side, and bade them touch him, that they should not take him for a ghost or a spirit; [θ [Luke xxiv, 39-43: John xx, 27.]] sometime he also did eat with them; but ever he was talking with them of the everlasting kingdom of God, to assure the truth of his resurrection. For *then he opened their understanding, that they might perceive the Scriptures, and said unto them, Thus it is written, and thus it behoved Christ to suffer, and to rise from death the third day, and that there should be*[o] *preached openly in his name penance*[p] *and remission of sins to all the nations of the world.* [Luke xxiv, [45-47.]]

Ye see, good Christian people, how necessary this article of our faith is, seeing it was proved of Christ himself by such evident reasons and tokens, by so long time and space. Now therefore, as our Saviour was diligent for our comfort and instruction to declare it, so let us be as ready in our belief to receive it to our comfort and instruction. As he died not for himself, no more did he rise again for himself. *He was dead,* saith St. Paul, *for our sins, and rose again for our justification.* [Rom. iv, 25.] O most comfortable word, evermore to be borne in remembrance! He died, saith he, to put away sin; he arose again to endow us with righteousness. His death took away sin and malediction; his death was the ransom of them both; his death destroyed death, and overcame *the devil, which had the power of death* in his subjection; [Hebr. ii, 14.] his death destroyed hell with all the damnation thereof. Thus *is death swallowed up by Christ's victory;* thus is hell spoiled for ever. [1 Cor. xv, [54, 57.]]

If any man doubt of this victory, let Christ's glorious resurrection declare him the thing[q]. If death could not keep Christ under his dominion and power, but that he arose again, it is manifest that his power was overcome. If death be conquered, then must it follow that sin, wherefore *death* was appointed as *the wages*, must be also destroyed. [Rom. vi, 23.] If death and sin be vanished away, then is the devil's tyranny vanquished[r], *which had the power of death*, and was the author and brewer of sin, and the

[o] that there should be] to have TAV. [p] penance] pardon 1623. [q] the thing] that thing TAV. [r] vanquished] vanished *from* 1571, resisted TAV.

ruler of hell. If Christ had the victory of them all by the power of his death, and openly proved it by his most victorious and valiant resurrection, as it was not possible for his great might to be subdued of them; and then this[s] true, that Christ *died for our sins, and rose again for our justification;* why may not we, that be his members by true faith, rejoice, and boldly say with the Prophet Osee and the Apostle Paul, *Where is thy dart, O death? Where is thy victory, O hell? Thanks be unto God,* say they, *which hath given us the victory by our Lord Christ Jesus.*

[Hos. xiii, 14:] 1 Cor. xv, [55, 57.]

This mighty conquest of his resurrection was not only signified afore[t] by divers figures of the Old Testament, as by Samson[ι] when he slew the lion, out of whose mouth came out sweetness[u] and honey; and as David[κ] bare his figure when he delivered the lamb out of the lion's mouth, and when he overcame and slew the great giant Goliath; and as when Jonas[λ] was swallowed up of[x] the whale's mouth, and cast up again on land to live[y]; but was also most clearly prophesied by the Prophets of the Old Testament, and in the New also confirmed by the Apostles. *He hath spoiled,* saith St. Paul, *rule and power* and all the dominion of our spiritual enemies; *he hath made a shew of them openly, and hath triumphed over them in his own person*[1].

ι Judg. xiv, [5–8.]
κ 1 Sam. xvii, [34, 35, 49, 50.]
λ [Jon. i, 17;] ii, [10.]
Col. ii, [15.]

This is the mighty power of the Lord whom we believe on. By his death hath he wrought for us this victory, and by his resurrection hath he purchased everlasting life and righteousness for us. It had not been enough to be delivered by his death from sin, except by his resurrection we had been endowed with righteousness. And it should not avail us to be delivered from death, except he had risen again, to open for us the gates of heaven, to enter into life everlasting. And therefore St. Peter thanketh *God the Father of our Lord Jesu*[z] *Christ for his abundant mercy, because he hath begotten us,* saith he, *unto a lively hope by the resurrection of Jesus Christ from death, to enjoy an inheritance immortal, that shall never*[a] *perish, which is laid up in heaven for them that be kept by the power of God thorough faith*[b]. Thus hath his resurrection wrought for us life and righteousness. He passed through death[c] and hell, to the in-

1 Pet. i, [3–5.]

[s] then this] it is 1623. [t] afore] before *from* 1567. [u] came out sweetness] came sweetness *from* 1567. [x] up of] up in *from* 1582. [y] on land to live] to land on live 1570, on land alive *from* 1571. [z] Jesu] Jesus *from* 1567. [a] shall never] never shall *from* 1567. [b] thorough faith] through faith *from* 1563 C. [c] through death] thorow death TAV.

[1] Triumphans illos in semetipso. *Vulg.*

tent to put us in good hope that by his strength we shall do the same. He paid the ransom of sin, that it should not be laid to our charge. He destroyed the devil and all his tyranny, and openly triumphed over him, and took away from him all his captives, and hath raised[μ] and set them with himself amonges[d] the heavenly citizens above. He died to destroy the rule of the devil in us; and he arose[e] again to send down his Holy Spirit to rule in our hearts, to endow us with perfect righteousness. Thus is it[f] true that David songe[g], *Veritas de terra orta est, et justitia de coelo prospexit*[h]: the truth of God's promise is in earth to man declared, or *from the earth is the* everlasting *Verity*, God's Son, *risen* to life; and the true *righteousness* of the Holy Ghost *looking*[i] *out of heaven*, and[i] is in[k] most liberal largess dealt upon all the world. Thus is *glory* and praise rebounded[l] upward[m] *to God above* for his mercy and truth; and thus is *peace* come down from heaven *to men* of good and faithful hearts[2]. Thus *is mercy and truth*, as David writeth, *together met*; thus *is peace and righteousness* imbracing and *kissing each other*.

[μ Ephes. ii, [6.]]

[Ps. lxxxiv [lxxxv, 11.]]

[Eph. iv, [8:] *Captivam duxit captivitatem.*]

[Luke ii, [14.]]

[Ps. lxxxiv [lxxxv, 10:] *Misericordia et veritas obviaverunt sibi, &c.*[n]]

If thou doubtest of so great wealth and felicity that is wrought for thee, O man, call to thy mind that therefore hast thou received into thine own possession the everlasting Verity, our Saviour Jesus Christ, to[o] confirm to thy conscience the truth of all this matter. Thou hast received him, (if in true faith and repentance of heart thou hast received him, if in purpose of amendment thou hast received him,) for an everlasting gage or pledge of thy salvation. Thou hast received his body which was once broken and his blood which was shed for the remission of thy sin. Thou hast received his body, to have within thee the Father, the Son, and the Holy[p] Ghost for to dwell with thee, to endow thee with grace, to strength thee against thy enemies[q], and to comfort thee with their presence. Thou hast received his body to endow thee with everlasting righteousness, to assure thee of everlasting bliss and life of thy soul. For with Christ by true faith art thou quickened again, saith St. Paul, from death of sin to life of grace, and in hope translated from corporal and everlasting death to the everlasting life of glory in

[Eph. ii, [5–8.]]

[d] amonges] amongst 1567–1574, among *from* 1582. [e] arose] rose *from* 1570. [f] is it] it is *from* 1567. [g] songe] sung *from* 1582. [h] prospexit] perspexit TAV., *but* prospexit *in other copies.* [i] looking *and* and] *so in all.* [k] and is in] and in *from* 1582. [l] rebounded] rebounding TAV. [m] upward] upwards *from* 1582. [n] sibi &c.] sibi. *from* 1563 G. [o] Christ, to] Christ, in form of bread, to TAV. [p] and the Holy] and Holy TAV. [q] thy enemies] thine enemies *from* 1563 G.

2 Gloria in altissimis Deo, et in terra pax hominibus bonae voluntatis. *Luc.* II, 14, *Vulg.*

heaven, where now thy conversation should be, and thy heart and desire set. Doubt not of the truth of this matter, how great and high soever these things be. It becometh God to do no little[r] deeds, how impossible soever they seem to thee. Pray to God that thou mayest have faith to perceive this great mystery of Christ's resurrection, that by faith thou mayest certainly believe *nothing* to be *impossible with God*[v]. Only bring thou faith to Christ's holy word and sacrament. Let thy repentance shew thy faith; let thy purpose of amendment and obedience of thy heart to God's law hereafter declare thy true belief. Endeavour thyself to say with St. Paul from henceforth, *Our conversation is in heaven, from whence we look for a Saviour, even the Lord Jesus Christ; which shall change our vile bodies, that they may be fashioned like to his*[s] *glorious body; which he shall do by the same power* whereby he rose from death, and *whereby he shall be able to subdue all things unto himself.*

[v] Luke [i, 37;] xviii, [27.]

Phil. iii, [20, 21.]

Thus, good Christian people, forasmuch as ye have heard these so great and excellent benefits of Christ's mighty and glorious resurrection, as how that he hath ransomed sin, overcome the devil, death, and hell, and hath victoriously gotten the better hand of them all, to make us free and safe from them; and knowing that we be by this benefit of his resurrection risen with him by our faith unto life everlasting; being in full surety of our hope, that we shall have our bodies likewise raised again from death, to have them glorified in immortality and joined to his glorious body; having in the mean while his Holy[t] Spirit within our hearts as a seal and pledge of our everlasting inheritance, by whose assistance we be replenished with all righteousness, by whose power we shall be able to subdue all our evil affections rising against the pleasure of God; these things, I say, well considered, let us now in the rest of our life declare our faith that we have to this[u] most fruitful article by framing ourselves thereunto in rising daily from sin to righteousness and holiness of life. *For what shall it avail us,* saith St. Peter, *to be escaped and delivered from the filthiness of the world through*[x] *the knowledge of the Lord and Saviour Jesus Christ, if we be intangled again therewith, and be overcome again? Certainly it had been better,* saith he, *never to have known the way of righteousness, than, after it is known and received, to turn backward*[y] *again from the holy commandment of God given unto us. For so*

2 Pet. ii, [20-22.]

[r] little] small 1623. [s] like to his] like his *from* 1567. [t] his Holy] this Holy *from* 1574. [u] to this] in this *from* 1574. [x] through] thorough TAV. [y] backward] back 1623.

shall the proverb have place in us where it is said, The dog is returned to his vomit again, and the sow that was washed to her wallowing in the mire again. What a shame were it for us, being thus so clearly and freely washed from our sin, to return to the filthiness thereof again! What a folly were it, thus endowed with righteousness, to lose it again! What madness were it to lose the enheritance that we be now set in for the vile and transitory pleasure of sin! And what an unkindness should it be, where our Saviour Christ of his mercy is come to us to dwell within[z] us as our guest, to drive him from us, and to banish him violently out of our souls, and instead of him, in whom is all grace and virtue, to receive the ungracious spirit of the devil, the founder of all naughtiness and mischief! How can we find in our hearts to shew such extreme unkindness to Christ, which hath now so gently called us to mercy and offered himself unto us, and he now entered within us? Yea, how dare we be so bold to renounce the presence of the Father, the Son, and the Holy Ghost, (for[a], where one is, there is God all whole in Majesty together with all his power, wisdom, and goodness,) and fear not, I say, the danger and peril of so traitorous a defiance and departure[b]?

Good Christian brethren and sisters, advise yourselves: consider the dignity that ye be now set in. Let not folly[c] lose[d] the thing that grace hath so preciously offered and purchased. Let not wilfulness and blindness put out so great light that is now shewed unto you. Only take good hearts unto you, and *put*[ξ] *upon you all the armour of God, that ye may stand against* [ξ Eph. vi, [11, 12.]] *your enemies*, which would again subdue you and bring you into their thraldom. Remember *ye be bought*[o] *from your vain conversation*, [o 1 Pet. i, [18–21.]] and that your freedom is purchased *neither with gold nor silver, but with the price of the precious blood of that most*[e] *innocent Lamb Jesus Christ; which was ordained to the same*[f] *purpose before the world was made, but he was so declared in the latter*[g] *time of grace for your sakes, which by him have your faith in God, who hath raised him from death and hath given him glory, that you should have your faith and hope toward*[h] *God.* Therefore, as ye[i] have hitherto followed the vain lusts of your minds, and so displeased God to the danger of your[k] souls, so now, *like obedient children*[π], thus purified by faith, give your- [π [Ibid. 14.]]

[z] dwell within] dwell with 1623. [a] Ghost, (for] Ghost, now received in this holy Sacrament, (for TAV. [b] and departure] *not in* TAV. [c] not folly] no folly 1623. [d] lose] loose 1623. [e] most] *omitted* 1623. [f] the same] this same TAV. [g] latter] later TAV. [h] toward] towards 1623. [i] Therefore, as ye] Therefore, as you *from* 1563 D. [k] danger of your] danger of our 1582, 1623.

selves to walk that way which God moveth you to, that ye may (ρ Ibid. [9.]) receive *the end of your faith, the salvation of your souls*[ρ]. And, *as* (σ Rom. vi, [19.]) *ye have given*[σ] *your bodies to unrighteousness, to sin after sin, so now give yourself*[l] *to righteousness, to be sanctified therein.*

If ye delight in this article of your faith[m], that Christ is risen again from death to[n] life, then follow you the example of his (Rom. vi, [2–4.]) resurrection, as St. Paul exhorteth us, saying, *As we be buried with Christ by our baptism into death, so let us* daily *die to sin,* mortifying and killing the evil desires and motions thereof; and, *as Christ was raised up from death by the glory of the Father, so let us rise to a new life, and walk continually therein;* that we may likewise, as natural children, live a conversation to move (τ Matt. v, [16.]) men to *glorify our Father which is in heaven*[τ]. *If we then*[υ] *be* (υ Col. iii, [1, 2.]) *risen with Christ* by our faith to the hope of everlasting life, let us rise also with Christ, after his example, to a new life, and leave our old. We shall then be truly risen, if we *seek for things that be heavenly,* if we *have our affection upon*[o] *things that be above, and not on things that be on earth*[p]. If ye desire to know what these earthly things be which ye should put off, and what be the heavenly things above that ye should seek and ensue, St. Paul in the Epistle to the Colossians declareth, when he ex- ([Ibid. 5–10.]) horteth us thus: *Mortify your earthly members* and old affections[q] of sin, as *fornication, uncleanness, unnatural lust, evil concupiscence, and covetousness, which is worshipping of idols; for which*[r] *things the wrath of God is wont to fall on the children of unbelief; in which things once ye walked, when ye lived in them. But now put ye also away from you wrath, fierceness, maliciousness, cursed speaking, filthy speaking, out of your mouths. Lie not one to another, that the old man with his works be put off, and the new put*[s] *on.* These be the earthly things which St. Paul moveth[t] you to cast from you, and to pluck your hearts from them. For[u] in following these ye declare yourselves earthly and worldly. These be the fruits of the earthly Adam. These should ye[x] daily kill by good diligence in withstanding the desires of them, that ye might rise to righteousness. *Let your affection* from henceforth *be set on heavenly things.* Sue and search for (φ [Ibid. 12, 13.]) *mercy*[φ], *kindness, meekness, patience, forbearing one another, and forgiving one another, if any man have any quarrel*[y] *to another: as Christ forgave you, even so do ye.* If these and such other hea-

[l] yourself] yourselves *from* 1582. [m] of your faith] of our faith *from* 1582. [n] from death to] from the death to 1623. [o] upon] on *from* 1567. [p] on earth] on the earth *from* 1563 G. [q] affections] affection *from* 1574. [r] for which] for the which *from* 1567. [s] new put] new be put *from* 1567. [t] moveth] moved 1623. [u] from them. For] from. For TAV. [x] should ye] should you *from* 1571. [y] any quarrel] a quarrel *from* 1582.

venly virtues ye ensue in the residue of your life, ye shall shew plainly that *ye be risen with Christ*, and that ye be the heavenly *children of your Father in heaven*[χ], from whom[ψ], as from the Giver, cometh these graces and gifts. Ye shall prove by this manner that *your conversation is in heaven*[ω], where your hope is, and not on earth, following the beastly appetites of the flesh.

χ [Matt. v, 45.]
ψ James i, [17.]
ω Phil. iii, [20.]

Ye must consider that ye be therefore cleansed and renewed, that ye should from henceforth *serve*[α] *God in holiness and righteousness all the days of your lives,* that ye may reign with him[z] in everlasting life. If ye refuse so great grace, whereto ye be called, what other thing do ye than heap up your[a] damnation more and more, and so provoke God to cast his displeasure unto you, and to revenge this mockage of his holy Sacraments in so great abusing of them? Apply yourselves[b], good friends, to live in Christ, that Christ may still live in you: whose favour and assistance if ye have, then have ye[β] everlasting life already within you, then can nothing hurt you. Whatsoever is hitherto done and committed, Christ, ye see, hath offered you pardon, and clearly received you to his favour again: in full surety whereof ye have him now inhabiting and dwelling within you. Only shew yourselves[c] thankful in your lives: determine with yourselves[d] to refuse and avoid all such things in your conversations as should offend his eyes of mercy[γ]. Endeavour yourselves[e] that way to rise up again, which way ye fell into the well or pit[f] of sin. If by your tongue ye[g] have offended, now thereby rise again, and glorify God therewith. Accustom it to laud and praise the Name of God, as ye have therewith dishonoured it. And, as ye have hurt the name of your neighbour, or otherways[h] hindered him, so now entend to restore it to[i] him again. For without restitution God accepteth not your confession[k], nor yet your repentance. It is not enough to *forsake evil*[δ], except ye[l] set your courage to *do good.* By what occasion soever ye[m] have offended, turn now the occasion to the honouring of God and profiting[n] of your neighbour.

α Luke i, [74, 75.]
β John v, [24.]
γ Col. iii, [5, 6.]
Restitution.
δ Ps. xxxvi [xxxvii, 27.]

Truth it is that sin is strong, and affections unruly. Hard it is to subdue and resist our nature, so corrupt and leavened with the sour bitterness of the poison which we received by the inheritance of our old father Adam. *But yet take good courage,* saith our Saviour Christ[ε], *for I have overcome the world* and all

Matth. vi.[o]
ε [John xvi, 33.]

[z] with him] with them *from* 1571. [a] up your] to your 1563 C—1571, to you *from* 1574. [b],[c],[d],[e] yourselves] yourself TAV. [f] or pit] and pit TAV. [g] tongue ye] tongue you *from* 1582. [h] otherways] otherwise TAV. *and from* 1567. [i] it to] *not in* TAV. [k] confession] shrift TAV. [l] except ye] except you *from* 1571. [m] soever ye] soever you *from* 1563 C. [n] profiting] profit *from* 1563 G. [o] Matth. vi] *so in* TAV. *and all.*

[Rom. vi, [14.]] other enemies for you. *Sin shall not have power over you, for ye be now under grace,* saith St. Paul. Though your power be weak, yet[ς] *Christ is risen again* to strength[p] you in your battle; *his Holy Spirit shall help your infirmities.* [ς Rom. viii, [11, 26, 34.]] In trust of his mercy[q], take you in hand to *purge*[η] *this old leaven* of sin, that [η 1 Cor. v, [7, 8.]] corrupteth and soureth the sweetness of your life[r] before God; *that ye may be as new* and fresh *dough,* void of all sour *leaven of wickedness:* so shall ye shew yourself[s] to be sweet bread to God, that he may have his delight in you. I say, kill and offer you up the worldly and earthly affections of your bodies: *for Christ our Easter lamb is offered up for us,* to slay[t] the power of sin, to deliver us from the danger thereof, and to give us example to die to sin in our life[u]. As the Jews did eat their Easter[3] lamb and kept[x] their feast in remembrance of their deliverance out of Egypt, even so *let us keep our Easter feast* in the thankful remembrance of Christ's benefits, which he hath plentifully wrought for us by his resurrection and passing to his Father, whereby we be[y] delivered from the captivity and thraldom of all our enemies. Let us in like manner pass over the affections of our old conversation, that we may be delivered from the bondage thereof, and rise with Christ. The Jews kept their feast in abstaining[θ] from leavened bread by the space of seven days: [θ Exod. xii, [15-20.]] *let us* Christian folk *keep our holyday* in spiritual manner, that is, *in abstaining,* not from material leavened bread, but *from the old leaven* of sin, *the leaven of maliciousness and wickedness.* Let us cast from us the leaven of corrupt doctrine[ι], that will infect our souls. [ι [Matt. xvi, 6, 12.]] *Let us keep our feast* the whole term of our life *with eating the bread of pureness* of godly life *and truth* of Christ's doctrine. Thus shall we declare that Christ's gifts and graces have their effect in us, and that we have the right belief and knowledge of his holy resurrection: where truly, if we apply our faith to the virtue thereof, and in our life[z] conform us to the example and signification meant thereby, we shall be sure to rise hereafter to everlasting glory by the goodness and mercy of our Lord Jesus Christ. To whom with the Father and the Holy Ghost be all glory, thanksgiving, and praise in infinita seculorum secula. Amen.

[p] strength] strengthen 1587, 1595, 1623. [q] mercy] confidence TAV. [r] your life] our life *from* 1574. [s] yourself] yourselves *from* 1563 G. [t] slay] flea TAV. *by error for* slea, *which is in other copies.* [u] our life] our lives 1623. [x] kept] keep 1623. [y] we be] we are *from* 1582. [z] and in our life] in our life and *from* 1582.

3 *Easter* is used for the Feast of the Passover in our Authorised Version, *Acts* XII, 4.

AN HOMILY

OF THE WORTHY RECEIVING AND REVERENT[a] ESTEEMING OF THE SACRAMENT OF THE BODY AND BLOOD OF CHRIST.

THE great love of our Saviour Christ towards mankind, good Christian people, doth not only appear in that dear bought benefit of our redemption and salvation by his death and passion, but also in that he so kindly provided that the same most merciful work might be had in continual remembrance, to take some place in us, and not be frustrate of his end and purpose. For, as tender parents are not content to procure for their children costly possessions and livelihood, but take order that the same may be conserved and come to their use; so our Lord and Saviour thought it not sufficient to purchase for us his Father's favour again (which is that deep fountain of all goodness), and eternal life, but[b] also invented the ways most wisely whereby they might redound to our commodity and profit. Amongst the which means is the public celebration of the memory of his precious death at the Lord's table: which although it seem of small virtue to some, yet, being rightly done by the faithful, it doth not only help their weakness, who be by their poisoned nature readier to remember injuries than benefits, but strengtheneth and comforteth their inward man with peace and gladness, and maketh them thankful to their Redeemer with diligent care of godly[c] conversation. And, as of old time God decreed[α] his wondrous benefits of the deliverance of his people to be kept in memory by the eating of the passover with his rites and ceremonies, so our loving Saviour hath ordained[β] and established the remembrance of his great mercy expressed in his passion in the institution of his heavenly Supper: where every one of us must be guests and not gazers, eaters and not lookers, feeding ourselves and not hiring other to feed for us; that we may live by our own meat, and not perish[d] for hunger while[e] others[f] devour all. To this his commandment forceth

[α] Exod. xii, [14–27.]

[β] Matt. xxvi, [26–28:] 1 Cor. xi, [23–26.]

[a] REVERENT] REVEREND 1623. [b] goodness), and eternal life, but] goodness and eternal life), but *from* 1563 G. [c] of godly] and godly *from* 1571. [d] not perish] not to perish *from* 1582. [e] while] whiles *from* 1563 B. [f] others] other *from* 1571.

Luke xxii, [19, 20:] 1 Cor. xi, [24, 25:] Matt. xxvi, [27.]

us, saying, *Do ye thus*[g], *Drink ye all of this.* To this his promise enticeth us[h]: *This is my body, which is given for you; This is my blood, which is shed for you.*

1 Cor. xi, [29.] Matt. xxii, [12.] 1 Cor. xi, [28.]

So then, as of[i] necessity we must be ourselves partakers of this table, and not beholders of other, so we must address ourselves to frequent the same in reverent and due[k] manner; lest, as physic provided for the body, being misused, more hurteth than profiteth, so this comfortable medicine of the soul, undecently received, tend[l] to our greater harm and sorrow. As[m] St. Paul saith: *He that eateth and drinketh unworthily eateth and drinketh his own damnation.* Wherefore, that it be not said to us, as it was to the guest of that great supper, *Friend, how camest thou in not having the marriage garment?* and that we may fruitfully use St. Paul's counsel, *Let a man prove himself, and so eat of that bread and drink of that cup,* we must certainly know that three things be requisite in him which would seemly, as becometh such high mysteries, resort to the Lord's table: that is, a[n] right and a worthy[o] estimation and understanding of this mystery; secondly, to come in a sure faith; and thirdly, to have newness or pureness of life to succeed the receiving of the same.

But, before all other things, this we must be sure of specially[p], that this Supper be in such wise done and ministered as our Lord and Saviour did and commanded to be done, as his holy Apostles used it, and the good fathers in the primitive Church frequented it. For, as that worthy man St. Ambrose saith[1], "he is unworthy the[q] Lord that otherways[r] doth celebrate that mystery than it was delivered by him; neither can he be devout that otherways[s] doth presume than it was given by the Author." We must then take heed, lest, of the memory, it be made a sacrifice; lest, of a communion, it be made a private eating; lest, of two parts, we have but one; lest, applying it for the dead, we lose the fruit that be alive. Let us rather in these matters follow the advice of Cyprian in the like cases; that is, cleave fast to the first beginning; hold fast the Lord's

g thus] this *from* 1582. h enticeth us:] enticeth: *from* 1567. i then, as of] then of *from* 1582. k due] comely 1623. l tend] tendeth *from* 1567. m As] And *from* 1563 C. n that is, a] That is the first, a 1563 B–F; That is, first, a *from* 1563 G. o and a worthy] and worthy 1623. p specially] especially *from* 1571. q unworthy the] unworthy of the *from* 1563 G. r otherways (*line* 27)] otherwise *from* 1567. s otherways (*line* 29)] otherwise *from* 1582.

1 Indignum dicit esset Domino qui aliter mysterium celebrat quam ab eo traditum est. Non enim potest devotus esse, qui aliter praesumit quam datum est ab Auctore. *Hilar. Diac. Comment. in Epist.* I *ad Cor.* XI, 27; *Ambros. Opp.* II, *Append.* 149 E.

tradition; do that in the Lord's commemoration which he himself did, he himself commanded, and his Apostles confirmed [2].

This caution or foresight if we use, then may we see to those[t] things that be requisite in the worthy receiver; whereof this was the first, that we have a right understanding of the thing itself. As concerning which thing, this we may assuredly persuade ourselves, that the ignorant man can neither worthily esteem nor effectually use those marvellous graces and benefits offered and exhibited in that Supper, but either will lightly regard them to no small offence, or utterly contemn[u] them to his utter destruction; so that by his negligence he deserveth the plagues of God to fall upon him, and by contempt he deserveth everlasting perdition. To avoid then these harms, use the advice of the Wise Man, who willeth thee, *when thou sittest at an earthly king's table*, to *take diligent heed what things are set before thee*. Prov. xxiii, [1.] So now much more, at the King of kings' table, thou must carefully search and know what dainties are provided for thy soul: whither thou art come, not to feed thy senses and belly to corruption, but thy inward man to immortality and life; not to consider[w] the earthly creatures which thou seest, but the heavenly graces which thy faith beholdeth. "For this table is not," saith Chrysostom[3], "for chattering jays, but for eagles," who flee "*thither, where the dead body lieth*[γ]." γ [Matt. xxiv, 28.] And, if this advertisement of man cannot persuade us to resort to the Lord's table with understanding, see the counsel of God in the like matter, who charged[δ] his people to teach their posterity, δ [Exod. xii, 26, 27; xiii, 8.] not only the rites and ceremonies of his Passover[x], but the cause and end thereof: whence we may learn, that both more perfect knowledge is required at this time at our hands, and that the ignorant cannot with fruit and profit exercise himself

[t] see to those] see those 1623. [u] contemn] condemn *from* 1567. [w] not to consider] nor to consider *from* 1571. [x] his Passover] the Passover *from* 1567.

2 Ad radicem atque originem traditionis Dominicae revertatur...... Dominica traditio servetur, neque aliud fiat a nobis quam quod pro nobis Dominus prior fecerit...... Et a Domino praecipitur, et ab Apostolo ejus hoc idem confirmatur et traditur, ut quotiescunque biberimus in commemorationem Domini hoc faciamus quod fecit et Dominus. *Cyprian. Epist.* LXIII *ad Caecil. pp.* 148, 152, *ed. Oxon., pp.* 104, 107, *ed. Paris.* See also *Epist.* LXXIV *ad Pompeium,* Nam si ad divinae traditionis caput —— origo surrexit, *p.* 215 *Oxon., p.* 141 *Paris.*

3 Ὅπου γὰρ τὸ πτῶμά, φησιν, ἐκεῖ καὶ οἱ ἀετοί, πτῶμα καλῶν τὸ σῶμα διὰ τὸν θάνατον.... ἀετοὺς δὲ καλεῖ, δεικνὺς ὅτι καὶ ὑψηλὸν εἶναι δεῖ τὸν προσιόντα τῷ σώματι τούτῳ, καὶ μηδὲν πρὸς τὴν γῆν κοινὸν ἔχειν, μηδὲ κάτω σύρεσθαι καὶ ἕρπειν, ἀλλ' ἄνω πέτεσθαι διηνεκῶς, καὶ πρὸς τὸν Ἥλιον τῆς δικαιοσύνης (Mal. iv, 2) ἐνορᾷν, καὶ ὀξυδερκὲς τὸ ὄμμα τῆς διανοίας ἔχειν· ἀετῶν γάρ, οὐ κολοιῶν, αὕτη ἡ τράπεζα. Chrysost. in Epist. I ad Cor. Homil. XXIV; Opp. X, 216 C.

in the Lord's Sacraments. But to come nigher to the matter: St. Paul, blaming the Corinthians for the profaning of the Lord's Supper, concludeth that ignorance both of the thing itself and the signification thereof was the cause of their abuse; for they came thither unreverently, *not discerning the Lord's body.* Ought not we then, by the monition of the Wise Man, by the wisdom of God, by the fearful example of the Corinthians, to take advised heed, that we thrust not ourselves to this table with rude and unreverent ignorance, the smart whereof Christ's Church hath rued and lamented these many days and years? For what hath been the cause of the ruin of God's religion, but the ignorance hereof? What hath been the cause of this gross idolatry, but the ignorance hereof? What hath been the cause of this mummish[4] massing, but the ignorance hereof? Yea, what hath been, and what is at this day, the cause of this want of love and charity, but the ignorance hereof? Let us therefore so travail to understand the Lord's Supper, that we be no cause of the decay of God's worship, of no[y] idolatry, of no[z] dumb massing, of no[a] hate and malice: so may we the boldlier have access thither to our comfort.

1 Cor. xi, [29.]

Neither need we to think that such exact knowledge is required of every man, that he be able to discuss all high points in the doctrine thereof. But thus much he must[b] be sure to hold, that in the Supper of the Lord there is no vain ceremony, no bare sign, no untrue figure of a thing absent, but, as the Scripture saith, *the table of the Lord, the bread and cup of the Lord, the memory of Christ, the annunciation of his death,* yea, *the communion of the body and blood of the Lord* in a marvellous incorporation, which by the operation of the Holy Ghost, the very bond of our conjunction with Christ, is through faith wrought in the souls of the faithful, whereby not only their souls live to eternal life, but they surely trust to win to their[c] bodies a resurrection to immortality[5]. The true understanding

Matt. xxvi, [26, 27:] 1 Cor. x, [16, 21;] xi, [24, 26, 27.]

Iren. Lib. iv, cap. 34.

y z a of no] *so in all.* b he must] we must *from* 1582. c win to their] win their 1623.

4 mummish: silent, without speech, like mummers; nearly equivalent to "dumb" in line 18. See *Tyndale's Obedience of a Christian Man,* "What helpeth it also—at such mumming," *pp.* 226, 227, *ed. Park. Soc.*

5 Πῶς τὴν σάρκα λέγουσιν εἰς φθορὰν χωρεῖν, καὶ μὴ μετέχειν τῆς ζωῆς, τὴν ἀπὸ τοῦ σώματος τοῦ Κυρίου καὶ τοῦ αἵματος αὐτοῦ τρεφομένην; . . . ὡς γὰρ ἀπὸ γῆς ἄρτος προσλαμβανόμενος τὴν ἔκκλησιν τοῦ Θεοῦ οὐκέτι κοινὸς ἄρτος ἐστὶν, ἀλλ' Εὐχαριστία, ἐκ δύο πραγμάτων συνεστηκυῖα, ἐπιγείου τε καὶ οὐρανίου· οὕτως καὶ τὰ σώματα ἡμῶν μεταλαμβάνοντα τῆς Εὐχαριστίας μηκέτι εἶναι φθαρτὰ, τὴν ἐλπίδα τῆς εἰς αἰῶνας ἀναστάσεως ἔχοντα. Iren. contra Haeres. IV, xviii (*al.* xxxiv), 5; Opp. I, 251, ed. Venet. 1734.

of this fruition and union, which is betwixt the[d] body and the head, betwixt the true believers and Christ, the ancient catholic fathers both perceiving themselves, and commending to their people, were not afraid to call this Supper[6], some of them, "the salve of immortality, a sovereign[e] preservative against death;" other, "a deifical communion;" other, "the sweet dainties of our Saviour;" "the pledge of eternal health, the defence of faith, the hope of the resurrection;" other, "the food of immortality," "the healthful grace," and "the conservatory to everlasting life." All which sayings, both of the holy Scripture and godly men, truly attributed to this celestial banquet and feast, if we would often call to mind, O how would they inflame our hearts to desire the participation of these mysteries, and oftentimes to covet after this bread, continually to thirst for this food; not as specially regarding the terrene and earthly creatures which remain, but always holding fast and cleaving by faith to the *Rock* whence we may *suck the sweetness of* everlasting *salvation*. And, to be brief, thus much more[f] the faithful see, hear[g], and know, the favourable mercies of God sealed, the satisfaction by Christ towards us confirmed, the[h] remission of sin stablished[i]. Here they may feel wrought the tranquillity of conscience, the increase of faith, the strengthening of hope, the large spreading abroad of brotherly kindness, with many other sundry graces of God; the taste whereof they cannot attain unto who be drowned in the deep dirty lake of blindness and

Ignat. Epist. ad Ephes. Dionysius. Origenes. Optatus. Cyprian. de Coen. Dom. Athan. de Pecc. in Spir. Sanc.

[Deut. xxxii, 4, 13, 15: 1 Cor. x, 4.]

[d] is betwixt the] is the *till* 1623. [e] a sovereign] and sovereign *from* 1563 B. [f], [g] more, hear] *so in all. Did the author write* thus much may the faithful see here, and know the—? [h] confirmed, the] confirmed, and the *from* 1563 G. [i] stablished] established *from* 1571.

6 Ἕνα ἄρτον κλῶντες, ὅς ἐστιν φάρμακον ἀθανασίας, ἀντίδοτος τοῦ μὴ ἀποθανεῖν. Ignat. Epist. ad Ephes. c. XX.

Μετασχὼν δὲ καὶ μεταδοὺς τῆς θεαρχικῆς κοινωνίας κ. τ. λ. Pseudo-Dionys. Areop. de Eccles. Hierarch. III, ii.

Si contemnimus dapes Salvatoris nostri &c. *Origen. in Luc. Homil.* XXXVIII, *Opp.* III, 977 b, F.

Quid enim tam sacrilegum quam altaria Dei ... frangere, ... unde a multis et pignus salutis aeternae et tutela fidei et spes resurrectionis accepta est? *Optat. de Schism. Donatist.* VI, 1.

Immortalitatis alimonia datur, a communibus cibis differens. *Arnold. de Coena Domini, ad calc. Cyprian. Opp. p.* 39 *ed. Oxon., col. cix ed. Paris.*

Alius ... maculatus ... sanctum Domini edere et contrectare non potuit, cinerem ferre se apertis manibus invenit. Documento unius ostensum est Dominum recedere cum negatur, nec immerentibus ad salutem prodesse quod sumitur, quando gratia salutaris in cinerem sanctitate fugiente mutatur. *Cyprian. de Lapsu, Opp. p.* 133 *ed. Oxon., p.* 189 *ed. Paris.*

Ἃ γὰρ **λελάληκά**, φησιν (Joan. VI, 63), **ὑμῖν, πνεῦμά ἐστι καὶ ζωή**· ἴσον τῷ εἰπεῖν, Τὸ μὲν δεικνύμενον καὶ διδόμενον ὑπὲρ τῆς τοῦ κόσμου σωτηρίας ἐστὶν ἡ σάρξ ἣν ἐγὼ φορῶ, ἀλλ' αὕτη ὑμῖν καὶ τὸ ταύτης αἷμα παρ' ἐμοῦ πνευματικῶς δοθήσεται τροφὴ, ὥστε πνευματικῶς ἐν ἑκάστῳ ταύτην ἀναδίδοσθαι καὶ γίνεσθαι πᾶσι φυλακτήριον εἰς ἀνάστασιν ζωῆς αἰωνίου. Athanas. Epist. IV ad Serap. §. 19; Opp. I, 710 C, ed. Paris. 1698.

ignorance. From the which, O beloved, wash yourselves with the living waters of God's word, whence you may perceive and know both the spiritual food of this costly Supper and the happy trustings and effects that the same doth bring with it.

Now it followeth to have with this knowledge a sure and constant faith, not only that the death of Christ is available for the redemption of all the world, for the remission of sins, and reconciliation with God the Father, but also that he hath made upon his cross a full and sufficient sacrifice for thee, a perfect cleansing of thy sins; so that thou acknowledgest no other Saviour, Redeemer, Mediator, Advocate, Intercessor, but Christ [Gal. ii, 20.] only, and that thou mayest say with the Apostle, that he *loved thee and gave himself for thee.* For this is to stick fast to Christ's promise made in his institution, to make Christ[k] thine own, and to applicate[l] his merits unto thyself. Herein thou needest no other man's help, no other sacrifice or oblation, no sacrificing priest, no mass, no means established by man's invention. That faith is a necessary instrument in all these holy ceremonies Heb. xi, [6.] we may thus assure ourselves, for that, as St. Paul saith, *without faith it is unpossible to please God.* When a great number e [1 Cor. x, 5.] of the Israelites *were overthrown in the wilderness*[e], "Moyses, Aaron, and Phinees did eat manna, and pleased God, for that In Joan. Hom. 6. they understood," saith St. Augustine[7], "the visible meat spiritually: spiritually they hungered it; spiritually they tasted it; that they might be spiritually satisfied." And truly, as the bodily meat cannot feed the outward man, unless it be let into a stomach to be digested which is healthsome and sound, no more can the[m] inward man be fed, except his meat be received into his soul and heart, sound and whole in faith. Therefore De Coen. Dom. saith Cyprian[8], "when we do these things, we need not to whet our teeth, but with sincere faith we break and divide that holy[n] bread." It is well known that the meat we seek for in this Supper is spiritual food, the nourishment of our soul, a heavenly refection and not earthly, an unvisible meat[o] and not bodily, a

k make Christ] make of Christ 1563 A–C. l applicate] apply 1623. m can the] can thy *till* 1574. n that holy] that whole *from* 1582. o unvisible] invisible *from* 1567.

7 Manducavit manna et Moyses, manducavit manna et Aaron, manducavit manna et Phinees, manducaverunt ibi multi qui Domino placuerunt, et mortui non sunt. Quare? Quia visibilem cibum spiritaliter intellexerunt, spiritaliter esurierunt, spiritaliter gustaverunt, ut spiritaliter satiarentur. *Augustin. in Joan. Evang.* VI, 49, *Tractat.* XXVI, § 11; *Opp. Tom.* III, *Par.* II, 498 B.

8 Haec quotiens agimus, non dentes ad mordendum acuimus, sed fide sincera panem sanctum frangimus et partimur. *Arnold. de Coena Domini ad calc. Cyprian. Opp. p.* 44 *ed. Oxon., col. cxviii ed. Paris.*

ghostly sustenance[p] and not carnal: so that to think that without faith we may enjoy the eating and drinking thereof, or that that is the fruition of it, is but to dream a gross carnal feeding, basely abjecting[q] and binding ourselves to the elements and creatures; whereas, by the advice of the Council of Nicene, we ought to "lift up our minds by faith[9]," and, leaving these inferior and earthly things, there seek it where *the Sun of righteousness* ever shineth. Take then this lesson, O thou that art desirous of this table, of Emissenus, a godly father, that[10] "when thou goest up to the reverend[r] Communion to be satisfied with spiritual meats, thou look up with faith upon the holy Body and Blood of thy God, thou marvel with reverence, thou touch it with thy mind[s], thou receive it with the hand of thy heart, and thou take it fully with thy inward man."

Concilium Nicen.

[Mal. iv, 2.]

Euseb. Emiss. Serm. de Euchar.

Thus we see, beloved, that, resorting to this table, we must pluck up all the roots of infidelity, all distrust in God's promises, we must make[t] ourselves living members of Christ's body. For the unbelievers and faithless cannot feed upon that precious Body: whereas the faithful have their life, their abiding, in him; their union, and as it were their incorporation, with him. Wherefore[u] let us prove and try ourselves unfeign-

p sustenance] substance *from* 1563 B. q abjecting] objecting *from* 1563 G. r reverend] reverent *till* 1582. s thy mind] the mind *from* 1582. t we must make] we make 1574, that we make *from* 1582. u him. Wherefore] him. Whereof thus saith St. Augustine: He which is at discord with Christ doth neither eat his flesh nor drink his blood, although he receive, to the judgment of his destruction, daily the outward Sacrament of so great a thing. Wherefore 1563 A I, *with* Lib. 4 de Trinit. *in the margin*[11].

9 Ἐπὶ τῆς θείας τραπέζης πάλιν κἀνταῦθα (here too, as well as in Baptism) μὴ τῷ προκειμένῳ ἄρτῳ καὶ τῷ ποτηρίῳ ταπεινῶς προσέχωμεν· ἀλλ' ὑψώσαντες ἡμῶν τὴν διάνοιαν πίστει νοήσωμεν κεῖσθαι ἐπὶ τῆς ἱερᾶς ἐκείνης τραπέζης **τὸν ἀμνὸν τοῦ Θεοῦ, τὸν αἴροντα τὴν ἁμαρτίαν τοῦ κόσμου** (Joan. I, 29), κ.τ.λ. Gelas. Hist. Concil. Nicaen. Lib. II, cap. XXX; Concil. Labbe II, 233 C, Mansi II, 888 C. See Jewell, Reply to Harding, Art. V, Div. 8; and Defence of Apology, Part II, Ch. XIV, Div. 4.

10 Cum reverendum altare cibis spiritualibus satiandus ascendis, sacrum Dei tui Corpus et Sanguinem fide respice, honora, mirare (*al.* honore mirare), mente continge, cordis manu suscipe, et maxime totum haustu interioris hominis assume. These are the concluding words of a passage placed by Gratian in the *Decretum* (III *De Consecr.*, ii, 35, *Quia corpus*), and ascribed by him to Eusebius Emesenus. In the collection of Homilies, fifty six in number, first published at Paris in 1547 under the name of Eusebius, they occur, with some variation, in Hom. V. de Pascha at fol. 45 a: but critics have long been agreed that Eusebius cannot have been the author, and the whole of that collection is confidently assigned to Faustus Reiensis or Regiensis, Bishop of Riez in the latter part of the fifth century, by *Oudin de Scriptor. Eccles. Antiq.* The Homily to which the passage here cited belongs is comprised in several of the editions of the Works of St. Jerome under the title *De Eucharistia* or *De Corpore et Sanguine Christi.*

11 Nam qui discordat a Christo nec carnem ejus manducat nec sanguinem bibit, etiam si tantae rei sacramentum ad judicium suae praesumtionis quotidie indifferenter accipiat. *Prosper. Lib. Sententt. ex Augustin. Delibatt.* § 341, *Au-*

[ς] [Rom. xi, 17, 24: John xv, 1-6: Eph. v, 30, 32.]

edly, without flattering ourselves, whether we be plants [ς] of that fruitful [x] olive, living *branches of the true Vine, members* indeed *of Christ's mystical body;* whether God hath purified our hearts by faith to the sincere acknowledging of his Gospel and imbracing of his mercies in Christ Jesu [y]: that so [z] at this his table we receive, not only the outward Sacrament, but the spiritual thing also; not the figure, but the truth; not the shadow only, but the body; not to death, but to life; not to destruction, but to salvation. Which God grant us to do thorough [a] the merits of our Lord and Saviour: to whom be all honour and glory for ever. Amen.

[x] that fruitful] the fruitful 1623. [a] Jesu] Jesus 1623. [y] that so] so that 1587, 1595, 1623. [a] thorough] through *from* 1571.

gustin. Opp. X *Append.* 247. But the Homilist took the sentence at second hand from Gratian, *Decret.* III *De Consecr.*, ii, 65, *Qui discordat,* where *perditionis* was printed instead of *praesumtionis* until the corrected edition of Pope Gregory XIII in 1582. And this will account for the wrong reference to the *Fourth Book de Trinitate:* for that portion of the Decretum has many chapters in succession taken from Augustine, and in all the early editions of it *c.* 60, *Corpus et Sanguinem,* is thus cited, "Item in li. iiii de Trinitate," and then each of the next six chapters, 61–66, is cited by the single word "Item" with nothing to shew that any of them come from any other part of Augustine's Works.

The sentence itself is not found in Augustine. Prosper seems to have formed it by abridgment from two sentences in *Tractat.* XXVI *in Joan. Evang.* §§15 and 18 (*Augustin. Opp. Tom.* III, *Par.* II, 500 D and 501 A), Hujus rei sacramentum—particeps fuerit, and, Ac per hoc—Deum videbunt; with which should be compared *De Civ. Dei* XXI, and XXV, 4 (*Opp.* VII, 646 G, 647 A).

The second of those two sentences is the one from which our 29th Article is framed; and the suppression of that Article after it had been approved by both Houses of Convocation in 1563 seems to give a peculiar significance to the omission of this passage from all published copies of the Homilies. See *Cardwell's Synodalia, No.* III, *Vol.* I, *p.* 38. An account of the single copy in which the passage remains is given in the Preface to this volume.

THE SECOND PART OF THE HOMILY OF THE WORTHY RECEIVING AND REVERENT[a] ESTEEMING OF THE SACRAMENT OF THE BODY AND BLOOD OF CHRIST.

IN the Homily of late rehearsed unto you ye have heard, good people, why it pleased our Saviour Christ to institute that heavenly memory of his death and passion, and that every one of us ought to celebrate the same at his table in our own persons, and not by other. You have heard also with what estimation and knowledge of so high mysteries we ought to resort thither, you have heard with what constant faith we should clothe and deck ourselves, that we might be fit and decent partakers of that celestial food. Now followeth the third thing necessary in him that would not eat of this bread nor drink of this cup unworthily, which is newness of life and godliness of conversation.

For newness of life, as fruits of faith, are[b] required in the partaker[c] of this table. We may learn by the eating[d] of the typical lamb, whereunto no man was admitted but he that was a Jew, that was circumcised, that was before sanctified. Yea, St. Paul testifieth, that, although all the[e] people were partakers 1 Cor. x, [1–11.] of the Sacraments under Moses, yet, for that some of them were still worshippers of images, whoremongers, tempters of Christ, murmurers, and coveting after evil things, God overthrew those in the wilderness, and that for our example; that is, that we Christians should take heed we resort unto our Sacraments with holiness of life, not trusting in the outward receiving of them, and infected with corrupt and uncharitable manners. For this sentence of God must always be justified, [Hos. vi, 1: Matt. ix, 13.] *I will have mercy, and not sacrifice.* "Wherefore," saith Basil[1], De Bapt. Lib. i, cap. 3.

[a] REVERENT] REVEREND 1623. [b] are] *so in all.* [c] partaker] partakers *from* 1582. [d] by the eating] by eating 1623. *Did the author write* For, that newness of life—of this table, we may learn by the eating *&c.*? [e] although all the] although the *from* 1563 G.

1 Δεῖ οὖν τὸν προσιόντα τῷ σώματι καὶ τῷ αἵματι τοῦ Χριστοῦ, εἰς ἀνάμνησιν (1 Cor. XI, 24, 25) αὐτοῦ τοῦ ὑπὲρ ἡμῶν ἀποθανόντος καὶ ἐγερθέντος (2 Cor. V, 15), μὴ μόνον καθαρεύειν ἀπὸ παντὸς μολυσμοῦ σαρκὸς καὶ πνεύματος (2 Cor. VII, 1), ἵνα μὴ εἰς κρίμα φάγῃ καὶ πίῃ, ἀλλὰ καὶ ἐνεργῶς δεικνύειν τὴν μνήμην τοῦ ὑπὲρ ἡμῶν ἀποθανόντος καὶ ἐγερθέντος, ἐν τῷ νενεκρῶσθαι μὲν τῇ ἁμαρ-

"it behoveth him that cometh to the Body and Blood of Christ, *in commemoration of him that died and rose again*,[f] not only to be pure *from all filthiness of the flesh and spirit*, lest he eat and drink to his[g] condemnation[h], but also to shew out evidently a memory of *him that died and rose again for us*, in this point, that he be[i] *mortified to sin* and *the world*, to *live* now *to God in Christ Jesu our Lord*." So then we must shew outward testimony in following the signification of Christ's death: amongst the which this is not esteemed least, to render thanks to Almighty God for all his benefits briefly comprised in the death, passion, and resurrection of his dearly beloved Son.

The which thing because we ought chiefly at this table to solemnize, the godly fathers named it Eucharistia, that is, Thanksgiving[2]: as if they should have said, Now above all other times ye ought to laud and praise God; now may ye[j] behold the matter, the cause, the beginning, and the end of all thanksgiving; now if ye[k] slack, ye shew yourselves most unthankful, and that no other benefit can ever stir you to thank God, who so little regard here so many, so wonderful, and so profitable benefits. Seeing then that the name and thing itself
Heb. xiii, [15.] doth monish us of thanks, *let us*, as St. Paul saith, *offer always to God the host* or sacrifice *of praise*[3] *by Christ, that is, the*
Ps. l, [23.] *fruit of the lips which confess his Name*. For, as David singeth, *he that offereth to God thanks and praise honoureth him*. But how few be there of thankful persons in comparison to the un-
a Luke xvii, [12–18.] thankful! Lo, ten lepers in the Gospel[a] were healed, and but one only returned to give thanks for his health. Yea, happy it were, if among forty communicants we could see two unfeignedly to give[l] thanks. So unkind we be, so oblivious we be, so proud beggars we be, that partly we care not for our own commodity, partly we know not our duty to God, and chiefly we will not confess all that we receive. Yea, and if we be forced by God's power to do it, yet we handle it so coldly, so drily, that our lips praise him, but our hearts dispraise him; our tongues bless him, but our life curseth him; our words wor-

[f] rose again,] *so in all, without* for us. [g] drink to his] drink his 1623. [h] his condemnation] his own condemnation *from* 1582. [i] he be] ye be 1623. [j] may ye] may you *from* 1567. [k] if ye] if you *from* 1571. [l] unfeignedly to give] unfeignedly give *from* 1567.

τίᾳ καὶ τῷ κόσμῳ καὶ ἑαυτῷ, ζῆν δὲ τῷ Θεῷ, ἐν Χριστῷ Ἰησοῦ τῷ Κυρίῳ ἡμῶν (Rom. VI, 11; Gal. VI, 14; 2 Cor. V, 15). Basil. de Baptismo I, iii, 3; Opp. II, 651 E. The Benedictine editor questions the genuineness of this treatise: see his Preface to Tom. II, pp. lxxvii–lxxxv.

2 See for example Irenaeus cited before, p. 442, n. 5. See also *Bingham, Eccles. Orig.* XV, iii, 9.

3 Offeramus hostiam laudis. *Vulg.*

ship him, but our works dishonour him. O let us therefore learn to give God here thanks aright, and so to agnize his exceeding graces poured upon us, that they, being shut up in the treasure house of our heart, may in due time and season in our life and conversation appear to the glorifying of his holy Name.

Furthermore, for newness of life, it is to be noted that St. Paul writeth, that *we being many are one bread and one body, for all be partakers of one bread;* declaring thereby not only our communion with Christ, but that unity also wherein they that eat at this table should be knit together. For by dissension, vainglory, ambition, strife, envying, contempt, hatred, or malice they should not be dissevered, but so joined by the bond of love in one mystical body, as the corns of that bread in one loaf. In respect of which strait knot of charity the true Christians in the tender time of Christ's[m] Church called this Supper Love[4]; as if they would say[n], none ought to sit down there that were out of love and charity, who bore[o] grudge and vengeance in his heart, who also did not profess his kind affection by some charitable relief for some part of the congregation. And this was their practice. O heavenly banquet, then so used! O godly guests, who so esteemed this feast! But O wretched creatures that we be at these days, who be without reconciliation of our brethren whom we have offended, without satisfying them whom we have caused to fall, without any kind thought[p] or compassion toward them whom we might easily relieve, without any conscience of slander, disdain, misreport, division, rancour, or inward bitterness; yea, being accombred with[β] the cloaked hatred of Cain, with the long covered[q] malice of Esau, with the dissembled falsehood of Joab, dare yet[r] presume to come up to these sacred and fearful mysteries. O man, whither rushest thou unadvisedly? It is a table of peace, and thou art ready to fight. It is a table of singleness, and thou art imagining mischief. It is a table of quietness, and thou art given to debate. It is a table of pity, and thou art unmerciful. Dost thou neither fear God, the maker of this feast? nor reve-

[1 Cor. x, 17.]

β Gen. iv, [5–8;] xxvii, [41:] 2 Sam. iii, [27.]

m tender time of Christ's] primitive 1623. n would say] should say *from* 1563 B. o bore] bare *from* 1582. p kind thought] kind of thought *from* 1571. q covered] coloured 1623. r yet] ye *from* 1563 G.

4 Perhaps the Homilist says this on the strength of Tertullian's statement in *Apol.* c. 39. Coena nostra de nomine rationem sui ostendit. Id vocatur quod dilectio penes Graecos. But the context there shews that Tertullian is not speaking of the Eucharist, but of the Feast of Charity or Love Feast of the early Christians, just as the Ἀγάπη is distinguished from the Εὐχαριστία in *Ignat. Epist. ad Smyrn.* c. 8. See *Bingham, Eccles. Orig.* xv, vii, 6, 7.

rence his Christ, the refection and meat? nor regardest his spouse, his beloved[s] guest? nor weighest thine own conscience, which is sometime thine inward accuser? Wherefore, O man, tender thine own salvation; examine and try thy good will and love towards the children of God, the members of Christ, the heirs of the heavenly heritage; yea, towards the image of God, the excellent creature thine own soul. If thou have offended, now be reconciled. If thou have caused[t] any to stumble in the way of God, now set them up again. If thou have disquieted thy brother, now pacify him. If thou have wronged him, now relieve him. If thou have defrauded him, now restore to him. If thou have nourished spite, now imbrace friendship. If thou have fostered hatred and malice, now openly shew thy love and charity; yea, be prest[5] and ready to procure thy neighbour's health of soul, wealth, commodity, and pleasure[u], as thine own. Deserve not the heavy and dreadful burden of God's displeasure for thine evil will towards thy neighbour, so unreverently to approach to this table of the Lord.

Chrysost. ad Pop. Ant. Hom. 60.

Last of all, as there is here "the mystery of peace"[6] and the Sacrament of Christian society, whereby we understand what sincere love ought to be betwixt the true communicants, so here be the tokens of pureness and innocency of life, whereby we may perceive that we ought to purge our own soul from all uncleanness, iniquity, and wickedness, "lest, when we receive the mystical bread," as Origen saith[7], "we eat it in an unclean place, that is, in a soul defiled and polluted with sin." In Moyses' law[y] the man that did eat of the sacrifice of thanksgiving with his uncleanness upon him should be destroyed from his people: and shall we think that the wicked and sinful person shall be

In Levit. cap. xxiii, Hom. 14. Luke xvii.[8]

y [Numb. v, 2; ix, 6; xix, 15.]

s beloved] wellbeloved *from* 1582. t have caused] hast caused *till* 1582. u pleasure] pleasures *from* 1574.

5 prest: at hand, prompt, an old French word.

He maketh his spirits as heralds to go,
And lightnings to serve we see also prest:
His will to accomplish they run to and fro,
To save or consume things, as seemeth him best.

Ps. CIV, 4, *Old Version.*

6 Τοῦτο γὰρ τὸ μυστήριον οὐ μόνον ἁρπαγῆς ἀλλὰ καὶ ψιλῆς ἔχθρας καθαρεύειν κελεύει διὰ παντός· καὶ γὰρ εἰρήνης ἐστὶ μυστήριον τοῦτο τὸ μυστήριον. Chrysost. in Matth. Hom. L (*al.* LI); Opp. VII, 517 C: Ad Pop. Ant. Hom. LX Lat., Opp. ed. Basil. 1530 Tom. IV p. 583 A.

7 Unde simili modo etiam tibi lex ista proponitur, ut, cum acceperis panem mysticum, in loco mundo manduces eum; hoc est, ne in anima contaminata et peccatis polluta Dominici Corporis Sacramenta percipias. *Origen. in Levit. Hom.* XIII, 5; *Opp.* II, 257 b, E.

8 It does not appear to what this reference, "Luke xvii," belongs.

excusable at the table of the Lord? We both read in St. Paul[8] [8 1 Cor. xi, [30.]] that the Church at Corinth[x] was scourged of the Lord for misusing the Lord's Supper; and we may plainly see Christ's Church these many years miserably vexed and oppressed for the horrible profanation of the same. Wherefore let us all, universal and singular, behold our own manners and lives, to amend them. Yea, now at the least let us call ourselves to an account, that it may grieve us of our former evil conversation, that we may hate sin, that we may sorrow and mourn for our offences, that we may with tears pour them out before God, that we may with sure trust desire and crave the salve of his mercy, bought and purchased with the blood of his dearly beloved Son Jesus Christ, to heal our deadly wounds withal. For surely, if we do not with earnest repentance cleanse the filthy stomach of our soul, it must needs come to pass that[9], "as wholesome meat [Chrysost. ad Pop. Ant. Hom. 61.] received into a raw stomach corrupteth and marreth all, and is the cause of further sickness," so we shall[y] eat this healthsome[z] bread and drink this cup to our eternal destruction. Thus we, and not other, must throughly[a] examine, and not lightly look over, ourselves, not other men; our own conscience, not other men's lives; which we ought to do uprightly, truly, and with just correction. "O," saith St. Chrysostom[10], "let no Judas [Ad Pop. Ant. Hom. 60.] resort to this table; let no covetous person approach. If any be a disciple, let him be present. For Christ saith, *With my* [Matt. xxvi, [18.]] *disciples I make my passover.*" Why cried the deacon in the primitive Church, "If any be holy, let him draw near"?[11] Why did they celebrate these mysteries, the choir door being shut? Why were the public penitents and learners in religion com-

[x] at Corinth] of Corinth *from* 1582. [y] we shall] shall we *from* 1563 EF. [z] healthsome] wholesome *from* 1582. [a] throughly] thoroughly 1623.

9 Ὥσπερ γὰρ ἡ τροφὴ, φύσει οὖσα θρεπτικὴ, ἐὰν εἰς κακόσιτον ἐμπέσῃ, πάντα ἀπόλλυσι καὶ διαφθείρει, καὶ γίνεται νόσου ἀφορμή· οὕτω δὴ καὶ ταῦτα τὰ τῶν φρικτῶν μυστηρίων. Chrysost. in Epist. ad Hebr. Hom. XVII; Opp. XII, 169 C: Ad Pop. Ant. Hom. LXI Lat., Opp. ed. Basil. 1530 Tom. IV p. 587 A.

10 Μηδεὶς τοίνυν Ἰούδας παρέστω, μηδεὶς φιλάργυρος. εἴ τις μὴ μαθητὴς, παραχωρείτω· οὐ δέχεται τοὺς μὴ τοιούτους ἡ τράπεζα· μετὰ γὰρ τῶν μαθητῶν μου, φησὶ, ποιῶ τὸ πάσχα. Chrysost. in Matth. Hom. LXXXII (*al.* LXXXIII); Opp. VII, 789 A. Nullus itaque Judas assistat, nullus avarus. Si quis est discipulus, adsit. Nam tales mensa non suscipit: ait enim, *Cum discipulis meis facio pascha.* Ad Pop. Ant. Hom. LX Lat., Opp. ed. Basil. 1530 Tom. IV p. 582 C.

11 It does not appear that exactly this proclamation was made by the deacon. The words are rather an interpretation put upon the proclamation, Ἅγια τοῖς ἁγίοις, which was actually made. See *Chrysost. in Epist. ad Hebr. Hom.* XVII, *Opp.* XII, 170, 171: *Bingham, Orig. Eccles.* XV, iii, 31.

On the next two sentences see *Chrysost. in Matth. Hom.* XXIII (al. XXIV), *Opp.* VII, 288 C: *Constitt. Apost.* VIII, 6–9, 12: *Bingham, ibid.* 5.

manded at this time to avoid? Was it not because this table receiveth[b] no unholy, unclean, or sinful guests? Wherefore, if servants dare not presume[c] to an earthly master's table whom they have offended, let us take heed we come not with our sins unexamined into this presence of our Lord and Judge. If they be worthy blame who[d] kiss the prince's hand with a filthy and unclean mouth, shalt thou be blameless, which with a filthy stinking[e] soul, full of covetousness, fornication, drunkenness, pride, full of wretched cogitations and thoughts, dost[f] breathe out iniquity and uncleanness on the bread and cup of the Lord?

Epilog. Thus you have[g] heard how you should come reverently and decently to the table of the Lord, having the knowledge out of his word of the thing itself and the fruits thereof, bringing a true and constant faith, the root and wellspring of all newness of life, as well in praising God, loving[h] our neighbour, as purging our own conscience from filthiness. So that neither the ignorance of the thing shall cause us to contemn it, nor unfaithfulness make us void of fruit, nor sin and iniquity procure us God's plagues; but shall[i], by faith in knowledge, and amendment of life in faith, be here so united to Christ our Head in his mysteries to our comfort, that after we shall have full fruition of him indeed to our everlasting joy and eternal life. To the [1 John ii, 1.] which he bring us that died for us, and redeemed us, *Jesus Christ the righteous:* to whom with the Father and the Holy Ghost, one true and eternal God, be all praise, honour, and dominion for ever. Amen.

[b] receiveth] received *from* 1563 B. [c] not presume] not to presume 1623. [d] who] which *from* 1563 B. [e] a filthy stinking] a stinking *from* 1582. [f] dost] doth 1563 B–1567. [g] you have] have you *from* 1563 EF. [h] God, loving] God, and loving *from* 1567. [i] but shall] *so in all.*

AN HOMILY

CONCERNING THE COMING DOWN OF THE HOLY GHOST AND THE MANIFOLD GIFTS OF THE SAME.

FOR WHITSUNDAY.

BEFORE we come to the declaration of the great and manifold gifts of the Holy Ghost, wherewith the Church of God hath been evermore replenished, it shall first be needful briefly to expound unto you whereof this feast of Pentecost or Whitsuntide had his first beginning. You shall therefore understand that the feast of Pentecost was always kept the fiftieth day after Easter[1], a great and solemn feast among the Jews, wherein they did celebrate the memorial of their deliverance out of Egypt, and also the memorial of the publishing of the Law, which was given unto them in the mount Sinai upon that day. It was first ordained and commanded to be kept holy, not by any mortal man, but by the mouth of the Lord himself; as we read in Levit. xxiii and Deut. xvi. The place appointed for the observation thereof was Jerusalem, where was great recourse of people from all parts of the world; as may well appear in the second chapter of the Acts, wherein[α] mention is made of Parthians, Medes, Elamites, inhabiters of Mesopotamia, inhabiters of Jewry, Cappadocia, Pontus, Asia, Phrygia, Pamphylia, and divers other such places; whereby we may also partly gather what great and royal solemnity was commonly used in that feast.

α [Acts ii, 5-11.]

Now, as this was given in commandment to the Jews in the old Law, so did our Saviour Christ as it were confirm the same in the time of the Gospel, ordaining after a sort a new Pentecost for his disciples; namely[β], when he sent down the Holy Ghost visibly in form of cloven tongues like fire, and gave them power to speak in such sort, that every one might hear them, and also understand them, in his own language. Which miracle,

β [Acts ii, 1-11.]

1 See before, p. 438, n. 3.

that it might be had in perpetual remembrance, the Church hath thought good to solemnize and keep holy this day, commonly called Whitsunday. And here is to be noted, that, as the Law was given to the Jews in the mount Sinai the fiftieth day after Easter, so was the preaching of the Gospel through the mighty power of the Holy Ghost given to the Apostles in the mount Sion the fiftieth day after Easter. And hereof this feast hath his name, to be called Pentecost, even of the number of the days. For, as St. Luke writeth in the Acts of the Apostles, *when fifty days were come to an end*[2], the disciples being *all together with one accord in one place*, the Holy Ghost *came suddenly* among them, *and sat upon each of them, like as it had been cloven tongues of fire.* Which thing was undoubtedly done, to teach the Apostles and all other men, that it is he which giveth eloquence and utterance in preaching the Gospel; that it is he which openeth the mouth to declare the mighty works of God; that it is he which engendereth a burning zeal toward[a] God's word, and giveth all men a tongue, yea, a fiery tongue, so that they may boldly and cheerfully profess the truth in the face of the whole world: as Esay was indued with this Spirit. *The*
Isa. l, [4.] *Lord,* saith Esay, *gave me a learned* and a skilful *tongue, so that I might know to raise up them that are fallen with the word*[3].
Ps. l [li, 15.] The Prophet David crieth to have this gift, saying, *Open thou my lips, O Lord, and my mouth shall shew forth thy praise.* For
Matt. x, [20.] our Saviour Christ also in the Gospel saith to his disciples, *It is not you that speak, but the Spirit of your Father which is within you.* All which testimonies of holy Scripture do sufficiently declare, that the mystery of[b] the tongues betokeneth the preaching of the Gospel, and the open confession of the Christian faith, in all them that are possessed with the Holy Ghost. So that, if any man be a dumb Christian, not professing his faith openly, but cloaking and colouring himself for fear of danger in time to come, he giveth men occasion, justly and with good conscience, to doubt lest he have not the grace of the Holy Ghost within him, because he is tongue tied, and doth not speak.

Thus then have ye heard the first institution of this feast of Pentecost or Whitsuntide, as well in the old Law among the Jews, as also in the time of the Gospel among the Christians.

[a] toward] towards *from* 1563 B.

[b] mystery of] mystery in *from* 1563 B.

2 Cum complerentur dies Pentecostes. *Vulg.*

3 Dominus dedit mihi linguam eruditam, ut sciam sustentare eum qui lassus est verbo. *Vulg.*

Now let us consider what the Holy Ghost is, and how consequently he worketh his miraculous works towards mankind.

The Holy Ghost is a spiritual and divine substance, the third Person in the Deity, distinct from the Father and the Son, and yet proceeding from them both. Which thing to be true, both the Creed of Athanasius beareth witness, and may be also easily proved by most plain testimonies of God's holy word. When Christ was baptized of John in the river Jordan, we read[γ] that the Holy Ghost came down in the form of a dove, and that the Father thundered *from heaven, saying, This is my dear and well beloved Son, in whom I am well pleased.* Where note three divers and distinct Persons, the Father, the Son, and the Holy Ghost; which all notwithstanding are not three Gods, but one God. Likewise, when Christ did first institute and ordain the Sacrament of Baptism, he sent[δ] his disciples into the whole world, willing them to baptize *all nations in the name of the Father, the Son, and the Holy Ghost.* Also[c] in another place he saith[ε], *I will pray unto my Father, and he shall give you another Comforter.* Again, *When the Comforter shall come, whom I will send from my Father,* &c. These and such other places of the New Testament do so plainly and evidently confirm the distinction of the Holy Ghost from the other Persons in the Trinity, that no man can possibly doubt[d] thereof, unless he will blaspheme the everlasting truth of God's word. As for his proper nature and substance, it is altogether one with God the Father and God the Son, that is to say, spiritual, eternal, uncreated, incomprehensible, almighty; to be short, he is even God and Lord everlasting. Therefore he is called the Spirit of the Father; therefore he is said to proceed from the Father and the Son; and therefore he was equally joined with them in the commission that the Apostles had to baptize all nations.

γ Matt. iii, [16, 17.]

δ Matt. xxviii, [19.]

ε John xiv, [16; xv, 26.]

But, that this may appear more sensibly to the eyes of all men, it shall be requisite to come to the other part, namely, to the wonderful and heavenly works of the Holy Ghost, which plainly declare unto the world his mighty and divine power. First, it is evident that he did wonderfully govern and direct the hearts of the Patriarchs and Prophets in old time, illuminating their minds with the knowledge of the true Messias, and giving them utterance to prophesy of things that should come to pass long time after. For, as St. Peter witnesseth, *the prophecy came*

2 Pet. i, [21.]

c Also] And *from* 1563 G.

d man can possibly doubt] man possibly doubt 1563 C–H, man possibly can doubt *from* 1567.

not in old time by the will of man, but the holy men of God spake as they were moved inwardly by the Holy Ghost. And of Zachary Luke i, [64, 67.] the high priest it is said in the Gospel, that *he, being full of the Holy Ghost, prophesied and praised God.* So did also Simeon, Anna, Mary, and divers other, to the great wonder and admiration of all men.

Moreover, was not the Holy Ghost a mighty worker in the conception and the nativity of Christ our Saviour? St. Matthew Matt. i, [18.] saith that the blessed Virgin *was found with child of the Holy Ghost, before Joseph and she came together.* And the angel Gabriel did expressly tell her that it should come to pass, saying, Luke i, [35.] *The Holy Ghost shall come upon thee, and the power of the most High shall overshadow thee.* A marvellous matter, that a woman should conceive and bear a child without the knowledge of man. But, where the Holy Ghost worketh, there nothing is unpossible: as may further also appear by the inward regeneration and sanctification of mankind.

John iii, [3-5.] When Christ said to Nicodemus, *Unless a man be born anew, of water and the Spirit, he cannot enter into the kingdom of God,* he was greatly amazed in his mind, and began to reason with Christ, demanding *how a man might be born which was old? Can he enter,* saith he, *into his mother's womb again, and so be born anew?* Behold a lively pattern of a fleshly and carnal man. He had little or no intelligence of the Holy Ghost, and therefore he goeth bluntly to work, and asketh how this thing were possible to be true: whereas otherwise, if he had known the great power of the Holy Ghost in this behalf, that it is he which inwardly worketh the regeneration and new birth of mankind, he would never have marvelled at Christ's words, but would have rather taken[e] occasion thereby to praise and glorify God. For, as there are three several and sundry Persons in the Deity, so have they three several and sundry offices proper unto each of them, the Father to create, the Son to redeem, the Holy Ghost to sanctify and regenerate. Whereof the last, the more it is hid from our understanding, the more it ought to move all men to wonder at the secret and mighty working of God's Holy Spirit, which is within us. For it is the Holy Ghost, and no other thing, that doth quicken the minds of men, stirring up good and godly motions in their hearts, which are agreeable to the will and commandment of God, such as otherwise of their own crooked and perverse nature they should never have. *That*

[e] have rather taken] rather take 1623.

which is born of the flesh, saith Christ, *is flesh, and that which is born of the*[f] *Spirit is spirit.* (John iii, [6.]) As who should say, Man of his own nature is fleshly and carnal, corrupt and naught, sinful and disobedient to God, without any spark of goodness in him, without any virtuous or godly motion, only given to evil thoughts and wicked deeds: as for the works of the Spirit, the fruits of faith, charitable and godly motions, if he have any at all in him, they proceed only of the Holy Ghost, who is the only worker of our sanctification, and maketh us new men in Christ Jesus[g]. Did not God's Holy Spirit miraculously work in the child David[ζ], (ζ 1 Sam. xvii, [33–37.]) when of a poor shepherd he became a princelike[h] Prophet? Did not God's Holy Spirit miraculously work in Matthew, *sitting at the receipt of custom*, (Matt. ix, [9.]) when of a proud publican he became an humble and lowly Evangelist? And who can choose but marvel, to consider that Peter should become of a simple fisher a chief and mighty Apostle, Paul of a cruel and bloody persecutor a faithful disciple of Christ to teach the Gentiles?

Such is the power of the Holy Ghost to regenerate men, and as it were to bring them forth anew, so that they shall be nothing like the men that they were before. Neither doth he think it sufficient inwardly to work the spiritual and new birth of man, unless he do also dwell and abide in him. *Know ye not*, saith St. Paul[η], *that ye are the temple of God, and that his Spirit dwelleth in you? Know ye not that your bodies are the temples of the Holy Ghost, which is within you?* (η 1 Cor. iii, [16; vi, [19.]) Again he saith[θ], *You are not in the flesh, but in the spirit; for why*[4] *the Spirit of God dwelleth in you.* (θ Rom. viii, [9.]) To this agreeth the doctrine of St. John, writing on this wise: *The anointing which ye have received* (he meaneth the Holy Ghost) *dwelleth in you.* (1 John ii, [27.]) And the doctrine of Peter saith the same, who hath these words: *The Spirit of glory and of God resteth upon you.* (1 Pet. iv, [14.]) O what a comfort[i] is this to the heart of a true Christian, to think that the Holy Ghost dwelleth within him! *If God be with us*, as the Apostle saith[ι], *who can be against us?* (ι Rom. viii, [31.])

O but how shall I know that the Holy Ghost is within me? some man perchance will say. Forsooth, as[κ] *the tree is known by his fruit*, (κ [Matt. xii, 33.]) so is also the Holy Ghost. *The fruits of the Holy Ghost*, (Gal. v, [19–23.]) according to the mind of St. Paul, are these; *love, joy, peace*,

[f] flesh, saith Christ, is flesh, and that which is born of the] *omitted* 1623. [g] Jesu] Jesus 1623. [h] princelike] princely 1623. [i] what a comfort] what comfort *from* 1570.

4 for why: εἴπερ: si tamen, *Vulg.* See before, p. 343, n. 3.

longsuffering, gentleness, goodness, faithfulness, meekness, temperancy[k], &c. Contrariwise *the deeds of the flesh are these; adultery, fornication, uncleanness, wantonness, idolatry, witchcraft, hatred, debate, emulation, wrath, contention, sedition, heresy, envy, murder, drunkenness, gluttony, and such like.* Here is now that glass wherein thou must behold thyself, and discern whether thou have the Holy Ghost within thee, or the spirit of the flesh. If thou see that thy works be virtuous and good, consonant to the prescript rule of God's word, savouring and tasting not of the flesh but of the Spirit, then assure thyself that thou art endued with the Holy Ghost: otherwise in thinking well of thyself thou doest nothing else but deceive thyself.

The Holy Ghost doth always declare himself by his fruitful and gracious gifts, namely[λ], by *the word of wisdom*, by *the word of knowledge,* which is the understanding of the Scriptures, by *faith,* in *doing of miracles*, by *healing* them that are diseased, by *prophecy,* which is the declaration of God's mysteries, by *discerning of spirits, diversity*[l] *of tongues, interpretation of tongues,* and so forth. All which gifts, as they proceed from one Spirit, and are severally given to man according to the measurable distribution of the Holy Ghost, even so do they bring men, and not without good cause, into a wonderful admiration of God's divine power. Who will not marvel at that which is written in the Acts of the Apostles, to hear their bold confession before the council at Jerusalem, and to consider that they went away with joy and gladness, *rejoicing that they were counted worthy to suffer rebukes* and checks *for the Name* and faith *of Christ Jesus?* This was the mighty work of the Holy Ghost; who, because he giveth patience and joyfulness of heart in temptation and affliction, hath therefore worthily obtained this name in holy Scripture, to be called a *Comforter.* Who will not also marvel to read the learned and heavenly sermons of Peter and the other disciples[m], considering that they were never brought up in school of learning, but called even from their nets to supply rooms of Apostles? This was likewise the mighty work of the Holy Ghost; who, because he doth instruct the hearts of the simple in the true knowledge of God and his holy word[n], is most justly termed by this name and title, to be *the Spirit of*

λ 1 Cor. xii, [7–11.]

Acts v, [29–32, 41.]

John xiv, [16.]

Ibid. [17.]

k temperancy] temperance *from* 1563 B.

l diversity] diversities *from* 1563 G, *except* 1595.

m the other disciples] the disciples *from* 1567.

n his holy word] his word 1623.

truth. Eusebius in his Ecclesiastical History[5] telleth a strange story of a certain learned and subtile philosopher, who, being an extreme adversary to Christ and his doctrine, could by no kind of learning be converted to the faith, but was able to withstand all the arguments that could be brought against him with little or no labour. At length there started up a poor simple man, of small wit and less knowledge, one that was reputed among the learned as an idiot; and he on God's Name would needs take in hand to dispute with this proud philosopher. The bishops and other learned men standing by were marvellously abashed at the matter, thinking that by his doings they should be all confounded and put to open shame. He notwithstanding goeth on, and, beginning in the Name of the Lord Jesus, brought the philosopher to such point in the end, contrary to all men's expectation, that he could not choose but acknowledge the power of God in his words, and to give place to the truth. Was not this a miraculous work, that one seely soul, of no learning, should do that which many bishops, of great knowledge and understanding, were never able to bring to pass? So true is that saying[o] of Bede[6]: "Where the Holy Ghost doth instruct and teach, there is no delay at all in learning." Much more might here be spoken of the manifold gifts and graces of the Holy Ghost, most excellent and wonderful in our eyes: but, to make a long discourse through all, the shortness of time will not serve; and, seeing ye have heard the chiefest, ye may easily conceive and judge of the rest.

Lib. x cap. 3.

Hom. 9 super Lucam.

Now were it expedient to discuss this question, whether all they which boast and brag that they have the Holy Ghost do truly challenge this unto themselves, or no? Which doubt, because it is necessary and profitable, shall, God willing, be dissolved in the next part of this Homily. In the mean season let us, as we are most bound, give hearty thanks to God the Father

o that saying] the saying *from* 1567.

5 See *Eccles. Hist. Lib.* x *cap.* iii *Rufino Autore, ad calc. Euseb. Eccles. Hist. Rufino Interprete.* Sozomenus, *Hist. Eccles.* I, 18, took the story from Rufinus.

6 Nulla quippe in discendo mora est ubi Spiritus Sanctus doctor adest. *Bed. Hom. in Luc.* i, 39–47, In illo tempore exsurgens Maria &c., *Aestiv. de Sanct., in Fest. Visitat. B. M. V.* (*Jul.* 2); *Opp.* VII, 143, 33, *ed. Basil.* 1563. This is the *ninth* Homily in the Collection, "Homilie hoc est Conciones populares sanctissimorum ecclesie doctorum Hieronymi, . . . Bede presbyteri, . . . et aliorum," printed at Basle by Frobenius in 1516 in folio; and the sentence quoted occurs in *col.* 1 of *fol.* 7 a.

and his Son Jesus Christ for sending down this Comforter[p] into the world; humbly beseeching him so to work in our hearts by the power of this Holy Spirit, that we, being regenerate and newly born again in all goodness, righteousness, sobriety, and truth, may in the end be made partakers of everlasting life in his heavenly kingdom through Jesus Christ our only[q] Lord and Saviour. Amen.

[p] this Comforter] his Comforter 1623. [q] only] *omitted after* 1563 F.

THE SECOND PART OF THE HOMILY CONCERNING THE HOLY GHOST, DISSOLVING THIS DOUBT, WHETHER ALL MEN DO RIGHTLY[a] CHALLENGE TO THEMSELVES THE HOLY GHOST, OR NO.

OUR Saviour Christ, *departing*[α] *out of the world unto his Father*, promised[β] his disciples to send down *another Comforter, that should continue with them for ever*, and *direct them into all truth*. Which thing to be faithfully and truly performed, the Scriptures do sufficiently bear witness. Neither must we think that this Comforter was either promised or else given only to the Apostles, but also to the universal Church of Christ, dispersed through the whole world. For, unless the Holy Ghost had been always present, governing and preserving the Church from the beginning, it could never have sustained so many and so great[b] brunts of affliction and persecution with so little damage and harm as it hath. And the words of Christ are most plain in this behalf, saying that[γ] *the Spirit of truth should abide with them for ever*, that[δ] *he would be with them always* (he meaneth by grace, virtue, and power) *even to the world's end*. Also in the prayer that he made to his Father a little before his death he maketh intercession, not only for himself and his Apostles, but indifferently[ε] *for all them that should believe in him through their words*, that is to wit, for his whole Church. Again, St. Paul saith, *If any man have not the Spirit of Christ, the same is not his*. Also in the words following, *We have received the spirit of adoption, whereby we cry, Abba, Father*. Hereby then it is evident and plain to all men, that the Holy Ghost was given, not only to the Apostles, but also to the whole body of Christ's congregation, although not in like form and majesty as he came down at the feast of Pentecost.

α [John xiii, 1.]
β John xiv, [16, 26;] and xv, [26; xvi, 7, 13.]
γ John xiv, [16, 17.]
δ Matt. xxviii, [20.]
ε John xvii, [20.]
Rom. viii, [9, 15.]

But now herein standeth the controversy, whether all men do justly arrogate to themselves the Holy Ghost, or no. The Bishops of Rome have for a long time made a sore challenge

a MEN DO RIGHTLY] MEN RIGHTLY *from* 1563 D. b and so great] and great *from* 1570.

thereunto, reasoning for themselves after this sort. The Holy Ghost, say they, was promised to the Church, and never forsaketh the Church: but we are the chief heads and the principal part of the Church: therefore we have the Holy Ghost for ever; and whatsoever things we decree are undoubted verities and oracles of the Holy Ghost. That ye may perceive the weakness of this argument, it is needful to teach you first what the true Church of Christ is, and then to confer the Church of Rome therewith, to discern how well they agree together.

[g] Eph. ii, [20.]

The true Church is an universal congregation or fellowship of God's faithful and elect people, *built*[g] *upon the foundation of the Apostles and Prophets, Jesus Christ himself being the head corner stone.* And it hath always three notes or marks, whereby it is known; pure and sound doctrine, the Sacraments ministered according to Christ's holy institution, and the right use of ecclesiastical discipline. This description of the Church is agreeable both to the Scriptures of God and also to the doctrine of the ancient fathers, so that none may justly find fault therewith.

Now, if ye will compare this with the Church of Rome, not as it was at[c] the beginning, but as it is presently and hath been for the space of nine hundred years and odd, you shall well perceive the state thereof to be so far wide from the nature of the true Church, that nothing can be more. For neither are they *built upon the foundation of the Apostles and Prophets,* retaining the pure and sound[d] doctrine of Christ Jesu; neither yet do they order either[e] the Sacraments or else the ecclesiastical keys in such sort as he did first institute and ordain them, but have so intermingled their own traditions and inventions, by chopping and changing, by adding and plucking away, that now they may seem to be converted into a new guise. Christ commended to his Church a Sacrament of his Body and Blood: they have changed it into a sacrifice for the quick and the dead. Christ did minister to his Apostles, and the Apostles to other men, indifferently under both kinds: they have robbed the lay people of the cup, saying that for them one kind is sufficient. Christ ordained no other element to be used in Baptism but only water,

Augustine.

whereunto when the word is joined, it is made, as St. Augustine saith[1], a full and perfect Sacrament: they, being wiser in their

[c] at] in *from* 1571. [d] pure and sound] sound and pure *from* 1563 G. [e] either] *omitted* 1623.

[1] Detrahe verbum, et quid est aqua nisi aqua? Accedit verbum ad elementum, et fit Sacramentum, etiam ipsum tanquam visibile verbum. *Augustin. in Joan. Evang. Tractat.* LXXX, § 3; *Opp. Tom.* III, *Par.* II, 703 B.

own conceit than Christ, think it is not well nor orderly done, unless they use conjuration; unless they hallow the water; unless there be oil, salt, spittle, tapers, and such other dumb ceremonies, serving to no use, contrary to the plain rule of St. Paul[f], who willeth *all things* to be *done* in the Church *unto edification*. Christ ordained the authority of the keys to excommunicate notorious sinners, and to absolve them which are truly penitent: they abuse this power at their own pleasure, as well in cursing the godly with bell, book, and candle[g] [2], as also in absolving the reprobate, which are known to be unworthy of any Christian society; whereof he that[h] lust to see examples, let him[i] search their lives. To be short, look what our Saviour Christ pronounced[η] of the Scribes and the Pharisees[k] in the Gospel, the same may we[l] boldly and with safe conscience pronounce[m] of the Bishops of Rome, namely, that they have forsaken, and daily do forsake, the commandments of God, to erect and set up their own constitutions. Which thing being true, as all they which have any light of God's word must needs confess, we may well conclude, according to the rule of Augustine, that the Bishops of Rome and their adherents are not the true Church of Christ, much less then to be taken as chief heads and rulers of the same. "Whosoever," saith he[3], "do dissent

1 Cor. xiv, [26.]

η [Matt. xv, 3, 6: Mark vii, 9, 13.]

August. contr. Petil. Donat. Epist. cap. 4.

f of St. Paul] of Paul *till* 1563 G. g candle] candles *from* 1570. h he that] they that *from* 1582. i him] them *from* 1571. k and the Pharisees] and Pharisees *from* 1571. l may we] may be 1563 B–F, *and from* 1574. m pronounce] pronounced 1563 C–F, *and from* 1574.

2 To curse "with bell, book, and candle" was to curse formally and solemnly, as appears by the following extract from a rubric which follows the General Sentence or Great Curse (Articuli Generales Majoris Excommunicationis) on *fol.* 157 a of a Sarum *Manual* printed at Rouen in 1510, (Bodl. "4° Z, 12, Th. Seld.") Potest denunciator quotienscunque eam denunciat, si viderit expedire ad terrorem audientium, uti illa debita solennitate qua . . . utitur Ecclesia in aliis articulis majoris excommunicationis sententias fulminando, videlicet, cum cruce erecta, pulsatis campanis, candelis accensis et in terram projectis et extinctis.

That General Sentence included "alle heretikes and alle tho that mayntene heresie," and was appointed to be read to the people four times in the year in the mother tongue. Of it, and of the actual curse with which it ended, Becon has preserved several forms in his *Reliques of Rome*. One of them ends thus: Et sicut extinguitur haec lucerna hominum, ita extinguatur lumen eorum in secula seculorum, nisi ad emendationem et satisfactionem venerint. Fiat, Fiat. Amen. Another, which was found in St. Paul's Church in Canterbury, and which is all in English, ends thus: "They be accursed of God and of holy Church fro the soole of theyr foote unto the crown of her head, sleaping and waking, sittinge and standinge, and in al her words, and in all her workes: and but if they have grace of God for to amende hem here in this life, for to dwel in the payne of hel for ever withouten end. Fiat. Fiat. Do to the boke. Quench the candle. Ring the bel. Amen. Amen." *Becon's Works*, III, 378 a, 382 a, *ed.* 1563.

3 Quicunque de ipso Capite ab Scripturis sanctis dissentiunt, etiam si in omnibus locis inveniantur in quibus Ecclesia designata est, non sunt in Ecclesia. *Augustin. contra Donatist.* (vulgo *de Unit. Eccles.*) § 7; *Opp.* IX, 341 G.

from the Scriptures concerning the Head, although they be found in all places where the Church is appointed, yet are they not in the Church." A plain place, concluding directly against the Church of Rome.

Where is now the Holy Ghost, which they so stoutly do claim to themselves? Where is now *the Spirit of truth*[θ], that will not suffer them in any wise to err? If it be possible to be there where the true Church is not, then is it at Rome: otherwise it is but a vain brag, and nothing else. St. Paul, as ye have heard before, saith, *If any man have not the Spirit of Christ, the same is not his.* And, by turning the words, it may be as truly[n] said, If any man be not of Christ, the same hath not his Spirit[o]. Now, to discern who are truly his and who not, we have this rule given us, that[ι] *his sheep do always hear his voice.* And St. John saith[κ], *He that is of God heareth God's word.* Whereof it followeth, that the Popes, in not hearing Christ's voice, as they ought to do, but preferring their own decrees before the express word of God, do plainly argue to the world that they are not of Christ nor yet possessed with his Spirit.

θ [John xvi, 13.]
[Rom. viii, 9.]
ι John x, [27.]
κ John viii, [47.]

But here they will allege for themselves, that there are divers necessary points not expressed in holy Scripture, which were left to the revelation of the Holy Ghost; who being given to the Church, according to Christ's promise, hath taught[λ] *many things* from time to time, which the Apostles *could not then bear.* To this we may easily answer by the plain words of Christ, teaching us that the proper office of the Holy Ghost is, not to institute and bring in new ordinances, contrary to his doctrine before taught, but to expound[p] and declare those things which he had before taught, so that they might[q] be well and truly understood. *When the Holy Ghost*, saith he[μ], *shall come, he shall lead you into all truth.* What truth doth he mean? any other than he himself had before expressed in his word? No. For he saith, *He shall take of mine, and shew it unto*[r] *you.* Again[ν], *He shall bring you in remembrance of all things that I have told you.* It is not then the duty and part of any Christian, under pretence of the Holy Ghost, to bring in his own dreams and phantasies into the Church; but he must diligently provide that his doctrine and decrees be agreeable to Christ's holy Testament: otherwise, in making the Holy Ghost the author thereof, he doth blaspheme and belie the Holy Ghost to his own condemnation.

λ John xvi, [12.]
μ Ibid. [13, 14.]
ν John xiv, [26.]

n be as truly] be truly *from* 1582. o not his Spirit] not the Spirit *from* 1582. p to expound] shall come 1623. q they might] it might 1623. r shew it unto] shew unto *from* 1582.

Now to leave their doctrine, and come to other points. What shall we judge or think[s] of the Pope's intolerable pride? The Scripture saith[ξ], that *God resisteth the proud, and sheweth grace to the humble.* Also it pronounceth[o] them *blessed which are poor in spirit*, promising that *they which humble themselves shall be exalted.* And Christ our Saviour willeth[π] all his to *learn of him, because he is humble and meek.* As for pride, St. Gregory saith[4] "it is the root of all mischief[ρ]." And St. Augustine's judgment is this, that it maketh men devils[5]. Can any man then, which either hath or shall read the Popes' lives, justly say that they had the Holy Ghost within them? First, as touching that they will be termed Universal Bishops and Heads of all Christian Churches through the world, we have the judgment of Gregory expressly against them; who, writing to Mauritius the Emperor, condemneth John Bishop of Constantinople in that behalf, calling him[6] the prince of pride, Lucifer's successor, and the forerunner of Antichrist. St. Bernard also agreeing thereunto saith[7], "What greater pride can there be, than that one man should prefer his own judgment before the whole Congregation, as though he only had the Spirit of God?" And Chrysostom pronounceth a terrible sentence against them, affirming plainly[9], that "whosoever seeketh to be chief in earth shall find

ξ [James iv, 6.]
o Matt. v, [3;] xxiii, [12.]
π [Matt. xi, 29.]
ρ Ecclus. [x, 13.]
Lib. iv, Epist. 76, 78.
Serm. 3 de Resur. Dom.
Dialogorum Lib. iii.[8]
Chrysost. sup. Matt.

s judge or think] think or judge *from* 1567.

4 Radix quippe cuncti mali superbia est. *Gregor. I Moral. Lib.* XXXI, § 87; *Opp. ed. Paris.* 1705, I, 1035 D.

5 Humilitas homines sanctis angelis similes facit, et superbia ex angelis daemones fecit. *Paulin. Aquilei. Lib. Exhort.* vulgo *De Salutar. Docum. c.* 18; *Augustin. Opp.* VI *Append.* 196 D. In the *Liber Epistolarum Beati Augustini* published by *Amerbach at Basle* in 1493, in which the treatise is printed as *Epist.* CXI, the last word in this passage is *facit*, not *fecit;* and the passage is so cited in many collections of extracts from the Fathers.

6 Doctores humilium, duces superbiae, ovina facie lupinos dentes abscondimus.... Sed in hac ejus superbia quid aliud nisi propinqua jam Antichristi esse tempora designatur? Quia illum videlicet imitatur qui, spretis in sociali gaudio angelorum legionibus, ad culmen conatus est singularitatis erumpere, dicens &c. *Gregor. I Epist.* V, 20, 21 (*al.* IV, 32, 34), *Opp.* II, 747 E, 751 C. The former only of these Epistles is addressed to Mauritius; the other was written to the Empress Constantia. In the edition of Gregory's Works printed at Paris in 1523, and possibly in others, the Epistles are numbered as "Capitula"; and the two here cited are Chapters 76 and 78, as in the marginal reference. On the matter of them see *Jewel's Reply to Harding, Art.* IV, *Div.* iv.

7 Et quae major superbia quam ut unus homo toti Congregationi judicium suum praeferat, tanquam ipse solus habeat Spiritum Dei? *Bernard. in Temp. Resurrect. Serm.* III, 4; *Opp.* I, 911 A.

8 It does not appear to what the reference "Dialogorum Lib. iii" belongs.

9 Quicumque ergo desiderat primatum coelestem sequatur humilitatem terrestrem; quicumque autem desiderat primatum in terra inveniet confusionem in coelo: ut jam inter servos Christi non sit de primatu certamen. *Opus Imperf. in Matth. Hom.* XXXV, *ad calc. Chrysost. Opp. Tom.* VI, *p.* CLIII C.

confusion in heaven," and that he which striveth for the supremacy shall not be reputed among the servants of Christ. Again he saith[10], "To desire a good work, it is good; but to covet the chief degree of honour, it is mere vanity." Do not these places sufficiently convince their outrageous pride in usurping to themselves a superiority above all other, as well ministers and bishops, as kings also and emperors?

Sabellic. Ennead. 9, Lib. 7.

But, as the lion is known by his claws, so let us learn to know these men by their deeds. What shall we say of him that made the noble king Dandalus to be tied by the neck with a chain, and to lie flat down before his table, there to gnaw bones like a dog? Shall we think that he had God's Holy Spirit within him, and not rather the spirit of the devil? Such a tyrant was Pope Clement the Sixth[11]. What shall we say of him that proudly and contemptuously trod Frederic the Emperor under his feet, applying that verse[t] of the Psalm unto himself: *Thou shalt go upon the lion and the adder; the young lion and the dragon thou shalt tread under thy foot?* Shall we say that he had God's Holy Spirit within him, and not rather the spirit of the devil? Such a tyrant was Pope Alexander the Third[12]. What shall we say of him that armed and animated the son against the father, causing him to be taken, and to be cruelly famished to death, contrary to the law both of God and also nature[u]? Shall we say that he had God's Holy Spirit within him, and not rather the spirit of the devil? Such a tyrant was Pope Paschal the Second[13]. What shall we say of

Ps. xc [xci, 13.]

[t] that verse] the verse *from* 1567. [u] also nature] also of nature *from* 1563 D.

[10] Et opus quidem bonum desiderare bonum est; primatum autem honoris concupiscere vanitas est. *Ibid.* CLii E.

[11] This abject submission was made by Francisco Dandolo to Pope Clement the Fifth in 1313. Dandolo, though afterwards Doge of Venice, was then only a private citizen, and came as ambassador to obtain a release from the Pope's interdict. His wearing of the chain was in some measure voluntary, and it does not appear that he actually had to gnaw bones. But the surname of Dog remained with him. *Sabellic. Rer. Venet. Dec.* II, *Lib.* i. *Raynald. Annal. an.* 1313, *xxxiv.* See *Jewel's Defence of the Apology, Part* IV, *Ch.* vii, *Div.* 4, "*Franciscus Dandalus.*"

[12] *Carion. Chron.* (really written by Melancthon) *Lib.* III, *Frid. Barbar.* See *Jewel, ibid. Ch.* viii, *Div.* 1. The interview between the Emperor Frederic Barbarossa and Pope Alexander III took place at Venice in July 1177; but this story of the Pope's insolence is rejected by modern historians as a fable. See *Milman's History of Latin Christianity,* VIII, ix, *vol.* III, *p.* 536, *note* p.

[13] See *Jewel, ibid. Ch.* vii, *Div.* 6, and the authorities cited by him. Prince Henry, afterwards the Emperor Henry V, revolted from his father Henry IV in December 1104. Milman says there is no evidence to shew that the Pope suggested this unnatural rebellion, but he certainly sanctioned it and gave it his blessing as soon as it was made. *History of Latin Christianity,* VIII, i.

him that came into his popedom like a fox, that reigned like a lion, and died like a dog? Shall we say that he had God's Holy Spirit within him, and not rather the spirit of the devil? Such a tyrant was Pope Boniface the Eighth[14]. What shall we say of him that made Henry the Emperor, with his wife and his young child, to stand at the gates of the city in the rough winter barefooted and barelegged, only clothed in linsey woolsey, eating nothing from morning to night, and that for the space of three days? Shall we say that he had God's Holy Spirit within him, and not rather the spirit of the devil? Such a tyrant was Pope Hildebrand[15], most worthy to be called a firebrand[16], if we shall term him as he hath best deserved.

Many other examples might here be alleged; as of Pope Jone the harlot, that was delivered of a child in the high street, going solemnly in procession[17]; of Pope Julius the Second, that wilfully cast St. Peter's keys into the river Tiberis[18]; of Pope Urban the Sixth, that caused five cardinals to be put in sacks and cruelly drowned[19]; of Pope Sergius the Third, that persecuted the dead body of Formosus his predecessor, when it had been buried eight years[20]; of Pope John, the Fourteenth of that name, who, having his enemy delivered into his hands, caused him first to be stripped stark naked, his beard to be shaven, and to be hanged up a whole day by the hair, then to be set upon an ass with his face backward towards[x] the tail, to

x towards] toward *from* 1582.

14 De quo fertur: Intravit ut vulpes, regnavit ut lupus, mortuus est ut canis. *Paralip. ad calc. Chron. Abbat. Ursperg. (Conrad von Lichtenau), Bonif. VIII.* De quo dicitur, quod intravit ut vulpes, vixit ut leo, et moritur ut canis. *Rolewinck, Fasciculus Temporum, an.* 1294. See *Jewel, ibid. Ch.* vi, *Div.* 1, "*Bonifacius VIII.*"

15 *Platina de Vit. Gregor. VII. Chron. Abbat. Ursperg., Hist. Henr. IV, an.* 1076. *Sabellic. Rhaps. Hist. Enn. IX, Lib.* iii. *Jewel, ibid. Ch.* vii, *Div.* 4 and *Div.* 6. *Milman, ibid.* VII, ii.

16 There is a coarser allusion to the name of Hildebrand in *Bishop Pilkington's Confutation of an Addition on the Burning of Paul's, sect.* VIII, *p.* 565, *ed. Park. Soc.*

17 See *Jewel, ibid. Ch.* I, *Div.* I, "*Dame Joan the Pope.*" She was said to have succeeded Leo IV, who died in 855; but the whole story has long been abandoned by historians as a fable. See *Gibbon, Ch.* XLIX, *notes* 129–132.

18 Veniatque in mentem Julii secundi Papae, egregii bellatoris et cruenti; qui aliquando cum exercitu egrediens urbem clavem Petri projecit in Tiberim cum hisce verbis: Quiā clavis S. Petri non amplius valet, valeat gladius S. Pauli. *Theod. Bibliandri ad German. Principes Oratio, p.* 81, *ed. Basil.* 4to. *s. a.*

19 *Theodoric. a Niem, Schism.* I, 60. *Sabellic. Rhaps. Hist.* IX, ix. See *Jewel, ibid. Part* I, *Ch.* X, *Div.* 2; and *Milman, ibid.* XIII, ii.

20 Platina and other writers attribute this to Sergius III, but it was really the act of Stephen IV, and Platina himself says that it was related of him. *Baron. Annal. an.* 897, ii. *Concil. Labbe* IX, 502 E; *Mansi* XVIII, 223 B. See *Jewel, ibid.*

be carried round about the city in despite, to be miserably beaten with rods, last of all to be thrust out of his country, and to be banished for ever[21]. But, to conclude and make an end, ye shall briefly take this short lesson: wheresoever ye find the spirit of arrogancy and pride, the spirit of envy, hatred, contention, cruelty, murder, extortion, witchcraft, necromancy, &c., assure yourselves that there is the spirit of the devil, and not of God; albeit they pretend outwardly to the world never so much holiness. For, as the Gospel teacheth us, the Spirit of Jesus is a good Spirit, an holy Spirit, a sweet Spirit, a lowly Spirit, a merciful Spirit, full of charity and love, full of forgiveness and pity, *not rendering evil for evil*, extremity for extremity, but *overcoming evil with good*, and *remitting* all offence even *from the heart*. According to which rule, if any man live uprightly, of him it may be safely pronounced, that he hath the Holy Ghost within him; if not, then it is a plain token that he doth usurp the name of the Holy Ghost in vain.

[1 Pet. iii, 9: Rom. xii, 21: Matt. xviii, 35.]

Therefore, dearly beloved, according to the good counsel of St. John, *believe not every spirit, but first try them whether they be of God or no. Many*[σ] *shall come in my name*, saith Christ, and shall *transform themselves into angels of light, deceiving, if it be possible, the very elect. They shall come*[τ] *unto you in sheep's clothing, being inwardly cruel and ravening wolves.* They shall have an outward shew of great holiness and innocency of life, so that ye shall hardly or not at all discern them. But the rule that ye must follow is this[υ], to *judge them by their fruits.* Which if they be wicked and naught, then is it unpossible that the tree of whom they proceed should be good. Such were all the popes and prelates of Rome for the most part, as doth well appear in the story of their lives; and therefore they are worthily accounted among the number of *false prophets and false Christs*[φ] which deceived the world a long while.

1 John iv, [1.]

σ Matt. xxiv, [5, 24: 2 Cor. xi, 13–15.]

τ Matt. vii, [15–20.]

υ Luke vi, [43–45.]

φ [Matt. xxiv, 24.]

The *Lord of heaven and earth*[χ] defend us from their tyranny and pride, that they never enter into his vineyard again to the disturbance of his seely poor flock, but that they may be utterly confounded and put to flight in all parts of the world. And he of his great mercy so work in all men's hearts by the mighty power of the Holy Ghost, that the comfortable Gospel of his Son Christ may be truly preached, truly received, and truly fol-

χ [Matt. xi, 25.]

21 This vengeance was taken on Peter, Prefect of Rome, by the Emperor Otho the Great and Pope John XIII, whom Platina reckons as John XIV. *Baron. Annal. an.* 966, ii.

lowed in all places, to the beating down of sin, death, the pope, the devil, and all the kingdom of Antichrist; that, the scattered[y] and dispersed sheep being at length gathered into *one fold*[ψ], we may in the end rest all together in the bosom[ω] of Abraham, Isaac, and Jacob, there to be partakers of eternal and everlasting life, through the merits and death of Jesus Christ our Saviour. Amen.

ψ [John x, 16.]

ω [Luke xvi, 22: Matt. viii, 11.]

y the scattered] like scattered *from* 1571.

AN HOMILY

FOR THE DAYS OF ROGATION WEEK.

THAT ALL GOOD THINGS COMETH FROM GOD.

I AM purposed this day, good devout Christian people, to declare unto you the most deserved praise and commendation of Almighty God; not only in consideration [a] of the marvellous creation of this world, or for the conservation [b] and governance thereof, wherein his great power and wisdom might excellently appear, to move us to honour and dread him; but most specially in consideration of his liberal and large goodness, which he daily bestoweth on us his reasonable creatures, for whose sake he made this whole [c] universal world with all the commodities and goods therein: which his singular goodness, well and diligently remembered on our [d] part, should move us, as duty is again, with hearty affection to love him, and with word and deed to praise him and serve him all the days of our life. And to this matter, being so worthy to entreat of, and so profitable for you to hear, I trust I shall not need with much circumstance of words to stir you to give your attendance, to hear what shall be said. Only I would wish your affection inflamed in secret wise within yourself to raise up some motion of thanksgiving to the goodness of Almighty God in every such point as shall be opened by my declaration particularly unto you. For else what shall it avail us to hear and know the great goodness of God towards [e] us, to know that whatsoever is good proceedeth from him, as from the principal fountain and the only author, or to know that whatsoever is sent from him must needs be good and wholesome, if the hearing of such matter moveth us no further but to know it only? What availed [f] it the wise men of the world to have a [g] knowledge of *the power and divinity of God* by the secret inspiration of him, where *they did not* honour and *glorify him* in their knowledges *as God?*

[Rom. i, 19-22.]

[a] only in consideration] only in the consideration *from* 1571. [b] for the conservation] for conservation 1571, 1574; for conversation *from* 1582. [c] this whole] the whole *from* 1571. [d] on our] of our *Ed.* 1. [e] towards] toward 1563 G–1582. [f] availed] availeth 1623. [g] a] *omitted* 1623.

What praise was it to them, by the consideration of the creation of the world to behold his goodness, and yet *were not*[i] *thankful* to him again for his creatures? What other thing deserved this blindness and forgetfulness of them at God's hands, but utter forsaking of him? And so forsaken of God they could not but fall into extreme ignorance and error. And, although they much esteemed themselves in their wits and knowledge, and gloried in their wisdom, yet *vanished they away blindly in their thoughts*[1], *became fools,* and perished in their folly. There can be none other end of such as draweth nigh to God by knowledge, and yet depart from him in unthankfulness, but utter destruction. This experience saw David in his days. For in his Psalm he saith, *Behold, they which withdraw themselves from thee shall perish; for thou hast destroyed them all that are strayed from thee.* (Ps. lxxii [lxxiii, 27.]) This experience was perceived to be true of that holy Prophet Hieremy. *O Lord,* saith he, *whatsoever they be that forsake thee shall be confounded; they that depart from thee shall be written in the earth*[2], and soon forgotten. (Jer. xvii, [13.]) It profiteth not, good people, to hear the goodness of God declared unto us, if our hearts be not inflamed thereby to honour and thank him. It profited not the Jews, which were God's elect people, to hear much of God, seeing that he was not received in their hearts by faith, nor thanked for his benefits bestowed upon them. Their unthankfulness was the cause of their destruction. Let us eschew the manner of these before rehearsed, and follow rather the example of that holy Apostle St. Paul, which when[k] in a deep meditation he did behold the marvellous proceedings of Almighty God, and considered his infinite goodness in the ordering of his creatures, he brast[l] out into this conclusion: *Surely,* saith he, *of him, by him, and in him*[3] *be all things.* (Rom. xi, [36.]) And, this once pronounced, he stack[m] not still at this point, but forthwith thereupon joined to these words, *To him be glory and praise for ever. Amen.*

Upon the ground of which words of St. Paul, good audience, I purpose to build my exhortation of this day unto you. Wherein I shall do my endeavour, first to prove unto you, that all good things *cometh*[n] *down to us*[o] *from above, from the Father of light;* (James i, 17.) secondly, that Jesus Christ, his Son and our Saviour,

[i] yet were not] not to be 1623. [k] which when] who when 1623. [l] brast] burst 1623. [m] stack] stuck 1623. [n] cometh] come *from* 1582. [o] to us] unto us *from* 1563 G.

1 Ἐματαιώθησαν ἐν τοῖς διαλογισμοῖς αὐτῶν. Rom. i, 21. Evanuerunt in cogitationibus suis: *Vulg.*

2 Recedentes a te in terra scribentur. *Vulg.*

3 Εἰς αὐτόν. In ipso: *Vulg.*

is the mean by whom we receive his liberal goodness; thirdly, that in the power and virtue of the Holy Ghost we be made meet and able to receive his gifts and graces: which things, distinctly and advisedly considered in our minds, must needs compel us in most low reverence, after our bounden duty, always to render him thanks again in some testification of our good hearts for his deserts unto us. And, that the intreating of this matter in hand may be to the glory of Almighty God, let us in one faith and charity call upon the Father of mercy, from whom [Ibid.] *cometh every good gift and every perfect gift*, by the mediation[p] of his wellbeloved Son our Saviour, that we may be assisted with the presence of his Holy Spirit, and wholesomely[q] on both our parts[r] to demean ourselves in speaking and hearing[s], to the salvation of our souls.

In the beginning of my speaking unto you, good Christian people, suppose not that I do take upon me to declare unto you the excellent power or the incomparable wisdom of Almighty God, as though I would have you believe that it might be expressed unto you by words. Nay, it may not be thought that that thing may be comprehended by man's words that is incomprehensible. And too much arrogancy it were for *dust and ashes*[a] to think that he could[t] worthily declare his Maker. It passeth far the dark understanding and wisdom[u] of a mortal man, to speak sufficiently of that divine Majesty which the angels cannot understand. We shall therefore lay apart to speak of that profound[x] and insearchable[y] nature of Almighty God, rather acknowledging our weakness than rashly to attempt that is above all man's capacity to compass. It shall better suffice us in low humility to reverence and dread his Majesty, which we cannot comprise, than by overmuch curious searching to be overcharged with the glory.

a [Gen. xviii, 27.]

We shall rather turn our whole contemplation to answer a while his goodness towards us; wherein we shall be much more profitably occupied, and more may we be bold to search. To consider this great[z] power he is of can but make us dread and fear; to consider his high wisdom might utterly discomfort our frailty to have any thing ado[a] with him: but in consideration of his inestimable goodness we take good heart again to trust well unto him; by his goodness we be assured to take him for

p mediation] meditation *Ed.* 1, 1563 C–H, 1567, 1595. q wholesomely] profitably 1623. r both our parts] both parts 1623. s hearing] hearkening 1623. t could] can *from* 1574. u and wisdom] of wisdom 1567–1582, of the wisdom 1587, 1595. x that profound] the profound 1623. y insearchable] unsearchable *from* 1563 B. z this great] the great 1623. a ado] to do 1623.

our refuge, our hope and comfort, our merciful Father, in all the course of our lives. His power and wisdom compelleth us to take him for God omnipotent, invisible, having rule[β] in heaven and in earth[b], having all things in his subjection, and will have none in council with him, nor any to ask the reason of his doing: for he may do what liketh him, *and none can resist him*[4]. For *he worketh all things* in his secret judgment *to his own pleasure, yea, even the wicked to damnation,* saith Salomon. By the reason of this nature he is called[γ] in Scripture[c] *consuming fire,* he is called *a terrible* and *fearful God.* Of this behalf therefore we may[d] have no familiarity, no access unto him: but his goodness again tempereth[e] the rigour of his high power, and maketh us bold, and putteth us in hope that he will be conversant with us and easy unto us.

β Dan. iv, [35.]
Prov. xvi, [4.]
γ Heb. xii, [29: Deut. iv, 24; x, 17: Exod. xv, 11.]

It is his goodness that moveth him to say in Scripture[δ], *It is my delight to be with the children of men.* It is his goodness that moveth him to call us unto him, to offer us his friendship and presence. It is his goodness that patiently suffereth our straying from him, and suffereth us long, to win us to repentance. It is of his goodness that we be created reasonable creatures, where else he might have made us brute beasts. It was his mercy to have us born among the number of Christian people, and thereby in a much more nighness to salvation, where we might have been born (if his goodness had not been) among the paynims, clean void from God and the hope of everlasting life. And what other thing doth his loving and gentle voice, spoken in his word, where he calleth us to his presence and friendship, but declare his goodness only, without regard of our worthiness? And what other thing doth stir him to call us to him when we be strayed from him, to suffer us patiently, to win us to repentance, but only his singular goodness, no whit of our deserving?

δ Prov. viii, [31.]

Let them all come together that be now glorified in heaven, and let us hear what answer they will make in these points afore rehearsed, whether their first creation was of[f] God's goodness or of themselves. Forsooth David would make answer for them all, and say, *Know ye for surety, even the Lord is God; he hath made us, and not we ourselves.* If they were asked again, who should be thanked for their regeneration, for their justifi-

Ps. c, [3.]

b and in earth] and earth *from* 1563 G. c called in Scripture] called in the Scripture 1563 B–F. d we may have] we have 1623. e tempereth] temper *Ed.* 1, 1563 G *and* H, 1567. f was of] was in *from* 1570.

4 Non est qui resistat manui ejus. *Vulg.*

cation, and for their salvation, whether their deserts or God's goodness only; although in this point every one confess sufficiently the truth of this matter in his own person, yet let David answer by the mouth of them all at this time; who cannot[g] [Ps. cxv, 1.] choose but say, *Not to us, O Lord, not to us, but to thy Name give all the thank for thy loving mercy and for thy truth's sake.* If we should ask again, from whence came their glorious works and deeds, which they wrought in their lives, wherewith God was so highly pleased and worshipped by them, let some other [e] [Matt. xviii, 16.] witness be brought in to testify this matter, *that*[e] *in the mouth of two or three* may the truth be known. Verily that holy Pro- [Is. xxvi, [12.]] phet Esay beareth record, and saith, *O Lord, it is thou* of thy goodness *that hast wrought all our works in us,* not we of ourselves[h]. And, to uphold the truth of this matter against all justiciaries and hypocrites, which rob Almighty God of this honour[i], and ascribe it to themselves, St. Paul bringeth in his [2 Cor. iii, [5:] Acts xvii, [28.]] belief. *We be not,* saith he, *sufficient of ourselves, as of ourselves, once to think any thing, but all our ableness is of God's goodness. For he it is in whom we have all our being, our living, and moving.* If ye will know furthermore where they had their gifts and sacrifices, which they offered continually in their lives to Almighty God, they cannot but agree with David, where he [ζ 1 Chron. xxix, [14.]] saith[ζ], *Of thy* liberal *hand, O Lord, we have received that we gave unto thee*[5].

If this holy company therefore confesseth[k] so constantly, that all the goods and graces wherewith they were indued in soul came of the goodness of God only, what more can be said to prove that all that is good cometh from Almighty God? Is it meet to think that all spiritual goodness cometh from God above only, and that other good things, either of nature or of fortune (as we call them), cometh of any other cause? Doth God of his goodness adorn the soul with all the powers thereof, as it is? and cometh the gifts of the body, wherewith it is indued, from any other? If he doeth the more, cannot he do the less? To justify a sinner, to new create him from a wicked person to a righteous man, is a greater act, saith St. Augustine[6], than to

[g] who cannot] he cannot *Ed.* 1. [h] we of ourselves] we ourselves *from* 1563 B. [i] this honour] his honour *from* 1563 C. [k] confesseth] confess *from* 1582.

[5] Quae de manu tua accepimus dedimus tibi. *Vulg.*

[6] Prorsus majus hoc esse dixerim quam est coelum et terra et quaecunque cernuntur in coelo et in terra. . . . Non hic audeo praecipitare sententiam: intelligat qui potest, judicet qui potest, utrum majus sit justos creare quam impios justificare. *Augustin. in Joan. Tractat.* LXXII, § 3; *Opp. Tom.* III, *Par.* II, 688 A, B.

make such a new heaven and earth as is already made. We must needs agree, that whatsoever good thing is in us, of grace, of nature, of[l] fortune, is of God only, as the only Author and Worker.

And yet it is not to be thought that God hath created all this whole universal world as it is, and, thus once made, hath given it up to be ruled and used after our own wits and device, and so take[m] no more charge therefore: as we see the shipwright, after he hath brought his ship to a perfect end, then delivereth he it[n] to the mariners, and take[o] no more cure[p] thereof. Nay, God hath not so created the world, that he is careless of it; but he still preserveth[q] it by his goodness, he still stayeth[r] it in his creation: for else, without his special goodness, it could not stand long in his condition. And therefore St. Paul saith[η], that he preserveth all things and beareth them up still in his word, lest they should fall without him to their nothing again, whereof they were made. If his special[s] goodness were not every where present, every creature should be out of order, and no creature should have his property, wherein he was first created. He is therefore invisibly[t] every where and in every creature, and *fulfilleth both heaven and earth*[θ] with his presence; in the fire, to give heat; in the water, to give moisture; in the earth, to give fruit; in the heart, to give his strength; yea, in our bread and drink he is[u], to give us nourishment; where without him the bread and drink cannot give sustenance, nor the herb health, as the Wise Man plainly confesseth it, saying, *It is not the increase of fruits that feedeth men, but it is thy word, O Lord, which preserveth them that trust in thee.* And Moses agreeth to the same, when he saith, *Man's life resteth not in bread only, but in every word which proceedeth out of God's mouth. It is neither the herb nor the plaster that giveth health* of themselves, *but thy word, O Lord,* saith the Wise Man, *which healeth all things.* It is not therefore the power of the creatures which worketh their effects, but the goodness of God which worketh in them. In his word truly doth all things consist. By that same word that heaven and earth were made, by the same are they upholden, maintained, and kept in order, saith St. Peter, and shall be till Almighty God shall withdraw his power from them, and speak their dissolution.

η Heb. i, [3;] iii, [4.]

θ [Jer. xxiii, 24.]

Wisd. xvi, [26.]

Deut. viii, [3.]

Wisd. xvi, [12.]

2 Pet. iii, [7.]

[l] nature, of] nature, or of *from* 1570. [m] so take] so taken 1570, so taketh *from* 1571. [n] delivereth he it] delivereth it 1623. [o] and take] and taketh *from* 1570. [p] cure] care *from* 1582. [q] preserveth] preserve *Ed.* 1. [r] stayeth] stay *Ed.* 1. [s] special] especial *Ed.* 1, *and from* 1582. [t] invisibly] invisible *from* 1563 G. [u] he is] is he *from* 1582.

If it were not thus, that the goodness of God were effectually in his creatures to rule them, how could it be that the main sea, so raging and labouring to overflow the earth, could be kept [Job xxviii, 11.] within his bonds[x] and banks, as it is? That holy man Job evidently spied the goodness of God in this point, and confessed, that[y], if he had not a special goodness to the preservation of the earth, it could not but shortly be overflowed of the sea. How could it be that the elements, so diverse and contrary as they be among themselves, should yet agree and abide together in a concord, without destruction one of another, to serve our use, if it came not only of God's goodness so to temper them? How could the fire not burn and consume all things, if it were left[z] loose to go whither it would, and not stayed in his sphere by the goodness of God, measurably to heat these inferior creatures to their riping? Consider the huge substance of the earth, so heavy and great as it is: how could it so stand stably in the place[a] as it doth, if God's goodness reserved it not so for us to Ps. ciii [civ, 5.] travail on? *It is thou, O Lord,* saith David, *which hast founded the earth in his stability;* and during thy word *it shall never reel* or fall down. Consider the great strong beasts and fishes, far passing the strength of man: how fierce soever they be and strong, yet by the goodness of God they prevail not against us, but are under our subjection, and serve our use. Of whom came the invention thus to subdue them and make them fit for our commodities? Was it by man's brain? Nay, rather this invention came by the goodness of God, which inspired man's [Job xxxviii, 36.] understanding to have his purpose of every creature[b]. *Who was it,* saith Job, *that put will and wisdom in man's head* but God only of his goodness? And as the same saith again, *I perceive* Job xxxii, [8.] *that every man hath a mind, but it is the inspiration of the Almighty that giveth understanding.* It could not be verily, good Christian people, that man of his own wit unholpen[c] should invent so many and diverse devices in all crafts and sciences, except the goodness of Almighty God had been present with men, and had stirred their wits and studies of purpose to know the natures and disposition of all his creatures to serve us sufficiently in our needs and necessities, yea, not only to serve our necessities, but to serve our pleasures and delight, more than necessity requireth. So liberal is God's goodness to us, to provoke us to thank him, if any hearts we have.

[x] bonds] bounds *from* 1582. [y] confessed, that] confessed it: that *Ed.* 1. [z] left] let *from* 1574. [a] the place] the space 1582, 1623, that space 1587, 1595. [b] Nay, rather—creature.] or rather—creature? *Ed.* 1. [c] unholpen] upholden *from* 1582.

The Wise Man, in his contemplation by himself, could not but grant this thing to be true, that I reason unto you. *In his hands*, saith he, *be we, and our words, and all our wisdom, and all our sciences and works of knowledge. For it is he that gave me the true instruction of his creatures, both to know the disposition of the world, and the virtues of the elements, the beginning and end of times, the change and diversities of them, the course of the year, the order of the stars, the natures of beasts, and the powers of them, the power of the winds*[7]*, and thoughts of men, the differences of plants*[d]*, the virtue of roots; and, whatsoever is hid and secret in nature, I learned it. The artificer of all these taught me this wisdom.* And further he saith, *Who can search out the things that be in heaven? For it is hard for us to search such things as be on earth and in daily sight afore us. For our wits and thoughts,* saith he, *be imperfect, and our policies uncertain. No man can therefore search out the meaning in these things, except thou givest wisdom, and sendest thy Spirit from above.* If the Wise Man thus confesseth all these things[e] to be of God, why should not we acknowledge it, and by the knowledge of it to consider[f] our duty to Godward to give[g] him thanks for his goodness?

Wisd. vii. [16–21.]

Wisd. ix. [16, 14, 17.]

I perceive that I am far here overcharged with the plenty and copy[8] of matter, that might be brought in for the proof of this cause. If I should enter to shew how the goodness of Almighty God appeared[h] every where in the creatures of the world, how marvellous they be in their creation, how beautified[i] in their order, how necessary they be to our use, all with one voice must needs grant their author to be none other but Almighty God; his goodness must they needs extol and magnify every where. To whom be all honour and glory for evermore.

[d] plants] planets *all except* 1582, 1587, 1595. [e] all these things] all things *from* 1582. [f] it to consider] it consider *from* 1571. [g] to give] and give *from* 1571. [h] appeared] appear *Ed.* 1. [i] beautified] beautiful *from* 1582.

7 Πνευμάτων βίας. Vim ventorum: *Vulg.*

8 copy: a literal rendering of *copia.* "We cannot follow a better pattern for elocution than God himself: therefore, he using divers words in his holy writ and indifferently for one thing in nature, we, if we will not be superstitious, may use the same liberty in our English versions out of Hebrew and Greek for that copy or store that he hath given us." *Preface to the Authorised Version of the Bible,* near the end. The very phrase, "copye of mattre," occurs in *Hall's Chronicle, Hen. VII an.* 17, *fol.* 53 b *ed.* 1548.

THE SECOND PART OF THE HOMILY

FOR ROGATION WEEK[a].

IN the former part of this Homily, good Christian people, I have declared to your contemplation the great goodness of Almighty God in the creation of this world with all the furniture thereof for the use and comfort of man, whereby we might the rather[b] be moved to acknowledge our duty again to his Majesty. And I trust it hath wrought not only credit[c] in you, but also it hath moved you to render your thanks secretly in your hearts to Almighty God for his lovingkindness.

But yet peradventure some will say that they can agree to this, that all that is good pertaining to the soul, or whatsoever is created with us in body, should come from God, as from the Author of all goodness, and from none other; but for[d] such things as be without them both, I mean such good things which we call goods of fortune, as riches, authority, promotion, and honour, some men may think that they should come of our industry and diligence, of our labour and travail, rather than supernaturally.

Now then consider, good people, if any author there be of such things concurrent with man's[e] labour and endeavour, were it meet to ascribe them to any other than to God? As the paynim[f] philosophers and poets did err, which took fortune and made her a goddess, to be honoured for such things. God forbid, good Christian people, that this imagination should earnestly be received of us, that be worshippers of the true God, whose works and proceedings be expressed manifestly in his word. These be the opinions and sayings of infidels, not of true Christians. For they indeed, as Job maketh mention, believe and say

Job xxii, [14.]

that *God hath his residence* and resting place *in the clouds, and consider*[g] *nothing of our matters*[1]. Epicures they be that imagine

[a] THE HOMILY FOR ROGATION WEEK] THIS HOMILY *Ed.* 1, *and* 1563 A–F. [b] might the rather] might rather 1623. [c] credit] belief 1623. [d] but for] but of *from* 1563 C. [e] with man's] to man's 1587, 1595; of man's 1623. [f] paynim] paynims *from* 1582. [g] and consider] and considereth *from* 1582.

[1] Nubes latibulum ejus, nec nostra considerat, et circa cardines coeli perambulat. *Vulg.*

that *he walketh about the coasts of the heavens*, and have[h] no respect to these[i] inferior things; but that all these things should proceed either by chance and at[k] adventure, or else by disposition of fortune, and God to have no stroke in them. What other thing is this to say than[α], as *the fool supposeth in his heart, There is no God?* Whom we shall none otherwise reprove than with God's own words by the mouth of David. *Hear, my people,* saith he, *for I am thy God, thy very God. All the beasts of the wood are mine, sheep and oxen that wandereth*[l] *on*[m] *the mountains. I have the knowledge of all the fowls of the air; the beauty of the field is my handywork. Mine is the whole circuit of the world, and all the plenty that is in it.* And again by the[n] Prophet Jeremy: *Thinkest thou that I am a God of the place nigh me, saith the Lord, and not a God far off? Can a man hide himself in so secret a corner that I shall not see him? Do not I fulfil* and replenish *both heaven and earth? saith the Lord.* Which of these two should be most believed? fortune, whom they paint to be blind of both eyes, ever unstable and unconstant in her wheel, in whose hands they say these things be? or God, in whose hands and[o] power these things be indeed, who for his truth and constance[p] was yet never reproved? For his sight looketh thorough heaven and earth, and seeth all things presently with his eyes. Nothing is too dark or hidden from his knowledge, not the privy thoughts of men's minds. Truth it is that of God[r] is all riches, all power, all authority, all health, wealth, and prosperity; of the which we should have no part without his liberal distribution, and except it came from him above. David first testifieth it of[s] riches and possessions: *If thou givest good luck, they shall gather; and, if thou openest thy hand, they shall be full of goodness*[t] [2]*: but, if thou turnest thy face, they shall be troubled.* And Salomon saith, *It is the blessing of the Lord that maketh rich men.* To this agree[u] that holy woman Anne, where she saith in her song[β], *It is the Lord that maketh the poor, and maketh the rich: it is he that promoteth and pulleth down: he can raise a needy man from his misery, and from the dunghill he can lift up a poor personage, to sit with princes and have the seat of glory: for all the coasts of the earth be his.*

α Ps. xiv, [1.]
Ps. xlix [1, 7, 10–12.]
Jer. xxiii, [23, 24.]
Ps. civ, [28, 29.]
Prov. x, [22.]
β 1 Sam. ii, [7, 8.]

h and have] and hath 1623. i to these] of these *from* 1582. k and at] or at *from* 1570. l wandereth] wander *from* 1582. m on] in *from* 1570. n again by the] again the 1623. o hands and] hand and *from* 1563 G. p constance] constancy *from* 1582. r that of God] that God 1623. s testifieth it of] testifieth of *from* 1570. t goodness] goodes *Ed.* 1. u agree] agreeth *from* 1563 G.

2 Aperiente te manum tuam omnia implebuntur bonitate. *Vulg.*

Now, if any man will ask what shall it avail us to know that [γ [James i, 17.]] *every good gift*[γ], as of nature and fortune (so called), *and every perfect gift*, as of grace, concerning the soul, to be[x] of God, and that it is his gift only, forsooth for many causes is it[y] convenient for us to know it. For so shall we know, if we confess the truth, who ought justly to be thanked for them. Our pride shall be thereby abated, (perceiving naught to come of ourselves but sin and vice,) if any goodness be in us, to refer all laud and praise for the same to Almighty God. It shall make us not to[z] avaunce[a] ourselves before our neighbour, to despise him for that he hath fewer gifts, seeing God giveth his gifts where he will: it shall make us by the consideration of our gifts not to extol ourselves before our neighbours: it shall make *the wise* [δ Jer. ix, [23.]] *man*[δ] *not to glory in his wisdom*[b], *nor the strong man in his strength, nor the rich to glory in his riches*, but in the living God, which is Author[c] of all these: lest, if we should do so, we [1 Cor. iv, [7.]] might be rebuked with the words of St. Paul, *What hast thou that thou hast not received? and, if thou hast received it, why gloriest in*[d] *thyself, as though thou haddest not received it?*

To confess that all good things cometh from Almighty God is a great point of wisdom, my friends. For so confessing we [James i, [5.]] know whither to resort, for to have them if we want; as St. James bid[e] us, saying, *If any man wanteth the gift of wisdom, let him ask it of God, that gives*[f] *it, and it shall be given him.* As the Wise Man, in the want of such a like gift, made his recourse to [Wisd. viii, [21.]] God for it, as he testifieth in his book. *After I knew*, saith he, *that otherwise I could not be chaste*[3], *except God granted it*, (*and this was*, as he there writeth, *high wisdom, to know whose gift it was*,) *I made haste to the Lord, and earnestly besought him, even from the roots of my heart, to have it.* I would to God, my friends, that in our wants and necessities we would go to God, as St. James bids[g], and as the Wise Man teacheth us that he did. I would we believed steadfastly that God only gives[h] them. If we did, we would not[i] seek our want and necessity of the devil and his ministers so oft as we do, as daily experience declareth it. For, if we stand in necessity of corporal health, whither go

[x] that every good gift—to be] *so in all.* [y] is it] it is *from* 1574. [z] us not to] us to 1623. [a] avaunce] advaunce 1571, 1582; advance 1574, 1623. [b] in his wisdom] of his wisdom *from* 1582. [c] is Author] is the Author *from* 1582. [d] gloriest in] gloriest thou in *from* 1582. [e] bid] biddeth *from* 1582. [f], [h] gives] give *Ed.* 1. [g] bids] bid *Ed.* 1, biddeth *from* 1563 G. [i] we would not] we should not *from* 1582.

3 Γνοὺς δὲ ὅτι οὐκ ἄλλως ἔσομαι ἐγκρατής. Ut scivi quoniam aliter non possem esse continens: *Vulg.*

the common people but to charms, witchcrafts, and other delusions of the devil? If we knew that God were the Author of this gift, we would only use his means appointed, and bide his leisure, till he thought it good for us to have it given. If the merchant and worldly occupier knew that God is the Giver of riches, he would content himself with so much as by just means, approved of God, he could get to his living, and would be no richer than truth would suffer him; he would never procure his gain and ask his goods at the devil's hand. God forbid, ye will say, that any man should take his riches of the devil. Verily so many as increase themselves by usury, by extortion, by perjury, by stealth, by deceits and craft, they have their goods of the devil's gift. And all they that give themselves to such means, and have renounced the true means that God hath appointed, have forsaken him, and are become worshippers of the devil, to have their lucres and advantages[k]. They be such as kneel down to the devil at his bidding, and worship him; for he promiseth them for so doing, that he will give them the world and the goods therein. They cannot otherwise better serve the devil than to do his pleasure and commandment. And his motion and will it is to have us forsake the truth, and betake us to falsehood, to lies, and perjuries. They therefore which believed[l] perfectly in their heart, that God is to be honoured and requested for the gift of all things necessary, would use no[m] other means to relieve their necessities but truth and verity, and would serve God to have competency of all things necessary. The man in his need would not relieve his want by stealth: the woman would not relieve her necessity and poverty by giving her body to other in adultery for gain. If God be the Author indeed of life, health, riches, and welfare, let us make our recourse to him, as to the[n] Author, and we shall have it, saith St. James. Yea, *it is high wisdom* by the Wise Man therefore *to know whose gift it is.*

For many other skills[4] it is[o] wisdom to know and believe that all goods[p] and graces be of God, as the Author. Which thing well considered must needs make us think that we shall make

[k] advantages] avauntages 1563 A—F. [l] believed] believeth 1567–1574, believe *from* 1582. [m] use no] use none *from* 1574. [n] as to the] as the *from* 1567. [o] skills it is] skills is it *Ed.* 1. [p] goods] goodness *from* 1571.

[4] skills: reasons, causes. "Sothli we han schewid by skile" (causati enim sumus, *Vulg.*) "Jewis and Greekis alle for to be undir synne." *Wycliffe, Rom.* iii, 9. "And in lijk manere also Joon the Apostle, for humblenesse, in his Epistle for the same skile sette not his name tofore." *Ibid. Prol. to Hebr.* in the later version, the earlier having "by the same resoun" instead of "for the same skile."

account for that which God giveth us to occupy[q], and therefore shall make us to be more diligent well to spend them to God's glory and to the profit of our neighbour; that we may make a good account at the last, and be praised for good stewards; that we may hear these words of our Judge, *Well done, good servant and faithful: thou hast been faithful in little, I will make thee ruler over much: go into*[r] *thy Master's joy.*

Matt. xxv, [21.]

Besides, to believe certainly God to be the Author of all the gifts that we have shall make us to be in silence and patience when they be taken again from us. For, as God of his mercy doth grant us them to use, so otherwhiles he doth justly take them again from us, to prove our patience, to exercise our faith, and by the means of the taking away of a few, to bestow the more warily those that remain, to teach us to use them the more to his glory after he giveth them to us again. Many there be that with mouth can say that they believe that God is the Author of every good gift that they have, but in the time of temptation they go back from this belief. They say it in word, but deny it in deed. Consider me[s] the usage[t] of the world, and see whether it be not true. Behold the rich man, that is indued with substance: if by any adversity his goods be taken from him, how fumeth and fretteth he! how murmureth he[u] and despaireth! He that hath the gift of good reputation, if his name be any thing touched by the detractor, how unquiet is he! how busy to revenge his despite! If a man hath the gift of wisdom, and fortune to be taken of some evil willer for a fool, and is so reported, how much doth it grieve him to be so esteemed! Think ye that these believe constantly that God is the Author of these gifts? If they believed[w] it verily, why should they not patiently suffer God to take away his gifts again, which he gave them freely, and lent for a time?

But ye will say, I could be content to resign to God such gifts, if he took them again from me; but now are they taken from me by evil chances and false shrews[5], by naughty wretches; how should I take this thing patiently? To this may be an-

q occupy] possess 1623. r go into] go in into *from* 1567. s me] *omitted* 1587, 1595, 1623. t usage] custom 1623. u murmureth he] doth he murmur *Ed.* 1. w believed] believe *from* 1570.

5 shrews: wicked, mischievous persons, of either sex. *Wycliffe in Job* v, 13, IX, 20, *Prov.* X, 31, uses the word for *pravus* of the Vulgate. He also uses the verb *to beshrew* for *depravare*. And he has *shrewid* for *nefarius* in *Gen.* XXXIX, 8, and *shrewidnes* for *iniquitas* in *Gen.* VI, 11, XV, 16, *Wisd.* IV, 14, and for *nequitia* in *Psalm* LIV, 16; but the later or Purvey's version substitutes some other word in these five places.

swered, that Almighty God is of his nature invisible, and cometh to no man visibly[x], after the manner of man, to take away his gifts that he lent; but in this point, whatsoever God doeth, he bringeth it about by his instruments ordained thereto. He hath good angels, he hath evil angels; he hath good men, and he hath evil men; he hath hail and rain, he hath wind and thunder, he hath heat and cold; innumerable instruments hath he, and messengers, by whom again he asketh such gifts as he committeth to our trust. As the Wise Man confesseth, the *creature* [Wisd. xvi, [24.]] must needs wait to *serve his Maker,* to be *fierce against unjust men to their punishment:* for, as the same author saith, *he* [[Ibid. v, 17.]] *armeth the creature to revenge his enemies.* And otherwhiles to the probation of our faith stirreth he up such storms. And therefore, by what mean and instrument soever God takes[y] from us his gifts, we must patiently take God's judgment in worth[6], and acknowledge him to be the Taker and Giver; as Job saith, *The Lord gave, and the Lord took,* [Job i, [21.]] when yet his enemies drove[z] his cattle away, and when the devil slew his children, and afflicted his body with a grievous[a] sickness. Such meekness was in that holy King and Prophet David[*], [* 2 Sam. xvi, [5–12.]] when he was reviled of Semei in presence[b] of all his host: he took it patiently, and reviled not again; but, as[c] confessing God to be the author of his innocency and good name, and offering it to be at his pleasure, *Let him alone,* saith he to one of his knights[d], that would have revenged such despite, *for God hath commanded him to curse David, and peradventure God intendeth*[e] *thereby to render me some good turn for this curse of him today.* And, though the minister otherwhiles doeth evil in his act, proceeding of malice, yet, forsomuch[f] as God turneth his evil act to a proof of our patience, we should rather submit ourself in patience than to have indignation at God's rod; which peradventure, when he hath corrected us to our nurture[7], he will cast it into the fire, as it deserveth.

[x] visibly] visible 1623. [y] takes] take *Ed.* 1. [z] drove] drave *from* 1567. [a] with a grievous] with grievous 1623. [b] in presence] in the presence *from* 1563 G. [c] but, as] but said, as *Ed.* 1. [d] knights] servants 1623. [e] intendeth] intend *Ed.* 1. [f] forsomuch] forasmuch 1563 C—F, *and from* 1567.

6 "I take in worthe, or I take in good worthe: Je prens en gré, and Je supporte." *Palsgrave, Lesclarcissement de la Langue Francoyse.* See note 37 on the Homily of Matrimony. Or will the following sentence explain the phrase better? "He took it patiently: he thought himself worthy of God's rod." *Hutchinson, The Image of God, ch.* XV, *p.* 74, *ed. Park. Soc.* In the Office for the Visitation of the Sick the second part of the Exhortation began "Take therefore in good worth" previously to the revision of the Prayer Book in 1661.

7 nurture: training, discipline, παιδεία, as in *Ephes.* VI, 4.

Let us in like manner truly acknowledge all our gifts and prerogatives to be so God's gifts, that we shall be ready to resign them up at his will and pleasure again. Let us throughout[g] our whole lives confess all good things to come of God, of what name and[h] nature soever they be; not of these corruptible things only whereof I have now last spoken, but much more of all spiritual graces behovable for our soul. Without whose goodness no man is called to faith, or stayed therein, as I shall hereafter in the next part of this Homily declare to you. In the mean season forget not what hath already been spoken to you, forget not to be comformable[i] in your judgments to the truth of this doctrine[k], and forget not to practise the same in the whole state of your[l] life; whereby ye shall obtain that blessing[m] promised by our Saviour Christ, *Blessed be they which hear the word*[n] *of God, and fulfilleth*[o] *it* in life. [Luke xi, 28.] Which blessing he grant to us all who reigneth over all, one God in Trinity, the Father, the Son, and the Holy Ghost: to whom be all honour and glory for ever. Amen.[p]

[g] throughout] thoroughout *Ed.* 1. [h] name and] name or 1623. [i] comformable] comfortable *from* 1582. [k] this doctrine] his doctrine *from* 1582. [l] state of your] state your 1563 A. [m] that blessing] the blessing *from* 1563 G. [n] the word] to word 1563 A. [o] fulfilleth] fulfil *from* 1582. [p] Amen.] *not in Ed.* 1, 1563 A—F.

THE THIRD PART OF THE HOMILY

FOR ROGATION WEEK[a].

I PROMISED to you to declare that all spiritual gifts and graces cometh[b] specially from God. Let us consider the truth of this matter, and hear what is testified first of the gift of faith, the first entry into the Christian life, *without which*[c] *no man can please God*[α]. First[d], St. Paul confesseth it plainly to be God's gift, saying[β], *Faith is the gift of God*. And again, St. Peter saith *it is of God's power that ye be kept through faith to salvation*. It is of the goodness of God that we falter not in our hope unto him. It is verily God's work in us, the charity wherewith we love our brethren. If after our fall we repent, it is by him that we repent, which reacheth forth his merciful hand to raise us up. If any will we have to rise, it is he that preventeth our will, and disposeth us thereto. If after contrition we feel our conscience at peace with God thorough[e] remission of our sin, and so be reconciled again to his favour, and hope to be his children and inheritors of everlasting life, who worketh these great miracles in us? our worthiness? our deservings and endeavours? our wits and virtue? Nay verily: St. Paul will not suffer flesh and clay to presume to such arrogancy, and therefore saith, *All is of God, which hath*[f] *reconciled us to himself by Jesus Christ; for God was in Christ when he reconciled the world unto himself*. God the Father of all mercy wrought this high benefit unto us, not by his own person, but by a mean, by no less mean than his only beloved Son, whom he spared not from any pain and travail that might do us good. For upon him he put our sins; upon him he made our ransom; him he made the mean betwixt us and himself: whose mediation was so acceptable to God the Father through his profound[g] and perfect obedience, that he took his act for a full satisfaction of all our disobedience and rebellion; whose righteousness he took to weigh against our sins; whose redemption he would have stand against our damnation.

α [Heb. xi, 6.]
β Ephes. ii, [8.]
1 Pet. i, [5.]
[2 Cor. v, 18, 19.]

[a] THE HOMILY FOR ROGATION WEEK] THIS HOMILY *Ed.* 1, *and* 1563 A—F. [b] cometh] come *from* 1582. [c] without which] without the which *from* 1563 G. [d] First] For *from* 1571. [e] thorough] through *from* 1563 G. [f] which hath] which have *Ed.* 1. [g] profound] absolute 1623.

In this point what have we to muse within ourselves, good friends? I think, no less than that which St. Paul said in the remembrance of this wonderful goodness[h] of God, *Thanks be to Almighty God thorough*[i] *Christ Jesus our Lord.* For it is he[γ] for whose sake we received this high gift of grace. For, as by him, being the everlasting Wisdom, he wrought all the world and that is contained therein, so by him only and wholly would he have all things restored again in heaven and in earth. By this our heavenly Mediator therefore do we know the favour and mercy of God the Father. By him know we his will and pleasure towards us: for he is[δ] *the brightness of his Father's glory, and a* very clear *image* and pattern *of his substance.* It is he whom the Father in heaven delighteth to have for his *wellbeloved Son*[ε], whom he authorised to be our Teacher, whom he charged us to hear, saying, *Hear him.* It is he by whom the Father of heaven doth bless[ζ] us with all spiritual and heavenly gifts, for whose sake and favour, writeth St. John[η], *we have received grace* and favour. To this our Saviour and Mediator hath God the Father given the power[θ] of heaven and earth, and the whole jurisdiction and authority to distribute his goods and gifts committed to him. For so writeth the Apostle[ι]: *To every one of us is grace given according to the measure of Christ's giving.* And thereupon to execute his authority committed, after that he had brought sin and the devil to captivity, to be no more hurtful to his members, he ascended up to his Father again; and from thence sent liberal gifts to his wellbeloved servants; and hath still the power till[k] the world's end to distribute his Father's gifts continually in his Church to the establishment and comfort thereof. And by him hath Almighty God decreed to dissolve the world[l], to call all before him, to judge both the quick and the dead. And finally by him shall he condemn the wicked to eternal fire in hell, and give the good eternal life, and set them assuredly in presence with him in heaven for evermore. Thus ye see how[κ] *all is of God* by his Son Christ our Lord and Saviour. Remember, I say once again, your duty of thanks: let them be never to want: still join[m] yourself to continue in thanksgiving: ye can offer to God no better sacrifice; for he saith himself[λ], *It is the sacrifice of praise* and thanks *that shall honour me*[1]. Which thing was well perceived of that holy Pro-

Rom. vii, [25.]
γ Ephes. i, [3–10.]
δ Heb. i, [3.]
ε Matt. iii, [17;] xvii, [5.]
ζ Ephes. i, [3.]
η John i, [16.]
θ [Matt. xxviii, 18.]
ι Ephes. iv, [7, 8.]
κ [2 Cor. v, 18.]
λ Ps. l, [23.]

h goodness] goodnes *Ed.* 1, 1563 D, *and from* 1563 F; goodes 1563 A—C *and* E. i thorough] through *from* 1563 C. k till] to *from* 1567. l the world] to world 1563 A *and* B. m join] enjoin 1623.

1 Sacrificium laudis honorificabit me. *Vulg.*

phet David, when he so earnestly spake to himself thus: *O my soul, bless thou the Lord; and all that is within me, bless his holy Name. I say once again, O my soul, bless thou the Lord, and never forget his manifold rewards*[2]. Ps. ciii, [1, 2.]

God give us grace, good people, to know these things, and to feel them in our hearts! This knowledge and feeling is not in ourself; by ourself it is not possible to come by it; and great[n] pity it were that we should lose so profitable knowledge. Let us therefore meekly call upon that bountiful Spirit the Holy Ghost, which proceedeth from our Father of mercy and from our Mediator Christ, that he would assist us and inspire us with his presence, that in him we may be able to hear the goodness of God declared unto us to our salvation. For without his lively and secret inspiration can we not once so much as speak the name of our Mediator, as St. Paul plainly testifieth: *No man can once name our Lord Jesus Christ but in the Holy Ghost.* (1 Cor. xii, [3.]) Much less should we be able to believe and know these great mysteries that be opened to us by Christ. St. Paul saith that *no man can know what is of God, but the Spirit of God. As for us,* saith he, (1 Cor. ii, [11, 12.]) *we have received, not the spirit of the world, but the Spirit which is of God,* for this purpose, *that* in that holy Spirit *we might know the things that be given us* by Christ.

The Wise Man saith that in the power and virtue of the Holy Ghost resteth[o] all wisdom, and all ability to know God and to please him; for he writeth thus[μ]: *We know that it is not in man's power to guide his goings: no man can know thy pleasure, except thou givest wisdom, and sendest thy Holy Spirit from above. Send him down*[3], therefore prayeth he to God, *from thy*[p] *holy heavens and from the throne of thy Majesty, that he may be with me and labour with me, that so I may know what is acceptable before thee.* Let us with so good heart pray as he did, and we shall not fail but to have his assistance. For[ν] *he is soon seen of them that love him; he will be found of them that seek him:* for very liberal and gentle is *the Spirit of wisdom.*

μ [Jer. x, 23:] Wisd. ix, [14–17, 10.]

ν [Wisd. vi, 12; vii, 7.]

In his power shall we have sufficient ability to know our duty to God. In him shall we be comforted and couraged to walk in our duty. In him shall we be meet vessels to receive the grace of Almighty God. For it is he that purgeth and purifieth

n and great] a great *from* 1571. o resteth] rested *Ed.* 1, *and* 1563 A—F. p from thy] from the *from* 1582.

2 Et noli oblivisci omnes retributiones ejus. *Vulg.*

3 Ἐξαπόστειλον αὐτὴν, sc. τὴν σοφίαν.

the mind by his secret working, and he only is present everywhere by his invisible power, and *containeth all things*[ξ] in his dominion. He lighteneth[q] the heart to conceive worthy thoughts of[r] Almighty God. He sitteth in the tongue of man to stir him to speak his honour. No language is hid from him, for *he hath the knowledge of all speech*[o]. He only ministereth spiritual strength to the powers of our soul and body. To hold the way which God hath prepared[s] for us, to walk rightly in our journey, we must acknowledge that it is in the power of his *Spirit, which helpeth our infirmity*[π]. That we may boldly come in prayer, and call upon Almighty God as *our Father*[ρ], it is by this Holy Spirit, which *maketh intercession for us with continual sighs*. If any gift we have, wherewith we may work to the glory of God and profit of our neighbour, all is wrought[σ] by *this one*[t] *and selfsame Spirit, which maketh*[u] *his distributions peculiarly to every man as he will.* If any wisdom we have, it is not of ourselves; we cannot glory therein, as begun of ourselves; but we ought to glory in God, from whom it came to us, as the Prophet Hieremy writeth: *Let him that rejoiceth rejoice in this, that he understandeth and knoweth me; for I am the Lord which sheweth*[x] *mercy, judgment, and righteousness in the earth; for in these things I delight, saith the Lord.* This wisdom cannot be attained but by the direction of the Spirit of God, and therefore it is called spiritual wisdom.

ξ [Wisd. i, 7.]
o [Ibid.]
π [Rom. viii, 26.]
ρ Gal. iv, [6:] Rom. viii, [15, 26.]
σ 1 Cor. xii, [7-11.]
Jer. ix, [24.]

And nowhere can we more certainly search for the knowledge of this will of God, by the which we must direct all our works and deeds, but in the holy Scriptures: for, *they be they that testify of* him, saith our Saviour Christ. It may be called knowledge and learning that is otherwhere gotten out of[y] the word; but the Wise Man plainly testifieth that *they all be but vain which have not in them the wisdom of God.* We see to what vanity the old philosophers came, which[z] were destitute of this science, gotten and searched for in his word. We see what vanity the School doctrine is mixed with, for that in this word[a] they sought not the will of God, but rather the will of reason, the trade[4] of custom, the path of the Fathers, the practice of the Church. Let us therefore read and revolve the holy Scripture both *day and night*[τ]; for *blessed is he that hath his whole*

John v, [39.]
Wisd. xiii, [1.]
τ Ps. i, [1, 2.]

[q] lighteneth] illightneth *Ed.* 1. [r] thoughts of] thoughts to *from* 1563 G. [s] hath prepared] had prepared *from* 1570. [t] this one] his own *from* 1563 G. [u] maketh] make *Ed.* 1. [x] sheweth] shew 1623. [y] out of] without 1623. [z] came, which] came unto, which *Ed.* 1; came, who 1623. [a] this word] this world 1571-1595.

4 trade: trodden way. See before, p. 64, n. 23.

meditation therein. It is that that giveth[υ] *light to our feet to walk by.* It is that which[φ] *giveth wisdom to the simple* and ignorant. In it may we find[χ] *eternal life.* In the holy Scriptures find we Christ: in Christ find we God; for he it is that is *the express image*[ψ] of the Father; *he that seeth Christ seeth the Father.* And contrariwise, as St. Hierome saith[5], "the ignorance of Scripture is the ignorance of Christ." Not to know Christ is to be in darkness in the middes[b] of our worldly and carnal light of reason and philosophy. To be without Christ is to be in foolishness: for he is the only Wisdom of the Father; *in whom*[ω] *it pleased him that all fulness* and perfection *should dwell.* With whom whosoever is indued[α] *in heart by faith,* and *rooted fast in charity,* hath laid a sure foundation to build on, whereby he *may be able to comprehend with all saints what is the breadth and length*[c] *and depth, and to know the love of Christ.* This universal and absolute knowledge is that wisdom which St. Paul[β] wished[d] these Ephesians to have, as under heaven the greatest treasure that can be obtained. For of this wisdom the Wise Man writeth thus of his experience: *All good things came to me together with her, and innumerable riches through her hands.* And addeth moreover in that same place, *She is the mother of all these things. For she is an infinite treasure unto men, which whoso use become partakers of the love of God.*

υ Ps. cxix, [105.]
φ Ps. xix, [7.]
χ John v, [39.]
ψ Heb. i, [3:] John xiv, [9.]
Hierome.
ω Col. i, [19;] ii, [3, 9.]
α Eph. iii, [17-19.]
β [Eph. i, 15-19; iii, 14-19.]
Wisd. vii, [11, 12, 14.]

I might with many words move some of this audience to search for this wisdom, to sequester their reason, to follow God's commandment, to cast from them the wits of their brains, to savour[e] this wisdom, to renounce the wisdom and policy of this fond world, to taste and savour that whereunto the favour and will of God hath called them, and willeth us finally to enjoy by his favour, if we would give ear. But I will haste to the third part of my text[6], which as it followeth in words more plentifully[f] in the text which I have last cited unto you, wherein is expressed further in Sapience[γ] how God giveth his elect an understanding[g] of the motions of the heavens, of the[h] alterations and circumstances of time[i], so it must needs follow in them

γ [Wisd. 17-19.]

[b] middes] middest 1587, 1595. [c] breadth and length] breadth, length *from* 1567. [d] wished] wisheth *from* 1567. [e] to savour] to favour *from* 1563 B. [f] plentifully] plentiful *from* 1567. [g] elect an understanding] elect in understanding *Ed.* 1, elect understanding 1623. [h] heavens, of the] heavens, the *Ed.* 1. [i] of time] of the time *Ed.* 1.

5 Ignoratio Scripturarum ignoratio Christi est. *Hieron. Prolog. ad Isaiam, Opp.* IV, 1.

6 "The third part of my text" seems to be *Eph.* v, 16, cited below, p. 490, l. 29. Observe the expression "these Ephesians" in line 17 above.

that be indued with this spiritual wisdom.[k] For, as they can search where to find this wisdom, and know of whom to ask it, so know they again that in time it is found, and can therefore attemper themselves[l] to the occasion of the time, to suffer no time to pass away wherein they may labour for this wisdom and to increase therein. They[m] know how God of his infinite mercy and lenity giveth[6] all men here time and *place of repentance;* and they see how the wicked, as Job writeth[7], *abuse the same to their pride:* and therefore do the godly take the better hold of the time, to redeem it out of such use as it is spoiled in by the wicked. They which have this wisdom of God can gather by the diligent and earnest study of the worldlings of this present life, how they wait their times, and apply themselves to every occasion of time, to[n] get riches, to increase their lands and patrimony. They see the time pass away, and therefore take hold on it in such wise that otherwhiles they will with the loss[o] of their sleep and ease, with suffering many pains, catch the offer of their time, knowing that that which is once[p] past cannot be returned again: repentance may follow, but remedy is none[q]. Why should not they then that be spiritually[r] wise in their generation wait their time, to increase as fast in their state, to win and gain everlastingly? They reason what a brute forgetfulness it were in man, indued with reason, to be ignorant of their times and tides, when they see the turtledove, the stork, and the swallow to wait their times, as Hieremy saith: *The stork in the air knoweth her appointed times; the turtle and the*[s] *crane and the swallow observe the time of their coming; but my people knoweth not the judgment of the Lord.*

6 Job xxiv, [23.]

Jer. viii, [7.]

Eph. v, [16.]

St. Paul willeth us to *redeem the time, because the days are evil.* It is not the counsel of St. Paul only, but of all other that ever gave precepts of wisdom. There is no precept more seriously given and commanded than to know the time. Yea, Christian men, for that they hear how grievously God complaineth and threateneth in the Scriptures them which will not know the time of his visitations, are learned thereby the rather

k But I will haste——spiritual wisdom.] *so in Ed.* 1, *except as shewn in notes* g, h, i. *All other editions give the passage thus, except as shewn in notes* f, g: But I will haste to the third part of my text, wherein is expressed further in Sapience how God giveth his elect an understanding of the motions of the heavens, of the alterations and circumstances of time. Which as it followeth in words more plentifully in the text which I have last cited unto you, so it must needs follow in them that be indued with this spiritual wisdom. l attemper themselves] attemper themself *Ed.* 1. m wisdom and to increase therein. They] wisdom. And to increase therein they *all editions.* n time, to] time, and to 1623. o with the loss] with loss *from* 1563 EF. p once] *omitted* 1623. q is none] in none 1623. r spiritually] spiritual 1623. s turtle and the] turtle, the *from* 1567.

7 Dedit ei Deus locum poenitentiae, et ille abutitur eo in superbiam. *Vulg.*

earnestly to apply themselves thereunto. After our Saviour Christ had prophesied with weeping tears of the destruction of Jerusalem, at the last he putteth the cause, *For that thou hast not known the time of thy visitation.* [Luke xix, [44.]] O England, which canst not nor will not ponder the time of God's merciful visitation, shewed thee from day to day, and yet wilt[t] not regard it, neither wilt thou with his punishment be driven to thy duty, nor with his benefits be provoked to thanks; if thou knewest what may fall upon thee for thine[u] unthankfulness, thou wouldest provide for thy peace.[x]

Brethren, howsoever the world in generality is forgetful of God, let us particularly attend to our time, and win the time with diligence, and apply ourselves to that light and grace that is offered us. Let us, if God's favour and judgments, which he worketh in our time, cannot stir us to call home to ourself to do that belong[y] to our salvation, at the least way let the malice of the devil, the naughtiness of the world, which we see exercised in these perilous and last times wherein we see our days so dangerously set, provoke us to watch diligently to our vocation, to walk and go forward therein. Let the misery and short transitory joys spied in the casualty of our days move us while we have them in our hands, and seriously stir us, to be wise, and to expend the gracious good will of God to usward; which *all the day long stretcheth out his hands* (as the Prophet saith) [Isai. lxv, [2.]] unto us, for the most part his merciful hands, sometime his heavy hands; that we, being learned thereby, may escape the danger that must needs fall on the unjust, who[ε] *lead*[z] *their days in felicity* and pleasure without the knowing of God's will toward them, but *suddenly they go down into hell*[8]. [ε Job xxi, [13.]]

Let us be found watchers, found in the peace of the Lord; that[a] at the last day we may be[ζ] *found without spot and blameless.* [ζ [2 Pet. iii, 14.]] Yea, let us endeavour ourselves, good Christian people, diligently to keep the presence of his Holy Spirit. Let us renounce all uncleanness; for he is the Spirit of purity. Let us avoid all hypocrisy; for this[η] *Holy Spirit will flee from that* [η Wisd. i, [5.]]

[t] yet wilt] yet wyl *Ed.* 1. [u] for thine] for thy *Ed.* 1. [x] O England——thy peace.] *so in Ed.* 1, *except as shewn in notes* t, u. *But all editions of the Homilies entire give the passage thus:* O England, ponder the time of God's merciful visitation, which is shewed thee from day to day, and yet wilt not regard it. Neither wilt thou with his punishment be driven to thy duty, nor with his benefits be provoked to thanks. If thou knewest what may fall upon thee for thine unthankfulness, thou wouldest provide for thy peace. *Except that all from* 1563 G *throw the first two sentences into one by printing* O England——regard it, neither——to thanks. [y] belong] belongeth 1563 F, belonging *from* 1582. [z] lead] leadeth *Ed.* 1. [a] Lord; that] Lord: and that *Ed.* 1.

8 Ducunt in bonis dies suos, et in puncto ad inferna descendunt. *Vulg.*

which is feigned. Cast we off all malice and evil[b] will; for this Spirit[θ] *will never enter into an evil-willing soul.* Let[c] us[ι] *cast away all the whole lump of sin that standeth about us*[9]*;* for he[κ] *will never dwell in that body that is subdued to sin.* We cannot be seen thankful to Almighty God, and *work*[λ] such *despite to the Spirit of grace,* by whom we be sanctified. If we do our endeavour, we shall not need to fear, we shall be able to overcome all our enemies that fight against us. Only let us apply ourself[d] to accept the grace[e] that is offered us. Of Almighty God we have comfort by his goodness; of our Saviour Christ's mediation we may be sure; and this Holy Spirit will suggest unto us that shall be wholesome, and confirm us in all things. Therefore it cannot be but true that St. Paul affirmeth[μ], *Of him, by him, and in him*[10] *be all things:* and in him, after this transitory life well passed, shall we have all things. For St. Paul saith[ν], *When the Son of God shall subdue all things unto him, then shall God be all in all.*

θ Wisd. i, [4.]
ι Heb. xii, [1.]
κ Wisd. i, [4.]
λ Heb. x, [29.]
μ [Rom. xi, 36.]
ν 1 Cor. xv, [28.]

If ye will know how God shall be *all in all*, verily after this sense may ye understand it. In this world ye see that we be fain to borrow many things to our necessity of many creatures: there is no one thing that sufficeth all our necessities. If we be an hungred, we lust for bread. If we be athirst, we seek to be refreshed with ale[f] or wine. If we be cold, we seek for cloth. If we be sick, we seek to the physician. If we be in heaviness, we seek for comfort of our friends or of company. So that there is no one creature by itself[g] that can content all our wants and desires. But in the world to come, in that everlasting felicity, we shall no more beg and seek our particular comforts and commodities of divers creatures, but we shall possess all that we can ask and desire in God, and God shall be to us all things. He shall be to us both father and mother; he shall be bread and drink, cloth, physicians, comfort[h]; he shall be all things to us, and that of much more blessed fashion and more sufficient contentation than ever these creatures were unto us, with much more delectation[i] than ever man's reason[k] is able to conceive. *The eye of man is not able to behold, nor his ear can hear, nor it*

1 Cor. ii, [9.]

[b] and evil] and all evil *from* 1563 EF. [c] soul. Let] soul. And let *Ed.* 1. [d] ourself] ourselves 1623. [e] the grace] that grace *from* 1567. [f] with ale] of ale *Ed.* 1. [g] itself] himself *Ed.* 1. [h] physicians, comfort] *so in all, but with no point between the two words. Perhaps the author wrote* physician & comfort. [i] delectation] declaration *from* 1563 C. [k] man's reason] man's declaration than ever man's reason 1623.

[9] Deponentes omne pondus et circumstans nos peccatum. *Vulg.*

[10] See before, p. 471, n. 3.

can be compassed in the heart of man, what joy it is that God hath prepared for them that love him.

Let us all conclude then with one voice with the words of St. Paul: *To him which is able abundantly to do*[1] *beyond our desires and thoughts, according to the power working in us, be glory and praise in his Church by Christ Jesus for ever, world without end. Amen.* Ephes. iii, [20, 21.]

[1] abundantly to do] to do abundantly *from* 1563 G.

AN EXHORTATION

TO BE SPOKEN TO SUCH PARISHES WHERE THEY USE THEIR PERAMBULATIONS[a] IN ROGATION WEEK FOR THE OVERSIGHT OF THE BOUNDS AND LIMITS OF THEIR TOWNS[b].

ALTHOUGH we be now assembled together, good Christian people, most principally to laud and thank Almighty God for his great benefits, by beholding the fields replenished with all manner fruit[c], to the maintenance of our corporal necessities, for our food and sustenance; and partly also to make our humble suits in prayers to his fatherly providence, to conserve the same fruits, in sending us seasonable weather, whereby we may gather in the said fruits to that end for which his merciful[d] goodness hath provided them; yet have we occasion secondarily given us in our walks on these[e] days to consider the old ancient bounds and limits belonging to our own township and to other our neighbours bordering about us, to the intent that we should be content with our own, and not contentiously strive for other's, to the breach of charity, by any encroaching one upon another, or claiming[f] one of the other further than that in ancient right and custom our forefathers have peaceably laid out unto us for our commodity and comfort.

Surely a great oversight it were in us, which be Christian men in one profession of faith, daily looking for that heavenly inheritance which is bought for every one of us by the bloodshedding of our Saviour Jesus Christ, to strive and fall to variance for the earthly bounds of our towns, to the disquiet of our life betwixt ourselves, to the wasting of our goods by vain expenses and costs in the law. We ought to remember that our habitation is but transitory and short in this mortal life. The more shame it were to fall out into immortal hatred among ourselves for so brittle possessions, and so to lose our eternal inheritance in heaven. It may stand well with charity for a

[a] PERAMBULATIONS] PERAMBULATION 1563 C–F, 1570–1595; PREAMBULATION 1623. [b] TOWNS] TOWN *from* 1570. [c] manner fruit] manner of fruit 1623. [d] merciful] fatherly *from* 1567. [e] these] those 1623. [f] or claiming] for claiming *from* 1582.

Christian man quietly to maintain his right and just title; and it is the part of every good townsman to preserve, as much as lieth in him, the liberties, franchises, bounds, and limits of his town and country. But yet so to[g] strive for our very rights and duties with the breach of love and charity, which is the only livery of a Christian man, or with the hurt of godly peace and quiet, by the which we be knit together in one general fellowship of Christ's family, in one common household of God, that is utterly forbidden, that doth God abhor and detest; which provoketh Almighty God's wrath otherwhiles[h] to deprive us quite of our commodities and liberties, because we do so abuse them for matter[i] of strife, discord, and dissension. St. Paul blamed the Corinthians for such contentious suing among themselves, to the slander of their profession before the enemies of Christ's religion, saying thus unto them: *Now there is utterly a fault among you, because ye go to law one with another. Why rather suffer ye not wrong? why rather suffer ye not harm?* [1 Cor. vi, [7.]]

If St. Paul blameth the Christian men, whereof some of them for their own right went contentiously[k] so to law, commending thereby the profession of patience in a Christian man; if Christ our Saviour would have us rather to suffer wrong, and to turn[a] our left cheek to him which hath smitten the right, to suffer one wrong after another, rather than by breach of charity to defend our own; in what state be they before God who do the wrong? what curses do they fall into which by[l] false witness defraud either neighbour[m] or township of his due right and just possession? which will not let to take an oath by the holy Name of God, the Author of all truth, to set out a falsehood[n] and a wrong? *Know ye not*, saith St. Paul, *that the unrighteous shall not inherit the kingdom of God?* [1 Cor. vi, [9.]] What shall he[o] then win, to increase a little the bounds and possessions of the earth, and lose the possession[p] of the inheritance everlasting? Let us therefore take such heed in maintaining of our bounds and possessions, that we commit not wrong by incroaching upon other. Let us beware of sudden verdict in things of doubt. Let us well advise ourselves, to advouch that certainly whereof either we have no good knowledge or remembrance, or to claim that we have no just title to.

[a Matt. v, [39.]]

Thou shalt not, commandeth Almighty God in his Law, *re-* [Deut. xix, [14.]]

[g] yet so to] yet to *from* 1582. [h] otherwhiles] otherwhile *from* 1570. [i] matter] matters *from* 1563 C. [k] contentiously] contentiousness 1563 B–D *and* F, of contentiousness 1563 E. [l] which by] who by 1623. [m] either neighbour] either their neighbour *from* 1567. [n] out a falsehood] out falsehood 1623. [o] shall he] shall we *from* 1563 EF. [p] possession] possessions *from* 1582.

move thy neighbour's mark, which they of old time have set in Prov. xxii, [28.] *thine*[q] *inheritance. Thou shalt not,* saith Salomon, *remove the ancient bounds which thy fathers have laid.* And, lest we should esteem it to be but a light offence so to do, we shall understand that it is reckoned among the curses of God pronounced upon Deut. xxvii, [17.] sinners. *Accursed be he,* saith Almighty God by Moses, *who removeth his neighbour's doles and marks*[1]*: and all the people shall say, answering Amen* thereto, as ratifying that curse upon whom it doth light. They do much provoke the wrath of God upon themselves, which use to grind up the doles and marks which of ancient time were laid for division[r] of meres[2] and balks[3] in the fields, to bring the owners to their right. They do wickedly which do turn up the ancient terries[4] of the fields, that old men beforetime[s] with great pains did tread out; whereby the lord's records, (which be the tenant's evidences,) be perverted and translated, sometime to the disheriting of the right owner, to the oppression of the poor fatherless or the poor widow. These covetous men know not what inconveniences they be authors[t] of. Sometime by such craft and deceit be committed great discords[u] and riots in the challenge of their lands, yea, sometime[w] murders and bloodshed; whereof thou art guilty, whosoever thou be that givest the occasion thereof.

This covetous practising therefore with thy neighbour's 1 Thess. iv, [6.] lands and goods is hateful to Almighty God. *Let no man subtilly compass or defraud his neighbour,* biddeth St. Paul, *in any manner of cause. For God,* saith he, *is a revenger of all such.* God is the God of all equity and righteousness, and therefore forbiddeth all such deceit and subtilty in his Law by these Deut. xix[x] [Levit. xix, 35, 36.] words: *Ye shall not do unjustly*[y] *in judgment, in line, in weight,*

[q] thine] their 1623. [r] for division] for the division *from* 1582. [s] beforetime] beforetimes *from* 1563 C. [t] be authors] be the authors *from* 1582. [u] discords] disorders *from* 1582. [w] yea, sometime] yea, sometimes *from* 1563 G. [x] Deut. xix] *so in all.* [y] not do unjustly] not unjustly 1582, 1587, 1595; not deal unjustly 1623.

[1] Maledictus qui transfert terminos propinqui sui. *Vulg.* Rendered, *Cursed be he which translateth the bounds and doles of his neighbour,* in Queen Eliz. Injunct. XIX; *Cardwell's Document. Ann. No.* XLIII, *Vol.* I, *p.* 188, 1. The word "dole," which properly means a portion dealt out or assigned to any one, is here used for a low post or stone set in the ground to mark the division of properties. See Mr. Albert Way's note on the word in his edition of the *Promptorium Parvulorum, p.* 126.

[2] meres: boundaries. In some parts of England the word is nearly synonymous with "balks," as here: see Albert Way on "meer," *ibid. p.* 333. In others it has a larger application, according to its use by *Spenser, Faerie Queene,* III, ix, 46.

[3] balks: narrow strips of land left unploughed between two pieces of arable in a common field. Spenser makes a forcible metaphor of it in the *Faerie Queene,* VI, xi, 16. See note 6 below.

[4] The word "terries" has not been discovered elsewhere.

or measure: you[z] *shall have just balances, true weights, and true measures. False balance*, saith Salomon, *are an abomination unto the Lord.* Prov. xi, [1;] xx, [23.] Remember what St. Paul saith, *God is the revenger* of all wrong and injustice; as we see by daily experience, however it thriveth ungraciously which is gotten by falsehood and craft. We be taught by experience, how Almighty God never suffereth the third heir to enjoy his father's wrong possessions[5]; yea, many a time they are taken from himself in his own lifetime. God is not bound to defend such possessions as be[a] gotten by the devil and his counsel. God will defend all such men's goods and possessions which by him are obtained and possessed, and will defend them against the violent oppressor. So witnesseth Salomon: *The Lord will destroy the house of the proud man; but he will stablish the borders of the widow.* Prov. xv, [25.] *No doubt of it*, saith David, *better is a little truly gotten to the righteous man, than the innumerable riches of the wrongful man.* Ps. xxxvi [xxxvii, 16.] Let us flee therefore, good people, all wrong practices in getting, maintaining, and defending our possessions, lands, and livelodes[b], our bounds and liberties, remembering that such possessions be all under God's revengeance.

But what do I[c] speak of house and land? nay, it is said in Scriptures[d], that God in his ire doth root up whole kingdoms for wrongs and oppressions, and doth translate kingdoms from one nation to another for unrighteous dealing, for wrongs and riches gotten by deceit. This is the practice of the Holy One, saith Daniel, Dan. iv, [17.] *to the intent that living men may know, that the Most High hath power on the*[e] *kingdoms of men, and giveth them to whomsoever he will.* Furthermore, what is the cause of penury and scarceness, of dearth and famine? any[f] other thing but a token of God's ire, revenging our wrongs and injuries one done[g] to another? *Ye have sown much*, upbraideth God by his Prophet Aggei, Haggai i, [6, 9.] *and yet bring in little; ye eat, but ye be not satisfied; ye drink, but ye be not filled; ye clothe yourselves, but ye be not warm; and he that earneth his wages putteth it in a bottomless purse. Ye look*[h] *for much increase, but lo, it came to little; and, when ye brought it home into your barns, I did blow it away, saith the Lord.* O consider therefore the ire of God against

[z] you] ye *from* 1574. [a] as be] as are *from* 1582. [b] livelodes] *so in all, but* livelordes *by error in* 1623. *See page* 125, *note* g. [c] do I] do we *from* 1563 C. [d] in Scriptures] in Scripture 1563 C–1574, in the Scripture *from* 1582. [e] on the] over the 1623. [f] famine? any] famine? is it any 1623. [g] one done] done one 1623. [h] look] looked *from* 1582.

5 De male quaesitis non gaudet tertius haeres. *Adag. Gilb. Cognati*, 497. Cited (but with *vix* for *non*) by *Sanderson*, *Serm.* III *ad Pop.*, *Works* III, 85, 86, *ed Jacobson.*

gleaners, gatherers, and incroachers upon other men's lands and possessions!

It is lamentable to see in some places, how greedy men use to plough and grate upon their neighbour's land that lieth next them; how covetous men nowadays plough up so nigh the common balks and walks, which good men beforetime made the greater and broader, partly for the commodious walk of his neighbour, partly for the better shack[6] in harvest time to the more comfort of his poor neighbour's cattle. It is a shame to behold the insatiableness of some covetous persons in their doings; that where their ancestors left of their land a broad and sufficient bierbalk to carry the corpse to the Christian sepulture[i], how men[k] pinch at such bierbalks, which by long use and custom ought to be inviolably kept for that purpose; and now they either quite ear[7] them up, and turn the dead body to be borne further about in the high streets, or else, if they leave any such mere, it is too strait for two to walk on. These strange incroachments, good neighbours, should be looked upon, these should be considered, in these days of our perambulations; and afterward[l] the parties monished[m] and charitably reformed, who be the doers of such private gaining to the slander of the township and to the[n] hinderance of the poor.

Your highways should be considered in your walks, to understand where to bestow your days' works according to the good statutes provided for the same[8]. It is a good deed of mercy to amend the dangerous and noisome ways, whereby thy[o] poor neighbour, sitting on his seely weak beast, foundereth not in

[i] sepulture] sepulchre 1563 B–F. [k] how men] *so in all.* [l] afterward] afterwards *from* 1574. [m] monished] admonished *from* 1570. [n] and to the] and the *from* 1582. [o] thy] the 1563 B–F.

6 The word "shack" is commonly used in Norfolk and Suffolk with reference to the turning of swine into stubble fields to pick up the grain that has been shaken out of the ripe ears, or into oak or beech woods to pick up acorns or mast. Richardson says it is "applied generally to *feed among stubble,*" and cites in proof this sentence of the Homily. No doubt the practice of turning cattle of all kinds into open fields as soon as the corn has been got in is common in many parts of England, but this word does not seem to be in use concerning it; and it is not till after harvest that cattle and swine are so turned out to feed, whereas the "shack" of the Homily was something "in harvest time." Unable to offer a satisfactory explanation of the word here, I will only add, as possible materials for one, that in Rutland, at least in the parish of South Luffenham (as the Master of Balliol College informs me), a balk considerably broader than others in the same field, so broad as to allow a cart to travel along it, is called a "shocky balk," and that in the second edition of *Carr's Glossary of the Craven Dialect* "shacket" is explained as "a small cart load."

7 ear: plough; as in *Deut.* XXI, 4, 1 *Sam.* VIII, 12, *Is.* XXX, 24.

8 See *Stat.* 2 & 3 *Philip and Mary,* c. 8, requiring parishioners to give four days' work every year towards the repair of the highways.

the deep thereof, and so the market the[p] worse served for discouraging of poor victuallers to resort thither for the same cause.

If now therefore ye will have your prayers heard before Almighty God for the increase of your corn and cattle, and for the defence thereof from unseasonable mists and blasts, from hail and other such tempests, love equity and righteousness, ensue mercy and charity, which God most requireth at our hands. Which Almighty God respected[q] chiefly in making his civil laws for his people the Israelites, in charging[β] the owners not to gather up their corn too nigh at harvest season, nor the grapes and olives in gathering time, but to leave behind some ears of corn for the poor gleaners. By this he meant to induce them to pity the poor, to relieve the needy, to shew mercy and kindness. It cannot be lost which for his sake is distributed to the poor. For[γ] *he which ministereth seed to the sower* and *bread to the hungry*, which sendeth down *the early and latter rain* upon your fields, so to fill up *the barns with corn* and *the winepresses with wine and oil;* he, I say, who recompenseth all kind benefits[r] *in the resurrection of the just;* he will assuredly recompense all merciful deeds shewed to the needy, howsoever unable the poor is upon whom it is bestowed. *O*, saith Salomon, *let not mercy and truth forsake thee. Bind them about thy neck*, saith he, *and write them on the table of thy heart: so shalt thou find favour at God's hand.* Thus *honour thou the Lord with thy riches, and with the firstfruits*[s] *of thine increase: so shall thy barns be filled with abundance, and thy presses shall brust*[t] *with new wine.* Nay, God hath promised[δ] to *open the windows of heaven* upon the liberal righteous man, that he shall want nothing. He will repress the devouring caterpillar, which should devour your fruits. He will give you peace and quiet to gather in your provision, that ye may[ε] *sit every man under his own vine* quietly, without fear of the foreign enemies to invade you. He will give you, not only food to feed on, but stomachs and good appetites to take comfort of your fruits, whereby in all things ye may have sufficiency. Finally, he will bless you with all manner abundance in this transitory life, and endue you with all manner benediction[x] in the next world, in the kingdom of heaven, through the merits of our Lord and Saviour. To whom with the Father and the Holy Ghost be all honour everlastingly[y]. Amen.

β Levit. xix, [9, 10:] Deut. xxiv, [19–21.]

γ 2 Cor. ix, [10: Ps. cxlvi, 7:] Joel ii, [23, 24: Luke xiv, 14.]

Prov. iii, [3, 4, 9, 10.]

δ [Prov. xi, 25: Mal. iii, 10, 11.]

ε 1 Mach. iv[u] [Mic. iv, 4.]

p market the] market is the 1563 B–F. q respected] respecting *from* 1582. r kind benefits] kind of benefits 1563 D–F, *and from* 1570. s the firstfruits] thy firstfruits 1563 A–C. t brust] burst *from* 1574. u 1 Mach. iv] *so in all till* 1623, *then omitted.* x manner benediction] manner of benediction 1623. y everlastingly] everlasting *from* 1582.

AN HOMILY

OF THE STATE OF MATRIMONY.

THE word[1] of Almighty God doth testify and declare whence the original beginning of matrimony cometh, and why it is ordained. It is instituted of God, to the intent that man and woman should live lawfully in a perpetual friendly fellowship[a], to bring forth fruit, and to avoid fornication: by which means[b] a good conscience might be preserved on both parties in bridling the corrupt inclinations of the flesh within the limits of honesty; for God hath straitly forbidden all whoredom and uncleanness, and hath from time to time taken grievous punishments[c] of this inordinate lust, as all stories and ages hath[d] declared. Furthermore, it is also ordained, that the Church of God and his kingdom might by this kind of life be conserved and enlarged, not only in that God giveth children by his blessing, but also in that they be brought up by the parents godly in the knowledge of God's word; that thus[e] the knowledge of God and true religion[2] might be delivered by succession from one to another, that finally many might enjoy that everlasting immortality.

Wherefore, forasmuch as matrimony serveth as[f] well to avoid sin and offence as to encrease the kingdom of God, you, as all other which enter that state[g], must acknowledge this benefit of God with pure and thankful minds, for that he hath so ruled

a friendly fellowship] friendship 1623. b means] mean *from* 1582. c punishments] punishment *from* 1582. d ages hath] ages have *from* 1582. e thus] this *till* 1571. f serveth as] serveth us as *from* 1582. g that state] the state *from* 1582.

1 As much as half of this Homily, namely, all from the beginning of it to the end of the quotation from *Psalm* cxxviii on page 506, and the concluding paragraph from "Whereupon do your best endeavour" on page 514, is translated with very little alteration from an Address of Veit Dietrich or Theodor, a preacher of great celebrity at Nuremberg; of which there is a Latin Version under the title, *Adhortatio ad Pios Conjuges Germanice scripta a M. Vito Theodoro piae memoriae,* on signn. C c 3–7 of Selneccer's work upon the Epistles of St. Peter, *In Divi Petri Apostoli Epistolas Carmen Paraphrasticum et Homiliae, seu Conciones, Authore M. Nicolao Selneccero, cum Indice praecipuorum locorum,* an octavo volume printed at *Jena* in 1567. But the Address in German has not been found, nor any earlier copy of a Latin Version of it.

For the better understanding of the Homily, a few passages from Selneccer's translation are given in footnotes.

2 Dei agnitio et verus Dei cultus. *Seln.*

your hearts[h] [3] that ye follow not the example of the wicked world, who set their delight in filthiness of sin, where both[i] of you stand in the fear of God, and abhor all filthiness. For that is surely the singular gift of God, where the common example of the world declareth how the devil hath their hearts bound and entangled in divers snares, so that they in their wifeless state run into open abominations without any grudge of their conscience. Which sort of men that liveth[k] so desperately and filthily[l], what damnation tarrieth for them St. Paul describeth it to them, saying, *Neither whoremongers*[m] *neither adulterers shall inherit the kingdom of God.* This horrible judgment of God ye be escaped thorough[n] his mercy[4], if so be that ye live inseparately according to God's ordinance.

1 Cor vi, [9, 10.

But yet I would not have you careless, without watching. For the devil will assay to attempt all things to interrupt and hinder your hearts and godly purpose, if ye will give him any entry. For he will either labour to break this godly knot once begun betwixt you, or else at the least he will labour to encomber it with divers griefs and displeasures. And this is his[o] principal craft, to work dissension of hearts of the one from the other; that, whereas now there is pleasant and sweet love betwixt you, he will in the stead thereof bring in most bitter and unpleasant discord. And surely that same adversary of ours doth, as it were from above, assault man's nature and condition. For this folly is ever from our tender age grown up with us, to have a desire to rule, to think highly by ourself[p], so that none thinketh it meet to give place to another. That wicked vice of stubborn will and self love is more meet to break and to dissever the love of heart, than to preserve concord. Wherefore married persons must apply their minds in most earnest wise to concord, and must crave continually of God the help of his Holy Spirit, so to rule their hearts and to knit their minds together, that they be not dissevered by any division of discord.

This necessity of prayer must be oft in the occupying[q] and using of married persons, that ofttime[r] the one should pray for the other, lest hate and debate do arise betwixt them. And because few do consider this thing, but more few do perform it,

[h] your hearts] our hearts 1571–1595. [i] where both] but both 1623. [k] liveth] live *from* 1582. [l] filthily] filthy 1623. [m] whoremongers] whoremonger *from* 1582. [n] thorough] through *from* 1563 B. [o] is his]-is the 1623. [p] by ourself] of ourself 1623. [q] occupying] practice 1623. [r] ofttime] ofttimes *from* 1570.

[3] Agere gratias pro hoc beneficio, quod animum ejusmodi vobis dedit. *Seln.*
[4] Dei beneficio. *Seln.* See note 3.

(I say, to pray diligently,) we see how wonderfully[s] the devil deludeth and scorneth this state, how few matrimonies there be without chidings, brawlings, tauntings, repentings, bitter cursings, and fightings. Which things whosoever doth commit[t], they do not consider that it is the instigation of the ghostly enemy, who taketh great delight therein: for else they would with all earnest endeavour strive against these mischiefs, not only with prayer, but also with all possible diligence; yea, they would not give place to the provocation of wrath, which stirreth them either to such rough and sharp words or stripes, which is surely compassed by the devil: whose temptation, if it be followed, must needs begin and weave the web of all miseries and sorrows. For this is most certainly true, that of such beginnings must needs ensue the breach of true concord in heart, whereby all love must needs shortly be banished. Then cannot it[u] be but a miserable thing to behold, that yet they are of necessity compelled to live together, which yet cannot be in quiet together. And this is most customably every where to be seen. But what is the cause[x] thereof? Forsooth, because they will not consider the crafty trains of the devil, and therefore giveth[y] not themselves to pray to God, that he would vouchsafe to repress his power. Moreover, they do not consider how they promote the purpose of the devil, in that they follow the wrath of their hearts, while they threat one another, while they in their folly turn all upside down, while they will never give over their right, as they esteem it, yea, while many times they will not give over the wrong part indeed. Learn thou therefore, if thou desirest to be void of all these miseries, if thou desirest to live peaceably and comfortably in wedlock, how to make thy earnest prayer to God, that he would govern both your hearts by his[z] Holy Spirit, to restrain the devil's power, whereby your concord may remain perpetually.

But to this prayer must be joined a singular diligence, whereof
1 Pet. iii, [7.] St. Peter giveth his precept[a], saying, *You husbands, deal[b] with your wives according to knowledge*[5], *giving honour to the wife, as unto the weaker vessel, and as unto them that are heirs also of the grace of life, that your prayers be not hindered.* This precept

[s] wonderfully] wonderful *from* 1563 G. [t] doth commit] do commit 1567–1574. [u] cannot it] can it not 1563 F, *and from* 1570. [x] the cause] he cause 1623. [y] giveth] give *from* 1582. [z] by his] by the 1623. [a] his precept] this precept *from* 1571. [b] deal] *so in all. But no doubt the Homilist wrote* dwel. *See note* 5 *below.*

5 *Οἱ ἄνδρες ὁμοίως, συνοικοῦντες κατὰ γνῶσιν.* Viri, cohabitate uxoribus cum ratione: *Seln.*

doth peculiarly[c] pertain to the husband: for he ought to be the leader and author of love in cherishing and encreasing concord; which then shall take place, if he will use measureableness[d] and not tyranny, and if he yield some things to[e] the woman. For the woman is a weak creature, not endued with like strength and constancy of mind: therefore they be the sooner disquieted, and they be the more prone to all weak affections and dispositions of mind, more than men be; and lighter they be and more vain in their fantasies and opinions. These things must be considered of the man, that he be not too stiff; so that he ought to wink at some things, and must gently expound all things, and to forbear.

Howbeit, the common sort of men doth judge that such moderation should not become a man: for they say that it is a token of a womanish[f] cowardness; and therefore they think that it is a man's part to fume in anger, to fight with fist and staff. Howbeit, howsoever they imagine, undoubtedly St. Peter doth better judge what should be seeming to a man, and what he should most reasonably perform. For he saith reasoning should be used[6], and not fighting. Yea, he saith more, that the woman ought to have a certain *honour* attributed to her; that is to say, she must be spared and borne with, the rather for that she is *the weaker vessel,* of a frail heart, inconstant, and with a word soon stirred to wrath. And therefore, considering these her frailties, she is to be the rather spared. By this means thou shalt not only nourish concord, but shalt have her heart in thy power and will; for honest natures will sooner be retained to do their duty[g] rather by gentle words than by stripes. But he which will do all things with extremity and severity, and doth use always rigour in words and stripes, what will that avail in the conclusion? Verily nothing but that he thereby setteth forward the devil's work; he banisheth away concord, charity, and sweet amity, and bringeth in dissension, hatred, and irksomeness, the greatest griefs that can be in the mutual love and fellowship of man's life. Beyond all this, it bringeth another evil therewith; for it is the destruction and interruption of prayer. For in the time that the mind is occupied with dissension and discord there can be no true prayer used. For the Lord's Prayer hath not only a respect to particular persons, but

[c] peculiarly] particularly *from* 1563 C. [d] measurableness] moderation 1623. [e] things to] thing to *from* 1582. [f] of a womanish] of womanish *from* 1567. [g] their duty] their duties 1623.

6 Utere, inquit, ratione. *Seln.* See note 5.

to the whole universal; in the which we openly pronounce that we will forgive them which hath[h] offended against us, even as we ask forgiveness of our sins of God. Which thing how can it be done rightly, when their hearts be at dissension? How can they pray each for other, when they be at hate betwixt themselves? Now, if the aid of prayer be taken away, by what means can they sustain themselves in any comfort? For they cannot otherwise either resist the devil, or yet have their hearts stayed in stable comfort in all perils and necessities, but by prayer. Thus all discommodities, as well worldly as ghostly, follow this froward testiness and comberous fierceness in manners; which be more meet for brute beasts than for reasonable creatures. St. Peter doth not allow these things, but the devil desireth them gladly. Wherefore take the more heed. And yet a man may be a man, although he doth not use such extremity, yea, though[i] he should dissemble some things in his wife's manners. And this is the part of a Christian man, which both pleaseth God, and serveth also in good use to the comfort of their marriage state.

Now as concerning the wife's duty. What shall become her? Shall she abuse the gentleness and humanity of her husband, and at her pleasure turn all things upside down? No surely; for that is far repugnant against God's commandment. For
1 Pet. iii, [1.] thus doth St. Peter preach to them: *Ye wives, be ye in subjection to obey your own husbands*[k]. To obey is another thing than to control or command; which yet they may do to their children and to their family; but as for their husbands, them must they obey, and cease from commanding, and perform subjection. For this surely doth nourish concord very much, when the wife is ready at hand at her husband's commandment, when she will apply herself to his will, when she endeavoureth herself to seek his contentation and to do him pleasure, when she will eschew all things that might offend him. For thus will most truly be verified the saying of the poet, "A good wife by obeying her husband shall bear the rule[7]": so that he shall have a delight

[h] which hath] which have *from* 1582. [i] though] although 1582, 1623. [k] husbands] husband *till* 1582.

7 Casta ad virum matrona parendo imperat.
From the *Sententiae* of *Publius Syrus*.

It does not appear that Dietrich quoted Syrus or any other poet here: at least Selneccer's Latin version is merely this; Sic enim cor ipsius [*sc.* mariti] lucrifacit, ut laetetur quoties domum sibi ad uxorem redeundum est. And perhaps our English Homilist made his quotation from the *Christiani Matrimonii Institutio*

and a gladness the sooner at all times to return home to her. But on the contrary part, when the wives be stubborn, froward, and malapert, their husbands are compelled thereby to abhor and flee from their own houses, even as they should have battle with their enemies.

Howbeit, it can scantly be but that some offences shall sometime chance betwixt them: for no man doth live without fault; specially for that the woman is the more frail part[l]. Therefore let them beware that they stand not in their faults and wilfulness; but rather let them acknowledge their follies, and say, My husband, so it is, that by my anger I was compelled to do this or that: forgive it me, and hereafter I will take better heed. Thus ought women[m] the more[n] readily to do, the more they be ready to offend. And they shall not do this only to avoid strife and debate, but rather in the respect of the commandment of God, as St. Paul expresseth it in this form of words: *Let women be subject to their husbands, as to the Lord: for the husband is the head of the woman, as Christ is the Head of the Church.* [Eph. v, [22, 23.]] Here you understand that God hath commanded that ye should acknowledge the authority of the husband, and refer to him the honour of obedience. And St. Peter saith in that same place[o] afore[p] rehearsed, that *holy matrons did sometimes*[q] *deck themselves*, not with gold and silver, but in *putting their whole hope in God*, and in *obeying their husbands; as Sara obeyed Abraham, calling him lord: whose daughters ye be*, saith he, if ye follow her example. [1 Pet. iii, [3-6.]] This sentence is very meet for women to print in their remembrance. Truth it is, that they must specially feel the griefs[r] and pains of their matrimony, in that they relinquish the liberty of their own rule, in the pain of their travailing, in the bringing up of their children; in which offices they be in great perils, and be grieved with great afflictions, which they might be without, if they lived out of matrimony. But St. Peter saith that this is the chief ornament of *holy matrons*, in that they *set their hope* and trust *in God*; that

[l] frail part] frail parte 1567–1570, frail partie *from* 1571. [m] ought women] ought the women 1571, ought the woman *from* 1574. [n] women the more] woman more 1623. [o] that same place] that place *from* 1563 G. [p] afore] before *from* 1571. [q] sometimes] sometime 1570–1595, in former time 1623. [r] feel the griefs] feel the grief *from* 1567.

of *Erasmus*, who, although he gave the line correctly in his own edition of the *Sententiae*, (the first in which they were assigned to Syrus, whereas before they were printed among the Works of Seneca,) yet in that treatise cites it thus:

Bona mulier parendo apud virum imperat.

Erasm. Opp. v, 573, *ed.* 1540.

is to say, in that they refused not from marriage for the business thereof, for the griefs[s] and perils thereof, but committed all such adventures to God, in most sure trust of help, after that they have called upon his aid. O woman, do thou the like, and so shalt thou be most excellently beautified before God and all his angels and saints. And thou needest not to seek further for doing any better works. For, obey thy husband, take regard of his requests, and give heed unto him to perceive what he requireth of thee; and so shalt thou honour God, and live peaceably in thy house. And, beyond this[t], God shall follow thee with his benediction, that all things shall well prosper

[Ps. cxxviii, 1-4.] both to thee and to thy husband, as the Psalm saith. *Blessed is the man which feareth God, and walketh in his ways. Thou shalt have the fruit of thine own hands: happy shalt thou be, and well shall it*[u] *go with thee. Thy wife shall be as a vine plentifully spreading about thy house. Thy children shall be as the young springs of the olives about thy table. Lo, thus shall that man be blessed,* saith David, *that feareth the Lord.*

This let the wife have ever in mind, the rather admonished thereto by the apparel of her head, whereby is signified that she is under covert and[v] obedience of her husband. And, as that apparel is of nature so appointed to declare her subjection, so

α [1 Tim. ii, 9.] biddeth St. Paul[α] that all other of her raiment should express both *shamefastness and sobriety*. For, if it be not lawful[8] for

β [1 Cor. xi, 10.] the woman to have her head bare, but to bear thereon[β] the sign of her power[9], wheresoever she goeth, more is it required that she declare the thing that is meant thereby. And therefore

s for the griefs] for the gifts 1623. t beyond this] beyond all this *from* 1571. u shall it] it shall *from* 1571. v covert and] covert or *from* 1574.

8 So much of this Homily as is comprised within these words, "For, if it be not lawful," and these in p. 514, l. 6, "in one concord of heart and mind," is translated, with some abridgment here and there, from the latter part of Chrysost. in Epist. I ad Cor. Homil. XXVI, Εἰ γὰρ γυμνὴν οὐ δεῖ κ. τ. λ., Opp. X, 235–240. In the sentence next before Chrysostom cites the text from 1 Tim. which our Homilist also quotes; and a little further back he argues that as the long hair of a woman is a natural sign, so her veil is a conventional sign, of her subjection and obedience to the man.

But the translation was made from the Latin version of his works put forth at Basle in 1530 by Erasmus, in which all the Homilies on 1 Cor. after the first twenty were done by Fisher, Bishop of Rochester. This passage, beginning Nam si nudum caput, is in Tom. I, pp. 284–286, of that edition. Between the two translations the sense of Chrysostom has suffered; and a few passages both of his Greek and of Bishop Fisher's Latin are therefore given in footnotes, where it seemed needful, either to elucidate the sense, or to justify our own Homilist.

9 Τῆς ὑποταγῆς τὸ σύμβολον. Potestatis signum: *Erasm.* Potestatem is the word in the *Vulgate* for ἐξουσίαν in 1 *Cor.* XI, 10.

these ancient women of the old world called their husbands lords, and shewed them reverence in obeying them.

But peradventure she will say that those men loved their wives indeed. I know that well enough, and bear it well in mind. But, when I do admonish you of your duties, then call not to consideration what their duties be. For, when we ourselves do teach our children to obey us as their parents, or when we reform our servants, and tell them that they should obey[γ] their masters, not only at the eye, but as to the[w] Lord; if they should tell us again our duties, we would[x] not think it well done. For, when we be admonished of our duties and faults, we ought not then to seek what other men's duties be. For, though a man had a companion in his fault, yet should not he[y] thereby be without his fault. But this must be only looked on, by what means thou mayest make thyself without blame. For Adam[δ] did lay the blame upon the woman, and she turned it unto the serpent; but yet neither of them was thus excused. And therefore bring not such excuses to me at this time, but apply all thy diligence to hear[z] thine obedience[10] to thy[a] husband. For, when I take in hand to admonish thy husband to love thee and to cherish thee, yet will I not cease to set out the law that is appointed for the woman[11], as well as I would require of the man what is written for his law. Go thou therefore about such things as becometh thee only, and shew thyself tractable to thy husband. Or rather, if thou wilt obey thy husband for God's precept, then allege[12] such[b] things as be in his duty to do, but perform thou diligently those things which the Lawmaker hath charged thee to do: for thus is it most reasonable to obey God, if thou wilt not suffer thyself to transgress his law[13]. He that loveth his friend seemeth to do no great thing; but he that honoureth him that[c] is hurtful and hateful to him, this man is worthy much[d] condemnation. Even so think thou[e], if thou canst suffer an extreme husband, thou shalt

γ [Eph. vi, 5–7.]

δ [Gen. iii, 12–19.]

[w] as to the] as the 1623. [x] would] should 1623. [y] not he] he not 1623. [z] hear] *so in all. Perhaps the Homilist wrote* bear. *See note* 10. [a] to thy] to thine *from* 1582. [b] allege such] *so in all. Perhaps the Homilist wrote* allege not such. *See note* 12. [c] honoureth him that] honoureth that *from* 1582. [d] much] most *from* 1574. [e] think thou] think you *from* 1582.

10 Παρέχειν ἅπερ ὀφείλεις. Debitum exhibere: *Erasm.*

11 Οὐκ ἀφίημι αὐτὸν προενεγκεῖν εἰς μέσον τὸν τῇ γυναικὶ κείμενον νόμον. Non omitto quin legem mulieri positam in medium adducam: *Erasm.*

12 Καὶ γὰρ εἰ διὰ τὸν Θεὸν πείθῃ τῷ ἀνδρὶ, μή μοι πρόφερε κ. τ. λ. Vel potius si propter Deum viro parueris, noli mihi proponere &c.: *Erasm.*

13 Τοῦτο γάρ ἐστι μάλιστα Θεῷ πείθεσθαι, τὸ καὶ ἐναντία πάσχουσαν μὴ παρακινεῖν τὸν νόμον. Hoc enim maxime est Deo parere, si legem praevaricari non patieris: *Erasm.*

have a great reward therefore; but, if thou lovest him only because he is gentle and curtess[f] [14], what reward will God give thee therefore? Yet I speak not these things, that I would wish the husbands to be sharp towards their wives; but I exhort the women, that they would patiently bear the sharpness of their husbands. For, when either parts do their best to perform their duties the one to the other, then followeth thereon great profit to their neighbours for their example's sake[15]. For when the woman is ready to suffer a sharp husband, and the man will not extremely entreat his stubborn and troublesome wife, then be all things in quiet, as in a most sure haven.

Even thus was it done in old time, that every one did their own duty and office, and was not busy to require the duty of their neighbours. Consider, I pray thee, that Abraham took[ε] to him his brother's son: his wife did not blame him therefore. He commanded him[g] to go with him a long journey[16]: she did not gainsay it, but obeyed his precept. Again, after all those great miseries, labours, and pains of that journey, when Abraham was made as lord over all, yet did he give place[ϛ] to Lot of his superiority. Which matter Sara took so little to grief, that she never once suffered her tongue to speak such words as the common manner of women is wont to do in these days: when they see their husbands in such rooms to be made underlings, and to be put under their youngers, then they upbraid them with comberous talk, and call them fools, dastards, and cowards for so doing. But Sara was so far from speaking any such thing, that it came never into her mind and thought so to say, but allowed the wisdom and will of her husband. Yea, beside[h] all this, after the said Lot had thus his will, and left to his uncle the lesser[i] portion of land, he chanced[j] to fall into[ζ] extreme peril: which chance when it came to the knowledge of this said Patriarch, he incontinently put all his men in harness[17], and prepared himself with all his family and friends against the host of the Persians[18]. In which case Sara did not counsel him to

ε [Gen. xii, 4, 5.]

ϛ [Gen. xiii, 8–11.]

ζ [Gen. xiv, 12–14.]

f curtess] courteous *from* 1582. g commanded him] *so in all. See note* 16. h beside] besides *from* 1567. i lesser] less *from* 1574. j chanced] chanceth 1563 G–1574.

14 curtess: curteis in *Chaucer, Cant. Tales, Prol. The Squier* 99; and in *Wycliffe, Wisd.* VII, 23, and *Prol. to Isai.*; from Fr. *courtois*, courteous.

15 Ταχέως καὶ τὰ τοῦ πλησίον ἕψεται· οἷον, ὅταν ἡ γυνὴ κ.τ.λ. Etiam proximi utilitas sequitur, ut exempli gratia. Quando mulier &c.: *Erasm.*

16 Ἐκέλευσεν αὐτὴν ὁδὸν ὁδεῦσαι μακράν. Jussit ut longum iter faceret: *Erasm.*

17 harness: armour; as in 1 *Kings* XX, 11; XXII, 34.

18 *Persae* apud Nostrum audiunt As-

the contrary, nor did say, as then might have been said, My husband, whither goest thou so unadvisedly? Why runnest thou thus on head? Why dost thou offer thyself to so great perils, and art thus ready to jeopard thine own life, and to peril the lives of all thine, for such a man as hath done thee such wrong? At least[k] way, if thou regardest not thyself, yet have compassion on me, which for thy love have forsaken my kinred and my country, and have the want both of my friends and kinsfolks, and am thus come into so far countries with thee. Have pity on me, and make me not here a widow, to cast me to such[l] cares and troubles. Thus might she have said: but Sara neither said nor thought such words, but she kept herself in silence in all things. Furthermore, all that time when she was barren, and took no pain[m], as other women did, by bringing forth fruit in his house, what did he? He complained not to his wife, but[η] to Almighty God[19]. And consider how either of them did their duties as became them; for neither did he despise Sara because she was barren, nor never did cast it in her teeth. Consider again how Abraham expelled[θ] the handmaid out of his house[n], when she required it: so that by this I may truly prove that the one was pleased and contented with the other in all things. But yet set not your eyes only in this[o] matter, but look further what was done before this, that Agar[ι] used her mistress despitefully, and that Abraham himself was somewhat provoked against her[20]; which must needs be an intolerable matter and a painful to a freehearted woman and a chaste. Let not therefore the woman be too busy to call for the duty of her husband, where she should be ready to perform her own[21]; for that is not worthy any great commendation[p]. And even so again let not the man only consider what longeth[q] to the woman, and to stand

η [Gen. xv, 2, 3: xvi, 1, 2.]

θ [Gen. xxi, 9–14.]

ι [Gen. xvi, 4–6.]

k At least] At the least *from* 1563 G. l to such] into such *from* 1582. m pain] pains *from* 1567. n his house] the house *from* 1563 G. o in this] on this *from* 1563 G. p commendation] commendations 1623. q longeth] belongeth *from* 1582.

syrii, Babylonii, et Orientales fere omnes, etiam qui ante diluvium vixerunt. Quin et ipse Abrahamus *Persa* dicitur Tom. v, p. 301 D, et *ex Persis* Tom. IX, p. 120 E. *Field in loc. Chrysost.*

19 Μετὰ ταῦτα τῆς γαστρὸς ἀγόνου μενούσης αὕτη μὲν οὐ πάσχει τὰ τῶν γυναικῶν, οὐδὲ ἀποδύρεται· ἐκεῖνος δὲ θρηνεῖ, ἀλλ' οὐχὶ πρὸς τὴν γυναῖκα, ἀλλὰ πρὸς τὸν Θεόν. Praeterea, cum sterilis esset, minime mulierum labores perpessa, neque partu distracta, ille flet, non ad uxorem, sed ad Deum: *Erasm.*

20 Τὰ πρότερα ἐξέταζε, ὅτι ὕβριζεν αὐτήν, ὅτι κατηλαζονεύετο τῆς κυρίας. Priora inquire, quod contumelia eam affecit, quod in uxorem est irritatus: *Erasm.*

21 Μὴ τοίνυν τοῦ ἀνδρὸς τὴν ἀρετὴν ἀναμενέτω ἡ γυνή, καὶ τότε τὴν ἑαυτῆς παρεχέτω. Ne igitur viri virtutem expectet mulier, inde suam exhibeat: *Erasm.*

too earnestly gazing thereon[22]; for that is not his part or duty. But, as I have said, let either parts[r] be ready and willing to perform that which belongeth specially[s] to themself[t]. For, if we be bound to hold out[κ] our left cheek to strangers which will smite us on the right cheek, how much more ought we to suffer an extreme and unkind husband!

κ [Matt. v, 39.]

But yet I mean not that a man should beat his wife. God forbid that; for that is the greatest shame that can be, not so much to her that is beaten, as to him that doeth the deed. But, if by such fortune[u][23] thou chancest upon such an husband, take it not too heavily; but suppose thou that thereby is laid up no small reward hereafter, and in this lifetime no small commendation to thee, if thou canst be quiet. But yet to you that be men thus I speak: let there be none so grievous fault to compel you to beat your wives. But what say I your wives? No, it is not to be borne with that an honest man should lay hands on his maidservant to beat her. Wherefore, if it be a great shame for a man to beat his bondservant, much more rebuke it is to lay violent hands upon his freewoman. And this thing may we[v] well understand[w] by the laws which the paynims hath made[x], which doth discharge her any longer to dwell with such an husband, as unworthy to have any further company with her, that doth smite her[24]. For it is an extreme point thus so vilely to entreat her like a slave, that is fellow to thee of thy life, and so conjoined[y] unto thee beforetime in the necessary matters of thy living. And therefore a man may well liken such a man, if he may be called a man rather than a wild beast, to a killer of his father or his mother. And, whereas we be commanded[λ] to forsake our father and mother for our wife's sake, and yet thereby do work them none injury, but do fulfil the law of God, how can it not appear then to be a point of extreme madness to intreat her despitefully for whose sake God

λ [Gen. ii, 24: Matt. xix, 5.]

[r] parts] partes 1563 A–F, parties 1563 G–1567, partie 1570–1574, party *from* 1582. *See before, page* 508, *line* 6. [s] specially] especially *from* 1582. [t] themself] themselves *from* 1582. [u] such fortune] *so in all. Perhaps the Homilist wrote* some fortune. *See note* 23. [v] may we] may be *from* 1571. [w] understand] understood 1623. [x] hath made] have made *from* 1582. [y] conjoined] joined *from* 1567.

22 Καὶ τότε φιλοσοφείτω. Et inde philosophetur: *Erasm.*

23 Ἀπὸ περιστάσεώς τινος. Casu aliquo: *Erasm.*

24 Καὶ τοῦτο καὶ ἐκ τῶν ἔξωθεν ἄν τις ἴδοι νομοθετῶν, οἳ τὴν τὰ τοιαῦτα παθοῦσαν οὐκέτι ἀναγκάζουσι συνοικεῖν τῷ τυπτήσαντι, ἅτε ἀναξίῳ ὄντι τῆς πρὸς αὐτὴν ὁμιλίας. It does not appear who were the heathen lawgivers here intended by St. Chrysostom. In the year 449, more than forty years after his death, such relief was granted to the outraged wife by a law of the Emperor Theodosius II; but it was afterwards withdrawn by Justinian. See *Cod. Justin.* v, xvii, 8.

hath commanded thee to leave parents? Yea, who can suffer such despite? Who can worthily express the inconvenience that is, to see what weepings and wailings be made in the open streets, when neighbours run together to the house of so unruly an husband, as to a Bedlem[z] man who goeth about to overturn all that he hath at home? Who would not think that it were better for such a man to wish the ground to open and to swallow[a] him in, than once ever after to be seen in the market?

But peradventure thou wilt object that the woman provoketh thee to this point. But consider thou again that the woman is a frail vessel, and thou art therefore made the ruler and head over her, to bear the weakness of her in this her subjection. And therefore study thou to declare the honest commendation of thine authority; which thou canst no ways[b] better do than to forbear to utter[c] her in her weakness and subjection[25]. For, even as the king appeareth so much the more noble, the more excellent and noble he maketh his officers and lieutenants, whom if he should dishonour, and despise the authority of their dignity, he should deprive himself of a great part of his own honour; even so, if thou dost despise her that is set in the next room beside thee, thou dost much derogate and decay the excellency and virtue of thine own authority. Recount all these things in thy mind, and be gentle and quiet. Understand that God hath given thee children with her, and art made a father, and by such reason appease thyself. Dost not thou[d] see the husbandmen, what diligence they use to till that ground which once they have taken to farm, though it be never so full of faults? As for an example, though it be dry, though it bringeth forth weeds, though the soil cannot bear too much wet, yet he tilleth it[26], and so winneth fruit thereof. Even in like manner, if thou wouldest use like diligence to instruct and order the mind of thy spouse, if thou wouldest diligently apply thyself to

[z] Bedlem] bedlime 1563 A–E, Bedlym 1563 F, bedlem *or* Bedlem *from* 1563 G. [a] and to swallow] and swallow *from* 1582. [b] no ways] no way *from* 1563 G. [c] utter] urge 1623. [d] not thou] thou not *from* 1574.

25 Ὅταν τὸ ἀρχόμενον μὴ ἀτιμάζῃς. Si subditae non insultaveris: *Erasm.*

The verb *to utter* has not been found elsewhere in this sense. It seems to be from the French *outrer*, which is thus explained in the *Dictionnaire de Trévoux*: "Piquer au vif, faire un cruel affront, offenser griévement, pousser la patience à bout: asperioribus verbis vellicare, inurere; graviter offendere, vellicare." Jamieson, in the *Supplement* to his *Scottish Dictionary*, says *to outray* means *to treat outrageously*. The remote source is clearly the Latin *ultra*.

26 Τοῦτο καὶ σὺ ποίει. Colit tamen: *Erasm.*

weed out by little and little the noisome weeds of uncomely manners out of her mind with wholesome precepts, it could not be but in time thou shouldest feel the pleasant fruit thereof to both your comforts. Therefore, that this thing chance not so, perform this thing that I do here counsel thee. Whensoever[e] any displeasant matter riseth at home, if thy wife hath done aught amiss, comfort her, and increase not the heaviness. For, though thou shouldest be grieved with never so many things, yet thou shalt[f] find nothing more grievous than to want the benevolence of thy wife at home; what offence soever thou canst name, yet shalt thou find none more intolerable than to be at debate with thy wife. And for this cause most of all oughtest thou to have this love[27] in reverence. And, if reason moveth thee to bear any burden at any other men's hands, much more at thy[g] wife's[28]. For, if she be poor, upbraid her not; if she be simple, taunt her not, but be the more curteous[29]: for she is thy body, and made *one flesh* with thee.

[Gen. ii, 24: Eph. v, 28, 31.]

But thou peradventure wilt say, that she is a wrathful woman, a drunkard, a beastly[h], without wit and reason. For this cause bewail her the more. Chafe not in anger, but pray to[i] Almighty God. Let her be admonished and holpen[j] with good counsel, and do thou thy best endeavour that she may be delivered of all these affections. But, if thou shouldest beat her, thou shalt increase her evil affections; for frowardness and sharpness is not amended with frowardness, but with softness and gentleness. Furthermore, consider what reward thou shalt have at God's hand: for, where thou mightest beat her, and yet for the respect of the fear of God thou wilt abstain and bear patiently her great offences, the rather in respect of that law which forbiddeth that a man should cast out his wife, what fault soever she be combred with, thou shalt have a very great reward. And before the receipt of that reward thou shalt feel many commodities; for by this means she shall be made the more obedient, and thou for her sake[k] shalt be made the more meek. It is written in a story of a certain strange philosopher, which had a

[e] Whensoever] Whatsoever 1563, 1567; Whansoever 1570. [f] yet thou shalt] yet shalt thou *from* 1563 D *except* E. [g] at thy] of thy *till* 1563 G. [h] a beastly] and beastly *from* 1563 G. [i] pray to] pray unto *from* 1582. [j] holpen] helped *from* 1582. [k] her sake] his sake *till* 1563 G.

27 Ἡ ταύτης ἀγαπή. Hujusmodi dilectio: *Erasm.*

28 Εἰ γὰρ ἀλλήλων τὰ βάρη δεῖ βαστάζειν (Gal. vi, 2), πολλῷ μᾶλλον τῆς γυναικός. Quod si invicem onera ferenda sunt, multo magis uxoris: *Erasm.*

29 Ἀλλὰ ῥύθμισον μᾶλλον. Sed esto modestior: *Erasm.* On the word "curteous," which all the editions have here, see note 14.

cursed[30] wife, a froward, and a drunkard; when he was asked for what consideration he did so bear her evil manners, he made answer, "By this means," said he, "I have at home a schoolmaster, and an example how I should behave myself abroad: for I shall," saith he, "be the more quiet with other[l], being thus daily exercised and taught in the forbearing of her." Surely it is a shame that paynims should be wiser than we; we, I say, that be commanded to counterfeit[m] angels, or rather God himself thorough[n] meekness[31]. And for the love of virtue[o] this said philosopher Socrates[32] would not expel his wife out of his house; yea, some say that he did therefore marry his wife, to learn this virtue by that occasion. Wherefore, seeing many men be far behind the wisdom of this man, my counsel is, that first and before all things, that man[p] do his best endeavour to get him a good wife, indued with all honesty and virtue; but, if it so chance that he is deceived, that he hath chosen such a wife as is neither good nor tolerable, then let the husband follow this philosopher, and let him instruct his wife in every condition, and never lay these matters to sight. For the merchant man, except he first be at composition with his factor to use his interaffairs[q] quietly[33], he will neither stir his ship to sail, nor yet will lay hands upon his merchandise[34]. Even so let us do all things that we may have the fellowship of our wives, which is the factor of all our doings at home, in great quiet and rest. And by these means all things shall prosper quietly[35], and so shall we pass through the dangers of the troublous sea of this

[l] with other] with others *from* 1582. [m] counterfeit] resemble 1623. [n] thorough] through *from* 1563 C. [o] of virtue] *so in all. Perhaps the Homilist wrote* of this virtue, *as below in line* 11. [p] that man] a man 1623. [q] interaffairs] interfairs *from* 1582.

30 cursed: spiteful, mischievous, ill tempered, perverse; specially said of a woman, but usually written *curst* in this sense.

"They [bears] are never curst but when they are hungry.
Shakespeare, Winter's Tale III, 3.

I was never curst,
I have no gift at all in shrewishness.
Midsummer Night's Dream III, 2.

As curst and shrewd
As Socrates' Xanthippe. *Taming of the Shrew* I, 2.

31 Αὐτὸν τὸν Θεὸν ζηλοῦν κατὰ τὸν τῆς ἐπιεικείας λόγον (Luc. vi, 36: Eph. v, 1). Imitari ... ipsum Deum per mansuetudinem: *Erasm.*

32 Chrysostom does not name Socrates, but see *Xenoph. Sympos.* II, 10, or *Aul. Gell.* I, 17.

33 Πρὶν ἢ πρὸς τὸν κοινωνὸν συνθήκας θέσθαι τὰς δυναμένας εἰρήνην πρυτανεύειν. Nisi cum socio pacta faciat quibus pacifice inter se vivant: *Erasm.* The word "interaffairs" has not been found elsewhere.

34 Οὐδὲ τῆς ἄλλης ἅψεται ἐμπορίας. Neque alias tangit merces: *Erasm.*

35 Πάντα ἡμῖν ἔσται γαληνά. Omnia tranquilla succedent: *Erasm.*

world. For this state of life will be more honourable and comfortable than our houses, than servants, than money, than lands and possessions, than all things that can be told[36]. As all these, with sedition and discord, can never work us any comfort; so shall all things turn to our commodity and pleasure, if we draw this yoke in one concord of heart and mind.

Whereupon do your best endeavour that after this sort ye use your matrimony, and so shall ye be armed on every side. Ye have escaped the snares of the devil and the unlawful lusts of the flesh, ye have the quietness of conscience, by this institution of matrimony ordained by God: therefore use oft prayer to him, that he would be present by you, that he would continue concord and charity betwixt you. Do the best ye can of your parts to custom yourselves to softness and meekness, and bear well in worth such oversights as chance[37]; and thus shall your conversation be most pleasant and comfortable. And although (which can no otherwise be) some adversities shall follow, and otherwhiles now one discommodity, now another, shall appear, yet in this common trouble and adversity lift up both your hands unto heaven; call upon the help and assistance of God, the Author of your marriage; and surely the promise of relief is at hand. For Christ affirmeth in his Gospel, *Where two or three be gathered together in my Name, and be agreed, what matter soever they pray for, it shall be granted them of my heavenly Father.* Why therefore shouldest thou be afeard[r] of the danger, where thou hast so ready a promise and so nigh an help? Furthermore, you must understand how necessary it is for Christian folk to bear Christ's cross; for else we shall never feel how comfortable God's help is unto us.

[Matt. xviii, 19, 20.]

Therefore give thanks to God for his great benefit, in that ye have taken upon you this state of wedlock; and pray you instantly that Almighty God may luckily defend and maintain you therein, that neither ye be overcomed[s] with any tempta-

[r] afeard] afraid *from* 1563 G. [s] overcomed] overcome 1623.

36 Τοῦτο καὶ πρὸ οἰκίας καὶ ἀνδραπόδων καὶ χρημάτων καὶ ἀγρῶν καὶ αὐτῶν τῶν πολιτικῶν πραγμάτων ἄγωμεν· καὶ πάντων ἡμῖν προτιμότερον ἔστω τὸ ιὴν μεθ' ἡμῶν ἐπὶ τῶν οἴκων (but οἰάκων in Field's edition from the *Codex Monacensis*) καθημένην μὴ στασιάζειν μηδὲ διχοστατεῖν πρὸς ἡμᾶς. Haec nobis domo, servis, pecuniis, agris, civilibus, et omnibus denique rebus honorabilior sit, neve ipsa nobiscum domi in seditione et discordia vivat: *Erasm.*

37 Vobismetipsis invicem condonetis. *Seln.* See before, p. 483, n. 6. "I trust in God's grace I shall bear all personal injuries and slanders well in worth, as hitherto I have done." *Abp. Parker to Dr. Stokes circ.* 1539, *Correspondence, No.* x, *p.* 13, *ed. Park. Soc.*

tion[t] nor with any adversity. But before all things take good heed that ye give no occasion to the devil to let and hinder your prayers by discord and dissension. For there is no stronger defence and stay in all our life than is prayer: in the which we may call for the help of God, and obtain it; whereby we may win his blessing, his grace, his defence, and protection, so to continue therein to a better life to come. Which grant us he that died for us all: to whom be all honour and praise for ever and ever. Amen.

[t] temptation] temptations 1623.

AN HOMILY
AGAINST IDLENESS.

FORASMUCH as man, being not born to ease and rest, but to labour and travail, is by corruption of nature through sin so far degenerated and grown out of kind, that he taketh idleness to be no evil at all, but rather a commendable thing, seemly for those that be wealthy; and therefore is[a] greedily imbraced of most part of men, as agreeable to their sensual affection, and all labour and travail is diligently avoided, as a thing painful and repugnant to the pleasure of the flesh; it is necessary to be declared unto you, that, by the ordinance of God which he hath set in the nature of man, every one ought, in his lawful vocation and calling, to give himself to labour; and that idleness, being repugnant to the same ordinance, is a grievous sin, and also, for the great inconveniences and mischiefs which spring thereof, an intolerable evil; to the intent that, when ye understand the same, ye may diligently flee from it, and on the other part earnestly apply yourselves, every man in his vocation, to honest labour and business; which as it is enjoined unto man by God's appointment, so it wanteth not his manifold blessings and sundry benefits.

Almighty God, after that he had created man, put him into Paradise, that he might dress and keep it: but, when he had transgressed God's commandment, eating the fruit of the tree which was forbodden[b] him, Almighty God forthwith did cast him out of Paradise[a] into this woful vale of misery, enjoining him to labour the ground that he was taken out of, and to eat his bread in the sweat of his face all the days of his life. It is the appointment and will of God, that every man, during the time of this mortal and transitory life, should give himself to some[c] honest and godly exercise and labour, and every one to do[d] his own business, and to walk uprightly in his own calling. *Man*, saith Job, *is born to labour*[1]. And we are commanded by

[a] Gen. iii, [17-24.]

Job v, [7.]

[a] and therefore is] *so in all.* [b] forbodden] forbidden *from* 1563 EF. [c] some] such 1623. [d] one to do] one follow 1623.

[1] Homo nascitur ad laborem. *Vulg.*

Jesus Sirach, *not to hate painful works, neither husbandry,* or other such misteries of travail, *which the Highest hath created.* (Ecclus. vii, [15.]) The Wise Man also exhorteth us to *drink the waters of our own cistern, and of the rivers that run out of the middes of our own well;* (Prov. v, [15.]) meaning thereby that we should live of our own labours, and not devour the labours of other. St. Paul, hearing that among the Thessalonians there were *certain that lived* dissolutely and *out of order,* that is to say, *which did not work, but were busybodies,* (2 Thess. iii, [6–14.]) not getting their own living with their own travail, but eating other men's bread of free cost, did command the said Thessalonians, not only *to withdraw themselves* and abstain from the familiar company of such inordinate persons, but also that, *if there were any such amonges theme*[e] *that would not labour, the same should not eat,* nor have any living at other men's hands. Which doctrine of St. Paul, no doubt, is grounded upon the general ordinance of God, which is, that every man should labour; and therefore it is to be obeyed of all men, and no man can justly exempt himself from the same.

But when it is said, all men should labour, it is not so straitly meant that all men should use handy labour: but, as there be divers sorts of labour[f], some of the mind, and some of the body, and some of both, so every one, (except by reason of age, debility of body, or want of health he be unapt to labour at all,) ought, both for the getting of his own living honestly and for to profit others, in some kind of labour to exercise himself, according as the vocation whereunto God hath called him shall require. So that whosoever doeth good to the common weal and society of men with his industry and labour, whether it be by governing the common weal publicly, or by bearing public office or ministry, or by doing any common necessary affairs of his country, or by giving counsel, or by teaching and instructing others, or by what other means soever he be occupied, so that a profit and benefit redound thereof unto others, the same person is not to be accounted idle, though he work no bodily labour, nor is to be denied his living, (if he attend his vocation,) though he work not with his hands. Bodily labour is not required of them which by reason of their vocation and office are occupied in the labour of the mind to the profit[g] and help of others.

St. Paul exhorteth Timothy to eschew and *refuse idle widows, which go about from house to house,* (1 Tim. v, [11, 13.]) because they are *not only*

[e] amonges] among *from* 1563 G. [f] of labour] of labours *from* 1582. [g] the profit] the succour 1623.

idle, but prattlers also and busybodies, speaking things which are not comely. The Prophet Ezechiel, declaring what the sins of the city of Sodom were, reckoneth idleness to be one of the Ezek. xvi, [49.] principal. *The sins,* saith he, *of Sodom were these; pride, fulness of meat, abundance, and idleness: these things had Sodom and her daughters*[2]; meaning the cities subject to her. The horrible and strange kind of destruction of that city and all the β [Gen. xix, 24, 25.] country about the same, which was[β] fire and brimstone raining from heaven, most manifestly declareth what a grievous sin idleness is, and ought to admonish us to flee from the same, and embrace honest and godly labour. But, if we give ourselves to idleness and sloth, to lurking and loitering, to wilful wandering and wasteful spending, never settling ourselves to honest labour, but living like drone bees by the labours of other men, then do we break the Lord's commandment, we go astray from our vocation, and incur the danger of God's wrath and heavy displeasure, to our endless destruction, except by repentance we turn again unfeignedly unto God.

The inconveniences and mischiefs that come of idleness, as well to man's body as to his soul, are more than can in short time be well rehearsed. Some we shall declare and open unto you, that by considering them ye may the better with your- γ Prov. x, [4.] selves gather the rest. *An idle hand,* saith Salomon[γ], *maketh* δ Prov. xii, [11;] and xxviii, [19.] *poor, but a quick labouring hand maketh rich.* Again[δ]: *He that tilleth his land shall have plenteousness of bread; but he that floweth in*[h] *idleness is a very fool, and shall have poverty* ε Prov. xx, [4.] *enough*[3]. Again[ε]: *A slothful body will not go to plough for cold of the winter: therefore shall he go a begging in summer, and have nothing.* But what shall we need to stand much about the proving of this, that poverty followeth idleness? We have too much experience thereof (the thing is the more to be lamented) in this realm. For a great part of the beggary that is among the poor can be imputed to nothing so much as to idleness, and to the negligence of parents; which do not bring up their children either in good learning, honest labour, or some commendable occupation or trade, whereby, when they come to age, they might get their living. Daily experience also teacheth, that

[h] floweth in] *so in all. Perhaps the Homilist wrote* followeth. *See note* 3.

2 Haec fuit iniquitas Sodomae..., superbia, saturitas panis et abundantia, et otium ipsius et filiarum ejus. *Vulg.*

3 Qui autem sectatur otium stultissimus est. Qui autem sectatur otium replebitur egestate. *Prov.* xii, 11; xxviii, 19; *Vulg.*

nothing is more enemy or pernicious to the health of man's body, than is idleness, too much ease and sleep, and want of exercise.

But these and such like incommodities, albeit they be great and noisome, yet, because they concern chiefly the body and external goods[i], they are not to be compared with the mischiefs and inconveniences which through[k] idleness happen to the soul: whereof we will recite some. Idleness is never alone, but hath always a long tail of other vices hanging on, which corrupt and infect the whole man after such sort, that he is made at length nothing else but a lump of sin. *Idleness*, saith Jesus Sirach, (Ecclus. xxxiii, [27.]) *bringeth much evil and mischief*. St. Bernard calleth it "the mother of all evils, and stepdame of all virtues;" adding moreover, that it doth prepare and as it were tread the way to hell-fire[4]. Where idleness is once received, there the devil is always[l] ready to set in his foot, and to plant all kind of wickedness and sin, to the everlasting destruction of man's soul. Which thing to be most true we are plainly taught in the thirteenth of Matthew, where it is said, that *the enemy came while men were asleep,* (Matt. xiii, [25.]) *and sowed naughty tares among the good wheat*. In very deed the best time that the devil can have to work his feat is when men be asleep, that is to say, idle: then is he most busy in his work; then doth he soonest catch men in the snare of perdition; then doth he fill them with all iniquity, to bring them, without God's special favour, unto utter destruction.

Hereof we have two notable examples most lively set before our eyes. The one in King David[ζ], who, tarrying at home idly, (ζ 2 Sam. xi.) as the Scripture saith, *at such times as* other *kings go forth to battle*, was quickly seduced of Satan to forsake the Lord his God, and to commit two grievous and abominable sins in his sight, adultery and murder. The plagues that ensued these offences[η] were horrible and grievous, as it may easily appear to (η 2 Sam. xii, [10, 11.]) them that will read the story. Another example of Samson[θ], (θ Judges xvi, [1–25.]) who, so long as he warred with the Philistines, enemies to the

[i] external goods] external goodes 1563 A, B, *and* G; eternal goodnes 1563 C—F; eternal goodes 1563 H. [k] through] thorough *from* 1582. [l] always] *omitted* 1623.

4 Fugienda proinde otiositas, mater nugarum, noverca virtutum. *Bernard. De Consid.* II, 13; *Opp.* I, 431 B. Effoeminari quidem otio et torpere pigritia nihil aliud est quam suffocare virtutem, nutrire superbiam, viamque construere ad gehennam. *Petr. Blesens. Epist.* IX, *sub fin.* These two sentences, with some abridgment or modification, are placed together, and referred to "*Bern. in ser.*", in several of the old Collections which bear such names as *Flores Sententiarum*, *Polyanthea*, *Repertorium* or *Speculum Morale*; and the whole has thence been cited as St. Bernard's by other writers besides our Homilist.

people of God, could never be taken or overcome; but, after that he gave himself to ease and idleness, he not only committed fornication with the strumpet Dalila, but also was taken of his enemies and had his eyes miserably put out, was put in prison and compelled to grind in a mill, and at length was made the laughingstock of his enemies. If these two, who were so excellent men, so well beloved of God, so endued with singular and divine gifts, the one namely of prophecy, and the other of strength, and such men as never could by vexation, labour, or trouble be overcome, were overthrown and fell into grievous sins by giving themselves for a short time to ease and idleness, and so consequently incurred miserable plagues at the hands of God; what sin, what mischief, what inconvenience and plague is not to be feared of them which all their life long give themselves wholly to idleness and ease?

Let us not deceive ourselves, thinking little hurt to come of doing nothing. For it is a true saying, When one doeth nothing, he learneth to do evil. Let us therefore always be doing of some honest work, that the devil may find us occupied[5].
[1 Pet. v, 8, 9.] He himself is ever occupied, never idle; but *walketh* continually *seeking to devour* us. Let us *resist him* with our diligent watching in labour and in welldoing. For he that diligently exerciseth himself in honest business is not easily catched in the devil's snare. When man through idleness, or for default of some honest occupation or trade to live upon, is brought to poverty and want of things necessary, we see how easily such a man is induced for his gain to lie, to practise how he may deceive his neighbour, to forswear himself, to bear false witness, and oftentimes to steal and murder, or to use some other ungodly mean to live withal; whereby not only his good name, honest reputation, and a good conscience, yea, his life, is utterly lost, but also the great displeasure and wrath of God, with divers and sundry grievous plagues, are procured. Lo here the end of the idle and sluggish bodies whose hands cannot away with honest labour; loss of name, fame, reputation, and life here in this world, and, without the great mercy of God, the purchasing of everlasting destruction in the world to come. Have not all men then good cause to beware and take heed of idleness, seeing they that imbrace and follow it have commonly of their pleasant idleness sharp and sour displeasures?

5 Facito aliquid operis, ut te semper diabolus inveniat occupatum. *Hieron. Epist.* 125 (al. 4) *ad Rust. Mon.* § 11; *Opp.* I, 933 D.

Doubtless, good and godly men, weighing the great and manifold harms that come by idleness to a commonweal, have from time to time provided with all diligence that sharp and severe laws might be made for the correction and amendment of this evil. The Egyptians had a law, that every man should weekly[m] bring his name to the chief rulers of the province, and therewithal declare what trade of life he occupied[n], to the intent that idleness might be worthily punished, and diligent labour duly rewarded[6]. The Athenians did chastise sluggish and slothful people no less than they did heinous and grievous offenders, considering, as the truth is, that idleness causeth much mischief. The Areopagites called every man to a strait account, how he lived; and, if they found any loiterers, that did not profit the commonweal by one means or other, they were driven out and banished, as unprofitable members, that did only hurt and corrupt the body[7]. And in this realm of England good and godly laws have been divers times made[8], that no idle vagabonds and loitering runagates should be suffered to go from town to town, from place to place, without punishment; which neither serve God nor their Prince, but devour the sweet fruits of other men's labour, being common liars, drunkards, swearers, thieves, whoremasters, and murderers, refusing all honest labour, and give themselves to nothing else but to invent and do mischief, whereof they are more desirous and greedy than is any lion of his prey.

Herodotus.

To remedy this inconvenience, let all parents, and others which have the care and governance of youth, so bring them up either in good learning, labour, or some honest occupation or trade, whereby they may be able in time to come, not only to sustain themselves competently, but also to relieve and supply the necessity and want of others. And St. Paul saith, *Let him that hath stolen steal no more*, and he that hath deceived others,

Eph. iv, [25, 28.]

[m] weekly] *so in all.* [n] occupied] used 1623.

6 Νόμον δὲ Αἰγυπτίοισι τόνδε Ἄμασίς ἐστι ὁ καταστήσας· ἀποδεικνύναι ἔτεος ἑκάστου τῷ νομάρχῃ πάντα τινὰ Αἰγυπτίων ὅθεν βιοῦται· μηδὲ ποιεῦντα ταῦτα, μηδὲ ἀποφαίνοντα δικαίην ζόην, ἰθύνεσθαι θανάτῳ. Σόλων δὲ ὁ Ἀθηναῖος λαβὼν ἐξ Αἰγύπτου τοῦτον τὸν νόμον Ἀθηναίοισι ἔθετο· τῷ ἐκεῖνοι ἐς αἰεὶ χρέωνται, ἐόντι ἀμώμῳ νόμῳ. Herod. II, 177.

7 Plutarch says that by Draco's laws almost all offences were punished by death, ὥστε καὶ τοὺς ἀργίας ἁλόντας ἀποθνήσκειν. Solon, p. 87 E, ed. Francof. 1599. He also says that Solon, τῆς χώρας τὴν φύσιν ὁρῶν τοῖς γεωργοῦσι γλίσχρως διαρκοῦσαν, ἀργὸν τε καὶ σχολαστὴν ὄχλον οὐ δυναμένην τρέφειν, ταῖς τέχναις ἀξίωμα περιέθηκε, καὶ τὴν ἐξ Ἀρείου πάγου βουλὴν ἔταξεν ἐπισκοπεῖν ὅθεν ἕκαστος ἔχει τὰ ἐπιτήδεια, καὶ τοὺς ἀργοὺς κολάζειν. Ibid. p. 90 E.

8 See *Stat.* 22 *Hen. VIII*, *c.* 12; 3 & 4 *Edw. VI*, *c.* 16.

or used unlawful ways to get his living, leave off the same, *and labour rather, working with his hands that thing which is good, that he may have* that which is necessary for himself, and also be able *to give unto others that stand in need of his help.*

The Prophet David thinketh him happy that liveth upon his labour, saying, *When thou eatest the labours of thine hands, happy art thou, and well is thee.* This happiness or blessing consisteth in these and such like points. First, *it is the gift of God,* as Salomon saith, *when one eateth and drinketh, and receiveth good of his labour.* Secondarily[o], when one liveth of his own labour, so it be honest and good, he liveth of it with a good conscience; and an upright conscience is a treasure inestimable. Thirdly, he eateth his bread, not with brawling and chiding, but with peace and quietness, when he quietly laboureth for the same according to St. Paul's admonition. Fourthly, he is no man's bondman for his meat sake, nor needeth not for that to hang upon the good will of other men; but so liveth of his own, that he is able to give part to others. And, to conclude, the labouring man and his family, whiles they are busily occupied in their labour, be free from many temptations and occasions of sin which they that live in idleness are subject unto.

Ps. cxxviii, [2.]

Eccles. iii, [13.]

And here ought artificers and labouring men, who be at wages for their work and labour, to consider their conscience to God and their duty to their neighbour, lest they abuse their time in idleness, so defrauding them which be at charge both with great wages and dear commons. They be worse than idle men indeed, for that they seek to have wages for their loitering. It is less danger to God to be idle for no gain, than by idleness to win out of their neighbours' purses wages for that which is not deserved. It is true, that Almighty God is angry with such as do defraud[ι] the hired man of his wages: the cry of that injury ascendeth up to God's ear for vengeance. And as true it is, that the hired man who useth deceit in his labour is a thief before God. *Let no man,* saith St. Paul to the Thessalonians, *subtilly beguile his brother, let him not defraud him in his business: for the Lord is revenger*[p] *of such deceits*[9]. Whereupon he that will have a good conscience to God, that labouring man, I say, which dependeth wholly upon God's benediction ministering all things sufficient for his living, let him use his time in

ι [Deut. xxiv, 15: James v, 4.]

1 Thess. iv, [6.]

o secondarily] secondly *from* 1582.

p is revenger] is a revenger 1563 C—F, *and from* 1574.

9 Ne quis supergrediatur neque circumveniat in negotio fratrem suum: quoniam vindex est Dominus de his omnibus. *Vulg.*

faithful[q] labour; and, when his labour by sickness or other misfortune doth cease, yet let him think, for that in his health he served God and his neighbour truly, he shall not want in time of necessity. God upon respect of his fidelity in health will recompense his indigence, to move the hearts of good men to relieve such decayed men in sickness. Where otherwise whatsoever is gotten by idleness shall have no foison[r][10] to help in time of need. Let the labouring man therefore eschew for his part this vice of idleness and deceit, remembering that St. Paul exhorteth every man to *lay away* deceit, dissimulation, and *lying*, and to *use truth* and plainness *to his neighbour, because*, saith he, *we be members together* in one body, under one head, Christ our Saviour. Eph. iv, [25; and 4, 12, 15.]

And here might be charged the serving men of this realm, who spend their time in much idleness of life, nothing regarding the opportunity of their time, forgetting how service is no heritage, how age will creep upon them; where wisdom were they should expend their idle time in some good business, whereby they might increase in knowledge, and so the more worthy to be ready for every man's service. It is a great rebuke to them, that they study not either to write fair, to keep a book of account, to study the tongues, and so to get wisdom and knowledge in such books and works as be now plentifully set out in print of all manner languages[s]. Let young men consider the precious value of their time, and waste it not in idleness, in jollity, in gaming, in banqueting, in ruffians' company. Youth is but vanity, and must be accounted for before God. *How merry and glad soever thou be in thy youth, O young man*, saith the Preacher, *how glad soever thy heart be in thy young days*, how fast and freely soever thou *follow the ways of thine own heart and the lust of thine own eyes; yet be thou sure that God shall bring thee into judgment for all these things.* Eccles. xi, [9.]

God of his mercy put it into the hearts and minds of all them that have the sword of punishment in their hands, or have fami-

[q] in faithful] in a faithful 1623. [r] foison] means 1623. [s] manner languages] manner of languages 1623.

[10] foison, a French word, probably derived from the Latin *fusio*: indeed *fusion* occurs in old Scottish writers. It signifies, 1. abundance (as in *Shakespeare, Ant. and Cleop.* II, 7,

They know
By the height, the lowness, or the mean, if dearth,
Or foizon, follow ;)

2. sap, pith, substance, strength, as in this place, and in the adjective *foisonless*. See *Jamieson's Scottish Dictionary* and *Supplement*.

lies under their governance, to labour to redress this great enormity of all such as live idly and unprofitably in the commonweal, to the great dishonour of God and the grievous plague of his seely people! To leave sin unpunished, and to neglect the good bringing up of youth, is nothing else but to kindle the Lord's wrath against us, and to heap plagues upon our own heads. As long as the adulterous people were suffered to live licentiously without reformation, so long did the plague continue and increase in Israel, as ye may see in the book of Numbers. But, when due correction was done upon them, the Lord's anger was straightway pacified, and the plague ceased. Let all officers therefore look straitly to their charge. Let all masters of households reform this abuse in their families. Let them use the authority that God hath given them. Let them not maintain vagabonds and idle persons, but deliver the realm and their households from such noisome loiterers; that, idleness, the mother of all mischief, being clean taken away, Almighty God may turn his dreadful anger away from us, and confirm the covenant of peace upon us for ever, through the merits of Jesus Christ, our only Lord and Saviour. To whom with the Father and the Holy Ghost be all honour and glory world without end. Amen.

Numb. xxv, [1-8.]

AN HOMILY

OF REPENTANCE

AND OF TRUE RECONCILIATION UNTO GOD.

THERE is nothing that the Holy Ghost doth so much labour in all the Scriptures to beat into men's heads, as repentance, amendment of life, and speedy returning unto the Lord God of hosts. And no marvel why: for we do daily and hourly, by our wickedness and stubborn disobedience, horribly fall away from God, thereby purchasing unto ourselves, if he should deal with us according to his justice, eternal damnation. So that no doctrine is so necessary in the Church of God, as is the doctrine of repentance and amendment of life. And verily the true preachers of the Gospel of the kingdom of heaven, and of the glad and joyful tidings of salvation, have always in their godly sermons and preachings unto the people joined these two together, I mean repentance and forgiveness of sins; even as our Saviour Jesus Christ did appoint himself, saying, *So it behoved Christ to suffer, and to rise again the third day, and that repentance and forgiveness of sins should be preached in his Name among all nations.* And therefore the holy Apostle doth in the Acts speak after this manner: *I have witnessed both to the Jews and to the Gentiles the repentance towards God and faith towards our Lord Jesu*[a] *Christ.* Did not John Baptist, Zachary's son, begin his ministry with the doctrine of repentance, saying, *Repent, for the kingdom of God is at hand?* The like doctrine did our Saviour Jesus Christ preach himself[a], and commanded his Apostles to preach the same.

The doctrine of repentance is most necessary.

Luke xxiv, [46, 47.]

Acts xx, [21.]

Matt. iii, [2.]

a Matt. iv, [17.]

I might here allege very many places out of the Prophets, in the which this most wholesome doctrine of repentance is very earnestly urged, as most needful for all degrees and orders of men; but one shall be sufficient at this present time. These are the words of Joel the Prophet: *Therefore also now the Lord saith, Return unto me with all your heart, with fasting, weeping, and mourning; and rent*[b] *your hearts, and not your clothes, and*

Joel ii, [12, 13.]

[a] Jesu] Jesus *from* 1582. [b] mourning; and rent] mourning; rent *from* 1571.

return unto the Lord your God: for he is gracious and merciful, slow to anger, and of great compassion, and ready to pardon wickedness. Whereby[1] it is given us to understand, that we have here a perpetual rule appointed unto us, which ought to be observed and kept at all times; and that there is none other way whereby the wrath of God may be pacified and his anger assuaged, that the fierceness of his fury, and the plagues or[c] destruction which by his righteous judgment he had determined to bring upon us, may depart, be removed, and taken away.

A perpetual rule which all must follow.

Where he saith, *But now therefore saith the Lord, Return unto me*, it is not without great importance that the Prophet speaketh so. For he had afore set forth at large unto them the horrible vengeance of God, which no man was able to abide; and therefore he doth move them to repentance, to obtain mercy: as if he should say, I will not have these things to be so taken, as though there were no hope of grace left; for, although ye do by your sins deserve to be utterly destroyed, and God by his righteous judgments hath determined to bring no small destruction upon you, *yet, now* that[d] ye are in a manner on the very edge of the sword[2], if ye will speedily *return unto him*, he will most gently and most mercifully receive you into favour again. Whereby we are admonished that repentance is never too late, so that it be true and earnest. For, sith that God in the Scriptures will be called *our Father*, doubtless he doth follow the nature and property of gentle and merciful fathers, which seek nothing so much as[e] the returning again and amendment of their children, as Christ doth abundantly teach[β] in the parable of the Prodigal Son. Doth not the Lord himself say by the Prophet[γ], *I will not the death of the wicked, but that he turn from his wicked ways, and live?* And in another place[3]: *If we confess our sins*[f], *God is faithful and righteous to forgive us our sins, and to make us clean from all wickedness.* Which most comfortable promises are confirmed by many examples of the Scriptures. When the Jews did willingly receive and imbrace the wholesome counsel of the Prophet Esay, God by and by did reach

[Matt. vi, 9.]

β Luke xv, [11–32.]

γ Ezek. xviii, [23.]

Is. i, [18.]

1 John i, [9.]

Is. xxxvii.

c or] of 1623. d now that] know that 1623. e much as] much than 1563 A–F. f confess our sins] confess our sin *from* 1570.

1 About six pages beginning here, and ending "repent, turn, and amend" (p. 532, l. 8), are translated, almost verbatim, from Gualther's Sixth Homily on the Prophet Joel. A few passages from the original are given in footnotes.

2 Dum quasi in acie novaculae res vestrae sitae sunt. *Gualt.*

3 After the quotation from Ezekiel Gualther goes on thus. Item: *Si peccata vestra fuerint ut coccus, nive albiora reddentur; si rubeant instar purpurae, sicut lana nativa fient.* Et Joannes dicit: *Si confiteamur* &c. See note 8.

his helping hand unto them, and by his angel did in one night slay the most worthy and valiant soldiers of Sennacherib's camp. Whereunto may king Manasses be added, who after all manner of damnable wickedness returned unto the Lord, and therefore was heard of him, and restored again into his kingdom. The same grace and favour did[e] the sinful woman, Magdalene, Zaccheus, the poor thief, and many other feel[4]. All which things ought to serve for our comfort against the tentations[g] [5] of our consciences, whereby the devil goeth about to shake, or rather to overthrow, our faith. For every one of us ought to apply the same unto himself, and say, *Yet now return unto the Lord;* neither let the remembrance of thy former life discourage thee; yea, the more wicked that it hath been, the more fervent and earnest let thy repentance or returning be; and forthwith thou shalt feel *the ears of the Lord wide open unto thy prayers*[ζ].

δ 2 Chron. xxxiii, [1–13.]

e Luke vii, [48; viii, 2;] xix, [9; xxiii, 43.]

ζ [1 Pet. iii, 12.]

But let us more narrowly look upon the commandment of the Lord touching this matter. *Turn unto me*, saith he by his Prophet[h] Joel, *with all your hearts, with fasting, with weeping*[i], *and mourning; rent your hearts, and not your garments*, &c. In which words he comprehendeth all manner of things that can be spoken of repentance, which is a turning[j] again of the whole man unto God, from whom we be fallen away by sin. But, that the whole discourse thereof may the better be borne away, we shall first consider in order four principal points; that is, from what we must return, to whom we must return, by whom we may be able to convert, and the manner how to turn to God.

First, from whence or from what things we must return. Truly we must return from those things whereby we have been withdrawn, plucked, and led away from God. And these generally are our *sins*, which, as the holy Prophet Esay doth testify, *do separate God and us, and hide his face, that he will not hear us*. But under the name of sin [are reckoned[l]][6], not only those gross words and deeds which by the common judgment of men

From whence we must return[k].

Is. lix, [2.]

g tentations] temtations 1563 G, temptations *from* 1563 H. *See note* 5. h by his Prophet] by the holy Prophet 1623. i fasting, with weeping] fasting, weeping *from* 1567. j turning] returning *from* 1570. k whence we must return] whence we must turn 1623. l are reckoned] *wanting in all. See note* 6.

4 Eandem gratiam peccatrix illa Evangelica, Magdalene, Zacheus, latro Christi in cruce socius, et alii complures experti sunt. *Gualt.*

5 Adversus conscientiae tentationes. *Gualt.*

6 Sub peccati autem titulo censentur, non modo crassiora illa dicta aut facta quae communi hominum consensu pro turpibus et illicitis habentur, verum etiam cupiditates carnis, quae voluntati et Spiritui Dei (ut Paulus ait) reluctantur, et proinde serio coerceri et restingui debent. *Gualt.*

are counted to be filthy and unlawful, and so consequently abominable sins, but also the filthy lusts and inward concupiscences of the flesh, which, as St. Paul testifieth, do resist the will and Spirit of God, and therefore ought earnestly to be bridled and kept under. We must repent of the false and erroneous opinions that we have had of God, and the wicked superstition that doth breed of the same, the unlawful worshipping and service of God, and other like. All these things must they forsake that will truly turn unto the Lord and repent aright. For, sith that[η] *for such things the wrath of God cometh upon the children of disobedience,* no end of punishment ought to be looked for as long as we continue in such things. Therefore they be here condemned which will seem to be repentant sinners, and yet will not forsake their idolatry and superstition.

Gal. v, [17.]

η Eph. v, [6.]

Unto whom we ought to return.

Secondly, we must see unto whom we ought to return. *Revertimini usque ad me*[7], saith the Lord, that is, *Return as far as unto me.* We must then *return unto the Lord:* yea, we must return unto him alone; for he alone is the truth, and the fountain of all goodness. But we must labour that we do return *as far as unto* him, and that we do never cease and rest[m] till we have apprehended and taken hold upon him. But this must be done by faith; for, sith that[θ] *God is a spirit,* he can by none[n] other mean[o] be apprehended and taken hold upon. Therefore[p], first, they do greatly err which do not turn unto God, but unto the creatures, or unto the inventions of men, or unto their own merits; secondly, they that do begin to return unto the Lord, and do faint in the midway, afore[q] they come to the mark that is appointed unto them.

θ [John iv, 24.]

By whom we must return unto God.

Thirdly, because we have of our own selves nothing to present us to God, and do no less flee from him after our fall than our first parent Adam did, which, when[r] he had sinned, did seek[ι] to hide himself from the sight of God, we have need of a Mediator for to bring and reconcile us unto him, who for our sins is angry with us. The same is Jesus Christ: who, being true and natural God, equal and of one substance with the Father, did at the time appointed take upon him our frail nature in the blessed Virgin's womb, and that of her undefiled

ι [Gen. iii, 8.]

m and rest] nor rest *from* 1567. n none] no *from* 1563 G. o mean] means 1623. p Therefore] Wherefore *from* 1582. q afore] before 1623. r which, when] who, when 1623.

7 The text prefixed to Gualther's Homily is, *Sed et nunc dicit Dominus, Convertimini usque ad me in toto corde vestro* &c., being *Joel* ii, 12, 13, from the Zurich version published in 1543; and here he has, *Usque ad me,* inquit.

substance; that so he might be a Mediator betwixt[s] God and us, and pacify his wrath. Of him doth the Father himself speak from heaven, saying[κ], *This is my wellbeloved Son, in whom I am pleased*[t]. And he himself in his Gospel doth cry out and say[λ], *I am the way, the truth, and the life: no man cometh unto the Father but by me.* For he alone did with the sacrifice of his body and blood make satisfaction unto the justice of God for our sins[8]. The Apostles do testify[ν] that he was *exalted for to give repentance and remission of sins unto Israel:* both which things he himself did command[ξ] to be *preached in his Name*. Therefore they are greatly deceived that preach repentance without Christ, and teach the simple and ignorant that it consisteth only in the works of men. They may indeed speak many things of good works, and of amendment of life and manners; but without Christ[o] they be all vain and unprofitable. They that think that they have done much of themselves toward[u] repentance are so much more the further from God, because that they[x] do seek those things in their own works and merits which ought only to be sought in our Saviour Jesu[y] Christ, and in the merits of his death, passion[z], and bloodshedding.

κ Matt. iii, [17;] xvii, [5.]
λ John xiv, [6.]
John i; iii: 1 Pet. i.
ν Acts v, [31.]
ξ Luke xxiv, [47.]
o John xv, [4, 5.]

Fourthly, this holy Prophet Joel doth lively express the manner of this our returning or repentance, comprehending all the inward and outward things that may be here observed. First, he will have us to return unto God *with our whole heart;* whereby he doth remove and put away all hypocrisy, lest the same might justly be said unto us[π], *This people draweth near unto me with their mouth, and worshippeth*[b] *me with their lips, but their heart is far off from me.* Secondly, he requireth a sincere and pure love of godliness and of the true worshipping and service of God; that is to say, that, forsaking all manner of things that are repugnant and contrary unto God's will, we do give our hearts unto him, and all the[c] whole strength of our bodies and souls, according to that which is written in the Law, *Thou shalt love the Lord thy God with all thy heart, with all thy soul, and*

The manner of our returning[a].
π Isa. xxix, [13:] Matt. xv, [8.]
Deut. vi, [5.]

[s] betwixt] between *from* 1582. [t] am pleased] am well pleased *from* 1567. [u] toward] towards *from* 1567. [x] because that they] because they 1623. [y] Jesu] Jesus *from* 1567. [z] death, passion] death, and passion 1623. [a] of our returning] of our turning 1623. [b] worshippeth] worship *from* 1582. [c] and all the] and the 1623.

8 Is enim solus sui corporis et sanguinis sacrificio peccata nostra expiat, simulque ex verbi sui semine eos in Dei filios regenerat, et ad omne opus bonum idoneos reddit, qui natura filii irae nati fuerant. *Gualt.* Although our Homilist adopted no more than the first clause of this sentence, he transferred to his own margin three references to places in Scripture which belong to the remainder, *John* i, [12]; iii, [36]: 1 *Pet.* i, [23].

Halting on both sides.

True fast.[e]

Ps. xxv; xxxii; li; ciii; cxliii.

ρ Ps. lii, [1–5.]

with all thy strength. Here therefore nothing is left unto us that we may give unto the world and unto the lusts of the flesh. For, sith that the heart is the fountain of all our works, as many as do with their whole[d] heart turn unto the Lord do live unto him only. Neither do they yet repent truly that, halting on both sides, do otherwhiles[9] obey God, but by and by do think, that, laying him aside, it is lawful for them to serve the world and the flesh. And, because that we are letted by the natural corruption of our own flesh and the wicked affections of the same, he doth bid us also to return *with fasting;* not thereby understanding a superstitious abstinence and choosing of meats, but a true discipline or taming of the flesh, whereby the nourishments of filthy lusts and of stubborn contumacy and pride may be withdrawn and plucked away from it. Whereunto he doth add *weeping and mourning,* which do contain an outward profession of repentance; which is very needful and necessary, that so we may partly set forth the righteousness of God, when by such means we do testify that we deserved punishments at his hands, and partly stop the offence that was openly given unto the weak. This did David see, who, being not content to have bewept and bewailed his sins privately, would publicly in his Psalms declare and set forth the righteousness of God in punishing sin, and also stay them that mought[f] have abused his example to sin the more boldly. Therefore they are furthest from true repentance that will not confess and acknowledge their sins[g], nor yet bewail them, but rather[ρ] do most ungodly glory and rejoice in them.

Hypocrites do counterfeit all manner of things.

Now, lest any man should think that repentance doth consist in outward weeping and mourning only, he doth rehearse that wherein the chief of the whole matter doth lie, when he saith, *Rent your hearts, and not your garments, and turn unto the Lord your God.* For the people of the East part of the world were wont to rent their garments, if anything had happened[h] unto them that seemed untolerable[i]. This thing did hypocrites sometime counterfeit and follow, as though the whole repentance did stand in such outward gesture. He teacheth then, that another manner of thing is required; that is, that they must be contrite in their hearts, that they must utterly detest and abhor sins, and, being at defiance with them, return unto

[d] with their whole] with whole 1623. [e] True fast.] *omitted after* 1563. [f] mought] might *from* 1582. [g] their sins] their sin 1563 A–F. [h] had] *omitted* 1623. [i] untolerable] intolerable *from* 1571.

9 otherwhiles: interdum *Gualt.*

the Lord their God, from whom they went away before. For God hath no pleasure in the outward ceremony, but requireth *a contrite and humble heart;* which *he will never despise*, as David doth testify. [Ps. li, [17.]] There is therefore none other use of these[k] outward ceremonies, but as far forth as we are stirred up by them, and do serve to the glory of God and to the edifying of other[10].

How repentance is not unprofitable.

Now doth he add unto this doctrine or exhortation certain goodly[l] reasons, which he doth ground upon the nature and property of God, and whereby he doth teach that true repentance can never be unprofitable or unfruitful. For, as in all other things men's hearts do quail and faint, if they once perceive that they travail in vain, even so most specially in this matter must we take heed and beware that we suffer not ourselves to be persuaded that all that we do is but labour lost; for thereof either sudden desperation doth arise, or a licentious boldness to sin, which at length bringeth unto desperation. Lest any such thing then should happen unto them, he doth certify them of the grace and goodness of God, who is always most ready to receive them into favour again that turn speedily unto him. Which thing he doth prove with the same titles wherewith God doth describe and set forth himself unto Moses[σ], speaking on this manner: *For he is gracious and merciful, slow to anger, of great kindness, and repenteth him of the evil*, that is, such a one as is sorry for your affliction[m]. First, he calleth him gentle, and *gracious*, as he who of his own nature is more prompt and ready to do good than to punish. Whereunto this saying of Esay the Prophet seemeth to pertain, where he saith, *Let the wicked forsake his way, and the unrighteous his own imaginations, and return unto the Lord, and he will have pity on him, and to our God, for he is very ready to forgive.* [Isa. lv, [7.]] Secondly, he doth attribute unto him *mercy*, or rather, according to the Hebrew word, the bowels of mercies, whereby are signified[n] the natural affections of parents towards their children. Which thing David doth set forth goodly, saying, *As a father hath compassion on his children, so hath the Lord compassion on them that fear him: for he knoweth whereof we be made, he remembereth that we are but dust.* [Ps. ciii, [13, 14.]] Thirdly, he saith that he is *slow to anger*,

[σ] Exod. xxxiv, [6.]

[k] of these] to these *from* 1563 B. [l] goodly] godly *from* 1570. [m] affliction] afflictions *from* 1570. [n] are signified] he signified *from* 1563 G.

[10] Nisi quatenus et nos illis excitamur, et eadem gloriae Dei et aliorum aedificationi serviunt. *Gualt.*

that is to say, longsuffering and which is not lightly provoked to wrath. Fourthly, that he is *of much kindness:* for he is that bottomless well of all goodness, who rejoiceth to do good unto us. Therefore did he create and make men, that he might have whom he should do good unto, and make partakers of his heavenly riches. Fifthly, he *repenteth of the evil*, that is to say, he doth call back again and revoke the punishment which he had threatened, when he seeth men repent, turn, and amend.

Against the Novatians.

Whereupon we do not without a just cause detest and abhor the damnable opinion of them which do most wickedly go about to persuade the simple and ignorant people, that, if we chance, after we be once come to God and graffed[o] in his Son Jesu[p] Christ, to fall into some horrible sin, repentance[q] shall be unprofitable unto us, there is no more hope of reconciliation, or to be received again into the favour and mercy of God. And, that they may give the better colour unto their pestilent and pernicious error, they do commonly bring in the sixth and tenth chapters of the Epistle to the Hebrews and the second chapter of the second Epistle of Peter; not considering that in those places the holy Apostles do not speak of the daily falls that we, as long as we carry about this body of sin, are subject unto, but of the final falling away from Christ and his Gospel: which is a sin against[r] the Holy Ghost, that shall never be forgiven; because that they that do[r] utterly forsake the known truth do hate Christ and his word, they do crucify and mock him (but to their utter destruction), and therefore fall into desperation, and cannot repent. And, that this is the true meaning of the Holy Spirit of God, it appeareth by many other places of the Scriptures, which promiseth unto all true repentant sinners, and to them that with their whole heart do return[s] unto the Lord their God, free pardon and remission of their sins.

[Heb. vi, 4–6; x, 26–29; 2 Pet. ii, 20, 21.]

r Matt. xii, [31:] Mark iii, [29.]

The sin against the Holy Ghost.

Jer. iv, [1.]

For the probation hereof we read this: *O Israel,* saith the holy Prophet Hieremy, *if thou return, return unto me, saith the Lord; and, if thou put away thine abominations out of my sight, then shalt thou not be moved*[t]. Again, these are Esay's words: *Let the wicked forsake his own ways, and the unrighteous his own imaginations, and turn again unto the Lord, and he will have mercy upon him, and to our God, for he is ready to forgive.* And in the[u] Prophet Osee the godly do exhort one another after this manner: *Come, and let us turn again unto the Lord: for he hath*

Isa. lv, [7.]

Hos. vi, [1.]

o graffed] grafted 1623. p Jesu] Jesus 1587, 1595, 1623. q repentance] *omitted* 1623. r they that do] they do *from* 1582. s do return] do turn *from* 1574. t moved] removed 1623. u And in the] And the 1623.

smitten us, and he will heal us; he hath wounded us, and he will bind us up again. It is most evident and plain that these things ought to be understanded[x] of them that were with the Lord afore and by their sins and wickedness[y] were gone away from him; for we do not turn again unto him with whom we were never before, but we come unto him.

Note.

Now unto all them that will return unfeignedly unto the Lord their God the favour and mercy of God unto forgiveness of sins is liberally offered. Whereby it followeth necessarily, that, although we do, after we be once come to God and grafted[z] in his Son Jesu Christ, fall[a] into great sins, (*for*[v] *there is no righteous man upon the earth that sinneth not,* and, *if we say we have no sin, we deceive ourselves, and the truth is not in us,*) yet, if we rise again by repentance, and, with a full purpose of amendment of life, do flee unto the mercy of God, taking sure hold thereupon through faith in his Son Jesu Christ, there is an assured and infallible hope of pardon and remission of the same, and that we shall be received again into the favour of our heavenly Father.

v Eccles. vii, [20:] 1 John i, [8.]

It is written of David[φ], *I have found a man according to mine own heart;* or, *I have found David the son of Jesse, a man according to mine own heart, who will do all things that I will.* This is a godly[b] commendation of David. It is also most certain, that he did steadfastly believe the promise[χ] that was made him touching the Messias, who should come of him touching the flesh, and that by the same faith he was justified and grafted[c] in our Saviour Jesu Christ to come. And yet afterwards he fell horribly, committing[ψ] most detestable adultery and damnable murder: and yet, as soon as he cried, *Peccavi, I have sinned unto the Lord*[ω][11], his sin being forgiven, he was received into favour again.

φ [1 Sam. xiii, 14: Ps. lxxxix, 20:] Acts xiii, [22.]

χ 2 Sam. vii, [12–16, 28, 29.]

ψ 2 Sam. xi.

ω 2 Sam. xii, [13.]

Now will we come unto Peter, of whom no man can doubt but that he was grafted[d] in our Saviour Jesu Christ long[e] afore his denial. Which thing may easily be proved by the answer which he did, in his name and in the name of his fellow Apostles, make unto our Saviour Jesu Christ, when he said unto them[α], *Will ye also go away? Master,* saith he, *to whom shall we go? thou hast the words of eternal life; and we believe and know that thou art the Christ*[f]*, the Son of the living God.*

Peter.

α John vi, [67–69.]

x understanded] understood 1595, 1623. y wickedness] wickednesses 1582, 1587, 1623. z grafted] grafted 1623. a Jesu Christ, fall] Jesus Christ, fall *from* 1567. b a godly] a great 1623. c, d grafted] grafted 1623. e Jesu Christ long] Jesus Christ long *from* 1571. f the Christ] that Christ *from* 1574.

11 Peccavi Domino. *Vulg.*

Whereunto may be added the like confession of Peter, where Christ doth give this[g] most infallible testimony[β]: *Thou art blessed, Simon son*[h] *of Jonas; for neither flesh nor blood hath revealed this unto thee, but my Father which is in heaven.* These words are sufficient to prove that Peter was already justified through this his lively faith in the only begotten Son of God, whereof he made so notable and so solemn a confession. But did not he[γ] afterwards most cowardly deny his Master, although he had heard of him[δ], *Whosoever denieth me before men, I will deny him before my Father?* Nevertheless, as soon as with weeping eyes and with a sobbing heart he did acknowledge his offence, and with earnest[i] repentance did flee unto the mercy of God, taking sure hold thereupon through faith in him whom he had so shamefully denied, his sin was forgiven him, and, for a certificate and assurance thereof, the room of his Apostleship was not denied unto him. But now mark what doth follow. After the same holy Apostle had[ε] on Whitsunday with the rest of the disciples received the gift of the Holy Ghost most abundantly, he committed no small offence in Antiochia by bringing the consciences of the faithful into doubt by his example; so that Paul[ζ] was fain to rebuke him to his face, because that he *walked not uprightly*, or went not the right way, *in the Gospel.* Shall we now say, that after this grievous offence he was utterly excluded and shut out from the grace and mercy of God, and that this his trespass, whereby he was a stumbling-block unto many, was unpardonable? God forfend[k] we should say so.

β [Matt. xvi, 17.]
γ Matt. xxvi, [69–75.]
δ Matt. x, [33.]
ε Acts ii, [1, 4, 14, 37, 38.]
ζ Gal. ii, [11–14.]

What we must beware of.

But, as these examples are not brought in to the end that we should thereby take a boldness to sin, presuming on the mercy and goodness of God, but to the end that, if through the frailness of our own flesh and the temptation of the devil we fall into the like[l] sins, we should in no wise despair of the mercy and goodness of God; even so must we beware and take heed that we do in no wise think in our hearts, imagine, or believe, that we are able to repent aright, or to turn effectually unto the Lord, by our own might and strength. For this must be verified in all men[η], *Without me ye can do nothing.* Again[θ], *Of ourselves we are not able as much as to think a good thought.* And in another place[ι], *It is God that worketh in us both the will and the deed.* For this cause, although Hieremy had said be-

η John xv, [5.]
θ 2 Cor. iii, [5.]
ι Phil. ii, [13.]

g give this] give us 1623. h Simon son] Simon the son *from* 1567. i with earnest] with an earnest *from* 1582. k forfend] defend *from* 1563 G. l into the like] into like *from* 1574.

fore, *If thou return, O Israel, return unto me, saith the Lord,* yet afterwards he saith, *Turn thou me, O Lord, and I shall be turned; for thou art the Lord my God.* And therefore that holy writer and ancient father Ambrose doth plainly affirm that the turning of the heart unto God is of God [12]; as the Lord himself doth testify by his Prophet, saying, *And I will give thee*[m] *an heart to know me, that I am the Lord; and they shall be my people, and I will be their God; for they shall return unto me with their whole heart.*

Jer. iv, [1;] xxxi, [18.]

Ambros. de Vocat. Gent. Lib. 1, cap. 9.

[Jer. xxiv, 7.]

These things being considered, let us earnestly pray unto the living God, our heavenly Father, that he will vouchsafe by his Holy Spirit to work a true and unfeigned repentance in us; that, after the painful labours and travails of this life, we may[n] live eternally with his Son Jesus Christ. To whom be all praise and glory for ever and ever. Amen.

[m] thee] *so in all.* [n] life, we may] life, may 1623.

12 Omnis homo qui ad Deum convertitur Dei primum gratia commovetur. *De Vocatione Gentium,* I, 8. Concerning the author of this treatise see before, p. 50, n. 10.

THE SECOND PART OF THE HOMILY

OF REPENTANCE.

HITHERTO have ye heard, wellbeloved, how needful and necessary the doctrine of repentance is, and how earnestly it is, throughout[a] all the Scriptures of God, urged and set forth, both by the ancient Prophets, by our Saviour Jesu[b] Christ, and his Apostles; and that, forasmuch as it is the conversion or turning again of the whole man unto God, from whom we go away by sin, these four points ought to be observed; that is, from whence or from what things we must return, unto whōm this our returning must be made, by whose means it ought to be done, that it may be effectual, and, last of all, after what sort we ought to behave ourselves in the same, that it may be profitable unto us, and attain unto the thing that we do seek by it. Ye have also learned, that, as the opinion of them that deny the benefit of repentance unto those that, after they be come to God and graffed[c] in our Saviour Jesu[d] Christ, do, through the frailness of their flesh and the temptation of the devil, fall into some grievous and detestable sin, is most pestilent and pernicious; so we must beware that we do in no wise think, that we are able of our own selves and of our own strength to return unto the Lord our God, from whom we are gone away by our wickedness and sin. Now it shall be declared unto you, what be the true parts of repentance, and what things ought to move us to repent and to return unto the Lord our God with all speed.

There be four parts of repentance.

Repentance, as it is said before, is a true returning unto God, whereby men, forsaking utterly their idolatry and wickedness, do with a lively faith embrace, love, and worship the true living God only, and give themselves to all manner of good works, which by God's word they know to be acceptable unto him. Now there be four parts of repentance, which being set together may be likened unto an[e] easy and short ladde , whereby we may climb from the bottomless pit of perditio ,

[a] throughout] thoroughout 1623. [b] Jesu] Jesus 1587, 1595, 1623. [c] graffed] graf d 1623. [d] Jesu] Jesus 1623. [e] unto an] to an *from* 1570.

that we cast ourselves into by our daily offences and grievous sins, up into the castle or tower of eternal and endless salvation.

The first is the contrition of the heart. For we must be earnestly sorry for our sins, and unfeignedly lament and bewail that we have by them so grievously offended our most bounteous and merciful God; who *so* tenderly *loved us, that he gave* [John iii, 16.] *his only begotten Son* to die a most bitter death and to shed his dear heart blood for our redemption and deliverance. And verily this inward sorrow and grief, being conceived in the heart for the heinousness of sin, if it be earnest and unfeigned, is as a sacrifice to God: as the holy Prophet David doth testify, saying, *A sacrifice to God is a troubled spirit; a contrite and broken* Ps. li, [17.] *heart, O Lord, thou wilt not despise.* But, that this may take place in us, we must be diligent to read and hear the Scriptures and word[f] of God, which most lively do paint out before our eyes[g] our natural uncleanliness[h] and the enormity of our sinful life. For, unless we have a through[i] feeling of our sins, how can it be that we should earnestly be sorry for them? Afore David did hear[a] the word of the Lord by the mouth of the [a] 2 Sam. xii, [1–13.] Prophet Nathan, what heaviness, I pray you, was in him for the adultery and murder[k] that he had committed? So that it might be said right well, that he slept in his own sin. We read in the Acts of the Apostles that, when the people had heard the Acts ii, [37.] sermon of Peter, they were compunct and *pricked in their hearts.* Which thing would never have been, if they had not heard that wholesome sermon of Peter. They therefore that have no mind at all neither to read nor yet to hear God's word, there is but small hope of them, that they will as much as once set their feet or take hold upon the first staff or step of this ladder, but rather will sink deeper and deeper into the bottomless pit of perdition. For, if at any time through the remorse of their conscience, which accuseth them, they feel any inward grief, sorrow, or heaviness for their sins; forasmuch as they want the salve and comfort of God's word, which they do despise, it will be unto them rather a mean to bring them to utter desperation than otherwise.

The second is an unfeigned confession and acknowledging of our sins unto God; whom by them we have so grievously offended, that, if he should deal with us according to his justice,

[f] and word] and the word *from* 1582. [g] our eyes] your eyes 1571–1595. [h] uncleanliness] uncleanness *from* 1574. [i] a through] a thorough 1623. [k] and murder] and the murder *from* 1582.

we do deserve a thousand hells, if there could be so many. Y t, [β Ezek. xviii, [21, 22.]] if we will[β] with a sorrowful and contrite heart make an - feigned confession of them unto God, he will freely and fran ly forgive them, and so put all our wickedness out of remembra ce before the sight of his Majesty, that they shall no more be thought upon. Hereunto doth pertain the golden saying of he [Ps. xxxii, [5.]] holy Prophet David, where he saith on this manner: *Then I c- knowledged my sin unto thee, neither did I hide mine iniquity I said, I will confess against myself my wickedness unto the Lo d, and thou forgavest the ungodliness of my sin.* These are also he [1 John i, [9.]] words of John the Evangelist: *If we confess our sins, Go is faithful and righteous to forgive us our sins, and to make us cl an from all our wickedness.* Which ought to be understanded[l] of the confession that is made unto God. For these are St. u- [In Epist. ad Jul. Comit. 30.] gustine's words: That confession which is made unto Go is required by God's law; whereof John the Apostle speak h, saying, *If we confess our sins, God is faithful and righteous to forgive us our sins, and to make us clean from all our wickedne s:* for without this confession sin is not forgiven[1]. This is t en the chiefest and most principal confession that in the Scriptu es and word of God we are bidden to make, and without the wh ch we shall never obtain pardon and forgiveness of our sins.

Indeed besides this there is another kind of confession, wh ch is needful and necessary. And of the same doth St. James sp ak [James v, [16.]] after this manner, saying, *Acknowledge your faults one to n- other, and pray one for another, that ye may be saved:* as if he should say, Open that which grieveth you, that a remedy ay be found. And this is commanded both for him that compl in- eth and for him that heareth, that the one should shew his g ef to the other. The true meaning of it is, that the faithful ou ht to acknowledge their offences, whereby some hatred, ranc ur, grudge[m], or malice have risen[n] or grown among them on to another, that a brotherly reconciliation may be had; with ut

[l] understanded] understood 1595, 1623. [m] grudge] ground *from* 1574. [n] have risen] h ving risen *from* 1567.

[1] These words have not been found in St. Augustine nor in any of the writings which have been attributed to him. Nothing like them occurs in the treatise cited in the margin, first printed by Amerbach in 1493 as an Epistle (No. CXI) addressed "ad Julianum Comitem," afterwards entitled "De Salutaribus Documentis," and since assigned by the Benedictine editors to Paulinus of Aquileia, *Augustin. Opp.* VI *Append.* 193– 10. But the thought is contained in a Sermon on the text here quoted fro St. John, which used to pass as Augusti e's, but which has been displaced by the Benedictines as consisting of cc. 12 and 13 of Alcuin's treatise *De Virtutib et Vitiis: Augustin. Opp.* V *Append.* 417 D—G, *Serm.* 214, al. *de Temp.* 66.

the which nothing that we do can be acceptable unto God, as our Saviour Jesus Christ doth witness himself, saying, *When thou offerest thine offering at the altar, if thou rememberest that thy brother hath aught against thee, leave there thine offering, and go and be reconciled, and when thou art reconciled come and offer thine offering.* It may also be thus taken, that we ought to confess our weakness and infirmities one to another, to the end that, knowing each other's frailness, we may the more earnestly pray together unto Almighty God, our heavenly Father, that he will vouchsafe to pardon us our infirmities for his Son Jesus Christ's sake, and not to impute them unto us, when[y] *he shall render to every man according to his works.*

Matt. v, [23, 24.]

y [Matt. xvi, 27: Rom. ii, 6.]

And, whereas the adversaries go about to wrast[o] this place for to maintain their auricular confession withal, they are greatly deceived themselves, and do shamefully deceive others. For, if this text ought to be understanded[p] of auricular confession, then the priests are as much bound to confess themselves unto the lay people, as the lay people are bound to confess themselves to them. And, if to pray is to absolve, then the laity by this place hath as great authority to absolve the priests, as the priests have to absolve the laity. This did Johannes Scotus, otherwise called Duns[q], well perceive, who upon this place writeth on this manner[2]. "Neither doth it seem unto

Answer to the adversaries, which maintain auricular confession.

Joh. Scotus, Lib. iv Sent., Dist. xvii, Quaest. 1.

o wrast] wrest *from* 1567. p understanded] understood 1587, 1595, 1623. q Duns] Downs *or* Dounes *till* 1567.

2 After stating his opinion that confession is required by divine commandment, and then shewing that no express words of Christ to that effect are recorded by the Evangelists, Scotus goes on thus. Numquid dicemus . . . quod illud praeceptum habetur ex verbis alicujus Apostoli? Dicitur quod sic de illo verbo Jacobi quinto, *Confitemini alterutrum peccata* &c. Sed nec per hoc videtur mihi quod Jacobus praeceptum hoc dedit nec praeceptum a Christo promulgavit. Primum non. Unde enim sibi auctoritas obligandi totam Ecclesiam, cum esset Episcopus Ecclesiae Ierosolymitanae? Nisi dicas illam Ecclesiam in principio fuisse principalem, et per consequens ejus Episcopum principalem Patriarcham: quod non concederent Romani . . . Nec secundum videtur: quia &c. . . .

Utrumque etiam membrum simul probatur per illa verba annexa. Dicendo enim, *Confitemini alterutrum*, non magis dicit confessionem faciendam esse sacerdoti quam alii: subdit enim, *Et orate pro invicem, ut salvemini;* ubi nullus diceret ipsum instituisse nec promulgasse praeceptum divinum. Sed intellectus ejus est: [*ed.* est,] sicut in illo verbo, *Confitemini alterutrum*, persuasio ad humilitatem, ut scilicet generaliter nos confiteamur apud proximos peccatores (juxta illud, *Si dixerimus quia peccatum non habemus, nosmetipsos seducimus* &c.); ita per secundum persuadet ad charitatem fraternam, ut scilicet per charitatem fraternam subveniamus nobis invicem. *Duns Scot. in Sentent.* IV, xvii, *Quaest. Unic.*, §§ 15, 16.

But the Homilist seems to have taken the quotation, and two or three sentences preceding it, from the *Loci Communes* of Musculus: at least his translation agrees almost verbatim with the passage as given, not with scholar-like accuracy, by Musculus in that work, *De Poenit. p.* 258 *ed. Basil.* 1599.

me that James did give this commandment, or that he did set 't forth as being received of Christ. For, first and foremost, when e had he authority to bind the whole Church, sith that he w s only Bishop of the Church of Jerusalem? Except thou wilt sa , that the same Church was at the beginning the head Churc , and consequently that he was the head Bishop; which thing t e see of Rome will never grant." "The understanding of it th n is, as in these words, *Confess your sins one to another*, a persu - sion to humility, whereby he willeth us to confess ourselv s generally unto our neighbours, that we are sinners, accordi g to this saying[δ], *If we say we have no sin, we deceive ourselv s, and the truth is not in us.*"

δ [1 John i, 8.]

And, where that they do allege this saying of our Savio r Jesu[r] Christ unto the leper, to prove auricular confession o stand on God's word, *Go thy way, and shew thyself unto t e priest*, do they not see that the leper was cleansed from is leprosy afore he was by Christ sent unto the priest for to sh w himself unto him? By the same reason we must be cleans d from our spiritual leprosy, I mean, our sins must be forgiven s, afore that we come to confession. What need we then to t ll forth our sins into the ear of the priest, sith that they e already taken away? Therefore holy Ambrose, in his secon[s] Sermon upon the hundred and nineteenth Psalm, doth say f ll well[3]: "*Go shew thyself unto the priest:* who is the true Pri st but he which is[ε] *the Priest for ever after the order of Melchi e-dech?*" Whereby this holy father doth understand, that, *b th the priesthood and the law being changed*[ζ], we ought to ackno - ledge none other priest for deliverance from our sins but o r Saviour Jesus Christ; who, being our sovereign[t] Bishop, d h with the sacrifice of his body and blood, offered[η] once for e er upon the altar of the cross, most effectually cleanse the spirit al leprosy, and wash away the sins, of all those that with true c n-fession of the same do flee unto him.

Matt. viii, [4.]

Ambrose.

ε [Ps. cx, 4: Heb. v, 6; vi, 20.]

ζ Heb. vii, [12.]

η [Heb. ix, 12, 14; x, 10, 12, 14.]

It is most evident and plain that this auricular confessi n hath not his warrant of God's word; else it had not been law ul for Nectarius, Bishop of Constantinople, upon a just occasion to have put it down. For, when any thing ordained of God is y

Nectarius. Sozom. Eccles. Hist. Lib. vii, cap. 16.

r Jesu] Jesus *from* 1574. s second] *so in all.* t being our sovereign] being sovereign 162 .

3 Sed, ut plenius sanaretur, aperuit oculos ejus, dicens, *Vade, ostende te sacerdoti.* Multos sacerdotes habebat Synagoga: sed qui oculos aperit falsos non videt sacerdotes, verum adspicit. Quis est verus sacerdos, nisi ille qui est *Sacerdos in aeternum?* Ambros. in s. CXVIII (*Hebr.* CXIX) Serm. III, 30; p. I, 1003 D.

the lewdness of men abused, the abuse ought to be taken away, and the thing itself suffered to remain. Moreover, these are St. Augustine's words[4]: "What have I to do with men, that they should hear my confession, as though they were able to heal all my[u] diseases? A curious sort of men to know another man's life, and slothful[x] to correct or amend[y] their own. Why do they seek to hear of me what I am, which will not hear of thee what they are? And how can they tell, when they hear by me of myself, whether I tell the truth or not? sith that[θ] *no*[z] *mortal man knoweth what is in man, but the spirit of man which is in him.*" Augustine would not have written thus, if auricular confession had been used in his time. Being therefore not led with the conscience thereof, let us, with fear and trembling and with a true contrite heart, use that kind of confession that God doth command in his word; and then doubtless, as[ι] *he is faithful and righteous, he will forgive us our sins, and make us clean from all wickedness.* I do not say but that, if any do find themselves troubled in conscience, they may repair to their learned curate or pastor, or to some other godly learned man, and shew the trouble and doubt of their conscience to them, that they may receive at their hand the comfortable salve of God's word: but it is against the true Christian liberty, that any man should be bound to the numbering of his sins, as it hath been used heretofore in the time of blindness and ignorance.

Lib. x Conf. cap. 3.

θ [1 Cor. ii, 11.]

ι [1 John i, 9.]

The third part of repentance is faith, whereby we do apprehend and take hold upon the promises of God touching the free pardon and forgiveness of our sins; which promises are sealed up unto us with the death and bloodshedding of his Son Jesu Christ. For what should avail and profit us to be sorry for our sins, to lament and bewail that we have offended our most bounteous and merciful Father, or to confess and acknowledge our offences and trespasses, though it be done never so earnestly, unless we do steadfastly believe, and be fully persuaded, that God, for his Son Jesu Christ's[a] sake, will forgive us all our sins, and put them out of remembrance and from his sight? There-

u heal all my] heal my 1623. x slothful] slothfully *from* 1574. y or amend] and amend *from* 1563 G. z sith that no] sith no 1623. a Jesu Christ's] Jesus Christ's 1623.

4 Quid mihi ergo est cum hominibus, ut audiant confessiones meas, quasi ipsi sanaturi sint omnes languores meos? Curiosum genus ad cognoscendam vitam alienam, desidiosum ad corrigendam suam. Quid a me quaerunt audire qui sim, qui nolunt a te audire qui sint? Et unde sciunt, cum a meipso de meipso audiunt, an verum dicam? quandoquidem *nemo scit hominum quid agatur in homine, nisi spiritus hominis qui in ipso est.* Augustin. Confess. x, 3; Opp. I, 171 D.

fore they that teach repentance without a lively faith in our Saviour Jesu[b] Christ do teach none other but Judas' repentance; as all the Schoolmen do, which do only allow these three parts of repentance, the contrition of the heart, the confession of the mouth, and the satisfaction of the work[5]. But all these things we find in Judas' repentance, which in outward appearance did far exceed and pass the repentance of Peter. For, first and foremost, we read in the Gospel[κ] that Judas was so sorrowful and heavy, yea, that he was filled with such anguish and vexation of mind, for that which he had done, that he could not abide to live any longer. Did not he also, afore he hanged himself, make an open confession of his fault, when he said, *I have sinned, betraying the innocent blood?* And verily this was a very bold confession, which might have brought him to great trouble; for by it he did lay to the high priests' and elders' charge the shedding of innocent blood, and that they were most abominable murderers. He did also make a certain kind o satisfaction, when he did cast their money unto them again. No such thing do we read of Peter, although he had committed a very heinous sin and most grievous offence in denying of his Master. We find[λ] that *he went out, and wept bitterly:* whereo Ambrose speaketh on this manner[6]. "Peter was sorry and wept, because he erred as a man. I do not find what he said; I know that he wept. I read of his tears, but not of his satisfaction." But how chance that the one was received into favou again with God, and the other cast away, but because that the one did, by a lively faith in him whom he had denied, take hol upon the mercy of God, and the other wanted faith, whereby h did despair of the goodness and mercy of God? It is eviden and plain then, that, although we be never so earnestly sorr for our sins, acknowledge and confess them, yet all these thing shall be but means to bring us to utter desperation, except w do steadfastly believe that God our heavenly Father will, for hi Son Jesu[c] Christ's sake, pardon and forgive us our offences an trespasses, and utterly put them out of remembrance in hi sight. Therefore, as we said before, they that teach repentanc

The repentance of the Schoolmen.

Judas and his repentance.

κ Matt. xxvii, [3-5.]

Peter and his repentance.

λ [Matt. xxvi, 75.]

De Poenit. Dist. i, cap. Petrus.

b Saviour Jesu] Saviour Jesus *from* 1582. c Son Jesu] Son Jesus 1623.

5 So too *Concil. Trident. Sess.* VI, *Decr. de Justif., cap.* xiv; *Sess.* XIV, *cap.* iii, and *De Poenit. can.* iv.

6 Petrus doluit et flevit, quia erravit ut homo. Non invenio quid dixerit, invenio quod fleverit: lacrymas ejus lego satisfactionem non lego. *Ambros. Expos Luc.* X, 88; *Opp.* I, 1523 A: cited b Gratian in *Decret.* II, xxxiii, 3 *De Poenit. Dist.* i, *c.* I.

without Christ and a lively faith in the mercy of God do only teach Cain's or Judas' repentance.

The fourth is an amendment of life, or a new life, in bringing forth *fruits worthy of repentance.* For they that do truly repent must be clean altered and changed; they must become new creatures; they must be no more the same that they were before. And therefore thus said John Baptist unto the Pharisees and Sadducees that came unto his baptism: *O generation of vipers, who hath forewarned you to flee from the anger to come? Bring forth therefore fruits worthy of repentance.* Matt. iii, [7, 8.] Whereby we do learn, that, if we will have the wrath of God to be pacified, we must in no wise dissemble, but turn unto him again with a true and sound repentance, which may be known and declared by good fruits, as by most sure and infallible[d] signs thereof. They that do from the bottom of their hearts acknowledge their sins, and are unfeignedly sorry for their offences, will cast off all hypocrisy, and put on true humility and lowliness of heart. They will not only receive the physician of the soul, but also with a most fervent desire long for him. They will not only abstain from the sins of their former life and from all other filthy vices, but also flee, eschew, and abhor all the occasions of them. And, as they did before give themselves to uncleanness of life, so will they from henceforwards with all diligence give themselves to innocency, pureness of life, and true godliness.

We have the Ninivites for an example, which at the preaching of Jonas did not only proclaim a general fast, and that they should every one put on sackcloth, but they all did *turn from their evil ways and from the wickedness that was in their hands.* Jonah iii, [4–10.] But, above all other, the history of Zaccheus is most notable: for, being come unto our Saviour Jesu Christ, he did say, *Behold, Lord, the half of my goods I give to the poor; and if I have defrauded any man, or taken aught away by extortion or fraud, I do restore him fourfold.* Luke xix, 8. Here we see that after his repentance he was no more the man that he was before, but was clean changed and altered. It was so far off that he would continue and abide[e] still in his unsatiable covetousness, or take aught away fraudulently from any man, that rather he was most willing and ready to give away his own, and to make satisfaction unto all them that he had done injury and wrong unto. Here may we right well add the sinful woman[μ], which, when she

[μ] Luke vii, [37, 38.]

[d] infallible] fallible 1623.

[e] abide] bide *from* 1567.

came to our Saviour Jesu[f] Christ, did pour down such abun dance of tears out of those wanton eyes of hers, wherewith sh had allured many unto folly, that she did with them wash hi feet, wiping them with the hairs of her head, which she wa wont most gloriously to set out, making of them a net of th devil. Hereby we do learn what is the satisfaction that Go doth require of us, which is, that we *cease from evil, and d good*[ν], and, if we have done any man wrong, to endeavour our selves to make him true amends to the uttermost of our power; following in this the example of Zaccheus and of this sinfu woman, and also that goodly lesson that John Baptist, Zachary' son, did give unto them that came to ask counsel of him.

ν [Ps. xxxiv, 14: Is. i, 16, 17.]

This was commonly the penance that Christ enjoined sin ners[ξ], *Go thy way, and sin no more.* Which penance we shal never be able to fulfil without the special grace of him that dot say[o], *Without me ye can do nothing.* It is therefore our parts if at least we be desirous of the health and salvation of our ow selves, most earnestly to pray unto our heavenly Father to assis us with his Holy Spirit, that we may be able to hearken unt the voice of the true Shepherd, and with due obedience to fol low the same. Let us hearken to the voice of Almighty God, when he calleth us to repentance. Let us not harden ou hearts, as such infidels do who do abuse[g] the time given the of God to repent, and turn it to continue their pride and con tempt against God and man; which know not how much they *heap God's wrath upon themselves for the hardness of their hearts which cannot repent, at the day of vengeance.*[π] Where we hav offended the law of God, let us repent us of our straying from s good a Lord. Let us confess our unworthiness before him; bu yet let[h] us trust in God's free mercy for Christ's sake for th pardon of the same. And from henceforth let us endeavou ourselves to walk in a new life, *as newborn babes*[ρ], whereby w *may glorify*[σ] *our Father which is in heaven*[i], and thereby t bear in our consciences a good testimony of our faith; so at[k] the last to obtain the fruition of everlasting life through th merits of our Saviour. To whom be all praise and honour fo ever. Amen.

ξ John v, [14; viii, 11.]

o John xv, [5.]

π [Rom. ii, 5.]

ρ [1 Pet. ii, 2.]

σ [Matt. v, 16.]

f to ... Jesu] to ... Jesus *from* 1582. g who do abuse] who abuse *from* 1571. h but ye let] but let 1563 B—F. i is in heaven] is heaven 1623. k so at] so that at 1623.

THE THIRD PART OF THE HOMILY

OF REPENTANCE.

IN the Homily last spoken unto you, right well beloved people in our Saviour Christ, ye heard of the true parts and tokens of repentance; that is, hearty contrition and sorrowfulness of our hearts, unfeigned confession in word of mouth for our unowrthy living before God, a steadfast faith to the merits of our Saviour Christ for pardon, and a purpose of ourselves by God's grace to renounce our former wicked life, and a full conversion to God in a new life to glorify his Name, and to live orderly and charitably to the comfort of our neighbour in all righteousness, and to live soberly and modestly to ourselves by using abstinence and temperance in word and in deed in *mortifying our earthly members here upon earth.* [Col. iii, 5.] Now, for a further persuasion to move you to those parts of repentance, I will declare unto you some causes which should the rather move you to repentance.

The causes that should move us to repent.

First, the commandment of God, who in so many places of his holy[a] and sacred Scriptures doth bid us return unto him. *O ye children of Israel,* saith he[α], *turn again from your infidelity, wherein ye drowned yourselves*[1]. Again[β]: *Turn you, turn you, from your evil ways: for why will ye die, O ye house of Israel?* And in another place thus doth he speak by his holy Prophet Osee. *O Israel, return unto the Lord thy God; for thou hast taken a great fall by thine iniquity. Take unto you these words with you, when ye*[b] *turn unto the Lord, and say unto him, Take away all iniquity, and receive us graciously; so will we offer the calves of our lips unto thee.* In all these places we have an express commandment given unto us of God for to return unto him. Therefore we must take good heed unto ourselves, lest, whereas we have already by our manifold sins and transgressions provoked and kindled the wrath of God against us, we do by breaking this his commandment double our offences, and so heap still damnation upon our own heads. By our daily offences and trespasses, whereby we provoke the eyes of his Majesty, we do

α Isa. xxxi, [6.]

β Ezek. xxxiii, [11.]

Hos. xiv, [1, 2.]

a of his holy] of the holy *from* 1563 G. b when ye] when you *from* 1570.

1 Convertimini sicut in profundum recesseratis, filii Israel. *Vulg.*

well deserve, if he should deal with us according to his just ce, to be put away for ever from the fruition of his glory. ow much more then are we worthy of the endless torments of ll, if, when we be so gently called again after our rebellion, nd commanded to return, we will in no wise hearken unto the v ice of our heavenly Father, but walk still after the stubbornnes of our own hearts!

Secondly, the most comfortable and sweet promise that he Lord our God did of his mere mercy and goodness join unto his commandment. For he doth not only say[γ], *Return unto m O Israel;* but also, *If thou wilt return and put away all thine bominations out of my sight, thou shalt never be moved.* T ese words also have we in the Prophet Ezechiel: *At what t me soever a sinner doth repent him of his sin from the bottom o his heart, I will put all his wickedness out of my remembrance, s ith the Lord, so that they shall no more be*[c] *thought upon.* Thus re we sufficiently instructed that God will, according to his ro-mise, freely pardon, forgive, and forget all our sins, so that we shall never be cast in the teeth with them, if, obeying his c m-mandment, and allured by his sweet promises, we will unfei n-edly return unto him.

γ Jer. iv, [1.]

Ezek. xviii, [21, 22.]

Thirdly, the filthiness of sin: which is such that, as lon as we do abide in it, God cannot but detest and abhor us; neit er can there be any hope[δ] that we shall enter into the heav ly Hierusalem, except we be first made clean and purged fro it. But this will never be, unless, forsaking our former life, we do with our whole heart return unto the Lord our God, and, wi a full purpose of amendment of life, flee unto his mercy, taking s re hold thereupon through faith in the blood of his Son Jesu[d] Ch st. If we should suspect any uncleanness to be in us, where ore the earthly prince should lothe and abhor the sight of us, at pains would we take to remove and put it away! How m ch more ought we, with all diligence and speed that may be, to ut away that unclean filthiness that doth *separate* and make a di-vision *betwixt us and our God*, and that *hideth his face from us, that he will not hear us!* And verily herein doth appear ow filthy a thing sin is, sith that it can by no other means be washed away but by the blood of the only begotten Son of od. And shall we not from the bottom of our hearts detest nd abhor and with all earnestness flee from it, sith that it did st the dear heart blood of the only begotten Son of God, our Savi ur

δ [Rev. xxi, 27; xxii, 14, 15.]

Similitude.

Isa. lix, [2.]

[c] no more be] be no more *from* 1571.

[d] Jesu] Jesus 1623.

and Redeemer, to purge us from it? Plato doth in a certain place write, that, if virtue could be seen with bodily eyes, all men would wonderfully be inflamed and kindled with the love of it[2]. Even so on the contrary, if we might with our bodily eyes behold the filthiness of sin and the uncleanness thereof, we could in no wise abide it, but, as most present and deadly poison, hate and eschew it. We have a common experience of the same in them which, when they have committed any heinous offence or some filthy and abominable sin, if it once come to light, or if they chance to have a through feeling of it, they be so ashamed, their own conscience putting before their eyes the filthiness of their act, that they dare look no man on the face[e], much less that they should be able to stand in the sight of God. (Plato.)

Fourthly, the uncertainty and brittleness of our own lives: which is such, that we cannot assure ourselves that we shall live one hour or one half quarter of it. Which by experience we do find daily to be true in them that, being now merry and lusty, and sometimes feasting and banquetting with their friends, do fall suddenly dead in the streets, and otherwhiles under the board, when they are yet[f] at meat. These daily examples, as they are most terrible and dreadful, so ought they to move us to seek for to be at one with our heavenly Judge; that we may with a good conscience appear before him, whensoever it shall please him for to call us, whether it be suddenly or otherwise. For we have no more charter of our life than they have: but, as we are most certain that we shall die, so are we most uncertain when we shall die. For our life doth lie in the hand of God, who will take it away when it pleaseth him. And verily, when the highest somner[g] [3] of all, which is death, shall come, he will not be said nay, but we must forthwith be packing, to be presented[h] before the judgment seat of God, as he doth find us; according as it is written, *Where as the tree falleth, whether it be toward the south, or toward the north, there it shall lie.* Whereunto agreeth the saying of the holy Martyr of God, St. Cyprian, saying, "As God doth find thee when he doth call, so doth he judge thee[4]." Let us therefore follow the counsel of

(Death the Lord's somner.) (Eccles. xi, [3.]) (Contra Demetrianum.)

[e] on the face] in the face *from* 1563 C. [f] yet] *omitted* 1623. [g] somner] sumner 1587, 1595, 1623. [h] presented] present *from* 1563 G.

[2] Plato says this of Wisdom, φρόνησις, in *Phaedr.* p. 250 D; and he says nearly the same thing of the Beautiful, αὐτὸ τὸ καλόν, (the ipsa honestas of *Cic. de Fin.* v, 24), in *Sympos.* p. 211 D.

[3] somner: summoner.

[4] Qualem enim invenit Dominus cum hinc evocat, talem et judicat. *Expos. in Apocalyps. Hom.* XI, *Augustin. Opp.* III *Append.* 173 A. In *Jewel's Defence of*

[e] Ecclus. v, [7.]

the Wise Man, where he saith[e], *Make no tarrying to turn u to the Lord, and put not off from day to day; for suddenly shall he wrath of the Lord break forth, and in thy security thou shalt e*[i] *destroyed, and thou shalt*[j] *perish in time*[k] *of vengeance.* Wh ch words I desire you to mark diligently, because they do m st lively put before our eyes the fondness of many men, whic [l], abusing the longsuffering and goodness of God, do never th k on repentance or amendment of life. *Follow not,* saith he[ζ], *th ne own mind and thy strength, to walk in the ways of thy hea t; neither say thou, Who will bring me under for my works? or God the revenger will revenge the wrong done by thee. And ay not, I have sinned, and what evil hath come unto me? For he Almighty is a patient rewarder*[m], *but he will not leave thee n-punished. Because thy sins are forgiven thee, be not without ar to heap sin upon sin. Say not neither, The mercy of God is gr at, he will forgive my manifold sins. For mercy and wrath come f m him, and his indignation cometh upon unrepentant sinners.* s if he[n] should say, Art thou strong and mighty? art thou lu ty and young? hast thou the wealth and riches of the world? r, when thou hast sinned, hast thou received no punishment for t? let none of all these things make thee to be the slower to e-pent, and to return with speed unto the Lord; for in the da of punishment and of his sudden vengeance they shall not be a le to help thee. And specially, when thou art, either by the prea h-ing of God's word, or by some inward motion of his Holy Spi t, or else by some other means, called unto repentance, neg ct not the good occasion that is ministered unto thee; lest, w en thou wouldest repent, thou have[o] not the grace for to do it. or to repent is a good gift of God, which he will never grant u to them which[p], living in carnal security, do make a mock of his threatenings, or seek to rule his Spirit[q] as they list, as tho gh his working and gifts were tied unto their will.

ζ [Ibid. 2–6.]

Fifthly, the avoiding of the plagues of God and the utter de-struction that by his righteous judgment do hang[r] over he heads of them all that will in no wise return unto the Lord. *I*

[i] thou shalt be] shalt thou be *from* 1567. [j] and thou shalt] and shalt *from* 1563 G. [k] in time] in the time *from* 1582. [l] men, which] men, who 1623. [m] rewarder] rew ded 1563 A. [n] if he] if ye *from* 1582. [o] thou have] thou hast *from* 1563 B. [p] them w ich] them who 1623. [q] his Spirit] his spirits 1563 G–1595. [r] do hang] doth hang *from* 1563 B.

the Apology, Part II, *Ch.* xvi, *Div.* 2, this passage is cited as from Augustine, to whom the Exposition out of which it is taken used to be attributed. No doubt the writer of this Homily was quoting from memory, and had in his min the passage which is cited from Cypria in the Third Part of the Homily concer ing Prayer, p. 337, n. 5.

will, saith the Lord[η], *give them for a terrible plague to all the kingdoms of the earth, and for a reproach, and for a proverb, and for a curse in all places where I shall cast them, and will send the sword, the famine*[s], *and the pestilence among them, till they be consumed out of the land.* And wherefore is this? Because they hardened their hearts, and would in no wise *return*[θ] *from their evil ways,* nor yet forsake *the wickedness that was in their own hands,* that the fierceness of the Lord's fury might depart from them. But yet this is nothing in comparison of the intolerable and endless torments of hell fire, which they shall be fain to suffer who[ι] *after their hardness of heart, that cannot repent, do heap unto themselves wrath against the day of anger and of the declaration of the just judgment of God.* Whereas, if we will repent and be earnestly sorry for our sins[t], and with a full purpose of[u] amendment of life flee unto the mercy of our God, and, taking sure hold thereupon through faith in our Saviour Jesu[x] Christ, do *bring forth fruits worthy of repentance*[κ], he will not only pour his manifold blessings upon us here in this world, but also at the last, after the painful travails of this life, reward us with the inheritance of his children, which is the kingdom of heaven, purchased unto us with the death of his Son Jesu Christ our Lord. To whom with the Father and the Holy Ghost be all praise, glory, and honour world without end. Amen.

η Jer. xxiv, [9, 10.]

θ [Jonah iii, 8, 9.]

ι Rom. ii, [5.]

κ [Matt. iii, 8.]

s sword, the famine] sword of famine *from* 1570. t sins] sin *from* 1582. u purpose of] purpose and *from* 1574. x Saviour Jesu] Saviour Jesus *from* 1563 B.

AN HOMILY

AGAINST DISOBEDIENCE AND WILFUL REBELLION.

THE FIRST PART.

α Ps. xcvi, 8 [xcvii, 7;] and cii [ciii,] 20; and cxlviii, 2: Dan. iii, 58 [Song of the Three Holy Children 37;] and vii, 10: Matt. xxvi, 53: Col. i, 16: Heb. i, 4, 14: Rev. xix, 10.

β Gen. ii, 17.

γ Gen. i, 28.

As God the Creator and Lord of all things appointed[α] his angels[1] and heavenly creatures in all obedience to serve and to honour his Majesty, so was it his will that man, his chief creature upon the earth, should live under the obedience of him his[a] Creator and Lord; and for that cause God, as soon as he had created man, gave unto him a certain precept[β] and law, which he, being yet in the state of innocency and remaining in Paradise, should observe as a pledge and token of his due and bounden obedience, with denunciation of death if he did transgress and break the said law and commandment. And, as God would have man to be his obedient subject, so did he[γ] make all earthly creatures subject unto man; who kept their due obedience unto man so long as man remained in his obedience unto God. In the which obedience if man had continued still, there had been no poverty, no diseases, no sickness, no death, nor other miseries, wherewith mankind is now infinitely and most miserably afflicted and oppressed. So here appeareth the original kingdom of God over angels and man and universally over all things, and of man over earthly creatures, which God had made subject unto him; and withal the felicity and blessed state which angels, man, and all creatures had remained in, had they continued in due obedience unto God their King. For, as long as in this first kingdom the subjects continued in due obedience to God their King, so long did God embrace all his subjects with his love, favour, and grace; which to enjoy is perfect felicity. Whereby it is evident that obedience is the principal virtue of all virtues, and indeed the very root of all virtues, and the cause of all felicity.

But, as all felicity and blessedness should have continued with the continuance of obedience, so with the breach of obedience,

[a] of him his] of his *from* D.

1 Adorate eum, omnes angeli ejus. *Ps.* XCVI, 8, *Vulg.* Worship him, all ye gods. *Ps.* XCVII, 7, *Auth. Vers.*

and breaking in of rebellion, all vices and miseries did withal break in, and overwhelm the world. The first author[δ] of which rebellion, (the root of all vices and mother of all mischiefs,) was Lucifer, first God's most excellent creature and most bounden subject; who, by rebelling against the Majesty of God, of the brightest and most glorious angel is become the blackest and most foulest fiend and devil, and from the height of heaven is fallen into the pit and bottom of hell. Here you may see the first author and founder of rebellion and the reward thereof. Here you may see the grand captain and father of all rebels[b]: who, persuading[ε] the following of his rebellion against God, their Creator and Lord, unto our first parents Adam and Eve, brought[ζ] them in high displeasure with God; wrought their exile and banishment out of Paradise, a place of all pleasure and goodness, into this wretched earth and vale of all misery[c]; procured unto them sorrows of their minds, mischiefs, sickness, diseases, death of their bodies; and, which is far more horrible than all worldly and bodily mischiefs, he had wrought thereby their eternal and everlasting death[η] and damnation, had not God by the obedience of his Son Jesus Christ repaired that which man by disobedience and rebellion had destroyed, and so of his mercy had pardoned and forgiven him: of which all and singular the premises the holy Scriptures do bear record in sundry places. Thus you do[d] see, that neither heaven nor paradise could suffer any rebellion in them, neither be places for any rebels to remain in. Thus became rebellion, as you see, both the first and greatest[e] and the very root of all other sins, and the first and principal cause both of all worldly and bodily miseries, sorrows, diseases, sicknesses, and deaths; and, which is infinitely worse than all these, as is said, the very cause of death and damnation eternal also.

After this breach of obedience to God and rebellion against his Majesty, all mischiefs and miseries breaking in therewith and overflowing the world, lest all things should come unto confusion and utter ruin, God forthwith, by laws[θ] given unto mankind, repaired again the rule and order of obedience thus by rebellion overthrown: and, besides the obedience due unto his Majesty, he not only ordained[ι] that in families and households the wife should be obedient unto her husband, the children unto their parents, the servants unto their masters, but also, when

δ Matt. iv, 9; xxv. 41: John viii, 44: 2 Pet. ii, 4: Jude 6: Rev. xii, 7.

ε Gen. iii, 1 &c.: Wisd. ii, 24.

ζ Gen. iii, 8, 9 &c., 17, 23, 24.

η Rom. v, 12 &c., 19 &c.

θ Gen. iii, 17.

ι Gen. iii, 16: [Eph. vi, 1-5.]

b of all rebels] of rebels *from* 1582. c of all misery] of misery 1623. d you do] do you *from* 1582. e and greatest] and the greatest *from* 1582.

mankind increased and spread itself more largely over the world, he by his holy word did constitute and ordain in cities and countries several and special governors and rulers, unto whom the residue of his people should be obedient. As in reading of the holy Scriptures we shall find, in very many and almost infinite places[κ] as well of the Old Testament as of the New, that kings and princes, as well the evil[2] as the good, do reign by God's ordinance, and that subjects are bounden to obey them; that God doth give princes wisdom, great power, and authority; that God defendeth them against their enemies, and destroyeth their enemies horribly; that[λ] *the anger and displeasure of the prince is as the roaring of a lion, and the very messenger of death;* and that *the subject that provoketh him to displeasure sinneth against his own soul;* with many other things concerning both the authority of princes and the duty of subjects.

κ Job xxxiv, 30; and xxxvi, 7: Eccles. viii, 2; and x, 16, 17, 20: Ps. xviii, 50; and xx, 6; and xxi, 1; and cxliv, 1: Prov. viii, 15.

λ [Prov. xix, 12; xvi, 14; xx, 2.]

But here let us rehearse two special places out of the New Testament, which may stand in stead of all other. The first out of St. Paul's Epistle to the Romans, and the thirteenth chapter, where he writeth thus unto all subjects. *Let every soul be subject unto the higher powers. For there is no power but of God, and the powers that be are ordained of God. Whosoever therefore resisteth the power resisteth the ordinance of God; and they that resist shall receive to themselves damnation. For princes are not to be feared for good works, but for evil. Wilt thou then be without fear of the power? Do well; so shalt thou have praise of the same: for he is the minister of God for thy wealth. But, if thou do evil, fear: for he beareth not the sword for naught; for he is the minister of God, to take vengeance upon him that doeth evil. Wherefore ye must be subject, not because of wrath only, but also for conscience sake. For for this cause ye pay also tribute; for they are God's ministers, serving for the same purpose. Give to every man therefore his duty; tribute to whom tribute belongeth; custom to whom custom is due; fear to whom fear belongeth; honour to whom ye owe honour.* Thus far are St. Paul's words. The second place is in St. Peter's first[f] Epistle, and the second chapter, whose words are these. *Submit yourselves unto all manner ordinance*[g] *of man for the Lord's sake: whether it be unto the king, as unto the chief head; either unto rulers, as unto them that are sent of him for the punishment of evildoers, but for*

Rom. xiii, [1-7.]

1 Pet. ii, [13-18.]

[f] first] *omitted* 1623. [g] manner ordinance] manner of ordinances 1623.

2 Qui regnare facit hominem hypocritam propter peccata populi. *Job* XXXIV, 30, *Vulg.*

the cherishing of them that do well: for so is the will of God, that with well doing ye may stop the mouths of ignorant and foolish men: as free, and not as having the liberty for a cloak of maliciousness, but even as the servants of God. Honour all men: love brotherly fellowship[3]*: fear God: honour the king. Servants, obey your masters with fear; not only if they be good and courteous, but also though they be froward.* Thus far out of St. Peter.

By these two places of the holy Scriptures it is most evident that kings, queens, and other princes, (for he speaketh of authority and power, be it in men or women,) are ordained of God, are to be obeyed and honoured of their subjects; that such subjects as are disobedient or rebellious against their princes disobey God, and procure their own damnation; that the government of princes is a great blessing of God, given for the common wealth, specially of the good and godly, (for the comfort and cherishing of whom God giveth and setteth up princes,) and, on the contrary part, to the fear and for the punishment of the evil and wicked; finally, that if servants ought to obey their masters, not only being gentle, but such as be froward, as well, and much more, ought subjects to be obedient, not only to their good and courteous, but also to their sharp and rigorous princes. It cometh therefore neither of chance and fortune (as they term it), nor of the ambition of mortal men and women climbing up of their own accord to dominion, that there be kings, queens, princes, and other governors over men being their subjects; but all kings, queens, and other governors are specially appointed by the ordinance of God.

And, as God himself, being of an infinite majesty, power, and wisdom, ruleth and governeth all things in heaven and in earth[h], as the universal Monarch[μ] and only King and Emperor over all, as being only able to take and bear the charge of all; so hath he[ν] constitute[i], ordained, and set earthly princes over particular kingdoms and dominions in earth, both for the avoiding of all confusion, (which else would be in the world, if it should be without such[k] governors,) and for the great quiet and benefit of earthly men their subjects, and also that the princes themselves, in authority, power, wisdom, providence, and righteousness in government of people and countries committed to their charge, should resemble his heavenly governance, as the

μ Ps. x, 16; and xlv, 6 &c.; and xlvii, 2.
ν Ecclus. xvii, [17.]

h and in earth] and earth *from* 1582. i constitute] constituted *from* C. k without such governors] without governors *from* 1582.

3 Τὴν ἀδελφότητα: fraternitatem *Vulg.*

majesty of heavenly things may by the baseness of earthly things be shadowed and resembled. And for that similitude that is between the heavenly monarchy and earthly kingdoms well governed our Saviour Christ in sundry parables saith[ξ], that *the kingdom of heaven is resembled unto a man a king*[4]. And, as the name of *the King*[o] is very often attributed and given unto God in the holy Scriptures, so doth God himself in the same Scriptures sometime vouchsafe to communicate his name with earthly princes, terming them *gods*[π]; doubtless for that similitude of government which they have, or should have, not unlike unto God their King.

ξ Matt. xviii, 23; and xxii, 2.
o Ps. x, 16; and xlv; and xlvii, 2 &c.: Matt. xxii, 13; and xxv, 34.
π Ps. lxxxii, 6.

Unto the which similitude of heavenly government the nearer and nearer that an earthly prince doth come in his regiment, the greater blessing of God's mercy is he unto that country and people over whom he reigneth: and the further and further that an earthly prince doth swerve from the example of the heavenly government, the greater plague he is[1] of God's wrath, and punishment by God's justice, unto that country and people over whom God for their sins hath placed such a prince and governor. For it is indeed evident, both by the Scriptures and by daily[m] experience, that the maintenance of all virtue and godliness, and consequently of the wealth and prosperity of a kingdom and people, doth stand and rest more in a wise and good prince, on the one part, than in great multitudes of other men being subjects; and, on the contrary part, the overthrow of all virtue and godliness, and consequently the decay and utter ruin of a realm and people, doth grow and come more by an undiscreet and evil governor than by many thousands of other men being subjects. Thus say the holy Scriptures. *Well is thee, O thou land,* saith the Preacher[ρ], *whose king is come of nobles, and whose princes eat in due season, for necessity and not for lust.* Again[σ], *A wise and righteous king maketh his realm and people wealthy:* and, *A good, merciful, and gracious prince is as a shadow in heat, as a defence in storms, as dew, as sweet showers, as fresh watersprings in great droughts.* Again, the Scriptures, of undiscreet and evil princes, speak thus: *Woe*[τ] *be to thee, O thou land whose king is but a child, and whose princes are early at their banquets.* Again[υ], *When the wicked do reign, then men go to ruin*[5]. And again, *A foolish prince destroyeth*

ρ Eccles. x, 17.
σ Prov. xvi, [15; and xix, 12;] and xxix, [4:] Eccles. x, [17:] Is. xxxii, [1, 2.]
τ Eccles. x, 16.
υ Prov. xxviii, [12, 16;] and xxix, [4.]

[1] he is] is he 1623.   [m] by daily] daily by *from* 1582.

4 'Ανθρώπῳ βασιλεῖ: homini regi *Vulg.*
5 Regnantibus impiis ruinae hominum. *Prov.* xxviii, 12, *Vulg.*

the people: and, *A covetous king undoeth his subjects.* Thus speak the Scriptures, thus experience testifieth, of good and evil princes.

What shall subjects do then? Shall they obey valiant, stout, wise, and good princes, and contemn, disobey, and rebel against children being their princes, or against undiscreet and evil governors? God forbid. For first what a perilous thing were it to commit unto the subjects the judgment, which prince is wise and godly and his government good, and which is otherwise; as though the foot must judge of the head; an enterprise very heinous, and must needs breed rebellion. For who else be they that are most inclined to rebellion, but such haughty spirits? From whom springeth such foul ruin of realms? Is not rebellion the greatest of all mischiefs? And who are most ready to the greatest mischiefs, but the worst men? Rebels therefore, the worst of all subjects, are most ready to rebellion, as being the worst of all vices and furthest from the duty of a good subject; as, on the contrary part, the best subjects are most firm and constant in obedience, as in the special and peculiar virtue of good subjects. What an unworthy matter were it then to make the naughtiest subjects, and most inclined to rebellion and all evil, judges over their princes, over their government, and over their counsellors, to determine which of them be good or tolerable, and which be evil and so intolerable that they must needs be removed by rebels; being ever ready, as the naughtiest subjects, soonest to rebel against the best princes, specially if they be young in age, women in sex, or gentle and courteous in government; as trusting by their wicked boldness easily to overthrow their weakness and gentleness, or at the least so to fear the minds of such princes, that they may have impunity of their mischievous doings. But, whereas indeed a rebel is worse than the worst prince, and rebellion worse than the worst government of the worst prince, that hitherto hath been, both are rebels[n] unmeet ministers, and rebellion an unfit and unwholesome medicine, to reform any small lacks in a prince, or to cure any little griefs in government; such lewd remedies being far worse than any other maladies and disorders that can be in the body of a commonwealth.

But, whatsoever the prince be, or his government, it is evident that for the most part those princes whom some subjects do think to be very godly, and under whose government they

[n] are rebels] rebels are *from* 1582.

rejoice to live, some other subjects do take the same to be evil and ungodly, and do wish for a change. If therefore all subjects that mislike of their prince should rebel, no realm should ever be without rebellion. It were more meet that rebels should hear the advice of wise men, and give place unto their judgment, and follow the example of obedient subjects; as reason is that they whose understanding is blinded with so evil an affection should give place to them that be of sound judgment, and that the worse[p] should give place to the better: and so might realms continue in long obedience, peace, and quietness.

But what if the prince be undiscreet and evil indeed, and it[q] also evident to all men's eyes that he so is? I ask again, what if it be long of[6] the wickedness of the subjects that the prince is undiscreet or[r] evil? Shall the subjects both by their wickedness provoke God for their deserved punishment to give them an undiscreet or evil prince, and also rebel against him, and withal against God, who for the punishment of their sins did give them such a prince? Will you hear the Scriptures concerning this point? *God,* say the holy Scriptures[φ], *maketh a wicked man to reign for the sins of the people*[7]. Again[χ], *God giveth a prince in his anger*, meaning an evil one, *and taketh away a prince in his displeasure*, meaning specially when he taketh away a good prince for the sins of the people, as in our memory he took away our good Josias, King Edward, in his young and good years for our wickedness. And contrarily the Scriptures do teach[ψ], that God giveth wisdom unto princes, and maketh a wise and good king to reign over that people whom he loveth, and who loveth him. Again[ω], *If the people obey God, both they and their king shall prosper and be safe, else both shall perish,* saith God by the mouth of Samuel. Here you see that God placeth as well evil princes as good, and for what cause he doth both. If we therefore will have a good prince either to be given us or to continue, now we have such a one, let us by our obedience to God and to our prince move God thereunto. If we will have an evil prince (when God shall send such a one) taken away, and a good in his place, let us take away our

φ Job xxxiv, 30.
χ Hos. xiii, 11.
ψ 2 Chron. ii, [11, 12;] and ix, [8, 23:] Prov. xvi, [10.]
ω 1 Sam. xii, [14, 15, 25.]

p worse] worst *from* 1582. q and it] and is 1623. r is undiscreet or] is undiscreet and *from* 1571.

6 long of: caused by, owing to, more properly written along of.

O she was naught, and long of her it was
That we meet here so strangely.—*Shakespeare, Cymbeline,* v, 5.

7 See before, p. 552, n. 2.

wickedness, which provoketh God to place such an one over[s] us, and God will either displace him, or of an evil prince make him a good prince, so that we first will change our evil into good. For will you hear the Scriptures[a]? *The heart of the prince is in God's hand: which way soever it shall please him, he turneth it.* Thus say the Scriptures. Wherefore let us turn from our sins unto the Lord with all our hearts, and he will turn the heart of the prince unto our quiet and wealth. Else for subjects to deserve through their sins to have an evil prince, and then to rebel against him, were double and treble evil, by provoking God more to plague them. Nay, let us either deserve to have a good prince, or let us patiently suffer and obey such as we deserve.

a Prov. xxi, [1:] Ezra vii, [27.]

And, whether the prince be good or evil, let us, according to the counsel of the holy Scriptures, pray for the prince; for his continuance and increase in goodness, if he be good, and for his amendment, if he be evil.

Will[t] you hear the Scriptures concerning this most necessary point? *I exhort therefore,* saith St. Paul, *that, above all things, prayers, supplications, intercessions, and giving of thanks be had for all men, for kings and all that are in authority, that we may live a quiet and peaceable life with all godliness: for that is good and acceptable in the sight of God our Saviour,* &c. This is St. Paul's counsel. And who, I pray you, was prince over the most part of Christians[u], when God's Holy Spirit by St. Paul's pen gave them this lesson? Forsooth Caligula, Clodius[x], or Nero; who were not only no Christians, but pagans, and also either foolish rulers, or most cruel tyrants. Will you yet hear the word of God to the Jews, when they were prisoners under Nabuchodonozor king of Babylon, after he had slain their king, nobles, parents, children, and kinsfolks, burned their country, cities, yea, Hierusalem itself, and the holy temple, and had carried the residue remaining alive captives with him unto Babylon? will you hear yet what the prophet Baruch saith unto God's people being in this captivity? *Pray you,* saith the prophet, *for the life of Nabuchodonozor king of Babylon, and for the life of Balthasar his son, that their days may be as the days of heaven upon the earth; that God also may give us strength, and lighten our eyes, that we may live under the defence of Nabuchodonozor king of Babylon and*

1 Tim. ii, [1-3.]

Baruch i, 11[-13.]

s an one over] a one over *from* C. t Will] Well 1582, 1623. u of Christians] of the Christians 1623. x Clodius] Claudius 1623.

under the protection of Balthasar his son, that we may long do them service, and find favour in their sight[8]. *Pray for us also unto the Lord our God, for we have sinned against the Lord our God.* Thus far the prophet Baruch his words; which are spoken by him unto the people of God, of that king who was an heathen, a tyrant, and cruel oppressor of them, and had been a murderer of many thousands of their nation and a destroyer of their country, with a confession that their sins had deserved such a prince to reign over them.

And shall the old Christians, by St. Paul's exhortation, pray for Caligula, Clodius[y], or Nero? shall the Jews pray for Nabuchodonozor? these emperors and kings being strangers unto them, being pagans and infidels, being murderers, tyrants, and cruel oppressors of them, and the destroyers[z] of their country, countrymen, and kinsmen, the burners of their villages, towns, cities, and temples? and shall not we pray for the long, prosperous, and godly reign of our natural Prince, no stranger (which[β] is observed as a great blessing in the Scriptures)? of our Christian, our most gracious Sovereign, no heathen nor pagan prince? Shall we not pray for the health of our most merciful, most loving Sovereign; the preserver of us and our country in so long peace, quietness, and security; no cruel person, no tyrant, no spoiler of our goods, no shedder of our bloods[a], no burner and destroyer of our towns, cities, and country[b], as were those, for whom yet, (as ye have heard,) Christians, being their subjects, ought to pray? Let us not commit so great ingratitude against God and our Sovereign, as not continually to thank God for this[c] government, and for his great and continual benefits and blessings poured upon us by such government. Let us not commit so great a sin against God, against ourselves, and our country, as not to pray continually unto God for the long continuance of so gracious a ruler unto us and our country. Else shall we be unworthy any longer to enjoy those benefits and blessings of God which hitherto we have had by her, and shall[d] be most worthy to fall into all those mischiefs and miseries which we and our country have by God's grace through her government hitherto escaped.

β Deut. xvii, 15.

[y] Clodius] Claudius 1623. [z] and the destroyers] and destroyers *from* 1582. [a] of our bloods] of bloods 1623. [b] and country] and countries D, *and from* 1582. [c] this] his 1623. [d] her, and shall] her, shall 1623.

8 ... et ut det Dominus virtutem nobis, et illuminet oculos nostros, ut vivamus ..., et serviamus ..., et inveniamus gratiam in conspectu eorum. *Vulg.*

What shall we say of those subjects (may we call them by the name of subjects?) who neither be thankful nor make any prayer to God for so gracious a Sovereign; but also themselves take armour wickedly, assemble companies and bands of rebels, to break the public peace so long continued, and to make, not war, but rebellion; to endanger the person of such a gracious Sovereign; to hazard the estate of their country, for whose defence they should be ready to spend their lives; and, being Englishmen, to rob, spoil, destroy, and burn in England Englishmen; to kill and murder their own neighbours and kinsfolk, their own countrymen; to do all evil and mischief, yea, and more too than foreign enemies would or could do[9]? What shall we say of these men who use themselves thus rebelliously against their gracious Sovereign; who, if God for their wickedness had given them an heathen tyrant to reign over them, were by God's word bound to obey him and to pray for him? What may be spoken of them? So far doth their unkindness, unnaturalness, wickedness, mischievousness in their doings, pass and excel any thing and all things that can be expressed or uttered[e] by words. Only let us wish unto all such most speedy repentance, and with so grievous sorrow of heart as such so horrible sins against the Majesty of God do require, who in most extreme unthankfulness do rise, not only against their gracious Prince, against their natural country, but against all their countrymen, women, and children, against themselves, their wives, children, and kinsfolks, and, by so wicked an example, against all Christendom, and against whole mankind of all manner of people throughout the wide world; such repentance, I say, such sorrow of heart, God grant unto all such whosoever rise of private and malicious purpose, as is meet for such mischiefs attempted and wrought by them.

And unto us and all other subjects God of his mercy grant, that we may be most unlike to all such, and most like to good, natural, loving, and obedient subjects; nay, that we may be such indeed, not only shewing all obedience ourselves, but as many of us as be able to the uttermost of our power, ability, and understanding to stay and repress all rebels and rebellions

[e] or uttered] and uttered 1623.

9 This Homily was occasioned by the rebellion which broke out in the Northern counties under the Earls of Northumberland and Westmorland about the middle of November 1569. See *Camdeni Annales an.* 1569, *pp.* 164–168, *ed.* 1615: *Strype's Annals of the Reformation, ch.* LIV.

against God, our gracious Prince, and natural country, at every occasion that is offered unto us.

And, that which we all are able to do, unless we do it, we shall be most wicked, and most worthy to feel in the end such extreme plagues as God hath ever poured upon rebels. Let us all make[f] continual prayers unto Almighty God, even from the bottom of our hearts, that he will give his grace, power, and strength unto our gracious Queen Elizabeth, to vanquish and subdue all, as well rebels at home, as foreign enemies; that, all domestical rebellions being suppressed and pacified, and all outward invasions repulsed and abandoned, we may not only be sure and long continue in all obedience unto our gracious Sovereign, and in that peaceable and quiet life which hitherto we have led under her Majesty with all security; but also that both our gracious Queen Elizabeth, and we her subjects, may all together, in all obedience unto God the King of all kings[g] and unto his holy laws, lead our lives so in this world in all virtue and godliness, that in the world to come we may enjoy his everlasting kingdom. Which I beseech God to grant, as well to our gracious Sovereign, as unto us all, for his Son our Saviour Jesus Christ's sake. To whom with the Father and the Holy Ghost, one God and King immortal, be all glory, praise, and thanksgiving world without end. Amen.

Thus have you heard the First Part of this Homily: now, good people, let us pray.

THE PRAYER.[h]

O MOST mighty God, the Lord of hosts, the Governor of all creatures, the only Giver of all victories, who[i] alone art able to strengthen the weak against the mighty, and to vanquish infinite multitudes of thine enemies with the countenance of a few of thy servants calling upon thy Name, and trusting in thee; defend, O Lord, thy servant, and our Governor under thee, our Queen Elizabeth, and all thy people committed to her charge.

O Lord[k], withstand the cruelty of all those which be common enemies as well to the truth of thy eternal word, as to their own natural Prince and country, and manifestly to this crown and realm of England, which thou hast of thy divine providence

[f] us all make] us make *from* 1582. [g] of all kings] of kings *from* 1582. [h] The Prayer] The Prayer as in that time it was published 1623. [i] victories, who] victories, and who 1623 *after the third and the fourth Parts of the Homily, but not in the other places.* [k] charge. O Lord] charge, and especially at this time, O Lord A.

assigned in these our days to the government of thy servant, our Sovereign and gracious Queen.

O most merciful Father, if it be thy holy will, make soft and tender the stony hearts of all those that exalt themselves against thy truth, and seek either to trouble the quiet of this realm of England, or to oppress the crown of the same; and convert them to the knowledge of thy Son, the only Saviour of the world, Jesus Christ; that we and they may jointly glorify thy mercies.

Lighten, we beseech thee, their ignorant hearts to embrace the truth of thy word: or else so abate their cruelty, O most mighty Lord, that this our Christian region[1], with others that confess thy holy Gospel, may obtain by thine aid and strength surety from all enemies without shedding of Christian blood; whereby all they which be oppressed with their tyranny may be relieved, and they which be in fear of their cruelty may be comforted; and finally that all Christian realms, and specially this realm of England, may by thy defence and protection continue in the truth of the Gospel, and enjoy perfect peace, quietness, and security; and that we for these thy mercies, jointly all together with one consonant heart and voice, may thankfully render to thee all laud and praise; that we, knit in one godly concord and unity amongst ourselves, may continually magnify thy glorious Name; who, with thy Son our Saviour Jesus Christ and the Holy Ghost, art one eternal, almighty, and most merciful God. To whom be all laud and praise world without end. Amen.

[1] region] religion 1582, realm 1623.

THE SECOND PART OF THE HOMILY

AGAINST DISOBEDIENCE AND WILFUL REBELLION.[a]

AS in the First Part of this Treaty of obedience of subjects to their princes, and against disobedience and rebellion, I have alleged divers sentences out of the holy Scriptures for proof; so shall it be good, for the better both[b] declaration and confirmation of the said wholesome doctrine, to allege one example or two out of the same[c] holy Scriptures of the obedience of subjects, not only unto their good and gracious governors, but also unto their evil and unkind princes.

As king Saul was not of the best, but rather of the worst, sort of princes, as being out of God's favour[α] for his disobedience against God in sparing in a wrong pity the king Agag, whom Almighty God commanded to be slain according to the justice of God against his sworn enemy; and, although Saul of a devotion meant to sacrifice such things as he spared of the Amalechites to the honour and service of God, yet Saul was reproved for his wrong mercy and devotion, and was told that obedience would have more pleased him than such lenity; which sinful humanity, saith holy Chrysostom[1], is more cruel before God, than any murder or shedding of blood, when it is commanded of God. But yet how evil[β] soever Saul the king was, and out of God's favour, yet was he obeyed of his subject David, the very best of all subjects, and most valiant[γ] in the service of his prince and country in the wars, the most obedient[δ] and loving in peace, and always most true and faithful to his sovereign and lord, and furthest[d] off from all manner rebellion[e]. For the which his most painful, true, and faithful service king Saul yet rewarded him not only with great unkindness, but also sought his destruction and death[ε] by all means possible; so that David was fain to save his life, not by rebellion, nor any[f] re-

α 1 Sam. xv, 11, 22, 35.

Chrys. Tom. 1, Hom. 1 adversus Judaeos.

β 1 Sam. xvi, 14, 15; xviii, 10, 12; xix, 9, 20.

γ Ibid. xvii, 26 &c.; xviii, 27; xix, 5, 8; xxiii; xxvii.

δ Ibid. xvi, 23; xix, 4; xxiv, 9.

ε Ibid. xviii, 9, 25, 29.

a REBELLION.] REBELLION. The Second Part. A–E. b both] *omitted after* E. c same] *omitted after* 1574. d furthest] furdest A–D. e manner rebellion] manner of rebellion *from* 1582. f nor any] or any *from* 1582.

1 Κἂν φείσηταί τις καὶ φιλανθρωπεύσηται παρὰ τὸ δοκοῦν ἐκείνῳ [sc. τῷ Θεῷ], φόνου παντὸς ἀνοσιωτέρα γένοιτ' ἂν ἡ φειδώ. Chrysost. adv. Jud. Orat. IV, Opp. I, 617 B.

sistance, but by flight[ζ] and hiding himself from the king's sight. Which notwithstanding, when king Saul upon a time came alone into the cave where David was[η], so that David might easily have slain him, yet would he neither hurt him himself, neither suffer any of his men to lay hands upon him. Another time also David, entering by night with one Abisai[θ], a valiant and a fierce[g] man, into the tent where king Saul did lie asleep, where also he might yet more easily have slain him; yet would he neither hurt him himself, nor suffer Abisai, who was willing and ready to slay king Saul, once to touch him. Thus did David deal with Saul his prince, notwithstanding that king Saul continually sought his death and destruction.

ζ Ibid. xix, 19; xxi; xxii.
η Ibid. xxiv, 3–8.
θ Ibid. xxvi, 6, 9.

It shall not be amiss unto these deeds of David to add his words, and to shew you what he spake unto such as encouraged him[ι] to take his opportunity and advantage to slay king Saul, as his mortal enemy, when he might. *The Lord keep me,* saith David[κ], *from doing that thing, and from laying hands upon my lord, God's anointed. For*[λ] *who can lay his hand upon the Lord's anointed, and be guiltless? As truly as the Lord liveth, except that the Lord do smite him, or his days shall come to die, or that he go down to war, and be slain in battle, the Lord be merciful unto me, that I lay not my hand upon the Lord's anointed*[2]. These be David's words, spoken at sundry times to divers his servants provoking him to slay king Saul, when opportunity served him thereunto.

ι Ibid. xxiv, 4.
κ Ibid. 6 &c.
λ Ibid. xxvi, 9, 10, &c.

Neither is it to be omitted and left out, how, when an Amalechite had slain king Saul, even at Saul's own bidding and commandment[μ], (for he would live no longer now, for that he had lost the field against his enemies the Philistines[h],) the said Amalechite making great haste to bring first word and news thereof unto David, as joyous unto him for the death of his mortal enemy, bringing withal[ν] the crown that was upon king Saul's head, and the bracelet that was upon his[i] arm, both as a proof of the truth of his news, and also as fit and pleasant presents unto David, being by God appointed to be king Saul his successor in the kingdom; yet was that faithful and godly David so far from rejoicing at these news, that he rent his clothes, wept[ξ], and mourned, and fasted; and so far off from thanksgiving to the messenger, either for his deed in killing the king,

μ 2 Sam. i, 7, 9.
ν Ibid. 10.
ξ Ibid. 12.

g and a fierce] and fierce *from* 1582. h Philistines] Philistins 1582, Philistims 1623. i upon his] about his *from* 1582.

2 See before, p. 110, n. 5.

though his deadly enemy, or for his message and news, or for his presents that he brought, that he said unto him[o], *How happened it that thou wast not afraid to lay thy hands upon the Lord's anointed to slay him?* whereupon immediately he commanded one of his servants to kill the messenger, and said, *Thy blood be upon thine own head; for thine own mouth hath witnessed against thyself, in confessing that thou hast slain the Lord's anointed.*

This example, dearly beloved, is notable, and the circumstances thereof are well to be considered, for the better instruction of all subjects in their bounden duty of obedience, and perpetual fearing of them from attempting of any rebellion or hurt against their prince. On the one part, David was not only a good and true subject, but also such a subject as both in peace and war had served and saved his prince's honour and life, and delivered his country and countrymen from great danger of infidels, foreign and most cruel enemies, horribly invading the king and his country: for the which David was in singular[k] favour with all the people[π]; so that he might have had great numbers of them at his commandment, if he would have attempted any thing. Besides this, David was no common or absolute subject, but heir apparent to the crown and kingdom, by God appointed[ρ] to reign after Saul; which, as it increased the favour of the people that knew it towards David, so did it make David's cause and case much differing from the case of common and absolute subjects. And, which is most of all, David was highly and singularly in the favour of God[σ]. On the contrary part, king Saul was out of God's favour[τ] for that cause which is before rehearsed, and he as it were God's enemy, and therefore like in war and peace to be hurtful and pernicious unto the commonwealth; and that was known to many of his subjects, for that he was openly rebuked[υ] of Samuel for his disobedience unto God; which might make the people the less to esteem him. King Saul was also unto David a mortal and deadly enemy, though without David's deserving; who by his faithful, painful, profitable, yea, most necessary service had well deserved, as of his country, so of his prince: but king Saul far otherwise; the more was his unkindness, hatred, and cruelty towards such a good subject both odious and detestable. Yet would David neither himself slay nor hurt such an enemy, for that he was his prince and lord; nor would suffer any other to

o Ibid. 13–16.
π 1 Sam. xviii, 16, 30.
ρ Ibid. xvi, 12 &c.
σ Ibid. xviii, 12.
τ Ibid. xv, 11; xviii, 10, 12.
υ Ibid. xv, [19,] 22, 26.

k in singular] in a singular 1623.

kill, hurt, or lay hand upon him, when he might have been slain without any stir, tumult, or danger of any man's life.

Now let David answer to such demands as men desirous of rebellion do use to make. Shall not we, specially being so good The demand. men as we are, rise and rebel against a prince hated of God, and God's enemy, and therefore like not to prosper either in war or peace, but to be hurtful and pernicious to the commonwealth? No, saith good and godly David, God's and such a king's faith- The answer. ful subject, and so convicting such subjects as attempt any rebellion against such a king to be neither good subjects nor good men. But, say they, shall we not rise and rebel against so un- The demand. kind a prince, nothing considering or regarding our true, faithful, and painful service, or the safeguard of our posterity? No, The answer. saith good David, whom no such unkindness could cause to forsake his due obedience to his sovereign. Shall we not, say they, The demand. rise and rebel against our known, mortal, and deadly enemy, that seeketh our lives? No, saith godly David, who had learned The answer. the lesson that our Saviour afterward plainly taught[φ], that we φ [Matt. v, 44.] should do no hurt to our fellow subjects, though they hate us and be our enemies, much less[1] unto our prince, though he were our enemy. Shall we not assemble an army of such good fel- The demand. lows as we are, and by hazarding of our lives and the lives of such as shall withstand us, and withal hazarding the whole estate of our country, remove so naughty a prince? No, saith The answer. godly David; for I, when I might, without assembling force or number of men, without tumult or hazard of any man's life, or shedding of any drop of blood, have delivered myself and my country of an evil prince, yet would I not do it. Are not they, The demand. say some, lusty and courageous captains, valiant men of stomach, and good men's bodies, that do venture by force to kill or[m] depose their king, being a naughty prince and their mortal enemy? They may be as lusty, as[n] courageous, as they list, yet, saith The answer. godly David, they can be no good nor godly men that so do: for I not only have rebuked, but also commanded him to be slain as a wicked man, which slew king Saul mine enemy; though he, being weary of his life for the loss of the victory against his enemies, desired that man to slay him. What shall The demand. we then do to an evil, to an unkind prince, an enemy to us, hated of God, hurtful to the commonwealth, &c.? Lay no vio- The answer. lent hand upon him, saith good David; but let him live until

1 less] *so in all.*   m kill or] kill and *from* 1571.   n lusty, as] lusty, and as 1595, lusty and 1623.

God appoint and work his end, either by natural death, or in war by lawful enemies, not by traitorous subjects[o]. Thus would godly David make answer: and St. Paul, as ye heard before[3], willeth us to pray also[p] for such a prince.

If king David would make these answers, as by his deeds and words recorded in the holy Scriptures indeed he doth make, unto all such demands concerning rebelling against evil princes, unkind princes, cruel princes, princes that be to their good subjects mortal enemies, princes that are out of God's favour, and so hurtful or like to be hurtful to the commonwealth; what answer, think you, would he make to those that demand whether they (being naughty and unkind subjects) may not, to the great hazard of the life of many thousands and the utter danger of the state of the commonwealth and whole realm, assemble a sort of rebels, to put in fear, or to depose or destroy[q], their natural and loving Princess, enemy to none, good to all, even to them the worst of all other, the maintainer of perpetual peace, quietness, and security, most beneficial to the commonwealth, most necessary for the safeguard of the whole realm? What answer would David make to their demand, whether they may not attempt cruelly and unnaturally to destroy so peaceable and merciful a Princess[r]? What, I say, would David, so reverently speaking of Saul, and so patiently suffering so evil a king, what would he answer and say to such demands? What would he say, nay, what would he do to such high attempters, who so said and did, as you before have heard, unto him that slew the king his master, though a most wicked prince? If he punished with death, as a wicked doer, such a man, with what reproaches of words would he revile such, yea, with what torments of most shameful deaths would he destroy such, hellhounds rather than evil men, such rebels, I mean, as I last spake of? For, if they who do disobey an evil and unkind prince be most unlike unto David, that good subject, what be they who do rebel against a most natural and loving Prince? And, if David, being so good a subject that he obeyed so evil a king, was worthy of a subject to be made a king himself, what be they who are[s] so evil subjects that they will rebel against their gracious Prince

An unnatural and wicked question.

[o] either by——subjects] either in war by lawful enemies, not by traitorous subjects, or by natural death A. [p] to pray also] also to pray 1623. [q] to put in fear, or to depose or destroy] or to depose, to put in fear, or to destroy 1571–1595, either to depose——destroy 1623. [r] a Princess] a Prince 1623. [s] who are] which are 1623.

[3] See p. 557, ll. 19–29.

worthy of? Surely no mortal man can express with words[t], nor conceive in mind, the horrible and most dreadful damnation that such be worthy of, who, disdaining to be the quiet and happy subjects of their good prince, are most worthy to be the miserable captives and vile slaves of that infernal tyrant Satan, with him to suffer eternal slavery and torments.

This one example of the good subject David out of the Old Testament may suffice, and, for the notableness of it, serve for all.

In the New Testament the excellent example of the blessed Virgin Mary, the mother of our Saviour Christ, doth at the first offer itself. When proclamation[χ] or commandment was sent [χ Luke ii, 1 &c.] into Jewry from Augustus the Emperor of Rome, that the people there should repair unto their own cities and dwellingplaces, there to be taxed; neither did the blessed Virgin, though both highly in God's favour, and also being of the royal blood of the ancient natural kings of Jewry, disdain to obey the commandment of an heathen and foreign prince, when God had placed such a one over them; neither did she allege for an excuse, that she was great with child, and most near her time of deliverance; neither grudged she at the length and tediousness of the[u] journey from Nazareth to Bethlehem, from whence and whither she must go to be taxed; neither repined she at the sharpness of the dead time of winter, being the latter end of December, an unhandsome[x] time to travel[y] in, specially a long journey, for a woman being in her case; but, all excuses set apart, she obeyed, and came to the appointed place: where at her coming she found such great resort and throng of people, that, finding no place[ψ] in any inn, she was fain, after her long, [ψ Ibid. 7.] painful, and tedious journey, to take up her lodging in a stable, where also she was delivered of her blessed Child; and this also declareth how near her time she took that journey. This obedience of this most noble and most virtuous lady to a foreign and pagan prince doth well teach us, who in comparison to her[z] are most base and vile, what ready obedience we do owe to our natural and gracious Sovereign. Howbeit in this case the obedience of the whole Jewish nation[ω] (being otherwise a stubborn [ω Ibid. 3.] people) unto the commandment of the same foreign heathen prince doth prove, that such Christians as do not most readily obey their natural gracious sovereign are far worse than the

[t] with words] worth words E, 1571. [u] tediousness of the] tedious 1623. [x] unhandsome] unfit 1623. [y] travel] *so* A, travail B *and most others*. [z] to her] of her *from* 1574.

stubborn Jews, whom yet we[a] account as the worst of all people.

But no example ought to be of more force with us Christians than the example of Christ, our Master and Saviour: who, though he were the Son of God, yet did always behave himself most reverently to such men as were in authority in the world in his time; and he not rebelliously behaved himself, but[α] openly did teach the Jews to pay tribute unto the Roman Emperor, though a foreign and a pagan prince; yea, himself with his Apostles paid tribute unto him; and finally, being brought before Pontius Pilate[β], a stranger born and an heathen man, being lord president of Jewry, he acknowledged[γ] his authority and power to be given him from God, and obeyed patiently the sentence of most painful and shameful death, which the said judge pronounced and gave[δ] most unjustly against him, without any grudge, murmuring, or evil word once giving. There be many other[b] examples of the obedience to princes, even such as be evil, in the New Testament, to the utter confusion of disobedient and rebellious people: but this one may be an eternal example, which the Son of God, and so the Lord of all, Jesus Christ, hath given to us his Christians and servants; and such as may serve for all, to teach us to obey princes, though strangers, wicked, and wrongful, when God for our sins shall place such over us. Whereby it followeth unavoidably, that such as do disobey or rebel against their own natural gracious sovereigns, howsoever they call themselves or be named of others, yet are they indeed no true Christians, but worse than Jews, worse than heathens, and such as shall never enjoy the kingdom of heaven, which Christ by his obedience purchased for true Christians, being obedient to him the King of all kings, and to their prince, whom he hath placed over them. The which kingdom, the peculiar place of all such obedient subjects, I beseech God our heavenly Father, for the same our Saviour Jesus Christ's sake, to grant unto us. To whom with the Holy Ghost be all laud, honour, and glory now and for ever. Amen.

α Matt. xvii, 25 &c.: Mark xii, 17: Luke xx, 25.

β Matt. xxvii, 2: Luke xxiii, 1.

γ John xix, 11.

δ Matt. xxvii, 26: Luke xxiii, 24.

Thus have you heard the Second Part of this Homily: now, good people, let us pray.

The Prayer as before[c].

[a] yet we] we yet 1623. [b] many other] many and divers other *from* 1582. [c] as before] as in that time it was published 1623, *and then the Prayer itself.*

THE THIRD PART OF THE HOMILY

AGAINST DISOBEDIENCE AND WILFUL REBELLION.[a]

AS I have in the First Part of this Treatise shewed unto you the doctrine of the holy Scriptures as concerning the obedience of true subjects to their princes, even as well to such as be evil, as unto the good, and in the Second Part of the same Treaty confirmed the said[b] doctrine by notable examples, likewise taken out of the holy Scriptures; so remaineth it now, that I partly do declare unto you in this Third Part, what an abominable sin against God and man rebellion is, and how dreadfully the wrath of God is kindled and inflamed against all rebels, and what horrible plagues, punishments, and deaths, and finally eternal damnation doth hang over their heads; as how on the contrary part good and obedient subjects are in God's favour, and be partakers of peace, quietness, and security with other God's manifold blessings in this world, and, by his mercies, through our Saviour Christ, of life everlasting also in the world to come.

How horrible a sin against God and man rebellion is, cannot possibly[c] be expressed according unto the greatness thereof. For he that nameth rebellion nameth not a singular or one only sin, as is theft, robbery, murder, and such like; but he nameth the whole puddle and sink of all sins against God and man; against his prince, his country, his countrymen, his parents, his children, his kinsfolks, his friends, and against all men universally; all sins, I say, against God and all men heaped together nameth he that nameth rebellion.

The first table of God's law broken by rebellion and the sins of rebels against God.[d]

For, concerning the offence of God's Majesty, who seeth not that rebellion riseth first by contempt of God and of his holy ordinances and laws, wherein[a] he so straitly commandeth obedience, forbiddeth disobedience and rebellion? And, besides the dishonour done by rebels unto God's holy Name by their breaking of the oath[e] made to their prince with the attestation of God's Name and calling of his Majesty to witness, who hear-

[a] Rom. xiii, [1–7.]

[a] REBELLION.] REBELLION. The Second Part. A–E. [b] said] same *from* 1571. [c] possibly] possiblie A, possible *from* B *till* 1582. [d] The first table—God.] *omitted* 1623. [e] the oath] their oath *from* 1571.

eth not the horrible oaths and blasphemies of God's holy Name that are used daily amongst rebels, that is either amongst them or heareth the truth of their behaviour? Who knoweth not that rebels do not only themselves leave all works necessary to be done upon workdays undone, whiles they accomplish their abominable work of[f] rebellion, and do[g] compel others, that would gladly be well occupied, to do the same; but also how rebels do not only leave the Sabbath day of the Lord unsanctified, the temple and church of the Lord unresorted unto, but also do by their works of wickedness most horribly profane and pollute the Sabbath day, serving Satan and, by doing of his work, making it the devil's day instead of the Lord's day, besides that they compel good men, that would gladly serve the Lord, assembling in his temple and church upon his day as becometh the Lord's servants, to assemble and meet armed in the field to resist the fury of such rebels? Yea, and many rebels, lest they should leave any part of God's commandments in the first table of his law unbroken, or any sin against God undone, do make rebellion for the maintenance of their images and idols, and of their idolatry committed or to be committed by them; and in despite of God cut and tear in sunder his holy word, and tread it under their feet, as of late ye know was done[1].

The fifth commandment.

As concerning the second table of God's law, and all sins that may be committed against man, who seeth not that they be all contained[h] in rebellion? For first, the rebels do not only dishonour their prince, the parent of their country, but also do dishonour and shame their natural parents, if they have any, do shame their kinred and friends, do disherit[i] and undo for ever their children and heirs.

The sixth and the eighth[j] commandment.

Thefts, robberies, and murders, which of all sins are most lothed of most men, are in no men so much, nor so perniciously and mischievously, as in rebels. For the most errant[k] thieves and[l] cruellest murderers that ever were, so long as they refrain from rebellion, as they are not many in

[f] work of] worst of 1623. [g] and do] and to *from* 1571. [h] be all contained] be not contained 1571–1595, be contained 1623. [i] disherit] disinherit 1623. [j] and the eighth] and eighth *from* 1571. [k] errant] arrant 1623. [l] thieves and cruellest] thieves, cruellest 1623.

[1] The Earls of Northumberland and Westmorland published a Declaration stating that the main object of their enterprise was the restoring of "the true and catholic religion towards God" and of "all ancient customs and liberties to God's Church." *Strype, Ann.* 1, 583, 584. The tearing, insulting, and burning of Bibles and Prayer Books, especially at Durham, is recorded by Jewel on 1 Thess. v, 4–10, by Thomas Norton in his Address "to the Quenes Maiesties poore deceived Subiectes of the North Countrey, drawen into rebellion by the Earles of Northumberland and Westmerland" (8vo. 1569), and by Camden in his Annales, p. 166.

number, so spreadeth their wickedness and damnation unto a few; they spoil but a few, they shed the blood but of few[m], in comparison. But rebels are the cause of infinite robberies, and murders of great multitudes, and of those also whom they should defend from the spoil and violence of other; and, as rebels are many in number, so doth their wickedness and damnation spread itself unto many. And, if whoredom and adultery amongst such persons as are agreeable to such wickedness are (as they indeed be) most damnable, what are the forcible oppressions of matrons and men's wives, and the violating and deflowering of virgins and maids, which are most rife with rebels? how horrible and damnable, think you, are they? Now, besides that rebels, by breach of their faith given and oath[n] made to their prince, be guilty of most damnable perjury, it is wondrous to see what false colours and feigned causes, by slanderous lies made upon their prince and the counsellors, rebels will devise to cloak their rebellion withal, which is the worst and most damnable of all false witness bearing that may be possible. For what should I speak of coveting or desiring of other men's wives, houses, lands, goods, and servants in rebels, who by their wills would leave unto no man any thing of his own?

The seventh commandment.

The ninth commandment.

The tenth commandment.

Thus you see that all God's laws[o] are by rebels violated and broken, and that all sins possible to be committed against God or man be contained in rebellion: which sins if a man list to name by the accustomed names of the seven capital or deadly sins, as pride, envy, wrath, covetousness, sloth, gluttony, and lechery, he shall find them all in rebellion and amongst rebels. For first, as ambition and desire to be aloft, which is the property of pride, stirreth up many men's minds to rebellion, so cometh it of a Luciferian pride and presumption that a few rebellious subjects should set themselves up against the majesty of their prince, against the wisdom of the counsellors, against the power and force of all nobility and the faithful subjects and people of the whole realm. As for envy, wrath, murder, and desire of blood, and covetousness of other men's goods, lands, and livings, they are the inseparable accidents of all rebels, and peculiar properties that do usually stir up wicked men unto rebellion. Now such as by riotousness, gluttony, drunkenness, excess of apparel, and unthrifty games have wasted their own goods unthriftily, the same are most apt unto and most desirous

[m] of few] of a few 1623. [n] and oath] an oath 1587, 1595, and the oath 1623. [o] God's laws] good laws 1623.

of rebellion, whereby they trust to come by other men's goods unlawfully and violently. And, where other gluttons and drunkards take too much of such meats and drinks as are served to tables, rebels waste and consume in short space all corn in barns, fields, or elsewhere, whole garners[p], whole storehouses, whole cellars, devour whole flocks of sheep, whole droves of oxen and kine. And, as rebels that are married, leaving their own wives at home, do most ungraciously, so much more do unmarried men, worse than any stallands or horses, being now by rebellion set at liberty from correction of laws which bridled them before; which abuse[q] by force other men's wives and daughters, and ravish virgins and maidens, most shamefully, abominably, and damnably. Thus all sins, by all names that sins may be named, and by all means that all sins[r] may be committed and wrought, do all wholly upon heaps follow rebellion, and are to be found all together amongst rebels.

a 2 Sam. xxiv, 13.

Now, whereas pestilence, famine, and war are by the holy Scriptures[a] declared to be the greatest worldly plagues and miseries that lightly[s] can be, it is evident that all the miseries which all[t] these plagues have in them do wholly all together follow rebellion; wherein as all their miseries be, so is there much more mischief then in them all. For it is known that in the resorting of great companies of men together, (which in rebellion happeneth both upon the part of true subjects and of the rebels,) by their close lying together, and corruption of the air and place where they do lie with ordure and much filth in the hot[u] weather, and by[x] unwholesome lodging and lying often upon the ground, specially in cold and wet weathers[y] in winter; by their unwholesome diet and feeding at all times, and often by famine and lack of meat and drink in due time, and again by taking too much at other times; it is well known, I say, that as well plagues and pestilences, as all other kinds of sickness[z] and maladies, by these means grow upon and amongst[a] men, whereby mo men are consumed at the length, than are by dint of sword suddenly slain in the field. So that not only pestilences, but also all other sickness[b], diseases, and maladies, do follow rebellion; which are much more horrible

[p] garners] graners A–E. [q] before; which abuse] before) abuse 1623. [r] that all sins] that sins 1623. [s] lightly] likely 1623. [t] which all] that all *from* 1571. [u] hot] hoatte A–E, 1571. [x] weather, and by] weather, by A. [y] weathers] weather from 1582. [z] of sickness] of sicknesses *from* 1582. [a] grow upon and amongst] grow up and spring amongst] *from* 1582. [b] other sickness] other sicknesses *from* 1574.

than plagues, pestilences, and diseases sent directly from God, as hereafter shall appear more plainly.

And as for hunger and famine, they are the peculiar companions of rebellion. For, whiles[c] rebels do in short time spoil and consume all corn and necessary provision, which men with their labours had gotten and appointed upon for their finding the whole year after; and also do let all other men, husbandmen and others, from their husbandry and other necessary works, whereby provision should be made for times to come; who seeth not that extreme famine and hunger must needs shortly ensue and follow rebellion?

Now whereas the wise King and godly Prophet David judged[β] war to be worse than either famine or pestilence, for that these two are often suffered by God for man's amendment, and be not sins of themselves, but wars have always the sins and mischiefs of men upon the one side or other joined with them, and therefore is war the greatest of these worldly mischiefs; but of all wars civil war is the worst; and far more abominable yet is rebellion than any civil war, being unworthy the name of any war, so far it exceedeth all wars in all naughtiness, in all mischief, and in all abomination; and therefore our Saviour Christ denounceth[γ] desolation and destruction to that realm that by sedition and rebellion is divided in itself: now[d], as I have shewed before that pestilence and famine, so is it yet more evident that all the calamities, miseries, and mischiefs of war, be more grievous and do more follow rebellion than any other war, as being far worse than all other wars. For not only those ordinary and usual mischiefs and miseries of other wars do follow rebellion, as, corn and other things necessary to man's use to be spoiled; houses, villages, towns, cities to be taken, sacked, burned, and destroyed; not only many wealthy[e] men, but whole countries, to be impoverished and utterly beggared; many thousands of men to be slain and murdered; women and maids to be violated and deflowered: which[f] things, when they are done by foreign enemies, we do much mourn, (as we have great causes,) yet are all these miseries without any wickedness wrought by any our countrymen[g]. But, when these mischiefs are wrought in rebellion by them that should be friends, by countrymen, by kinsmen, by those that should defend their country and countrymen from such miseries, the misery is

β 2 Sam. xxiv, 14.

γ Matt. xii, 25.

c whiles] while *from* 1582. d therefore our Saviour——itself: now] *not in* A. e many wealthy] many very wealthy *from* 1571. f which] *not in* A. g any our countrymen] any of our own countrymen *from* 1574.

nothing so great as is the mischief and wickedness; when the subjects unnaturally do rebel against their prince, whose honour and life they should defend, though it were with loss[h] of their own lives; countrymen to disturb the public peace and quietness of their country, for defence of whose quietness they should spend their lives; the brother to seek and often to work the death of his brother, the son of the father; the father to[i] seek or procure the death of his sons, being at man's age; and by their faults to disherit[k] their innocent children and kinsmen their heirs for ever, for whom they might purchase livings and lands, as natural parents do take care and pains and be[l] at great costs and charges; and universally, instead of all quietness, joy, and felicity, (which do follow blessed peace and due obedience,) to bring in all trouble, sorrow, disquietness of minds and bodies, and all mischief and calamities[m]; to turn all good order upside down; to bring all good laws in contempt, and to tread them under feet; to oppress all virtue and honesty and all virtuous and honest persons, and to set all vice and wickedness and all vicious and wicked men at liberty to work their wicked wills, which were before bridled by wholesome laws; to weaken, to overthrow, and to consume the strength of the realm, their natural country, as well by the spending and wasting of the money[n] and treasure of the prince and realm, as by murdering of the[o] people of the same, their own countrymen, who should defend the honour[8] of their prince and liberty of their country against the invasion of foreign enemies; and so finally to make their country, thus by their mischief weakened, ready to be a prey and spoil to all outward enemies that will invade it, to the utter and perpetual captivity, slavery, and destruction of all their countrymen, their children, their friends, their kinsfolks left alive, whom by their wicked rebellion they procure to be delivered into the hands of foreign[p] enemies, as much as in them doth lie.

8 Prov. xiv, [28.]

In foreign wars our countrymen in obtaining the victory win the[q] praise of valiantness; yea, and though they were overcomed and slain, yet win they an honest commendation in this world, and die[r] in a good conscience, for serving God, their prince, and their country, and be children of eternal salvation. But in rebellion[s], how desperate and strong soever they be, yet

h with loss] with the loss *from* 1571. i father to] fathers to A, B. k disherit] disinherit 1623. l and be] and to be *from* 1582. m calamities] calamity *from* 1574. n of the money] of money 1623. o murdering of the] murdering the 1623. p of foreign] of the foreign *from* 1582. q win the] winneth the A. r die] dieth A. s in rebellion] the rebellion 1623.

win they shame here in fighting against God, their prince, and country, and therefore justly do fall headlong into hell if they die, and live in shame and fearful conscience, though they escape. But commonly they be rewarded with shameful deaths, their heads[t] and carcases set upon poles or[u] hanged in chains, eaten with kites and crows, judged unworthy the honour of burial; and so their souls, if they repent not, (as commonly they do not,) the devil harrieth[x 2] them into hell in the midst of their mischief. For which dreadful execution St. Paul[e] sheweth the cause of obedience, not only for fear of death, but also in conscience to Godward, for fear of eternal damnation in the world to come.

[e] Rom. xiii, [1-5.]

Wherefore, good people, let us, as the children of obedience, fear the dreadful execution of God, and live in quiet obedience, to be the children of everlasting salvation. For, as heaven is the place of good obedient subjects, and hell the prison and dungeon of rebels against God and their prince; so is that realm happy where most obedience of subjects doth appear, being the very figure of heaven; and contrariwise, where most rebellions and rebels be, there is the express similitude of hell, and the rebels themselves are the very figures of fiends and devils, and their captain the ungracious pattern of Lucifer and Satan, the prince of darkness: of whose rebellion as they be followers, so shall they of his damnation in hell undoubtedly be partakers; and as undoubtedly children of peace the inheritors of heaven with God the Father, God the Son, and God the Holy Ghost. To whom be all honour and glory for ever and ever. Amen.

Thus have you heard the Third Part of this Homily: now, good people, let us pray.

The Prayer as before[y].

[t] heads] hands 1623. [u] or] and *from* 1582. [x] harrieth] hurrieth 1623. [y] as before] as in that time it was published 1623, *and then the Prayer itself.*

2 harrieth, or harieth: draggeth. "Haryyn, or drawyn: Trahicio, pertraho." *Promptorium Parvulorum,* where see Alb. Way's note.

After Sir Roger Clifford, on the way to Tower Hill, had tried to escape, the sheriffs and their officers "constrayned hym to lye downe uppon the hardyll, and newly band hym, and so haryed hym to the sayde place of execucion." *Fabyan's Chronicle, an.* 1484–5.

THE FOURTH PART OF THE HOMILY

AGAINST DISOBEDIENCE AND WILFUL REBELLION[a].

FOR your further instruction, good people, to shew unto you how much Almighty God doth abhor disobedience and wilful rebellion, specially when rebels advance themselves so high that they arm themselves with weapon and stand in field to fight against God, their prince, and their country, it shall not be out of the way to shew some examples set out in Scriptures, written for our eternal erudition.

We may soon know, good people, how heinous offence the treachery of rebellion is, if we call to remembrance the heavy wrath and dreadful indignation of Almighty God against such subjects[b] as do only but inwardly grudge, mutter, and murmur against their governors; though their inward treason, so privily hatched in their breasts, come not to open declaration of their doings: as hard it is, whom the devil hath so far inticed against God's word, to keep themselves there; no, he meaneth still to blow the coal, to kindle their rebellious hearts to flame into open deeds, if he be not with grace speedily withstanded. Some of the children of Israel[α], being murmurers against their magistrates appointed over them by God, were stricken with foul leprosy: many were burnt up with fire suddenly sent from the Lord: sometime a great sort of thousands were consumed with the pestilence: sometime they were stinged to death with a strange kind of fiery serpents: and, which is most horrible, some of the captains with their band of murmurers, not dying by any usual or natural death of men, but[β] the earth opening, they, with their wives, children, and families, were swallowed quick down into hell. Which horrible destructions of such Israelites as were murmurers against Moyses, appointed by God to be their head and chief magistrate, are recorded in the book of Numbers and other places of the Scriptures, for perpetual memory and warning to all subjects how highly God is displeased with the murmuring and evil speaking of subjects against

α Numb. xi, [1;] xii, 10; xvi, [35, 46–49; xxi, 5, 6:] Ps. lxxvii [lxxviii, 31.]

β Numb. xvi, [27–33.]

a REBELLION.] REBELLION. The Fourth Part, A–E. b against such subjects] against subjects 1623.

their princes; for that, as the Scripture recordeth[γ], their *murmur* was *not against* their prince only, being a mortal creature, *but against God* himself also. Now, if such strange and horrible plagues did fall upon such subjects as did only murmur and speak evil against their heads, what shall become of those most wicked imps of the devil that do conspire, arm themselves, assemble great numbers of armed rebels, and lead them with them against their prince and country, spoiling and robbing, killing and murdering all good subjects that do withstand them, as many as they may prevail against? But those examples are written to stay us, not only from such mischiefs, but also from murmuring or[c] speaking once an evil word against our prince; which though any should do never so secretly, yet do the holy Scriptures shew[δ] that *the* very *birds of the air will bewray them*, and these so many examples before noted out of the same[d] holy Scriptures do declare that they shall not escape horrible punishment therefore.

γ Exod. xvi, 7 &c.

δ Eccles. x, [20.]

Now concerning actual rebellion, amongst many examples thereof set forth in the holy Scriptures, the example of Absolon[ε] is notable; who, entering into conspiracy against king David his father, both used the advice of very witty men, and assembled a very great and huge company of rebels. The which Absolon, though he were most goodly of person, of great nobility (being the king's son), in great favour of the people, and so dearly beloved of the king himself, so much that he gave commandment[ζ] that (notwithstanding his rebellion) his life should be saved; when for these considerations most men were afraid to lay their hands upon him, a great tree[η] stretching out his arm, as it were for that purpose, caught him by the great and long bush of his goodly hair, lapping about it as he fled hastily bareheaded under the said tree, and so hanged him up by the hair of his head in the air, to give an eternal document, that neither comeliness of personage, neither nobility, nor favour of the people, no, nor the favour of the king himself, can save a rebel from due punishment; God, the King of all kings, being so offended with him that, rather than he should lack due execution for his treason, every tree by the way will be a gallows or gibbet unto him, and the hair of his own head will be unto him instead of an halter to hang him up with, rather than he should lack one: a fearful example of God's punishment, good people, to consider. Now Achitophel, though otherwise an ex-

ε 2 Sam. xv, 12; and xvii, 1 &c., 11; and xviii, 7, 8.

ζ Ibid. xviii, 5.

η Ibid. 9.

Achitophel.

c or] and *from* 1582. d same] *omitted after* 1574.

θ 2 Sam. xv, 12; and xvi, 21, 23; and xvii, 23.

ceeding wise man, yet the mischievous counsellor[θ] of Absolon in this wicked rebellion, for lack of an hangman (a convenient servitor for such a traitor), went and hanged up himself: a worthy end of all false rebels, who, rather than they should lack due execution, will, by God's just judgment, become hangmen unto themselves. Thus happened it to the captains of that rebellion, beside[ι] forty thousand[e] of rascal[1] rebels slain in the field and in the chase. Likewise is it to be seen in the holy Scriptures, how that great rebellion[κ] which the traitor Seba moved in Israel was suddenly appeased, the head of the captain traitor (by the means of a seely woman) being cut off.

ι Ibid. xviii, 7, 8.

κ Ibid. xx.

And, as the holy Scriptures do shew, so doth daily experience prove, that the *counsels*[λ], conspiracies, and attempts of rebels never took effect[2], neither came to good, but to most horrible end. For, though God do[f] oftentimes prosper just and lawful enemies, which be no subjects, against their foreign enemies, yet did he never long prosper rebellious subjects against their prince, were they never so great in authority or so many in number. Five princes or kings[μ] (for so the Scripture termeth them) with all their multitudes could not prevail against Chodorlaomor, unto whom they had promised loyalty and obedience, and had continued in the same certain years; but they were all overthrown and taken prisoners by him: but Abraham with his family and kinsfolks, an handful of men in respect, owing no subjection unto Chodorlaomor, overthrew him and all his host in battle, and recovered the prisoners, and delivered them. So that, though war be so dreadful and cruel a thing as it is, yet doth God often prosper a few in lawful wars with foreign enemies against many thousands: but never yet prospered he subjects being rebels against their natural sovereign, were they never so great or noble, so many, so stout, so witty and politic; but always they came by the overthrow and to a shameful end: so much doth God abhor rebellion more than other wars, though otherwise being so dreadful and so great a destruction to mankind. Though not only great multitudes of the rude and rascal commons, but sometime also men of great wit, nobility, and

λ Ps. xx, 12 [xxi, 11.]

μ Gen. xiv.

e forty thousand] *so in all.* f God do] God doth *from* 1571.

1 rascal: a term of the forest for lean poor deer, of the common herd; thence applied, with no imputation of dishonesty, to people of the common sort, who are not *egregii*. So Spenser speaks of "the raskall many" running "in rude rablement", and of a "cruell Capitaine" employing "his raskall routs". *Faerie Queene*, I, xii, 9; II, ix, 15.

2 Cogitaverunt consilia quae non potuerunt stabilire. *Vulg.*

authority, have moved rebellions against their lawful princes, (whereas true nobility should most abhor such villainous, and true wisdom should most detest such frantic, rebellion;) though they would[g] pretend sundry causes, as the redress of the commonwealth, (which rebellion of all other mischiefs doth most destroy,) or reformation of religion, (whereas rebellion is most against all true religion;) though they have made a great shew of holy meaning by beginning their rebellions with a counterfeit service of God, (as did wicked Absolon begin[v] his rebellion with sacrificing unto God;) though they display and bear about ensigns and banners, which are acceptable unto the rude ignorant common people, great multitudes of whom by such false pretences and shews they do deceive and draw unto them: yet, were the multitudes of the rebels never so huge and great, the captains never so noble, politic, and witty, the pretences feigned to be never so good and holy, yet the speedy overthrow of all rebels, of what number, state, or condition soever they were, or what colour or cause soever they pretended, is and ever hath been such, that God thereby doth shew that he alloweth neither the dignity of any person, nor the multitude of any people, nor the weight of any cause, as sufficient for the which the subjects may move rebellion against their princes. Turn over and read the histories of all nations; look over the chronicles of our own country; call to mind so many rebellions of old time, and some yet fresh in memory; ye shall not find that God ever prospered any rebellion against their natural and lawful prince, but contrariwise that the rebels were overthrown and slain, and such as were taken prisoners dreadfully executed. Consider the great and noble families of dukes, marquesses, earls, and other lords, whose names ye shall read in our chronicles, now clean extinguished and gone; and seek out the causes of the decay; you shall find that not lack of issue and heirs male hath so much wrought that decay and waste of noble bloods and houses, as hath rebellion.

[v] 2 Sam. xv, 12.

And, for so much as the redress of the commonwealth hath of old been the usual feigned pretence of rebels, and religion now of late beginneth to be a colour of rebellion, let all godly and discreet subjects consider well of both, and first concerning religion. If peaceable king Salomon was judged of God to be more meet to build his temple, (whereby the ordering of religion is meant,) than his father king David, though otherwise a most

[g] would] should *from* 1582.

godly king, for that David was a great warrior, and had shed much blood[g], though it were in his wars against the enemies of God; of this may all godly and reasonable subjects consider, that a peaceable prince, specially our most peaceable and merciful Queen, who hath hitherto shed no blood at all, no, not of her most deadly enemies, is more like and far meeter either to set up or to maintain true religion than are bloody rebels, who have not shed the blood of God's enemies as king David had done, but do seek to shed the blood of God's friends, of their own countrymen, and of their own most dear friends and kinsfolk, yea, the destruction of their most gracious Prince and natural country, for defence of whom they ought to be ready to shed their blood, if need should so require. What a religion it is that such men and by[h] such means would restore may easily be judged; even as good a religion surely as rebels be good men and obedient subjects, and as rebellion is a good mean of redress and reformation, being itself the greatest deformation of all that may possibly[i] be. But, as the truth of the Gospel of our Saviour Christ, being quietly and soberly taught, though it do cost them their lives that do teach it, is able to maintain the true religion; so hath a frantic religion need of such furious maintenances as is rebellion, and of such patrons as are rebels, being ready, not to die for the true religion, but to kill all that shall or dare speak against their false superstition and wicked idolatry.

g [2 Chron. xxii, 7–10.]

Now concerning pretences of any redress of the commonwealth made by rebels, every man that hath but half an eye may see how vain they be, rebellion being, as I have before declared, the greatest ruin and destruction of all commonwealths that may be possible. And whoso looketh, on the one part, upon the persons and government of the Queen's most honourable counsellors, by the experiment of so many years proved honourable to her Majesty and most profitable and beneficial unto our country and countrymen; and, on the other part, considereth the persons, state, and conditions of the rebels themselves, the reformers (as they take upon them) of the present government; he shall find that the most rash and harebrained men, the most greatest[j] unthrifts, that have most lewdly wasted their own goods and lands, those that are over the ears in debt, and such as for thefts[k], robberies, and murders dare not in any

h men and by] men by *from* 1582. i possibly] possiblie A–C, possible *from* D. j the most greatest] the greatest 1623. k for thefts] for their thefts *from* 1571.

well governed commonwealth, where good laws are in force, shew their faces, such as are of most lewd and wicked behaviour and life, and all such as will not or cannot live in peace, are always most ready to move rebellion or to take[l] part with rebels. And are not these meet men, trow you, to restore the commonwealth decayed, who have so spoiled and consumed all their own wealth and thrift? and very like to mend[m] other men's manners, who have so vile vices and abominable conditions themselves? Surely that which they falsely call reformation is indeed not only a defacing or a deformation, but also an utter destruction, of all common wealth; as would well appear might the rebels have their wills, and doth right well and too well appear by their doing in such places of the country where rebels do rout; where though they tarry but a very little while, they make such reformation that they destroy all places and undo all men where they come, that the child yet unborn may rue it, and shall many years hereafter curse them.

Let no good and discreet subjects therefore follow the flag or banner displayed to rebellion and borne by rebels, though it have the image of the plough painted therein with GOD SPEED THE PLOUGH written under in great letters[3], knowing that none hinder the plough more than rebels, who will neither go to the plough themselves, nor suffer other that would go unto it. And, though some rebels bear the picture of the five wounds painted against those who put their only hope of salvation in the wounds of Christ, not those wounds which are painted in a clout by some lewd painter, but in those wounds which Christ himself bare in his precious body; though they, little knowing what the cross of Christ meaneth, which neither carver nor painter can make, do bear the image of the cross painted in a rag against those that have the cross of Christ printed[n] in their hearts[o]; yea[p], though they paint withal in

[l] or to take] or take *from* 1582. [m] mend] amend *from* 1582. [n] printed] painted *all except* A. *See before, page* 423, *line* 19. [o] And though——their hearts] And though some rebels, little knowing what the cross of Christ meaneth, which neither carver nor painter can make, do bear the image of the cross painted in a rag against those that have the cross of Christ printed in their hearts; though they bear the picture of the five wounds painted against those who put their only hope of salvation in the wounds of Christ, not those wounds which are painted in a clout by some lewd painter, but in those wounds which Christ himself bare in his precious body A. [p] yea] yet *all* 1574.

[3] No express statement of this motto, or of the ensign of the plough, being used by the rebels in the North has been discovered in any writer; but Norton's Address to them (cited in note 1 on the Third Part of this Homily) ends with these words: "And so yet till other errors be purged by God's grace working by the hearing of his word, we shall al goe under the gentle yoke of our naturall soveraigne, there let us draw lovingly together, and then say and sing merily, God spede the ploughe of England."

their flags, HOC SIGNO VINCES, By this sign thou shalt get the victory[4], by a most fond imitation of the posy of Constantinus Magnus[5] that noble Christian Emperor and great conqueror of God's enemies, a most unmeet ensign for rebels, the enemies of God, their prince, and country; or what other banner soever they shall bear[q]; yet let no good and godly subject, upon any hope of victory or good success[r], follow such standardbearers of rebellion. For, as examples of such practices are to be found as well in the histories of old as also of later[s] rebellions in our fathers' and our fresh memory; so, notwithstanding these pretences made and banners borne, are recorded withal unto[t] perpetual memory the great and horrible murders of infinite multitudes and thousands of the common people slain in rebellion, the dreadful[u] executions of the authors and captains, the pitiful undoing of their wives and children, and disheriting[x] of the heirs of the rebels for ever, the spoiling, wasting, and destruction of the people and country where rebellion was first begun, that the child then yet unborn might rue and lament it, with the final overthrow and shameful deaths of all rebels, set forth as well in the histories of foreign nations as in the chronicles of our own country; some thereof being yet in fresh memory, which, if they were collected together, would make many volumes and books; but on the contrary part all good luck, success, and prosperity that ever happened unto any rebels of any age, time, or country may be contained in a very few lines or words.

Wherefore, to conclude, let all good subjects, considering how horrible a sin against God, their prince, their country, and countrymen, against all God's and man's laws, rebellion is, being indeed not one several sin, but all sins against God and man heaped together; considering the mischievous life and

q yea, though they paint——shall bear *not in* A. r upon any hope of victory or good success] *not in* A. s later] latter *all except* A. t withal unto] withal to *from* 1582. u the dreadful] dreadful *from* 1582. x disheriting] disinheriting 1623.

4 Erle Percy there his ancyent spred,
The Halfe Moone shining all soe faire:
The Nortons ancyent had the crosse,
And the five wounds our Lord did beare.

The Rising in the North, vv. 105–108, in *Percy's Reliques of Ancient English Poetry, Vol.* 1, *p.* 293, *ed.* 4, 1794.

See also *Thomas Norton's Warning agaynst the dangerous practises of Papistes, and specially the parteners of the late Rebellion*, printed by John Daye without date, sign. H 2 *a*: and *Camd. Annal. p.* 166. Similar banners had been used in the Northern Rebellion in 1536. See *Speed's History of Great Britain*, IX, xxi, *p.* 1018, *ed.* 1632.

5 *Euseb. de Vit. Const.* I, 28.

deeds and the shameful ends and deaths of all rebels hitherto, and the pitiful undoing of their wives, children, and families, and disheriting[y] of their heirs for ever; and above all things considering the eternal damnation that is prepared for all impenitent rebels in hell with Satan, the first founder of rebellion and grand captain of all rebels; let all good subjects, I say, considering these things, avoid and flee all rebellion, as the greatest of all mischiefs, and embrace due obedience to God and our Prince, as the greatest of all virtues; that we may both escape all evils and miseries that do follow rebellion in this world, and eternal damnation in the world to come, and enjoy peace, quietness, and security with all other God's benefits and blessings which follow obedience in this life, and finally may enjoy the kingdom of heaven, the peculiar place of all obedient subjects to God and their prince, in the world to come. Which I beseech God, the King of all kings, grant unto us for the obedience of his Son our Saviour Jesus Christ. Unto whom with the Father and the Holy Ghost, one God and King immortal, all honour, service, and obedience of all his creatures is due for ever and ever. Amen.

Thus have you heard the Fourth Part of this Homily: now, good people, let us pray.

The Prayer as before[z].

[y] disheriting] disinheriting 1623.

[z] as before] as in that time it was published 1623, *and then the Prayer itself.*

THE FIFTH PART OF THE HOMILY

AGAINST DISOBEDIENCE AND WILFUL REBELLION.[a]

WHEREAS, after both doctrine and examples of due obedience of subjects to their princes, I declared lastly unto you what an abominable sin against God and man rebellion is, and what horrible plagues, punishments, and deaths, with death everlasting finally, doth hang over the heads of all rebels, it shall not be either impertinent or unprofitable now to[b] declare, who they be whom the devil, the first author and founder of rebellion, doth chiefly use to the stirring up of subjects to rebel against their lawful princes; that, knowing them, you may[c] flee them and their damnable suggestions, avoid all rebellion, and so[d] escape the horrible plagues and dreadful deaths[e] and damnation eternal finally due to all rebels.

Though[f] many causes of rebellion may be reckoned, and almost as many as there be vices in men and women, as hath been before noted, yet in this place I will only touch the principal and most usual causes, as specially ambition and ignorance. By ambition I mean the unlawful and restless desire in men to be of higher estate than God hath given or appointed unto them. By ignorance I mean no unskilfulness in arts or sciences, but the lack of knowledge of God's blessed will declared in his holy word; which teacheth both extremely to abhor all rebellion, as the[g] root of all mischief, and specially to delight in obedience, as the beginning and foundation of all goodness, as hath been also before specified. And, as these are the two chief causes of rebellion, so are there specially two sorts of men in whom these vices do reign, by whom the devil, the author of all evil, doth chiefly stir up all disobedience and rebellion. The restless ambitious having once determined by one means or other to achieve to their intended purpose, when

[a] REBELLION.] REBELLION. The Fifth Part. A–E. [b] now to] now lastly to A, *the Homily being then divided into five Parts only.* [c] you may] ye may *from* D. [d] and so] and to 1623. [e] deaths] death *from* 1582. [f] rebels. Though] rebels, and, embracing all obedience to God and your natural Prince, may enjoy God's blessings and your Prince's favour in all peace, quietness, and security in this world, and finally attain through Christ our Saviour life everlasting in the world to come; and so to conclude this whole treaty of due obedience and against damnable rebellion. Though A. [g] as the] as being the *from* 1582.

they cannot by lawful and peaceable means climb so high as they do desire, they attempt the same by force and violence; wherein, when they cannot prevail against the ordinary authority and power of lawful princes and governors themselves alone, they do seek the aid and help of the ignorant multitude, abusing them to their wicked purpose. Wherefore, seeing a few ambitious and malicious are the authors and heads, and multitudes of ignorant men are the ministers and furtherers, of rebellion, the chief point of this Part shall be as well to notify to the simple and ignorant men who they be that have been and be the usual[h] authors of rebellion, that they may know them, and also to admonish them to beware of the subtile suggestions of such restless ambitious persons, and so to flee them; that rebellions, though attempted by a few ambitious, through the lack of maintenance by any multitudes may speedily and easily, without any great labour, danger, or damage, be repressed and clearly extinguished.

It is well known, as well by all histories as by daily experience, that none have either more ambitiously aspired above emperors, kings, and princes, nor have more perniciously moved the ignorant people to rebellion against their princes, than certain persons which falsely challenge to themselves to be only counted and called spiritual. I must therefore here yet once again briefly put you, good people, in remembrance out of God's holy word, how our Saviour Jesus Christ and his holy Apostles, the heads and chief of all true spiritual and ecclesiastical men, behaved themselves towards the princes and rulers of their time, though not the best governors that ever were; that you be not ignorant whether they be the true disciples and followers of Christ and his Apostles, and so true spiritual men, that either by ambition do so highly aspire, or do most maliciously teach or most perniciously do execute rebellion against their lawful princes, being the worst of all carnal works and mischievous deeds. The holy Scriptures do teach[a] most expressly, that our Saviour Christ himself, and his holy[i] Apostles[k] St. Paul, St. Peter, with others, were unto the magistrates and higher powers, which ruled at their being upon the earth, both obedient themselves, and did also diligently and earnestly exhort all other Christians to the like obedience unto their princes and governors: whereby it is evident that men of the clergy and ecclesiastical ministers, as their successors, ought

[a] Matt. xvii, 25: Mark xii, 17: Luke xx, 25: Matt. xxvii: Luke xxiii: Rom. xiii, 1 &c.: 1 Tim. ii, 1, 2: 1 Pet. ii, 13.

[h] be the usual] be usual *from* 1582. [i] holy (*line* 35)] *omitted after* E. [k] Apostles] Apostle *till* 1582.

β John vi, 15; and xviii, 36.

γ Matt. xx, 25: Mark x, 42: Luke xxii, 25.

δ Matt. xxiii, 8: Luke ix, 46: 2 Cor. i, 24: 1 Pet. v, 3.

both themselves specially and before others[1] to be obedient unto their princes, and also to exhort all others unto the same. Our Saviour Christ likewise[β], teaching by his doctrine that *his kingdom was not of this world,* did by his example, in fleeing from those that would have made him king, confirm the same; expressly also forbidding[γ] his Apostles, and by them the whole clergy, all princely dominion over people and nations: and he, and his holy Apostles likewise, namely Peter and Paul, did forbid[δ] unto all ecclesiastical ministers dominion over the Church of Christ. And indeed, whiles that[m] ecclesiastical ministers continued in Christ's Church in that order that is in Christ's word prescribed[n] unto them, and in Christian kingdoms kept themselves obedient to their own princes, as the holy Scriptures[o] do[p] teach them, both was Christ's Church more clear from ambitious emulations and contentions, and the state of Christian kingdoms less subject unto tumults and rebellions.

ε Matt. xviii, 4; and xx, 28: Luke ix, 48; and xxii, 27.

Sext. Decre. Lib. iii, Tit. 16, cap. unico; et Lib. v, Tit. 9, cap. 5; in Glossa.

But, after that ambition and desire of dominion entered once into ecclesiastical ministers, (whose greatness, after the doctrine and example of our Saviour[ε], should chiefly stand in humbling of themselves[q],) and that the Bishop of Rome, (being by the order of God's word none other than the bishop of that one see and diocese, and never yet well able to govern the same,) did by intolerable ambition challenge, not only to be the head of all the Church dispersed throughout the world, but also to be lord of all the kingdoms[r] of the world, as is expressly set forth in the book of his own Canon Laws[1], most contrary to the doctrine and example of our Saviour Christ, whose vicar, and of his holy[s] Apostles, namely Peter, whose successor, he pretendeth to be; after this[t] ambition entered, and this challenge once made by the Bishop of Rome, he became at once

[1] before others] before other *from* 1574. [m] whiles that] whiles the 1587, 1595, 1623. [n] prescribed] ascribed 1587, 1595, 1623. [o] Scriptures] Scripture *from* D. [p] do] doth *from* 1582. [q] humbling of themselves] humbling themselves *from* 1582. [r] all the kingdoms] all kingdoms *from* 1582. [s] holy] *omitted* 1623. [t] after this] after his *from* D.

1 Totius enim orbis Papa tenet principatum. *Sext. Decretal.* III, xvi, *cap. unic.*, *Gloss.* Partibus.

Excipitur autem civitas Romana . . . , cum totius orbis Episcopus sit Romanus Pontifex. *Ibid.* v, ix, 5, *Gloss.* Privata.

Jewel cites both these passages concerning the Pope's claim to spiritual supremacy in his *Defence of the Apology, Part* v, *Ch.* vi, *Div.* 4. He likewise cites the former of the two concerning the claim to temporal supremacy in *Part* IV, *Ch.* vi, *Div.* 1, on "Deposing of Kings." See also on this point *Clementin.* II, xi, 2, where the Pope annuls certain proceedings, not only in virtue of the special supremacy which he claims over the Empire and over the Kingdom of Sicily, but also, as he says, ex illius plenitudine potestatis quam Christus *Rex regum et Dominus dominantium* [1 *Tim.* VI, 15, *Apoc.* XIX, 16] nobis licet immeritis in persona beati Petri concessit.

the spoiler and destroyer both of the Church, which is the kingdom of our Saviour Christ, and of the Christian Empire and all Christian kingdoms, as an universal tyrant over all. And, whereas before that challenge made there was great amity and love amongst the Christians of all countries, hereupon began emulation and much hatred between the Bishop of Rome and his clergy and friends on the one part, and the Grecian clergy and Christians of the East on the other part, for that they refused to acknowledge any such supreme authority of the Bishop of Rome over them; the Bishop of Rome, for this cause amongst others[u], not only naming them and taking them for schismatics, but also never ceasing to persecute them and the Emperors who had their see and continuance in Greece, by stirring of the subjects to rebellion against their sovereign lords, and by raising deadly hatred and most cruel wars between them and other Christian princes. And, when the Bishops[x] of Rome had translated the title of the Emperor and (as much as in them did lie) the Empire itself from their lord the Emperor of Greece, and of Rome also by right, unto the Christian princes of the West, they became in short space no better unto the West Emperors than they were before unto the Emperors of Greece. For the usual discharging of subjects from their oaths[y] of fidelity made unto the Emperors of the West, their sovereign lords, by the Bishops[z] of Rome; the unnatural stirring up of the subjects unto rebellion against their princes, yea, of the son against the father, by the Bishop of Rome; the most cruel and bloody wars raised amongst Christian princes of all kingdoms; the horrible murder of infinite thousands of Christian men, being slain by Christians; and, which ensued thereupon, the pitiful losses of so many goodly cities, countries, dominions, and kingdoms, sometime possessed by Christians in Asia, Africa, and Europa[a]; the miserable fall of the Empire and Church of Greece, sometime the most flourishing part of Christendom, into the hands of Turks[b]; the lamentable diminishing, decay, and ruin of Christian religion; the dreadful encrease of paganity[c], and power of the infidels and miscreants[2]; and all by the practice and procurement of the Bishop of Rome chiefly; is in the histories and chronicles

[u] others] other *from* C. [x] Bishops (*line* 17)] Bishop A. [y] oaths] oath *from* 1571. [z] Bishops (*line* 24)] Bishop A. [a] Africa, and Europa] Africa, Europa *from* 1582. [b] of Turks] of the Turks *from* 1582. [c] paganity] paganism 1623.

[2] miscreants: misbelievers, *méscréants*.

written by the Bishop of Rome's own favourers and friends to be seen, and is[d] well known unto all such as are acquainted with the said histories.

The ambitious intent and most subtile drifts of the Bishops of Rome in these their practices appeared evidently by their bold attempt in spoiling and robbing the Emperors of their towns, cities, dominions, and kingdoms in Italy, Lombardy, and Sicily, of ancient right belonging unto the Empire, and by the joining[e] of them unto their bishopric of Rome, or else giving them unto strangers to hold them of the Church and Bishops[f] of Rome as in capite, and as of the chief lords thereof, in which tenure they hold the most part thereof even at this day[g]. By[h] these ambitious and indeed traitorous means, and spoiling of their sovereign lords, the Bishops of Rome, of priests and none other by right than the bishops of one city and diocese, are by false usurpation become great lords of many dominions, mighty princes, yea, or emperors rather, as claiming to have divers princes and kings to their vassals, liegemen, and subjects; as in the same histories written by their own familiars and courtiers is to be seen. And indeed, since the time that the Bishops of Rome, by ambition, treason, and usurpation, achieved and attained to this height and greatness, they behaved themselves more like princes, kings, and emperors in all things, than remained like priests, bishops, and ecclesiastical or (as they would be called) spiritual persons in any one thing at all. For after this rate they have handled other kings and princes of other realms throughout Christendom, as well as their sovereign lords the Emperors, usually discharging[i] their subjects of their oath of fidelity, and so stirring them up to rebellion against their natural princes, whereof some examples shall in the last Part hereof be notified unto you.

Wherefore let all good subjects, knowing these the special instruments and ministers of the devil to the stirring up of all rebellions, avoid and flee them and the pestilent suggestions of such foreign usurpers and their adherents, and embrace all obedience to God and their natural princes and sovereigns; that they may enjoy God's blessings and their prince's favour in all[k] peace, quietness, and security[l] in this world, and finally attain, through Christ our Saviour, life everlasting in the world to

[d] and is] and as 1623. [e] by the joining] by joining 1623. [f] and Bishops] and Bishop *from* 1574. [g] in which tenure they hold the most part thereof even at this day] *not in* A. [h] By] But 1623. [i] usually discharging &c.] *See page* 590, *note* c. [k] favour in all] favour, all 1623. [l] quietness, and security] quietness, security 1623.

come. Which God the Father, for the same our Saviour Jesus Christ his sake, grant unto us all. To whom with the Holy Ghost be all honour and glory world without end. Amen.

Thus have you heard the Fifth[m] Part of this Homily: now, good people, let us pray.

The Prayer as before[n].

[m] fifth] sixth D, E, 1571. [n] as before] as in that time it was published 1623, *and then the Prayer itself.*

THE SIXTH AND LAST PART

OF THE HOMILY AGAINST DISOBEDIENCE AND WILFUL REBELLION.[a]

NOW, whereas the injuries, oppressions, raveny, and tyranny of the Bishops[b] of Rome, usurping as well against their natural lords the Emperors as against all other Christian kings and kingdoms, and their continual stirring of subjects unto rebellions against their sovereign lords, whereof I have partly admonished you before, were intolerable; and it may seem more than marvel that any subjects would after such sort hold with unnatural foreign usurpers against their own sovereign lords and natural country; it remaineth that I do declare the mean whereby they compassed these matters, and so to conclude this whole Treaty of due obedience and against disobedience and wilful rebellion.

Of ignorance of the simple people. The latter part.[d]

You shall understand[c] that by ignorance of God's word, wherein they kept all men, specially the common people, they wrought and brought to pass all these things, making them believe that all they[e] said was true, all that they did was good and godly, and that to hold with them in all things, against father, mother, prince, country, and all men, was most meritorious. And indeed what mischief will not blind ignorance lead simple men unto? By ignorance the Jewish clergy induced[α] the common people to ask the delivery of Barabbas the seditious murderer, and to sue for the cruel crucifying of our Saviour Christ, for that he rebuked the ambition, superstition, and other vices of the high priests and clergy. For, as our Saviour Christ testifieth[β] that those who crucified him wist not what they did, so doth the holy Apostle St. Paul say[γ], *If they had known*, if they had not been ignorant, *they would never have*

α Matt. xxvii, [20:] Luke xxiii, [18.]

β Luke xxiii, 34.

γ 1 Cor. ii, 8.

a REBELLION.] REBELLION. The Sixth Part. B–E. b Bishops] B. (*so shortened*) B–E, Bishop *in full from* 1571.

c the Emperors, usually discharging (*page* 588, *line* 28)—You shall understand] the Emperors. Now, where these things were intolerable, and it may seem more than marvel that any subjects would after such sort hold with unnatural foreign usurpers against their own sovereign lords and natural country; you shall understand A, *the Fifth and Sixth Parts of the Homily being then in one.*

d Of ignorance of the simple people. The latter part.] Of ignorance. The second part. A. *See before, page* 584, *lines* 18–22. e all they] all that they *from* 1582.

crucified the Lord of glory: but they knew not what they did. Our Saviour Christ himself also foreshewed[e] that it should come to pass by ignorance, that those who should persecute and murder his true Apostles and disciples should think they did God acceptable sacrifice and good service; as it also is[f] verified even at this day.

e John xv, 21; and xvi, 2, 3.

And in this ignorance have the Bishops of Rome kept the people of God, specially the common sort, by no means so much as by the withdrawing[g] of the word of God from them, and by keeping it under the veil of an unknown strange tongue. For, as it served the ambitious humour of the Bishops of Rome to compel all nations to use the natural language of the city of Rome, where they were Bishops, which shewed a certain acknowledging of subjection unto them; so yet served it much more their crafty purpose thereby to keep all people so blind, that they, not knowing what they prayed, what they believed, what they were commanded by God, might take all their commandments for God's. For, as they would not suffer the holy Scriptures or Church Service to be used or had in any other language than the Latin, so were very few even of the most simple people taught the Lord's Prayer, the Articles of the Faith, and the Ten Commandments, otherwise than in Latin, which they understood not: by which universal ignorance all men were ready to believe whatsoever they said, and to do whatsoever they commanded.

For, to imitate the Apostle's phrase, *if* the Emperor's subjects *had known* out of God's word their duty to their prince, they would not have suffered the Bishop of Rome to persuade them to forsake their sovereign lord the Emperor against their oath of fidelity, and to rebel against him, only for that he cast images (unto the which idolatry was committed) out of the churches[1], which the Bishop of Rome bare them in hand[2] to be heresy. *If they had known* of God's word but as much as the Ten Commandments, they should have found that the Bishop of Rome was not only a traitor to the Emperor his liege lord, but to God also, and an horrible blasphemer of his Majesty, in calling his holy word and commandment heresy; and that which the Bishop of Rome took for a just cause to rebel against his lawful prince, they might have known to be a doubling and

Si cognovissent. [1 Cor. ii, 8.]

Gregorius II, and III. Anno Dom. 726 &c.

In the second commandment.

f also is] is also *from* 1582. g by the withdrawing] by withdrawing *from* 1571.

1 See before, p. 198, nn. 35, 36.

2 bare them in hand: led them on to believe. See before, p. 211, n. 70.

tripling of his most heinous wickedness, heaped with horrible impiety and blasphemy. But, lest the poor people should know too much, he would not let them have as much of God's word as the Ten Commandments wholly and perfectly, withdrawing from them the Second Commandment, that bewrayeth his impiety, by a subtile sacrilege.

Henricus IV. Gregorius VII. Anno Dom. 1076. Paschalis II. Anno 1099.

Had the Emperor's subjects likewise *known* and been of any understanding in God's word, would they at other times have rebelled against their sovereign lord, and by their rebellion have holpen to depose[h] him, only for that the Bishop of Rome did bear them in hand that it was simony, and heresy too, for the Emperor to give any ecclesiastical dignities or promotions to his learned chaplains or other of his learned clergy, which all Christian Emperors before him had done without controlment?[3] Would they, I say, for that the Bishop of Rome bare them so in hand, have rebelled by the space of more than forty years together against him, with so much shedding of Christian blood and murder of so many thousands of Christians, and finally have deposed their sovereign lord, *had they known* and had in God's word any understanding at all? Specially, *had they known* that they did all this to pluck from their sovereign lord and his successors for ever their ancient right of the Empire, to give it unto the Romish clergy and to the Bishop of Rome, that he might for the confirmation of one archbishop and for a[i] Romish rag, which he calleth a pall[k], scarce worth twelve pence, receive many thousand crowns of gold, and of other bishops likewise great sums of money for their bulls, which is simony indeed; would, I say, Christian men and subjects by rebellion have spent so much Christian blood, and have deposed their natural, most noble, and most valiant prince, to bring the matter finally to this pass, *had they known* what they did, or had any understanding in God's word at all?

And, as these ambitious usurpers the Bishops of Rome have overflowed all Italy and Germany with streams of Christian blood, shed by the rebellions of ignorant subjects against their natural lords the Emperors[l], whom they have stirred thereunto

h depose] dispose D, E. i for a] for the 1623. k pall] Paul *all except* 1587 *and* 1595. l the Emperors] and Emperors *from* 1574.

3 See *Platina de Vitt. Greg. VII.*, *Paschal. II.* But to cover a "space of more than forty years" in the reign or life of the Emperor Henry IV we must go back to a period much before the actual elevation of Hildebrand to the pontificate; when however, with the title of Archdeacon, he was really Pope. See *Milman's History of Latin Christianity*, VI, iii; VII, iii–v; VIII, i.

by such false pretences, so is there no country in Christendom which by their like means and false pretences hath not been oversprinkled with the blood of subjects by rebellion against their natural sovereigns, stirred up by the same Bishops of Rome.

King John.

And to use one example of our own country. The Bishop of Rome did pick a quarrel to King John of England about the election of Stephen Langton to the bishopric of Canterbury, wherein the King had ancient right, being used by his progenitors, all Christian Kings of England before him; the Bishops of Rome having no right, but had begun then to usurp upon the Kings of England and all other Christian Kings, as they had before done against their sovereign lords the Emperors; proceeding even by the same ways and means, and likewise cursing King John, and discharging his subjects of their oath of fidelity unto their sovereign lord[4]. Now, *had* Englishmen at that time *known* their duty to their prince set forth in God's word, would a great many of the nobles[m] and other Englishmen, natural subjects, for this foreign and unnatural usurper his vain curse of the King, and for his feigned discharging of them of their oath of[n] fidelity to their natural lord, upon so slender or no ground at all, have rebelled against their sovereign lord the King? Would English subjects have taken part, against the King of England and against Englishmen, with the French King and Frenchmen, being incensed against this realm by the Bishop of Rome? would they have sent for and received the Dolphin of France, with a great army of Frenchmen, into the realm of England? would they have sworn fidelity to the Dolphin of France, breaking their oath of fidelity to their natural lord the King of England, and have stand[o] under the Dolphin's banner displayed against the King of England? would they have expelled their sovereign lord the King of England out of London, the chief city of England, and out of the greatest part of England upon the South side of Trent, even unto Lincoln, and out of Lincoln itself also, and have delivered the possession thereof unto the Dolphin of France, whereof he kept the possession a great while? would they, being Englishmen, have procured so great shedding of English blood and other infinite mischiefs and miseries unto England their natural country, as did

Innocentius III.

Philip, French King.

Lewes, Dolphin of France.

m of the nobles] of nobles *from* 1582. n oath of] oath and *from* 1582. o stand] stood *from* 1582.

4 See *Inett's Origines Anglicanae*, II, xx–xxv: *Milman, ibid.* IX, v.

follow those cruel wars and traitorous rebellion, the fruits of the Bishop of Rome's blessings? would they have driven their natural sovereign lord the King of England to such extremity, that he was inforced to submit himself unto that foreign false usurper, the Bishop of Rome, who compelled him to surrender up the crown of England into the hands of his legate; who in token of possession kept it in his hands divers days, and then delivered it again to King John upon that condition, that the King and his successors, Kings of England, should hold the crown and kingdom of England of the Bishop of Rome and his successors, as the vassals of the said Bishops of Rome for ever; in token whereof the Kings of England should also pay an[p] yearly tribute to the said Bishop of Rome, as his vassals and liegemen? would Englishmen have brought their sovereign lord and natural country into this thraldom and subjection to a false foreign usurper, *had they known* and had any understanding in God's word at all? Out of the which most lamentable case, and most miserable[q] tyranny, raveny, and spoil of the most greedy Romish wolves ensuing hereupon, the Kings and realm of England could not rid themselves by the space of many years after; the Bishop of Rome by his ministers continually not only spoiling the realm and Kings of England of infinite treasure, but also with the same money hiring and maintaining foreign enemies against the realm and Kings of England, to keep them in such his subjection, that they should not refuse to pay whatsoever those unsatiable wolves did greedily gape for, and suffer whatsoever those most cruel tyrants would lay upon them. Would Englishmen have suffered this? would they by rebellion have caused this, trow you, and all for the Bishop of Rome's causeless curse, *had they* in those days *known* and understanded[r], that God doth *curse*[e] *the blessings* and bless the cursings of such wicked usurping bishops and tyrants, as it appeared afterward in King Henry the Eighth his days, and King Edward the Sixth, and in our gracious Sovereign's days that now is, where neither the Pope's curses[5], nor God's manifold blessings, are wanting? But in King John's time the Bishop of Rome understanding

Pandulphus.

See the Acts of Parliament in King Edward the Third his days.

e Mal. ii, [2.]

p an] a *from* 1582. q and most miserable] and miserable *from* 1582. r understanded] understood 1595, 1623.

5 The famous bull of Pope Pius V against Queen Elizabeth bears date on February 25, 1570: but, in anticipation of it, Nicholas Morton had been sent over by the Pope in 1569 with authority to declare that Elizabeth was a heretic and therefore not entitled to the throne, and had actively promoted the Northern Rebellion by his statements. *Camd. Annal.* p. 165.

the brute blindness, ignorance of God's word, and superstition of Englishmen, and how much they were enclined to worship the babylonical beast of Rome, and to fear all his threatenings and causeless curses, he abused them thus; and by their rebellion brought this noble realm and Kings of England under his most cruel tyranny, and to be a spoil of his most vile and unsatiable covetousness and raveny for a long and a great deal too long a time.

And, to join unto the reports of histories matters of later[s] memory, could the Bishop of Rome have raised the late rebellions in the North and West countries in the times of King Henry and King Edward[6], our gracious Sovereign's father and brother, but by abusing of the ignorant people? Or is it not most evident that the Bishop of Rome hath of late attempted by his Irish patriarchs and bishops[7], sent from Rome with his bulls, (whereof some were deprehended[t],) to break down the bars and hedges of the public peace in Ireland, only upon confidence easily to abuse the ignorance of the wild Irishmen? Or who seeth not that upon like confidence yet more lately he hath likewise procured the breach of the public peace in England, (with the long and blessed continuance whereof he is sore grieved,) by the ministry of his disguised chaplains, creeping in laymen's apparel into the houses and whispering in the ears of certain Northen[u] borderers, being men[x] most ignorant of their duty to God and their[y] prince of all people of the realm; whom therefore, as most meet and ready to execute his intended pur-

[s] later] latter 1571–1587. [t] deprehended] apprehended *from* 1571. [u] Northen] Northren 1595, Northern 1623. [x] being men] being then 1623. [y] and their] and to their *from* 1582.

6 The rebellion in the North, known as "the Pilgrimage of Grace", was in 1536; the Western rebellion in 1549. See *Speed's History of Great Britain,* IX, xxi, *pp.* 1018–1026 *ed.* 1632: *Foxe, Acts and Monuments,* V, 730–737, *ed.* 1843–9.

7 Although the Homilist speaks of "patriarchs and bishops" in the plural number, history seems to have recorded only one such emissary from Rome, Richard Creagh, titular Primate of Ireland, who, after escaping from the Tower of London in 1565, returned to Ireland during the rebellion of Shane O'Niell in 1566 or 1567, was again apprehended and lodged in the Tower, and died there a prisoner in October 1585. See, in Roth's *Analecta de Rebus Catholicorum in Hibernia, De Processu Martyriali quorundam Fidei Pugilum, pp.* 1–47: O'Sullevan's *Historiae Catholicae Iberniae Compendium,* II, iv, 10: or Stuart's *Historical Memoirs of the City of Armagh, pp.* 249–251. It is not likely that Creagh or any other titular Primate took the title of Patriarch to himself; but Sir James Melvill (in his *Memoirs, p.* 9,) gives it in like manner to Robert Waucop in 1545, and perhaps it was in popular use.

To the sources of the information comprised in this note I have been directed by the Rev. Robert King's *Primer of the Church History of Ireland, Book* VI, *Chapters* i and v, and *Appendix, No.* xxvi, *edit.* 3.

pose, he hath by the said ignorant mass priests, as blind guides leading the blind, brought those seely blind subjects into the deep ditch of horrible rebellion, damnable to themselves, and very dangerous to the state of the realm, had not God of his mercy miraculously calmed that raging tempest, not only without any shipwrack of the commonwealth, but almost without any shedding of Christian and English blood at all.

And it is yet much more to be lamented that, not only common people, but some[z] other youthful or unskilful princes also suffer themselves to be abused by the Bishop of Rome his cardinals and bishops to the oppressing[a] of Christian men their faithful subjects, either themselves, or else by procuring the force and strength of Christian men to be conveyed out of one country to oppress true Christians in another country, and by these means open an entry unto Moors and infidels into the possession of Christian realms and countries[b]; other Christian princes in the mean time, by the Bishop of Rome's procuring also, being so occupied in civil wars, or so troubled[c] with rebellions, that they have neither leisure nor ability to confer their common forces to the defence of their fellow Christians against such invasions of the common enemies of Christendom, the infidels and miscreants. Would to God we might only read and hear out of histories of the old[d], and not also see and feel these new and present oppressions of Christians, rebellions of subjects, effusion of Christian blood, destruction of Christian men, decay and ruin of Christendom, increase of paganity[e], most lamentable and pitiful to behold, being procured in these our days, as well as in times past, by the Bishop of Rome and his ministers abusing the ignorance of God's word yet remaining in some Christian princes and people.

By which sour[f] and bitter fruits of ignorance all men ought to be moved to give ear and credit to God's word, shewing, as most truly, so most plainly, how great a mischief ignorance is, and again how great and how good a gift of God knowledge in God's word is. And to begin with the Romish[g] clergy, who though they do brag now, as did[ζ] sometime the Jewish clergy, that they cannot lack knowledge, yet doth God by his holy Prophets[η] both charge them with ignorance, and threaten them also, for that they have repelled the knowledge of God's word and law

ζ Jer. xviii, 18.

η Ezek. vii, 26: Hos. iv, 6.

z but some] by some *till* 1582. a to the oppressing] to oppressing *from* 1571. b realms and countries] realms countries 1582, 1623. c or so troubled] or troubled *from* 1571. d of histories of the old] of the histories of old *from* 1582. e paganity] paganism *from* 1582. f sour] sorrow *from* 1574. g Romish] *not in* A, B.

from themselves and from his people, that he will repel them, that they shall be no more his priests. God likewise chargeth[θ] princes as well as priests, that they should endeavour themselves to get understanding and knowledge in his word, threatening his heavy wrath and destruction unto them if they fail thereof. And the Wise Man saith[ι] to all men universally, princes, priests, and people, *Where is no knowledge, there is no good nor health to the soul*[8]; and that *all men be vain in whom is not the knowledge of God*[9] and his holy word; that[κ] *they who walk in darkness wot not whither they go*; and that the people that will not learn shall fall into great mischiefs; as did the people of Israel, who[λ], for their ignorance in God's word, were first led into captivity; and, when by ignorance afterward they would not[μ] *know the time of their visitation*, but crucified Christ our Saviour, persecuted[ν] his holy Apostles, and were so ignorant and blind that, when they did most wickedly and cruelly, they thought[ξ] they did God good and acceptable service, (as do many by ignorance think even at this day,) finally, through their ignorance and blindness, their country, towns, cities, Hierusalem itself, and the holy temple[h] of God were all most horribly destroyed, the most chiefest part of their people slain, and the rest led into most miserable captivity: for[ο] *he that made them had no pity upon them, neither would spare them*; and all for their ignorance[π]. And the holy Scriptures do teach[ρ] that the people that will not see with their eyes, nor hear with their ears, to learn and to understand with their hearts, cannot be converted and saved. And the wicked themselves, being damned in hell, shall confess ignorance in God's word to have brought them thereunto, saying[σ], *We have erred from the way of the truth, and the light of righteousness hath not shined unto us, and the sun of understanding hath not risen unto us. We have wearied ourselves in the way of wickedness and perdition, and have walked cumbrous and crooked ways: but the way of the Lord have we not known.* And as well our Saviour himself as his Apostle St. Paul do[i] teach[τ], that the ignorance of God's word cometh of the devil, is the cause of all error and misjudging, (as falleth out with ignorant subjects, who can rather espy[υ] a little mote in the eye of the prince or a counsellor than a great beam in their

θ Ps. ii, [10–12.]
ι Prov. xix, [2:] Wisd. xiii, [1.]
κ Prov. xvii, [24:] Eph. iv, [17, 18:] John xii, [35.]
λ Isa. v, 13.
μ Luke xix, 44; xxiii, 34.
ν Acts multis locis.
ξ John xvi, 2.
ο Isa. xxvii, [11.]
π Hos. iv, [6:] Bar. iii, [10–12, 28.]
ρ Isa. vi, 9: Matt. xiii, 14, 15: John xii, 40.
σ Wisd. v, [6, 7.]
τ Matt. xiii, 19: 2 Cor. iv, 3, 4.
υ Matt. vii, [3.]

h the holy temple] the temple 1623.

i Paul do] Paul doth *from* 1582.

8 Ubi non est scientia animae non est bonum. *Prov.* XIX, 2, *Vulg.*

9 Vani autem sunt omnes homines in quibus non subest scientia Dei. *Sap.* XIII, 1, *Vulg.*

own,) and universally it is the cause of all evil, and finally of eternal damnation; God's judgment being severe towards those who, when the *light*[φ] of Christ's Gospel *is come into the world, do delight more in darkness* of ignorance *than in the light* of knowledge in God's word. For all are commanded[χ] to read or hear, to search and study, the holy Scriptures, and are promised[ψ] understanding to be given them from God if they so do; all are charged[ω] not to believe either any dead man, nor if an angel should speak from heaven, much less if the pope do speak from Rome, against or contrary to the word of God; from the which[α] we may *not decline, neither to the right hand nor to the left*[10]. In God's word princes[β] must learn how to obey God and to govern men: in God's word subjects[γ] must learn obedience both to God and their princes. Old men and young[δ], rich and poor, all men and women, all estates, sexes, and ages, are taught their several duties in the word of God. For[ε] *the word of God is bright, giving light unto all men's eyes*[11], *the shining lamp directing all men's paths and steps.*

Let us therefore awake[ζ] from the sleep and darkness of ignorance, and open our eyes, that we may see the light: let us rise from *the works of darkness,* that we may escape eternal darkness, the due reward thereof: and let us *walk*[η] in the light of God's word *whiles we have light,* as becometh *the children of light;* so directing the steps of our lives in that way which leadeth to light and life everlasting, that we may finally obtain and enjoy the same. Which God *the Father*[θ] *of lights, who*[ι] *dwelleth in light* incomprehensible and *inaccessible,* grant unto us, through *the Light*[κ] *of the world* our Saviour Jesus Christ. Unto whom with the Holy Ghost, one most glorious God, be all honour, praise, and thanksgiving for ever and ever. Amen.

Thus have you heard the Sixth Part of this Homily: now, good people, let us pray.

The Prayer as before[k l].

φ John iii, [19.]
χ Matt. xi, 15; and xiii, 9, 43: Luke viii, 8: John v, 39.
ψ Ps. i, [1–3:] Matt. vii, 7: Luke xi, 9.
ω Luke xvi, 30, 31: Gal. i, 8.
α Deut. v, 32, 33.
β Deut. xvii, 14, 15 &c.
γ Rom. xiii, [1–7:] 1 Pet. ii, [13–17.]
δ Ps. cxviii [cxix, 9.]
ε Ps. xviii [xix, 8;] and cxviii [cxix, 105.]
ζ Eph. v, 14: 1 Thess. v, 4–6: [Rom. xiii, 11, 12.]
η John xii, 35, 36.
θ James i, 17.
ι 1 Tim. vi, 16.
κ John iii, [19; viii, 12; ix, 5.]

k Thus have you heard —— as before] *not in* A. 1623, *and then the Prayer itself.*

l as before] as in that time it was published.

10 Non declinabitis neque ad dexteram neque ad sinistram. *Deut.* v, 32, *Vulg.*

11 Praeceptum Domini lucidum, illuminans oculos. *Ps.* XVIII (*Hebr.* XIX), 8, *Vulg.*

A THANKSGIVING

FOR THE SUPPRESSION OF THE LAST REBELLION.

O HEAVENLY and most merciful Father, the Defender of those that put their trust in thee, the sure Fortress of all them that flee[a] to thee for succour; who, of thy most just judgments for our disobedience and rebellion against thy holy word, and for our sinful and wicked living, nothing answering to our holy profession, whereby we have given an occasion that thy holy Name hath been blasphemed amongst the ignorant, hast of late both sore abashed the whole realm and people of England with the terror and danger of rebellion, thereby to awake us out of our dead sleep of careless security; and hast yet, by the miseries following the same rebellion, more sharply punished part of our countrymen and Christian brethren, who have more nearly felt the same; and most dreadfully hast scourged some of the seditious persons with terrible executions, justly inflicted for their disobedience to thee and to thy servant their Sovereign, to the example of us all and to the warning, correction, and amendment of thy servants, of thine accustomed goodness turning always the wickedness of evil men to the profit of them that fear thee; who, in thy judgments remembering thy mercy, hast by thy assistance given the victory to thy servant our Queen, her true nobility and faithful subjects, with so little, or rather no, effusion of Christian blood, as also might justly have[b] ensued, to the exceeding comfort of all sorrowful Christian hearts; and that of thy fatherly pity and merciful goodness only, and even for thine own Name's sake, without any our desert at all: wherefore we render unto thee most humble and hearty thanks for these thy great mercies shewed unto us, who had deserved sharper punishment; most humbly beseeching thee to grant unto all us that confess thy holy Name, and profess the true and perfect religion of thy holy Gospel, thy heavenly grace, to shew ourselves in our living according to our profession; that we, truly knowing thee in thy blessed word, may obediently walk in thy holy commandments; and that we, being warned

[a] flee] fly 1623. [b] justly have] have justly *from* 1582.

by this thy fatherly correction, do provoke thy just wrath against us no more, but may enjoy the continuance of thy great mercies toward[c] us, thy right hand, as in this, so in all other invasions, rebellions, and dangers, continually saving and defending our Church, our realm, our Queen, and people of England; that all our posterities ensuing, confessing thy holy Name, professing thy holy Gospel, and leading an holy life, may perpetually praise and magnify thee, with thy only Son Jesus Christ our Saviour, and the Holy Ghost: to whom be all laud, praise, glory, and empire for ever and ever. Amen.

[c] toward] towards 1597, 1623.

INDEX OF TEXTS OF SCRIPTURE.

GENERAL INDEX.

Words obsolete or rare in form, meaning, or construction:

Words obsolete, &c., *continued.*

Words obsolete, &c., *continued.*

[Works,

BOOKS

PRINTED FOR THE UNIVERSITY OF OXFORD,

SOLD BY

JOHN HENRY PARKER, Oxford, and 377, Strand, London; and
E. GARDNER, 7, Paternoster Row, London.

At the following Prices in Boards.

BEVERIDGE'S Discourse upon the XXXIX Articles. The third complete edition. 1847. 8vo. 8*s.*

BINGHAM'S Works, edited by the Rev. R. BINGHAM, jun. M.A. *A new edition,* in 10 vols. 1855. 8vo. 5*l.* 5*s.*

BRAGGE'S Works, on the Miracles, Parables, &c. 5 vols. 1833. 8vo. 1*l.* 12*s.* 6*d.*

BULL'S Works, with Nelson's Life, by the Rev. E. BURTON, D.D. *A new edition.* 8 vols. 1846. 8vo. 2*l.* 9*s.*

BURNET'S History of the Reformation of the Church of England. *A new edition in the Press.*

—— Exposition of the XXXIX Articles. 1846. 8vo. 7*s.*

BURTON'S (Edward) Testimonies of the Ante-Nicene Fathers to the Divinity of Christ. *Second edition.* 1829. 8vo. 7*s.*

—— to the Doctrine of the Trinity and of the Divinity of the Holy Ghost. 1831. 8vo. 3*s.* 6*d.*

THE TWO BOOKS OF COMMON PRAYER, set forth by authority of Parliament in the Reign of King Edward the Sixth: compared with each other. *Third edition.* 1852. 8vo. 7*s.*

—— History of Conferences on the Book of Common Prayer from 1551 to 1690. *Third edition.* 1849. 8vo. 7*s.* 6*d.*

—— Reformatio Legum Ecclesiasticarum. The Reformation of the Ecclesiastical Laws as attempted in the reigns of King Henry VIII, King Edward VI, and Queen Elizabeth. 1850. 8vo. 6*s.* 6*d.*

CHILLINGWORTH'S Works. 3 vols. 1838. 8vo. 1*l.* 1*s.* 6*d.*

COMBER'S Companion to the Temple, &c. 7 vols. 1841. 8vo. 1*l.* 11*s.* 6*d.*

CRANMER'S Works, collected and arranged by the Rev. H. JENKYNS, M.A. Fellow of Oriel College. 4 vols. 1834. 8vo. 1*l.* 10*s.*

CYRIL (S.), Commentary on S. Luke, translated by R. PAYNE SMITH, M.A. 2 vols. 1859. 8vo. 14*s.*

FLEETWOOD'S (Bp.) Works. *A new edition.* 3 vols. 1854. 8vo. 1*l.* 1*s.* 6*d.*

FORMULARIES of Faith, put forth by authority in the reign of Henry VIII. *A new edition,* 8vo. 1856. 7*s.*

FULLER'S Church History of Britain, edited by the Rev. J. S. BREWER. 6 vols. 1845. 8vo. 1*l.* 19*s.*

HAMMOND'S Paraphrase and Annotations on the New Testament. 4 vols. 1845. 8vo. 1*l.* 10*s.*

—— Paraphrase on the Psalms, edited by the Rev. T. BRANCKER. 1850. 2 vols. 8vo. 1*l.* 1*s.*

HEURTLEY, (Dr. C. A.), Collection of Creeds, 1858. 8vo. *6s. 6d.*

HOOKER'S Ecclesiastical Polity, and other Works, with his Life by Walton, and additions, arranged by the Rev. JOHN KEBLE, M. A. Third edition. 3 vols. 1844. 8vo. *1l. 11s. 6d.*

HOOKER'S Works, (without Keble's Notes) 2 vols. 8vo. 1850. *11s.*

HOOPER'S, (Bishop George) Works. 2 vols. 8vo. 1855. *8s.*

INETT'S History of the English Church. By the Rev. J. GRIFFITHS, M. A. A new edition, in 2 vols. 1855. 8vo. *1l. 11s.*

JACKSON'S (Dr. Thomas) Works. 12 vols. 1844. 8vo. *3l. 6s.*

JEWEL'S Works. A new edition, edited by the Rev. R. W. JELF, D. D. 8 vols. 1847. 8vo. *2l. 10s.*

LESLIE'S (C.) Theological Works. 7 vols. 1832. 8vo. *2l.*

LIGHTFOOT'S Horæ Hebraicæ et Talmudicæ. A new edition, by the Rev. R. GANDELL, M. A. 4 vols. 1859. 8vo. *2l. 2s.*

NEWCOME'S (Abp.) Observations on our Lord's Conduct. 1852. 8vo. *5s.*

PATRICK'S (Bp.) Works, edited by the Rev. A. TAYLOR. 9 vols. 1859. 8vo. *3l. 14s. 6d.*

PEARSON'S Exposition of the Creed. A new edition, revised and corrected by the Rev. E. BURTON, D.D. 1847. 8vo. *10s. 6d.*

—— Minor Theological Works, now first collected, with a Memoir of the Author, Notes, and Index. By EDW. CHURTON, M.A. 2 vols. 1844. 8vo. *14s.*

SANDERSON'S Works, *now first collected* by W. JACOBSON, D.D. 6 vols. 1854. 8vo. *1l. 19s.*

SCOTT'S Christian Life, and other Works. 6 vols. 1826. 8vo. *1l. 7s.*

SHARP'S (Abp. John) Theological Works. 5 vols. 1829. 8vo. *1l. 2s. 6d.*

SIXTY SERMONS preached upon several occasions. By GEORGE SMALRIDGE, D.D. sometime Bishop of Bristol, and Dean of Christ Church, Oxford. A new edition. 1852. 2 vols. 8vo. *8s.*

SOUTH (Robert). Sermons Preached upon several Occasions. 5 vols. 1842. 8vo. *2l. 10s. 6d.*

STILLINGFLEET'S Origines Britannicæ: With Lloyd's Historical Account of Church Government. Edited by T. P. PANTIN, M. A. 2 vols. 1842. 8vo. *13s.*

—— Rational Account of the Grounds of Protestant Religion: being a Vindication of Abp. Laud's Relation of a Conference &c. 2 vols. 1844. 8vo. *10s.*

STUBBS (W.) Registrum Sacrum Anglicanum. Small 4to. 1858. *8s. 6d.*

WALL'S History of Infant Baptism, with Gale's Reflections, and Wall's Defence. A new edition, by the Rev. H. COTTON, D.C.L. 4 vols. 1845. 8vo. *1l. 12s.*

WATERLAND'S Works, with Life by W. VAN MILDERT, D.D. late Lord Bishop of Durham. A new edition, with copious indexes. 6 vols. 8vo. 1856. *2l. 11s.*

WYCLIFFE'S BIBLE, edited by FORSHALL and MADDEN. 4 vols. 1850. royal 4to. *5l. 15s. 6d.*

CATENA GRÆCORUM PATRUM in Novum Testamentum Tom. VIII. Ed. J. A. CRAMER, S.T.P. 1838–44. 8vo. *2l. 4s.*

PATRUM APOSTOLICORUM quæ supersunt opera; Gr. et Lat. Ed. GUL. JACOBSON, S.T.P. Tom. II. 1847. 8vo. *1l. 1s.*

Lightning Source UK Ltd.
Milton Keynes UK
UKHW011001200619
344740UK00001B/153/P